BUSINESS COMMUNICATIONS

11TH ED.

CAROL M. LEHMAN
Associate Professor
Mississippi State University

WILLIAM C. HIMSTREET
Professor Emeritus
University of Southern California

WAYNE MURLIN BATY
Professor Emeritus
Arizona State University

SOUTH-WESTERN College Publishing

An International Thomson Publishing Company

EC72KA
Copyright © 1996
by South-Western College Publishing
Cincinnati, Ohio

I(T)P
International Thomson Publishing
South-Western College Publishing is an ITP Company. The ITP trademark is used under
license.

ISBN: 0-538-84778-6

1 2 3 4 5 6 7 8 9 0 KI 4 3 2 1 0 9 8 7 6 5

Printed in the United States of America

Acquisitions Editor:	Randy G. Haubner
Developmental Editor:	Alice C. Denny
Freelance Developmental Editor:	Mary Lea Ginn
Production Editor:	Crystal Chapin
Production House:	DPS Associates, Inc.
Cover and Internal Designer:	Craig LaGesse Ramsdell
Cover Photo:	© Chuck Keeler
Photo Researcher:	Alix Roughen
Marketing Manager:	Stephen E. Momper

Library of Congress Cataloging-in-Publication Data

Lehman, Carol M.
    Business communications / Carol M. Lehman, William C. Himstreet,
Wayne Murlin Baty. — 11th ed.
      p. cm.
    Himstreet's name appears first on the earlier edition.
    Includes bibliographical references and index.
    ISBN 0-538-84778-6
    1. Commercial correspondence. 2. Business report writing.
3. Business communication. I. Himstreet, William C. II. Baty,
Wayne Murlin.
HF5721.H5   1996   95-12251
658.4'5—dc20   CIP

PREFACE

BUSINESS COMMUNICATIONS

The environment in which individuals communicate has changed significantly since the First Edition of *Business Communications* was published more than thirty years ago. Technology, globalization of our economy, flattening of the organizational structure of businesses, and legal and ethical concerns all affect the way people communicate in the business setting of the 1990s. To maintain its relevance in this dynamic environment, the Eleventh Edition of *Business Communications* addresses these concerns among other timely communications issues. Read on to find out how *Business Communications* will help your students master business communication skills for career success.

BUSINESS COMMUNICATIONS FACILITATES UNDERSTANDING AND DEVELOPS WRITING PROFICIENCY

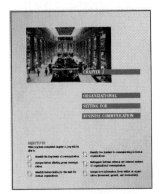

This text is carefully designed to facilitate students' understanding of crucial communication principles and to develop effective writing skills. Several new pedagogical features have been added to the Eleventh Edition, and all of the existing features have been thoroughly updated.

- A new pedagogical feature is introduced in this edition: the Integrated Learning System. The text and supplements are organized around the learning objectives presented at the beginning of each chapter. Numbered icons identify the objectives and appear next to the material throughout the text, *Study Guide, Instructor's Resource Manual,* and *Test Bank* where each objective is fulfilled. Within the text, end-of-chapter summaries and activities are provided for each learning objective. When students need further review to meet a certain objective, they can quickly identify the relevant material by simply looking for the icon. This integrated structure creates a comprehensive teaching and testing system.

- Important terms are now set in bold type for easy recognition and defined precisely in easy-to-understand language.

- Marginal questions and notes serve as handy self-checks that help students identify important concepts on each page. Students develop critical thinking skills as they apply their understanding in the new "Think It Over" marginal notes.

- Before-and-after writing examples, with sentence-by-sentence analysis, highlight common errors and help students see specific applications of effective writing principles. Many new examples have been added to the Eleventh Edition to ensure that models depict effective solutions to timely business problems.

1. New letters, memos, and e-mail messages demonstrate how to communicate about a range of issues. Topics include claims related to MIS documentation contracts, front-end charges for mutual funds, notice of company relocation to employees, and a procedural memo. Creative persuasive examples focus on promoting ideas rather than products; for example, an employee's appeal to a supervisor to approve a telecommuting work option, citizens to support a city's youth swim association, and a persuasive claim to a resort hotel to adjust the room rate because exercise facilities were not available to conference attenders as advertised.

2. Four excellent new annotated report examples enhance students' understanding of timely topics such as auditing a company's software policies and inventory, working in the Kuwaiti market, and electronic monitoring.

3. A new application letter, a follow-up letter, and thank-you letters to an interviewer and a reference illustrate how an applicant can identify and emphasize key qualifications that match company and job requirements.

4. Lively new examples of an effective table, various types of charts, and a flowchart reflect capabilities of advanced presentation graphics software.

Full-document format adds realism to letters, memos, resumes, and reports and reinforces students' understanding of standard business formats. These documents, complete with realistic letterheads, add visual appeal to the regular text discussion.

- "General Writing Guidelines" and "Check Your Writing" checklists let students quickly evaluate their documents. New checklists include (1) planning and delivering an oral presentation, (2) organizing and composing messages, (3) revising and proofreading messages, (4) interviewing, (5) preparing employment messages, and (6) handling performance appraisals.

- Completely new, engaging photos and relevant captions illustrate communication concepts and reinforce the text discussion. At least one photo in each chapter focuses on a real-world communication situation.

- Appealing graphics provide students a clear picture of the specific communication theory and concepts being discussed such as the communication process model taken from Chapter 1 shown here.

- Grammar and mechanics reviews in Appendix B provide clear examples and self-check quizzes to help students see where grammar review is needed. Basic style in writing is covered in Chapters 7 and 8. Appendix B provides a handy grammar reference for students.

- Extensive end-of-chapter activities let students solve realistic, challenging problems. You'll find review questions, exercises, an e-mail application, applications, and cases for analysis, 25 percent of which are new.

Activities are carefully written to portray business situations relevant in various business disciplines and require students to consider international, ethical, legal, and technological implications. Each writing application and case for analysis in Chapters 9-18 is classified so you can select applications and cases relevant to your students' interests and needs. Classifications identify the discipline and the specific implications inherent in the problem.

The activities also encompass a broad range of difficulty to meet various levels of student needs—a repeated request of reviewers and users. The level of each activity is clearly marked in the *Instructor's Resource Manual*. The four levels include

Level 1: Analyzing the strengths and weaknesses of a poorly written document and revising the document incorporating the critique.

Level 2: Composing a document based on the information provided in the case problem. Students may provide fictitious details if necessary. Includes all information students need to solve the writing problem. Challenging new cases require students to solve realistic business problems occurring in disciplines ranging from marketing to information systems and others.

Level 3: Conducting basic library research to locate relevant information needed to solve the problem.

Level 4: Analyzing a complex issue that may require extensive research to reach an informed decision. Critical thinking questions help students organize their thoughts. Students write appropriate document(s) to the intended audience(s). These analytical cases appear in a separate section entitled *Cases for Analysis.*

- Students build a strong theoretical foundation for writing (Chapters 1-8) before encountering the writing applications (Chapters 9-18). Reviewers and users have recommended this organizational pattern consistently. If you prefer to have your students write earlier, you can easily adapt the sequence and content of this flexible text.

Changes in the organization to the Eleventh Edition include a revised Chapter 1, "Interpersonal Communication and Listening" (formerly Chapter 2), that offers an engaging, highly relevant beginning for the study of business communications.

Part 3, "THE WRITING PROCESS," which covers the process of writing—determining the purpose and channel, envisioning the audience, adapting the message to the audience, organizing the message, writing the first draft, and revising and proofreading—has been streamlined for more focused coverage. Part 3 now includes Chapter 7, "Organizing and Composing Messages," and Chapter 8, "Revising and Proofreading Messages."

BUSINESS COMMUNICATIONS EXPOSES STUDENTS TO COMMUNICATION CHALLENGES IN REAL-WORLD COMPANIES

Advice from a panel of committed executives and exposure to communication dilemmas in real companies help students understand the relevance of effective oral and written communication in their career success. Throughout the text students learn to apply specific communication principles to real companies and situations.

- A Student Foreword, "Effective Communication Skills: Key Ingredients," challenges students to approach the course with added incentive. Examples from current literature and personal anecdotes of executives help students see the role of communication in the real world and the strong link to personal career success.

- Communication mentors give your students a priceless opportunity to "look over the shoulders" of a panel of communication mentors—six of the thirteen mentors are new to the Eleventh Edition. These corporate leaders represent numerous disciplines and various levels of management. As students study a particular principle, one or more of the communication mentors discuss how the principle actually works in today's dynamic business environment. They share related strategies for communicating effectively or provide concrete advice for developing the needed skill. To acquaint your students with the members of the communication mentor panel, refer them to the photos and brief profiles that appear at the end of the Student Foreword. A special format alerts students that they are learning from the real-life experiences of corporate executives.

- A *Communication in Action* (CIA) case for each chapter is built around an executive who addresses a communication dilemma in a real company. Cases are based on personal interviews with the executives. Each CIA case includes critical thinking questions and legitimate writing assignments (in chapters where writing has been introduced) that allow students to apply what they have learned. Answers to questions and applications appear in the *Instructor's Resource Manual*.

- Selected chapter openers, photographs, marginal notes, and text discussion also highlight communication issues in real companies.

- Six videotapes take students inside real companies to learn how business executives solve communication problems. Teaching and learning materials in the textbook and *Instructor's Resource Manual* help you use these videos to enliven your classroom presentation.

BUSINESS COMMUNICATIONS OFFERS COMPREHENSIVE COVERAGE OF TIMELY TOPICS

International, technological, ethical, legal, and interpersonal topics are integrated throughout the text to reinforce the importance of these factors in all phases of communication—oral and written. In addition to this comprehensive coverage, selected features further emphasize these important topics.

- A separate chapter on "Ethical and Legal Guidelines" (Chapter 6) builds awareness of ethical issues facing students now and on the job. Using a framework for analyzing ethical issues including legal aspects, students find solutions to ethical dilemmas that do not compromise their own personal values. Specific guidelines ensure students they are using effective communication ethically. Numerous examples from students' daily life, the business world, and cases offer ample opportunity to analyze complex issues where right and wrong may not be clear.

- Updated coverage on international and technology chapters (Chapters 4 and 5 respectively) reflect the latest issues including the Internet, online catalogs and information services, collaborative software, document conferencing, and detailed discussion of the ethical and legal implications of technology.

- End-of-chapter exercises and applications require students to solve problems with international, technological, ethical, legal, and interpersonal implications. The implications inherent in each application or case are clearly identified.

- An e-mail application at the end of each chapter develops proficiency in using this important tool in the workplace. Applications include sending the instructor an outline and bibliography of an upcoming oral or written report for approval, minutes of group meetings, and responses to cases where e-mail is an appropriate channel. Students message one another to apply specific communication theory and to facilitate collaborative writing projects. Advanced applications include querying an international agency through Gopher to seek firsthand information about international communication and performing an electronic search of a business research topic using the Internet.

BUSINESS COMMUNICATIONS
DEVELOPS CRITICAL THINKING SKILLS

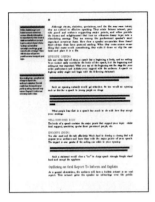

The ability to analyze complex issues, organize thoughts logically, and communicate these complex ideas concisely is essential for career success. The pedagogy of previous editions of *Business Communications* has involved teaching students to analyze and organize before beginning to write. Other features in the Eleventh Edition that foster the development of critical thinking skills include the following:

- Marginal notes marked "Think It Over" involve critical thinking and require students to analyze and apply the concepts presented in the text discussion.

- An ethical framework is presented to teach students to analyze ethical dilemmas from multiple perspectives and to identify solutions that conform to personal values.

- Cases for Analysis, the most challenging of the four ranges of difficulty available in the end-of-chapter activities, require students to analyze complex issues and communicate the analysis in logical, concise documents.

- Practical applications in the *Study Guide* provide critical thinking questions, or communication pointers, that help students analyze a situation and then organize their thoughts logically and concisely.

- Selected end-of-chapter activities, marked with a GMAT icon, can be used as a sample Analytical Writing Assessment (AWA) for students preparing for the Graduate Management Admission Test (GMAT). The AWA portion of the GMAT includes two writing tasks that assess the ability to think critically and communicate complex ideas. The *Instructor's Resource Manual* contains guidelines for scoring the AWA following the holistic scoring method used by GMAT graders.

GMAT

BUSINESS COMMUNICATIONS PROVIDES
EXCELLENT INSTRUCTIONAL RESOURCES

A complete package of instructional resources complement the textbook as well as your classroom presentations. Use these instructional materials to simplify and strengthen the study of business communication to make both in- and out-of-class time more effective.

Instructor's Resource Manual

The comprehensive *Instructor's Resource Manual* includes

- Suggestions for organizing the course in a semester and a quarter system, administering the course, managing collaborative writing projects, and integrating the six videotapes.

- Guidelines for grading letters, reports, and oral presentations and holistic scoring method for Analytical Writing Assessment (AWA) tasks required for the Graduate Management Admissions Test (GMAT).

- Chapter learning objectives, an outline, and teaching suggestions for each chapter.

- Answers to end-of-chapter review questions and suggested solutions to exercises, e-mail applications, Communication in Action cases, applications, and cases for analysis.

- Suggested Readings lists for each chapter that direct students to articles to supplement the text and expose them to real-world communication strategies.

- Transparency masters that contain solutions to exercises and cases, formatted for clear, easy projection.

Test Bank (Print and MicroExam)

The **Test Bank** includes approximately 1,000 test questions, 25 percent of which are new to the Eleventh Edition. Each test bank chapter includes a correlation table that classifies each question according to type and learning objective. There are 20 true-false, 30 multiple choice, and 5 short-answer questions for each chapter and Appendix A. Page references from the text are included. You can select factually and application oriented questions by referring to the marginal notation, *fact* or *appl* for the classification of each multiple choice question. About 75 percent of the questions are factual and 25 percent are application. These class-tested questions have been evaluated for clarity and accuracy.

South-Western's automated testing program, **MicroExam 4.0**, contains all the questions from the printed test bank, with a pull-down menu that allows you to edit, add, delete, or randomly mix questions for customized tests.

Color Acetate Transparencies and PowerPoint® Screens

In addition to the transparency masters included in the *Instructor's Resource Manual*, a package of approximately 100 fully developed one-, two-, and four-color overhead **transparencies** is available to adopters. The package is keyed to the text and includes many of the figures in the text, key communication concepts, activities designed to reinforce concepts presented in the text, and solutions to selected end-of-chapter activities.

The acetates are also available on a presentation disk that contains files created with **PowerPoint**®. (PowerPoint is a registered trademark of Microsoft Corporation.) You simply load the files pertaining to a specific lecture and display them as needed. You will need a personal computer and LCD technology to use the presentation disk in lieu of transparencies.

Study Guide

The **Study Guide** reinforces learning and includes three types of exercises:

- *Review Questions.* Students complete true/false and multiple choice questions for each chapter to help them master key principles. Twenty-five percent of the study guide questions are new. The feedback provided for each incorrect response clearly explains why the student's response is wrong and directs him or her to a page in the textbook for further study. Building this solid theoretical foundation will prepare your students for the applications (writing problems) in the text and will lead to improved scores on objective tests.

- *Practical applications for Chapters 9-18.* Students must solve three business-writing problems for each chapter, one of which is new to the Eleventh Edition. For the first two applications, students critique portions of texts (paragraphs within an entire letter or sections of letters that are difficult to write) and revise accordingly. Then, students compare their critiques and revisions to a succinct list of strengths, weaknesses, and suggested revisions. Before tackling the third application, students answer critical thinking questions that require them to analyze the situation and organize their thoughts. Comparing their work to the suggested answers allows students to compose the required document with increased confidence. Finally, they compare their document with the suggested solution and are prepared to write a similar document for evaluation.

- *Comprehensive review of major grammatical principles with exercises and answers.*

Videotapes with Teaching and Learning Materials

Six videotapes allow students to go inside real companies, meet business executives, and learn effective communication strategies. Each video ends with "Business Tips," a focused review of the major principles the executive explained. The videos have been carefully prepared to correspond with the major concepts presented in each of the six parts of *Business Communications*.

Teaching and learning materials are available to help you integrate these videotapes in your classroom. A full-page discussion of each tape appears in the appropriate place within the text. Each of these "Video Connections" previews the major points discussed in the film, includes five discussion questions that you can assign for homework or use to promote class discussion, and includes an application requiring students to apply key principles. (Students must write letters and memos for video applications in Parts 4-6 after writing has been introduced.)

The video segments include

- Part 1 (Chapter 3)   Public Speaking
                              Salsbury Communications, Inc.
                              Ventura County, California

- Part 2 (Chapter 4)   Intercultural Communication
                              Pacific Bell Directory
                              Orange County, California

- Part 3 (Chapter 8)   Revising and Proofreading
                              Amatulli and Associates
                              Cincinnati, Ohio

- Part 4 (Chapter 11)   Writing to Persuade
                              C. Pharr Marketing Communications
                              Dallas, Texas

- Part 5 (Chapter 14)   Communicating About Work and Jobs
                              Venture Stores, Inc.
                              St. Louis, Missouri

- Part 6 (Chapter 15)   Research Methods and the Report Process
                              Inteleco
                              Little Rock, Arkansas

ACKNOWLEDGMENTS

The authors express their sincere appreciation to all persons who have contributed to this textbook. These include

- The many faculty members with whom we have worked and the many professional educators who have reviewed, critiqued, and made significant contributions to each edition, and particularly to this one. These truly professional educators include

    Asberdine Alford   Linda L. Labin
    Suffolk Community College   Husson College

    Janice P. Burke   James A. Manos
    South Suburban College   California State University, Northridge

    Mildred S. Franceschi   Jolene D. Scriven
    Valencia Community College   Northern Illinois University

    Carolyn Hagler   Martha L. Soderholm
    University of Southern Mississippi York College

    Carrolle H. Kampermann
    Baylor University

- Instructors and other professionals who assisted in the preparation of special textual features and ancillary materials that coordinate with the content of the text. These individuals are Debbie DuFrene, Stephen F. Austin State University; Roger Conaway, University of Texas at Tyler; Mary Lea Ginn; Mona Casady, Southwest Missouri State University; and Mark Di Stasi, Paradigm Communication Group.

- Students in Dr. Lehman's classes, who completed many of the new exercises and suggested changes.

- Mark Lehman, who generously contributed his wealth of experience to aid in developing challenging business-world problems similar to those encountered in today's business environment; Lee Wilkins, for her creative contributions to portions of the text; and Julie Liddell, for her tireless assistance in various capacities.

We also appreciate the help provided by the various members of the South-Western College Publishing staff that made this edition possible. Lastly, we also thank our spouses, Mark Lehman, Maxine Himstreet, and Maxine Baty, and Dr. Lehman's young sons, Matthew and Stephen, for their constant support throughout such a lengthy and demanding project.

Carol M. Lehman   William C. Himstreet   Wayne Murlin Baty

BRIEF
CONTENTS

CONTENTS

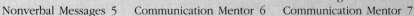

2 Organizational Setting for Business Communication 31

3 Public Speaking and Oral Reporting 51

PART 2

ANALYZING CRITICAL FACTORS INFLUENCING COMMUNICATION EFFECTIVENESS 79

4 Intercultural Communication 80

5 Business Communication Technology 107

PART 3

THE WRITING PROCESS 171

PART 4

COMMUNICATING THROUGH LETTERS, MEMORANDUMS, AND E-MAIL MESSAGES 239

9 Writing About the Pleasant and the Routine 240

10 Writing About the Unpleasant 281

11 Writing to Persuade 317

12 Writing Special Letters 367

PART 5

COMMUNICATING ABOUT WORK AND JOBS 397

17 Organizing and Writing
Short Reports and Proposals 551

18 Writing a Formal Report 589

APPENDICES

A Document Format and Layout Guide A-1

PHOTO CREDITS

p.1, Part 1 Opener, © Zigy Kalzuny/Tony Stone Images

p. 2, Chapter 1 Opener, © Roger Mear/Tony Stone Images

p. 15, © SWP

p. 17, © Tony Stone Images/Bruce Bosler

p. 31, Chapter 2 Opener, © Marc Pokempner/ Tony Stone Worldwide, Ltd.

p. 41, © The Stock Market/Chris Collins

p. 42, © Tony Stone Images, Dan Bosler

p. 51, Chapter 3 Opener, © Steve Allen/Liaison

p. 60, © Tony Stone Images/Tim Brown

p. 62, © Tony Stone Images/Robert E. Daemmrich

p. 81, Part 2 Opener, © Lois & Bob Schlowsky/ Tony Stone Images

p. 82, Chapter 4 Opener, © Mingasson/Liaison

p. 98, © Chicago Department of Aviation

p. 100, © Tony Stone Images/Charles Gupton

p. 107, Chapter 5 Opener, © Duclos-Guichard-Goover/Gamma-Liaison

p. 109, © Shooting Star/Gene Trindl

p. 111, © IBM

p. 145, Chapter 6 Opener, © Paramount/ Shooting Star

p. 147, © SWP

p. 157, © Liaison/Francis Apesteguy

p. 171, Part 3 Opener, © Pete McArthur/Tony Stone Images

p. 172, Chapter 7 Opener, © Gamma-Liaison

p. 188, © Saturn Corporation

p. 191, © Tony Stone Images/Henley & Savage

p. 211, Chapter 8 Opener, © Poulides/Thatcher/ Tony Stone Images

p. 214, © Tony Stone Images/Dan Bosler

p. 231, © NASA

p. 239, Part 4 Opener, © Tony Garcia/Tony Stone Images

p. 240, Chapter 9 Opener, © Bill Staley/Tony Stone Worldwide, Ltd.

p. 242, © Tony Stone Images/Roger Tully

p. 264, © Tony Stone Images/Jon Riley

p. 281, Chapter 10 Opener, © Tom Dietrich/Tony Stone Images

p. 283, © AP Wide World

p. 285, © David R. Frazier/Tony Stone Worldwide, Ltd.

p. 317, Chapter 11 Opener, © Daniel Bosler/ Tony Stone Images

p. 321, © Bob Krist/Tony Stone Images

p. 332, © UPI/Bettman Newsphotos

p. 367, Chapter 12 Opener, © Uniphoto, Inc.

p. 370, © Frank Herholdt/Tony Stone Images

p. 376, Courtesy NBC, The LeProvost

p. 383, © Andy Sacks/Tony Stone Images

p. 397, Part 5 Opener, © Ken Fisher/Tony Stone Images

p. 398, Chapter 13 Opener, © Erik Von Fischer/ Photonics Graphics

p. 409, © Olympia/Reuters/Bettman

p. 430, © DeWya/Sipa/Blecker

p. 449, Chapter 14 Opener, © 1995 Ron Forth Photography

p. 458, © SWP

p. 480, © John Madere/The Stock Market

p. 495, Part 6 Opener, © Bruce Ayers/Tony Stone Images

p. 496, Chapter 15 Opener, © D. E. Cox/Tony Stone Images

p. 502, © Don Smetzer/Tony Stone Worldwide, Ltd.

p. 511, © Ian O'Leary/Tony Stone Images

p. 527, Chapter 16 Opener, © Archive Photos

p. 532, © Dream Quest Images/Electric Images, Inc.

p. 544

p. 551, Chapter 17 Opener, © Wayne Williams/ Shooting Star

p. 563, © Tom Tracy/Tony Stone Images

p. 573, © Jim Pickerell/Tony Stone Images

P. 589, Chapter 18 Opener, © Reuter/Bettman

p. 596, © Steve Allen/Gama Liaison

STUDENT FOREWORD

EFFECTIVE COMMUNICATION SKILLS:

KEY INGREDIENTS IN CAREER SUCCESS

What is success? Is it graduating at the top of your class? Getting elected to an office? Being on a winning sports team? Inventing a new product? Getting a promotion?

Success means different things to different people. In the most general sense, success usually means achieving the goals you have set for yourself. For many people, goals for success involve having meaningful work, financial security, a family and home, and the ability to work for and contribute to the causes of your choice.

What goals you set, how you set them, and how you define your personal vision of success is up to you. Achieving success is then largely dependent on hard work and your commitment to developing the skills necessary to reaching the goals you set for yourself.

As a business student, your vision of success likely includes a career that will be filled with many challenges and responsibilities. Whether you aspire to be a manager, accountant, economist, financial analyst, computer programmer, market researcher, or any other professional, your ability to communicate effectively is essential. Good speaking and writing skills often are the only qualities that can bring your ability to the attention of others and put you first in line for a deserved promotion or challenging assignment.

Business leaders today adamantly support the relevance of communication skills to career success. In a survey of leading firms in the United States, executives disagreed on the relative importance of numerous managerial skills, but virtually all agreed that *communication and interpersonal skills* are second only to integrity (Smith, 1991). Communication skills are a common thread throughout many of the anecdotes of a professional's progress toward career success often included in *The Wall Street Journal* and other business publications. The following statements from executives indicate the importance they attach to communication skills:

> *Hugh B. Jacks, President and Owner, Potential Enterprises & Adventure Safaris:* Learning to communicate well should be a top priority for anyone aspiring to lead or advance in a career. Strong technical skills are needed, but technical ability alone will not result in career advancement. Those who develop only technical skills always will work *for* people who have both technical and leadership abilities, and communication is the key ingredient in leadership.

> *Dennis R. Beresford, Chairman, Financial Accounting Standards Board:* In accounting and all other professions, we must have the appropriate technical skills. But if we cannot communicate what we know, the value of the technical skills is lessened. For example, knowing how to compute corporate income taxes is a valuable skill. Being able to tell others how to do it magnifies the value of that technical skill. Others can capitalize on your knowledge only if you can communicate it.

> *Cynthia Pharr, President & CEO, C. Pharr Marketing Communications:* More than ever, sharp communication skills are essential to success. Ronald Reagan was called "the great communicator" and considered the "media president" because of his powerful ability to persuade via the media. Similar skills are required of today's business executives. Recent estimates are that chief executive officers of America's largest companies spend over 70 percent of their time on external affairs—communicating the messages of their companies. Businesspeople aspiring to top management slots should be increasingly eager to improve their ability to communicate, especially their public speaking skills.

Communication in today's business environment is becoming increasingly important because of rapidly changing computer technology and the highly competitive global economy. Businesses of all sizes—not just large corporations—are using computers to handle the large volume of information that must be processed quickly. Managers are turning to executive workstations to increase their productivity and save time. Primary applications include word processing, spreadsheets, data management, desktop publishing, graphics, and telecommunications. Business graduates who can communicate effectively using electronic communication technology will compete more favorably for available positions. Beginning businesspeople possessing these skills are more likely to earn respect, admiration, and positive performance appraisals from their supervisors.

APPLICANTS ARE SCREENED FOR COMMUNICATION SKILLS

Because the ability to communicate effectively plays an important part in a businessperson's success on the job, many employers have begun to view the ability to write and speak effectively as an important factor in selecting employees. Therefore, employers and professional certifying groups are screening applicants for skills in oral and written communication. For example:

- BellSouth Services requires applicants to complete an extensive questionnaire that includes essay questions. In addition, applicants are given a test similar to the ACT college entrance exam that includes a section on word usage.

- A small manufacturing firm requires applicants for all positions, including line workers, to write instructions for completing a typical task.

- Interviewers ask for specific evidence of applicants' communication and interpersonal skills. In other words, applicants are not asked, "Can you communicate well," but rather, "Give me a specific incident when you communicated effectively or worked well with others." This question is often followed with, "Good; now give me another example. . . ."

- The American Institute of Certified Public Accountants (AICPA) issued a statement presenting its view of communication skills (Roy and MacNeil, 1967, pp. 218-219):

  To [CPAs] the ability to express [themselves] well is more than the hallmark of educated [persons]; it is a professional necessity. Inability to express [their] findings in understandable, explicit, unambiguous, intelligible English can be self-defeating, potentially misleading, and possibly disastrous to clients, creditors, and investors. . . . We feel justified, therefore . . . in being unequivocal about this requirement of the common body of knowledge for beginning CPAs: *Candidates who cannot write the English language at least as well as a minimum-threshold should be denied admission to the profession, if need be on this account alone.*

The state boards of accountancy are standing behind this powerful statement. CPA exams are now evaluated for communication competence as well as the technical content. Business departments are revising their curricula and companies are providing in-service training with emphasis on refining communication and interpersonal skills.

THE VALUE OF GOOD COMMUNICATION SKILLS

Having good communication skills can give a job candidate an edge over other prospects. Once hired, developing these abilities can lead to promotions and advancements. However, people who have poor oral and written communication skills cannot expect to get the best jobs, nor can they expect to earn promotions if they do not make the effort to improve these vital skills. In some cases, employees have lost their jobs due to their inadequate communication skills. A high percentage of accounting firms reported poor writing skills as a major reason for terminating entry-level accountants (Cherry and Wilson, 1987). This list goes on and on.

How can poor communication skills alone merit such serious consequences? Xerox's response is concise but quite clear: "People who can't communicate aren't much use in a corporate environment." Exxon executives advise, "The world's best idea isn't any good if the originator can't explain it or work with others to make it a reality." Communication skills are also at the top of Kodak's list: "If someone has a good idea but can't sell it, how will that idea ever be any good to the company? Ideas must be sold to be used" ("Making It in the Corporate World," 1990, p. 9).

These executives and many more agree that employees with inadequate communication skills contribute very little to a company. Furthermore, employees' ineffective messages can cause costly mistakes and damage a company's reputation. For example, suppose a supervisor's unclear instructions caused employees to redo several tasks, which in turn delayed production three weeks. The production delay could cause customers to lose faith in the company and possibly to cancel their orders.

Production backups and lost customers are not the only fallout from this supervisor's inadequate communication. The frustrated employees are likely to have negative feelings toward the supervisor. Low morale often leads to reduced productivity. In addition to costly mistakes, unnecessary delays, and a frustrated workforce, the company must also bear the cost of selecting and training both the employees who are subsequently fired for poor writing skills and their replacements.

The message is becoming clear to more and more companies today. Companies facing today's intense competition *cannot afford* the costs of ineffective communication. In addition to screening employees for communication skills, some companies are providing writing and speaking instruction for their employees at all levels—including presidents and chief executive officers. These companies realize the value of good communication. They see that time and money are wasted and goodwill is damaged when communication is ineffective. Employees who possess good oral and written communication skills are valuable to their employers. They continue to practice and develop their skills and are rewarded for their efforts with recognition and advancement.

HOW CAN YOU DEVELOP EFFECTIVE COMMUNICATION SKILLS?

Completing this business communication course is an excellent way for you to begin acquiring the communication skills needed in today's highly competitive, automated business environment. The textbook is carefully designed to help you communicate effectively. You can

1. Read and study up-to-date discussions to master basic principles of communication (written and oral).
2. Study the numerous examples of poorly written and well-written messages and then incorporate effective writing techniques in your own writing.

3. Complete the end-of-chapter activities to gain necessary practice in applying the principles of good writing when communicating sound business decisions.

While learning important communication principles, you also will have a priceless opportunity to "look over the shoulders" of several successful business leaders who will serve as your "communication mentors." After you have studied a particular principle, one or more of your mentors will discuss how a communication principle actually works in today's dynamic business environment, share related strategies for communicating effectively, or simply provide concrete advice for developing a needed skill.

Your communication mentors represent various disciplines including accounting, finance, communications, public relations, and many others. When you see a *communication mentor photo and screen*, you will know you are "looking over the shoulder" of one of your mentors. To help you become acquainted with your communication mentors, read the brief introductions at the end of this section. Take a moment to connect the mentors' names with their photographs, the companies or organizations they represent, and their basic responsibilities. The better you know your mentors, the more closely you can relate to them as they contribute their valuable skills to your professional development.

Like many of the technical skills you have acquired, developing effective communication skills rests on your ability to reason logically and to make sound decisions. However, making the following commitments will facilitate your developing effective communication skills:

1. *Attempt to see things from your audience's perspective rather than from your own.* That is, have empathy for your audience. Being empathetic isn't as simple as it seems, particularly when dealing with today's diverse workforce. Erase the mind-set, "I know what *I* want to say and how *I* want to say it." Instead, ask, "How would my audience react to this message? How can I present this message so that my audience can easily understand it?"

2. *Revise your documents until you cannot see any additional ways to improve them.* Resist the temptation to think of your first draft as your last draft. Instead, look for ways to improve and be willing to incorporate valid suggestions once you have completed a draft. Remember that skilled speech writers might rewrite a script 15 or 20 times. Writers in public relations firms revise brochures and advertising copy until perhaps only a comma in the final draft is recognizable from the first draft. Your diligent revising will yield outstanding dividends. Specifically, the audience (your supervisor, your employees, or a client/customer, for example) is more likely to understand and accept your message. The dividend of diligent revising in this course is the increased probability that you will receive a favorable grade.

3. *Be willing to allow others to make suggestions for improving your writing.* Most people consider their writing very personal. That is, they are reluctant to share what they have written with others and are easily offended if others suggest changes. This syndrome, called *writer's pride of ownership*, can needlessly prevent you from seeking assistance from experienced writers—a proven method of improving communication skills. On the job, you will share your writing with the recipient (your supervisor, your employees, or a client/customer). Because a great deal of what is written in business today is written collaboratively, you will be required to subject your writing to review by others. To prepare for this workplace requirement, use this class to become

more comfortable with allowing others to read and critique your writing. You have nothing to lose but much to gain: exposure to successful techniques used by more seasoned writers and the chance to improve your writing skills.

To capitalize on the technical skills in your career field, you must begin developing effective communication skills. Once you are competent in your field *and* effective in communicating that knowledge to others, you can reap the rewards sure to come your way: increased ability to secure a job, to keep a job, and to earn deserved promotions to positions of higher visibility and responsibility.

REFERENCES

Cherry, A. A., & Wilson, L. A. (1987). A study of the writing skills of accounting majors in California. Unpublished study.

Making it in the corporate world. (1990, March). *Tomorrow's Business Leader*, pp. 8-10.

Roy, R. H., & MacNeill, J. H. (1967). *Horizons for a profession: The common body of knowledge for certified public accountants.* New York: American Institute of Certified Public Accountants.

Smith, K. V., & Savoian, R. (1991). Climbing to the top: Rising through the corporate ladder. *Review of Business, 13* (3), 34.

COMMUNICATION MENTOR

As chairman of the Financial Accounting Standards Board (FASB) since January 1987, I conduct meetings and public hearings of the FASB and act as its spokesperson before many groups, including government agencies and congressional committees. The FASB is the private-sector body that establishes standards for financial reporting by businesses and not-for-profit organizations.

Dennis R. Beresford
Chairman,
Financial Accounting Standards Board

COMMUNICATION MENTOR

My duties involve (a) supervising, directing, and controlling the affairs of the Appraisal Institute, (b) representing the Appraisal Institute with the directives, resolutions, and policies of the Board of Directors, and (c) acting on behalf of the Appraisal Institute when it is the sole voting member of another not-for-profit corporation.

Bernard J. Fountain, MAI, SRA
1993 President
Appraisal Institute

COMMUNICATION MENTOR

I oversee the audit, tax, and business advisory practices for Arthur Andersen's offices in Houston, New Orleans, San Antonio, Oklahoma City, Tulsa, and Denver. In this capacity, I am responsible for the quality and development of our practice in this region. The main components of this responsibility include recruiting and training talented professionals, meeting and exceeding our clients' expectations of service, and aggressively expanding our practice in the areas of our competence.

H. Devon Graham, Jr.
Southwest Regional Managing Partner
Arthur Andersen & Co.

COMMUNICATION MENTOR

As head of the Investor Relations and Corporation Communications Division, I am responsible for investor relations, financial public relations, and general media communications of California Federal Bank, one of the nation's largest savings institutions. I am a member of the Bank's Executive Management Committee and the Community Development Committee.

James F. Hurley
Executive Vice President
California Federal Bank

COMMUNICATION MENTOR

As president and owner of Potential Enterprises, I provide consulting services to various types of businesses. My major role at Adventure Safaris involves organizing and directing worldwide hunting and photographic safaris. I also serve on the board of directors of AmSouth Bancorporation, Provident Insurance Co., and Acme Cleveland Corporation.

Hugh B. Jacks
President and Owner
Potential Enterprises and Adventure Safaris

COMMUNICATION MENTOR

As president of INTELECO, I coordinate the work of a consulting group that specializes in the wireless telecommunications industry. Our clients are primarily outside of the United States; services include marketing and information management.

David Martin
President
INTELECO

COMMUNICATION   MENTOR

I direct the communications effort of the Professional Golfers' Association of America, the world largest working sports organization. My responsibilities include (1) supervising public relations efforts to promote the association; (2) coordinating media relations programs to assist the nation's media in their coverage of the PGA; and (3) overseeing internal and external communications vehicles such as books, programs, magazines, news releases, and speeches. I am also responsible for developing an effective corporate identification program.

Terence E. McSweeney
Director of Communications
PGA of America

COMMUNICATION   MENTOR

Maintaining banking relationships, bonding, and insurance is my chief responsibility. My duties also include developing, implementing, and updating the strategic plan. To promote community relations, I am required to speak publicly for civic and non-profit organizations.

Shirley F. Olson
Vice President & Chief Financial Officer
J. J. Ferguson Sand and Gravel/Prestress/Precast

COMMUNICATION   MENTOR

In my role as president and chief executive officer of a full-service public relations firm, I develop communication strategies for our clients, manage a firm composed of professional communicators, lead new business development activities, and provide senior-level counsel to executives.

Cynthia Pharr
President & CEO
C. Pharr Marketing Communications

COMMUNICATION   MENTOR

As a self-employed consultant, my primary activities consist of serving as an independent off-site Chief Financial Officer (CFO) to various companies and occasional engagements to provide litigation support and business valuation services. Previous experience includes developing professional staff at Price Waterhouse, supervising over 300 people while serving as CFO in a multi-location retail corporation, and serving as the primary business liaison to a large federal government agency.

R. D. Saenz
Business Consultant

COMMUNICATION   MENTOR

As a national bank examiner, I help to foster the safety and soundness of the national banking system. As part of the regulatory process, I aid in monitoring national banks' compliance with the law and promote the competitiveness, integrity, and stability of financial services. I either conduct examinations of national banks or function as a member of an examining team. I am also the local recruitment coordinator for my office and, therefore, conduct many of the initial interviews of potential examiners.

Gabriel Swan
National Bank Examiner
Office of the Comptroller of the Currency

COMMUNICATION   MENTOR

My primary duty is to make investments that have attractive risk-adjusted rates of return on behalf of the Prudential Insurance Company and its clients. This work involves evaluating the risks/rewards associated with investment strategies and structuring transactions to minimize risks and maximize returns. Currently, I am investigating investment opportunities in emerging markets such as Eastern Europe and Latin America.

Sajan K. Thomas
Vice President
Prudential Institutional Investors

C O M M U N I C A T I O N   M E N T O R

My responsibilities are to manage and oversee the firm's practice of accounting, audit, and business advisory services in the former Soviet Union, now referred to as the Confederation of Independent States (CIS). Our present offices include Moscow and St. Petersburg in Russia, Kiev in the Ukraine, and Almaty in Kazakhstan. I am responsible for the quality and development of our overall practice and serve numerous clients as engagement partner. I am involved in all areas of recruiting and training local personnel with the objective of eventually turning the practice over to national personnel.

Larry Wilson
Partner-in-Charge
Arthur Andersen, Moscow

PART 1

COMMUNICATION FOUNDATIONS

AND ORAL COMMUNICATION

CHAPTER 1

INTERPERSONAL

COMMUNICATION

AND LISTENING

OBJECTIVES

When you have completed Chapter 1, you will be able to

1 Define communication and describe the main purposes for communication in business.

2 Discuss the importance of nonverbal messages and explain the difficulties involved in interpretation.

3 Explain the communication process model and the ultimate objective of the communication process.

4 Explain how behavioral sciences and management theories (Maslow, McGregor's Theory X and Y, total quality management, stroking, and Johari Window) help management understand the role of communication in the workplace.

5 Discuss the benefits of good listening and identify causes of poor listening.

6 Identify the four styles of listening and specify strategies for improving listening for each style.

Embarking on a polar expedition is no casual decision. The scientists and adventurers who plan such an undertaking know the risks involved and have weighed the risks and the benefits. They know physical stamina and fitness are essential for survival and frequently exercise all major muscle groups in preparation for the ordeal. In addition, they must possess the proper equipment for such a venture: tents, warm sleeping bags and clothing, navigational instruments, food, fuel, and other necessities, including plans for emergencies. Finally, the adventurer knows that research is integral—a matter of life and death. He or she must know something of the terrain, the weather patterns, and the hazards that must be overcome. Learning from previous explorers' successes and failures is wise.

The true adventurer or explorer will not be daunted by sub-zero temperatures and icy mountains looming in his or her path. Instead, she or he will be driven to accept the challenge, anticipating the physical and emotional rush upon reaching the top of the world after pushing the body and mind to the limit. On each expedition, the explorer visualizes the thrill of getting past the barrier of ice, snow, and the elements to see the expanse of northern sky, knowing that he or she has accomplished a task that only few have done.

In some ways, communication can be similar to the challenge of a polar expedition. Developing good communication skills takes practice and the desire for challenge. Frequently, proper communication requires research and extra effort. Many barriers to effective communication exist and must be overcome. The successful manager tackles the obstacles head-on, looking forward to taking down communication barriers and reaping the rewards good communication skills bring. Studying this textbook is an excellent way to begin refining your oral and written communication skills so that you are prepared for the many communication challenges awaiting you.

PURPOSES OF COMMUNICATION

What is communication? For our purposes, **communication** is the process of exchanging information and meaning between or among individuals through a common system of symbols, signs, and behavior. Other words often used to describe the communication process are expressing feelings, conversing, speaking, corresponding, writing, listening, and exchanging.

LEARNING OBJECTIVE 1

Communication is the process of exchanging information and meaning between or among individuals through a common system of symbols, signs, and behavior.

People communicate to satisfy needs in both their work and nonwork lives. People want to be heard, appreciated, and wanted. They also want to accomplish tasks and achieve goals. Obviously, then, a major purpose of communication is to help people feel good about themselves and about their friends, groups, and organizations. Generally, people communicate for three basic purposes: to inform, to persuade, and to entertain.

Studies have shown that managers spend approximately 60 to 80 percent of their time involved in some form of communication:

How frequently does a manager communicate during a typical workday?

- Attending meetings and writing reports related to strategic plans and company policy.
- Presenting information to large and small groups.
- Explaining and clarifying management procedures and work assignments.
- Coordinating the work of various employees, departments, and other work groups.

- Evaluating and counseling employees.
- Promoting the company's products/services and image.

Understanding more about the process of communication will help you improve your communication skills. Then, an abundance of practice will allow you to refine verbal and nonverbal communication skills, which are used so frequently during a usual workday and are so critical to career success.

NONVERBAL COMMUNICATION

LEARNING OBJECTIVE 2

Distinguish between verbal and nonverbal communication.

Managers use verbal and nonverbal messages to communicate a message to a recipient. *Verbal* means "through the use of words," either written or spoken. *Nonverbal* means "without the use of words." Although most concern in communication study is given to verbal messages, studies show that nonverbal messages account for approximately 93 percent of the total meaning (Mehrabian, 1971). Nonverbal communication includes *metacommunication* and *kinesic* messages.

Metacommunication

A **metacommunication** is a message that, although *not* expressed in words, accompanies a message that *is* expressed in words. For example, "Don't be late for work" communicates caution; yet the sentence may imply (but not express in words) such additional ideas as "You are frequently late, and I'm warning you," or "I doubt your dependability" (metacommunications). "Your solution is perfect" may also convey a metacommunication such as "You are efficient," or "I certainly like your work." Whether you are speaking or writing, you can be confident that those who receive your messages will be sensitive to the messages expressed in words and to the accompanying messages that are present but not expressed in words.

Kinesic Communication

People constantly send meaning through **kinesic** communication, an idea expressed through nonverbal behavior. In other words, receivers gain additional meaning from what they see and hear—the visual and the vocal:

- Visual—gestures, winks, smiles, frowns, sighs, attire, grooming, and all kinds of body movements.
- Vocal—intonation, projection, and resonance of the voice.

Some examples of kinesic messages and the meanings they may convey follow:

Action	Possible Kinesic Message
A wink or light chuckle follows a statement.	"Don't believe what I just said."
A manager is habitually late for staff meetings.	"My time is more important than yours. You can wait for me."

The handshake, an important business custom, is an important part of your first impression. Does your handshake communicate warmth, sincerity, and credibility?

Action	Possible Kinesic Message
A supervisor lightly links his arm around an employee's shoulders at the end of a conference.	"Everything is fine; I'm here to help you solve this problem." Alternatively, the action may be considered paternalistic—a parent comforting a child after necessary discipline.
An employee smokes in areas other than those designated for smoking.	"I don't have to obey company rules that infringe on my personal rights. A little smoke won't hurt anyone."
A job applicant submits a resume containing numerous spelling and grammatical errors.	"My spelling and grammar skills are deficient." An alternative meaning is "For you I didn't care to do my very best."
A supervisor looks up but then returns her attention to her current project when an employee arrives for a performance appraisal interview.	"The performance appraisal interview is not an important process. You are interrupting more important work."
A group leader sits at a position other than at the head of the table.	"I want to demonstrate my equality with other members."

Overcoming Barriers Created by Nonverbal Messages

Metacommunications and kinesic communications have characteristics that all communicators should take into account:

1. *Nonverbal messages cannot be avoided.* Both written and spoken words convey ideas in addition to the ideas contained in the words used. All actions—and even the lack of action—have meaning to those who observe them.
2. *Nonverbal messages may have different meanings for different people.* If a committee member smiles after making a statement, one member may conclude that the speaker was trying to be funny; another may conclude that the speaker was pleased about having made such a great contribution; another may see the smile but have no reaction to it.
3. *Nonverbal messages may be intentional or unintentional.* "You are right about that" may be intended to mean "I agree with you" or "You are right on *this* issue, but you have been wrong on all others discussed." The sender may or may not intend to convey the latter and may or may not be aware of doing so.
4. *Nonverbal messages can contradict the accompanying verbal message and affect whether your message is understood or believed.* If the verbal and non-verbal messages contradict, which do you suppose the receiver will believe? Exactly—the old adage, "Actions speak more loudly than words" is correct. To illustrate the impact of the nonverbal message, Decker (1992, p. 85), a leading communication consultant, calls to mind a person who says, "'I'm happy to be here,' but looks at the floor, talking in a halting, tremulous voice, clasping his hands together in front of his body in an edgy, inhibited 'fig-leaf' posture." His verbal and nonverbal messages are contradictory; consequently, his audience may not trust his words. Likewise, consider:

COMMUNICATION MENTOR

Whether you are the sender or receiver, one skill will help you more than any other. Unfortunately, this skill only comes from experience. We're talking about developing an "ear" for nuance. Most of us say as much indirectly—through inflection, pauses, accelerations, and volume changes—as we do directly.

Learning from these subtle suggestions is not analytical detective work but requires making the extra effort to lean mentally into what the other person is saying or asking and truly participating in the feeling being expressed. Also, you must block out your own agenda for the time being. You will learn more from this skill than you will ever learn from so-called "body language."

James F. Hurley
Executive Vice President
California Federal Bank

- The detrimental effect spelling and grammar errors in job credentials might have on a job applicant's success in an interview. The verbal message communicates impeccable qualification. However, the interviewer receives the contradictory nonverbal message that implies the applicant is careless or has inadequate language skills.
- How speculatively a reader might react to "We appreciate your writing to us when you have a problem" when nothing has been done to solve the problem or to explain the lack of action.

5. *Nonverbal messages may get more attention than verbal messages.* If a supervisor rhythmically taps a pen while making a statement, the words may not register in the employee's mind. An error in basic grammar may get much more attention than does the idea that is being transmitted.

6. *Nonverbal messages provide clues about the sender's background and motives.* For example, excessive use of big words may suggest that a person reads widely or has an above-average education; it may also suggest a need for social recognition or insecurity about social background.

7. *Nonverbal messages are influenced by the circumstances surrounding the communication.* Assume that two men, Ward and Sam, are friends who work for the same firm. When they are together on the job, Ward sometimes puts his hand on Sam's shoulder. To Sam, the act may mean nothing more than "We are close friends." But suppose Ward becomes a member of a committee that subsequently denies a promotion for Sam. Afterward, the same act could mean "we are still friends"; but it could also arouse resentment. Because of the circumstances, the same act could now mean something like "Watch the hand that pats; it can also stab."

8. *Nonverbal messages may be beneficial or harmful.* Words or actions can be accompanied by nonverbal messages that help or hurt the sender's purpose.

COMMUNICATION MENTOR

Frequently the unintended misuse of a word, the inflection of a word, or a gesture can lead to misinterpretation. This can happen to even the most effective communicators. Eliciting feedback from an individual or an audience will ensure that the words you intend to communicate are being heard.

Terence E. McSweeney
Director of Communications
PGA of America

Metacommunications and kinesic communications can convey something like "I am efficient in my business and considerate of others," or they can convey the opposite. They cannot be eliminated, but they can be made to work for communicators instead of against them.

Although no one can give a set of rules for interpreting nonverbal messages, being aware of their presence and impact will improve your chances of using nonverbal messages effectively.

THE COMMUNICATION PROCESS

Effective communicators realize that communication is not an automatic process. That is, the message is not interpreted correctly just because the manager transmitted it. Rather than thinking, "*Anybody* could understand these instructions; they're crystal clear," the prudent manager anticipates possible breakdowns in the communication process—the unlimited ways the message can be misunderstood. This mind-set motivates the manager to design the initial message effectively and to be prepared to intervene at the appropriate time to ensure that the message received is as close as possible to the message sent.

Consider the simplified form of the communication process model presented in Figure 1-1. The stages of the model are as follows:

1. The sender encodes a message.
2. The sender selects an appropriate channel and transmits the message.
3. The receiver decodes the message.
4. The receiver encodes a message (feedback) to clarify any part of the message not understood. Feedback involves (a) the receiver's encoding a message, (b) the receiver's selecting a channel and transmitting the message, and (c) the sender's decoding the message. The sender and receiver continue to reverse roles until the message is understood.
5. The sender and receiver remove or minimize interferences that hinder the communication process.

LEARNING OBJECTIVE 3

An effective manager anticipates the unlimited ways a message can be misunderstood.

What are the stages of the communication process model?

FIGURE 1-1
*The communication process
model.*

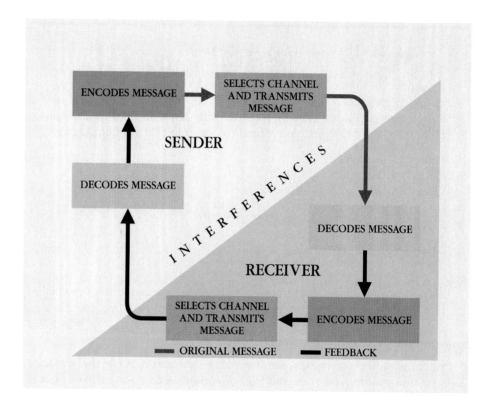

The Sender Encodes the Message

Selecting and organizing
the message is called
encoding.

Knowledge about the
receiver aids the sender in
encoding the message.
What type of information
could be helpful?

The message originates with the sender who transmits it to the receiver. The
sender carefully designs a message by selecting (1) words that clearly convey
the message and (2) nonverbal signals (gestures, stance, tone of voice, and so
on) that reinforce the verbal message. The process of selecting and organizing
the message is referred to as **encoding**. The sender's primary objective is to
encode the message in such a way that the message received is as close as
possible to the message sent. Knowledge of the receiver's educational level,
experience, viewpoints, and other information aid the sender in encoding the
message. If information about the receiver is unavailable, the sender can put
himself or herself in the receiver's position to gain fairly accurate insight for
encoding the message. Chapters 7 and 8 provide guidance in designing the
verbal message effectively; nonverbal communication was covered earlier in this
chapter.

THINK IT OVER
List at least three other
breakdowns in the encoding
process you have experienced.

Obvious breakdowns in the communication process at the encoding stage
occur if the sender uses

- Words not present in the receiver's vocabulary.
- Ambiguous, nonspecific ideas that distort the message.
- Nonverbal signals that contradict the verbal message.
- Expressions such as "uh" or grammatical errors, mannerisms (excessive hand
  movements, jingling keys), or dress that distracts the receiver.

Of course, this list is only a beginning of possible problems at the encoding
stage.

The Sender Selects an Appropriate Channel and Transmits the Message

To increase the likelihood that the receiver will understand the message, the sender carefully selects an appropriate channel for transmitting the message. Three typical communication channels are:

1. *Two-way, face-to-face.* Informal conversations, interviews, oral reports, speeches, and teleconferences.
2. *Two-way, not-face-to-face.* Telephone conversations and intercompany announcements.
3. *One-way, not-face-to-face.* Written documents such as letters, memos, reports, and press releases prepared traditionally or sent electronically (electronic mail, facsimile, voice mail).

Selecting an inappropriate channel can cause the message to be misunderstood and can adversely affect human relations with the receiver. For example, for a very complex subject, a sender might begin with a written document and follow up with a face-to-face discussion after the receiver has had an opportunity to study the document. Written documents are required when legal matters are involved and written records must be retained. A face-to-face meeting is a more appropriate channel for sending sensitive, unpleasant messages. For example, consider a supervisor calling an employee into a private office to discuss the employee's continual violation of safety regulations. A face-to-face meeting provides two distinct benefits: (1) The manager can solicit immediate feedback from the receiver to clarify misunderstandings and inaccuracies in the message. (2) In addition to hearing what the receiver is saying (the verbal message), the manager can "read" equally important nonverbal cues (tone of voice, body movements, and so on). The manager may feel comfortable with what the receiver is saying, but the nonverbal message may indicate that the receiver is overamplifying the problem or is underestimating the importance of the warning. The manager's discerning choice of a channel—meeting with the employee face to face rather than calling or writing a disciplinary memo—marks this manager as sensitive and empathetic, qualities that foster trust and open communication. The benefits of each channel are illustrated in Figure 1-2.

The Receiver Decodes the Message

The receiver is the destination of the message. The receiver's task is to interpret the sender's message, both verbal and nonverbal, with as little distortion as possible. The process of interpreting the message is referred to as **decoding**. Because words and nonverbal signals have different meanings to different people, countless problems can occur at this point in the communication process. Obvious breakdowns in communication occur at this stage if

- The sender inadequately encodes the original message. For example, the sender may use words not present in the receiver's vocabulary; use ambiguous, nonspecific ideas that distort the message; or use nonverbal signals that distract the receiver or contradict the verbal message.
- The receiver is intimidated by the position or authority of the sender. This tension may prevent the receiver from concentrating on the message

What are the three typical communication channels?

THINK IT OVER
Which channel would be the most appropriate for communicating the following messages? Justify your answer.
- Request from a client additional information needed to provide requested services.
- Inform a customer that an order cannot be delivered on the date specified in the contract.
- Inform the sales staff of a special sales incentive (effective six weeks from now).

What are the benefits of a face-to-face meeting?

Decoding is the process of interpreting the message.

Why is a decoded message sometimes different from an encoded one?

TWO-WAY, FACE-TO-FACE
- Instant feedback
- Nonverbal signals

TWO-WAY, NOT-FACE-TO-FACE
- Instant feedback
- Limited nonverbal signals

ONE-WAY, NOT-FACE-TO-FACE
- No instant feedback
- Minimal nonverbal signals

THINK IT OVER
Provide specific examples of breakdowns in decoding that you have experienced.

effectively enough to understand it clearly. Furthermore, an intimidated receiver may be afraid to ask for clarifications because of the perceived fear that questions might be associated with incompetence.

- The receiver is unwilling to attempt to understand the message because the topic is perceived to be too difficult to understand. Regardless of the clarity of a message explaining procedures for operating a computer software program, a receiver terrified of computers may be incapable of decoding the message correctly.

- The receiver is unreceptive to new and different ideas; that is, stereotypical visions and prejudices prevent the receiver from viewing the message with an open mind.

The infinite number of breakdowns possible at each stage of the communication process makes us marvel that mutually satisfying communication ever occurs. The complexity of the communication process amplifies the importance of the next stage in the communication process—feedback to clarify misunderstandings.

The Receiver Encodes a Message to Clarify Any Misunderstandings

Feedback is the receiver's response to the sender's message.

Is feedback sent verbally or nonverbally?

When the receiver responds to the sender's message, the response is called **feedback**. The feedback may prompt the sender to modify or adjust the original message to make it clearer to the receiver. Feedback may be verbal or nonverbal. A remark such as "Could you clarify . . ." or a perplexed facial expression provides clear feedback to the sender that the receiver does not yet understand the message. Conversely, a confident "Yes, I understand" and an upward nod of the head are likely to signal understanding or encouragement.

Interferences Hinder the Process

Senders and receivers must learn to deal with the numerous factors that interfere with the communication process. These factors are referred to as **interferences** or **barriers** to effective communication. Previous examples have illustrated some of the interferences that may occur at various stages of the communication process. Examples include

- Differences in educational level, experience, culture, and other characteristics of the sender and the receiver increase the complexity of encoding and decoding a message.
- Physical interferences occurring in the channel include loud talking near an area where a supervisor is explaining a work assignment, distracting and annoying static on a telephone line, or an overly warm room used for a lengthy staff meeting. Many companies schedule officer retreats at hotels or remote lodges to eliminate physical and mental interferences such as constant interruptions and other distractions present in workday surroundings. These retreats allow employees to disconnect themselves from routine responsibilities enough to participate effectively in strategic planning sessions, leadership development, cultural awareness workshops, and other executive meetings.
- A supervisor too rushed or too insecure to allow subordinates to ask questions or offer suggestions (feedback) creates a formidable barrier to effective communication. This supervisor loses time and money from errors made because unclear messages are not clarified and also generates negative feelings because employees perceive their opinions to be unwelcome.

Study carefully the barriers listed in Figure 1-3, and compile a list of other barriers that affect your ability to communicate with friends, teachers, co-workers, supervisors, and others. By being aware of these interferences, you can make concentrated efforts to remove these interferences whenever possible.

Consider another example to illustrate the stages in the communication process. While reading the following scenario, notice that the sender and receiver function in dual roles. That is, they both serve as sender and receiver, giving and receiving feedback (encoding and decoding messages) until the original receiver understands the message.

What are the consequences of refusing to permit feedback when communicating with others?

THINK IT OVER
Add to this list of interferences to effective communication. What suggestions can you offer for removing or minimizing each interference you listed?

THINK IT OVER
List three major mistakes Rick made while communicating with Allison.

Rick, an irate audit partner, barges into a senior accountant's work area (located in the center of a large, open office) wildly waving a file in his hand. Not seeming to notice that several others were standing nearby and without giving a greeting, Rick rudely throws a report on the desk. He says, "Just look at this report, Allison! Haven't you read any accounting pronouncements during the last two years?"

Startled at first, Allison takes just a few seconds to gain her composure and then replies, "Obviously, Rick, you have a major concern with the Krause report. Could you tell me exactly what the difficulty is?"

A little calmer now, Rick answers, "I've read through this report several times, and I just don't understand. Why doesn't the report contain a disclosure of market risks as required by SFAS No. 105?"

With a quiet sigh, Allison answers, "The industry specialists in our New York office assured me that a market risk disclosure is unnecessary in this case. I included their explanation with complete documentation in a memo placed in the Krause audit file."

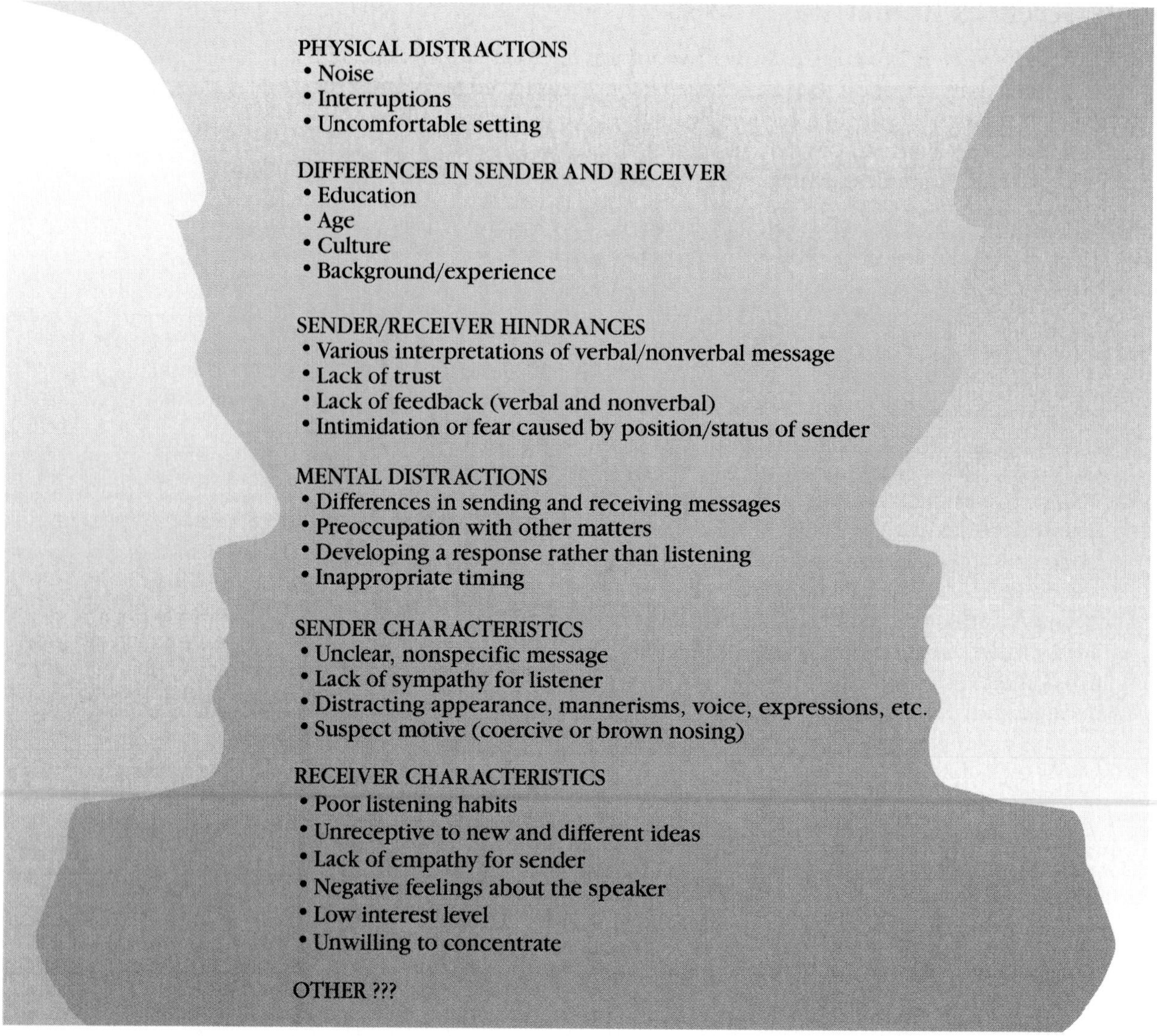

PHYSICAL DISTRACTIONS
• Noise
• Interruptions
• Uncomfortable setting

DIFFERENCES IN SENDER AND RECEIVER
• Education
• Age
• Culture
• Background/experience

SENDER/RECEIVER HINDRANCES
• Various interpretations of verbal/nonverbal message
• Lack of trust
• Lack of feedback (verbal and nonverbal)
• Intimidation or fear caused by position/status of sender

MENTAL DISTRACTIONS
• Differences in sending and receiving messages
• Preoccupation with other matters
• Developing a response rather than listening
• Inappropriate timing

SENDER CHARACTERISTICS
• Unclear, nonspecific message
• Lack of sympathy for listener
• Distracting appearance, mannerisms, voice, expressions, etc.
• Suspect motive (coercive or brown nosing)

RECEIVER CHARACTERISTICS
• Poor listening habits
• Unreceptive to new and different ideas
• Lack of empathy for sender
• Negative feelings about the speaker
• Low interest level
• Unwilling to concentrate

OTHER ???

FIGURE 1-3   Communication barriers.

Nodding his head, Rick says, "Fine; that particular disclosure was my only concern. Prepare the report for my signature, and let's try to get it to the client by tomorrow at the latest. Good work, Allison."

The communication process model will help identify the problems that the partner and accountant dealt with to reach an understanding, as shown in Figure 1-4.

BEHAVIORAL FACTORS AFFECTING COMMUNICATION

LEARNING OBJECTIVE 4   Behavioral scientists working in the fields of sociology and psychology have strongly influenced business management by stressing interpersonal communication problems in the business environment. Understanding these behavior

FIGURE 1-4   The communication process model in action.

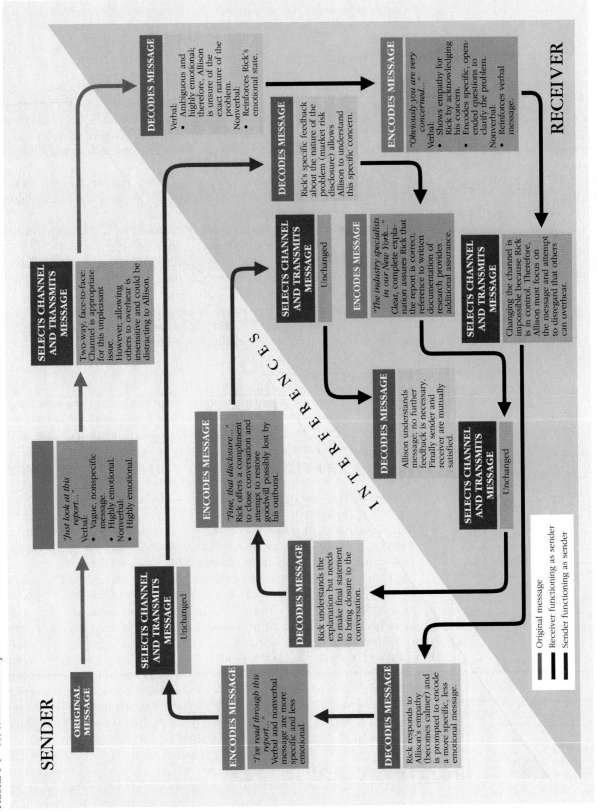

patterns provides supervisors valuable insights that facilitate communication with employees in today's information age.

Human Needs

Effective managers attempt to make each employee feel an important part of the company. Involving people in their work and "humanizing the work-place" appeal to the basic psychological and socio-logical needs of people.

Psychologist Abraham Maslow developed the concept of a hierarchy of needs through which people progress. In our society, most people have reasonably satisfied their lower-level physiological needs and security and safety needs (food, shelter, and protection from the elements and physical danger).

Beyond these two basic need levels, people progress to satisfy the three upper levels: (1) social needs for love, acceptance, and belonging; (2) ego needs to be heard, appreciated, and wanted; and (3) self-actualizing needs, including the need to achieve one's fullest potential through professional, philanthropic, political, educational, and artistic channels.

As people satisfy needs at one level, they move on to the next. The levels that have been satisfied still are present, but their importance diminishes.

Effective communicators are able to identify and appeal to need levels in various individuals or groups. Advertising is designed to appeal to need levels. Luxury car ads appeal to ego needs, toothpaste and deodorant ads appeal to social needs, and home security system ads appeal to security and safety needs. In business, efforts to help people satisfy needs are essential. A satisfied worker is generally more productive than a dissatisfied one.

Management Styles

Managers are empowering employees, the people who can do the most about providing quality goods and services.

Douglas McGregor, a management theorist, attempted to distinguish between the older, traditional view that workers are concerned only about satisfying lower-level needs and the modern view that production can be enhanced by assisting workers in satisfying higher-level needs.

Under the older view, management exercised strong control, empha-sized the job to the exclusion of concern for the individual, and sought to motivate solely through external incentives—a job and a paycheck. McGregor labeled this management style Theory X. Under the modern style, Theory Y, management strives to balance control and individual freedom. By treating the individual as a mature person, management lessens the need for exter-nal motivation: treated as adults, people will act as adults.

The total quality management movement draws on McGregor's assumptions about Theory Y management, creating a more responsible role for the worker in an organization. In a Total Quality Management environment, decision-making power is distributed to the people closest to the problem, those who usually have the best information sources and solutions. Each employee, from the president to the custodian, is expected to solve problems, participate in team-building efforts, and expand the scope of his or her role in the organization. "The goal of employee empowerment is to stop trying to motivate workers with extrinsic incentives as is in the case of traditional practices, and build a work environment in which all employees take pride in their work accomplishments and begin motivating themselves from within" (Hunt, 1993, p. 37).

Earlier efforts to develop greater job satisfaction have involved workers in "team" and "quality circle" programs. Voluntary groups of workers met with supervisors or management periodically to identify production prob-lems and propose solutions. Many quality circles did not receive support

Federal Express is consistently included in the listings of the best U.S. companies for which to work. Over the past five years, 91 percent of its employees responded that they were proud to work for Federal Express. Management policies and actions that foster this high level of job satisfaction include a "no layoff" philosophy, "guaranteed fair treatment procedure" for handling employee grievances (a model used by firms in many industries), and a well-developed recognition program for team and individual contributions to company performance (Hunt, 1993, p. 199).

from top management, however, and employees were not empowered to carry through with their solutions. In contrast, today the top managers of many companies understand that empowering employees to initiate continuous improvements is critical for survival. Only companies producing quality products and services will survive in today's world market.

Stroking and the Johari Window

People engage in communication with others in the hope that the outcome may lead to mutual trust, mutual pleasure, and psychological well-being. The communication exchange is a means of sharing information about things, ideas, tasks, and selves.

When two strangers first meet, their knowledge about each other might be nil. Assume, for example, that two employees meet at the vending machine in the company break room. After an introduction—"Hello, I'm John Robbins"; "Hello, I'm Susan Smith"—they know something about each other, if only the other's name and gender. They probably also gain an impression about the other person through appearance and dress. At this point, they know only superficial things about each other.

As the exchange continues, the two learn more and more about each other. Susan soon learns that John is the recently hired human resources manager. She says, "Yes, I'd heard that you were joining the company. Welcome aboard. I'm a data-entry operator in inventory control." John continues, "I'm glad to know you, Susan. If you have a couple of minutes, could you tell how you feel about the current flexible scheduling? Do you have any suggestions for making it work better?" As a result of this exchange, Robbins learns a little more about Smith—her knowledge and commitment to the company—as well as valuable information about a company procedure. Susan has learned that management cares about her opinion of a work-related issue.

This casual interaction becomes a definite *stroke* that is likely to enhance Susan's feelings about her work. Getting a pat on the back from the supervisor, receiving a congratulatory phone call or letter, and taking the time to listen to another person are other examples of everyday stroking. By paying attention to the importance of strokes, managers can greatly improve communication and people's feelings about their work.

As the relationship between John and Susan develops, they continue to learn more about each other. Their behavior leads to trust, and this trust leads to freer conversation. Sharing also allows people to learn about themselves. The Johari Window, shown in Figure 1-5, illustrates this concept. The upper left area, labeled "I," or "free area," represents what we know about ourselves and what others know about us. Area II, the blind area, designates those things others know about us but that we don't know about ourselves; for example, you cannot see yourself as you really are. Things we know about ourselves but that others don't know about us occupy the hidden or secret area, III. Area IV includes the unknown: things we don't know about ourselves and others don't know about us.

Each of these areas may vary in size according to the degree that we can learn about ourselves from others and to the degree that we are willing to disclose things about ourselves to others. Through reciprocal sharing people can learn about themselves and about others. In communication practice, such sharing occurs only when people develop *trust* in each other. Trust is something that must be earned. We are usually willing to tell people about our school records, our jobs, and other things that are not truly personal. But we share personal thoughts, ambitions, and inner feelings only with selected

Stroking is recommended in Blanchard's *The One-Minute Manager*: "Today, I'm going to walk around the work area and catch my people doing something right and let them know about it."

Adding an employee health club is on the list of things IBM's new CEO, Louis Gertsner, plans to do. This *stroke* should communicate concern for employees' health and well-being (Cauley, 1993).

Sharing information occurs only when people develop trust in one another.

FIGURE 1-5
The Johari Window.

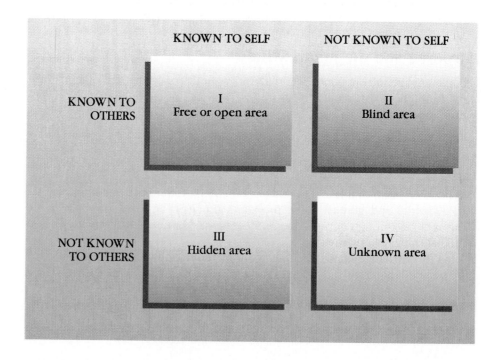

You must never assume that your messages are interpreted the same way by everyone. Instead, anticipate possible breakdowns in communication and try to overcome these gaps. What verbal and nonverbal cues can this doctor look for to determine whether the patient understands the information the doctor needs to make an accurate diagnosis?

others—those whom we have learned to trust. Trust is a quality we develop from experience with others. Through performance, we earn the trust of others. The relationships existing between supervisor and employee, doctor and patient, and lawyer and client are those of trust, but only in specific areas. In more intimate relationships—wife and husband, brother and sister, parent and child—deeper, personal feelings are entrusted to each other. When a confidant demonstrates that he or she can be trusted, trust is reinforced and leads to an expansion of the open area of the Johari Window. In business, the supervisor-employee relationship is often strengthened to the point where nonwork elements can be discussed freely.

The idea that trust and openness lead to better communication between two people also applies to groups. People engaged in organizational development (OD) are concerned with building large organizations by building effective small groups. They believe effectiveness in small groups evolves mostly from a high level of mutual trust among group members. The aim of OD is to open emotional as well as task-oriented communication. To accomplish this aim, groups often become involved in encounter sessions designed to enlarge the open areas of the Johari Window.

THINK IT OVER
Think about the types of information you (a) share freely, (b) share only with close friends, and (c) keep hidden. How does your decision to disclose information relate to the areas in the Johari Window and effective interpersonal communication?

LISTENING AS AN INTERPERSONAL SKILL

LEARNING OBJECTIVE 5

Listening involves much more than hearing or receiving. Once received, the message must be interpreted. Interpretation is a mental, not a physical, process. A final step is for the receiver to determine what action should be taken. The message might be stored for later use, as is done with educationally learned material; or it might be dismissed, as is often done with insignificant messages.

COMMUNICATION MENTOR

Listening is a powerful instrument that requires minimal physical energy and offers a lifetime of rewards. More of us should learn to master this simple form of common sense.

Terence E. McSweeney
Director of Communications
PGA of America

Most managers spend a major part of their day listening and speaking with supervisors, employees, customers, and a variety of business or industry colleagues and associates. Listening commonly consumes more of business employees' time than reading, writing, and speaking combined. Listening is an interpersonal skill as critical as the skill of speaking. Effective listening habits pay off in several ways:

What are the payoffs from good listening?

1. Good listeners are liked by others because they satisfy the basic human needs of being heard and being wanted.
2. Job performance is improved when downward oral messages are received and understood.
3. Accurate feedback from subordinates provides evidence of job performance.
4. Both superiors and subordinates may acquire greater job security from fewer mistakes or ignored messages.
5. People who listen well are able to separate fact from fiction, to cope with false persuasion effectively, and to avoid having others use them for personal gain. In other words, good listeners don't "get taken" very often.
6. Listening opens doors for ideas and thus encourages creativity.
7. Effective listeners are constantly learning—gaining knowledge and skills that lead to increased job performance, advancement, and increased job satisfaction.
8. Job satisfaction increases when people know what is going on, when they are heard, and when they participate in the mutual trust that develops from good communication.

Listening depends on your abilities to receive and decode both verbal and nonverbal messages. The best-devised messages and sophisticated communication systems will not work unless people on the receiving end of oral messages actually listen. Senders of oral messages must assume their receivers can and will listen, just as senders of written messages must assume their receivers can and will read.

Bad Listening Habits

Physicians cannot cure people of ailment unless their diagnoses reveal the nature of the ailment. In the same way, you can't improve your listening unless you understand some of the nonphysical ailments of your own listening. Most of us have developed bad listening habits in one or more of the following areas:

- *Faking attention.* Have you ever had an instructor call on you to respond to a question in class only to find you weren't listening? Have you ever had a parent, friend, or fellow worker ask you a question and find you weren't listening? Have you ever left a classroom lecture and later realized that you had no idea what went on? Have you ever been introduced to someone only to find that thirty seconds later you missed the name?

If you had to answer "yes" to any of these questions, join the huge club of "fakers of attention." The club is rather large because almost all people belong. Isn't it wonderful that we can look directly at a person, nod, smile, and pretend to be listening? We even fake giving feedback.

THINK IT OVER
Evaluate your own listening skills and work to improve at least three weaknesses. Record in a journal any effort you made to improve listening for at least 28 days—minimum time needed to change a habit. For example, write "I caught myself daydreaming in class today."

- *Welcoming disruptions.* Listening properly requires both physical and emotional effort. As a result, people welcome disruptions of almost any sort when they are engaged in somewhat difficult listening. The next time someone enters your classroom or meeting room during a lecture, notice how almost everyone in the room turns away from the speaker and the topic to observe the latecomer. Yielding to such disruptions begins early in life. Perhaps it is a form of curiosity.
- *Overlistening.* Overlistening occurs when listeners attempt to record in writing or in memory so many details that they miss the speaker's major points. Overlisteners "can't see the forest for the trees." Typical of this type of bad listening habit is the old story about college freshmen who, on the first day of class when the professor begins with, "Good morning," put it in their notes.
- *Stereotyping.* Most people use their prejudices and perceptions of others as a basis for developing stereotypes. As a result, people make spontaneous judgments about others based on their appearances, mannerisms, dress, speech delivery, and whatever other criteria play a role in their judgments. If a speaker doesn't come up to their standards in any of these areas, individuals simply turn off their listening and assume the speaker cannot have much to say.
- *Dismissing subjects as uninteresting.* People tend to use "uninteresting" as a rationale for not listening. Unfortunately, the decision is usually made before the topic is ever introduced. A good way to lose an instructor's respect is to ask, "Are we going to have anything important in class today?" if you have to (or want to) miss that day's class.
- *Failing to observe nonverbal aids.* Good listening requires use of eyes as well as ears. To listen effectively you must observe the speaker. Facial expressions and body motions always accompany speech and contribute much to messages. Unless you watch the speaker, you may miss the meaning.

In addition to recognizing bad listening habits and the variety of barriers to effective listening, you must recognize that listening is not easy. Many bad listening habits develop simply because the speed of spoken messages is far slower than your ability to receive and process them. Normal speaking speeds are between 100 and 150 words a minute. The human ear can actually distinguish words in speech in excess of 500 words a minute, and many people read at speeds well beyond 500 words a minute. Finally, your minds process thoughts at thousands of words a minute.

C O M M U N I C A T I O N   M E N T O R

No matter what role you play in business, you'll be a more valuable and effective manager—and a better servant to the organization—if you're an aggressive listener. No one has all the answers in today's business world, including the manager. In fact, the people closest to the work usually understand it best and are the best sources of ideas on how to improve work processes and procedures. Listening attentively and sincerely to people on all levels demonstrates that you respect them and believe their ideas are important.

If you're a good listener and ask good questions, people are likely to tell you the truth, offer worthwhile suggestions, and tell you what they need. If you don't listen or if you "shoot the messenger," you'll only hear what you want to hear.

One of the best ways to encourage people to communicate openly is to give them strokes, even when they bring bad news. The best way to give strokes is to keep the door open and not get upset.

Hugh B. Jacks
President and Owner
Potential Enterprises & Adventure Safaris

Who has the primary responsibility for making spoken communication effective? Why?

Because individuals cannot speak fast enough to challenge human listening equipment, listeners have the primary responsibility for making oral communication effective. People do seem to listen to gifted speakers, but they are rare. In everyday activities, good listening requires considerable mental and emotional effort.

Suggestions for Effective Listening

Feedback and nonverbal signs are two critical factors in face-to-face communication.

Because feedback and nonverbal signs are available, you can enhance the effectiveness of your face-to-face listening by following these suggestions:

1. *Watch the speaker.* Gestures, facial expressions, and eye movements can add much to the words used and the meaning intended. If the speaker cannot look you in the eye, the sincerity of the remarks may be questioned. Of course, the opposite is probably true: firm eye contact may indicate added sincerity or firmness.

2. *Provide feedback.* You can acknowledge understanding, agreement, disagreement, and a variety of other feedback responses through facial expressions, sounds, and gestures. This feedback allows the speaker to provide whatever restatement or added information may be necessary or continue with the discussion.

3. *Take time to listen.* Because people in a face-to-face communication are serving as senders and receivers simultaneously, they may become so preoccupied with thoughts about what to say that they fail to listen.

4. *Use your knowledge of speakers to advantage.* In most jobs, face-to-face oral communication occurs between people who already know each other. Through experience, you will begin to recognize others' speaking and organizing traits. Some people simply seem to run on and on with details

Effective listening habits build goodwill.

before making their point. Ask them what they had for dinner, and in reply you will probably be given recipes for each item and a description of the dining room's decor. With this type of speaker, you will learn to anticipate the major point but not pay much attention to the details. Other speakers give conclusions first and perhaps omit support for them. In this case, you will learn to ask feedback questions to obtain further information.

Listening for a Specific Purpose

Individuals listen to (1) interact socially, (2) receive information, (3) solve problems, and (4) share feelings with others. Each reason may call for a different style of listening or for a combination of styles.

LEARNING OBJECTIVE 6

CASUAL LISTENING

Listening for pleasure, recreation, amusement, and relaxation is **casual listening**. Some people have the radio on all day long; it provides background music and talk during daily routines and work periods, just as the car radio provides "companionship" for most commuters. Casual listening provides relaxing "breaks" from more serious tasks and supports our emotional health.

An interesting concept about all listening, but particularly true of casual listening, is that people are selective listeners. You listen to what you want to hear. In a crowded room in which everyone seems to be talking, you can block out all the noise and engage in the conversation you are having with someone. Casual listening doesn't require much emotional or physical effort, which is one of the reasons people engage in small talk.

LISTENING FOR INFORMATION

Listening for information is restricted to the search for data or material. In the classroom, for example, the instructor usually has a strategy for guiding the class

Listen for principles and methods—not minor details.

COMMUNICATION IN ACTION

Tim Smith, S & S Video

Starting a business is a daunting task even under the best of circumstances. Having enough capital to launch the business is only one of the considerations. Assuming one is able to open the doors of the enterprise, success is not a guarantee. Good communication skills can save a business and help it prosper.

Tim Smith saw his dream become a reality. He opened his video rental store in 1991. Although he was located in a rural area, he was not without competition. With major video franchises in the area, developing concepts and practices that would differentiate S & S from the other stores was vital. Smith asked himself several questions: "How can I compete with the big guys?" and "What can I offer that other video stores can't or don't?" He observed that personal involvement was lacking in many companies, especially large ones. He believed his advantage was personal communication with customers.

Smith started his business practicing open, honest communication with customers. He quickly learned that listening is a major component of good communication. He notes that many business owners "don't take the time to listen and ask what the customer wants. So many people are overbearing in conversation and focus on their own areas of knowledge." The tendency to be self-centered in conversation is strong, but Smith learned that customers appreciate others' interest in them and their activities. By engaging customers in conversation and learning more about them, Smith has earned their trust, and in turn, their business.

While his attempts at communication have not always been successful, Smith's policy has worked well. When customers are irate, he listens to their complaints and asks questions. He has learned that, in business, one must always be quick to take responsibility for mistakes. Instead of flatly telling the customer, "This is our policy in these cases," he asks, "What would you like me to do?" When customers know he cares about them and is willing to stand behind his product, they are likely to reward him with repeat business.

In addition to good verbal communication, Smith also spends a great deal of time on the telephone, informing patrons of new movies in stock or contacting customers who have not visited the store in several months and asking them how S & S may provide them with better service. He also writes announcements of arrivals or specials to mail to customers. By keeping in touch with customers and letting them know how much their business is valued, Smith establishes a strong personal link that sets him apart from larger businesses that do not invest as much time and energy in interpersonal communication with customers.

Open, honest communication with customers is essential to any business success. Smith's approach was clearly effective: in its first three years, S & S grew from eight to ten video rentals a day during its opening months of operation to 400 to 500 video rentals a weekend. Smith predicts that his business will continue to grow, and he credits the growth to successful interpersonal communication with customers. "Keep communication honest at all times," he emphasizes; "no exaggeration, no lies."

Applying What You Have Learned

1. Which of the three typical communication channels does Smith use primarily?
2. Identify some effective speaking and listening skills Smith uses when dealing with irate customers.
3. Assume that you are a small business owner. List several approaches you would take to practice open, honest communication with customers.
4. What are some payoffs Smith experiences for effective listening on the job?
5. When Smith states, "Keep communication honest at all times . . . no exaggeration, no lies," how does this ethical statement encourage that same ethical communication in his customers?

COMMUNICATION MENTOR

Often when someone in the workplace is ready to tell you something, you are not ready to listen. If the subject is important enough, don't hesitate to say, "Before I can pay full attention to you, I really need to finish this report (or whatever is distracting)." After clearing the decks, then give the communicator your full attention and listen intently.

When hearing a complex message, you may want to use the technique of "playing back" to the speaker what you have understood. When you can restate what you think someone said in your own words, you can be assured you have both heard and understood the message.

Cynthia Pharr
President & CEO
C. Pharr Marketing Communications

to desired goals. The instructor will probably stress several major points and use supporting evidence to prove or to reinforce them. When engaged in this type of listening, you could become so engrossed with recording every detail that you take copious notes without using an outline. The end result is a set of detailed notes without any organization.

Understand the outlining process. When you take notes, use a logical system such as the roman-numeral outline that uses I-A-1-a schemes to carry an outline to four levels (one major item with three degrees of subitems). If you find yourself with a lot of information beyond I-A levels, you are probably making notes of detailed information that is not essential to your success in the course.

In the process of listening for information, watch the speaker. Most speakers have developed a set of mannerisms composed of gestures and vocal inflections to indicate the degree of importance or seriousness they attach to portions of their presentation. Above all else, listening for information requires that listeners be able to separate fact from fiction, comedy from seriousness, and truth from untruth.

INTENSIVE LISTENING

When you listen to obtain information, solve problems, or persuade or dissuade (as in arguments), you are engaged in **intensive listening**. Intensive listening involves greater use of your analytical ability to proceed through problem-solving steps. You should have an understanding of the problem, recognize whatever limitations are involved, and know the implications of possible solutions. Intensive listening can be achieved by following these suggestions:

1. Try to become involved in the material by making written or mental notes that should be introduced as feedback to the speaker. Doodling can help you assemble your ideas for drawing a meaningful solution to the problem.

   Many "great minds" are doodlers.

2. Attempt to predict or anticipate the speaker's future points. Listen with the speaker but try to think ahead at times as well. Thinking ahead can help you develop a sense of the speaker's logic and future points.

3. Watch speakers for any nonverbal clues that will help you understand the speaker's point of view and emotional state.

   Involvement improves listening.

COMMUNICATION MENTOR

One morning a serious-looking associate came to my office door and asked to speak with me. Noticing the several stacks of paper I was working with, he said he would return after I had a chance to clear my desk. Quickly sweeping one arm from edge to edge, I literally "cleared my desk" onto the floor and invited him in. Any doubt he was convinced of my interest? The occasional dramatic gesture aside, develop a personal listening style that convinces the person that listening to him or her is your most important activity at that moment.

R. D. Saenz
Business Consultant

4. Try to avoid yielding to stereotypes, personal judgments, and distractions.
5. Provide listener feedback either orally or through nonverbal nods, facial expressions, or body movements to encourage further speaker comments and behavior adjustment.
6. Become a good summarizer. When your turn comes to respond, trace the development of the discussion and then take off from there with your own analysis. Don't be hesitant about "tailgating" on the ideas of others. Creative ideas are generated in an open discussion related to problem solving.

LISTENING FOR FEELINGS WITH EMPATHY

Empathetic listening is a strong stroke.

Empathy occurs when a person attempts to share another's feelings or emotions. Counselors attempt to use **empathetic listening** in dealing with their clients. Good friends often provide empathetic listening for each other. Empathy is a valuable trait developed by people who are skilled in interpersonal relations. The interesting thing about empathetic listening is that it more often than not results in **reciprocal listening**. When you take the time to listen to another, the courtesy is usually returned. Empathy leads to sharing.

Many people in positions of authority have developed excellent listening skills that apply to gaining information and to problem solving. However, a number of people have failed to develop good listening practices that work effectively in listening for feelings. For example, a meeting between a supervisor and an employee might go something like this:

THINK IT OVER
What bad listening habits prevented the supervisor from communicating with Maria? What steps would you recommend for overcoming these bad habits?

"Linda, I really need to talk to you about something important."

"That so, Maria? Well, take a seat and let me hear about it," the supervisor says in a friendly tone as she continues to stare in a perplexed way at a stack of papers on her desk.

As Maria takes a seat, Linda continues, "Maria, you think you have a problem, eh? How would you like to have the ones I'm faced with now? First, I'm right in the middle of union negotiations for the new three-year contract, I've had several problems with our supervisory crew in the Midland plant, and somebody has botched up our inventory procedure so we're running short and will have to back-order with several customers."

Finally Linda asks hastily, "Well, what's your problem, Maria?"

> Intimidated by her supervisor's preoccupation with her own problems and her abrupt manner, Maria decides today is not an appropriate time to get any assistance. To end the conversation without looking foolish, she quickly decides to ask a few questions about a routine procedure.
>
> Before Maria has a chance to speak, however, the supervisor suddenly signals the end of the discussion by saying, "Maria, I have another appointment now. If you'd like, we can continue our discussion later. I want to be of help, and my door is always open to you." She returns her attention to her work before Maria moves from her chair.
>
> Maria leaves completely frustrated, her problem still on her mind and unresolved.

Because of the supervisor's poor listening habits, Maria probably feels worse after the meeting than she did before. The supervisor learned nothing from the exchange. What if Maria's problem were company related? Good listening might have resulted in information helpful to solving the supervisor's own problems.

What specific effective listening techniques did the supervisor violate? First, the supervisor was too preoccupied with her own problems to take the time to listen for Maria's message—not to mention her feelings. Talking too much and giving strong nonverbal signals that she was not interested in what Maria had to say destroyed Maria's desire to talk. Despite the rough beginning, a gentle, empathetic, open-ended question might have encouraged Maria to share her information. Instead, the abrupt, emotion-laden question ("Well, what's your problem?") resembled a drilling question-and-answer session. (Remember, Maria did not use the word "problem" in her initial approach.)

Total empathy can never be achieved simply because no two people are exactly alike, and one can never really become the other person. The more similar our experiences, however, the better our opportunity to put ourselves in the other person's shoes. If two people have been skydiving, for example, one can appreciate how the other felt the first time. Listening with empathy involves some genuine tact along with other good listening habits. Remember that listening for feelings normally takes place in a one-to-one situation. Close friends who trust each other tend to engage in self-disclosure easily. Empathetic listening is enhanced when the participants exhibit trust and friendship. Here are some suggestions for empathetic listening:

Why can't individuals achieve perfect empathy?

1. *Get in step with the speaker.* Try to understand the speaker's background, prejudices, and points of view. Listen for emotionally charged words and watch for body language as clues to the speaker's underlying feelings.
2. *Do not interrupt the speaker.* Try to understand the speaker's full meaning, and wait patiently for an indication that you should enter the conversation. In addition, minimize environmental and mental distractions that serve as barriers to effective listening. For example, a supervisor's closing the office door to reduce distracting noise and refusing to accept phone calls during a performance appraisal interview enable the speaker and listener to concentrate more fully on the message.
3. *Let the speaker know you are interested in listening and are an active partner in the exchange of information.* Show genuine interest by remaining physically and mentally involved; for example, avoid daydreaming, yawning, frequently breaking eye contact, looking at your watch or papers on your desk, whispering to a person nearby, and allowing numerous interrup-

How can you let a speaker know you are listening and are involved?

tions (telephone calls or others breaking in to ask questions). Praise the speaker for his or her willingness to share information. As a result, you can realistically expect to receive additional information from this individual. Supervisors who show genuine interest will find that they receive valuable feedback from employees. In addition, the open, trusting work environment increases employee morale and productivity.

4. *Encourage the speaker to continue by providing appropriate, supportive feedback.* Develop your own encouraging signs such as a nod of the head, a throat-clearing sound, a smile, and even an encouraging grunt.

Reflective statements summarize or "reflect" the speaker's message. Why are they an important part of effective listening?

5. *Take advantage of your opportunity to speak to evaluate your understanding of the message and the speaker's feelings.* One way to check your level of understanding is to make reflective statements—an important part of effective listening. You simply restate in your own words what you think the other person has said. This paraphrasing will reinforce what you have heard and allow the speaker to correct any misunderstanding. For example, when Marcos says, "I really dislike the new production supervisor," an empathetic co-worker might summarize or reflect Marcos' message by saying, "You think he isn't a nice person?" Then Marcos might say, "Oh, I don't dislike him as a person, and as a supervisor he's quite good at giving instructions. The problem is he never stops long enough to find out whether I understand anything he's said. Then he's furious when the job isn't done correctly the first time." The reflective statement confirms that the listener has understood the message correctly. The statement also elicits a response that helps reveal the true source of the problem: frustration that the supervisor's communication style does not allow for feedback.

THINK IT OVER
Provide another probing prompt that might help Marcos understand his feelings.

6. *Use probing prompts to encourage the speaker to discuss a particular aspect of the message more thoroughly.* These prompts (statements or questions) help speakers define their problems more concretely and specifically. In the previous example of the disgruntled employee, the co-worker might say, "I realize that you aren't getting along with the new production supervisor, but I'm not entirely sure what Sam does that makes you so irritated." Like the reflective statement used previously, this probing prompt summarizes Marcos' message, but it also encourages him to explore his feelings and to identify the true source of the problem—inadequate feedback.

THINK IT OVER
List other situations (both personal and business related) that would require you to listen intensively while also listening for feelings with empathy.

Frequently you may have to combine listening intensively and listening for feelings. Performance appraisal interviews, disciplinary conferences, and other sensitive discussions between supervisors and employees require listening intensively for accurate understanding of the message and listening empathetically for feelings, preconceived points of view, and background. The interviewing process also may combine the two types of listening. Job interviewers must try to determine how someone's personality, as well as skill and knowledge, will affect job performance.

SUMMARY

1 Communication is the process of exchanging information and meaning between or among individuals through a common system of symbols, signs, and behavior. Managers spend most of their time in oral and written communication.

2 Managers communicate through verbal (use of words) and nonverbal (without use of words) communication. Nonverbal communication includes metacommunications, a message that, although not expressed in words, accompanies a message expressed in words; and kinesic communication, an idea expressed through body language (visual and vocal). Because a significant portion of meaning is expressed nonverbally, you must learn to interpret nonverbal messages accurately.

3 People engaged in communication encode and decode messages while simultaneously serving as both senders and receivers. In the communication process, feedback helps people resolve possible misunderstandings and thus improve communication effectiveness. Feedback and the opportunity to observe nonverbal signs are always present in face-to-face communication, the most effective of the three communication levels.

4 From the behavioral sciences and the work of several pioneering management theorists, we know that people
- Want to be heard, appreciated, and wanted.
- Like to be treated as adults, want to know that their ideas and suggestions have been considered, and want to be empowered to make decisions that will improve the quality of their work.
- Require "stroking" for their personal well-being.

5 Listening is crucial in interpersonal communication. Additionally, effective listening enhances organizational communication and leads to success in education and in careers. Bad listening habits include faking attention, welcoming distractions, stereotyping, dismissing topics as uninteresting, and ignoring nonverbal cues.

6 Individuals listen casually for pleasure, for information, intensively to solve problems, and empathetically to share feelings. All types of listening require being involved in the speaker's ideas, avoiding stereotypes and prejudices, watching for nonverbal cues, and providing timely, appropriate feedback. When listening for information, record *major* ideas using a logical outlining system. Intensively listening requires anticipating a speaker's future points, and being able to summarize and analyze major points and develop a viable solution. Techniques that facilitate empathetic listening include using reflective statements to evaluate your understanding of the speaker's feelings and probing statements to urge the speaker to discuss the issue more thoroughly.

REFERENCES

Blanchard, K., & Johnson, S. (1982). *The one-minute manager.* NY: Morrow.

Cauley, L. (1993, July 14). IBM chief cultivates quiet change. *USA Today,* pp. B1-2.

Decker, B. (1992). *You've got to be believed to be heard.* NY: St. Martin's Press.

Howell, A. (1991, December). Communicating for productivity, *Personnel Management*, pp. 20-21.

Hunt, V. D. (1993). *Managing for quality: Integrating quality and business strategy.* Homewood, IL: Business One Irwin.

Mehrabian, A. (1971). *Silent messages.* Belmont, CA: Wadsworth.

REVIEW QUESTIONS

1. What are the three purposes for which people communicate? What percentage of a manager's time is spent communicating? Give examples of the types of communication managers use.
2. Distinguish between the two primary components of a message. How much does each component contribute to the total meaning of a message?
3. When a manager says to the sales staff, "Let's try to make budget this year," what are some of the possible metacommunications?
4. List the five stages in the communication process using the following terms: (a) sender, (b) encode, (c) channel, (d) receiver, (e) decode, (f) feedback, and (g) interferences or barriers.
5. What are the three channels typically used to transmit messages? Provide several examples of each channel.
6. What types of differences between sender and receiver create barriers to communication?
7. How can managers use Maslow's need levels and McGregor's Theory X and Y to improve interpersonal communication with employees?
8. How has the total quality management movement extended the work of McGregor? How does this movement differ from the use of quality circles to increase job satisfaction popular in the 1980s?
9. What is meant by "stroking"? How does it affect interpersonal communication in the workplace?
10. The willingness of a person to self-disclose depends on what factor in a relationship?
11. What are some payoffs of effective listening on the job?
12. What is a primary cause of bad listening habits? Discuss six bad listening habits.
13. What is meant by "people listen selectively"?
14. How does "overlistening" occur? Discuss six guidelines for listening intensively.
15. Good listening for feelings depends on what listener trait? Discuss six guidelines for listening for feelings.

EXERCISES

1. Complete each of the THINK IT OVER activities that your instructor assigns.
2. Compile a list of situations during the next two days that illustrate the influence of metacommunication on the understanding of a message. Use the eight characteristics of nonverbal messages to describe specifically the overall effect of the metacommunication on the communication process.
3. Using the online database in your library, Chapter 4 of your textbook, or other resources, identify at least five nonverbal gestures that differ among cultures. Discuss how ignoring these differences in nonverbal communication might affect interpersonal communication with people from the cultures mentioned.
4. In groups of three, develop a list of 12 to 15 annoying habits of yours or of others that create barriers (verbal and nonverbal) to effective communication. Be prepared to present the list to the class.
5. In groups assigned by your instructor, develop a list of possible interferences (barriers) that may occur at each stage of the communication process. You may refer to the list of annoying habits generated in Exercise 4.

Stage of Communication Process

Interference

Encoding _____
Channel _____
Decoding _____
Feedback _____

Suggestion for Improvement

Encoding _____
Channel _____
Decoding _____
Feedback _____

6. Refer to the conversation between the supervisor and employee in the conversation on page 24.

Analyze the effectiveness of this conversation using the communication process model in Figure 1-1 as a guide. Identify problems (interferences or barriers) occurring at each stage of the communication process and provide suggestions for improvement. Be prepared to discuss your analysis with the class or in small groups assigned by your instructor.

7. Recall a recent conversation that you have had with a friend, teacher, co-worker, supervisor, or some other person. Write a brief scenario including the dialogue and a description of the nonverbal messages transmitted between the sender and receiver. Analyze the effectiveness of this conversation using the communication process model in Figure 1-1 as a guide. Identify problems (interferences or barriers) occurring at each stage of the communication process and provide suggestions for improvement. Be prepared to discuss your analysis with the class or in small groups assigned by your instructor.

8. Using the online database in your library or other resources, locate an article about companies, such as Federal Express, that have implemented total quality management programs that emphasize the important role of the worker. Write a brief summary outlining management actions that have led to high levels of job satisfaction.

9. Keep a log of strokes you receive and give in the next 24 hours. What was the apparent motive of each? How did the receiver react? Did the closeness of the relationship (relative, friend, stranger) affect the way the stroke was received? Did this communication exchange affect the relationship? Explain.

10. Discuss how a supervisor's understanding of the Johari Window could increase the effectiveness of performance appraisal interviews, disciplinary actions, and other difficult discussions with employees.

11. Prepare a record of your listening, speaking, reading, and writing activities and time spent in each during the hours of 8 a.m. to 5 p.m. for the next two days. You should attempt to record the time spent doing each activity for each one-hour time block in such a way that you obtain a total time for each activity. Be prepared to share your distribution with the class.

12. Critique your own listening skills. You may find it helpful to ask a friend to help you be objective in your assessment. Ask your instructor to provide a listening profile to guide your thinking. Prepare a three-column list. Label the first column *Listening Strength*, the second column *Listening Weakness,* and the third column *Strategy for Improvement.* In groups assigned by your instructor, discuss your ideas and plans for improving your listening skills.

13. Discuss a situation that you have faced that provides evidence of bad listening habits. Consider your experiences in school, employment, organizations, and interpersonal relationships. Based on the information gained from reading this chapter, give specific suggestions that would have improved listening in this situation.

14. In groups assigned by your instructor, select one of the business-related situations identified in Exercise 13.
   a. Role-play the communication exchange in a way that violates several of the effective listening techniques presented in the chapter. Repeat the role-playing activity and correct the bad listening habits.
   b. At your instructor's direction, present the ineffective listening version of the activity to the class. Ask the class to identify the bad listening habits and suggest ways for correcting them. If time permits, repeat the skit incorporating the suggestions from class members.

15. Read an article from a current magazine or journal about one of the concepts presented in a chapter in this book or select a topic assigned by your instructor. Give a short (two- or three-minute) oral presentation. Instruct the class to listen attentively but not to take notes. If your instructor directs, incorporate one or more of the distractions discussed in the chapter. Prepare three to five questions to ask the class about the material (either multiple choice, true-false, or short answer).

16. In groups of two assigned by your instructor, complete the following exercise:
    a. Write a 50- to 75-word response to the following statement or one provided by your instructor: "In an increasingly competitive global economy, the need for developing effective intercultural communication skills is imperative."
    b. Assign one group member to serve as reader and one group member to serve as respondent. The reader will read the short essay prepared in Step a. The respondent will complete the following activity: (i) summarize the message in 15 seconds, (ii) summarize the message in one sentence, (iii) summarize the message in one word used in the message, and (iv) summarize the message in one word *not* used in the message.
    c. Reverse roles and repeat Step b.

E-MAIL APPLICATION

Read an article from a current magazine or journal about one aspect of interpersonal communication presented in this chapter. Send your instructor a brief e-mail message discussing one specific idea presented in the article and your plan for using this suggestion to improve your own interpersonal communication skills. Include a complete bibliographic entry so that the instructor could locate the article (refer to pp. 602–604 for examples for formatting references).

CHAPTER 2

ORGANIZATIONAL

SETTING FOR

BUSINESS COMMUNICATION

OBJECTIVES

When you have completed Chapter 2, you will be able to

1 Identify the four levels of communication.

2 Discuss factors affecting group communication.

3 Identify factors leading to the need for formal organizations.

4 Identify two barriers to communicating in formal organizations.

5 Distinguish between external and internal systems of organizational communication.

6 Discuss how information flows within an organization (downward, upward, and horizontally).

Most Springfield residents do not think about Citizens' Bank every day. Many of them have checking or savings accounts there and only give the bank a second thought when they are considering obtaining a loan for a major purchase or making investment plans. When they think of the bank in an everyday context, most of the townspeople think of the three-story Greek revival building on the corner of First and Main, the building with the old clock in the center of the facade. They most likely do not give much thought to the people behind the scene: the bank president, the vice presidents, loan officers, and tellers. Yet, these people contribute largely to the success of the bank.

The success or failure of any business largely depends on the ability of people to work cooperatively toward a common goal: the success of the company. Keeping the lines of communication open is essential because all levels of the business are interdependent. When communication breaks down in one area, the effects often are felt at all levels, resulting in bad feelings among employees and loss of customers' trust. No one in this chain of communication is exempt:

- From the president who is responsible for communicating company goals and philosophy.
- To vice presidents who oversee various bank functions, explain work assignments, and evaluate performance objectively so employees are motivated to perform outstanding work.
- To employees who are willing to share ideas and suggestions for doing work more efficiently and improving the quality of life in the bank.

The following on-the-job scenes illustrate how inadequate communication skills might affect the success of Citizens' Bank:

Citizens' Bank decided to expand its services to include an in-house investment brokerage service. Marketing developed an impressive advertising campaign, including frequent ads promoting the new service in the local newspapers and an open house so potential investors could meet the newly hired investment broker. When frustrated investors began complaining about the broker's inability to provide timely investment information about specific stocks, an embarrassed investment broker was left to explain the problem: the EDP department had not anticipated the length of time required to implement an information system to connect the bank with the various stock exchanges. Therefore, marketing and EDP should have coordinated their efforts so that the information system was fully operational before any major advertising efforts were made.

After blistering criticism from the president saying the bank had too many loan foreclosures, the vice president of the lending and trust division ordered loan officers to turn down applications for loans that showed the least sign of risk. Realizing that the president was under pressure and clearly not open to discussion on the ramifications of the new loan policy, the loan officers decided to do as they were told. Unfortunately, the vice president's first indication that the explanation was insufficient occurred several weeks later when the chief loan officer reported that the bank's volume of new loans had decreased dramatically. Many of the loan applicants rejected because of the new, more stringent guidelines were loyal Citizens' Bank customers who had since sought and received loans from the bank's primary competitor.

Conversations all over the company—in the company break room, across the teller counters, and at the copy and fax machines—all seemed to lead to the same subject. The president has mandated new hours to compete with other banks with drive-through windows and extended hours. A number of the tellers, especially those who are single parents, have worked flexible daily schedules that permit them to work shorter schedules (20-30 hours a week), allowing them to arrive later and leave earlier to pick up their children from school and to work alternate Saturday mornings. The terse memo from the human resources director stated that no additional tellers would be hired to work the extended hours. Instead, all tellers must work at least eight hours a day—no exceptions would be made. The human resources director refused to listen to teller's concerns about the new extended work schedules and their discontent that the company has reneged on its longtime commitment to accommodate employees' personal needs. Recently, the human resources manager commented on excessive tardiness, sloppy work, and negative attitudes clearly visible to customers.

Effective communication could have prevented each of these costly mistakes. Imagine the positive results if

- The marketing and EDP managers had coordinated their efforts to offer the new investment service.
- The vice president had controlled her anger and focused first on providing clear, thorough information about controlling loan foreclosures and had made the buyers feel secure enough to clarify the confusing instructions.
- Management had tried to deal with the frequent, consistent information about the new work schedules coming to them through the grapevine—an informal, yet accurate indication of employees' major concerns.

Had you been involved in any of these situations, would you have possessed the communication skills needed to prevent the problem? Regardless of your career or your level within an organization, your ability to communicate will affect not only the success of the organization but also your personal success and your advancement within that organization.

LEVELS OF COMMUNICATION

The primary function of communication is to convey information and meaning through words, symbols, signs, or actions. People form messages by combining pieces or bits of information. This communicative process takes place on four levels:

1. **Intrapersonal communication** occurs when an individual processes information based on his or her own experiences. It is, in a sense, communication within one person. Communication may be impaired when the sender has significantly different experiences from the recipient because the recipient may be unable to process the information on an intrapersonal level.
2. **Interpersonal communication** takes place primarily when two people are involved in the process. As mentioned, they have two goals: (1) They want to accomplish whatever task confronts them, and (2) they want to feel better about themselves as a result of their interaction. These two goals are commonly referred as **task goals** and **maintenance goals**, respectively, and they exist side by side in varying degrees in most daily activities.
3. **Group communication** occurs among more than two people: a committee, a club, or all the students enrolled in a class. Groups are formed usually because the combined efforts of a number of people result in greater output than

What is the difference between a task goal and a maintenance goal?

the individual efforts of the same number of people. In other words, groups can do more for the individuals than the individuals can do for themselves.

4. **Organizational communication** arises when groups discover that they are unable to accomplish their goals without some kind of organization. Thus organizations are combinations of groups formed in such a way that large tasks may be accomplished.

Despite the differences in size and complexity, each of these levels of communication continues to have task and maintenance goals. The idea of maintenance goals can be divided into two distinct goals—self-maintenance and group maintenance:

- A **self-maintenance goal** describes an individual's need to maintain his or her personal worth or psychological well-being, and
- A **group maintenance goal** describes a group's need to maintain the nontask relationships they have developed through interacting with one another as a team.

COMMUNICATING IN GROUPS

Most of your oral communication in business will occur in one-to-one relationships (discussed in Chapter 1). You will probably also make oral reports and speeches (discussed in Chapter 3). Your second most frequent oral communication activity will likely occur when you participate in groups, primarily groups within the organizational work environment. Group and committee work have become crucial in most organizations. Group meetings can be productive when members understand something about groups and how they operate.

Purposes of Groups

Groups form for synergistic effects; that is, through pooling their efforts, group members can achieve more collectively than they could individually. At the same time, the social nature of groups contributes to the self-maintenance goals of members. Communication in small groups leads to group decisions that are generally superior to individual decisions. The group process can motivate members, improve thinking, and assist attitude development and change. The emphasis that groups place on task and maintenance activity is based on several factors in group communication.

Factors in Group Communication

As you consider the following factors in group communication, try to visualize their relationship to some groups to which you have belonged in school, religious organizations, athletics, and social activities.

LEADERSHIP
The ability of a group leader to work toward task goals while contributing to the development of group and individual maintenance goals is often critical to group success. In these group activities, leadership activities may be shared among several participants. Leadership may also be rotated, formally or informally.

COMMON GOALS
In effective groups, participants share a common goal, interest, or benefit. This goal focus allows members to overcome individual differences of opinion and to negotiate acceptable solutions.

How is an organization different from a group?

What are the benefits gained from forming a group?

LEARNING OBJECTIVE 2

ROLE PERCEPTION

People who are invited to join groups have perceptions of how the group should operate and what it should achieve. In addition, each member has a self-concept that dictates fairly well how he or she will behave. Those known to be aggressive will attempt to be confrontational and forceful, and those who like to be known as moderates will behave in moderate ways by settling arguments rather than initiating them. In successful groups, members play a variety of necessary roles and seek to eliminate nonproductive ones.

LONGEVITY

Groups formed for short-term tasks such as arranging a dinner and program will spend more time on the task than on maintenance. However, groups formed for long-term assignments such as an audit of a major corporation by a team from a public accounting firm may devote much effort to maintenance goals. Maintenance refers to division of duties, scheduling, recordkeeping, reporting, and assessing progress.

SIZE

The smaller the group, the more its members have the opportunity to communicate with one another. Conversely, large groups often inhibit communication because the opportunity to speak and interact is limited. When broad input is desired, large groups may be good. When expert opinion is the goal, smaller groups may be more effective. Interestingly, large groups generally divide into smaller groups for maintenance purposes, even when the large group is task oriented. Although much research has been conducted in the area of group size, no optimal number of members has been identified. Groups of five to seven members are thought to be best for decision-making and problem-solving tasks. An odd number of members is preferred because deciding votes are possible, and tie votes are infrequent.

Some congressional committees have over 50 members to ensure that various special interest groups and geographic regions are represented.

STATUS

Some group members will appear to be better qualified than others. Consider a group in which the chief executive of the organization is a member. When the chief executive speaks, members agree. When members speak, they tend to direct their remarks to the one with high status—the chief executive. People are inclined to communicate with peers as their equals, but they tend to speak upward to their supervisor and downward to lower-level employees. In general, groups require balance in status and expertise rather than homogeneity.

GROUP NORMS

A **norm** is a standard or average behavior. All groups possess norms. An instructor's behavior helps establish classroom norms. If an instructor is generally late for class, students will begin to arrive late. If the instructor permits talking during lectures, the norm will be for students to talk. People conform to norms because conformity is easy and nonconformity is difficult and uncomfortable. Conformity leads to acceptance by other group members and creates communication opportunities.

The performance of groups depends on several factors, but none is more important than leadership. The leader can establish norms, determine who can speak and when, encourage everyone to contribute, and provide the motivation for effective group activity.

THINK IT OVER
Recall a group of which you were a member. Why was the group formed? Was more time spent on task or maintenance goals? Why? How effective was the leader in facilitating the group's success (accomplishing the task and developing each individual's and the group's maintenance goals)? Explain.

COMMUNICATION   MENTOR

Any corporate team or group of employees is no different from a symphony orchestra. To function effectively, each individual in the group must work in harmony to achieve the group's goals. All members of the symphony must have the opportunity to contribute to the end product. The maestro—the stroker—must ensure that each member of the team receives equal recognition within the group. Fairhandedness is always the general rule. Soloists need not apply.

Terence E. McSweeney
Director of Communications
PGA of America

COMMUNICATING IN ORGANIZATIONS

LEARNING OBJECTIVE 3

A formal organization and a group are made up of individuals, and both have goals. However, organizations can accomplish some things individuals and groups cannot do by or for themselves. For example, the task goals of individuals and groups may generate such complicated and sizable endeavors that a more formal organizational structure is necessary to accomplish them.

Organizational structure is the overall design of an organization, much like a blueprint developed to meet the company's specific needs and to enhance its ability to accomplish goals. A company's organizational structure is depicted graphically in an organizational chart. It helps define the scope of the organization and assists people in getting a total view of a large, formal organization with employees performing specialized tasks yet working interdependently to accomplish common goals.

As goals expand, additional *specialization* is needed to achieve the goals. As specialization increases, individuals and units become more interdependent. A *functional organizational structure* is needed to coordinate efforts.

Consider the example of a small community bank that expands beyond the current management's ability to cope with it. In this case, the community bank concentrates on providing personal loan and mortgage financing. Suddenly this sleepy little town is awakened by an outburst of expansion—amusement parks, restaurants, hotels, outlet malls, and modern shopping centers. Soon, the bank is issuing multimillion dollar commercial loans. An in-house investment brokerage service is added to provide customers a convenient vehicle for investing in the stock market. Customers are demanding service at other locations. As a result, the bank opens a full-service branch in a newly developed shopping center in the center of the new-growth area.

Specialization of Individuals and Units

The expanded bank needs more employees and skills not currently available to handle the expanded business. Bank employees must be equipped to evaluate and manage corporate loans; provide up-to-the-minute, accurate investment advice; develop effective advertising campaigns for the bank's expanded services and new locations; and exercise control over a variety of other activities.

To exercise the necessary control over the wide range of activities, management has reorganized the large organization into a **functional organizational**

structure, as shown in Figure 2-1. Employees are grouped into smaller, separate departments on the basis of common tasks: lending and trust, operations, and fund-raising. Within these departments, further specialization of labor occurs. Lending and trust, for example, has specialists in three areas: commercial loans and mortgages, personal loans, and trusts. As the complexity of the undertaking increases, employees continue to become even more specialized.

Interdependence of Units and Individuals

Because of the specialization in a large functional organization, each of the smaller departments is dependent on the other units to some extent. Efforts by the lending and trust staff are very much dependent on the level of funds raised by the fund-raising department. A high degree of the bank's success rests on these departments' maintaining an appropriate spread between the interest rates charged on loans issued by the lending and trust department and interest earned on moneys raised by the fund-raising department. Regular reports from these units provide the basis for an efficient recordkeeping system that can, in turn, provide information to assist management in planning and decision making.

Within each of these departments, specialization of people leads to interdependence of individuals and among departments. All, however, are organized so that the goals of the organization can be achieved. In the everyday work of the organization, the task goals of the total organization exist side by side with the group maintenance goals of the departmental units and the self-maintenance goals of the individuals involved. The interdependence of units and individuals applies equally to both task goals and maintenance goals.

What factor created the need for Citizens' Bank to specialize? What benefits were gained from specializing into functional units?

Inadequate communication between interdependent departments can be detrimental to the financial health of a company. For example, the lending and trust and the fund-raising department at Citizens' can quickly "give the bank away" if they do not communicate frequently and accurately about the interest rates earned and received.

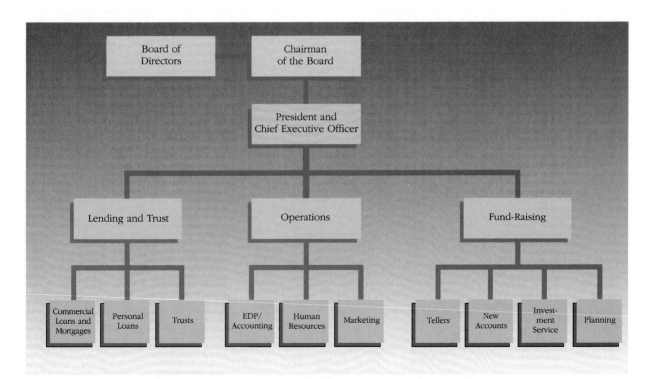

FIGURE 2-1   Organizational chart: Citizens' Bank.

To achieve its goals, the organization needs to direct and coordinate the interdependent units and individuals. The organizational structure develops to facilitate the communication networks needed to accomplish the goals. The original community bank in our example needs the functional organizational structure now that it has grown into a large full-service bank with numerous *specialized, interdependent* departments.

Many companies have realized that the traditional hierarchy organized around functional units is inadequate for coping or competing in the increasingly competitive global markets. Companies are organizing work teams that integrate work-flow processes rather than having specialists who deal with a single function or product. These cross-functional work teams break down the former barriers between isolated functional departments. Each employee, from the president to the custodian, is empowered to make decisions that will improve the quality of the company's products and services to satisfy the customer.

Communication Barriers Caused by a Functional Organizational Structure

Management designs organizational structures as a means of coordinating and controlling the behavior of members and units. However, communication problems are introduced by rigid organizational structure.

UNCLEAR INDICATION OF ROLE VS. STATUS

Traditionally, organizational charts have been used to describe the authority structure of the organization. People in higher positions in the chart appear to have greater authority than those at lower levels. If used to describe communication in the organization, however, the chart may be entirely inadequate. May people communicate only with those immediately above or below them; that is, only with those employees whose positions on the chart are connected to theirs by an uninterrupted line? Is each department on the chart autonomous and shielded from relationships with other departments? If units and individuals depend on one another, the chart does not define the communication structure.

The organizational chart does not necessarily define the relative importance of each department or individual participating in the organization. The chairman of the board occupies the highest spot on the chart, but the actual role may have little to do with the success or failure of the organization. The administrative assistant to an executive or someone in human resources, for example, may play a role considerably more authoritative and powerful than the position's status on the chart would indicate. **Role** is an informal part; **status** is a formal position based on the organizational chart or other prescribed functions.

EXCESSIVE COMPETITION

Organizational structure affects the behavior of individuals and units within the organization. Traditionally, organizations have had tall, pyramid-shaped organizational structures. The higher a person is on the pyramid, the greater the apparent authority and rewards. Most people probably strive for a higher position on the pyramid. This striving may determine relationships with peers, lower-level employees, and supervisors. Competition has become a characteristic of the North American way of life. People and organizations compete for a greater share of scarce resources, for a limited number of positions at the top of organizations,

THINK IT OVER
Businesses today are streamlining their operations, often referred to as *downsizing* or more recently as *rightsizing* and *re-engineering*. How is this process affecting the shape of organizational charts? the effectiveness of the communication process?

LEARNING OBJECTIVE 4

Does position on the organizational chart indicate an employee's impact on an organization?

What has been the typical organizational structure?

and for esteem in their professions. Such competition is a healthy sign of the human desire to succeed; and in terms of economic behavior, competition is fundamental to the private-enterprise system. At the same time, when excessive competition replaces the cooperation necessary for success, communication may be diminished, if not eliminated.

Just as you want to look good in the eyes of your peers, lower-level employees, and supervisors, units within organizations want to look good to one another. This attitude may cause behavior to take the competitive form, a "win/lose" philosophy. When excessive competition has a negative influence on the performance of the organization, everybody loses.

Most conflict among people and groups results from a lack of understanding. When one unit is uninformed about the importance or function of another, needless conflicts may occur as groups attempt to better themselves at the expense of others. Interestingly enough, a group engaged in competition tends to solidify and become cohesive with great internal group morale. As a consequence, the competitive spirit of the group may intensify and lead to further deterioration of communication with other groups.

> The basis for conflict within an organization is usually caused by *misunderstanding*.

Covey's (1989) experience with a company president illustrates this point. The president described his employees as selfish, uncooperative, and not producing as he believed they could. He insisted they had no reason not to cooperate. However, Covey found a chart behind a curtain on a wall of the president's office that contained a number of racehorses with the faces of the managers superimposed on the racehorses. At the end of the racetrack was a picture of Bermuda. Once a week the president would bring the managers in and ask them, "Now which of you is going to win a trip to Bermuda?" (Covey, 1989, p. 206). He wanted his people to benefit from working together, but he set them up in competition with one another so that one manager's success meant failure for the other managers.

Although competition is appropriate and desirable in many situations, management must take steps through open communication and information and reward systems to reduce competition and to increase cooperation. Cooperation is more likely when the competitors (individuals or groups within an organization) have an understanding of and appreciation for others' importance and functions. This cooperative spirit is characterized as a win/win philosophy. One person's success is not achieved at the expense or exclusion of another. Employees need to identify a solution that everyone finds satisfactory and is committed to achieving. Reaching this mutual understanding requires a high degree of trust and effective interpersonal skills, particularly empathetic and intensive listening skills and the willingness to communicate long enough to agree on an action plan that is acceptable to both.

> What do you believe would be the typical communication patterns of a manager working under a win/lose philosophy? a win/win philosophy?

FLAT ORGANIZATIONAL STRUCTURES

Businesses today are downsizing and eliminating layers of management. Companies implementing total quality management programs are reorganizing to distribute the decision-making power throughout the organization. As mentioned, the trend is to eliminate functional or departmental boundaries (e.g., lending and trust and fund-raising). Instead, work is reorganized in cross-disciplinary teams that perform broad core processes (e.g., product development and sales generation) and not narrow tasks such as forecasting market demand for a particular product. In a flat organizational structure, communicating across the organizational chart (among the cross-functional teams) becomes more important than

communicating up and down in a top-heavy hierarchy. Communication is enhanced because the message must travel shorter distances. Much of the communication involves face-to-face meetings with team members rather than numerous, time-consuming "handoffs" as the product moves methodically from one department to another.

The time needed to design a new card at Hallmark Cards decreased significantly when the company adopted a flat organizational structure. Team members representing the former functional areas (graphic artists, writers, marketers, and others) now work in a central area, communicating openly and frequently, solving problems and making decisions about the entire process as a card is being developed. For example, a writer, struggling with a verse for a new card, can solicit immediate input from the graphic artist working on the team rather than finalizing the verse and then "handing it off" to the art department (Hillkirk, 1993).

EXTERNAL AND INTERNAL SYSTEMS

LEARNING OBJECTIVE 5

Organizations impose *external communication* systems to get the work done; *internal communication* systems develop as people interact.

Two systems of organizational communication simultaneously influence human behavior. The **external communication** system is typified by the formal organizational chart, which is created by management to control individual and group behavior and to achieve the organization's goals. Essentially, the external system is dictated by the technical, political, and economic environment of the organization. Within this external system, people are required to behave in certain ways simply to get the work done. Because it is dictated by environmental forces existing outside the needs of the individuals in the organization, the system is called *external*.

The **internal communication** system develops as people interact within the formal, external system and certain behavior patterns emerge—patterns that accommodate social and psychological needs. To distinguish between the two systems, return to Citizens' Bank and its organizational chart. After the bank expansion, the president chose to continue working in the personal loans department, which is subordinate to and apparently has a reporting relationship to the operations department. Quite likely, however, the people in the operations department do not give the president a bad time. The behavior of these employees in the external system is minimal and just enough to get the work done. In the internal system, however, their behavior is adapted, depending on their personal perceptions of the president.

Passing the relay baton, a seemingly simple task, is accomplished only through precise communication and cooperation among team members. Likewise, teams in Motorola's Participative Management Program openly communicate ideas for improving products and processes; together, teams develop strategies to reduce defects and cycle time. This cooperative spirit has helped Motorola maintain its leadership position in the electronics industry (Hunt, 1993, p. 208).

Systems in Action

When employees rely almost entirely on the formal external communication system as a guide to behavior, the system might be identified as a *bureaucracy*. Procedures manuals, job descriptions, organizational charts, and other written materials dictate the required behavior. Communication channels are followed strictly, and red tape is abundant. Procedures are generally followed exactly; terms such as *rules* and *policy* serve as sufficient reasons for actions. Even the most formal organizations cannot function long without an internal communication system emerging. As people operate within the external system, they must interact on a person-to-person basis and create an environment conducive to satisfying their personal emotions, prejudices, likes, and dislikes.

> How can a supervisor's failure to address a teller's repeated cash shortage affect the external system?

In the college classroom, for example, the student behavior required to satisfy the external system is to attend class, take notes, read the text, and pass examinations. On the first day of class, this behavior probably is typical of almost all students, particularly if they did not know one another prior to attending the class. As the class progresses, however, the internal system emerges and overlaps the external system. Students become acquainted, sit next to people they particularly like, talk informally, and may even plan ways to beat the external system. Cutting class and borrowing notes are examples. Soon, these behaviors become norms for class behavior. Students who do not engage in the internal system may be viewed with disdain by the others. Obviously, the informality of the internal system is good for people because it helps satisfy maintenance goals. At the same time, it affects communication.

The Grapevine as an Internal System

The **grapevine**, often called the *rumor mill*, is perhaps the best-known internal communication system. It is actually a component of the internal system. As people talk casually during coffee breaks and lunch periods, the focus usually shifts from topic to topic. One of the topics most certainly would be work—job, company, supervisor, fellow employees. Even though the external system has definite communication channels, the grapevine tends to develop and operate within the organization.

As a communication channel, the grapevine is reputed to be speedy but inaccurate. In the absence of alarms, the grapevine may be the most effective

Businesspeople often speak informally about on-the-job issues. This communication network is referred to as "the grapevine"—a valuable source of accurate information as well as rumor.

way to let occupants know that the building is on fire. It certainly beats sending a written memorandum.

The grapevine often is thought of as a channel for inaccurate communication. In reality, it is no more or less accurate than other channels. Even formal communication may become inaccurate as it passes from level to level in the organizational hierarchy. The inaccuracy of the grapevine has more to do with the message input than with the output. For example, the grapevine is noted as a carrier of rumor, primarily because it carries informal messages. If the input is rumor, and nothing more, the output obviously will be inaccurate. But the output may be an accurate description of the original rumor.

For a college student, the grapevine carries much valuable information. Even though the names of the good instructors may not be published, students learn those names through the grapevine. How best to prepare for certain examinations, instructor attitudes on attendance and homework, and even future faculty personnel changes are messages that travel over the grapevine. In the business office, news about promotions, personnel changes, company policy changes, and annual salary adjustments often are communicated by the grapevine long before being disseminated by formal channels.

A misconception about the grapevine is that the message passes from person to person until it finally reaches a person who cannot pass it on—the end of the line. Actually, the grapevine works through a variety of channels. Typically, one person tells two or three others, who each tell two or three others, who each tell two or three others, and so on. Thus, the message may spread to a huge number of people in a very short time. Additionally, the grapevine has no single, consistent source. Messages may originate anywhere and follow various routes. More will be said about sources and routes later in this chapter.

An informal, internal communication system will emerge from even the most carefully designed formal, external system. Managers who ignore this fact are attempting to manage blindfolded. Carroll M. Perkins, former general manager of the Salt River Project in Phoenix, recommended that managers "learn to *use*

THINK IT OVER
Managers who ignore the grapevine will have difficulty achieving organizational goals. Think about a situation you have experienced where an instructor/adviser/employer ignored valid information coming to him/her through the grapevine. How did this situation affect your working relationship with the person?

the informal communication network rather than condemn or resist it. After two major workforce reductions at the Salt River Project, a rumor spread that a third layoff was imminent. The grapevine was as useful in counteracting the rumor as it was in spreading false information" (Himstreet, Baty, Lehman, 1993, p. 17).

Yet some managers do try to work exclusively with the external system. Achieving organizational goals must be extremely difficult for them. As long as people interact, the organization will have both systems.

COMMUNICATION FLOW IN ORGANIZATIONS

The flow of communication within the organization may be upward, downward, or horizontal, as shown in Figure 2-2. Because these three terms are used frequently in communication literature, they deserve clarification. Although the concept of flow seems simple, direction has meaning for those participating in the communication process.

LEARNING OBJECTIVE 6

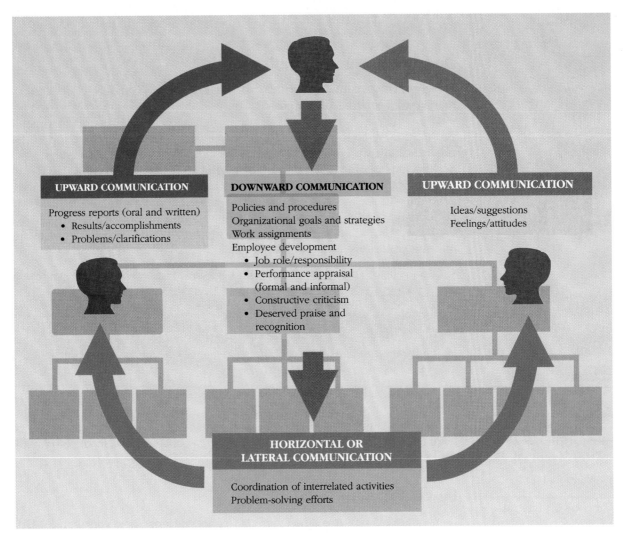

UPWARD COMMUNICATION

Progress reports (oral and written)
• Results/accomplishments
• Problems/clarifications

DOWNWARD COMMUNICATION

Policies and procedures
Organizational goals and strategies
Work assignments
Employee development
• Job role/responsibility
• Performance appraisal
  (formal and informal)
• Constructive criticism
• Deserved praise and
  recognition

UPWARD COMMUNICATION

Ideas/suggestions
Feelings/attitudes

HORIZONTAL OR
LATERAL COMMUNICATION

Coordination of interrelated activities
Problem-solving efforts

FIGURE 2-2   Flow of information within an organization.

COMMUNICATION MENTOR

In the Soviet/Russian culture, communication only flowed one way—down. Our challenge has been to reverse this pattern, teaching our Russian staff that to provide quality service to our clients, we must communicate with each other at least as much, if not more, than with our clients. This open communication flow (upward and downward) also builds trust and confidence, which are important as we develop this practice.

The "open-door" policy was also alien to the Russian culture; young staff would not consider walking into their Russian General Director's (similar to a president in the West) office to discuss a problem. In the former U.S.S.R., knowledge/information was power. Knowledge was shared only when doing so was personally beneficial—compartmentalization in its most specific and detailed form.

Larry E. Wilson, Managing Partner
Arthur Andersen, Moscow

Downward Communication

Why do messages seem to get longer as they move downward?

Downward communication flows from supervisor to employee, from policy makers to operating personnel, or from top to bottom on the organizational chart. As messages move downward through successive levels of the organization, they seem to get larger. A simple policy statement from the top of the organization may grow into a formal plan for operation at lower levels.

Teaching people how to do their specific tasks is an element of downward communication. Another element is orientation to a company's rules, practices, procedures, history, and goals. Employees learn about the quality of their job performance through downward communication.

Downward communication normally involves both written and oral methods and makes use of the following guidelines:

1. People high in the organization usually have greater knowledge of the organization and its goals than do people at lower levels.
2. Both oral and written messages tend to become larger as they move downward through organizational levels. This expansion results from attempts to prevent distortion and is more noticeable in written messages.
3. Oral messages are subject to greater changes in meaning than are written messages.

Management can obtain valuable suggestions from employees. The Egg McMuffin and all its clones originated from an idea generated by a lower-level McDonald's employee (Zaremba, 1991).

As discussed in Chapter 1, the receiver's reaction to a message is called **feedback**. When a supervisor sends a message to a lower-level employee who then asks a question or nods assent, the question and the nod are signs of feedback. Feedback may flow both downward and upward in organizational communication.

The receiver's reaction to a message is referred to as feedback.

Upward Communication

Communication upward, although necessary and valuable, does contain risks. **Upward communication** generally is feedback to downward communication.

When management requests information from lower organizational levels, the resulting information becomes feedback to that request. Employees talk to supervisors about themselves, their fellow employees, their work and methods of doing it, and their perceptions of the organization. These comments are feedback to the downward flow transmitted in both oral and written form by group meetings, procedures or operations manuals, company news releases, and the grapevine.

Accurate upward communication keeps management informed about the feelings of lower-level employees, taps the expertise of employees, helps management identify both difficult and potentially promotable employees, and paves the way for even more effective downward communication. Employees reporting upward are aware that their communications carry the risk of putting them on the spot. They might commit themselves to something they cannot handle, or they might communicate incorrectly.

Employees appreciate and welcome genuine opportunities to send information to management. They are likely to feel better about themselves and their purpose in the organization. On the other hand, they will likely resent and perhaps react harshly to any superficial attempt to provide an open communication network with management.

These factors, then, are important to consider when upward communication flow is involved:

1. Upward communication is primarily feedback to requests and actions of supervisors.
2. Upward communication may be misleading because lower-level employees often tell the superior what they think the superior wants to hear. Therefore, their messages might contradict their true observations and perceptions.
3. Upward communication is based on trust in the supervisor.
4. Upward communication frequently involves risk to an employee.
5. Employees will reject superficial attempts to obtain feedback from employees.

Horizontal or Lateral Communication

Horizontal or **lateral communication** describes interactions between organizational units on the same hierarchical level. These interactions reveal one of the major shortcomings of organizational charts. Charts do not allow

UNUM Corp. encourages employees to send questions and comments to the CEO using e-mail. Employee feedback led to a program to subsidize employee child-care expenses (Rice, 1991).

THINK IT OVER
Recall the human resources manager's ultimatum about new work hours at Citizens' Bank (opening scenario). What costs resulted from the human resources manager's refusal to seek feedback from the tellers? Discuss how this manager could have improved this communication and the results.

People communicate with others at their same level to coordinate activities within the organization.

COMMUNICATION MENTOR

Traditionally, most communication within American businesses has been downward communication. Until recent years, the majority of companies in this country followed a militaristic model with decisions made by the general and carried out by the privates.

Many people have become uncomfortable with this model because it tends to breed mediocrity and low employee morale. When information does not flow upward, employees justly feel that they are not being listened to or heard, and many good ideas never reach the top. When information does not flow sideways, various departments work in isolation, and the benefits of synergy are lost.

Any company that wants to remain competitive and successful in today's business environment must develop and use channels of communication that flow in all directions.

Hugh B. Jacks
President and Owner
Potential Enterprises & Adventure Safaris

much room for horizontal communication when they depict authority relationships by placing one box higher than another and define role functions by placing titles in those boxes. Yet horizontal communication is the primary means of achieving coordination in a functional organizational structure. At Citizens' Bank, for instance, the chart implies that people in operations cannot communicate directly with people in lending and trust, fund-raising, or operations without going through the chief executive officer. Obviously, that would be a rather difficult way to operate a complex organization.

Management must recognize that informal, horizontal communication takes place in any system or organization where people are available to one another. The informal communication and behavior that is not task oriented develop alongside formal task communication and behavior, contributing to morale, to improvements in ways to accomplish tasks, and to clarification of upward and downward communication. Formal horizontal communication serves a coordinating function in the organization. Units coordinate their activities to accomplish task goals just as adjacent workers in a production line coordinate their activities.

In an organization divided into cross-functional teams, horizontal communication among the team members is extremely important to achieve individual and team goals. Total quality management experts emphasize that honest, open communication is the single most important factor in successfully creating a Total Quality Management environment. "If people keep talking to one another, they can work through their problems, overcome barriers, and find encouragement and support from others involved in quality efforts" (Hunt, 1993, p. 121).

THINK IT OVER
Referring to the organizational chart in Figure 2-2, cite an example of *downward*, *upward*, and *horizontal* communication at Citizens' Bank (opening scenario). Next, discuss the flow of communication in an organization in which you belong or for which you have worked.

COMMUNICATION IN ACTION

Lonny Uzzell, Southside Bank

When Southside Bank opened its doors in October, 1960, as an independent and locally owned bank, its founders knew that responsiveness to customers was crucial to its success. Today, the bank has a strong community reputation for responsiveness to customers. Having kept the same name for over 30 years, the bank has maintained stability and demonstrated steady growth. The bank employs over 230 personnel and manages assets of over $400,000,000. What elements have been a key to this success? What role does business communication play in the bank's stability and growth?

Lonny Uzzell, senior vice president at Southside, believes key elements underlie Southside's success: responsiveness and sensitivity to customer's needs through effective listening and accurate feedback. Uzzell recounts the recent updating of the bank's computer system as an example. The system has undergone several major changes in recent months, requiring bank officers to inform customers of changes. Uzzell stated, "As a result of the transition between computer systems, customers received two bank statements one month: one from the old system and one from the new system. These changes created many questions and made communication with the customer extremely important." Letters were sent to customers about the change. Then, in response to questions, Southside organized incoming calls that

allowed customers to talk with individual officers about their accounts. As a bank officer who helps train and develop Southside employees, Uzzell knows well that good listening with customers is not just important to his work. It is essential to the bank's profitability.

Bank employees demonstrate responsiveness in other ways. When Uzzell meets someone in the lobby, telephones a customer, or responds to a bank customer through a letter, he listens to customers. He treats customers as if they are special. In doing so, he knows that customers receiving any less than special treatment may choose a competitor. When Uzzell talks with clients, he fully understands the concept of "relationship marketing." Personalized service at Southside is as important to customers as interest rates and investments. Today's bank customers demand better, more personalized service.

Not only must Uzzell listen well to customers, he must listen and respond to other bank employees. During a normal work day, he interacts with and listens to employees in different departments and throughout all levels of the bank's organization. Without good listening skills, he would not be successful at his work. Uzzell develops good relationships and quality service through good listening.

Applying What You Have Learned

1. During the working day, how does Uzzell experience listening in the four levels of communication?

2. Identify various directions in the flow of listening at the bank. How does good listening and timely, accurate feedback facilitate communication when a new computer system is installed?

3. Reflect on your own experiences with a bank. How did your interpersonal communication with bank employees make that experience positive or negative?

4. Using the organizational chart for Citizens' Bank of Springfield in Figure 2-1 as a sample, distinguish between formal and informal communication at Southside Bank. Provide several examples to illustrate the two distinct systems.

SUMMARY

1 Communication takes place at four levels: intrapersonal (communication within one), interpersonal (communication between two people), group (more than two people), and organizational.

2 Groups and organizations exist because people working together can accomplish more and make better decisions than can the same people working individually. The total is greater than the sum of the parts. Factors that affect the effectiveness of group communication include leadership, common goals, role perception, longevity, size, status, and group norms.

3 As tasks increase in size and complexity, specialization is required; thus, employees are grouped into smaller, separate departments. Because of the specialization, each department is interdependent on the other units. These *specialized, interdependent* departments are organized to achieve goals, and the resulting entity is an organization with a functional organizational structure.

4 Rigid organizational structure introduces two formidable communication barriers:
- The organizational chart may not define the relative importance of each department or individual in the organization; e.g., a person's role (actual importance in the company) may be greater than his or her status (formal position on the organizational chart).

- Excessive competition in traditional tall organizational structures impedes the cooperation and communication needed to succeed in today's workplace. Flat organizational structures that eliminate layers of management and departmental boundaries enhance horizontal communication and cooperation.

5 Communication helps control and coordinate the work of the organization through a formal, external system and an informal, internal system. The external system exists to accomplish tasks, and the internal system serves a personal-maintenance purpose that results in people feeling better about themselves and others. Because these systems operate simultaneously, a modified system emerges that combines qualities of both.

6 Communication flows upward, downward, and horizontally or laterally. These flows often defy the ability of management to describe them graphically. To cope with communication problems in organizations, management should (1) attempt to balance the external and internal systems, (2) use the systems for effective task accomplishment and maintenance purposes, and (3) indicate by example their concern for effective communication.

REFERENCES

Covey, S. (1989). *The seven habits of successful people: Powerful lessons in personal change.* NY: Simon & Schuster.

Hillkirk, J. (1993, November 9). More companies reengineering: Challenging status quo now in vogue. *USA Today,* p. 1b.

Himstreet, W. C., Baty, W. M., & Lehman, C. M. (1993). *Business communications.* Belmont, CA: Wadsworth.

Hunt, V. D. (1993). *Managing for quality: Integrating quality and business strategy.* Homewood, IL: Business One Irwin.

Rice, F. (1991). Champions of communication. *Fortune, 123,* 111-112, 114, 120.

Zaremba, A. (1989). The upward network. *Personnel Journal, 68,* 34, 36, 39.

REVIEW QUESTIONS

1. What is the difference between interpersonal and intrapersonal communication?
2. What are the two major goals of both interpersonal and group communication?
3. Synergy results from group work. What is synergy?
4. How does the longevity of a group task affect its attention to maintenance efforts?
5. Why is an odd number of group members frequently desirable?
6. Why do people conform to norms?
7. What two factors combine to characterize large, formal organizations?
8. List three barriers caused by formal organizational structure.
9. How might an organizational chart fail to indicate the relative importance of positions or individuals on the chart?
10. What is a possible cause of most conflict between or among groups?
11. How might the pyramid shape of an organizational chart affect individual and group performance?
12. Discuss how the win/win philosophy and effective communication skills can increase cooperation among individuals and units within an organization.
13. Discuss how a flat organizational structure affects communication.
14. What is the system of organizational communication called when it relies on rules, procedures, and formalities?
15. What is the system of organizational communication called when it is characterized by maintenance activities?
16. Does the grapevine lend itself to easy tracking? Why?
17. Why do downward messages tend to become larger as they travel through successive organizational levels?
18. Is organizational control achieved through horizontal communication or through upward-downward communication?
19. What technical term describes the receiver's reaction to a message?
20. Discuss the benefits and risks inherent in upward communication.

EXERCISES

1. Complete each of the "THINK IT OVER" activities your instructor assigns.
2. Describe the communication flow (external and internal) in a *group* with which you are familiar.
3. Draw an organizational chart to depict the external system of communication within an *organization* with which you are familiar. Using the terminology presented in the chapter, briefly explain your answer.
4. Using the same organization you selected in Exercise 3, distinguish between the external and internal systems of organizational communication. Provide several examples to illustrate the two distinct systems. How has management responded to the internal system you are describing (e.g., ignored or used it effectively)? Based on your reading of the chapter, what suggestions can you offer for improving the organizational communication structure of this organization?
5. Using the online database in your library, locate an article about a company that has adopted a flat organizational structure. Write a brief summary emphasizing the effect this change in organizational structure has had on the communication process.
6. In groups assigned by your instructor, complete the following activity:
   a. Select one group member to develop a short message (instructor may provide one). The first member whispers this message to the second member, the second member to the third member, and so on. Finally, the first member repeats the original message.
   b. As a group discussion, offer a few suggestions to managers for dealing with the grapevine.

E-MAIL APPLICATION

 Working with a student that your instructor designates, send your instructor a brief e-mail message about one of the following topics: (a) Provide a list of guidelines for effective group communication or (b) discuss the role of e-mail in organizational communica-tion. Elaborate on how e-mail is different from and superior or inferior to other means of communication such as memos, face-to-face meetings, telephone, etc. Discuss the factors that would lead you to select e-mail as an appropriate channel for a message.

CHAPTER 3

PUBLIC SPEAKING AND

ORAL REPORTING

OBJECTIVES

When you have completed Chapter 3, you will be able to

1. Analyze the audience for your oral presentations.

2. Plan and outline public speeches and oral reports.

3. Deliver speeches with increasing confidence.

4. Select, design, and use visual aids effectively.

Kimberly Clarice Aiken was a college sophomore when she became Miss America 1994. Both she and her high school adviser described Kimberly as shy. Kimberly says, "I was so shy I never did any public speaking [my junior year]." Giving speeches in senior English and practicing in front of a college-level communication class helped Kimberly overcome this shyness, and two years later she was confident enough of her public speaking skills to win a $35,000 scholarship as the new Miss America.

What are her strong points? She's "articulate," "honest," and "down-to-earth," say friends. "That could have been one of my advantages in the pageant," Kimberly says, "I probably wasn't too programmed or overly prepared." Being prepared, but also natural and open, is still important as she travels across the country representing young women in the United States.

Many prospective business leaders may expect that professional speechwriters will write speeches for them, but not even Miss America has that luxury. Although the Miss America Organization provides statistics, Miss America writes her own speeches, usually while on the airplane flying from one speaking engagement to another. Kimberly knows that adapting her message to the audience is necessary if the message is to have an impact. This goal becomes quite challenging, as she might be speaking to preschoolers in the morning and lawyers at a black-tie event in the evening (Sabo, 1994).

Throughout your career, you too will be judged by the effectiveness with which you communicate orally in your daily activities. You might make a presentation to your peers in committee work, to subordinates as part of a training or information program, or to senior management at a board of directors or shareholders meeting. In each case, your reputation is on the line. When you are effective, you gain status and earn respect. You find managing others easier, and you become promotable to increasingly higher levels. You may even take on a more attractive personal appearance as a by-product of your speaking ability.

You may accept that speaking with impact is important to your career; however, you are terrified of speaking before a group. You are not alone. Several surveys have placed public speaking at the top of lists of people's greatest fears. People fear public speaking more than any other threat in their lives—heights, insects, finances, deep water, sickness, or even death. Despite this intense fear of speaking before a group, Decker (1992) has found that the people who attempt to speak publicly succeed about 95 percent of the time.

If the success record for public speaking is so high, doesn't it seem senseless that many people exaggerate their fear, marking themselves failures *without* even attempting to speak? As you complete your college career, keep this success rate in mind and take advantage of every possible opportunity to speak in front of others. Start by sharing your ideas with one other person, speaking out at a committee meeting, presenting a report at a meeting, and finally making a formal presentation before a group. Each time you speak, attempt to improve your overall speaking impact. Identify major weaknesses and then develop strategies to eliminate them. This chapter will provide guidelines to get you started; you will learn to analyze your audience, plan and organize your topic; deliver your speech; and develop effective visual aids.

"You know what an audience thinks of a manager who can't effectively handle a 30-minute presentation? If this guy can't handle a 30-minute presentation, how can he handle a $30 million company?" (Rutter, 1993, p. 94). These opening remarks by Jerry Weissman, a professional trainer, emphasize the importance of public speaking to CEOs preparing to sell their company's first public offering.

THINK IT OVER
Recall a situation that required you to sell yourself or your ideas. Were you satisfied with the impression you made? Or were you nervous and totally ineffective?

COMMUNICATION MENTOR

A comfortable command of public speaking is one of the most empowering skills any businessperson can have. Whether they are physicians, engineers, politicians, or salespeople, the best speakers will always have a better chance of rising to a leadership position. All management hopefuls should begin training early and often for public speaking—through high school and college debate teams, speech classes, as Toastmasters, in professional and civic organizations—in fact, at any opportunity available to them.

Cynthia Pharr
President & CEO
C. Pharr Marketing Communications

KNOWING YOUR AUDIENCE

Because all audiences are not the same, speakers must be able to identify characteristics common to each audience. A research scientist should not deliver a speech to a lay audience in highly technical terms. A speech about acid rain to a farm group should address the farmers' problems, for example, and not focus on scientific causes of acid rain. People listen to speeches about things of interest to them. "What's in it for me?" is the question most listeners ask. Here are some important facts you can obtain about most audiences: ages, genders, occupations, educational levels, attitudes, values, broad and specific interests, and needs, if any.

LEARNING OBJECTIVE 1

Your analysis of most of these factors enables you to direct your speech specifically to your audience. In addition to these factors, you should also consider certain things about the occasion and location. Patriotic speeches to a group of military veterans will differ from speeches to a group of new recruits, just as Fourth of July speeches will differ from Memorial Day speeches. Seek answers to the following questions when you discuss your speaking engagement with someone representing the group or audience:

- What are the general characteristics of my audience (gender, age, culture(s), experience, attitude toward topic, and needs to be met through the speech)?
- How many will be in the audience?
- Will I be the only speaker? If not, where does my presentation fit in the program? What time of day?
- How much time will I be permitted? Minimum? Maximum?
- What are the seating arrangements? How far will the audience be from the speaker? Will a microphone be available?
- Is the audience required to attend?

Answers to these questions reveal whether the speaking environment will be intimate or remote, whether the audience is likely to be receptive and alert or nonreceptive and tired, and whether you will have to develop additional motivational or persuasive devices.

What factors about your audience affect the presentation you plan? What other facts might be helpful to know about your audience?

THINK IT OVER
How might you adapt an oral report you are delivering to a group of Japanese (or some other culture) businesspersons interested in a joint venture with your company? Locate articles, books, and review Chapter 4 to answer this question if necessary.

As a general observation, audiences *do* want to be in tune with a speaker. A well-prepared speaker can establish audience rapport easily. Your speaking goal is to have the audience react favorably to you and to your message. Keep in mind that your success will be judged by only one group: the audience. From planning your speech to practicing its delivery, focus your preparation on the audience.

As you plan and deliver your speech, keep this question in mind: "How will what I'm saying benefit this group of listeners?"

PLANNING YOUR SPEECH OR ORAL REPORT

LEARNING OBJECTIVE 2

What are the three purposes of speeches?

The process of planning your oral presentation evolves from your objective(s) for speaking. The traditional purposes of speeches are

1. *To entertain.* After-dinner speeches are generally designed to entertain. Although these speeches may have a secondary objective of informing or persuading through their messages, the content and delivery are developed with entertainment in mind.
2. *To inform.* When your major objective is to have the audience understand a body of information, concentrate on the logical presentation of content.
3. *To persuade.* Political speeches fall in the persuasive category because they attempt to influence or change the attitudes or actions of an audience.

Entertaining and informative speeches use the following types of organization:

1. *Narrative—telling a story.* Autobiographical stories and tales of adventure are examples of narration.
2. *Descriptive—describing a situation.* Speeches about how certain companies or industries handle problems of personnel, competition, new-product development, and similar topics are common at trade and industry association meetings.
3. *Explanatory—using a logical sequence.* Explanation is the basis for many talks *within* organizations. The talks are designed to explain existing or new policies and procedures to staff members.

Persuasive speeches succeed only when audiences react as the speaker intended. To obtain desired reactions, speakers must convince listeners of the benefits the desired action holds for them. Appeals to reason or to emotions such as pride, fear, love, economy, safety, health, and quality motivate human action.

List the benefits of oral reporting.

Within organizations, oral reporting is an important means of obtaining and exchanging information for decision making and policy development. Oral reporting is an efficient way to communicate because several people receive the message at the same time rather than individually at different times. It also constitutes an effective means of communicating because the audience is able to provide immediate feedback for clarification. As a result, oral reporting can significantly reduce message distortion and misunderstanding. Oral reports differ from stand-up, public speeches in several other ways:

How do oral reports differ from public speeches?

1. The primary purpose of an oral report is to inform, not to entertain. Oral reports should use narration, description, or explanation. Do not use appeals to emotion. Even a salesperson should not use emotional appeals when addressing a group of company officers about ways to solve problems and benefit the organization. Persuasion is an outcome of logical topic development.

COMMUNICATION   MENTOR

Accepting an invitation to speak is a wonderful opportunity and a major responsibility. Above all, make sure your speech is truly yours—that it reflects your sincere beliefs and your individual style—no matter who writes the first draft. Always edit and practice until you are comfortable with the individual words and the overall message. Members of the audience deserve to hear a speaker who is prepared, sincere, interested, and interesting.

They also deserve to hear a speech that was written with them in mind, so know your audience's interests and concerns. At the end of the speech, each listener should be able to answer the question: "Why is this message important to me?"

Public speaking is nerve-racking for most people, so start practicing now. Run for an office on campus; volunteer to introduce someone at a large gathering; or seek out any other worthwhile situation in which you'll be forced to stand before a crowd and speak.

Hugh B. Jacks
President & Owner
Potential Enterprises and Adventure Safaris

2. Much more usually is known about the audience for an oral report, and the speaker is probably known by most members of the audience. The oral report normally is given *within* the organization.
3. The setting for the oral report is more intimate than the setting for a formal speech because the audience is smaller.
4. The audience is more likely to ask questions during oral presentations.
5. The time allotted for an oral report tends to be short. Consequently, you must plan your presentation carefully so it covers the topic fully yet concisely.

Understanding your purpose is helpful in planning and outlining your speech.

Planning Your Strategy

With an understanding of the purpose of your oral presentation—why you are giving it, what you hope to achieve—and a conception of the size, interest, and background of the audience, you should arrive at the best type of speech organization to use.

Make a few written notes about your purpose and about the makeup of the audience, keeping in mind the time of day and the probable attitudes and mental alertness of the audience. These notes should assist you in selecting content for your presentation. To help you understand the process of outlining, consider two examples: an outline of a speech to gain support for a management training program and an outline of an oral report to recommend a site for a new branch office.

Outlining a Public Speech to Persuade

Assume that you are a promotional representative for Project COPE (Challenging Outdoor Personal Experiences), a personal development program. Through a weekend full of mentally and physically challenging events, participants develop self-confidence, trust, communication, and teamwork. Participants build these valuable managerial skills as they attempt to do things they have never done before and work together to develop creative ways to overcome the various obstacles. The "trust fall" (falling backwards to be caught by team members) and climbing a 30-foot tower and leaning out to catch a bar being held by team members below are examples of these demanding events.

Several of the senior executives of a large multinational company are sold on your program as a viable alternative for alleviating the company's slow response to the marketplace—a common problem with large companies. You have been invited to speak during the company's annual two-day management retreat. You are scheduled to speak at 10 a.m. and will have 30 minutes to present your message. About 300 managers—both men and women—will be your audience.

Your analysis indicates that a simple message about the company's need to respond to the marketplace with the same speed that small companies can would be well received. You want the audience to realize that (1) a slow response to the marketplace is an inherent problem with large companies, which places small companies at a competitive advantage and (2) COPE can prepare managers to deal effectively with this problem. How can you convince this audience that they will benefit by taking part in this program? You should appeal primarily to their desire to improve the quality of their work and the company's competitiveness. Your speech must be persuasive.

> **THINK IT OVER**
> Before developing your speech on COPE, answer these questions:
> - What is your purpose?
> - What do you know about your audience?
> - How will you adapt your speech to the time of day, place, and time allotment?

Selecting the Major Points

> Experienced speakers use simple outlines with only a few major points.

In a typical talk of 30 to 45 minutes, you can plan on two things. First, time permits development of only a few major points. Second, your audience can absorb only a few major points regardless of the length of the speech. Thus, you might outline your presentation about COPE as shown in Figure 3-1.

Making every statement in a talk into a major point—something to be remembered—is impossible, unless the talk lasts only two or three minutes.

Locating Support for Major Points

Once you have selected your major points, locate your supporting material. You may also reverse the process when you have a supply of major points from which to choose. In that case, use those for which you have a supply of supporting material. The best sources for supporting material will come from your everyday reading and listening. The broader your reading, the greater will be your supply of material.

To build the foundation for an emotional appeal, you may draw from several examples, methods, and techniques—first to ensure audience understanding and then to reinforce it. For example,

1. *Use statistical support.* Are statistics or other quantitative measures available to lend authority and believability to your points? Surely you can find

**COPE (Challenging Outdoor Personal Experiences):
Survival Skills Needed to Compete
in Today's Dynamic Workplace**

I. Introduction
   A. Purpose—Description of Cope
   B. Justification of or importance of the topic—COPE helps
      managers work together to respond quickly to the
      needs of the marketplace: (a) self-confidence, (b)
      communication, and (c) teamwork.

II. Body
   A. Major point 1 with support—Bolstering Self-Confidence
   B. Major point 2 with support—Developing Communication
      Skills
   C. Major point 3 with support—Working Effectively as a
      Team

III. Summary and Conclusion—Restate how COPE can benefit
      the individual manager and the company by developing
      self-confidence, communication, and teamwork and ask
      audience to participate.

FIGURE 3-1   Outline of a persuasive speech.

evidence to support your thesis that large companies are less responsive than smaller companies. Obtain statistics from companies that have participated in COPE related to reduced turnover and absenteeism, reduced time to develop products, increased responsiveness to the customer/client, and other measures of increased managerial effectiveness.

2. *Use anecdotes.* Anecdotes are stories having a relationship to the speech topic or a moral ending. Include stories about leading companies that have participated in COPE and can relate their firsthand experiences.

3. *Use quotes from prominent people.* Comments made by other authorities are always helpful. In the case of COPE, top management of leading companies represents a credible source of quotations.

4. *Use jokes and humor appropriately.* You know people like humor that is in good taste, so you incorporate a few amusing incidents that actually occurred during a COPE session. Each incident is relevant to your speech and appropriate to your audience. You believe these humorous accounts will make the audience more receptive to the idea of a weekend of intense activities.

5. *Use visual displays.* Slides, flip charts, and hand-held objects are effective in many speaking situations. Try to think of visual displays that will complement your oral presentation.

Case studies and specific personal incidents strengthen major points.

THINK IT OVER
Online databases give you instant access to numerous sources of timely information to support your points. Access a database available to you and key in a subject of your choice (perhaps an issue that currently is receiving a great deal of media coverage) Share with the class at least two possible sources to support your topic.

Although stories, statistics, quotations, and the like may seem trivial, they are critical to effective speaking. They retain listener interest, provide proof and evidence supporting major points, and often provide the humor and enlightenment that turn an otherwise dreary topic into a stimulating message. They are among the professional speaker's most important inventory items. How does a speaker accumulate these items? Most obtain them from personal reading. When they come across something that seems worth remembering, they write it down or clip the material and place it in a file.

EFFECTIVE OPENING

Like any other kind of story, a speech has a beginning, a body, and an ending. Your content really constitutes the body of the speech, but the beginning and ending are very important. What you say at the beginning sets the stage for your entire performance and initiates your rapport with the audience. A speech on highway safety might well begin with the following statement:

Just last year 15 young people from our community were killed in the prime of their lives by automobile crashes that could have been avoided.

Such an opening certainly would get attention. So too would an opening such as this for a speech to young people on drugs:

I live in a quiet, middle-class, comfortable neighborhood. That is, until just a few months ago—when four young people from three different families were killed in an automobile accident following a party at which drugs were used.

THINK IT OVER
In a small group, compile a list of ways to capture the audience's attention. You will recall ideas discussed in your public speaking class and may turn to Chapter 11 in this text to locate possible ideas.

What people hear first in a speech has much to do with how they accept your message.

WELL-SUPPORTED BODY

The body of a speech contains the major points that support your topic: statistical support, anecdotes, quotes from prominent people, etc.

EFFECTIVE ENDING

You also must end the talk effectively. Work hard to develop a closing that will impress your audience and leave them with the major points of your speech. The impact is even greater if the ending can relate to your opening:

So, my friends, make your community drug-free so you and your friends can grow up to enjoy the benefits of health, education, family, and freedom."

Such a statement would close a "no" to drugs speech strongly. Simply stand back and accept the applause.

Outlining an Oral Report to Inform and Explain

As a general observation, the audience will have a built-in interest in an oral report. This interest gives the speaker an advantage over the public speech in which the speaker must build audience interest as the talk develops.

A broad outline for an oral report should include the items listed in Figure 3-2.

> **CORNER OF MAIN AND FIRST IN WATSON**
> **IS OPTIMAL SITE FOR NEW**
> **BRANCH OFFICE**
>
> I.   Introduction (Purpose of the report)
>
> II. Body
>   A. Method of research and background material
>   B. Presentation of findings
>
> III. Summary/Conclusion (summarize major findings, discuss conclusions and implications and possible recommendations)

FIGURE 3-2   Outline of an oral report to inform and explain.

Many types of reports can be planned around this outline: reviews of economic conditions; summaries of new methods, practices, or policies; periodic reports of progress; studies of personnel; analyses of financial problems; and reports of research.

Support your ideas with factual information rather than emotional appeals.

INTRODUCTION

You might use one of the speech openings discussed for persuasive speeches if you believe it appropriate. However, because your purpose is to report, not to entertain, you should seek to stay with your subject. Consider an opening statement such as the following:

> When we were granted the approval to open a new branch office in Watson, we assigned a team to select the best possible inner-city location.

This opening introduces the subject immediately and sets the stage for the rest of the report. If you want to organize your report in a direct sequence, you might begin with

> I want to inform you about why and how we selected the corner of Main and First in Watson as the location for our newest branch office.

BODY

In speech organization, the major points are supported by anecdotes, statistics, and quotes. As you prepare your oral report, however, you will have to support your major points with factual information. The design of your paragraphs will become readily apparent to your listeners if you begin with a topic sentence and follow with the supporting material. For example,

> Three possible sites for the branch were available—Main and First, the Roseburg Mall, and the City National Bank building at Main and Twelfth. As this chart shows, pedestrian foot traffic is. . . .

THINK IT OVER
Effective oral reports have an **introduction** (speaker tells audience what will be discussed), a **body** (speaker tells the audience), and a **summary** (speaker restates what was told in the body).

THINK IT OVER
List two techniques a speaker might use to guide the audience from one major section of the report to another.

Oral reports are a common and often informal form of business communication. This manager has prepared a short, informative oral presentation supported by visual aids, and he has anticipated questions that his colleagues will ask about his findings.

Unlike a written report, your oral report does not have chapter headings and subheadings to guide the reader. Therefore, you should plan to use topic sentences to indicate when you change from one part of the report to another. Statements such as

Next, I will describe the two major problems that our proposal must address.

are helpful. You can also make a longer-than-normal pause between the end of one section and the beginning of the next. You may even indicate a change from topic to topic by changing your body position noticeably. Alternatively, you can list major topics on a posterboard or flip chart and can simply point to each one as you begin to talk about it. By using techniques that indicate a topic change, you will help your audience follow your presentation. If they make an effort, most will have a mental outline of your presentation.

SUMMARY

The summary section of the oral report is like that of the written report. State your conclusion and support it with the highlights from your supporting evidence:

In summary, we selected the Main and First location because it had. . . .

In a public speech, the ending is often an urgent plea for the members of the audience to take some action or to look on the subject from a new point of view.

DELIVERING YOUR ORAL PRESENTATION

All speeches fall into one of the following categories of delivery style:

1. *The impromptu speech.* Impromptu speaking may be frightening to most people because the speaker is called on without prior notice. In some cases, speakers can anticipate the request and formulate thoughts. In any case, impromptu speaking should be direct and frank. Someone not properly informed can simply say, "Thank you," for being called on and explain why the opportunity is being declined.

2. *The extemporaneous speech.* Extemporaneous speeches are planned, prepared, and rehearsed but not written in detail. Professionals use the extemporaneous style. Simple cues written on small index cards may provide enough material for the speaker to talk meaningfully for long periods. Familiarity with the material makes this style effective. Instructors use it because material may be adapted to different class situations, just as public speakers may adapt their material to different audiences.

3. *The memorized speech.* Memorization has the greatest limitations of the speech styles. Speakers are almost totally unable to react to feedback, and—as everyone who attended elementary school knows—the speaker who forgets a point and develops a mental block may lose the entire speech. Memorized speeches tend to sound monotonous, restrict natural body gestures and motions, and lack conviction. For short religious or fraternal rites, however, the memorized presentation is often impressive.

4. *The written-and-read speech.* For complex material and technical conference presentations, written-and-read speeches ensure content coverage. Additionally, this style protects speakers against being misquoted and also fits into exact time constraints, as in television or radio presentations. Written-and-read speeches often prevent speaker-audience rapport, particularly when speakers keep their eyes and heads buried in their manuscripts. If you use this method, write in large letters, avoid using difficult words that might cause you to stumble, and highlight in color items that need particular emphasis.

Electronic devices now make it possible to project manuscripts on transparent screens on each side of the speaker. The speaker may read the rolling manuscript but appear to be speaking extemporaneously.

Controlling Speech Qualities

Knowledge about and skill in three important qualities of speech—phonation, articulation, and pronunciation—are necessary to the development of effective speaking habits. Let's briefly look at each.

PHONATION

Phonation involves both the production and the variation of the speaker's vocal tone. You project your voice and convey feelings—even thoughts—by varying your vocal tones. Such elements as pitch (how high or low the tones are), intensity (how loud the tones are), and duration (how long the tones are held) are factors in phonation. These factors permit us to recognize other people's

LEARNING OBJECTIVE 3

What are the advantages and disadvantages of each delivery style? Which do you prefer? Explain.

How does the "voice of experience" and the "voice of authority" sound? Name at least two individuals who exhibit these voice qualities.

Sophisticated prompting devices assist public speakers; however, they are not a substitute for intense preparation. President Clinton learned this valuable lesson when the wrong speech for an important health-care address was cued into the prompting device. Clinton skillfully spoke from a written copy of the text for seven minutes while the error was being corrected.

Describe the qualities of a good voice.

voices over the telephone. Anyone who studies oral communication should also remember that changes in phonation occur with changes in emotional moods.

In general, good voices have medium or low pitch, are easily heard but are not too loud, carry smooth sounds, and are flexible in conveying emotional moods. Weak or poor voices generally have a very high or monotonous pitch, are too soft or too loud for comfortable listening, are jerky and distracting, or may lack flexibility.

Practicing the following exercises can be helpful to anyone trying to achieve good voice qualities:

1. *Breathe properly and relax.* Nervousness affects normal breathing patterns and is reflected in vocal tone and pitch. The better prepared you are, the better your phonation will be. Although relaxing may seem difficult to practice before a speech, a few deep breaths, just as swimmers take before diving, can help.

2. *Listen to yourself.* A tape recording of your voice reveals much about pitch, intensity, and duration. Most people are amazed to find their voices are not quite what they had expected. "I never dreamed I sounded that bad" is a common reaction. Nasal twangs usually result from a failure to speak from the diaphragm, which involves taking in and letting out air through the larynx, where the vocal cords operate. High pitch may occur from the same cause, or it may be a product of speaking too fast.

3. *Develop flexibility.* The good speaking voice is somewhat musical, with words and sounds similar to notes in a musical scale. Read each of the following sentences aloud and emphasize the <u>underscored</u> word in each. Even though the sentences are identical, emphasizing different words changes the meaning.

THINK IT OVER
Record your voice on a tape recorder or your answering machine. Evaluate the sound of your voice on the replay: Do you speak in a monotone with no rise or fall to emphasize meaning or express your emotion? Do you have a smile in your voice? Do you project your voice so that you can be heard easily? Repeat this exercise daily; concentrating on these voice qualities as you read aloud is another good exercise.

COMMUNICATION IN ACTION

Tom Watson, Watson Communications International, Inc.

Dr. Tom Watson stands confidently before the group of manufacturing employees, conducting management training. Working easily with flip chart, easel, and markers, his relaxed manner belies the fact that he once experienced severe communication anxiety before groups. His listeners see and hear a relaxed, clear communicator. However, he has struggled with communication anxiety as most speakers do, perhaps even more than most. Can the average speaker overcome communication anxiety? Are there some practical tips for managing anxiety?

Watson believes communication anxiety can be managed and even overcome. A professional trainer and experienced speaker, he typically appears confident and relaxed when speaking before groups. As founder and president of Watson Communications International, Inc., Watson directs a management consulting and training company headquartered in Texas with offices in California and Guam. He has consulted for government and business entities internationally, including the Government of Guam, the Bank of Hawaii, and the Government of Saipan; his clients include businesses such as AT&T, Texas Instruments, North American Coal Corporation, and TRW. His successful company grew as a result of hard work, but he first had to overcome the obstacle of communication anxiety before his company would grow.

As a youth, Watson so feared speaking that he avoided any situation which he would be required to speak, especially before groups. This fear, he says, was based in a childhood stuttering disorder that lasted through his high school years. Watson's story changed, however, when he enrolled as a college freshman in a beginning speech class and delivered his first presentation. The topic was amateur radio. Watson stuttered some before the class, but he slowly gained confidence, spoke more clearly, and finished the presentation. As the speech progressed, he became more "caught up" in his topic and spoke conversationally. The subject of amateur radio was one with which he was very familiar, and he had prepared and practiced his presentation thoroughly. The hard work paid off. He received an "A" from a professor who didn't give many. This first speaking success motivated Watson to try future presentations.

To become a confident speaker, Watson believes, a person must "have something to say, and say it well." Having a sincere, well-informed, and well-prepared message builds a speaker's confidence and greatly increases his or her ability to convince or move the audience to an action.

Watson believes that good public speaking does not come naturally for people but is a skill that must be cultivated. He admits some people have a "propensity" for public speaking—their personalities seem to "fit" the activity well. However, when comparing the so-called "born speaker" with the trained speaker, he has found the person with training will be more successful every time.

Applying What You Have Learned

1. Why is preparation so important in handling communication anxiety?
2. Does good public speaking come naturally for you? Give examples of your personal experiences in public speaking. What technique assisted Watson in overcoming his fear of speaking?
3. Assume that you are faced with giving a presentation to your class and are experiencing communication anxiety. What are some ways you can reduce this anxiety?

I̲ am happy you are here.	Maybe I'm the only happy one.
I a̲m̲ happy you are here.	I really am.
I am happy̲ you are here.	Happy best expresses my feeling.
I am happy yo̲u̲ are here.	Yes, you especially.
I am happy you a̲r̲e̲ here.	You may not be happy, but I am.
I am happy you are here̲.	Here and not somewhere else.

ARTICULATION

Avoid words and phrases like *gonna*, *gotta*, and *how come* that make you sound uneducated. Honestly evaluate the way you articulate words. Identify examples of carelessness and begin correcting them right away.

An articulate speaker produces smooth, fluent, and pleasant speech. **Articulation** is the way in which a speaker produces and joins sounds. Faulty articulation is usually caused by (1) organic disorders of the teeth, mouth, tongue, lips, and other speaking equipment; (2) lack of education; or (3) personal carelessness. *Snoo* for *What's new* is an example of carelessness. *Dis, wid,* and *dem* for *this, with,* and *them* may result from a lack of knowledge and education. Various forms of lisping may result from organic disorders. These examples should not be confused with *dialect*, which people informally call "an accent." A **dialect** is a variation in pronunciation, usually of vowels, from one part of the country to another. Actually, everyone speaks a dialect; and speech experts can often identify, even pinpoint, the section of the country from where a speaker comes. In the United States, people often describe dialects as New England, New York, Southern, Texan, Ozark, Midwestern, Mountain, and Western. Within each of these, minor dialects may arise regionally or from immigrant influence. The simple fact is that when people interact, they influence each other even down to speech sounds. Many prominent speakers may have developed a rather universal dialect that seems to be effective no matter who the audience is.

To improve your articulation, most authorities suggest that you become aware of common errors. Make your tongue, lips, and teeth do the jobs they should to produce proper sounds. Next, understand the speech sounds. Vowels, for example, are always sounded with the mouth open and the tongue clear of the palate. Consonants are responsible primarily for the distinctness of speech and are formed by an interference with or stoppage of outgoing breath.

PRONUNCIATION

Learn the vowel sound symbols used in dictionaries and work on pronouncing words correctly. To get started, what is the preferred pronunciation of *status, data, economics,* and *envelope*?

A dictionary provides the best source to review pronunciation. People may articulate perfectly but still mispronounce words. Perhaps the best rule is to pronounce words in the most natural way. The dictionary often gives two pronunciations for a word. The first one is the desired pronunciation and the second, an acceptable variation. For example, to adopt a pronunciation commonly used in England such as *shedule* for *schedule* or *a-gane* for *again* could be considered affected speech. In other cases, the dictionary allows some leeway. The first choice for pronouncing *data* is to pronounce the first *a* long, as in *date*; but common usage is fast making pronunciation of the short *a* sound, as in *cat*, acceptable. Good speakers use proper pronunciation and refer to the dictionary frequently in both pronunciation and vocabulary development.

When preparing for a speech, do not just read it quietly; practice it aloud. Hearing your speech helps you identify impersonal expressions that would be fine on paper but not in a speech. Reading also alerts you to any "verbal potholes," word combinations that would cause you to stumble. Practice projecting a competent, interesting voice.

When your voice qualities combine to make your messages pleasingly receptive, your primary concerns revolve around developing an effective delivery style.

Using Style in Speeches

Although all of the following suggestions are appropriate for formal public speaking, most also apply to oral reporting and other speaking situations.

1. Expect a few "butterflies" before you speak. A touch of nervousness probably means you will be a success.
2. Insist on a proper, impressive introduction if the audience knows little about you. Providing your status lends credibility to your speeches. Professional speakers prepare their own introductions. You should do the same. Thank the person who made the introduction. "Thank you, Mr. President" after the introduction for an oral report and "Thank you for your kind introduction, Ms. Garcia" for a speech are adequate. Then you follow with your own introduction to your presentation. For a public speech, use the opening as an effort to capture the attention of the audience. Startling statements, jokes or humor related to the topic, famous quotations, and anecdotal stories are familiar speech openings.
3. Select a few friendly faces in the audience. Speak to them because it is easier to speak to a few than to the audience as a whole. A sea of nondescript faces is a difficult audience. When you make eye contact with a few, as shown in Figure 3-3, you will appear to be speaking to each person in the audience.
4. Use gestures naturally to communicate confidence and warmth.
   a. Try to eliminate any nervous gestures that can distract the audience. Names have been coined to describe the common positions people assume when they are speaking and do not have anything to grasp:

"Fig leaf"	Hands together in front of body (one hand on top of the other)
"Napoleon"	Stiff body with hand in coat
"Praying hands"	Hands held together in front of body in praying position
"Jangler"	Stuffing hands in pockets and perhaps jingling keys

   b. Move hands and arms to make a point and then let hands fall naturally to your side.

THINK IT OVER
In a small group, discuss common anxieties caused when giving a speech. What makes you uncomfortable when you speak before a group? Generate possible ways of overcoming this natural nervousness and work to control it.

Why prepare your own introduction?

THINK IT OVER
Have someone videotape you giving a speech or just making a brief statement before a small group. View the videotape and identify your nervous gestures and any other distracting gestures or annoying speech habits.

FIGURE 3-3
Selecting listeners for eye contact.

    c.   Smile genuinely and maintain steady eye contact (long enough to finish a complete thought or sentence) to involve the listener.

    d.   Stand tall with your shoulders back and your stomach in to communicate confidence and high self-esteem.

    e.   Stand in the "ready position." Keep weight forward with knees slightly flexed so you are ready to move easily rather than rooted rigidly in one spot, probably hiding behind the lectern (Decker, 1992, p. 94).

THINK IT OVER
In small groups, generate a list of gestures that differ among cultures to share with the class. Develop sensitivity to cultural differences and be prepared to adapt your delivery style when communicating with other cultures.

5. Avoid "nonwords" that irritate the listener and destroy your effectiveness. Common nonwords include

uhh	so
ahh	like I said
umm	sort of
well	okay
you know	basically

Identify nonwords that you frequently use and then work on replacing them with a three- to five-second pause. This brief gap between thoughts gives you an opportunity to think about what you want to say next and time for your audience to absorb your idea. Presenting an idea (sound bite) and then pausing briefly is similar to two people talking across a desk and is just as effective. The listener will not notice the slight delay, and the absence of meaningless words will make you appear more confident and polished.

6. Avoid other annoying speech habits such as clearing your throat or uttering a soft cough constantly, which will shift audience's attention from the speech to the speaker.

7. Use a lectern to hold your notes and to steady a shaky hand, at least until you gain some confidence and experience. Keep in mind, though, that weaning yourself from the lectern will eliminate a physical barrier between you and the audience. Without the lectern, you will speak more naturally. If you are using a microphone, ask for a cordless, portable microphone so that you can move freely.

THINK IT OVER
Recall a speech where the speaker used humor inappropriately. How did this incident affect the presentation, the audience's attitude toward the speaker, and the topic? Contrast this situation to one where you felt the speaker used humor effectively.

8. Use jokes or humor appropriately. If you cannot tell a joke well, do not use one or *you* may be the joke! Humor should be related to your speech content. Good speakers use humor to create a special bond with the audience, to make them appear friendly, warm, and likable. They often emphasize words in such a way so as to generate laughter, share amusing things that happen to them, or poke fun at themselves. They refrain from any humor that may reflect negatively on race, color, religion, the opposite sex, age, and nationality.

9. Avoid jargon or technical terms that the listeners may not understand. Instead, use plain English that the audience can easily understand. Make your speech more interesting and memorable by using word pictures to make your points. Hughes (1990, p. 58) provides this example: If your message is a warning of difficulties ahead, you could say: "We're climbing a hill that's getting steeper, and there are rocks and potholes in the road." Drawing analogies between new ideas and familiar ones is another technique for generating understanding. For example, comparing the power supply of a computer to the horsepower of an automobile engine, floppy disks to a briefcase, and a hard drive to a filing cabinet would help a computer novice comprehend complex concepts easily.

THINK IT OVER
Provide three examples of broad terms (rather than specific data) and/or word pictures that would help an audience understand a concept in your field or discipline.

10. Do not overwhelm your audience with excessive statistics. Instead, use broad terms or word pictures that the listener can remember. Instead of

"68.2 percent," say "over two thirds"; instead of "112 percent rise in production," say "our output more than doubled." Hearing that computer hard drives hold "four times as much as a floppy disk" is less confusing and more memorable than hearing the exact number of megabytes for each medium. Choose novel, interesting word pictures such as "McDonald's has sold enough burgers to make a cow five miles high" rather than trite images such as the number of football fields or how many times around the world (Hughes, 1990, p. 58).

11. Watch your audience. They will tell you how you are doing and whether you should shorten your speech. Be attentive to negative feedback in the form of talking, coughing, moving chairs, and other signs of discomfort.

12. Work particularly hard on your closing remarks. A good closing serves to leave the audience in a good mood and may help overcome some possible mistakes made during the speech.

13. Dress carefully and tastefully. Appropriate clothing and good grooming affect audiences positively.

14. Appear confident and appear to enjoy making the speech. "Your listeners won't care how much you know until they know how much you care," is pertinent advice from an anonymous source Decker (1992, p. 137) quoted.

Focus on feedback from your audience and adapt your presentation as needed.

Public speaking is both an art and a skill. Careful planning and practice are essential for building speaking skills. If you feel more confident when reading from a manuscript, do so. A poor extemporaneous speech is worse than a properly delivered written-and-read speech. In addition, learning to use visual aids effectively will increase your chances of delivering a speech with a high degree of impact.

Keeping Within Time Limits

If your presentation is part of a busy program, be prepared to complete the presentation within the allotted time. In many organizations, speakers have one or more rehearsals before making reports to groups such as a board of directors. These rehearsals, or dry runs, are made before other executives and are critiqued, timed, revised, and rehearsed again. In some organizations, sessions are videotaped so participants can see how they come across.

Questions often disrupt carefully laid plans. At the same time, questions provide feedback, clarify points, and ensure understanding. More often than not, people ask questions that will be answered in a later part of the presentation. In these cases, you should say something like, "I believe the next slide will clarify that point. If not, we will come back to it." If the question can be answered quickly, the speaker should do so while indicating that it will also be covered later in the presentation. If necessary, the speaker might also indicate that questions will be answered following a certain portion of the presentation. In any case, rehearsal should include a session on questions that might be raised. Then, the talk can be altered to anticipate the questions.

Explain two techniques for handling questions asked during a presentation.

USING VISUAL AIDS

Visual aids are important to oral reports because they reinforce the spoken word. Through the use of visuals, a speaker hits the listener (receiver) with double

LEARNING OBJECTIVE 4

COMMUNICATION MENTOR

Never be afraid to ask for help if you're preparing for an important presentation. Ask someone to help you rehearse, get feedback, and pay attention to it. If you feel you need extra help, get professional assistance. The time and money you spend can make a difference in your presentations.

H. Devon Graham, Jr.
Southwest Regional Managing Partner
Arthur Andersen & Co.

How do visuals improve an oral presentation?

impact—through the eyes and the ears. An ancient Chinese proverb says, "Tell me, I'll forget. Show me, I may remember. But involve me and I'll understand." Research confirms this common-sense idea, indicating that using visual aids

- Reduces the time required to present a concept.
- Increases retention from 14 percent to 38 percent.
- Results in speaker's achieving goals 34 percent more often than when visuals are not used.
- Increases group consensus by 21 percent when used in meetings (Decker, 1992, p. 85).

Skilled speakers generally develop a set of visual aids before they determine exactly what they will say about each one. Typical visuals include

- *Text.* Helps an audience visualize major ideas and follow the flow of the presentation more easily; for example, the outline of the presentation or a list of major considerations in a feasibility study.
- *Graphics, pictures, or models.* Illustrate complex information or major points so they can be understood more easily than if they were presented orally; for example, a pie chart depicting sales trends or a picture or replica of a new product line.

The text chart (left) in Figure 3-4 displays the benefits of expansion for a retail store. The pie chart (right) summarizes data; exploding the slice adds emphasis to an important point.

Many speakers will go to a great deal of effort to prepare a good visual—and then not use it effectively! Inexperienced speakers often ignore the visual altogether or fall into the habit of simply nodding their heads toward the visual. Neither of these techniques is adequate for involving the audience with the visual. In fact, if the material is complex, the speaker is likely to lose the audience completely.

To enhance the impact of your presentations, follow these guidelines for preparing and using visual aids:

Why are you advised to limit the number of visuals used in a single presentation?

1. *Limit the number of visual aids used in a single presentation.* Too many visuals can overwhelm, bore, and tire the audience. Although the audience values being able to "see" your points, they also welcome the variety provided by listening and the break from concentrating on visuals, especially if they are being displayed in a darkened room. Take a thorough look at the

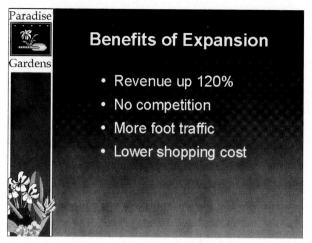 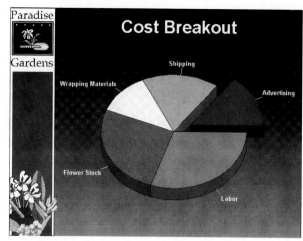

FIGURE 3-4   Speakers use text (left) and graphic visuals (right) to enhance presentations.

entire presentation and prepare visuals needed to (a) direct the reader's attention to major points and (b) clarify or illustrate complex information.

2. *Include only one major idea on each visual.* This rule requires you to keep the visual simple and allows you to make the print large enough for the audience to see. Include only the major point you want the listener to remember—not everything you intend to say about the idea. Too much detail may lead the audience to concentrate on unimportant items and results in letters and figures too small to be read from a distance. Keep the text lines short so the eye can follow them easily. Shortening the text lines has the added benefit of opening up the page with more white space, thus giving the eye a break and making the visual look more appealing.

3. *Design the graphic to avoid distorting facts and relationships.* Using inappropriate scales or designing confusing graphics that hide significant information are unethical ways to communicate. Chapter 16 presents the principles of designing graphics (e.g., line, bar, and pie charts) to enhance readability of information.

4. *Keep the design simple and clean.* Resist the temptation to clutter the page with too many colors, fonts (type styles), and graphics. "Less is more" is a cardinal rule when preparing an effective visual. Computer technology has raised the standards for presentation materials; however, inexperienced designers are likely to use the power of the technology to make visuals overly complex and difficult to understand. For example, squeezing too many ideas or too much data into a text chart or a graph and using every available font, color, texture, clip-art (predrawn art available on disk, scanned art, or company logos), cartoon, or decorative border defeats the purpose of a visual. Your goal is to provide the audience with at-a-glance comprehension. After spending time experimenting with numerous features available on presentation software (few companies provide training in graphic design), experienced users usually learn that the most effective visuals are simple and clean, not colorfully chaotic. Consider carefully the following practical presentation design strategies compiled by Kupsh, Jones, & Graves (1990):

   • *Design horizontal (landscape) rather than vertical (portrait) visuals.* The landscape design leads the eye across the page left to right and is more soothing.

THINK IT OVER
Is it ethical for a company to overstate an insignificant change in unit sales by using a graph with inappropriate scales?

Keep visuals simple and easy to read—provide at-a-glance comprehension.

THINK IT OVER
Assume that you are giving a talk on preparing effective visuals. Prepare a visual(s) to support your major points.

- *Develop a standard design to appear on each visual.* This design creates a sense of continuity or theme (e.g., a logo in one corner or the heading in a shaded box). Templates available with presentation graphics software, such as those in Figure 3-5, provide ideas for standard designs.
- *Be concise and limit words to key points.* Include no more than four words in a heading and no more than seven lines or points on a visual.
- *Keep the use of capital letters to a minimum.* Reading uppercase is slower because most reading material is in lowercase.
- *Avoid abbreviations that might confuse the reader.* Generally, eliminate punctuation.
- *Use graphic devices—borders, boxes, shadows, lines, bullets (circles, squares, pointers of some sort) to separate items and direct attention.* Use numbers only if the sequence is important; otherwise, they clutter the visual.
- *Use clip-art, scanned art, or cartoons to illustrate important points and break the monotony of a series of visuals containing only text.*

5. *Be sure that the visual is large enough to be seen by everyone in the audience.* For text charts, use large, bold lettering that is large enough for the audience to read. As a general rule of thumb, use font sizes of at least 24 points for headings and no less than 14 points for subpoints (72 points = 1-inch high). Sans serif letters—letters without the tails and squiggles—are easier to read. Using larger print may reduce the number of words that will fit on the visual. If necessary, create a separate visual for the idea you were forced to omit.

Misspellings in visuals are inexcusable.

6. *Proofread the visual carefully following the same systematic proofreading procedures used for printed letters and reports.* Misspellings in handouts or displays can be very embarrassing and can adversely affect your credibility. Many presentation software programs have built-in spellcheckers to help ensure complete accuracy. When preparing visuals that are customized for a prospective client/customer, double-check to be certain that names of people, companies, and products are spelled correctly.

Small notes placed on visuals provide discreet prompts as you discuss the visual.

7. *Paraphrase the visual rather than read it line for line.* To increase the quality of your delivery, develop a workable method of recording what you

FIGURE 3-5
Designing visuals with templates available with the software.

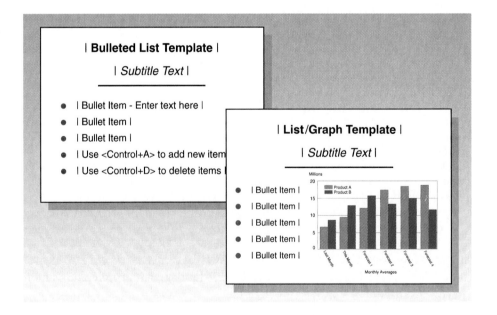

plan to say about each graphic. For example, record your statements on a small index card for each visual. As you proceed from one visual to another, simply move to the next card. Sometimes you may write notes lightly in pencil directly on the back of posters or the borders framing transparencies. You can then refer to these notes without the audience's seeing them. If you are using a computer and the appropriate software to display your visual aids, you can input your notes directly on the screen containing the visual. When you display the visual, the audience sees only the visual while you conveniently (and discreetly) refer to the notes on the computer monitor.

8. *Step to one side of the visual so the audience can see it.* Use a pointer if necessary. Direct your remarks to the audience, not the graphic; in other words, maintain eye contact with the audience.

Let's examine some of the visual devices available to speakers. (Graphics are discussed in more detail in Chapter 16.) The most common are (1) handouts; (2) chalkboards and whiteboards; (3) flip charts and posters; (4) projected visuals; (5) videotapes, audiotapes, filmstrips, and films; and (6) models and physical objects.

Handouts

Printed handouts are the dominant type of presentation materials used; about 47 percent of presenters surveyed in a study of 900 participants used handouts (Antonoff, 1990). Even though you can fit more information on a printed page than on other visuals, avoid doing so. Keep handouts simple. Summarize major points, but do not provide the audience with your entire presentation. If possible, distribute the handout when it is needed rather than at the beginning of the presentation. Otherwise, the audience may read the handout while you are explaining background information needed to understand the idea presented in the handout.

What type of visual is used most often to support oral presentations?

Chalkboards and Whiteboards

Chalkboards and whiteboards are useful for preparing informal visuals to small groups. Some major problems presented by the chalkboard or whiteboard are the slickness and lack of cleanliness of some boards, poor penmanship of the user, and the failure of the user to erase items once they have been considered. If you plan to use a board, practice and make certain the equipment is satisfactory before your presentation. If your visual is sizable or complex, you will find it helpful to place it on the board before your presentation. Many portable chalkboards or whiteboards have two sides, thus permitting you to keep your material from view until you need it.

Flip Charts and Posters

Flip charts consist of a pad of paper with sheets about 2' x 3', fastened at the top and mounted on an easel with a tray for markers. Posters are prepared on single sheets of posterboard of various sizes and colors and displayed on an easel. Poster paints, markers, and various types of press-on letters can be used to prepare professional-looking flip charts and posters.

COMMUNICATION   MENTOR

Here are a few tips on graphic presentation, complex or simple:

1. Bring your audience to some interim conclusion before proceeding to your next chart or slide.
2. Try to determine how members of your audience will be listening (for broad concepts, biases, fine points, conclusions), and cater to those areas in your text and graphics.
3. Use color cautiously, whether you're using the nearly limitless palette of a computer software program or marker pens. If your colors are too "hot," they will be distracting to your content or, worse yet, will trivialize it in the eyes of your audience. Notice the colors on television commercials that vitalize words and images.
4. Make sure everyone can see and hear you.

James F. Hurley
Executive Vice President
California Federal Bank

What advantage does a flip chart or poster have over a chalkboard or whiteboard?

A speaker can prepare a series of visuals before the presentation and simply "flip" from one visual to the next as the speech progresses. Additionally, flip charts and posters often are used to record ideas generated during a discussion or to display material (such as an outline of the presentation) for a long time. Although they serve many of the same purposes as a chalkboard or whiteboard, flip charts and posters permit the speaker to use color to advantage and to prepare material in advance, factors not always available with a chalkboard or whiteboard.

Projected Visuals

Visuals that can be projected on a large screen are effective for both large and small audiences. Examples include transparencies, slides, and computer-generated visuals. During your presentation, you can refer to specific parts of the visual by pointing to them on the screen. In addition, you can move from one visual to another quickly and easily. An advantage of projected visuals is their adaptability to overlay presentations. For example, a speaker can display only the headings and projected sales line in the first visual. The second visual, overlaid on the first, adds the actual sales line. This technique is effective because the speaker wants to talk about projected sales before getting the audience involved in actual sales and the reasons for the discrepancies.

TRANSPARENCIES

Transparencies can be made of anything from freehand drawings to printed pages by simply running the original copy through a copying machine capable of copying onto transparent acetate. Additionally, you can write on transparencies with specially designed pens; in this way, a blank transparency serves the same purpose as a chalkboard, whiteboard, or flip chart. If you use presentation graphics software to prepare your visuals, you can simply generate a transparency from the visual displayed on the computer screen.

SLIDES

Presentations built around 35-millimeter slides usually involve several visuals in a planned sequence and are displayed with a carousel or other slide projector. A major disadvantage is that the room usually is darkened. However, for presentations involving ordinary photography (depicting persons, places, and things), the slide method is the most appropriate. For example, colorful photographs of Hawaii's beautiful sandy beaches and scenes of happy tourists enjoying the entertainment and experiencing the Polynesian culture are effective means to attract tourists to Hawaii.

> **THINK IT OVER**
> Provide another example of an oral report that would require a photographic slide.

Another way to produce slides is to use presentation graphics software programs. These programs allow you to generate slides from the visuals displayed on the computer screen. Computer-generated visuals, projected with a computer and an overhead projection panel (connected to an ordinary overhead projector), provide the same sophistication as 35-millimeter slides. A major advantage is that you save the expense and effort required to prepare photographic slides.

> A computer with appropriate software and a laser printer are valuable tools for preparing professional visuals for a speech.

COMPUTER PRESENTATIONS

Increasing numbers of speakers are preparing highly professional presentation materials using computers and presentation graphics software. To illustrate the process of preparing computer-generated visuals, consider the steps for preparing a series of text visuals for a presentation: (1) Input your ideas into a built-in outliner that will help you organize your thoughts; (2) select features for displaying the text (font, type size, color, texture, border, clip-art, captions, and others); (3) view and edit each visual, indicating the exact sequence of each visual and the special effects (graphics, sound, and motion) between visuals if they are to be projected using the computer; and (4) generate printed handouts, slides, transparencies, or a slide show for an onscreen presentation. A series of slides developed for an oral presentation is shown in Figure 3-6. With all slides displayed side by side on one screen, you can easily rearrange the order or zoom in on a particular slide to make changes.

Many programs provide templates (prepared designs) that suggest features and even colors that work well together. You simply select the template, and your information (text or graphics) is formatted automatically. After viewing the results, you can revise the format if you wish. These templates help the novice presenter resist the temptation to create overwhelmingly complex visuals simply because the technology is available.

An automated onscreen presentation that runs unattended is quite effective for a booth in a trade show where you must attract the attention of passersby. Another effective use of automated onscreen presentations is a customized presentation for a potential client/customer or employees working in remote locations. The clients or employees can run the presentation on their own personal computers privately at their convenience and are able to repeat the presentation as many times as necessary (the software used to create the presentation is not needed to run it).

> Name two situations where an automated onscreen presentation would be effective.

FIGURE 3-6
Sequencing slides for an on-screen presentation.

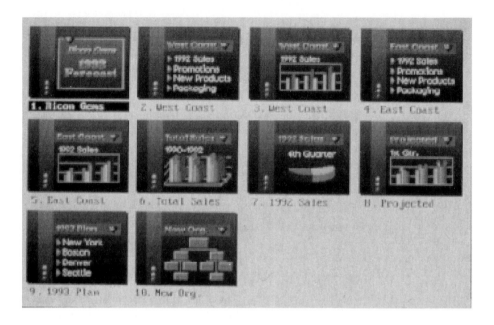

Explain how projecting visuals from a computer improves the quality of feedback.

On the other hand, using an automated onscreen presentation may overwhelm a smaller, face-to-face audience. This captive audience may be distracted by the special effects used to move from one idea to another. In addition, the fully automated onscreen presentation limits the human interaction important in typical meetings or presentations. Automation eliminates one of the major advantages of projecting visuals directly from the computer screen—the capability of adapting the visual to accommodate the audience.

Videos, Films, and Audiotapes

Videos, films, and audiotapes can be used to illustrate major points. For example, a video showing mock interviews would be an effective aid in illustrating effective interviewing strategies in a human resources management training seminar. In today's visual age, an audience relates well to the color and professional quality of these visuals. Many speakers, however, allow a videotape or film to become the entire presentation. This practice violates a central principle in using visuals: The visual is intended to supplement your speech and is *not* a substitute for it.

Because more and more companies are recognizing the value of employee training and development, public relations agencies report that the production of training videos is becoming a larger part of their total work. Highly professional training videos carry expensive price tags; a conservative estimate is $1,500 per minute. Videotapes, like computer presentations, can be mailed to potential customers/clients and employees in remote locations.

Models and Physical Objects

A sample of a product or a replica to exact scale allows the audience to visualize and become involved with the idea being presented. For example, an airline manager involved in a training seminar wanted to convince the airline to replace foil food containers with fiber containers. The manager brought some pastry packed in one of the fiber containers to the seminar. As the participants bit into the sweet, moist pastry, they became "instant believers" (Rockey, 1977).

Before planning a public speech or an oral report and designing effective visual aids, study carefully the specific suggestions in the "Check Your Public Speaking" checklist that follows the chapter summary. Practice your delivery at least once, and then compare your style with the points listed in the delivery section of the checklist; make necessary improvements as you continue to polish your presentation.

SUMMARY

1 **Knowing your audience will enable you to direct your public speech or oral presentation to the specific needs and interests of your audience.** Identify general characteristics (age, gender, experience, etc.), size, and receptiveness of the audience. The audience for an oral report is generally smaller, better known to the speaker, and more likely to create a less formal, more intimate speaking environment.

2 **After you have identified the audience, determine your purpose: to entertain, inform, and persuade.** Entertaining and informative speeches can be organized in one of three ways: narrative, descriptive, or explanatory. Oral reporting is an efficient means for exchanging information for decision making and policy development with several people at the same time.

Next, select the major points to support your idea. Locate supporting material for each point; e.g., statistical support, anecdotes, quotes from prominent people, appropriate humor, and visual displays. Focus on preparing an effective beginning to create rapport with the audience and an effective ending to leave the audience with a strong summary thought to remember. The summary of an oral report will include the conclusion and highlight the evidence to support the conclusion.

3 **Learn to deliver your speech with confidence by following these guidelines:** Choose an appropriate delivery style: impromptu, extemporaneous, memorized, and written-and-read. Control vocal qualities such as phonation, articulation, and pronunciation. Good voices have medium or low pitch, are easily heard, carry smooth sounds, and vary to reflect moods. Articulate speakers produce smooth, fluent, and pleasant speech. Good speakers refer to a dictionary frequently to ensure proper pronunciation.

Suggestions for improving delivery style for public speakers and oral reporters include expecting some nervousness, insisting on a proper introduction, speaking to a few friendly faces to ensure good eye contact, using gestures naturally, avoiding nonwords and annoying speech habits, using a lectern to hold notes but not to hide behind, using jokes appropriately, avoiding jargon or excessive statistics, and looking to the audience for feedback.

4 **Using visual aids reduces the time required to present a concept and increases retention because the audience can visualize major ideas and follow the presentation more easily.** Guidelines for preparing visual aids include limiting the number of visuals; including one major idea in simple, easy-to-understand design and large enough for the audience to read; and proofreading to eliminate all errors. To use a visual aid effectively, paraphrase rather than read the visual and step to one side so the audience can see the visual.

Visual aids available to speakers include handouts; chalkboards and whiteboards; flip charts and posters; projected visuals (transparencies, slides, and computer presentations); videos, films, and audiotapes; and models and physical objects. Each type provides specific advantages and should be selected carefully.

REFERENCES

Antonoff, M. (1990). Presentations that persuade. *Personal Computing, 14* (7), 60-65, 67-68.

Decker, B. (1992). *You've got to be believed to be heard.* New York: St. Martin's Press.

Hughes, M. (1990). Tricks of the speechwriter's trade. *Management Review, 9* (11), 56-58.

Kupsh, J., Jones, C. L., & Graves, P. R. (1990). Presentation design strategies. *Business Education Forum, 45* (3), 28-31.

Rockey, E. H. (1977). *Communicating in organizations.* Cambridge, MA: Winthrop Publishers.

Rutter, N. (1993, September 13). Jerry's CEO charm school. *Forbes,* pp. 94, 98, 102, 104, 108.

Sabo, S. (1994, March/April). Here she is . . . *Tomorrow's Business Leader,* pp. 7-8.

REVIEW QUESTIONS

1. Who is an excellent speaker currently on the national political scene? What qualities make this speaker effective?
2. What are some of the things a speaker should attempt to learn about the potential audience? What is the best source for this information?
3. How does the scheduled time of a speech play a part in speech preparation?
4. How many major points should a speaker plan to develop? Explain.
5. What are the traditional purposes of speeches?
6. List four categories of examples a speaker can use to support the major points of a persuasive speech.
7. How might too much persuasion on the part of a speaker affect an audience when the purpose of the speech is to inform or to entertain? How is persuasion developed in oral reporting?
8. Why is oral reporting an effective and efficient way to communicate? How does oral reporting differ from public speaking?
9. What items, materials, or methods might a speaker use to assist or to reinforce audience understanding?
10. Why are the opening and ending portions of a speech so important?
11. What is the key element in the opening of a public speech and an oral report?
12. How might the ending of an oral report differ from the ending of a public speech?
13. Why is memorization a hazardous speech style?
14. What speaking style is used most often by professional speakers?
15. How do articulation and pronunciation differ? List three suggestions for controlling speech qualities to improve the effectiveness of an oral presentation.
16. What suggestions would you give to a prospective speaker about the use of gestures?
17. What suggestions would you give to a prospective speaker about the use of jokes or humor?
18. Summarize the guidelines provided for developing an effective delivery style.
19. Discuss three guidelines for preparing and using visual aids.
20. What are the chief advantages of using chalkboards and whiteboards?
21. List at least three guidelines for preparing visuals that provide "at-a-glance comprehension."
22. What advantages does using a flip chart or poster have over using a chalkboard or whiteboard?
23. Discuss the advantages gained from using projected visuals—transparencies, slides, or computer-generated visuals—to enhance your speech or oral report.
24. Describe at least two situations in which an automated onscreen presentation would be (a) an effective choice of visual aids and (b) an ineffective choice of visual aids.
25. Describe at least two situations in which a model or physical object could be used to supplement your speech or oral report.

EXERCISES

1. Complete each of the THINK IT OVER activities that your instructor assigns.
2. List a topic on which you believe you are qualified to give a five- or ten-minute talk. Write an outline indicating the introduction, major points (body), and the summary.
3. Evaluate the speaking skill of a well-known television newscaster or commentator. What are the strengths? Weaknesses? Offer suggestions for improving the person's oral communication skills. Pay special attention to speech qualities, audience eye contact, rapport, and organization.
4. Critique your own speaking skills. Ask a friend to help you be objective in your assessment. Prepare a three-column list. Label the columns *Speaking Strength, Speaking Weakness,* and *Strategy for Improvement.* In groups assigned by your instructor, discuss your improvement plan in an effort to gain additional ideas for enhancing your speaking skills.
5. In groups of four assigned by your instructor, select four topics related to effective business communication or some other business-related topic. A group leader may randomly assign a topic to each member or allow the members to select a topic. You may select the following questions or use them as a guide for developing similar ones:
   a. Why are communication skills a key ingredient in your career (specify a career)?
   b. Why are effective cross-cultural communication skills imperative in an increasingly competitive global economy?
   c. How has rapidly changing technology revolutionized communication in business organizations?
   d. What would business be like if legality were a company's only ethical benchmark or criterion?
   e. Are business organizations less (or more) ethical today than they were a decade ago?

   Following a brief preparation time, each member will give a one- to two-minute oral report to the group. After all oral reports are given, the group will briefly discuss the strengths and weaknesses of each report and attempt to provide each member with a few specific suggestions for improvement.
6. Read an article from a current magazine or journal about one of the concepts presented in this chapter or in another chapter in the textbook, or select a topic of your choice or one assigned by your instructor. Give a short (two- to three-minute) oral presentation. Design at least one visual following the guidelines presented in the chapter and use it effectively in your presentation.
7. As a part of a team of four, present a mock annual shareholders' meeting before the class. You should work from an annual report of a major company. One person should be the chief executive officer, one the chief operating officer, one the financial officer, and one the chief marketing officer.

   Each will speak for two to three minutes. The CEO should preside and introduce each of the others appropriately before each speaks. Your report should include a review of the year's activities, plans for the next year, and information about the firm's role in the community. Design effective visuals and use them effectively in your presentation.

E-MAIL APPLICATION

Your instructor has provided specific instructions for preparing an oral presentation. Using an online database, locate several resources on your topic from the campus library or an external library. Using these resources, develop an outline for your presentation. Send your instructor an e-mail message containing the outline and a list of the sources you intend to use.

Fear of public speaking is reported to be the number one fear of American adults. This enormous fear results primarily from the typical lack of experience in public speaking situations. Practice is the most effective antidote for fear, and the speaker who can overcome the fear of public speaking certainly possesses a marketable skill.

An accomplished speaker gives careful attention to the nonverbal dimensions, articulation of words, topic selection, and content structuring. When the verbal and nonverbal channels match, the speaker has a much greater chance of having the audience believe the message.

Discussion Questions

1. What five characteristics does Greg Salsbury mention as nonverbal dimensions of oral communication? Why are they considered nonverbal?
2. What does Salsbury say is the best way to overcome nervousness in public speaking? How much of this technique is desirable?
3. What is the most critical part of an oral presentation? Why?
4. What role does humor play in public speaking?
5. Salsbury uses the 1984 presidential race between Reagan and Mondale as an example of the importance of having "everything in sync." Explain the concept, referring to the two candidates for examples.

Applications

You have been asked to give a brief oral presentation to a group of high school students at a career day. Your topic is on why students should consider a career in your chosen field.

1. Prepare a three-point outline for the talk that includes an introduction, body, and summary.
2. Be prepared to make your presentation to the class (maximum length of three minutes).

PLANNING A SPEECH OR AN ORAL REPORT

- ☐ Identify characteristics common to the audience and the speech setting (number in audience, seating arrangements, time of day).
- ☐ Identify your purpose: entertain, inform, or persuade.
  - ☐ Public speech—attempt to influence the attitudes or actions of the audience.
  - ☐ Oral report—obtain or exchange information for decision making.
- ☐ Develop an effective opening that presents the purpose and initiates rapport with the audience.
- ☐ Select a few major points and locate support for each point: statistics, anecdotes, quotes, and appropriate humor.
- ☐ Develop an effective ending that calls for the audience to accept your ideas (speech) or provides a conclusion with recommendations (oral report).

DELIVERING A SPEECH OR AN ORAL REPORT

- ☐ Expect some nervousness.
- ☐ Insist on a proper, impressive introduction.
- ☐ Select a few friendly faces in the audience to ensure good eye contact.
- ☐ Use gestures naturally to communicate confidence and warmth.
- ☐ Avoid irritating "nonwords."
- ☐ Avoid other annoying speech habits.
- ☐ Use a lectern to steady your hands only until you gain confidence.
- ☐ Use jokes or humor appropriately.
- ☐ Avoid jargon or technical terms that the listeners may not understand.
- ☐ Do not overwhelm your audience with excessive statistics.
- ☐ Watch your audience for important feedback.
- ☐ Dress carefully and tastefully.
- ☐ Appear confident and appear to enjoy making the speech.
- ☐ Keep within the time limits.

DESIGNING AND USING VISUAL AIDS

- ☐ Limit the number of visual aids used in a single presentation.
- ☐ Include only one major idea on each visual.
- ☐ Design the graphic to avoid distorting facts and relationships.
- ☐ Keep the design simple and clean.
  - ☐ Design horizontal (landscape) rather than vertical (portrait) visuals.
  - ☐ Develop a standard design to appear on each visual.
  - ☐ Be concise and limit words to key points.
  - ☐ Keep the use of capital letters to a minimum.
  - ☐ Avoid abbreviations that might confuse the reader.
  - ☐ Use graphic devices—borders, boxes, shadows, lines, bullets—to separate items and direct attention.
  - ☐ Use clip-art, scanned art, or cartoons to illustrate important points and break the monotony of a series of visuals containing only text.
- ☐ Be sure that the visual is large enough to be seen by everyone in the audience.
- ☐ Proofread the visual carefully to eliminate any errors.
- ☐ Paraphrase the visual rather than read it line for line.
- ☐ Step to one side of the visual so the audience can see it.

SELECTING APPROPRIATE VISUAL AIDS (check more than one)

- ☐ Chalkboard and whiteboards—convenient for small audiences in an informal setting, can erase and reuse the surface, and no special equipment needed.
- ☐ Flip charts and posters—same advantages as chalkboards, can flip from one visual to another, can use color, and can prepare in advance.

- ☐ Projected visuals
    - ☐ Transparencies—same advantages as chalkboards, can write on them with pens and can be prepared from a visual displayed on a computer.
    - ☐ Slides—excellent for presentations requiring photography; can be prepared from visuals displayed on computer, can be arranged in a planned sequence, and require darkened room.
    - ☐ Computer presentations—excellent for large audiences such as trade shows or for customized presentations to be mailed to potential customers. Limit human interaction.
- ☐ Videos, films, and audiotapes—illustrate major points in engaging manner; should be used to supplement a presentation, not replace it.
- ☐ Models and physical objects—allow the audience to visualize and experience the idea being presented.

PART 2

ANALYZING CRITICAL FACTORS

INFLUENCING COMMUNICATION

EFFECTIVENESS

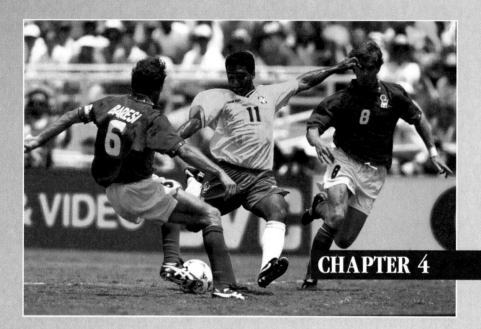

CHAPTER 4

INTERCULTURAL

COMMUNICATION

OBJECTIVES
When you have completed Chapter 4, you will be able to

1 Discuss the importance of communicating effectively across cultures, genders, and ages.

2 Identify how culture affects patterns of behavior and communication effectiveness.

3 Identify five potential barriers to intercultural communication.

4 Apply specific guidelines for effective written and oral communication with an intercultural audience.

Understanding how to communicate effectively with people from other cultures is becoming more integral to the work environment as many U.S. companies increasingly conduct business with international companies or become multinational. Successful communication must often span barriers of language and almost always requires a person to consider differing world views resulting from societal, religious, or other cultural factors. If a person fails to consider these factors, communication suffers, and the result is often embarrassing and potentially costly.

McDonald's is an example of a large U.S. company that has expanded its operations to include most major countries in the world. To be successful on an international scale, McDonald's managers had to be aware of cultural differences and be willing to work to ensure that effective communication occurred despite these barriers. The results so far have been overwhelmingly positive for McDonald's; for example, their store in Moscow reports healthy sales despite the ailing economy in the former Soviet Union.

Occasionally, however, a whopper of an intercultural communication *faux pas* occurs. That is just what happened when McDonald's began its promotional campaign in Britain for the World Cup soccer championship. It seemed like a clever (and harmless) idea to reproduce the flags of the 24 nations participating in the event and print them on packaging—two million Happy Meal bags, to be exact. What marketing personnel failed to consider was that words from the *Koran* are printed on the Saudi flag. The *Koran*, the holy book of Islam, which contains the teaching of Mohammed, is viewed as sacred by Muslims. The idea that these words were mass-printed to sell a product with the knowledge that the packages would be thrown into the trash angered and offended many Muslims, who immediately complained. McDonald's apologized for the gaffe and agreed to cooperate with the Saudis in finding a solution to the problem (McGarry, 1994).

This error serves as an example of how much "homework" is involved in maintaining good relations with customers or clients from other cultures. The potential barrier of language is obvious; however, successful managers know that much more is involved in communicating with everyone—across cultures, genders, ages, abilities, and other differences. Before you attempt to sell a product, train employees, or even attend a banquet or meeting with representatives from other countries, brush up on the customs and learn a little about the culture and any other differences. The result will be positive communications, and you will have earned a positive reputation for yourself and your company.

INTERCULTURAL COMMUNICATION OPPORTUNITIES

As world markets expand, U.S. employees at home and abroad will be doing business with more people from other countries. You may find yourself working abroad for a large American company, an international company with a plant in the United States, or a company with an ethnically diverse workforce. Regardless of the workplace, your **intercultural communication** skills, that is, your ability to communicate effectively with women and people of other cultures, will affect your success in today's culturally diverse, global economy.

Working for a Multinational Company Abroad

Worldwide telecommunications and intense international business competition have forced many industries to expand into world markets. During the past four

COMMUNICATION   MENTOR

Traveling internationally, American businesspeople see strong evidence of pervasive American influence—from familiar department stores in Mexico to golden arches in Eastern Europe. They should not also assume that American customs and habits are acceptable worldwide. Businesspeople operating internationally can save themselves and their companies a great deal of embarrassment by learning as much as possible about the culture and customs of their host countries.

Cynthia Pharr
President & CEO
C. Pharr Marketing Communications

decades, U.S. firms have established plants in Europe, Central and South America, and Asia. At many U.S. corporations, such as Dow Chemical, Gillette, and IBM, more than 40 percent of total sales have come from international operations in a recent year.

Sweeping changes taking place throughout the world promise to continue to expand international business. The passage of NAFTA (North American Free Trade Agreement), the unification of East and West Germany, the formation of independent republics from the former Soviet Union, and the restructuring of the European Economic Community (EEC) will significantly alter the international marketplace.

Even prior to NAFTA many U.S. companies, especially retailers such as Wal-Mart, J.C. Penney, and Neiman Marcus, had already begun to "pursue the pesos" in Mexico. Merchants are finding their Mexican stores outperform their U.S. stores—about $100 more per square foot than the average U.S. store. Although the U.S. retail market is overdeveloped, a huge Mexican market is eager to gobble up U.S. goods. One mall developer described Mexico City as "the city of 20 million with only enough malls to serve Toledo, Ohio" (Neuborne, 1993, p. B2).

Also, the standardization of Europe's diverse national markets in the 12-nation European Community will open up a vast, single market—areas long dominated by national monopolies and multiple standards and regulations. American companies, many competing with Japanese companies at home, are positioning themselves to reap the benefits of rich European markets. "Whoever wins Europe will win the war," a statement made by a European marketing vice president, accurately describes the intense competition ahead among Japan, the United States, and Europe (Toy et al., 1991).

Working for a Foreign-Owned Company

Over the past decade, Asians (primarily Japanese) and Europeans have built plants in the United States. Operating three auto-assembly facilities and an engine plant in the United States, Honda boasts that two-thirds of the 855,000 Hondas sold in America are made in America with 75 percent domestic content (Magnusson, Treece, & Symonds, 1991). In 1992 foreign investment was over $419 billion a year, about 86 percent of the value of U.S. investment abroad (Schlesinger, 1994). Japan is a major source of the growth of foreign ownership

How are NAFTA and the EEC affecting foreign investment?

THINK IT OVER
Locate a recent article discussing a U.S. company's venture into a world market. Choose a company related to your career field if possible.

THINK IT OVER
List companies from other countries that have plants in the United States.

What is the level of foreign investment in the U.S. today?

of U.S. businesses, with four of the largest international employers in the U.S.—Honda, Bridgestone/Firestone, Sony, and Toyota Motor (Hoerr, Spiro, Armstrong, & Treece, 1990).

Additionally, periods of a weakened dollar on international markets have encouraged other countries to buy pieces of the United States. For example, by purchasing CBS Records, Inc., and Columbia Pictures Entertainment, Inc., Sony, the Japanese electronics giant, now provides movies and soundtracks for its customers to play on Sony VCRs and CD players. Mitsubishi Estate Co. purchased approximately 60 percent of the Rockefeller Center, an American land-mark, and most of Verbatim from Eastman Kodak. In addition, the bright green BP stations are constant reminders of the familiar orange and white American-owned Gulf stations bought out by British Petroleum.

Did you know that a Japanese-owned company owns the rights to Michael Jackson's music?

Working in a Culturally Diverse Workforce

Changing demographics in the United States are requiring American- and foreign-owned companies to face ethnic diversity in the workplace. Several fac-tors contribute to the dramatic change in the composition of the workforce.

The United States traditionally has accepted individuals from other lands. Rather than being a melting pot, the United States created an environment in which people of varying cultures could live. People with a common heritage generally formed their own neighborhoods and worked intently at retaining their traditional customs and language, while still sharing in the common culture to an extent. Consequently, *mosaic* seems to be a more accurate term than *melting pot* to reflect the changing demographics (Solomon, 1990). As in a mo-saic, small distinct groups are combined to form the pattern or design of the U.S. population and workforce.

What term accurately describes the changing demographics in the U.S.?

The rise in new immigrants is not the only recent demographic trend that affects business. The maturing of the "baby-boom" generation, a relatively low birthrate, and increasing life spans have led to a higher average age in the popu-lation. Predictions are that by the year 2020, more than one-third of the total population will be older than 50 (Holland, 1991). Additionally, the flood of females entering the job market has substantially changed the American workforce. According to the Hudson Institute's *Workforce 2000* report, native-born white males will make up only 15 percent of those entering the workforce in the year 2000 (Miller, 1991). The labor pool will consist primarily of women, African-Americans, Hispanics, and other minorities, as shown in Figure 4-1.

The white-male dominated workforce is changing.

People from such different backgrounds as today's workers invariably bring different values, attitudes, and perceptions to the workplace. This diversity can lead to misunderstandings, miscommunications, and missed opportunities to improve both the workers and the organizations. Thus, managers must be prepared to communicate effectively with workers of different nationalities, genders, races, ages, abilities, etc.

Companies such as Digital, AT&T, and PepsiCo offer training programs that help employees appreciate working with others who are different from them.

Many American companies are addressing the issues raised by diversity. Because more than half its employees are international, Esprit de Corp, a women's clothier, added English classes to its training program. At times, limited knowledge of English creates problems. Slang and hurried instructions can make minority workers' lives miserable. Cultural customs can inter-

FIGURE 4-1   Changing demographics.
By the turn of the century, the labor "pool" will consist primarily of women, African-Americans, Hispanics, Asians, and other minorities—not white-male dominated as it has been in the past.

fere as well. For example, a Korean administrative assistant nodded her head as her supervisor gave instructions about a computer spreadsheet program. Her nod indicated only that she had been listening. When she failed to do as instructed, she was crestfallen. She had not *understood* what had been said. When miscommunication occurs, both sides are frustrated and often angry. In addition, increasing numbers of companies are providing diversity training seminars to help workers understand and appreciate gender differences and the cultures of co-workers.

Several generations will undoubtedly be required to learn to deal effectively with the ethnic minority workforce. As these changes evolve, subtle changes will probably occur in the dominant culture as well. Such changes have occurred throughout America's history as people of different backgrounds have joined and contributed to the culture. Whether you are a male or a female; a member of a racial minority; a native or an immigrant; or a member of any other demographic group or work group that shares values, meanings, and behaviors (doctors/nurses), your ability to reach out to members of other groups is critical. Managing a diverse workforce effectively will require you to communicate with *everyone* and to help all employees reach their fullest potential and contribute to the company's goals.

CULTURE AND COMMUNICATION

Managers with the *desire* and the *skill* to conduct business in these new international markets and to manage a diverse workforce effectively will confront problems created by cultural differences. The way messages are decoded and encoded is not just a function of the experiences, beliefs, and assumptions of the person sending or receiving those messages but also are shaped by the society in which he or she lives.

People learn patterns of behavior from their culture. The **culture** of a people is the product of their living experiences within their own society. Culture could be described as "the way of life" of a people and includes a vast array of behaviors and beliefs. These patterns affect how people perceive the world, what they value, and how they act. These patterns can create barriers to communication if you encounter a person whose behavior follows different patterns.

Culture has three key characteristics:

1. *Culture is learned by people over time.* Individuals are not born knowing their culture but acquire it through interactions with others. The family; schools; social institutions such as churches, clubs, and businesses; and the media all play a part in teaching each member of a society the expectations and norms of behavior.
2. *Components of culture are interrelated.* In the United States, for instance, the high value placed on material goods is related to the use of economic well-being as a measure of success and happiness. These values provide support for the approval placed on independence of mind and action, which in turn is connected to the existence of a relatively fluid class structure. The list of connections could go on, but these examples alone make it clear that each of these components of American culture is connected to other components.
3. *Culture is shared.* That is, the various aspects of culture are common to many individuals. No country has one unified culture, however. Human societies

THINK IT OVER
What changes do you see companies making in an effort to accommodate the needs of a diverse workforce? For example, The Opryland Hotel picks up Asian-American workers with private buses and runs a child-care center 21 hours a day, 365 days a year; Marriott offers an English-as-a-second language program (Jesitus, 1991). Discuss the programs you have seen in operation and others you have read about in the current literature.

THINK IT OVER
Identify and attend a cultural diversity program offered on your campus.

LEARNING OBJECTIVE 2

THINK IT OVER
Where do you fit in the mosaic? What is your ethnic or cultural background, social or economic class/status, educational level? What interests and inspires you? What do you value the most?

are so large and diverse that many different cultures can exist within them; these are called **subcultures**. Although each subculture differs from others, they often share some traits that derive from the main or dominant culture.

What are the three
characteristics of culture?

Each society exhibits its culture in many ways. Certainly customs, the accepted way of interacting with others, are expressions of the culture. The American practice of shaking hands reflects the value that is placed on the individual. Indians greet each other with a slight bow to honor the divine spark that they believe resides in each person. Each culture has certain objects, gestures, sounds, or images that contain special meaning for that culture. The American flag symbolizes the nation's independence and strength; a red, white, and blue package tries to associate itself with those meanings. Advertising, which in some respects is the use of cultural symbols, requires sensitivity to the specific meanings of the symbols employed.

The structures and roles of religious institutions, schools, social organizations, businesses, and governments all reflect the way the people of that culture see the world. These institutions, in turn, develop cultures of their own that influence the people within the institution.

What other language is
used differently in
different countries?

Finally, how people communicate in speaking and writing as well as nonverbally is shaped by culture. Culture enables people to acquire a language that they may use in common with others of the same culture and as a medium for passing culture from one generation to the next. The language also reflects cultural values and norms. English is the language of Australia, Jamaica, and South Africa, as well as Great Britain, Canada, and the United States. However, all of these cultures are very different; in fact, even their forms of English differ.

THINK IT OVER
What does your culture value the most? What thinking patterns and problem-solving approaches do you prefer?

Culture provides individuals with the standards for behavior and gives them a feeling of identification and belonging; they feel a part of something larger than themselves. Problems occur between people of different cultures primarily because people tend to assume that their own cultural norms are the right way to do things. They wrongly believe that the specific patterns of behavior desired in their own cultures are universally valued.

Typical stereotypes are that all Irish and red heads have short tempers, all Italians are in the Mafia, all Puerto Ricans are gang members, all older people are feeble and forgetful, and all teenagers are irresponsible. Can you add to this list?

BARRIERS TO INTERCULTURAL COMMUNICATION

Because cultures give different definitions to such basics of interaction as values and norms, people reared in two different cultures may clash. Let us explore some of the main areas in which those clashes take place: stereotypes, timing, personal space, body language, and translation limitations.

LEARNING OBJECTIVE 3

THINK IT OVER
Television shows and movies promote stereotypes of nationalities, age groups, disabilities, and professions. *Mrs. Doubtfire* centers around a stereotypical career woman —devoted to her job but has no time for her children, home, or marriage. Accountants are typically characterized as boring, unappealing males. Recall the IRS agent in *For Love or Money* and the accountant in *Ghostbusters*. What are other examples?

Stereotypes

One group often forms a mental picture of the main characteristics of another group, creating preformed ideas of what people in this group are like. These pictures, called **stereotypes**, influence the way members of the first group interact with members of the second. When members of the first group observe a behavior that conforms to that stereotype, the validity of the preconceived notion is reinforced. They view the other person as a representative of a class of people rather than as an individual.

All cultures have stereotypes about other cultures they have encountered. These stereotypes can get in the way of communication when people interact on the basis of the imagined representative and not the real individual. One way of exploring the force of stereotypes is to review those held about North Americans.

The North American stereotype does exist although it may undergo drastic change as their previously unchallenged world dominance in international trade fades. The abundance of natural resources, industrial strength, and consumer economy have made North Americans appear affluent and wasteful in the eyes of other cultures. Visitors to the U.S. "are often astonished to see cars less than ten years old heaped in junk yards. These cars would probably still be on the road in most countries, because other cultures seem more inclined to foster an awareness of the need for conserving resources and preserving material goods" (Phatak, 1995, p. 55).

North Americans attempt to control nature; many other cultures worship it as part of their religions. North Americans also seem to seek status through the acquisition of material things—automobiles, imported shoes, designer jeans— whereas many other cultures can get along with mass transportation, ordinary footwear, and any pair of pants.

North Americans are also looked upon by many others as strong individualists, and aggressive. These traits have been fostered and reinforced by the movies they export and by their taking on the role of an international police force.

Additional elements in the North American stereotype are their attitudes toward formality, time, and change. North Americans generally act informally, perhaps in keeping with their reputation of rugged individualism. Many other cultures place a high value on formality, rituals, and social rules. They also place the family, group, and organization before individuals. To North Americans, "time is money." In certain other cultures, time is the cheapest commodity and an inexhaustible resource. Time represents the person's life span on earth, which is only part of eternity. North Americans look on change as inevitable but also attempt to initiate and control it. In many other cultures, change is seen as inevitable, but no attempt is made to initiate it.

If much of the world looks at North Americans according to these stereotypes, how do North Americans look at the rest of the world? Rather than attempting to describe stereotypes North Americans have of other peoples, recognize that North Americans all engage in some stereotyping, both individually and collectively.

Stereotyping is a barrier to communication in international relations—political, economic, and social. The problems of being seller or buyer, employee or employer, or based at home or in another country are all affected by a person's culture and the stereotypes the person learns from his or her culture.

Timing

Although they live in the same hemisphere, Latin Americans have a different attitude toward time than do North Americans or Europeans. Anyone who has visited Mexico and arranged taxi service to arrive at a certain time can attest to the two time frames of Mexico—clock time and "Mexican" time.

This observation is not made to denigrate Mexicans. It simply explains the different values the two cultures place on time. North Americans, like some northern Europeans who are also concerned about punctuality, make appointments, keep them, and do not waste time completing them.

In some cultures—such as Latin America—the language of time says that important things take longer than unimportant ones. An interesting thing about

THINK IT OVER
Some television shows and movies dispel stereotypes: *Murder She Wrote* portrays a senior citizen as healthy, active, intelligent, and financially independent. *Shindler's List* shows that all Jews are not rich, and all Germans are not bad. Can you think of other exceptions?

Generally, North Americans value the efficient use of time, prefer speaking over writing as a means of exchanging information, and focus on the individual vs. the group.

Cultural behaviors vary widely, and they can be misinterpreted easily.

People are often "late" in Latin America because time is not a priority in their cultures. North Americans may consider this behavior rude.

cultures that pay little attention to appointment keeping is that once the appointment begins, the host will probably spend more than the agreed-on time and show more hospitality and generosity than North Americans generally expect. The next visitor may be kept waiting interminably, but that visitor will also receive the same cordial, considerate treatment.

The language of time is based on cultural factors often not understood by others. In the Middle East and in many countries of Asia, life on earth is considered to be only a tiny portion of a person's total time, including life after death. In that perspective, what difference does an hour or so make?

Personal Space

Space operates as a language just as time does. In North America, large offices frequently are reserved for executives as status symbols. In many parts of the world, large offices are for clerical workers and smaller ones for executives. Not much space is required for thinking and planning, so large areas are reserved as working spaces.

People with northern European backgrounds tend to find discussing business with someone in close proximity invasive or unpleasant.

In all cultures, the distance between people functions in communication as "personal space" or "personal territory." In the United States, for example, for intimate conversations with close friends and relatives, individuals are willing to stay within about a foot and a half of each other; for casual conversations, up to two or three feet; for job interviews and personal business, four to twelve feet; and for public occasions, more than twelve feet. The next time you are on an elevator in a public building, notice how uncomfortable most people appear. They usually stare either at the floor or at the ceiling because their personal territory has been invaded and they must stand shoulder to shoulder with strangers.

However, in many cultures other than the U.S., close personal contact is accepted. Men customarily kiss each other on the cheek when they are introduced or when they meet. To many North Americans, this situation is normally embarrassing; to the international, it is no more personal than shaking hands. As a rule, North Americans tend to move away when someone enters their personal territory. By observing the behavior of others, you can gain some idea of their concept of personal territory, which can assist you in your attempts to communicate.

Body Language

The adage "Things are not always what they seem" accurately describes the difficulty in interpreting nonverbal behavior in a single culture or across other cultures.

THINK IT OVER
List at least three different interpretations for a rising tone of voice in a business discussion.

The familiar North American symbol for "okay" or "everything is all right" is made by forming a circle with the thumb and forefinger. In other cultures the same gesture may mean zero, as in France; money, as in Japan; or a vulgarity, as in Brazil. The familiar symbol of "V" for victory formed by the index and middle fingers is an insulting sign in much of Europe, particularly in the United Kingdom, unless the palm faces the receiver of the message.

North Americans nod their heads up and down to indicate agreement or "yes." In other parts of the world, the nod indicates only that the person heard what was said. In Bulgaria and some other Eastern European countries, the up-and-down head motion means "no" and the side-to-side motion "yes"—just the opposite of the meanings for North Americans. Other cultures indicate "no" by a jerk of the head or a back-and-forth waving of a finger, as people sometimes do when saying "no-no" to a child.

COMMUNICATION MENTOR

The majority of agreements between Western firms and Russian firms are first written in English and then translated into Russian because Russian law, especially contract law, is evolving. Because of the command economy of the past 75 years, many words—especially financial and accounting terms—have no Russian equivalent. Therefore, concepts like net income, return on equity, payout, return on investment, pre-tax, etc., have no meaning to the majority of Russian partners. This lack of understanding has led to numerous difficulties between partners as ventures progress and terms of agreements are implemented. As a result, agreements must be extremely specific and defined in simple, detailed terms.

Larry E. Wilson, Managing Partner
Arthur Andersen, Moscow

You can have your appointment or interview cut short in most Arabian countries if you sit in such a way that the sole of your shoe is visible—an insulting symbol. The solution is to sit with feet flat on the floor.

The "business lunch" is an American tradition; much business is transacted on the golf course, on tennis courts, and at social functions as well. However, in most parts of the world, dining and recreation are social functions and not the place or time to conduct business. So, "When in Rome. . . ."

Translation Limitations

Words in one language do not always have an equivalent meaning in other languages, and the concepts the words describe are often different as well. A study of how Japanese and North American business students understood the concept of profit concluded this way: "It is important for the American to understand that his definition of *profit* as solely corporate gain—involving as it will the maximization of short-term gains—conflicts with the Japanese definition, which necessarily involves a long-term view of things" (Sullivan & Kameda, 1982, p. 38). When the meaning of a word is not agreed on in advance, later misunderstanding is a strong possibility.

In a humorous and helpful book about marketing overseas, Ricks (1983) highlights the problems of translating with several examples of U.S. advertising and product labels that resulted in different meanings when translated. General Motors promoted its cars in Belgium with "Body by Fisher," a phrase familiar to North Americans; but in Flemish, the translation was "Corpse by Fisher." "Come alive with Pepsi" became "Come out of the grave . . ." in German and "Bring your ancestors back from the dead" in parts of Asia. Some products did not succeed: Pet milk failed in France because *pet* means, among other things, to break wind. A U.S. product failed in Sweden because its name translated to enema, which the product was not.

Even within English-speaking countries, words can vary greatly in meaning. A U.S. manager, who recently transferred to the United Kingdom operations of a major U.S. corporation, was disarmed by the mixed reactions (perplexed and

Cultural differences affect advertising. A French cognac producer planned to photograph a dusty bottle to symbolize the age and quality of the product. But to the Japanese, a dusty bottle is a dirty bottle. The company dusted the bottle and photographed it against a backdrop of a certain white wood associated with prestige in Japan (Berger, 1987).

THINK IT OVER
List other business blunders you have read about. Obtain a copy of Ricks' book and be prepared to share at least one blunder with the class.

A U.S. manager learned quickly that a "flyover" in the U.K. is actually an "overpass" and that many other words have different meanings in the U.K.

COMMUNICATION IN ACTION

Jim Bice, APV plc

Traveling internationally presents many challenges for business executives. Adapting to changes in time zones, different foods, and different cultures can be formidable. Perhaps no challenge is as great as learning to communicate with someone from a different culture. An employee who possesses knowledge and experience in communicating with a different culture becomes a rich asset to a company operating in a global marketplace.

Jim Bice seems to take the challenge of international travel in stride. Living in the United States, Bice travels throughout Europe, China, and other parts of the world to conduct marketing shows for his company. He is Vice President of Marketing International for APV plc, an engineering group headquartered in London that operates throughout the world. The company provides a wide range of products and services to the food and beverage processing industry. APV reported gross revenues of 947.3 million pounds in 1992, or approximately $1.6 billion in U.S. dollars. Bice believes that good communication with other cultures makes him successful when traveling internationally.

To show the importance of communication when first meeting businesspeople from other cultures, Bice describes the exchange of business cards with the Chinese. North Americans typically greet other businesspeople by shaking hands and exchanging names while making initial greetings. North Americans exchange business cards, if appropriate, after initial greetings. In contrast, Chinese businesspeople typically exchange business cards first, exchange names, and then shake hands. At first, they slightly bow while observing the other person's business card. To adapt to their greeting, Bice holds his business card, printed in Chinese on one side and English on the other, in front of him with both hands. After reading the card, the Chinese businessperson will then sound out Bice's name in English. Bice makes any corrections to the way his name was pronounced. After saying Bice's name correctly, the Chinese presents his or her card and follows the American custom of shaking hands. When the Chinese know that Bice understands their cultural greeting well, their business transactions progress smoothly. Bice's marketing success depends on this basic knowledge of communication in the initial greeting.

When marketing a show in Beijing, Bice relies on basic interpersonal communication skills such as eye contact, listening, and feedback. He realizes that newcomers to the country must speak slowly and deliberately, pausing between words when addressing the Chinese in English. Bice stresses the importance of having not only good verbal communication skills but also knowledge of nonverbal communication with the Chinese.

Bice received his intercultural training informally. Most of what he has learned came from fellow employees who had conducted business in China before him, but he learned many basics through trial and error. However employees receive training today, he believes companies will require greater knowledge and experience of their employees. "Get all the formal training in intercultural communication you can," he emphasizes. "In doing so, you'll be a more valuable employee to a company."

Applying What You Have Learned

1. During an initial greeting with a Chinese businessperson, list several guidelines that help facilitate good communication.
2. Do you feel Mr. Bice's training adequately prepared him to communicate cross-culturally? Explain why.

amused) he received when he used the familiar expression "Get back to me at your leisure." Later a fellow worker explained the intercultural blunder: the word *leisure* as well as *water closet* is commonly used to refer to the *restroom*. In addition, the familiar reference to James Bond, Agent 007 (*double 0 - 7*), is typical of references to double numbers and letters in the United Kingdom. For example, in the United States, the phone number "555-6733" would most often be stated number by number, "*5 5 5 - 6 7 3 3*," and "Dunwoody," a street name, would be spelled aloud letter by letter. In contrast, in the United Kingdom, you would commonly hear "*triple 5 - 6 7 double 3.*" Likewise, Dunwoody Drive would be spelled "*D u n - double o - d y.*"

Translators can be helpful, but keep in mind that a translator is working with a second language and must listen to one language, mentally cast the words into another language, then speak them. This process is difficult and opens the possibility that the translator will fall victim to one or more of the cultural barriers.

Knowing the language of the host country demonstrates your sincere interest in the culture. Learning the language will provide insight into some of the culture's central concepts embedded in the language. For example, knowing that the Japanese concept of "indebtedness" is expressed in a word that has no direct English equivalent will help a stranger understand this important concept in context of the Japanese language (Marquardt and Engel, 1993).

Carroll Perkins, former general manager of the Salt River Project, in Phoenix, Arizona, made an interesting observation and recommendation about learning a second language:

> We recruit employees who can conduct conversations in Spanish and translate written materials from Spanish to English or English to Spanish. However, many of our applicants place little emphasis on their knowledge of a second language.
>
> So that you can compete for the many jobs that involve communication with people of different cultures, reserve some of your elective courses for taking a series of foreign language courses (enough to gain some degree of fluency) or a refresher course in the foreign language you studied in high school. Then, above all, when preparing your resume, be certain to exploit your ability to communicate in other languages—especially if you know the job sought requires such skills (Himstreet, Baty, & Lehman, 1993).

For a number of reasons, learning a second language may not be feasible—you are completing a short-term assignment, you must leave immediately, or the language is extremely difficult to learn (e.g., Japanese and Arabic) and you have no previous training. However, even if you cannot speak their language fluently, people from other cultures will appreciate simple efforts to learn a few common phrases.

GUIDES TO GOOD INTERCULTURAL COMMUNICATION

With so many barriers to communication, communicating with people of another culture is difficult. Communicating between genders, through the generation gap, among races, and through other differences present unique challenges as well. Anyone who enters the business world today must be aware of these potential trouble spots and of ways of avoiding them.

THINK IT OVER Generate a list of at least five other words with meanings that vary in English-speaking countries.

To increase your marketability, take foreign language courses and exploit this capability on your resume.

Assume that you have been assigned as an expatriate to Saudi Arabia. Should you learn to speak the language of the country?

LEARNING OBJECTIVE 4

General Principles

A good guideline for someone about to engage in business with a person from another country is to learn about that person's culture. Many sources of useful information are available. Experienced businesspeople have written books recounting some of the subtle but important ways that people in other countries communicate. Networking can generate the names of other businesspeople who have made contact with another culture. A telephone conversation or a lunch meeting may provide pointers on what to do and what not to do. Large corporations with frequent and extensive dealings in other lands often establish workshops in which employees receive briefing and training before accepting overseas assignments. Learning the language is an invaluable way of becoming more familiar with another culture.

Another basic guideline for communicating is to have patience—with yourself and the other person. Conversing with someone from another country, when one of you is likely to be unfamiliar with the language being used, can be difficult and time consuming. By being patient with mistakes, making sure that all questions are answered, and not hurrying, you are more likely to make the outcome of the conversation positive. You must also learn to be patient and tolerant of ambiguity. Being able to react to new, different, and unpredictable situations with little visible discomfort or irritation will prove invaluable. The author Howard Schuman writes "a sense of humor is indispensable for dealing with the cultural mistakes and *faux pas* you will certainly commit" (Marquardt and Engel, 1993).

The third basic guideline for communicating is to get help when you need it. If you are not sure what is being said—or why something is being said in a certain way—ask for clarification. If you feel uneasy about conversing with someone from another culture, bring along someone you trust who understands that culture. You will have a resource if you need help.

Written Communication

When writing for intercultural audiences, keep in mind some of these suggestions:

1. Write naturally but avoid abbreviations, slang, acronyms, technical jargon, sports and military analogies, and other devices. Many of these expressions help you clarify an idea and personalize your messages; however, they may be confusing to those unfamiliar with American usage. Those speaking English as a second language learn English from a textbook; therefore, they may have difficulty understanding directions to complete a project "ASAP" (as soon as possible) or to convert to "WYSIWYG" (what you see is what you get) software. They may be mystified when you reject bid proposals that are "out of the ball park" or "way off target," recruit job applicants who are "sharp as brass tacks," or refer to the supervisor as "the top gun."

2. Avoid words that trigger emotional responses such as anger, fear, or suspicion. Such words are often referred to as "red flag" words because they elicit the same response as a red flag waved in front of a raging bull. "Hot buttons," the term used in a popular training film, *Communicating Across Cultures* (1987), conveys a similar connotation. Regardless of the term, using words such as "gal," "boy," "handicapped," and "foreigner" is a sure way to shut a reader's mind to your message, to make understanding practically impossible, and to destroy any chance of trust and cooperation.

Libraries contain a wealth of material on cultural differences because of the increase in international business. Two excellent sources are Managing a Diverse Work Force by Fernandez and Going International by Copeland and Griggs.

THINK IT OVER
To get a sense of what being "different" is like, imagine what it would be like to be new in this country, not to speak or understand English well or at all, to have a disability, etc. Ask an international student on campus to share his or her experience in adapting to a new culture.

THINK IT OVER
Provide examples of figurative expressions, jargon, and analogies that might be misunderstood by other cultures.

THINK IT OVER
List several words you would label "red flag."

COMMUNICATION   MENTOR

"Globalization" is a reality in the business world. The fall of communism in the former Soviet Union and Eastern Europe, the passage of the North American Free Trade Agreement (NAFTA), and the opening of China are just a few of the events that will lead to increased international interaction for U.S. businesses. To be better prepared to succeed in this environment, you should learn a foreign language and become fluent in it. To be better prepared to succeed in this environment, try to spend some time in a foreign country if possible. This experience will not only expose you to different cultures and peoples but help develop an appreciation of how things are done in other countries. In international communications—written or oral—keep in mind the following hints:

- Keep your communication simple and straightforward. Avoid jargon and colloquialisms. Do not assume your international audience will understand common U.S. expressions. Even highly educated foreigners may not pick up on the meaning. Always use proper grammar.
- Be polite and formal and use proper designations when addressing someone (i.e., Dr., Professor, Director). Never call business contacts by their first names unless you have permission. Unlike in the U.S., in many countries, men do not remove their jackets during meetings. If you are unsure, err on the side of being too formal.
- Be aware of your contacts' culture and traditions. In Japan, bow when you give your business card and always read the card you receive. Develop an interest and appreciation for your contacts' culture and traditions; they will appreciate your sincerity.
- Do not put your contacts in embarrassing situations, especially in front of others. In many countries, a rather lengthy relationship-building period ensues prior to decisions being made. You should not demand immediate decisions.

International business can be interesting and rewarding. It can also be frustrating and confusing. Keeping these simple rules in mind can help you prevent costly and embarrassing mistakes.

Sajan K. Thomas
Vice President
Prudential Institutional Investors

3. Use simple terms but attempt to be specific as well. Some of the simplest words might be interpreted within the context of each situation in which they are used (e.g., *fast* has several meanings). Likewise, avoid use of superlatives such as *fantastic* and *terrific* because they may be misinterpreted as overly dramatic or insincere. Also avoid overly formal and difficult expressions that may be confusing or considered pompous; e.g., *pursuant to your request* or *ostentatious*.

4. Follow the same techniques for increasing readability you would use in writing to someone fluent in English: (a) Write short, simple sentences containing only one idea, and (b) construct short paragraphs that focus on developing one major idea.

Do all cultures communicate bad news in the same way?

5. Use the message planning principles you will learn in this course. In addition, learn the subtle differences in the ways different cultures organize messages, especially those presenting bad news. For example, Germans tend to be more direct with bad news, but other cultures avoid negative messages or camouflage them so expertly that the reader might not recognize them.
6. Use graphics, visual aids, and forms whenever possible because they simplify the message.
7. Use figures for numbers. This system is almost universal. Keep in mind, however, that most people in the world use the metric system. Be aware of differences in the way numbers are written. For example, $2,400.00 in the United States is written as 2400,00 in other countries.
8. Write out the name of the month in international correspondence to avoid misunderstandings. When using a number to represent the month, many countries state the date before the month; for example, 10.2 1992 for February 10. Readers from the United States might easily interpret this message to mean October 2, 1992, because in the United States the month is written first (2/10/92).
9. Become familiar with the traditional format of letters in the country of the person to whom you are writing and adapt your format as much as possible. Note the differences in the
   a. *Formality of the salutation and complimentary close.* The Germans, who prefer a formal salutation such as "Very Honored Mr. Professor Jones," might be offended by your choice of an informal "Dear Jim," a salutation you believed was appropriate because you had met and done prior business with Professor Jones.
   b. *Position of various letter parts such as the letter address and the writer's name and title.* For example, in German letters the company name follows the complimentary close and the signature block is omitted, leaving the reader responsible for deciphering the writer's signature (Varner, 1987).

Why use figures for numbers and spell out the month of the year when communicating with an international audience?

Oral Communication

In face-to-face communication, attempt to be natural while at the same time being aware of intercultural issues. Rely on these suggestions when communicating orally with an intercultural audience:

1. Avoid any actions—even subtle ones—that could be perceived to mean you believe your culture does things better than another. Instead, remind yourself constantly that the lifelong programming that guides a person's values and identity *differs* from culture to culture. One simple example clarifies this point. Although in the United States, some people might believe that senior citizens would probably be happier retiring to the temperate climate in Arizona, other cultures might view this practice as scandalous: "Look how they treat older people in this country—its awful" (McCaffrey & Hafner, 1985). Rather than chiding Asians for their formalities and seemingly meaningless fillers, open-minded U.S. managers understand that Asians highly value developing long-term relationships.

   Other intercultural insensitivities that reduce a manager's effectiveness include refusing to exchange (or learn to exchange correctly) bilingual business cards with the Japanese, failing to learn that "yes" really means "no" in some cultures, and presuming that all workers in a U.S. foreign

THINK IT OVER Obtain a copy of a business letter written by someone from another culture. Identify the major differences between this letter and a traditional U.S. letter. Share your letter with the class or small groups.

THINK IT OVER Based on your own experience interacting with someone from another culture, list several customs that are different from your own. Do you appreciate that his or her culture differs from your own or do you insist that your customs are better (more practical and sensible) than the customs of other cultures?

Showing empathy for others goes a long way toward opening up communication.

COMMUNICATION   MENTOR

A great deal of time is spent by both Western and Russian partners in the "courtship" stage to ensure that everyone fully understands the contributions/ objectives of the other. We recommend this procedure to both our Western and Russian clients and work with them to eliminate these very basic communication problems.

Larry E. Wilson, Managing Partner
Arthur Andersen, Moscow

subsidiary speak passable English. Interculturally naive managers, who continue to insist that culture does not affect international business, will make many intercultural mistakes. Unfortunately, this poor performance, in turn, will make it difficult for the company to capitalize on international business opportunities: prospective expatriates will be reluctant to accept overseas assignments, and the company's reputation in other countries will be damaged (McCaffrey & Hafner, 1985).

2. Minimize your stereotype of a culture. Instead, focus on the other person as an individual. Empathize with the audience; that is, view the situation from the audience's viewpoint rather than your own.

3. Try to understand some of the cultural elements that distinguish you from others in the communication process. To "see ourselves as others see us"— the gift Robert Burns asked for—is excellent advice for communicating with any audience and especially one from a different culture (Marcus, 1991). Strive to see yourself as the audience sees you and not as you see yourself.

4. Avoid slang, jargon, figurative expressions, "red flag" words, and other devices peculiar to American usage.

5. Enunciate words carefully and speak somewhat more slowly when communicating with those who speak English as a second language. However, avoid the temptation to speak in a very loud voice to get your point across.

6. Introduce frequent feedback to determine whether the listener has understood. Avoid asking "Is that clear?" or "Do you understand?" Both of these direct statements might elicit a "yes" answer if the person thinks saying "no" may be interpreted as incompetence or if the person's culture advocates saying "yes" to save face. Consider the following subtle, yet effective, techniques of verifying understanding.

   a. Observe the other person carefully throughout the conversation for signs of misunderstanding. You might ask, for example, if you or the listener might restate the idea in another way; rephrasing the message is far superior to repeating the same words more loudly.

   b. Conclude meetings or telephone calls with a clear understanding of what has been agreed on and what actions are necessary. Immediately following the oral meeting (telephone or face-to-face), send a letter or facsimile outlining these points.

7. Resist the temptation to interrupt the speaker before the message is complete. Your interruption would be considered rude in any culture. Moreover,

THINK IT OVER
Describe yourself as you believe others see you.

Ask questions but do not interrupt needlessly.

THINK IT OVER
A Japanese manager instructed an American worker to "ship any job lots of more than 25 units" and was enraged when he learned she had failed to ship 40 lots—all of 25 units. After an intense discussion, the manager learned that North Americans' interpretation of "more than 25" does not include 25, as it does for the Japanese (Sullivan, Kameda, & Nobu, 1991). What could the Japanese manager have done when giving the initial instructions to prevent the delay of the shipment and the hard feelings created by the miscommunication?

Judging a person by how you feel about his or her race, class, ethnic background, or age is stereotyping, a serious threat to effective communication. Communicating effectively to everyone in a diverse workforce requires you to treat each person that you meet as an individual.

the speaker may be intimidated by attention focused on his or her English skills. Of course, the obvious negative effect is that you may misinterpret the message if you do not hear the speaker's entire message.

THINK IT OVER
What is the appropriate protocol for greetings and introductions in the United States?

8. Become familiar with appropriate conventions for greetings and introductions in various cultures. For example, should you use the traditional American handshake or some other symbol of greeting? Is using the person's given name acceptable? Can you introduce yourself, or must you have someone else who knows the other person introduce you? Are business cards critical, and what rules should you follow when presenting a business card? Gaining competence in greetings and introductions will enable you to make a positive initial impression and thus to concentrate on the purpose of your meeting rather than agonize over an awkward, embarrassing slip in protocol. Your audience will appreciate your willingness to learn and value their customs.

    A business card printed in two languages is an efficient and effective tool. The two business cards in Figure 4-2 are the front and back sides of the same card. One side is printed in English; the other, in Russian.

THINK IT OVER
How familiar are you with geography and current and past events in other countries?

9. Research the participants' country or countries when you have advance notice about a meeting. A 1988 study by the National Geographic Society found that North Americans—youths and adults—were unable to locate countries on a world map. North Americans ranked below both Asians and Europeans in this simple task. Nothing would be more embarrassing and offensive than to reveal total ignorance about others. In other words, lack of preparation is not *smart* for business. In an article about negotiating with the Japanese, Flannigan (1990, p. 52) chided North Americans for depending on the other side for advice. "A Japanese company would never negotiate with North Americans without having at least one member of its team who speaks proficient English. Expect to face a negotiator who has read Hemingway and can tell you Babe Ruth's batting average. Conversely, if you go to the table with people who can't speak Japanese or find Yamaguchi-ken on a map and

FIGURE 4-2   *Proper introductions require presenting business cards in cultures such as the Chinese and Japanese with respect.   Because these cultures consider the business card an extension of the self, damage to the card is damage to the individual.*

have never heard of Isao Harimoto or Natsume Sosecki—you may get taken to the cleaners. It's the oldest rule in the book: Know your opponent.

10. Expect to spend extra time communicating with people from other cultures, especially people who are not time conscious and who believe that personal relationships are the basis of business dealings. Be patient with what you may consider time-consuming formalities and courtesies and lengthy decision-making styles when you would rather get right down to business or move on to the next point. Be patient and attentive during long periods of silence; in many cultures people are inclined to stay silent unless they have something significant to say or if they are considering (not necessarily rejecting) an initial offer. In fact, some Japanese have asked how North Americans can think and talk at the same time. Understanding this pattern of conversation can prevent you from making unnecessary concessions such as selling the store before the other side even has a chance to reply. Understanding can help you feel more comfortable during these seemingly endless moments of silence and less compelled to fill the gaps.

11. Become familiar with the subtle differences in nonverbal communication and adapt your own practices to avoid creating barriers to effective communication. Nonverbal areas to investigate include gestures, posture, body language, eye contact, dress, emotional expression, and time (relative importance, length of work day, holidays). Some nonverbal behavior of other countries is well known by now. For instance,

   • The Japanese greet with a respectful bow rather than the traditional handshake.

   • North Americans, who believe that maintaining eye contact is the hallmark of a person to be trusted, may consider the Japanese to be impolite when they keep their eyes lowered, not knowing this gesture is a sign of respect. Some cultures and ethnic groups, including Asian females and African-Americans, listen without direct eye contact, which is often frustrating to North American Caucasians who inaccurately perceive that the listener is uninterested and not listening.

   • The time-conscious North American can expect to be kept waiting for an appointment in Central America, the Middle East, and other countries where the North American sentiment "time is money" is not accepted.

THINK IT OVER
How might a Caucasian perceive these nonverbal expressions: (a) an African-American employee responds to the supervisor with eyes diverted, (b) a Japanese scientist working in the U.S. returns home to a less challenging position, or (c) Asian employees refuse to take part in quality improvement discussions?

THINK IT OVER
Can you list other differences in nonverbal behavior that could affect your ability to communicate effectively with someone from another culture or ethnic or age group?

Before speaking with persons from different cultures, you need to prepare by studying those cultures. In addition, when speaking across cultural and language gaps, remember to be courteous, speak clearly, and avoid using slang or regionalisms.

THINK IT OVER
Using at least two current sources, supplement the guidelines for intercultural communication provided here.

- North Americans, who often slap each other on the back or put an arm around the other as a sign of friendship, receive disapproval from the Japanese, who avoid physical contact. Japanese shopkeepers place change on a plastic plate to avoid physical contact with customers (Flannigan, 1990).

Being aware of differences in nonverbal behavior minimizes unnecessary embarrassment as well as confusion that can be detrimental to achieving the goal desired.

SUMMARY

1 **The business school graduate of today will almost certainly work for a multinational firm or in a culturally diverse workplace.** For many people, the growing area of international business will require them to work overseas as their careers progress. Their success will likely depend on their ability to communicate effectively across cultures, genders, ages, abilities, and other differences.

2 **Patterns of behavior learned from your culture (language, values, attitudes, customs) affect your actions and perceptions.** These patterns create barriers to communication when you communicate with people whose behavior follows different cultural patterns. Problems occur primarily when

people of one culture assume their cultural patterns of behavior should be valued by everyone.

3 **Five potential barriers to effective intercultural communication exist.** Stereotyping is a major barrier to intercultural communication; workers and employers can improve communication by recognizing cultural factors and by considering people as individuals rather than as members of stereotypical groups. Differences in timing, personal space, body language, and translations also create barriers to effective communication. General principles for overcoming these barriers include learning about the other person's culture (or other differences), having patience with yourself and the other person, being tolerant of ambiguity, and seeking outside assistance when necessary.

4 **Specific suggestions for improving written and oral communication include many of the same practices recommended for communication within a culture.** Important differences, however, are to avoid the use of terms peculiar to a language or terms open to several interpretations, write figures as numbers and write out the name of months to avoid confusion, and become familiar with the traditional formats of letters in the country of the person to whom you are writing. To facilitate oral communication, learn effective strategies for determining whether your message has been understood, keeping in mind that people from some cultures may not admit any misunderstandings. Avoid interrupting the speaker having difficulty with the language. Be familiar with major differences in greetings/introductions and nonverbal communication.

REFERENCES

Berger, M. (1987, July/August). Building bridges over the cultural waters. *International Management,* pp. 61-62.

Copeland L., & Griggs, L. (1985). *Going international: How to make friends and deal effectively in the global marketplace.* New York: Random House.

Flannigan, T. (1990). Successful negotiating with the Japanese. *Small Business Reports, 15* (6), 47-52.

Himstreet, W. C., Baty, W. M., & Lehman, C. M. (1993). *Business communications* (10th ed.). Belmont, CA: Wadsworth.

Holland, J. R. (1991, May). Reaching older audiences: Aging America presents communications challenges and opportunities. *Public Relations Journal,* pp. 14-15, 20-21.

Hoerr, J., Spiro, L. N., Armstrong, L., & Treece, J. B. (1990, December 17). Cultural shock at home: Working for a foreign boss. *Business Week,* pp. 80-81, 84.

Jesitus, J. (1991). The new labor pool. *Hotel and Motel Management, 206* (21), 23-24.

Jones, D., & Neuborne, E. (1993, November 16). Made in USA means sales in Mexico. *USA Today,* p. B1.

Marquardt, M. J., & Engel, D. W. (1993). HRD competencies for a shrinking world. *Training and Development, 47* (5), 59-64.

McCaffrey, J. A., & Hafner, C. R. (1985, October). When two cultures collide: Doing business overseas. *Training Development Journal,* pp. 26-31.

McGarry, M. J. (1994, June 9). Short cuts. *Newsday,* p. A50.

Magnusson, P., Treece, J. B., & Symonds, W. C. (1991, November 18). Honda, is it an American car? *Business Week,* pp. 105-107, 109, 112.

Marcus, B. W. (1991). Cross-cultural concerns. *New Accountant, 6* (6), 21, 42.

Miller, W. H. (1991, May 6). A new perspective for tomorrow's workforce. *Industry Week,* p. 6.

Neuborne, E. (1993, November 16). NAFTA or not, U.S. retailers pursue pesos. *USA Today,* p. 2B.

Phatak, A. V. (1995). *International dimensions of management* (4th ed.). Cincinnati, OH: South-Western College Publishing.

Ricks, D. A. (1983). *Big business blunders.* Homewood, IL: Dow Jones-Irwin.

Schlesinger, A. M., Jr. (Ed.). (1994). *The world almanac and book of facts.* Mahwah, NJ: Funk & Wagnalls Corporation.

Solomon, J. (1990, September 12). Learning to accept cultural diversity. *The Wall Street Journal,* p. B1.

Sullivan, J. H., & Kameda, N. (1982). The concept of profit and Japanese-American business communication problems. *Journal of Business Communication, 19* (1), 33-39.

Sullivan, J. H., Kameda, N., & Nobu, T. (1991). Bypassing in managerial communication. *Business Horizons, 34* (1), 71-80.

Toy, S., Levine, J. B., Maremont, M., & Miller, K. L. (1991, June 3). The battle for Europe. *Business Week,* pp. 44-50, 52.

U.S. Bureau of the Census. (1993). *Statistical abstract of the United States: 1993* (111th ed.). Washington, DC: Author.

Valuing diversity part III: Communicating across cultures. (1987). [Film]. San Francisco: Copeland Griggs Productions, Inc.

Varner, I. I. (1987). Internationalizing business communication courses. *Bulletin of the Association for Business Communication, 50* (4), 11.

Note: Exercise 8 was extracted with permission from Lehman, C. M., & Taylor, G. S. (1994). A role-playing exercise for analyzing intercultural communication. *Bulletin of the Association for Business Communication, 57* (2), 23-32.

REVIEW QUESTIONS

1. Provide evidence to support the statement that chances are great that you will be involved in international business activities or have to communicate across cultural gaps.
2. What recent world events have affected the level of international investment?
3. What factors have caused and are causing the decline in the dominance of the white male in the workforce in the United States?
4. What are companies doing to address the issue of multiculturalism in the workplace?
5. How does a culture benefit a people?
6. Explain how a society exhibits its culture.
7. What dangers are inherent in the stereotyping of a people, genders, age groups, work groups, or people who share other differences?
8. What effect might religion have on "the language of time"?
9. What is meant by "We view everything through the prism of our own experience"?
10. List the three *general* guidelines for communicating with intercultural audiences.
11. How do technical jargon, slang expressions, and "red flag words" endanger intercultural communication?
12. Stereotyping is considered both bad and good. What are some helpful or good aspects of stereotypes? What precautions can you take to minimize stereotyping as you prepare to communicate with someone from another culture?
13. How can you elicit accurate feedback in intercultural communication?
14. Discuss three guidelines for writing to an intercultural audience.
15. Discuss three guidelines for communicating orally to an intercultural audience.

EXERCISES

1. Complete each of the THINK IT OVER activities that your instructor assigns.
2. Identify the extent that increasing diversity affects you in your current affiliations. Consider your classes, part-time employment, organizations, and other activities. With what cultures are you in contact?
3. Melby Enterprises has not yet sought global markets for its products. Its president believes that international sales involve too many complexities and would, therefore, not be profitable. As a new manager, you must convince the president to reconsider the company's position on international sales. Using specific incidents from current newspapers and magazines, show how other businesses are profitably expanding their markets through international trade. Be prepared to share your ideas with the class.
4. Assess your adaptability to other cultures. Ask a friend to help you be objective in your assessment. Ask your instructor to provide an assessment sheet to guide your thinking. Prepare a three-column list and label the columns *Strength, Weakness,* and *Strategy for Improvement.* In groups assigned by your instructor, discuss your improvement plan in an effort to gain additional

insight for enhancing your intercultural communication skills.
5. Interview an international student, professor, or businessperson in your area. Your purpose is to learn about this person's culture and customs, communication practices in his or her country, and general advice for adapting to other cultures. Encourage the interviewee to share specific problems he or she faces and ways of addressing those problems. Summarize your findings in a short report and be prepared to share it with the class.
6. Interview a businessperson returning from an assignment in another country or one who has experience working in a foreign-owned company in the United States. Ask this person to describe his or her preparation for the assignment and to discuss specific problems in communicating and how those problems were addressed. Summarize your findings in a short report and be prepared to share it with the class.
7. Read an article in a newspaper, journal, or magazine about intercultural communication. Write a brief summary of the article and be prepared to share it with the class.
8. Assume that a Japanese vendor has just arrived at

FTE Enterprises (a major manufacturer of CD players) for an appointment to negotiate the delivery date for an order placed by the buyer, who is a Caucasian female. The vendor has been escorted to the shop floor where the buyer is trying to determine why a critical piece of machinery had broken for the third time in three weeks. Your task is to evaluate the buyer's and vendor's communication skills as you observe their conversation.

a. Two students will role-play the communication exchange between the vendor and the buyer (instructor will provide the script). A third student should read the lines marked "Thinking," which reveal what is going on in the minds of the others.

b. Identify any message or action that facilitated communication (breakthrough) or created a barrier to effective communication (breakdown). Make a comment about the appropriateness of the communication channel at the beginning of the conversation and whenever it changes. Be certain to analyze the nonverbal signals dramatized during the role-play. From your analysis, generate a list of at least three strengths and weaknesses in the vendor's and the buyer's communication style.

9. In groups of three, discuss each of the following critical incidents. Identify how you think the different cultures will interact.

a. A U.S. engineer working with a subsidiary in Asia begins a general meeting of the professional staff by praising one manager for outstanding work on a report.

b. A U.S. manager sees two Arab-American employees arguing and decides to stay out of it.

c. While the American supervisor waits, a Latino manager starts a budget-planning meeting by chatting casually and taking care of other "formalities."

d. After carefully presenting the benefits of the company's product, a sales representative from the United States presses an Indonesian buyer for a sales decision and eventually asks directly whether the buyer wishes to place an order.

e. A human resources manager becomes irate when an Asian woman does not maintain direct eye contact during a performance appraisal interview—or any other time.

f. Two managers have applied for an overseas assignment in Asia. One is a highly aggressive marketing expert with proven managerial experience; the other is a good team worker with a high degree of interpersonal skill. Which one would you choose and why?

g. As negotiations with Malaysian business executives become quite lengthy, a group of U.S. businesspersons become less formal, repeatedly crossing their legs in such a way that the soles of their shoes are visible.

h. A U.S. executive, committed to preparing reports with the most up-to-date information possible, required that all periodic reports be submitted approximately two days before the composite report was to be submitted to the president. The executive has been transferred to the Mexico operation and plans to follow this same practice.

i. Discouraged about the slow pace of negotiations with the Japanese, a U.S. manager suggested that the senior-level people from each side meet alone to attempt to work out the differences.

j. Eager to finalize negotiations with a group of United Kingdom (U.K.) business executives, a U.S. manager agreed to play golf the following day with a number of the U.K. executives. The U.S. manager diplomatically introduces one of the points of discussion between holes.

k. A female executive is being considered for transfer to a Middle Eastern country to negotiate the location of a new plant.

l. Arriving at the first meeting with a Japanese executive, a U.S. manager hurriedly pulls out a business card. Disregarding the fact that the card had bent slightly as it was pulled from the pocket, the manager hands the card to the Japanese executive with the name and title facing away from the executive. Politely, the manager accepts a business card from the Japanese executive. Holding the card with one hand, the U.S. manager quickly skims the name and title on the card while placing a briefcase on the table, signaling a desire to begin the meeting.

10. Recall a recent conversation you have had with a person from another culture or another region within the United States—a friend, teacher, coworker, supervisor, or some other person. Write a brief scenario including the dialogue and a description of the nonverbal messages transmitted. Analyze the effectiveness of this conversation

using the communication process model; use Figure 1-4 as a guide. Identify problems (interferences or barriers) occurring at each stage of the communication process and provide suggestions for improvement. Considering the barriers you have identified and the information gained from reading this chapter, give specific suggestions for improving this communication exchange. Be prepared to discuss your analysis with the class or in small groups assigned by your instructor.

11. In groups assigned by your instructor, select one of the critical incidents described in Exercise 9 or the situation identified in Exercise 10.
   a. Role-play the communication exchange violating intercultural communication principles. Repeat the role-playing exercise, correcting the communication errors.
   b. Present the ineffective intercultural exchange to the class at your instructor's direction. Ask the class to identify the problems and suggest ways for correcting them. If time permits, repeat the skit incorporating the suggestions.

12. Prepare a checklist of factors to guide a businessperson in researching the culture of another country. To begin your checklist, consider the broad ideas discussed in this chapter (values, symbols, language, and nonverbal communication); but include specific factors within each broad category. For example, the broad idea of nonverbal communication might include factors such as gestures, time, space, handshake or other greeting, touching, and others.

13. Select a country other than the U.S. or an ethnic culture in the United States that you know little about. Using the checklist prepared in Exercise 12, perform one or more of the following tasks:
   a. Develop a culture profile of the country or culture you selected. Briefly provide guidelines about each factor included in your checklist.
   b. Write a report designed to provide managers with specific guidelines for integrating successfully into this culture without suffering from culture shock.
   c. Develop your information (or selected portions) into a training program for managers preparing to do business with this culture. Prepare appropriate visual aids and handouts to support your ideas. Present the training program to your class if directed by your instructor.

14. Technology has increased the amount and speed of global communication. Increased globalization has affected various disciplines in unique ways. Identify one area (issue) in your own discipline that has been significantly influenced by globalization. Prepare a short report explaining the issue and its effect on the discipline.

E-MAIL APPLICATION

 This application will acquaint you with the Gopher service and its global connections. Gopher, developed at the University of Minnesota in 1991, is a distributed document delivery system. It allows campuses to disseminate news, announcements, and other kinds of information and to link with other campuses and government agencies. The system provides access to many networks and thousands of services around the world. Menus provide a single interface to all Gopher groups. Direct links are available to many electronic telephones and e-mail directories, as well as to full-text searches of major libraries and archived documents.

1. Acquire from your instructor a basic instruction sheet about how to access Gopher through your university computer.

2. Select a specific country or international agency from the Gopher service (e.g., Australian National University, UNESCO, etc.). Your instructor may assign a particular country or agency.

3. Obtain the e-mail directory of the users of the agency selected in Step 2 and then select an individual from the listing.

4. Message the individual selected (or possibly more than one to assure a response) requesting their opinion on a topic of interest to business communication. Topics might include the importance of speaking several languages; international telecommunication; ways to improve international communication; differences in verbal, nonverbal, or written communication among countries or cultures, etc.

5. Print your response and submit it to your instructor or share it with the class.

The United States is a nation of cultural diversity. Each wave of immigration, whether prompted by religious, political, or economic reasons, has added new facets to our distinct culture. The term *eclectic* has been used to describe this diversity; it refers to that which is made up of components from various sources and implies that the result is the sum of many perspectives.

As businesses attempt to serve the diverse needs of an eclectic community, recognizing and respecting cultural differences becomes increasingly important. The management of Pacific Bell Directory discusses this vital concept in terms of the unique characteristics of the Southern California intercultural environment. While the particular cultural components may vary, the same communication challenges exist.

Discussion Questions

1. Stephanie Dollschnieder refers to an important ingredient in successful intercultural communication as "cutting each other slack." What does she mean? Give examples of how this strategy can be accomplished.
2. What part do respect and trust play in intercultural communication? How are they related concepts?
3. To what extent is courtesy a universal concept?
4. How does the "salad bowl" concept of culture differ from the traditional "melting pot" idea?
5. Jan Birkelbach discusses the wide array of behavior within cultural groups and cautions against generalizing that all members of a specific group fit a certain stereotype. Give examples of several such stereotypes.

Application

You must make a short presentation to your company's staff concerning the cultural diversity of your community and the importance of effective intercultural communication.

1. Determine what cultural groups are present in your community and in what proportions. (Your chamber of commerce or city offices may be of help.)
2. Interview one or more persons from each of the major cultural groups in your community. Identify what is unique about their language, nonverbal communication, perception of time, customs, family life, etc.
3. Prepare an outline for your talk, emphasizing the importance of intercultural communication and including several suggestions for improving intercultural communication in your community.

CHAPTER 5

BUSINESS COMMUNICATION

TECHNOLOGY

OBJECTIVES

When you have completed Chapter 5, you will be able to

1 Identify the benefits of using organizational databases and online information services and spreadsheets to collect and analyze data.

2 Identify the benefits of using word-processing, spellchecks, thesauruses, and writing-analysis software to write and organize text.

3 Explain how printers and desktop publishing and presentation graphics are useful to enhance the overall effectiveness of a document.

4 Discuss how e-mail, voice mail, facsimile machines, cellular telephones, telecommuting, teleconferences, and videoconferences facilitate sharing data effectively.

5 Identify ethical and legal implications associated with technology.

The sprinter warms up before the race. He stretches, breathes deeply, and concentrates on winning. At the command to line up, he walks to his starting block, crouches into place, and waits to hear the gunshot signaling the beginning of the fifty-yard dash. But when he hears the loud bang, he remains frozen at the starting point, watching the other sprinters race toward the finish.

This scenario is literally a nightmare for professional runners. They train, work hard, practice, diet, lift weights, sacrifice personal time to work toward their goals, and try not to let anything interfere with their achievement of those goals. In some ways, business managers face the same situation. They have studied, completed internships, and made many sacrifices to get closer to their ultimate goals. Unless they can use electronic tools to access, assemble, and communicate information in a timely manner, however, they may end up like the sprinter—stuck in the blocks, left behind at the start.

Electronic tools have not eliminated the need for basic communications skills. If anything, these electronic tools, like all new tools and techniques, create new obstacles or barriers to communication that must be overcome. These tools, however, also create opportunities, which range from the kinds of communications that are possible to the quality of the messages themselves. Electronic tools for communication can help people

Name three general ways computers can be used to improve the quality of messages.

1. Collect and analyze information for messages.
2. Shape their messages to be clearer and more effective.
3. Communicate quickly and efficiently with others over long distances.

One chapter cannot cover all aspects of electronic tools in detail but can focus on those tools that expedite the quick and accurate flow of communication. The chapter also will outline some of the problems that can arise in messages created with these electronic tools and describe some techniques to avoid these pitfalls. These tools are grouped into four broad categories: collecting and analyzing, writing, presenting, and transmitting data.

COLLECTING AND ANALYZING DATA

LEARNING OBJECTIVE 1

Knowing how to collect information and communicate in a networked world is critical if you and your company are to be competitive. The "information superhighway," a part of the National Information Infrastructure, is predicted to bring vast amounts of data into our homes and businesses. However, online information services currently available provide a wide range of sources and services to facilitate our research.

Generally, electronic communication provides researchers with two distinct advantages:

What benefits does electronic communication provide?

1. Electronic searches of organizational databases and electronic networks can be done in a fraction of the time required to conduct manual searches of printed sources.
2. The vast amount of information available allows researchers to develop better solutions to problems.

Internal databases enable decision makers to obtain information from their own company records quickly and accurately. External databases (networks) allow users to access information from remote locations literally around the world and in an instant transfer that information to their own terminals for further manipulation and storage.

Innovations in computer and communication technology are developing rapidly. Successful executives stay abreast of what new technologies are available and how they can improve their businesses, and they are not afraid to learn new skills.

The purpose of this section is to familiarize you with the major types of electronic information available and whet your appetite to gain additional experience. Begin refining your electronic research skills by creating a database and accessing specific information. Go to your library to access its card catalog and indexed material; learn to access the library's database from a remote location. Once you have mastered these electronic research skills, begin exploring the Internet or any other online information services available at your college.

Organizational Databases

All businesses have a number of databases that constantly must be created, updated, and maintained. An **organizational database** is a computer file containing intracompany information such as financial, sales, or production data. Database information often is vital to the production of certain reports. Because the best report is useless if it is not timely, information in a database must be easy to retrieve and must be accurate. A database for a wholesaler, for example, might contain all possible retailers in different geographic locations. From these data, a list of retailers in the Midwest could be compiled and printed in a few minutes.

Databases organize data in meaningful ways, permit them to be updated, and allow them to be retrieved in a variety of report formats that can be used for decision making or other purposes. For example, the list of retailers could be transferred into a table to be included in a report, eliminating the need to rekey this information. In addition, the list could be merged with a form letter to produce a personalized letter and envelope or mailing label for each retailer. *Paradox*[1] and *dBase*[2] are well-known database programs.

What is an organizational database?

THINK IT OVER
Describe one database application you have created or know about that allows a decision maker to access and organize information quickly.

1   *Paradox* is a registered trademark of Ansa Software, a Borland Company.
2   *dBase* is a registered trademark of Borland International, Inc.

COMMUNICATION   MENTOR

The time you spend establishing hands-on familiarity with the technological tools available in your business will be an investment, not an expense. You don't need to become an expert but know enough to exploit the potential of those tools in ways that enhance the effectiveness of your communication.

R. D. Saenz
Business Consultant

What three benefits do organizational databases provide report writers?

Databases offer these advantages:

1. **Data organization**, the ability to organize large amounts of data.
2. **Data integrity**, assurance that the data will be accurate and complete.
3. **Data security**, assurance that the data are secure because access to a database is controlled through several built-in data security features.

Data security exists because users must enter an identification code or a password to gain access to a database, thus protecting it from unauthorized personnel. In addition, a system can be devised that permits only certain authorized workers to change information in the database, even though a broader range of workers can access the data. The ethical responsibility associated with privacy and data security is discussed later in this chapter.

Online Library Catalogs and Other Databases

Turn to Chapter 15, "Library Research" section, and study the printout of an electronic search to locate information about intercultural communication.

THINK IT OVER
Access your library's database and conduct a search to learn more about one of the topics in this chapter; e.g., information superhighway, online information services, videoconferences, or ethical implications of technology.

Many libraries now provide online databases of their card catalogs and indexed material. Rather than searching laboriously through card catalog drawers or individual indexes, you can conduct an electronic search using terminals in the library or in computer labs on campus. If the library permits, you may also connect with the library database from your computer at home or some other location using communications software and a modem. Useful electronic business research tools are *ABI/Inform*® [3] and *Business Dateline*® [4]. Visit your library or business computer lab and identify the electronic research tools available and begin learning to use them effectively. In Chapter 15, which discusses business research methods, you will learn more about electronic searches of library card catalogs and indexed material.

Online Information Services

People use online services for two basic purposes: to communicate with others and to obtain information. The communication aspect involves

- Sending electronic messages and computer files across the world.
- Participating in discussion groups (forums) to get answers to questions and to benefit generally from the information generated by a group interested in a

3   *ABI/Inform* is a registered trademark of American Business Information, Inc.
4   *Business Dateline* is a registered trademark of University Microfilms, Inc.

Companies are developing significant uses for the Internet as more people connect and the Internet becomes easier to use. For example, doctors at hospitals with Internet connections consult with faraway specialists by transmitting 3-D brain scans that can be rotated and examined onscreen. Panasonic communicates quickly with its suppliers and customers and its U.S. and Japanese labs.

specific interest or browsing occasionally through the "network news" generated by other discussion groups to read the latest discussions in these areas.

People use online services to communicate with others and to obtain information.

The quest for information involves

- Downloading software available on the service.
- Accessing vast amounts of information from a wide range of sources.

Using a modem, the appropriate communication software, and an assigned password, you can obtain information from around the world by subscribing to the Internet or a commercial online service.

A modem is becoming an important professional tool.

THE INTERNET

The **Internet** is a loose collection of millions of computers at thousands of sites around the world (universities, government offices, and businesses) whose users can pass along information and share files. For example, users have access to NASA-funded computers, transcriptions of the U.S. Supreme Court opinions, software, card catalogs from many libraries, immense archives of indexed materials, and the list goes on and on. The Internet was intended to be used for academic and research purposes; however, about 63 percent of the networks worldwide are registered to corporations whose primary use is electronic mail. / The Internet is growing phenomenally with about 150,000 new members joining each month (Kantor, 1994).

To help you understand how an Internet connection facilitates research by college faculty, consider this scenario:

THINK IT OVER
React to the statement that the "Internet will be a *ramp* onto the information superhighway." Locate some current information on the topic if necessary.

A U.S. professor collaborating with a Finnish professor on a research project locates information about the project using a number of Internet capabilities (Gopher, Wais, World-Wide Web, and others). The American professor submits several questions about the research underway to an electronic discussion group and "drops in" on several other groups to browse through discussions related to the topic. After compiling the information and generating a tentative outline, the American professor saves the information in a computer file and sends it electronically, along with an electronic mail message, to the coauthor in Finland. Within seconds, the Finnish professor is retrieving the computer file and making revisions, which are returned to the American coauthor with an e-mail message discussing the revisions and progress of the research. The electronic transfer of information continues until the project is completed.

Communicating through Internet connections is especially helpful when communicating with people in different time zones (especially in other countries) or with conflicting schedules.

THINK IT OVER
In small groups, generate a list of ways you can use the Internet to communicate and obtain information for your classes or other academic purposes.

With an Internet connection and the Internet address of other users, you can collaborate with students in your class or other universities in a similar way. Accessing the vast amount of information on the Internet and sending electronic mail messages and computer files to students involved in a class project will speed up research time and provide timely, relevant information that should lead to a better project. In addition, if you work or have schedules that conflict with group members, you will find Internet an excellent way to coordinate the work of the group efficiently. You too can become involved in discussion groups to learn more about topics in which you are interested; e.g., business, computers, software, and business communication.

COMMERCIAL ONLINE INFORMATION SERVICES

Private information services are another means for accessing business information quickly and relatively inexpensively. Consider this scenario of a typical manager working online:

"Going on line is like walking into a giant library, post office, shopping mall, and nightclub all at once. Everywhere you turn, there's something new or useful" (Kantor, 1994).

"You can move from tracking your stocks, to writing the president, to chatting with a group of eminent physicians, to troubleshooting a PC problem, to researching NAFTA, to booking a flight for your next business trip—without ever disconnecting from your online service" (Kantor, 1994, p. 110).

The five major national commercial information services are *America Online*[5], *CompuServe*[6], *Dow Jones News/Retrieval with MCI Mail*[7], *GEnie*[8], and *Prodigy*[9]. Basically, CompuServe, Dow Jones with MCI Mail, and GEnie offer a suite of services for business users; whereas, America Online and Prodigy offer less-expensive personal services. All of these networks charge a monthly fee for basic services and may add hourly charges for other services; some charge for each electronic mail message.

List some of the major types of information and services provided by commercial online information services. Do you have access to any of these services?

The information services contain information on general news, stocks, financial markets, sports, travel, weather, and a variety of publications (some allow you to retrieve the full text). An online encyclopedia is a standard service; one service updates its encyclopedia quarterly to keep it current. A "clipping" service that finds all articles on a specific topic from the various news services is

5   *America Online* is a registered trademark of America Online, Inc.
6   *CompuServe* is a registered trademark of CompuServe Incorporated and H & R Block, Inc.
7   *Dow Jones News/Retrieval with MCI Mail* is a registered trademark of Dow Jones & Company, Inc.
8   *GEnie* is a registered trademark of General Electric Information Services.
9   *Prodigy* is a registered service mark and trademark of Prodigy Services Company.

a time-efficient way to stay abreast of important topics. The major information services allow you to access the Internet so you can take advantage of the in-depth information located there. However, until user-friendly interfaces to the Internet become available, searching a library on America Online or CompuServe is much easier assuming these commercial services are on your desktop.

The information services as well as local services provide discussion forums. For instance, vendors such as Microsoft Corporation, Novell, Inc., and WordPerfect Corporation have provided online support to their customers through CompuServe or their own local bulletin board services. Vendors encourage users to refer to the online service before calling for technical support. Therefore, they post driver updates, software patches, and frequently asked questions (FAQs), saving technical support time on the voice lines for more urgent problems. Companies also provide electronic bulletin boards within a company to provide employees and customers up-to-date information about their products and services rather than having to wait several days for information to be communicated (Kantor, 1994).

Hurdles Involved in Using Online Services

Obviously, using online services can provide valuable information for making informed decisions quickly. However, knowing which service is likely to contain the information you need and then learning to "tunnel" through the vast amount of information *productively* can be an overwhelming experience. The experience can also be expensive in terms of time spent and charges incurred for online time.

Conducting a database search requires that you know the search procedures and how to construct a search strategy. Searching a library on the commercial services is relatively simple. However, conducting searches on the Internet has been referred to as "doing research in a vast archive with thousands of incomplete catalogs and no librarian" (Tetzeli, 1994, p. 86). Now that the demand for online services is increasing so rapidly, companies are developing graphical interfaces to help users locate information more easily.

With a general understanding of the types of online services available, invest the time and energy to learn to use the online services available for your use at your school or employment. Enroll in courses or workshops that provide hands-on training on using online services; Internet courses should be readily available. As you broaden your experience, collecting data electronically will become productive and enjoyable.

Spreadsheets

For preparing reports containing any analysis of numbers, an electronic spreadsheet is invaluable. An **electronic spreadsheet** is a forecasting and decision-making tool that can manipulate and analyze data easily. The spreadsheet's forecasting ability allows the user to ask, for instance, how profits would change if costs and sales were reduced by 10 percent or increased by 5 percent. The ability to calculate these variable forecasts—called "what-if" questions—quickly is one of the main benefits of spreadsheets.

The spreadsheet can transform a vast amount of numerical data into information that can be used in decision making. By condensing data into organized tables, the spreadsheet greatly assists the manager in meaningfully interpreting the data. For example, the spreadsheet in Figure 5-1 contains numerous

Companies are using online services to enhance customer support. How does providing quick, instant information about products and answers to questions facilitate communication and build trust?

"Information surfing" and "navigating" are jargon expressions associated with learning your way through the vast amounts of information in available online services.

THINK IT OVER
In small groups, share your experience with online information services. What problems have you encountered? What strategies have you used to gain proficiency in communicating in a "networked" world?

Describe two specific business applications for a spreadsheet. What benefits would they provide a business?

FIGURE 5-1
Spreadsheet simplifies computing of projected change in composition of billable hours.

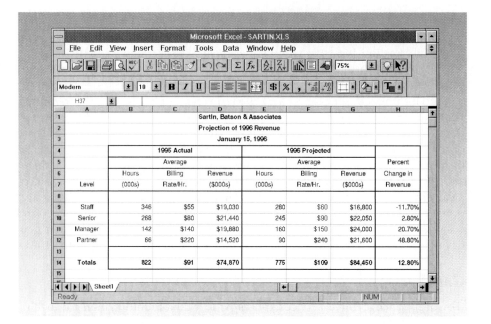

formulas that automatically calculate the projection of 1996 revenue. When a value is entered in F11 (average billing rate), the corresponding value of cell G11 (revenue) is automatically recomputed. By supplying a new number in cell G11, the program recalculates the values in three other cells and displays new results: H11 (percent change in manager revenue), G14 (total revenue), and H14 (percent change in total revenue). Such formulas are the key to "what-if" analysis.

Once it has been created, a spreadsheet can be inserted into a document with word-processing software. To depict complex data more clearly, the manager can also quickly construct a graphic using the prepared spreadsheet, as shown in Figure 5-2. The manager inserts the stacked-bar chart in a memo to the managing partner to reinforce her explanation of the change in the composition of billable hours. Using the same spreadsheet, the manager can easily generate a visual aid (transparency, slide, or printed handout) to support an oral report. Popular spreadsheet programs include *Lotus 1-2-3*® [10], *Excel*® [11], and *Quattro Pro*® [12].

The main barrier to good communication with a spreadsheet is the use of incorrect formulas for manipulating data. Whenever you create a template for a particular spreadsheet, be sure to check the validity of the formulas by running a sample test with some data.

Another barrier stems from the confidence that people develop in the results produced by a spreadsheet. Because the computer has such vast capabilities, users assume that a computer-generated report must be correct. However, the results are only as good as the data that are entered in the first place. To gain confidence in the results, take these steps:

1. *Verify data entered into the spreadsheet against the source.*
2. *Evaluate results to be certain that they are reasonable.* If the results seem

Spreadsheets are not infallible; a person with judgment must verify the accuracy of the computations.

Describe the procedures for verifying the accuracy of a spreadsheet.

10   *Lotus 1-2-3* is a registered trademark of Lotus Development Corporation.
11   *Excel* is a registered trademark of Microsoft Corporation.
12   *Quattro Pro* is a registered trademark of Borland International, Inc.

TO: Juan Perez, Managing Partner

FROM: Karen Paradiso, Human Resources Manager   *KP*

DATE: January 15, 1995

SUBJECT: PROJECTION OF 1996 REVENUE

The projected revenue for 1996 has been calculated as shown in the graph. To review the spreadsheet containing these calculations, you may access CONRAD.XLS.

The following factors were considered in preparing these projections: (1) The business downturn has developed into a prolonged recession, thus reducing our clients' willingness to entertain consulting engagements. (2) Our typical staff turnover is declining primarily because of reductions in hirings at competing companies. (3) Increased client expectations are demanding the use of staff with extensive business experience.

The amount of work is expected to be about the same as in 1995. Fewer professional hours will be required because more experienced accountants will perform a larger portion of the work. Staff hours will decline as we hire fewer college graduates. Increased billing rates and a different mix of hours among the levels will result in a 12.8 percent increase in total revenues.

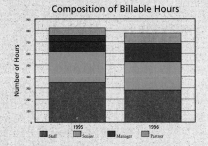

Please inform me of any changes you wish to incorporate in this projection. With your approval, I will prepare a final projection of 1996 revenue.

FIGURE 5-2
Stacked bar graph clarifies complex relationship and reinforces manager's major points.

questionable, begin by rechecking the accuracy of formulas and data input into the spreadsheet.

3. *Check to ensure that the assumptions behind "what-if" projections are reasonable.*

4. *Critique the spreadsheet design carefully to be certain that it **reinforces** the accuracy of your data.* Misspelled words, inconsistent formats (for example, some headings are centered and parallel headings appear flush left), and illogical or unattractive arrangement of data could create a serious question in the reader's mind: "Because these errors are present, *how* can I be confident that the data are correct?" Today's highly sophisticated spreadsheet software may be intimidating to some novice users. As a result, these users may underutilize spreadsheets or avoid them altogether. As an important first step, reluctant users must resolve to overcome the forceful tendency to

THINK IT OVER
Are you responsible for the accuracy of the information you gather and manipulate? What are possible consequences of communicating inaccurate information about other people? Have you ever experienced any repercussions?

avoid topics that appear to be difficult. With an open mind, they can commit the time and energy needed to develop a marketable skill: the ability to process information quickly and accurately. If necessary, they should seek adequate training by asking for help from co-workers who are experienced spreadsheet users, attending in-house computer training sessions, or enrolling in college computer application classes.

WRITING AND ORGANIZING DATA

Word-processing software expedites the production of a document and also improves the quality of the message. Other electronic tools that improve writing are electronic spellchecks, thesauruses, and writing-analysis software.

Word-Processing Software

Explain how word-processing improves the quality of writing.

Using word-processing, you can draft a document, store it on magnetic medium, and retrieve and revise it as many times as necessary to produce a clear, understandable document. Word-processing software also allows you to format the document using indentations, print features (**boldface**, <u>underline</u>, shadow, outline, or *italics*), graphic lines and boxes, and various typefaces, etc., and then print a highly professional copy. Reports and longer documents become less tedious to produce because of features that facilitate writing and editing:

1. *Insert and delete.* The insert feature allows you to enter new copy—from one character to several paragraphs—anywhere in the document. The delete feature allows you to remove text, from a single character to many pages.
2. *Block.* The block feature allows you to identify any portion of the document as a block, which can then be deleted, moved to another location, or copied from one position to another. If after keyboarding a long report, you decide that a paragraph makes more sense in another location, you can create a block and use the move feature. You can use the block and copy features to repeat a complicated table in more than one part of a report.
3. *Search and replace.* The search-and-replace feature is helpful when you have consistently misspelled a word throughout a document or decide to change a word throughout a report. For example, with just a few keystrokes, you can use the search-and-replace feature to change "multicultural" to "intercultural" every time it appears in your 50-page report. In addition to the time saved, an important benefit is the increased confidence in the accuracy of your work.

   Revisions that significantly enhance the quality of the memorandum in Figure 5-3 can be made efficiently using word-processing features. Because revisions are simple, writers using word-processing software are much more likely to revise a document than writers using traditional methods.
4. *Redline and document comment.* The redline feature and document comment features are beneficial when several people contribute to one document, a common practice in business. Traditionally, one author uses a red pen to edit drafts before passing them to another author. Today, authors often share disks or send computer files electronically to authors in remote locations; redline marks text that has been added, deleted, or edited. These marks are removed from the file when each author has approved the changes.

THINK IT OVER
Look at Figure 5-3 carefully. Using the block-move feature to reverse the order of the first and second paragraph is simple and improves the coherence of this memo significantly (begins with an overview and then leads into discussion of FASB 106). Read the original and the revised memo and note the improvement.

Convince other group members working on a class project to use the redline and document comment features so that each person can approve changes and insert reminders and queries.

Replace full name of statement with FASB106 except for first occurrence.

TO: O. S. Townsend, Human Resources Director

FROM: Krista Deweese, President

DATE: June 5, 19--

SUBJECT: *RENEGOTIATION OF UNION CONTRACT TO ELIMINATE* POSTRETIREMENT HEALTH-CARE BENEFITS

A recent statement from the Financial Accounting Standards Board has changed the way we account for postretirement benefits. Statement No. 106, Employers' Accounting for Postretirement Benefits Other Than Pensions *(FASB 106)* requires that the cost of providing future medical benefits to be accounted for on the accrual basis.

In 1976, you recall, we agreed to provide health care to qualified retirees as a part of a revised employment contract signed that year. At that time, ~~providing~~ postretirement health-care ~~was~~ *costs were* relatively inexpensive. *However, several factors have changed the picture significantly.*

No ¶ This change in accounting principle has made us realize the magnitude of providing these postretirement benefits. Estimates of future costs based on ~~Statement No. 106, Employers' Accounting for Postretirement Benefits Other Than Pensions~~ *FASB 106* could severely inhibit our ability to remain competitive with firms who are not providing postretirement benefits.

So that the company can cope with this issue, I authorize you to begin renegotiating the union contract immediately. My initial thought is that we could offer employees a pay increase in exchange for these postretirement health-care benefits. *Please consult with corporate finance to determine an acceptable pay increase.*

FIGURE 5-3
Word-processing features (insert and delete, block, and search-and-replace) simplify revisions of documents.

Uses search-and-replace feature to input acronym for full name of statement.

Inserts a more descriptive subject line.

Uses block and move features to reposition the second paragraph to create a more logical sequence.

Deletes wordy expressions.

Inserts an appropriate action ending.

Asked to approve the memorandum in Figure 5-4, the production manager changes the delivery date and authorizes a discount for a partial order. The proposed additions are displayed in red, and a line is drawn through the proposed deletions. On a printed copy of this document, the additions appear in bold. The exact appearance may vary depending on the setup of the system.

Document comments allow writers to insert reminders and notes to themselves and co-authors. These comments can be displayed for easy reference or hidden to eliminate distractions. The production manager's explanation for the delayed delivery date appears in the comment box in Figure 5-4. Collaborative software programs that assist users in writing collaboratively are also available. Each author marks revisions and inserts document comments in much the same way as with word-processing software and then sends the computer file to the co-author. Some collaborative software programs allow multiple authors to work on a document at the same time.

THINK IT OVER
If you have an Internet connection, attach a computer file to an electronic message directed to your instructor (or person specified by your instructor). Explain in the e-mail that you are learning to transfer files electronically. Ask your instructor or lab assistant for help if necessary.

FIGURE 5-4
Redline and a document comment alert co-author of proposed changes and provide needed feedback.

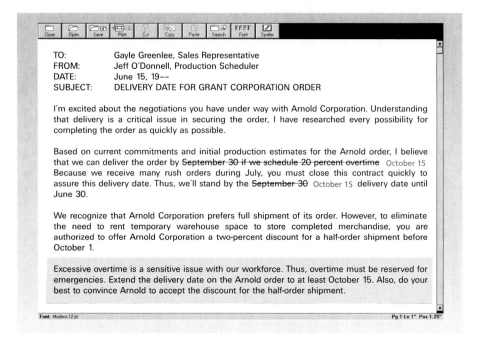

TO: Gayle Greenlee, Sales Representative
FROM: Jeff O'Donnell, Production Scheduler
DATE: June 15, 19--
SUBJECT: DELIVERY DATE FOR GRANT CORPORATION ORDER

I'm excited about the negotiations you have under way with Arnold Corporation. Understanding that delivery is a critical issue in securing the order, I have researched every possibility for completing the order as quickly as possible.

Based on current commitments and initial production estimates for the Arnold order, I believe that we can deliver the order by ~~September 30 if we schedule 20 percent overtime~~ October 15 Because we receive many rush orders during July, you must close this contract quickly to assure this delivery date. Thus, we'll stand by the ~~September 30~~ October 15 delivery date until June 30.

We recognize that Arnold Corporation prefers full shipment of its order. However, to eliminate the need to rent temporary warehouse space to store completed merchandise, you are authorized to offer Arnold Corporation a two-percent discount for a half-order shipment before October 1.

Excessive overtime is a sensitive issue with our workforce. Thus, overtime must be reserved for emergencies. Extend the delivery date on the Arnold order to at least October 15. Also, do your best to convince Arnold to accept the discount for the half-order shipment.

Font: Modern 12 pt   Pg 1 Ln 1" Pos 1.25"

Turn to Figure 18-3 to study the simple procedures for creating and updating footnotes using word-processing software.

5. *Automatic contents page, index, and document references.* Most of the sophisticated word-processing programs include a feature that generates a contents page, index, and document references automatically. This feature saves time in the initial creation of these pages and in their updating if pagination changes during editing. You will learn more about this timesaving feature when you study the report-writing chapters (Chapters 17-18).

Describe the general procedure for producing form letters using word-processing software.

6. *Mail merge.* This feature facilitates large-scale mailings of form letters. The text of a form letter is basically the same for all recipients, but the letter is personalized by adding variables—information that is different for each recipient. For example, the variables shown in parentheses in the standard text in Figure 5-5 are the client's name, address, salutation, and conference attended. The personalized letter is prepared by combining the standard text with a list of variables for each letter. Special codes instruct the software to insert the variables in the appropriate location in the standard text. With this feature, each client receives an original letter instead of a photocopy of the standard text with his or her name individually keyed in—a laborious task that creates a less-than-favorable impression. In addition, you can use the sort feature to arrange the addresses in numeric order according to ZIP Code. Printing the letters and envelopes or mailing labels in this order will eliminate the time-consuming task of sorting mass mailings according to U.S. Postal Service regulations.

The most frequent complaint about the mail-merge feature is that form letters are impersonal. Many people simply refuse to read such letters for that reason. Constructing a good standard letter that does not sound like a form letter can circumvent this problem. To make a form letter more personal,

What steps can be taken to make a form letter more personal?

1. Add more variables to the standard text to tailor it to the individual.
2. Use personalized envelopes instead of mass-produced mailing labels.

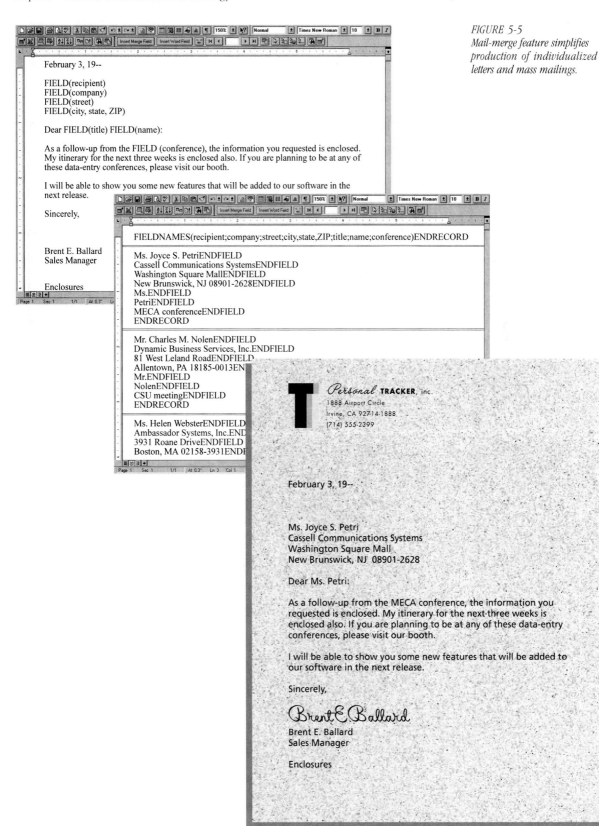

FIGURE 5-5
Mail-merge feature simplifies production of individualized letters and mass mailings.

3. Be sure to spell names correctly.
4. Produce a higher-quality document by using a better grade of paper and better-quality printers.

Spellcheck, Thesaurus, and Writing-Analysis Software

Spellchecks, *thesauruses,* and *writing-analysis software* aid in producing an effective message. With spellcheck, you can automatically check the spelling of every word in a document against the program's dictionary. The words misspelled or not included in the dictionary are highlighted. You simply select the correct spelling from a list provided by the computer or input the correct spelling if it does not appear in the list. Some programs allow you to add words to the dictionary. Overreliance on spellchecks, however, can be a costly mistake. In Chapter 8, you will learn to apply systematic proofreading, which involves understanding the limitations of spellchecks.

The thesaurus feature automatically generates a list of synonyms and antonyms for any word. You may choose one word from the list to substitute for the original. This feature can help you find words with very precise meanings and add freshness and variety to your writing.

Writing-analysis software used in conjunction with word-processing software helps writers improve their writing style and locate grammatical errors. After the writer composes a document using word-processing software, the writing-analysis software checks the document against the grammar and style principles stored in the program and generates a list of suggestions for improving the document. A popular writing-analysis program that may be included with a word-processing software program is *Grammatik*® [13]. Using software to analyze writing is ineffective if the writer accepts the software's critique without evaluating whether the suggestion is appropriate for the particular message being written. A writer should ask, "Does the technique suggested achieve my desired objectives?" For example, using active voice to achieve clear, vivid images is an effective writing principle, but it is not recommended when conveying bad news. Chapter 8 provides additional information about the specific assistance these programs provide and their limitations.

PRESENTING DATA

Being able to access and manipulate data is not enough; the course of daily business often requires that these data be communicated to others. Various kinds of computer software, along with some specialized hardware, make very effective tools for creating convincing presentations.

Printing

The printed page remains one of the main vehicles for business communication. The quality of appearance of a printed document depends not only on the software but on the printer as well. The two most prominent types of printers

---

13   *Grammatik* is a registered trademark of Novell, Inc.

are dot matrix and laser. To distinguish between these printers, consider four factors that affect your decision of which printer to purchase: (1) print quality, (2) speed, (3) graphics capability, and (4) price.

DOT MATRIX PRINTERS

A dot matrix printer is the least expensive printing alternative. These printers have a mechanism called a *printhead* with a number of points called *pins* that strike the ribbon in various combinations to create characters (patterns of dots) on the paper. The closer the dots, and the greater the number of dots in the same space, the better the quality of the printed character.

Dot matrix printers generally have at least two printing modes that produce different print qualities. In the draft mode, the dots forming each character are clearly visible, and the output is not appropriate for external correspondence. The draft mode is suitable for preparing internal correspondence; routine business documents; and drafts of proposals, reports, and letters/memos at high speeds.

In the near-letter-quality mode, each character is printed twice, which reduces the visible space between dots. Unfortunately, the print speed is significantly reduced in this mode. Although more expensive dot matrix printers produce characters with exceptional quality, the print quality remains inadequate for external business correspondence.

Dot matrix printers can also be used to print certain graphic images, a capability that makes them versatile. Dot matrix printers are currently available in 9-pin and 24-pin models. The 24-pin model produces better character quality and is more expensive.

List two benefits of a dot matrix printer.

LASER PRINTER

A laser printer produces characters of the highest quality available for printers that are commonly used in business. These printers use lasers and a process similar to photocopying to produce a page of characters at a time. Because the characters can be shaped in the form of the letters traditionally supplied by professional typesetters for publishing, these printers are considered near-typeset quality. Laser printers also possess the capability of handling sophisticated graphic images.

Print speed is a significant advantage of laser printing. Manufacturers advertise laser printers with print speeds of 4 to 17 pages per minute. The disadvantage of laser printers is the cost: approximately three times as much as dot matrix printers.

Laser printers offer a number of typefaces that can be enlarged (scaled) within a wide range, from tiny letters to letters larger than a standard sheet of paper. The typeface can be varied to emphasize specific information. Some of these variations include italic, boldface, shadow, and outline.

List several reasons that would convince a business to buy a laser printer.

Note the quality of the bar chart shown in Figure 5-6, a newsletter produced using desktop publishing capabilities and a laser printer. In addition, special models of both dot matrix and laser printers are capable of printing in color. Color can be used to emphasize specific information and to increase the visual appeal of the message.

Desktop Publishing Software

Desktop publishing software helps managers and other workers surpass simple word-processing capabilities by using typography, design elements, and even graphic images to create communications that are persuasive and professional

What is desktop publishing and what benefits does it provide?

FIGURE 5-6   *Desktop publishing creates highly professional business documents.*

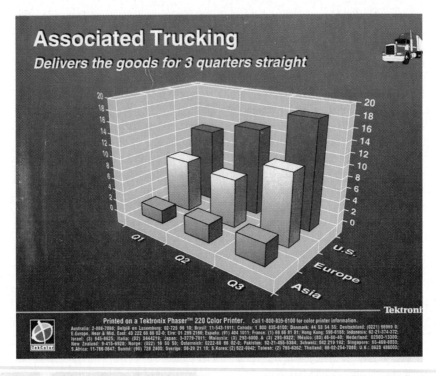

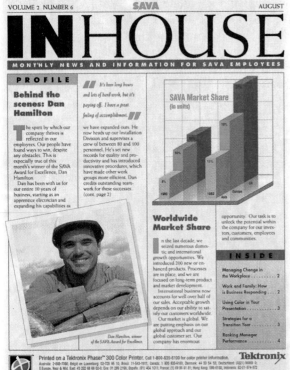

looking. Using desktop publishing software and a high-quality printer, one person can create important publications such as prospectuses, annual reports, and newsletters.

In the typical flow of desktop publishing, a document (or a number of documents) is created, edited, and proofread in a word-processing program. The document is then brought into a page-layout, or desktop publishing, program such as *PageMaker*® [14] or *Ventura Publisher*® [15], where the text can be styled with different typefaces, sizes, and other enhancements such as rules, boxes, and other graphic devices.

By using desktop publishing, you can create a company image at a fraction of the cost once required. This software can be used to create business cards, letterheads, forms, in-house newsletters, direct-mail advertising, catalogs, manuals, sales reports, and countless other publications. Some of these documents can be created through the use of top-of-the-line word-processing programs.

Graphic images can range from a pie chart showing sales distribution to the picture of a building to supplement a newsletter article announcing the opening of a new division. Text and graphics are combined electronically to make a complete presentation. When printed on a laser printer, the result can be a convincing newsletter and other graphic images as shown in Figure 5-6.

Graphics are available from several sources:

1. Electronic spreadsheet and presentation graphics software are used to generate graphics.
2. Limited clip-art (predrawn graphics stored on disk or CD-ROM) comes with top-of-the-line word-processing software, and additional clip-art can be purchased separately.
3. Drawing software such as *CorelDRAW*™ [16] and *Adobe Illustrator*® [17] allows desktop publishers to draw their own images (flowcharts, pictograms, scaled drawings of products, and so on).
4. Scanners convert printed images (graphics, photos, signatures, letterhead, and text) to electronic files that can be integrated into a document.

Presentation Graphics Software

Pie charts, bar graphs, and line graphs can be generated by graphics software to help readers grasp a point more readily than they can interpret a narrative or even a table. Communication professionals who use graphics in newspapers and television news reports are aware of the direct impact that pictures can have on the reader or viewer.

Decision makers who do not have the time to wade through pages of written text searching for key information are among the primary beneficiaries of graphic presentations. A manager may win the day by supporting a case for expansion with a line graph showing the resulting increase in profits. A salesperson might close a deal by backing up a proposal with five bar graphs illustrating the superiority of a product over the competition's.

The use of graphics in presentations has grown greatly in recent years because of the development of increasingly capable programs for generating

THINK IT OVER
Collect several samples of correspondence, newsletters, annual reports, and brochures from businesses. Discuss in groups how desktop publishing techniques have been used to improve the appearance of each document.

Which of these sources of graphics are available to you?

The stacked bar chart in Figure 5-2 was created using a spreadsheet program, saved in a graphics format, and imported into the memo. Next year the manager can input the new projections into the same spreadsheet and generate a new graphic in a matter of seconds. If you have not imported graphics into documents, find someone to help you learn.

14 *PageMaker* is a registered trademark of Aldus Corporation.
15 *Ventura Publisher* is a registered trademark of Ventura Software, Inc.
16 *CorelDRAW* is a trademark of Corel Systems, Inc.
17 *Adobe Illustrator* is a trademark of Adobe Systems, Incorporated.

graphs on personal computers. Such packages as *Harvard Graphics*® [18] and *Microsoft Chart*® [19] create standard graph types that work as templates within which data are placed to produce a polished, professional-looking image. The images can be produced quickly and efficiently as well. Chapter 16 and the reports in Chapters 17 and 18 contain numerous graphics created with presentation graphics software. Chapter 3 includes specific guidelines for producing and using visuals for oral presentations.

You can convert a graphic to a transparency or color slide to support an oral report.

Graphic Design Principles

How does too much variety get in the way of communicating?

Type, design, and graphics introduce new considerations that were once the concern of only graphic artists or typesetters. Desktop publishing puts a very useful tool in the hands of the untrained user; unfortunately, the results often show the lack of training. Having the tools to design does not make you a designer. Newcomers to desktop publishing, enchanted with the effects that can be created with type, rules, shadows, and boxes, clutter documents with too many type styles or with too many lines. The result is not an effective presentation but a jumble of words and graphic elements that confuse and alienate the reader.

By following some simple principles of design, however, the budding desktop publisher can effectively use the tools at his or her disposal:

1. *Keep it simple.* The more variety included on a page, the more difficulty the reader will have in following the message. Restricting the document to no more than two or three typefaces and just a few special effects is often the best approach.
2. *Keep it consistent.* Treat comparable elements in the same way. All the headlines in a newsletter with five articles should be in the same typeface and style. Save special treatments for material that is special.
3. *Design graphics to avoid distorting or obscuring facts and relationships.* A graphic designed to obscure negative information deliberately is shown in Chapter 6, Figure 6-8.
4. *Let form follow function.* A document should be styled in such a way that it looks like what it is. A purchase order need not be elegant; the menu of an expensive restaurant should look more dignified than the price list of a dry-cleaning service.

SHARING DATA

LEARNING OBJECTIVE 4

Computers have added another kind of communication to the practice of business—electronic communications. You have already seen that a modem can link someone with a personal computer to a large database, allowing the computer user to access important and up-to-date information such as stock and bond prices. Computerized communications can also link individuals in other ways.

What is electronic mail? Do you have access to e-mail at your school? If so, do you use it to facilitate communication with your instructor and class members? Ask about e-mail capabilities if you are not using it already.

Electronic Mail

Offices use a number of traditional methods for sending a document, depending on the time constraints and the cost of the method. The U.S. Postal Service can be

18 *Harvard Graphics* is a registered trademark of Software Publishing Corporation.
19 *Microsoft Chart* is a registered trademark of Microsoft Corporation.

COMMUNICATION MENTOR

Of all the technological tools available, e-mail is my favorite. Frequently, I must communicate with examiners who are working in banks hundreds of miles away. They are able to receive my e-mail messages and respond immediately.

Gabriel Swan
Federal Bank Examiner

relied on for two- to four-day delivery or overnight service within the United States. Many private carriers provide overnight or second-day service. For messages that must be sent faster than those methods can manage, electronic mail is used.

Electronic mail, or *e-mail*, as it is often called, is most commonly defined as person-to-person communication in which the transmission and receipt of the message takes place through a computer. Electronic mail can be used to distribute memos, reports, and documents without sending them through the mailroom.

E-mail helps solve the problem of "telephone tag." Approximately 70 percent of business telephone callers *do not* reach the person they called on the first try. The result is a game of tag, as the caller and the person called keep trying to reach the other unsuccessfully. With electronic mail, the caller simply keys in a message and sends it to an electronic mailbox. Receivers are notified that a message awaits them, and they respond to the caller as soon as the message is read. When it is delivered and read quickly, electronic mail can be almost as convenient and articulate as a personal conversation.

For example, the electronic message in Figure 5-7 is the partner's response to the memo shown earlier in Figure 5-2. The partner sent his reactions to the human resources manager's projection electronically for three reasons: (1) The electronic message will reach the manager more quickly than a printed memo and thus will expedite the completion of the revenue projections. (2) Because the response is relatively brief and simple, the manager will not need a printed copy of the message; the electronic message can be read and immediately discarded. (3) The electronic message prevents the partner from playing "telephone tag" to deliver a message that is unlikely to require a verbal response.

E-mail systems that operate on a company's existing computer system are relatively inexpensive. In fact, some in-house systems send messages for as little as five to seven cents each. When a single message is sent to several recipients, the savings are even greater compared with the cost of traditional communication methods. For example, suppose the vice president of production must inform six regional sales managers, located in offices across the country, that they must postpone sales of a particular model immediately because of complaints of defective workmanship. Obviously, timely delivery is a critical factor because the purpose of the message is to prevent the shipment of any more orders. Mail service is too slow, and the telephone system is inconvenient because the regional offices are located within several time zones. In fact, East Coast offices

What is telephone tag? Explain how e-mail minimizes this problem.

E-mail is especially useful when communicating a single message to several people or over different time zones.

THINK IT OVER
Can you think of another example when e-mail is an appropriate message medium? inappropriate medium?

FIGURE 5-7
*Instant feedback provided in
electronic-mail message expedites
the completion of an assignment.*

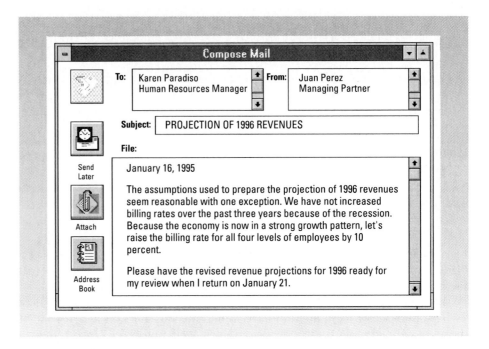

have already closed for the day. E-mail is the appropriate medium for this message. With only a few keystrokes, the vice president sends one electronic message that reaches all managers instantly at a low cost.

E-mail usage will continue to gain widespread use, especially as it becomes the foundation for more advanced corporate applications. One such application already available is referred to as the *forms definition feature*. For example, using this feature, a sales rep can select a form such as an expense form, complete it, and send it to his/her supervisor who will electronically sign it and send copies to the appropriate persons. Additionally, intelligent rules based on content can be encoded, which will instruct the form to route itself automatically. For example, if a claim is more than $10,000, the form will forward itself to a senior bank officer (Mailman 1.0, 1991).

Voice Mail

Voice mail allows you to use your telephone to dial a voice mail service and store an oral message. The message is then delivered to the person or list of persons you are calling. Recipients can retrieve messages when they return to the office or dial in from remote locations to listen to their messages. Voice mail provides many of the benefits of e-mail but does not require a computer.

Facsimile Machine

A **facsimile machine** or a *fax* is a flexible and inexpensive form of electronic mail. A fax machine reads a document that has been inserted into the machine and transmits the document (text, pictures, and graphics) over telephone lines to another fax machine that receives the message and prepares a printed copy of the document. Because increasing numbers of companies of all sizes are using fax machines, entrepreneurs are putting fax machines that take credit cards into airport lounges, hotel lobbies, and convention centers. To use them, you simply insert your credit card in the machine, dial the number you want to reach, and send your document.

The advantage of fax transmission is speed. For example, a high-speed fax machine can transmit a page in about 20 seconds. Improved machines offer print quality comparable to that of a copy machine. In addition, fax machines are easy to operate. Because they can be programmed, the cost of transmission can be cut by sending a message in evening hours to take advantage of lower telephone rates. Sending faxes also facilitates communicating with people in different time zones.

Telecommuting

Telecommuting allows individuals to work in their homes and use electronic mail to transmit work from their homes to the office. The major advantages of telecommuting are the reduced time and expense of commuting and the increased flexibility of working hours. Rather than spending two to three hours a day commuting to work in an urban area, for example, employees use a modem, telephone lines, and a remote workstation to transmit their work electronically. Memos, reports, even entire books can be transmitted in this way.

In addition, practitioners from various disciplines are using modems and telephone lines to transmit information quickly and cost effectively. For example:

- Accountants transmit income tax returns to the Internal Revenue Service.
- Private investors transmit investment transactions to stockbrokers.
- Sales representatives calling on customers in remote locations transmit orders to the home office to facilitate quick delivery (and foster good customer relations).
- Professionals working away from their offices (for example, in clients' offices or other remote sites) transmit information back to their offices. For instance, an engineer transmits detailed production information so that personnel in the home office can begin analyzing the data. Auditors transmit financial information collected while working in clients' offices to expedite completion of the final audit report.

Transmitting information and computing from remote locations have become more prevalent because of the availability of *laptop* and *notebook computers*. Laptops, which are about the size of a large book, and smaller notebook computers, give professionals access to computing power regardless of where they are—hotel room, airplane, taxi, or client's office. These portable systems are battery operated and generally contain secondary storage (a floppy disk drive, a hard disk drive, or both), a screen, and a keyboard. Newer innovations include palmtop computers, tiny hand-held computers that rest on the palm of the hand, lapbody computers that can drape from the neck, and "wearable" computers (e.g., wrap around the forearm to facilitate recording inventory).

Managers use portable computers for two major reasons: (1) to make every minute of a busy schedule count and (2) to generate and communicate up-to-the-minute information without returning to their desktop computers. As technology improves, manufacturers are enhancing the quality of the images displayed on the monitor and the quality of the printouts. Poor-quality images and printouts have been the major disadvantages of portable systems.

What are the advantages of a fax machine?

Computers equipped with fax/modem software can now send and receive faxes. Managers review incoming faxes on the screen and print only pertinent ones—a significant cost savings.

Are practitioners in your field telecommuting? Provide at least one example.

THINK IT OVER
Locate an article discussing how businesses are using "wearable" computers. Do you have personal knowledge of such an application?

How do portable computers benefit users?

Cellular Telephones

Efficient use of time and closer contact with co-workers, clients, and customers are convincing reasons to use a cellular telephone.

Cellular telephones, often called *mobile phones*, are cellular radios that transmit messages over airways. Cellular telephones are a powerful communication tool, especially for managers who are on the move (those who spend several hours commuting to and from work, travel from one meeting or work site to another, or work at sites with no access to a telephone) and must stay in immediate reach of the home office at all times. The increased productivity resulting from the more efficient use of time justifies the use of cellular service. Cellular telephones also help managers stay in closer contact with co-workers and with current and prospective clients and customers. Quick, courteous responses build strong interpersonal relations, which in turn lead to increased employee commitment and an edge over competitors. As cellular service expands to reach remote areas as well as urban areas, cellular telephones will soon become a standard business tool.

What general factors determine whether an employee could profit from a cellular phone? List several job categories that you believe could profit from cellular telephones.

Scanning cellular messages transmitted across public airways is difficult because frequencies change so often; however, it can be done. Therefore, to protect the privacy of cellular telephone conversations, follow these general practices:

THINK IT OVER
Using electronic search tools available, locate an article or book discussing the etiquette related to the use of cellular telephones. (Hint: Consult Letitia Baldrige's *New Complete Guide to Executive Manners*.) Compile a brief list of do's and don'ts.

- Let your caller know you are speaking from a cellular telephone.
- Use discretion when discussing confidential, sensitive information. For example, avoid reciting credit card numbers, calling card numbers, or similar information. Select words carefully, stick to first names, and avoid specifics, if possible ("Is anybody listening," 1993).

Scrambling devices and enhanced privacy services are available for those needing added protection.

Electronic Meetings

Teleconferences and videoconferences are alternatives to face-to-face meetings that allow several people at different locations to communicate electronically. These electronic conferences can eliminate or reduce the high costs of face-to-face meetings: travel, hotels, food, and time lost in transit.

TELECONFERENCES

A telephone conference call, in which several people in different geographic locations are on the same line at the same time, is an example of teleconferencing. Teleconferences facilitate decision making because all involved in a decision are involved in the discussion; the expense and time involved in traveling are saved.

VIDEOCONFERENCES

Some give Saddam Hussein credit for the increased use of the videoconference. When he invaded Kuwait, businesspeople searched for ways to have meetings without jumping on airplanes (Hogan, 1994).

The **videoconference** takes advantage of all media—audio, graphics, and video. Speakers provide the audio feedback, facsimile devices send graphics, and cameras transmit the video portion of the conference in a specially equipped room. Participants engage in group discussions while observing one another's facial expressions and gestures.

Some personal computer companies have introduced inexpensive personal **desktop videoconferencing systems** that allow users to hold electronic meetings and share and annotate files and images across existing local area

COMMUNICATION MENTOR

Technology allows companies to deliver instantly the same message to different audiences in ways that meet their special needs. For instance, a company may announce a breakthrough new product to financial analysts using a national wire service and internationally via a satellite news conference. Key customers may receive a technical briefing through a controlled direct broadcast satellite network while employees at remote facilities receive and play videotapes of a presentation by their company's CEO. All of this, through technology and adequate planning, can happen during one business day.

Cynthia Pharr
President & CEO
C. Pharr Marketing Communications

networks and telephone lines in real time. Desktop videoconferencing restores the nonverbal elements of interpersonal communication that are lost over the telephone and is more personal than a "disembodied" voice at the other end of a telephone line. More important than the visual dimension, however, is the ability to "document conference." Using collaborative software with the desktop technology, users in remote locations can see each other as they work together on computer files (share text files, graphics, and images) at the same time. For example, an engineer in one location can share design diagrams with a marketing associate at a distant site, allowing the two to collaborate on the design without traveling ("Low-priced," 1993). An ad agency and client make changes on proposed ads; a doctor sends an x-ray to a remote expert, gets an opinion, and saves lives (Tucker, 1993).

As the cost of videoconferencing capability declines, electronic meetings will become a common communication medium. Oral communication, especially within small groups, will be critical to interacting effectively in this environment.

> A projected 45,000 to 50,000 videoconferencing systems are expected to be installed by 1995 as compared with 15,000 in operation in 1993 (Tucker, 1993).

Guidelines for Communicating Electronically

Electronic communication (including voice mail) is a handy way to communicate quickly and conveniently with another worker or with a database. Problems can arise if the system is used inappropriately or if messages are too long or poorly organized. The following guidelines will help you use electronic communication effectively:

1. *Send messages on electronic systems that are related to business and not designed to give the recipient a good laugh.* Resist the urge to "personalize" the message that identifies your voice mailbox and informs callers that you are unavailable. Keep the message highly professional, giving the caller a clear indication of when you will return the call.
2. *Do not flood the system with "junk mail."* One of the key benefits of electronic mail is to allow workers to communicate more effectively than with

> Discuss general guidelines for using electronic communication effectively.

traditional means. If the system is clogged with unnecessary messages that the receiver feels compelled to answer, productivity will be lost, not gained.

3. *Be conscientious in checking and responding to electronic messages to avoid missing important information needed to complete your assignments.* Ignoring electronic messages from co-workers can erode efforts to create an open, honest work environment.

4. *Remember you are responsible for the content of an e-mail message.* Because e-mail moves so quickly between people and often becomes very informal, more like a conversation, individuals may not realize (or forget) their responsibility. If a person denies commitments made via e-mail, someone involved may produce a printed copy of the e-mail message in question as verification.

5. *Read each message very carefully before you send it.* Often writers hold a particularly sensitive letter or one written in anger and mail it the next day if they still deem the message appropriate. Unfortunately, once you press the simple keystrokes to transmit an e-mail message, you cannot get it back.

6. *Avoid sending confidential information because the security of e-mail is low compared with other media.* Undeliverable messages are delivered to a mail administrator, and e-mail messages are frequently caught in system backups and sit on tapes in machine rooms for years. Thus, an old message can be "resurrected" with little effort (Krol, 1992). Likewise, computer glitches can also result in voice mail messages being delivered to incorrect voice mailboxes.

7. *Decide whether the electronic system is an appropriate channel for your message.* These systems are intended for information typically sent through printed memos, *not* for formal communication such as performance appraisals or disciplinary action. As the sender, you are responsible for choosing the most effective channel for your message; technology simply increases your choices of channels. You may elect to schedule a face-to-face meeting if a message is sensitive, highly emotional, or subject to misinterpretation. Actually, choosing an appropriate channel is an important aspect of communicating ethically. After all, if the recipient loses dignity as a result of the channel used to convey the message, you have acted unethically. How humiliated Bo Schembechher must have felt when he was notified by fax that he had been dismissed from his position as president of the Detroit Tigers. Including this detail as part of this major sports story must have increased the embarrassment (Sports News, 1992).

8. Organize your message carefully just as you would a traditionally prepared message. Present information in the order it is likely to be needed. For example, describe the nature and purpose of an upcoming meeting before giving the specifics (date, place, time). Otherwise, the reader or listener may have to reread portions of an electronic memo or review an entire voice mail message to extract the details. Busy managers will appreciate your using empathy (putting yourself in the receiver's position) to determine a logical, efficient sequence of information.

9. *Avoid lengthy, detailed information.* Requiring the receiver to remember or to write down a significant amount of information indicates that you lack empathy for your audience, who may be struggling to take notes from the monitor or listening and relistening to a recorded message. Lengthy messages are likely

The security of e-mail is very low. Much of Oliver North's connection to the Iran-Contra affair was documented through old e-mail files found in system backups.

THINK IT OVER
Generally for what types of messages is electronic communication appropriate? What ethical implications are involved in choosing an appropriate channel for a message? Provide an example—a personal one, if possible.

C O M M U N I C A T I O N   M E N T O R

In the past ten years, the development and use of various electronic tools for communication have increased significantly. Although technology has made communication more efficient, it has reduced the human element involved, thereby reducing effectiveness in certain situations. My suggestions regarding electronic communication follow:

- Become proficient with the technologies that will be used in your school and businesses. These may include word-processing, electronic mail, facsimiles, and even satellite videoconferencing.
- Understand when a more human approach may be more effective. For example, conveying bad news or communicating a strong disagreement should be done face to face if possible. Also, a personal handwritten note of congratulations may be far more meaningful than an electronic note. Experience and corporate culture will help you in making these decisions.
- Use proper grammar in electronic mail. Your notes could be forwarded to many people whom you have not met, and these notes could make your first impressions on them.
- Do not overuse voice mail, especially during office hours. Customers and superiors usually want to talk with humans when they call.

Sajan K. Thomas
Vice President
Prudential Institutional Investors

to become distorted and thus cause costly delays and mistakes. When sending a voice mail message, follow these general procedures:

- Identify yourself and state the purpose of the call. Then describe the specific information you need so that the receiver can gather that information before returning the call.
- Repeat important information to give the receiver a second chance to hear it or to confirm what he or she heard the first time. For example, you will probably introduce yourself at the beginning of the message. If you leave a telephone number at the end, repeat your name and state the telephone number twice very slowly.
- Avoid a monotone or "reading" voice and nonwords such as "uh," "well," and "and-a." Instead, speak in a natural, well-paced, audible tone, using appropriate voice inflection that makes your message more interesting and conveys accurate nonverbal signals, adding to the overall clarity of your message.

10. *Use the following style guidelines to make e-mail easier to read (Krol, 1992):*
    - Keep the line length reasonably short (no more than 60 characters) so the entire line will display on the monitor.
    - Use both uppercase and lowercase letters because such a style is easier to read than using only uppercase or lowercase letters exclusively.

Give specific guidelines for leaving a good voice mail message. Write an example.

- Do not use special print features (bold, italics, etc.) because the terminal receiving the message may not be able to interpret them. Use uppercase letters to emphasize an important idea instead.

LEGAL AND ETHICAL IMPLICATIONS OF TECHNOLOGY

LEARNING OBJECTIVE 5

"Computer technology, like any other invention, has the potential to exalt or debase the people who use it" (Connell, 1993, E1). However, it is our responsibility "to ensure that information technology and the information it handles are used to enhance the dignity of mankind" (Mason, 1986, p. 54). This discussion will focus on issues related to privacy and accessibility, property rights, and accuracy.

Privacy and Accessibility

What are the common invasions of our privacy caused by technology?

Technology threatens our privacy, our right to be left alone, free from surveillance or interference from other individuals or organizations. Common invasions of privacy caused by technology include collecting excessive amounts of information for decision making and maintaining too many files, monitoring the exact time employees spend on a specific task and between tasks and exact number and length of breaks, and supervisors' or co-workers' reading other employees' electronic mail and computer files. Integrating computer files containing information collected from more than one agency without permission is a major threat to privacy. Although an individual may have authorized the collection of the individual information, merging the information may reveal things the individual may want to remain private (Mason, 1986).

Our right to privacy is protected primarily by the First Amendment (guarantees freedom of speech and association) and the Fourth Amendment (protects against unreasonable search and seizure of one's personal documents or home and due process). However, the Fair Information Practices (FIP) form the basis of 13 federal statutes that ensure the security and integrity of personal information collected by governmental and private agencies. Set forth in the FIP are conditions for handling information about individuals in such areas as credit reporting, education, financial records, newspaper records, cable communications, electronic communications, and video rentals. Study the following principles carefully (Laudon and Laudon, 1994):

What are the five Fair Information Practices?

FAIR INFORMATION PRACTICES PRINCIPLES

1. There should be no personal record systems whose existence is secret.
2. Individuals have rights of access, inspection, review, and amendment to systems that contain information about them.
3. There must be no use of personal information for purposes other than those for which it was gathered without prior consent.
4. Managers of systems are responsible and can be held accountable and liable for the damage done by systems and for their reliability and security.
5. Governments have the right to intervene in the information relationships among private parties.

Employee privacy concerns have been called the "workplace issue of the 1990s."

Despite this federal legislation and state laws passed to enhance and strengthen it, most Americans feel they have less privacy today than ever. According to a recent Harris poll, 76 percent of Americans believe they have lost all control over personal information, and 67 percent believe that computers must be restricted in the future to preserve privacy (Equifax, 1992). Those statistics are not surprising, for many of us have experienced an invasion of privacy over personal information in today's highly computerized society.

As one example, consider the privacy of e-mail messages. Many firms claim they have the right to monitor the electronic mail of their employees because they own the facilities and intend them to be used for job-related communication only (Rifkin, 1991). On the other hand, employees expect that their e-mail messages would be kept private. However, the Electronic Communications Privacy Act (ECPA) of 1986 favors employers:

- Employers may read their employees' mail as long as the monitoring is done in the ordinary course of the employer's business.
- Communication monitoring is permissible with the express or implied consent of one of the parties to the conversation.

Thus, to protect themselves against ECPA liability, employers simply provide a legitimate business reason (preventing computer crime, retrieving lost messages, regulating employee morale) for the monitoring and obtain written consent to e-mail interception or at least notify employees. Employees who use the system after the notification may have given implied consent to the monitoring (Casarez, 1992). Federal and state laws related to employee privacy are being introduced. The Privacy for Consumers and Workers Act has been introduced into Congress and would cover most forms of electronic surveillance, requiring employers to notify present and prospective employees of any monitoring policies and forbidding secret monitoring (Bowers, 1991; Casarez, 1992).

In the past the courts have agreed that employers have the right to monitor their workers while on the job, but pending lawsuits should address the growing concern that present laws do not protect employee privacy rights. Alana Shoars, e-mail administrator, told 700 Epson employees that only e-mail messages captured through routine network administration and troubleshooting would be read. When she later discovered all employee e-mail originating from outside the company was being read, she complained and was fired for "gross misconduct and insubordination" ("Epson E-mail," 1990). Shoars sued Epson for invasions of privacy on behalf of herself and other Epson employees. Epson asserts Shoars was fired for good cause but has since notified employees that it cannot guarantee e-mail privacy because of its need to protect against computer crime (Casarez, 1992). Although litigation related to these new privacy issues is already underway, the development of law is lagging far behind technology; nevertheless, employers can expect changes in the laws as technology continues to develop.

As you collect and access information, adopt the following ethical practices:

1. *Collect only information that is* **needed** *as opposed to what you would* **like** *to know.* Resist the urge to add a few additional questions to a survey instrument with the idea you might use that information later.
2. *Develop (and use) safeguards for the security of information and instill in data handlers the values of privacy and the importance of confidentiality.*
   a. Require employees to use passwords to gain access to the system and enforce routine changes of passwords on a periodic basis. Also, provide guidance in assigning a password that cannot be easily broken; e.g., never

THINK IT OVER
Have you ever felt your privacy was threatened by technology? Give examples of invasions of privacy of which you have personal knowledge.

What steps can you take to ensure that information is collected and accessed ethically?

use birth dates or names. Krol (1992) summarizes the criteria for selecting a good password:

- Is at least six characters long.
- Has a mixture of uppercase, lowercase, and numbers.
- Is not a word or a set of adjacent keys (e.g., QWERTY).

An easy way to meet all of these criteria is to pick the first letters of a favorite phrase, like, *MtFbwyYS* (May the Force be with you, Young Skywalker).

What types of information can you access from your university's computer? Ask your instructor what additional information a faculty member is allowed to access.

b. Require users to "sign off" or "logout" of e-mail when they leave their terminals. This procedure would prevent a person from sending a harassing message or committing a computer crime with no fear of being caught—the offender's name and e-mail identification would not be displayed on an unattended terminal.

c. Assign user identification passwords that limit information a person can observe and change. Consider access to information stored on your college's computer. A user identification number and password limit the types of information various personnel at the university—registrar, faculty, administrators, and students—can access about students and university employees.

d. Consider the use of encryption facilities if you are sending extremely confidential information. Through **encryption**, users can encode their messages so that only the intended recipient can read them. Reading or changing encrypted messages is virtually impossible, which, of course, limits the employer's ability to monitor e-mail for business purposes.

3. *Develop a clear privacy policy that complies with the law and does not unnecessarily compromise the interests of the employees or employer.* Be certain employees understand whether e-mail is considered private or corporate property. Explain exactly how employees will be monitored and the limits. For example, "we will canvass all e-mail if we suspect criminal activity, such as drug trafficking. But no, your supervisor will not be told you're seeing a psychotherapist twice a week" (Smith, 1993, p. 88). Open communication will circumvent litigation but more importantly build trust and thus improve employee relations.

Electronic monitoring may also destroy creativity. For example, a CEO tapping into a database to determine the progress of a project can also judge the quality of the work at any point. "Teams assigned to new undertakings won't take chances because they will worry not about how the project will look in the end, but how it will look at 3 p.m. on Tuesday" (Smith, 1993, p. 88).

Property Rights

Several serious legal and ethical implications relate to the protection of intellectual property and the use (and abuse) of technology.

SOFTWARE AND INTELLECTUAL PROPERTY

Why is the protection of intellectual property so difficult?

Several substantial economic and ethical concerns surround the question of intellectual property rights. Regardless of how costly it is to create in its original form, information is easy to reproduce and share with others without destroying the original. Therefore, protecting information once it is communicated to another is virtually impossible.

Trade secret laws, copyrights, and patents have provided some protection for intellectual property such as software. Because perfect copies of software can be made so easily, Laudon and Laudon (1994) conclude we are becoming a society of lawbreakers, citing surveys in which people report that they violate minor laws such as speeding, taking paper clips from the office, and *copying*

COMMUNICATION IN ACTION

Al Walea, USAA

Fast-changing electronic technology poses a challenge for business and industry today. One company, USAA (formally United Services Automobile Association) of San Antonio, Texas, is a leader in using technology to its advantage while serving its 2.6 million customers. USAA provides insurance and full financial services to commissioned military officers and their dependents.

Al Walea, USAA's executive director in claims analysis and design, specializes in keeping current with the latest technological changes. He works in USAA's information services division and understands well how the sharing and exchanging of data in his company have made it a success. "Because we conduct nearly all our business over the phone," Walea explains, "it is extremely important that information be processed accurately and promptly."

When USAA receives a customer's written correspondence, that correspondence is "imaged" (electronically photographed) and stored in a database. Each authorized employee has access to the database and can instantly access the customer's records. "Our systems are extremely automated," Walea says. "Typically, most customers do not write letters when corresponding with USAA. They prefer to call one of our 800 numbers. These calls must be routed properly to one of the 10,000 employees housed in the San Antonio central office building." When an employee makes changes in the database, those changes are available instantly to every other authorized employee throughout the country. Such instant service meets customers' needs and demonstrates how to exploit technology to business advantage.

According to Walea, "Technology is not an objective. Technology is really not a driver. Technology is an enabler. You first have to understand the business need, which should determine which technology is used." Walea believes that the most successful technologies are invisible to the customer. The customer may not really care about sophisticated technology and how it works but wants claims or policies processed quickly and accurately.

Technology not only helps USAA's customers, it also protects the privacy of their information. USAA is one of the few companies that never sells its information. "Information is simply not released," Walea explains. "Our information is not shared with others and is never sold. If you give information to USAA, that information stays with USAA." The USAA database contains sensitive information on almost all active duty and retired commissioned military officers, including information about each military officer's background, length of stay in assigned locations, and job classification.

Sharing of information internally is protected because the system tracks whoever accesses a customer's record. If an unauthorized individual attempts to access a customer's record, the system automatically locks the station's keyboard. USAA requires that definitive action be taken when such unauthorized access is attempted, and a letter of reprimand is placed in the offending employee's file. In some cases, dismissal may be required. Walea states, "Privacy of information is taken very seriously at USAA."

Applying What You Have Learned

1. Why is a current, accurate database so important to USAA's business?

2. Describe USAA's advantage of conducting most business by telephone. What are some disadvantages?

3. Assume that you are a customer of USAA. What privacy-of-information concerns do you have about personal information existing in a large company's databanks?

software. One in every five copies of business software used today is reported to be an unauthorized copy. Although professors are perceived to have ethical standards superior to business executives, Shim and Taylor (1991) found that many professors justify copying software for education and research purposes—the ends-justify-the-means argument. Consequently, this topic may have been omitted from your discussion of information systems; thus, a review of software legalities is important here. Read your copyright agreement carefully; however, general guidelines provided by the Computer Software Copyright Act passed by Congress in 1990 are as follows:

What do copyright agreements generally prohibit?

- You are generally prohibited from modifying, transferring, adapting, leasing, or loaning entire programs or parts of programs. Companies can and will obtain damages if infringements are detected. Monetary penalties may be as high as $100,000 for each occurrence.
- Recently many software companies have modified their agreements to permit the installation of an authorized copy on more than one computer system in your office or home or on a portable. However, you cannot run the software *legally* on more than one computer simultaneously. This philosophy interprets the use of software as similar to the use of a book; we might read it at the office and then take it home to read as well.

Wang issued clear guidelines to users that would protect Wang's intellectual property. The company has filed a copyright infringement lawsuit against a customer who refused to pay an operating system license fee (Stedman, 1994).

THINK IT OVER
Try to obtain information about your university's software policy. What steps are taken to enforce the policy? If you own software, read your license agreement carefully and be certain that you are not in violation.

Despite the lax attitude toward software pirating, take a strong ethical stand. Adhere strictly to software copyright agreements and encourage co-workers to do the same. If you are responsible for computers, clearly communicate the company's expectations related to copyright violations. Then develop a systematic means of monitoring the software use. For example, many companies conduct periodic software checks. These checks should be announced in advance to give employees a chance to "clean up their act" and to dispel employees' fear that they are being monitored. Studies and comments from monitored employees clearly indicate that employees feel monitoring is an invasion of privacy, which eventually lowers morale, trust for supervisors, and increases work-related stress (Nussbaum, 1989).

COMPUTER CRIME AND ABUSE

Computer crime is the commission of illegal acts through the use of or against a computer. **Computer abuse** is the commission of acts involving a computer that may not be illegal but are considered unethical. Computer crime is estimated to cost business over $1 billion. Yet to avoid embarrassment, many companies will not report computer crimes caused by their employees. The most economically damaging computer crimes are introducing viruses, theft of services, disruption of computer services, and theft of telecommunication services (Laudon & Laudon, 1994).

The FBI estimates that the average armed robbery nets about $10,000, but computer crimes bring in more than $1 million (Aldag and Stearns, 1992).

THINK IT OVER
What forms of computer abuse have you witnessed at college or work? Who was hurt by these unethical actions and how? What did you do to oppose these actions?

What can you do to combat computer crime and abuse? First, report any incidents involving employees you suspect might be using the computer illegally (transferring funds, stealing files, etc.). Many users hack (use a computer illegally) as a prank; disgruntled employees may sabotage a computer system to get even with the company. Second, honestly evaluate your own work habits to ensure that you are not using the computer unethically. For example, using a computer system (including the Internet and online services) to operate a profit-generating business during "off hours" is certainly unethical. However, using the company's computer for playing games, balancing the checkbook, sending electronic messages about personal matters, researching a child's research project, or making personal travel arrangements may seem insignificant; and, unfortunately, the "everyone-is-doing-it" mentality is a compelling argument. Lost productivity of the employee and the computer and additional charges for online information services are costs companies incur when employees use company equipment and company time to complete these personal activities. In addition, increased traffic on the Internet may cause poor performance for many legitimate users. Using the computer to transmit hateful, harassing, obscene messages or computer files is abusive as this antisocial behavior violates the rights of others.

Accuracy

Because communicating inaccurate information can adversely affect a person's life, you should take precautions to ensure accuracy and make reparations for any harm caused. As you read, one of the FIPs requires managers of systems to be "responsible, accountable, and liable for the damage done by systems and for their reliability and security." People are suing and receiving financial settlements for irreparable harm caused and dignity lost because of inaccurate information. One noteworthy case involved a couple who had made regular payments on a long-term loan from a bank. When the computer indicated that the account was delinquent, the bank refused to consider the payments Louis Marches had *insisted* the bank clerk record in his coupon book. When informed the bank was foreclosing on the loan, Mrs. Marches suffered a near-fatal stroke and became paralyzed. The Marches sued the bank and won. Yet, all the bank president could say was "Computers make mistakes; banks make mistakes, too" (Mason, 1986, p. 50).

> You are responsible for communicating accurate information and can be held accountable for any harm caused when you communicate inaccurate information.

As you use information for decision making,

1. *Be certain the information is **relevant**, **current**, and **verified***. Consider the source of the information to ensure that it is appropriate and unbiased. Delete information on a regular basis to ensure that "old" information is not used inappropriately. Allow people access to their own records so they can verify the accuracy of the data.
2. *Do not assume information is correct simply because it was generated by a computer.* Take systematic steps to verify the accuracy of information input into an information system against the source; proofread names and amounts very carefully. Evaluate the results of any computation to be sure it is reasonable.
3. *Design computer routines that automate verification checks of computer files.*

With the continued development of technology, especially the information superhighway, these and many other ethical dilemmas must be addressed. The question of equal access to information technology arises as technology becomes increasingly important to succeed in our society. Some argue that inattention to this question could lead to a society of information dropouts—illiterate information have-nots (Mason, 1986; Laudon & Laudon, 1994). Major ethical issues related to the information superhighway already being discussed include information overload and overreliance on information, detachment from reality caused by "virtual reality," and the effects of prolonged exposure

> **THINK IT OVER**
> What ethical issues will unfold as technology becomes increasingly important and the eventual introduction of the information superhighway takes place? In small groups, discuss these issues; locate additional resources and read more about these possible future dilemmas.

to violent entertainment and various other types of questionable information that can be accessed interactively from the home. Others question what will happen to the national character when users cluster into special-interest groups as they listen to 500 channels rather than tune in to a central arena such as network television (Takahasi, 1993).

SUMMARY

1 **Some people mistakenly think of electronic tools for business communication as substitutes for basic communication skills.** However, they are tools that augment and enhance each phase of the communication process—from collecting and analyzing, writing and organizing, presenting, and transmitting data.

Collecting and analyzing—Organizational databases, library databases, the Internet, and commercial online information services provide quick access to vast amounts of information needed for decision making. Spreadsheets allow decision makers to manipulate and analyze data easily.

2 **Writing and organizing**—Word-processing software expedites the process of writing, revising, and formatting documents using special features such as insert and delete, block, search and replace, automatic report pages, and mail merge. Redline and document comment features aid in collaborative writing projects; mail merge simplifies mass mailings and enables the writer to personalize a form letter for individual receivers. Spellchecks and writing-analysis software assist writers in preparing well-written, mechanically correct documents that portray a positive image for the company.

3 **Presenting**—High-quality printers, desktop publishing, and graphics programs improve the overall effectiveness of the document, making the

document "look" as good as it sounds. Simple procedures for designing an effective document include (1) keeping the design simple, (2) maintaining consistency with comparable design elements, (3) designing honest graphics that do not distort or obscure facts and relationships, and (4) choosing a design that is compatible with the function the document serves.

4 **Sharing**—Electronic mail, voice mail, facsimile machines, portable computers, and cellular telephones enable mangers to send and receive information instantaneously, minimizing the cost and alleviating the time-consuming delays caused by traditional transmission methods. Electronic meetings—teleconferences and videoconferences—allow individuals at remote locations to communicate electronically, eliminating the time and costs involved in travel for face-to-face meetings.

5 **As you handle information, you must be certain that information technology does not violate basic rights of individuals and that you abide by all laws related to the use of technology.** These ethical and legal responsibilities include (1) avoiding any invasions of an individual's privacy, (2) adhering strictly to software copyright license agreements, (3) reporting unauthorized use of the computer, and (4) ensuring that all information disclosed is accurate. Other major ethical issues are predicted as the information superhighway becomes a reality.

REFERENCES

Aldag, R. J., & Stearns, T. M. (1992). *Management*, 2nd ed., Cincinnati: South-Western.

Bowers, D. K. (1991) The privacy challenge on Capitol Hill. *Marketing Research*, *3* (4), 60.

Casarez, N. B. (1992). Electronic mail and employee relations: Why privacy must be considered. *Public Relations Quarterly*, *37* (2), 37.

Connell, J. (1993, December 10). Cyberethics: Innovations raise questions about who should be allowed to do what with the information superhighway. *The San Diego Union-Tribune*, pp. 1-9.

Epson E-mail: Private or company information. (1990, October 22). *InfoWorld*, p. 66. In Shannon, J. H., & Rosenthal, D. A. (1993). Electronic mail and privacy: Can the conflicts be resolved? *Business Forum*, (p. 31).

Equifax report on consumers in the information age, a national survey. (1992). In Laudon, K. C., & Laudon, J. P. (1994). *Management information systems: Organization and technology*, 3rd ed., (p. 711). New York: Macmillan.

Hogan, M. (1994). Videoconferencing now. *PC Computing, 7*(4), 80.

"Is anybody listening: Ensuring cellular privacy. (1993). *Computing Canada, 19*(2), 37.

Kantor, A. (1994). Making on-line service work for you. *PCMagazine, 13*(5), 110-114, 120, 122.

Krol, E. (1992). *The whole INTERNET*. Sebastopol, CA: O'Reilly & Associates.

Laudon, K. C., & Laudon, J. P. (1994). *Management information systems: Organization and technology*, 3rd ed., New York: Macmillan.

Low-priced electronic meetings. (1993). *Software Industry Report, 25*(24), 7.

Mailman 1.0, Reach Software. (1991). *PC World, 9*(8). In Shannon, J. H., & Rosenthal, D. A. (1993). Electronic mail and privacy: Can the conflicts be resolved? *Business Forum*, (p. 31).

Mason, R. O. (1986). Four ethical issues of the information age. In Dejoie, R., Fowler, G., & Paradice, D. (1991), *Ethical issues in information systems* (pp.

46-55). Boston: Boyd & Fraser.

Nussbaum, K. (1989). Computer monitoring: A threat to the right to privacy. In Dejoie, R., Fowler, G., & Paradice, D. (1991), *Ethical issues in information systems* (pp. 134-139). Boston: Boyd & Fraser.

Rifkin, G. (1991, October 14). The ethics gap. *Computerworld*, p. 83.

Shim, J. P., & Taylor, G. S. (1991). A comparative study of unauthorized software copying: Information systems faculty members' vs. practicing managers' perceptions. In Dejoie, R., Fowler, G., & Paradice, D. (1991), *Ethical issues in information systems* (pp. 189-198). Boston: Boyd & Fraser.

Smith, L. (1993, August 9). Can the boss look into my head? *Fortune*, p. 88.

Sports News. (1992, August 7). *Los Angeles Times*, p. C5.

Stedman, C. (1994, January 31). Wang slaps user with lawsuit. *Computerworld*, p. 31.

Takahashi, D. (1993, December 21). Trouble ahead on the information superhighway. *Los Angeles Times*, p. 8.

Tetzeli, R. (1994, March 8). The INTERNET and your business. *Fortune*, p. 86.

Tucker, T. (1993). Videoconferencing's getting personal. *Teleconnect, 11*(9), 50.

REVIEW QUESTIONS

1. Name three general ways computers can be used to improve the quality of messages and facilitate the quick and accurate flow of information.

2. What two distinct advantages does electronic communication provide?

3. Why are organizational databases important in business? Identify a number of different types of databases a company might have. Give an example of a database that would help you.

4. Discuss the major reasons people use online databases. Provide a detailed example, showing several ways the Internet or one of the commercial information services can be used to collect information for decision making. Be prepared to discuss your experience with these services.

5. What obstacles may hinder your use of the Internet or other online information services?

6. Provide an example of how an electronic spreadsheet or graphics generated from a spreadsheet can be used to reinforce or clarify major points presented in a business document. Perhaps you can share a situation encountered in your part-time employment, student activities, or another class.

7. List the two major barriers faced when creating a spreadsheet. List general guidelines for verifying the accuracy of a spreadsheet.

8. Review the following word-processing features: insert; delete; block and move; block and copy; search and replace; redlining and document comment; spellcheck; thesaurus; writing-analysis software; automatic contents page, index, and document references; and mail merge. Which feature would you select for each example?

   a. Two lines of copy were omitted.

   b. Words were misspelled.

   c. One sentence needs to be removed.

   d. The product number was incorrect twelve times.

e. Three paragraphs on the first page need to be moved to page 10.

f. Because last-minute data were required to ensure accuracy and usefulness, a lengthy report was prepared with only two to three hours remaining to complete the preliminary and addenda parts (all parts except the report itself).

g. Because of a backlog in production, 25 orders of Model XL-100 will be delayed for approximately three weeks. A letter must be sent informing customers of the delay.

h. A complicated table on page 2 needs to be used again on page 14.

i. Software developers prepared a description of a new software program and submitted it to the sales department on disk. After revising the description for inclusion in a consumer catalog, the advertising manager returned the disk to the software developers for revisions and approval.

j. You cannot think of a word to use in place of "advent."

k. You earned low ratings on the "Written Communication Skills" section in two previous performance appraisals. Your supervisor said that simply "trying harder" was not sufficient; you must locate some means for identifying and overcoming your problems before your next review.

9. Discuss how word-processing features or collaborative software can aid in producing a document that is written collaboratively (composed by more than one writer or at least requiring the input and approval of another person). Provide an example of a business document that would logically involve collaborative writing.

10. Explain how word-processing software makes preparing form letters more efficient than traditional communication methods. List four guidelines for personalizing form letters.

11. What advantages do spellchecks, thesauruses, and writing-analysis programs provide writers? What are the limitations of each of these three programs?

12. Briefly describe the differences between the two major types of printers, keeping in mind the four factors that affect the decision to buy a printer.

13. Describe the general process of preparing a document using desktop publishing. How does this process affect communication?

14. What contributions do graphics make to the effectiveness of a business document? What effect has technology had on the use of graphics? Explain.

15. What are the four sources of graphics to be integrated into desktop published documents? Discuss any experience you have had working with any of these sources.

16. Give an example of how desktop publishing or graphics-generating software can be a barrier to communication.

17. List the three basic principles for graphic design presented in this chapter. Turn to the "Visual Aids" section of Chapter 3, and list the seven guidelines for preparing and using visual aids.

18. What advantages are provided by (a) electronic mail, (b) facsimile machine, (c) portable computers, and (d) cellular telephones? Discuss your experience with each type of electronic communication.

19. What is telecommuting and what are its major advantages? Provide an example from your experience or knowledge of a practitioner's use of modems and telephones to transmit information quickly and cost effectively.

20. Briefly discuss the general guidelines for using electronic communication tools effectively.

21. List and briefly discuss the four legal and ethical issues related to technology discussed in this chapter.

22. List the five Fair Information Practices. Discuss any personal experience where you believe privacy was threatened by technology.

23. What steps can you take to safeguard a person's privacy as you collect information needed for decision making? the accuracy of the information you collect?

24. What guidelines related to the use of computer software are provided in the Computer Software Copyright Act of 1980?

25. Define computer crime and abuse and provide several examples of each. Provide an example of a computer crime reported in the media or discussed in a computer class or an example of computer abuse of which you are aware. Who was hurt by these illegal or unethical actions and how? What could be done to deter such actions?

EXERCISES

1. Complete each of the THINK IT OVER activities that your instructor assigns.
2. As a communication consultant, you deliver training seminars designed to increase the communication skills of employees at all levels of the organizations engaging your services. In addition to presenting communication concepts and issues, you involve the employees in open discussion, role-playing, and other hands-on activities. You have kept your seminars current and practical by sharing information from current articles in business and practitioner magazines.

   From many of these articles, you have shared anecdotes about communication successes or problems faced by other companies and practical guidelines for improved communication. Employees are eager to hear that their problems are not unique, and the anecdotes are carefully selected to support a particular point you wish to make. In honest, simple terms, these real-world incidents help you keep the employees' attention and make you look *good*.

   You have a two-week break between consulting engagements, and you plan to use this time to update your current readings. You are eager to find "a few good gems" that will help these employees grasp an important communication and/or give them the commitment to go the extra mile to overcome barriers to effective communication and, thus, career advancement.

   Required:
   a. Access your library's database, the Internet, or another online information service to locate a current article that
      • Pertains to a communication topic to be studied in this chapter (refer to contents page) or a topic assigned by your instructor.
      • Appears in a business or business practitioner magazine—no academic journals. For example, look for articles in *The Wall Street Journal, Business Week, Forbes, Training and Development Journal*, and others.
      • Appears in an issue no earlier than 1992.
      • Contains practical guidelines for communicating more effectively in the business

   environment. You are confident that the content of this article will make a positive impact on the communication skills of your clients' workers. For example, avoid "data heavy" articles that would be interesting to academic types or top-level managers wanting quantitative evidence that a particular design is effective. Select articles with anecdotes of good things happening in real companies and providing specific, beneficial tips for dealing with particular communication issues.
   b. Submit a *copy* of the article and a *printout* of the citation and abstract of the article generated in your search. Highlight the bibliographical information for the article. Refer to the sample printout in Figure 15-5.
3. Study carefully the spreadsheet on the top of page 142 designed to compute payroll for Artistic Expressions. Identify any errors and explain how each error could influence the effective transfer of this information.
4. Perform an automatic search-and-replace procedure on any word in a one-page document using any word-processing program. Be prepared to discuss any problems that occur as a result of the automatic search-and-replace feature.
5. Keyboard the memo on page 142 and perform a spellcheck using any word-processing software. Proofread a printed copy of the memo. Use the standard proofreaders' marks shown in Appendix A to mark any corrections. Write a brief report summarizing your observations about this process.
6. Keyboard a one-page document using any word-processing program or compose a brief message, depending on your instructor's guidelines. Use a writing-analysis program to generate a critique of the document. Outline the major writing improvements suggested by the computer. List any observations you can make about these suggestions. For example, do you believe the suggestions are valid, or should you overrule some of them? Explain.
7. Bring to class samples of documents produced on printers of varying quality. Discuss the effect the quality of print has on the message.

```
Artistic Expressions
Payroll Summary

                                  Hourly  Gross     With-        Net
Employee        Dept.      Hrs.    Wage    Pay       oldings      Pay
--------------------------------------------------------------------
Day, Bart       Sales       45     13.5    641.25    243.60    397.65
Harden, Lisa    Delivery    40      8.5    340.00    125.00    215.00
Lambert, Matt   Maintanance 25      5.5    137.50     50.50     87.00
Dollar, Janice  Sales       48        5    280.00     98.80    161.20
Jones, Alan     Delivery    40      8.25   330.00    125.45    204.55
Kelly, Melanie  Sales       48     12.5    650.00    247.90    402.10
Patterson, Kim  Sales       40       15    600.00    228.00    372.00
Sanford, Jon    Sales       41       14    581.00    220.75    360.25
                                           ----------------------------
                                         3,539.75  1,119.25  2,199.75
                                           ============================
```

Exercise 3

October 5, 19--

Lorenzo Koch, Vice President of Sales

INSTALLATION OF CELLULAR SERVICE BY NOVEMBER 15

At last the time is right for giving our sales staff cellular telephones.

During last years budgeting process, we determined that cellular telephones would not be cost effective until cellular service reached our Western sales region. Yesterday at the Chamber of Commerce meeting, the sales manager of Berling Cellular Services announced that their service territory would be extend as of January 1. The expanded territory will include our Western region.

Let's procede immediately with the installation of cellular facilities. I am convinced that having our system full operable by November 1 will provide our sales staff a advantage over our competitors. You have the authority to acquire the neccesssary equipment and to schedule training seminar to educate the sales representatives on the most affective use of this technology.

Despite the large capitol investment, I am very supportive of this investment. Berling Cellular Services have assured me that the increased productivity of our staff will permit us to recoup our investment with a couple of months. For that reason, I will be quite eager to reveiw you periodic progress reports.

Wallace R. Slocum
President

Exercise 5

8. After consulting advertising and design books and periodicals, write a two-page report presenting principles of effective page layout and design.

9. Indicate whether you believe e-mail or voice mail would be an appropriate medium for sending the following messages. Justify your answer.

   a. The company is expecting a visit from members of a committee evaluating your bid for this year's Malcolm Baldrige National Quality Award. All employees must be notified of the visit.

   b. After careful deliberation, the management of a mid-sized pharmaceutical company is convinced the only way to continue its current level of research is to sell the company to a larger company. The employees must be informed of this decision.

   c. Lincoln Enterprises is eager to receive the results of a drug test on a certain employee. The drug testing company has been asked to send the results as quickly as possible.

   d. Juan Perez, the recipient of the memo in Figure 5-2, requested a revised analysis of the projections. He has asked you to send the spreadsheet so that he can manipulate the data himself.

   e. The shipping department has located the common carrier currently holding a customer's shipment that should have been delivered yesterday. Inform the customer that the carrier has promised delivery by tomorrow morning.

10. Complete the e-mail application (on page 144), except send voice mail messages in response to the scenarios. If voice mail equipment or a recorder is not available, pair with a student your instructor designates and alternate sending these messages.

11. Describe a communication obstacle you have encountered when using an electronic communication tool. If you do not have a personal experience, describe one that could happen. How did (would) you deal with the barrier? What insights did (might) you gain from this experience? What have you learned from reading this chapter that could have aided (could aid) you in overcoming this barrier?

12. Management has asked you to suggest ways to improve office productivity. You conduct interviews with several employees. What are your solutions to the following problems?

   a. A memo takes two or three days to get from one department to another.

   b. Sales executives are frustrated about the excessive time spent in air travel for regional product information meetings.

   c. Telephone tag is a problem for many employees.

   d. Proposals with misspelled words often reach supervisors.

   e. Information is lost in crowded file cabinets and cannot be retrieved in time to assist in decision making.

   f. Administrative assistants become upset when asked to make changes or revisions in documents because they have to spend hours retyping entire documents.

   g. Co-workers, contractors, and bank loan officers frequently need to reach the vice president of a land development company readily so that they can make or implement decisions. However, reaching the vice president is nearly impossible as he is often away from the home office visiting building sites, meeting with contractors, negotiating bank loans, or traveling between these various locations.

   h. A producer in a California film studio is irritated when filming is stopped to wait for a scriptwriter working in a remote location to rewrite and mail a portion of script. These delays are the major cause of a film's exceeding budget, a common occurrence for this producer recently.

E-MAIL APPLICATION

Plan and send e-mail messages in response to the following scenarios:

1. You must inform employees of the specific dates for repaving the company parking lot. One-half of the normal parking spaces will be available on any given day during this process.

2. You are part of a committee planning a reception/banquet for the company's annual alumni event. You want to give the committee a report on the menu choices available in the price range agreed on at the initial planning meeting.

3. Notify all employees that the youth sports team (soccer, baseball, basketball) your company sponsors is playing for the league championship game. Provide a list of the players and encourage the employees to support the team (whatever you believe is appropriate).

4. As Gayle Greenlee, the sales representative who received the memo in Figure 5-4, you send the production scheduler an e-mail message with another alternative for managing overtime. Explain that hiring and training students to fill these rush orders would be less expensive than paying the excessive overtime and would avoid the sensitive issue of overtime for regular employees.

5. Encourage employees to take part in the state-wide "Trash Bash" scheduled for later this month. Announce you have issued a friendly challenge to one of the company's local competitors in an effort to promote active participation in this worthy community effort.

6. Write an e-mail message for each scenario in Exercise 9 that you identified as appropriate for e-mail.

CHAPTER 6

ETHICAL AND LEGAL

GUIDELINES

OBJECTIVES
When you have completed Chapter 6, you will be able to

1 Define *ethics* and identify the process by which individuals develop a foundation for making ethical decisions.

2 Identify the common causes for unethical behavior in the workplace.

3 Use an ethical decision-making framework to facilitate identifying and effectively communicating solutions that conform to your personal values.

4 Apply the guidelines for taking moral responsibility for all communication (oral and written) transmitted and actions taken.

John Grisham's best-selling novel *The Firm*, which was also a big hit at the box office, is a story of good guys versus bad guys. Although the concept is rather simple, it does address a number of issues that businesspeople face, no matter what their career fields. How can you be sure that your company engages only in ethical and legal practices? What should you do if you suspect it is not?

Mitchell McDeere, the main character in Grisham's tale, was not born wealthy. He worked hard, played by all the rules, and graduated at the top of his class from a prestigious Ivy League law school. His dreams were coming true; his future seemed certain and bright. Mitch was sure he would get a good job; however, when Bendini, Lambert & Locke offered him a position with their firm in Memphis, Tennessee, he was shocked at his good fortune. The firm paid him an unbelievable salary, furnished him with a luxury imported car, a fine home, and even arranged for his wife to get a teaching job at a local school. Things simply seemed too good to be true.

As Mitch soon discovered, it *was* too good to be true. To his dismay, he discovered that the firm was involved in a crime syndicate, party to a number of illegal activities. To compound the problem, he couldn't think of a safe or conclusive means of proving the involvement. Finally, he remembered seeing where certain lawyers had deliberately overcharged clients for services. As a result, he was able to collect evidence needed for authorities to begin an investigation.

Had Mitch not had an ethical sense of judgment and strong personal values, he might have chosen to "go with the flow" and not pursue the corrupt lawyers. After all, he was set for life in a prestigious law firm with the opportunity for even further material success. But he knew that in the end, justice would win (Grisham, 1991).

You may never find yourself in the same situation as Mitch, but ethical issues do arise frequently in most areas of business. "Real" examples of unethical conduct include General Motors' managers accused of stealing documents when they "defected" to Volkswagen (Maynard, 1993) and CIA agent Aldrich Ames's smuggling top-secret information to the Russians. Incidents of sexual harassment in the workplace, such as the well-publicized Tailhook scandal involving U.S. naval officers, are increasing. Savings and loan officers have used depositors' funds for speculative investments, and investment bankers have used inside information to gain an advantage over traders in the stock market. These are just a few of the numerous unethical acts reported by the press almost daily. Indeed, one research study revealed that six out of ten of those surveyed admitted that they would probably trade six months' probation for an illegal $10 million (Reinemund, 1992).

Matters of ethics are seldom clear-cut issues of right versus wrong and often contain many ambiguous elements. In addition, the pressure appears to be felt most strongly by lower-level managers who are least experienced doing their jobs. Many of these managers are recent business school graduates.

What can you do now to prepare for dealing with pressure to compromise personal values? First, remember that only if you have definite beliefs on a variety of issues and the courage to practice them will you be able to make sound ethical judgments. Putting ethical business practices first will also benefit the company for whom you work as its reputation for fairness and good judgment retains long-term clients or customers and brings in new ones. Second, learning to analyze ethical dilemmas (identify the consequences of your actions) will help you make decisions that conform to your own value system. Thus, unless you know what you stand for and how to analyze the ethical issue, you become a puppet, controlled by the motives of others, too weak to make a decision on your own. What will you do?

THINK IT OVER
Take time to watch *Silkwood*, the inspiring true story of Karen Silkwood, a young woman who did what she believed was right when she discovered what appeared to be dangerous weaknesses in the way deadly plutonium was contained. What were the costs and benefits of her ethical stand?

Unethical behavior in the workplace is reported by the press almost daily.

THINK IT OVER
In groups, discuss a current example of an unethical act by a business organization or its employee(s).

The Tailhook sexual harassment scandal, insider trading by investment bankers, and Blue Cross/ Blue Shield's questionable salaries and perks for executives while maintaining nonprofit status are all widely publicized examples of unethical conduct. Frequently, ethical issues are tied together with business decisions. As a manager, you must be aware of the pressure to make unethical choices and know how to make sound decisions instead.

THE FOUNDATION FOR ETHICAL BEHAVIOR

Although ethics is a common point of discussion, many might find defining ethics quite challenging. Most people immediately associate ethics with standards and rules of conduct, morals, right and wrong, values, and honesty. Dr. Albert Schweitzer defined *ethics* as "the name we give to our concern for good behavior. We feel an obligation to consider not only our own personal well-being, but also that of others and of human society as a whole" (Slayton, 1980, p. 5). In other words, **ethics** refers to the principles of right and wrong that guide us in making decisions that affect others.

   Although the recorded accounts of ethical misconduct would seem to indicate that businesses are dishonest and unscrupulous, keep in mind that millions of business transactions are made daily on the basis of honesty and concern for the welfare of others. Why should a business make ethical decisions? What difference will it make? James E. Perrella, executive vice president of Ingersoll-Rand Company, has a powerful reply to these questions (Slayton, 1991, p. 7):

> Our question of today should be, what's the right thing to do, the right way to behave, the right way to conduct business? Don't just ask, is it legal?
>
> Have you ever considered what business would be like if we all did it? If every businessman and businesswoman followed the Golden Rule?

COMMUNICATION MENTOR

Being faced with questions of ethics during your career is a very real possibility. Now is the time to prepare yourself. Decide now what your values are, what you believe in, what honesty and integrity and fairness really mean to you. Write it all down on a sheet of paper; keep the paper in a safe place. Making these judgments now will prepare you to handle a difficult situation if it occurs later on, because you'll already know what kind of person you are, and you'll know what you should do.

H. Devon Graham, Jr.
Southwest Regional Managing Partner
Arthur Andersen & Co.

Many people including many business leaders would argue that such an application of ethics to business would adversely affect bottom-line performance. I say nay. . . Good ethics, simply, is good business. Good ethics will attract investors. Good ethics will attract good employees. . .

You can do what's right. Not because of conduct codes. Not because of rules or laws. But because you know what's right.

How are our basic morals and values developed?

Just how do we know what's right? Obviously many of our basic morals and values are developed during our early, formative years, from birth through high school. The pervasive influence of parents, relatives, leaders/teachers/coaches in religious institutions and schools, and other significant individuals have contributed to our sense of honesty and integrity and led us to cultivate other values that mold ethical decisions. For example, consider how the following actions might affect a young person's moral development:

- Parents thoughtlessly violate laws, especially when they believe they will not be caught—driving at speeds significantly above the speed limit, littering highways and other property, or "pirating" computer software.
- Parents and others you respect routinely cheat on their income taxes by overstating the value of contributions or claiming vacation expenses as deductible business expenses.
- Parents routinely complete a child's homework to ensure that the child earns a high grade or perhaps just to minimize the amount of time spent completing homework each evening.

THINK IT OVER
What other actions might affect a young person's moral development?

- Parents or older siblings neglect to tell a sales clerk of an error made in their favor; for example, if they received too much change, were charged the sale price for an item not on sale, or were not charged for an item.
- Teachers copy audiotapes, records, videotapes, sheet music, or computer software, rationalizing that the action is all right because these copyrighted materials are being used for educational purposes.
- Community and religious leaders, coaches, parents, and others make derogatory remarks and off-color jokes about minorities, the handicapped, or other groups.

Each of these actions advocates self-interest with total disregard for the law or the welfare of other people. Continual exposure to this "me-for-me" interest communicates the belief that this behavior is acceptable; unfortunately, this value system is the one taken to the workplace.

Throughout our lives, individuals continue to reevaluate and set new priorities and thus adjust their basic value system, for better or for worse. For example, whenever you make a difficult ethical decision, you reinforce your basic values of honesty and integrity and build your character. However, making even small compromises in ethical behavior can lead to more serious unethical behavior and perhaps even to illegal actions.

Sometimes individuals commit unethical acts because they do not identify a particular situation as an ethical issue. The problem is that many ethical issues are unapparent or seemingly benign. Further inspection of the issue, however, reveals a discrete, but very real, compromise of personal values. In some instances, individuals are being pressured to act unethically by individuals such as employers, peers, parents, and coaches or leaders who may not have a malicious or calculating motive. Examine the following commonplace unethical behaviors:

- Copying from another student's test paper to achieve a certain grade point average (pressure to meet parents' expectations or to pass a course).
- Not contributing your share to a group project.
- Plagiarizing on a term paper.
- Copying a computer software program so that you can complete class assignments on your own computer rather than endure the inconvenience of using a computer lab.
- Not reporting a student you witnessed cheating on an exam.
- Listing false qualifications on a resume to increase your chances of securing a job, scholarship, or internship.

Likewise, identifying ethical issues in typical workplace situations may be difficult, and co-workers and superiors may apply pressure for seemingly logical reasons. To illustrate, examine each of the following workplace situations for a possible ethical dilemma:

- A law clerk is instructed to disassemble a client's accounting records to hinder the IRS from detecting the client's fraudulent tax reporting.
- A salesperson who travels extensively feels cheated that personal telephone calls are not reimbursed travel expenses. Consequently, the salesperson overstates car mileage to cover the cost of the telephone calls.
- To protect his job, a transportation manager decides not to question an international shipment of goods that the manager believes is prohibited by governmental trade sanctions (that is, shipping high-technology or military equipment to specified countries).
- To increase the revenues generated from its service departments, a company intentionally increases the complexity of its product. As a result of these changes, repairs are more likely to be made by an authorized service department.
- Angry at a superior for an unfavorable performance appraisal, an employee leaks confidential information (for example, trade secrets such as a recipe or product design, marketing strategies, or product development plans) to an acquaintance who works for a competitor.

Your fundamental morals and values provide the foundation for making ethical decisions; however, even minor concessions in day-to-day ethical deci-

Many people abandon their principles, believing it is the best way to get ahead.

Basic values may gradually erode if you make even small compromises in your ethical behavior.

Why do individuals commit unethical acts?

THINK IT OVER
Examine your own daily life. Can you provide other examples of temptations to be unethical?

THINK IT OVER
Is it ethical for a company to reduce the safety and environmental standards in a plant in a developing nation below those used in its U.S. plants in an effort to reduce construction and operation cost?

THINK IT OVER
Have you experienced any pressure to perform unethical acts at your job? How did you handle the situation?

COMMUNICATION   MENTOR

Succeeding will be much easier if you approach your business career knowing that very few short-term rewards exist for ethical behavior within the workplace (within the worker, yes, but not within the workplace). The exact opposite is true for unethical behavior.

Your manager probably will not say, "I'm pleased to note that over the past six months you have consistently exceeded our expectations by not cheating on your expense accounts. You're looking good for a bonus!" Meanwhile, by "padding" expense accounts over the same six months, an unethical co-worker may be defrauding the company of enough money to cover, let's say, a pair of good shoes and a great Italian dinner.

This irony of ethics in one or more of its many forms will be frustrating and maddening when you experience it. You will have to call on your instinct and experience to understand that long-term results of ethical behavior will *absolutely* be better than the short-term results of unethical behavior. Walking in a stolen pair of shoes with a bad taste in your mouth isn't worth it.

James F. Hurley
Executive Vice President
California Federal Bank

sions can gradually weaken this foundation. One way to safeguard your ability and willingness to act ethically and responsibly is to be keenly aware of common pressures to compromise your personal value system.

CAUSES OF UNETHICAL BEHAVIOR IN THE WORKPLACE

LEARNING OBJECTIVE 2

What are the major causes of unethical behavior in the workplace?

Understanding the major causes of unethical behavior in the workplace will help you become sensitive to signals of escalating pressure to compromise your values. Research on unethical corporate behavior has identified several potential causes of unethical behavior. These causes include excessive emphasis on profits, misplaced corporate loyalty, obsession with personal ambition, expectation of not getting caught, unethical tone set by top management, uncertainty about whether the action is wrong, and unwillingness to take an ethical stand.

Excessive Emphasis on Profits

The first, and probably most important, cause of unethical behavior appears to be an excessive emphasis on corporate profits. In the case of Beechnut's selling infant apple juice without a trace of apple in the ingredients (Traub, 1988), corporate executives first bought the suspicious but inexpensive juice concentrate at a time when profits were down. Nestlé, their corporate parent, was demanding both improved profits and a positive cash flow. Given Beechnut's recent performance, these goals were unreasonable, at least in the short term. To keep their jobs, however, and to do what was best for the company, the Beechnut executives may have felt compelled to cut corners wherever possible.

Heavy emphasis on profits may send a message to many managers that the end justifies the means. In other words, if only the amount of earnings per share matters in assessing managerial performance, the message to managers is "do whatever is necessary to increase the bottom line." Thus, managers justify unethical acts because they are in the "best interest" of the company.

THINK IT OVER
What would you do if your supervisor asked you to do something you believe is unethical?

Misplaced Corporate Loyalty

The response by Beechnut's executives to unrealistic profit goals may have revealed another factor that contributes to unethical acts: a misplaced sense of corporate loyalty. Hence, managers may actually believe that their actions, however questionable, are for the good of the company.

Obsession with Personal Advancement

Managers who wish to outperform their peers or are working for the next promotion may feel that they cannot afford to fail. They may do whatever it takes to achieve the objectives assigned to them. To ensure favorable measures of success, managers may attempt to minimize controllable expenses long enough to earn a promotion. For example, a manager may neglect preventive maintenance of equipment, reduce or postpone essential research and development, or bypass selected quality control points. These actions may make the manager (and even the company) look good in the short run, but continued disregard for these critical factors is detrimental to the long-term well-being of a company.

Expectation of Not Getting Caught

Managers who believe that the end justifies the means often believe that the unethical activity will never be discovered. Unfortunately, a great deal of improper behavior escapes detection in the business world. Therefore, this cause of unethical behavior is a difficult one to correct.

Under intense pressure to meet production quotas, a production manager may cut corners on certain quality control measures. For example, the manager may bypass inspecting bolts to ensure that they meet specifications (size and resistance) or may ship finished merchandise without completing the exact inspection agreed to in the sales contract (such as a requirement that *every* unit, not a random sample, be inspected).

Believing no one will ever find out, employees are tempted to falsify records such as expense accounts. They may overstate the cost of meals to compensate for unauthorized expenses (telephone calls, entertainment, laundry service) or include expenses not incurred (meals paid for by others or nonexistent taxi fares). Similarly, sales representatives may overreport the number of sales contacts made during a certain period if they believe no control measure will reveal the true effort they expended. Employees who call in sick and spend the day conducting personal business or enjoying an extra-long weekend have little fear that management will discover this unethical activity.

Turncoat CIA agent Aldrich H. Ames says smuggling was easy because of a lax security system. He could freely access information because of available databases and the CIA's policy that "everybody has to coordinate with everything" (Ames: Smuggling was easy, 1994).

What are other examples of unethical behavior that may go undetected?

Unethical Tone Set by Top Management

Another cause of unethical behavior relates to the corporate culture. If top managers are not perceived as highly ethical, lower-level managers may be less ethical as a result. Employees have little incentive to act ethically if their superiors do

How does the ethical behavior of top management affect the ethical behavior of other employees in the company?

COMMUNICATION   MENTOR

If you are ever, at any stage of a business career, unlucky enough to find yourself in a routinely unethical environment, you will discover quite rapidly that there is a seductive quality to it. Whether practiced on a company-wide or departmental scale, there will be a "team spirit" among the unethical group that subtly states: "Look at the impunity with which we ignore certain ethical standards and get such good results. Come on, our success can be yours."

If your personal ethical principles are extremely strong and uncompromised up to this point, you can be a holdout and, depending on the level of your job and degree of influence, try to become an agent of change. This route is courageous and perilous, along which you will certainly need increased authority, responsibility, and decision-making powers. If you are relatively inexperienced and your business ethics are largely untested, you will soon feel the magnetic pull of your fellow workers. Before this situation happens and potentially ruins your chance for a solid career and a sense of personal contentment, the best solution is to run, not walk, to a job where ethical behavior prevails.

James F. Hurley
Executive Vice President
California Federal Bank

THINK IT OVER
Ethical decisions are especially difficult to make when we cross national borders. For example, in Saudi Arabia, hiring female managers for most jobs is illegal; but for an American company with operations there, is it unethical not to do so (Donaldson, 1994)?

THINK IT OVER
List other ethical issues related to computer technology. (Review the discussion of privacy and access, intellectual property rights, and accuracy in Chapter 5.)

Is an action always clearly right or wrong?

not set an example and encourage and reward ethical behavior. The following actions by top management clearly set the tone for unethical behavior:

- A sales manager requires sales representatives to promise delivery of orders on the date required by a potential customer—even if the representatives know the production schedule is backlogged and will not permit prompt delivery.
- A vice president of finance requires the purchasing agent to buy all supplies and office equipment from a company owned by the vice president's brother, even though the purchasing agent can document that the supplies could be purchased for a lower price elsewhere.
- A staff development director routinely copies articles, entire software documentation manuals, training guides, and preview copies of training films for distribution at staff development seminars. Although several employees have brought these infringements of copyright laws to the attention of the company president, no action has been taken.
- Although management reports that only undeliverable e-mail messages will be read, managers routinely access and read employees' e-mail messages.

Uncertainty About Whether an Action is Wrong

Many times, managers are placed in situations in which the line between right and wrong is not clearly defined. When caught in this grey area, the perplexed manager asks, "How far is too far?" The following situations place managers in such a quandary:

- A company bids for a job that requires expertise the company does not have but would acquire if the bid is ultimately received. For example, a computer

systems company bids to install a sophisticated network system even though the company has no experience in installing networks. A construction company with no experience in building high-security correctional facilities bids to build a jail or state prison.
- A firm bills a client the amount quoted, but the actual time required to complete the project was significantly less than estimated or other savings reduced the actual cost.
- A consulting firm performs similar consulting jobs for competing companies and is, therefore, privy to confidential information.

Unwillingness to Take an Ethical Stand

Often employees know what is right or wrong but are not willing to take the risk of challenging a wrong action. Furthermore, employees may lack the confidence or the skill needed to confront others with sensitive ethical issues. They may remain silent and then justify their unwillingness to act. Consider the risk involved in speaking out on each of the following workplace situations:

- You report that you are being sexually harassed or that you are aware that another employee is being sexually harassed.
- You inform management that the public relations director is violating copyright laws by scanning copyrighted designs and cartoons for use in in-house publications and in promotional material prepared for distribution outside the company.
- You report that co-workers are using the company long-distance telephone service and computer (including expensive online information services) for personal use.

THINK IT OVER
Why do you think some people are unwilling to take an ethical stand? Can you think of other situations to add to this list?

FRAMEWORK FOR ANALYZING ETHICAL DILEMMAS

After you have determined that an ethical issue is part of a situation you are facing, the next step is to select the appropriate analytical tools to help you handle the situation. By analyzing ethical dilemmas from multiple perspectives, you may be able to find a solution that better conforms to your own personal values. The flow chart shown in Figure 6-1 represents a framework for making an ethical decision and for supporting that decision in a written or oral message. The framework instructs you (the decision maker) to complete the following five-step process after you have identified a possible course of action:

LEARNING OBJECTIVE 3

1. Identify the legal implications of the alternative and determine whether the alternative adheres to contractual agreements and company policy. If yes. . .
2. Determine whether the alternative is consistent with company or professional codes of ethics. If yes. . .
3. Use ethical principles and theories to assess whether the alternative judged to be legal (Step 1) and in compliance with codes of ethics (Step 2) is ethical. If yes. . .
4. Implement the alternative.
5. Communicate ethical decisions to appropriate individuals inside or outside the organization.

If the result of any of the first three steps is No, select another alternative. The following sections discuss each step in the process in detail.

FIGURE 6-1
Framework for analyzing ethical
issues.

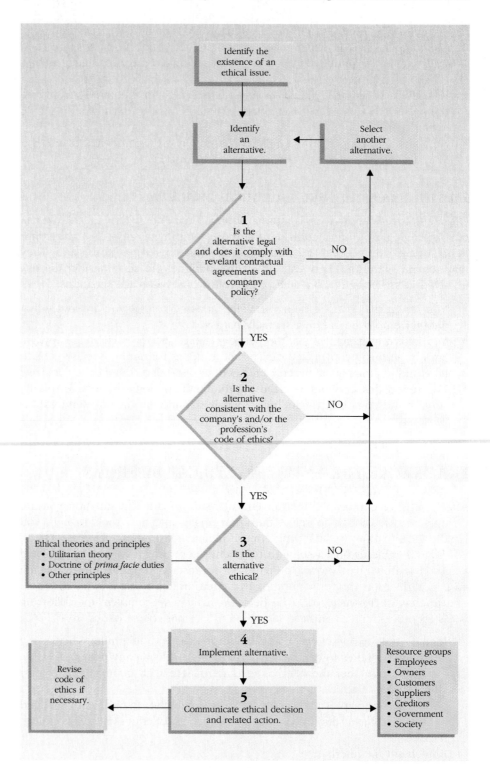

Legal Considerations

The first step in making ethical decisions involves identifying possible legal implications. In other words, is the alternative legal? Does it comply with relevant contractual agreements or company policy? The law specifically outlines the "black" area—those alternatives that are clearly wrong. Obviously, obeying the law is in the best interest of all concerned: you as an individual, your company, and society. In addition, contractual agreements between the organization and another group provide explicit guidance in selecting an ethically responsible alternative.

If the alternative is legal and complies with pertinent contractual agreements and company policy, you may advance to the next decision point in the framework. On the other hand, if the alternative is illegal or violates contractual agreements or company policy, you must select and evaluate another alternative.

For example, suppose you have discovered that products recently shipped contained component parts that had not been subjected to your company's standard quality inspection. You are confident that an ethical issue is involved. What are the legal implications of this action? To answer that question, suppose the uninspected component was

What action is taken if the alternative is legal and complies with pertinent contractual agreements? If the alternative violates the law and contractual agreements?

Type of Product	Legal Implications
A part for the engine of an Air Force fighter jet.	Federal laws may govern contracts between the Department of Defense and its contractors. Obey the law. Select another alternative.
The paint used in the production of a child's toy.	Product safety laws may govern the quality and content of this component. Obey the law. Select another alternative.
The paper used in the production of a textbook.	No laws have been violated; however, a breach of contract may be involved. Consult the contract and abide by it. Select another alternative if necessary.

An organization may exchange information or make financial transactions with a variety of resource groups. Consequently, when interacting with any of these resource groups, the employee must identify the legal implications affecting the appropriate resource group(s). For example, a variety of laws and contractual agreements apply to an organization's interaction with its employees. Laws have been enacted to protect employee rights related to equal opportunity, sexual harassment, workplace safety, benefits, privacy, performance appraisal, and employee recommendations. Likewise, laws and contracts affect interactions with owners, customers, suppliers, creditors, government, society, and others.

General legal guidelines for topics related to business communications (e.g., illegal interview questions and employee recommendations) are included in this textbook. However, this textbook is not intended to serve as a comprehensive legal reference.

Your employer will require you to become an expert in the laws that affect your particular area. When you encounter an unfamiliar area, you must investigate any

THINK IT OVER
What are the major legal areas affecting interactions with customers? Owners? Suppliers? Creditors? Government? Society?

THINK IT OVER
What level of legal expertise in your area of competence will your employer expect you to have?

possible legal implications. Suppose an advertising manager of an auto dealership decides to use film footage of a family arriving at a local festival in a make of minivan sold by the dealer. To identify specific legal guidelines related to using a person's likeness, the manager researches this unfamiliar topic. The research provides the basis for the content of a letter to the family seeking their permission to use the footage in a television advertisement. Examine every oral and written message sent to resource groups inside and outside of the organization to ensure that it adheres to applicable laws and pertinent contractual agreements and company policy. Your meticulous research will give you necessary evidence and confidence in your ability to defend your message if required.

Company and Professional Codes of Conduct

If the alternative is legal and complies with relevant contractual agreements and company policy, your next step is to consult your company's or profession's **code of ethics**. This written document summarizes the company's or profession's standards of ethical conduct. Some companies refer to this document as a *credo* or *standards of ethical conduct*.

THINK IT OVER
More and more companies and professions have issued codes of ethics. If you have access to a copy, share its major principles with the class.

Increasing numbers of companies and professional organizations have issued codes of ethics. However, in the formative years of many major companies, founders had to uphold their high ethical principles without the support of published codes of ethical conduct. For example:

- Bristol and Myers listened as a chemist talked with them about a quinine pill that could contain a third as much quinine as the genuine item but looked the same. Bristol said to Myers: "Make out a check to this man; he's through" (Oliverio, 1990, p. 19).
- Samuel Price (one of the founders of the public accounting firm that became Price Waterhouse) was pressured to undertake work on the guarantee of a fee to be charged only if the report were favorable. With no clearly stated principles to back him up, he explained, "Our charges must in no way be dependent upon the result of the examination and the only way to impress this upon them is simply to refuse to proceed until charges and outlays are provided for" (Oliverio, 1990, p. 19).

What action should you take if the alternative does not adhere to the standards of ethical conduct presented in your company's or profession's code of ethics?

These founders firmly believed that ethical behavior was a definite way to ensure the success of their companies. They set the tone for ethical standards at the top and established practices that supported their views.

Carefully review the code of ethics to determine whether the alternative is contrary to the standards set forth in the code. In addition, the code of ethics may provide suggestions for resolving the issue. If the alternative violates the code of ethics, you must evaluate another alternative beginning with the first step in the framework, the legality of the alternative.

To become aware of the ethical behavior advocated by your intended profession, locate its code of ethics. You may find the code printed in a professional or practitioner journal in your field. In addition, talking with professors or practitioners in your field and reading articles in professional journals will acquaint you with basic ethical views held by your profession.

THINK IT OVER
What ethical conduct does your profession advocate? What major responsibilities does it place on its practitioners?

What benefits do ethics awareness programs provide?

Many companies provide comprehensive ethics awareness programs designed to help employees understand and adhere to the company's ethical standards. These programs should help management identify breakdowns in the system and then develop solutions to correct these problems. In addition, the United States Sentencing Commission has issued sentencing guidelines that impose tough

Corporations are constantly working to earn higher profits than competing companies. The computer and software industries have been noted for their fierce competition. In 1994, Microsoft, headed by owner Bill Gates, was ordered to pay over $100 million to Stac Electronics for patent infringement while Stac was penalized $13.7 million (to be paid to Microsoft) for "misappropriating a trade secret" (Reuters, 1994). This recent example illustrates the need for creating a corporate culture where unethical actions are not rewarded.

sentences for corporate white-collar crime and provide strong incentives for companies to establish meaningful compliance programs to deter and report criminal conduct by their employees (Slayton, 1991).

Ethical Principles and Theories

At this point, assume that your alternative has passed the first two tests; that is, it (1) is legal and complies with contractual agreements and company policy and (2) adheres to the company's or the profession's code of ethics. Contrary to the views of many decision makers, your analysis is not yet complete. Recall the powerful statement by James Perrella, Ingersoll-Rand's corporate leader: "What's the right thing to do, the right way to behave, the right way to conduct business? Don't just ask, is it legal?" (Slayton, 1991, p. 7). Thus, the final—and extremely important—test your alternative must satisfy is the test of integrity. Is it ethical? If, after careful analysis, you judge the alternative to be ethical, you may implement it; otherwise, you must evaluate another alternative.

Numerous principles and ethical theories are available to help individuals and companies analyze ethical issues. A simple and ancient principle, the Golden Rule, "Do unto others as you would have them do unto you," is still an effective yardstick for measuring ethical conduct. Perrella referred to the improved quality of business if everyone followed the Golden Rule. The Quakers' uncomplicated approach also has merits: "In all your dealings, leave the other people at least as well off as you found them."

Somewhat more sophisticated but still straightforward are the six points in the Pagano Model for determining whether a proposed action is ethical (Mathison, 1988, p. 781). You must answer the following six questions honestly:

1. Is the proposed action legal—the core starting point?
2. What are the benefits and costs to the people involved?
3. Would you want this action to be a universal standard, appropriate for everyone?
4. Does the action pass the light-of-day test? That is, if your action appeared on television or others learned about it, would you be proud?

Why is your ethical analysis not complete after you have determined that an alternative is legal, contractual, and complies with existing codes of ethics? What is the next step in your analysis?

5. Does the action pass the Golden Rule test? That is, would you want the same to happen to you?
6. Does the action pass the ventilation test? Ask the opinion of a wise friend with no investment in the outcome. Does this friend believe that the action is ethical?

Pizza Hut applies the "Rose Bowl" test. Managers ask "How would a new marketing strategy be viewed, not in the comfort of internal meetings but on the 50-yard line of the Rose Bowl before 100,000 people?" (Reinemund, 1992).

Various theories and principles of ethical behavior have been proposed. You must evaluate them and choose the one (or several) that most closely parallels your own moral system. Two ethical theories that have received widespread acceptance in both the philosophical and the business communities are the utilitarian theory and the doctrine of *prima facie* duties. These theories can serve as analytical tools to help you analyze complex ethical situations and evaluate alternative actions.

UTILITARIAN THEORY

THINK IT OVER
Which principles or theories do you apply when evaluating an ethical decision?

The major premise of the **utilitarian theory** is that in all situations one ought to do that which provides the greatest balance of good over harm for everyone. Thus, an ethical decision maker must estimate the impact of each alternative action on all organizational **stakeholders** (the persons or groups who will be affected by the decision) and then select the one that optimizes the satisfaction of the greatest number of people.

The utilitarian theory involves selecting the alternative that brings the greatest good to the greatest number.

For simplicity, the major stakeholders of any organization consist of five groups: owners, employees, customers, local communities, and society at large. Applying the utilitarian theory in an organization involves carefully elaborating the costs and benefits imposed by a particular decision or action on each of these five groups. The decision imposing the fewest costs and most benefits across all groups is the one that should be selected.

Who are the major stakeholders in an organization?

As an example, consider the decision that Weyerhaeuser Company might make about whether to continue to manufacture disposable diapers or to get out of the business. The production of disposable diapers has been labeled unethical by some people because of the undesirable effects of disposable diapers on the environment. Indeed, some groups are pushing for legislation that would either ban the use of disposable diapers or impose a usage tax on them. Analyzing this ethical situation using utilitarian theory requires you to assess the costs and benefits created by the production of these diapers for all key stakeholders. This analysis is shown in Figure 6-2.

THINK IT OVER
What do you think Weyerhaeuser should do?

This simplified utilitarian analysis shows why Weyerhaeuser's decision is such a difficult one. The major short-term benefits of diaper production for the company, its employees, and its customers all appear to be quite positive. However, in the long run, the costs of using this convenient product may be quite significant at the societal level. Whenever such tradeoffs exist, analyzing an issue using a second ethical theory, the theory of duties, is useful.

DOCTRINE OF *PRIMA FACIE* DUTIES

What are Ross's *prima facie* duties?

In simplest terms, a *duty* is an obligation to take specific steps (Freeman & Gilbert, 1988). Ross's **doctrine of *prima facie*** (self-evident) **duties** include (1) not harming innocent people, (2) keeping promises, (3) showing gratitude, (4) acting in a just way, and (5) providing reparations to those who have been harmed by one's actions. These duties are not ethical absolutes but are considered to be highly desirable moral tenets that should be honored whenever possible (Beauchamp & Bowie, 1979).

Stakeholder	Cost(s)	Benefit(s)
Owners		Disposable diaper business is currently highly lucrative.
Employees		Increased production allows employees to continue to be employed and to earn wages.
Customers		Weyerhaeuser's diapers are sold under private labels (e.g., Kroger or Revco) and tend to be cheaper than the major brands, thereby saving the customer money.
		Babies benefit because disposable diapers keep them dryer longer than cloth diapers.
		Busy parents benefit from the convenience.
Local Communities	No impact different from costs imposed on society.	
Society	Bulky diapers require 100 years to degrade.	
	Disposable diapers create huge amounts of trash in valuable landfill space. The diaper industry argues that these products comprise only two percent of landfill space; others argue that even this small amount is too much because landfill space is at a premium.	

FIGURE 6-2   *Analysis of disposable diaper production using the utilitarian theory.*

To use this doctrine as an ethical decision tool, you must again consider the organization's major stakeholders: owners, employees, customers, local communities, and society. Then determine which of Ross's five duties are relevant to the decision under consideration, and of these, which may be violated for any of the stakeholders.

Applying the doctrine of *prima facie* duties to the disposable diaper dilemma leads to new insights on the issue, as shown in Figure 6-3.

As these assessments show, applying ethical theories is not an easy task. The analytical process, however, enhances your critical thinking about the consequences of any action. Even if no right answer is possible, clear thinking will help you and any ethically conscious manager better understand the nature of the issue at hand.

COMMUNICATION IN ACTION

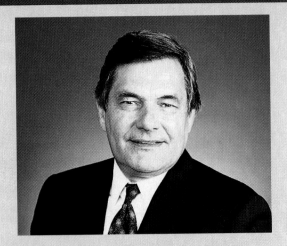

James F. Hurley, California Federal Bank

Information about a company's merger or acquisition is a valuable commodity for the media, financial analysts, or investors interested in those discussions. Keeping such information confidential, while communicating with those constituencies as fully as possible, poses ethical challenges for a company's communication executives who have insider information. James F. Hurley, Executive Vice President of California Federal Bank, one of the nation's largest publicly traded savings institutions, has encountered such ethical situations. Based in Los Angeles, California Federal Bank currently maintains approximately $14 billion in assets and $8.4 billion in deposits.

Working in investor relations, financial public relations, and general media communications, Hurley has faced "moments of truth" in conversations about mergers, acquisitions, and other highly sensitive corporate developments. He communicates regularly with top securities analysts and institutional investors on Wall Street. Those opinion and decision makers carry billions and billions of dollars of investment power. He also speaks with top editors of national media such as *The Wall Street Journal, Fortune,* and *Business Week.*

"There are probably no more highly classified secrets in a company than in the merger and acquisitions area," Hurley says. Those who work in communications will be challenged to hold fast to an ethical standard when pressed for information by media and investor representatives, who are expert at probing for such activities. Hurley understands those "I heard" calls. "We all like to probe for secrets; secrets hold seductive power," Hurley explains.

The Security and Exchange Commission files contain examples of those who have been prosecuted for deciding to profit from or enjoy "the power of secret knowledge" rather than maintain ethical standards.

When a discussion of a company's activities touches a confidential area, Hurley and his associates must employ their communications skills to deftly shift the conversation away from the sensitive area while continuing to communicate openly on other aspects of the company's business strategy.

In the late 1980s, Hurley's bank and another large bank were in discussions about a "merger of equals." The banks were involved in intense, highly secret conversations with each other. At one point, word "leaked out" about the discussions. Hurley received calls from editors, competitors, and highly placed investors for information. He had to maintain total ethical balance in his conversations.

What analysts write based on their conversations with Hurley can be extraordinarily important as to how investors value California Federal Bank's shares. These analysts, whom Hurley knows are the gatekeepers on the buy-and-sell side of Wall Street, help form investor opinion. What they write influences major firms like Merrill Lynch, Prudential, CS First Boston, Sanford Bernstein, or Smith Barney Shearson. When investors or others who seek corporate information get on the line, Hurley has to have his ethical standards well in hand.

"That's a lot of power talking to you on the other end of the line," Hurley explains. "These investors can make your day or ruin it. Without the appropriate ethics and experience, a business communicator can be placed in a position to compromise his or her personal ethical standards in exchange for the moment of glory that comes with sharing a secret."

That is why a business communicator is not just a writer or speaker, Hurley believes. The communicator is often in a position to make instantaneous value judgments. Hurley states, "The higher a person goes in communications, the more instantaneous his or her ethical reactions and judgments have to be. Greater responsibilities and greater pressures follow each rise in position."

Applying What You Have Learned

1. Why do you think Hurley feels he must be particularly alert when asked to give information that would give the caller an undue advantage?
2. What might occur if Hurley revealed secret information about a possible merger or acquisition between California Federal Bank and another large bank?
3. Review the six points of the Pagano Model for ethical decision making. How does Hurley's reaction to requests for information pass point four, the light-of-day test?

Stakeholder	Obligation(s)
Owners	Keeps promise to earn profits, as diaper production earns more money than a comparable investment in another product.
Employees	Keeps promise to provide employment.
Customers	Keeps promise to provide demanded product at fair price.
Local Communities	No duties different from those imposed on society.
Society	May not meet promise of protecting the environment. Manufacturers argue diapers are degradable; however, critics contend only under ideal conditions where sunshine and air can exert their effects.

Harm to innocent people living in future generations resulting from excess trash is unknown. Uncertain of the cost of cleaning up the environment and how quality of life will be affected.

Could make reparations for harm by setting up recycling centers for its diapers, but at the expense of profits for its shareholders. |

FIGURE 6-3
Analysis of disposable diaper production using the doctrine of prima facie duties.

COMMUNICATING DECISIONS ETHICALLY AND RESPONSIBLY

The in-depth analysis required by the ethical framework presented in Figure 6-1 will help you critically examine relevant issues and identify an ethically acceptable alternative. The analysis also will provide you with the logical reasoning needed to write a convincing report to support your decision. Equally important is your ability to communicate your ethical decision and related action to appropriate resource groups—the final step in the framework.

The effective communicator will reap unlimited benefits from communicating an ethical decision to a customer, owner, employee, or top management. These benefits include

- Increased likelihood that the message will yield the desired response from the receiver.
- Courage to deal with ethical issues otherwise ignored because of insecurity in communicating about sensitive or unpleasant issues.
- Positive business relationships built on honest disclosure of information.
- Justified respect from superiors as an honest, sensitive, highly effective communicator worthy of challenging and rewarding opportunities.

LEARNING OBJECTIVE 4

What are the benefits of being able to communicate ethical decisions effectively?

THINK IT OVER
What are other benefits of being an effective communicator?

Language is a powerful
tool that must be used
responsibly and ethically.

This partial list of the benefits of effective communication emphasizes the power language can provide. The familiar directive "with power comes responsibility" applies especially to your use of communication skills. Because effective communication is such a powerful tool, you must accept responsibility for using it for *one and only one* purpose: to uphold your own personal values and your company's standards of ethical conduct.

Before speaking or writing, use the following guidelines to help you filter your message to ensure that you are using effective communication skills responsibly and ethically:

1. *Is the information stated as truthfully, honestly, and fairly as possible?* Have you included all information relevant to the receiver even if it is contrary to your argument? Consider the enticing error of omission in the following workplace dilemma:

> In a letter to an investor, an investment manager enthusiastically reports that the client's stock portfolio has experienced 24-percent growth. The letter omits the fact that the stock market as a whole has increased 32 percent in the same period.

   Is it ethical for the stock investor to withhold the overall stock market growth so that the client is unable to compare his or her stock growth to a standard? Likewise, suppose a company president decides to disclose the financial benefits of a plant closing. When writing the company's annual report to the stockholders, is it ethical for the manager to omit the downside of the plant closing—3,000 employees were laid off in a town where the plant was the primary employer? Gaining a reputation for sending messages that disclose complete and accurate information (regardless of whether it supports your views) builds a solid foundation for strong, long-lasting relationships.

2. *Are the ideas expressed clearly and understandably?* In other words, if a message is to be classified as honest, you must be reasonably confident that the reader can understand the message accurately. To accomplish this goal, select words that convey the exact meaning intended and that are within the

THINK IT OVER
Rewrite the dialogue in the
cartoon to include complete
and honest information about
the plant closing.

A plumber did not understand the following responses to his query: "The effect of HCL is incompatible with metallic piping" and "We cannot assume responsibility for the production of toxic and noxious residues with HCL." Finally, the Bureau of Standards wrote a message its audience could understand: "Don't use HCL. It eats the heck out of pipes!" (Reinemund, 1992).

Ethical messages disclose complete information—both positive and negative.

reader's vocabulary. To illustrate this point, evaluate the explanation shown in Figure 6-4 that a computer representative gave to a customer who was having difficulty transferring data between two microcomputer systems. The clear, easy-to-understand message in Figure 6-5 builds goodwill.

Your computer has high-density secondary storage devices that have antiquated the format utilized by older computers. The sectors on high-density disks have been condensed and thus cannot be recognized by earlier generation hardware. To facilitate the transfer of data between the two systems, format the storage medium using the syntax prescribed in your documentation manual.

FIGURE 6-4
Highly technical message damages goodwill.

Your new computer has high-density disk drives that allow your computer to store more data on a disk than many older computers. These older computers format disks in double-density format and, therefore, cannot read disks formatted in high-density format. However, newer computers with high-density disk drives *can* read disks in double-density format. To prepare a disk for use in either of your microcomputers, simply format the disk in double-density format. To do this, input the following DOS command at the C> prompt: format /4.

FIGURE 6-5
Clear, easy-to-understand message builds goodwill.

When using **euphemisms** (words that make an idea seem better than it is), be sure your motive is to cushion the blow of the negative information and not to ridicule the receiver or prompt the receiver to misconstrue the true message. For example, is it ethical for a politician to talk about *tax enhancements* rather than *tax increases* if the intent is to distort the voters' perceptions? Is it truthful for a military spokesperson to speak of *friendly casualties* to minimize and, in some cases, avoid the negative publicity inherent in reporting the number of soldiers killed accidentally by the military's own weapons? Chapters 7 and 8 provide techniques for using words and style effectively and expressing a message from the receiver's viewpoint.

3. *Are unpleasant ideas stated tactfully and positively to preserve the receiver's self-worth and to build future relationships?* Becoming adept at communicating negative information will give you the confidence needed to handle sensitive situations in a positive, constructive manner rather than to ignore them until they get out of control. For example, a supervisor, uncertain how to approach an employee about low productivity, may (1) intimidate or antagonize the employee if the negative information is not carefully presented or (2) continually postpone the confrontation until the only recourse is to terminate the employee. Consider the negative tone reflected in the memorandum in Figure 6-6.

Even though Josh is clearly responsible for the problem, the revised memo shown in Figure 6-7 is more tactful and offers suggestions for solving the problem. The memo ends with a final offer of help rather than a threat.

Obviously, being able to say "no" without alienating others is a priceless tool when you must take a stand on a difficult ethical issue. Chapter 10 and portions of Chapter 12 will help you gain skill in conveying negative information while retaining the goodwill of the receiver.

> **THINK IT OVER**
> Generate a list of euphemisms you believe might misconstrue the true message and a list of euphemisms you consider appropriate for softening unpleasant information.

> Ability to convey negative information tactfully increases a manager's effectiveness.

TO: Josh Martin

FROM: Lee Sanford

DATE: January 5, 19--

SUBJECT: ACCOUNTS RECEIVABLE MUST BE CONTROLLED

Accounts receivable are out of control.

What has happened to the credit checks that are supposed to control such grotesque delinquency? The company has provided you with staff to perform these credit checks and to contact overdue accounts. Maybe it would be a good idea if you started using them.

Josh, this problem is inexcusable, and I expect to see improvement right away.

FIGURE 6-6   Negative tone damages goodwill.

Executives suspect that one job candidate in three lies or omits relevant information from his or her resume, a practice that seems to be increasing in today's tight job market (Gaines, 1994).

THINK IT OVER
Do you think "inflating a job title, lengthening the dates of employment, or exaggerating responsibilities to make you look better in the job market" is unethical? What are the consequences of these "resume enhancements"?

4. *Does the message embellish or exaggerate the facts?* Legal guidelines related to advertising provide clear guidance for misrepresentation of products or services; however, overzealous sales representatives or imaginative writers can use language skillfully to create less-than-accurate perceptions in the minds of the readers. Businesses have learned the hard way that overstating the capabilities of a product or service (promising more than can be delivered) is not good for business in the long run.

Persuading the reader to take a particular action (buy a product or service, provide an adjustment on a nonroutine claim, or agree to grant a favor) is covered in Chapter 11. Developing skill in writing persuasively will be important throughout your profession. Using effective persuasion techniques to write a winning resume and application letter, the topic of Chapters 13 and 14, will be especially helpful as you begin your career. These techniques should *not* be used, however, if your motive is to exploit the receiver.

5. *Is your viewpoint supported with objective facts? Are facts accurately documented to allow the reader to judge the credibility of the source and to give credit where credit is due? Can opinions be clearly distinguished from facts?* Do you have a conflict of interest that will prevent you from preparing an unbiased message? Suppose a company has determined it must close one of its plants because of excess capacity. The controller has been appointed to a committee to evaluate the plant sites and determine which should be closed. Questions such as these must be answered: Which plant is least efficient? Which plant closing will have the least negative impact on the community? Which plant is least desirably located? Which plant is least adaptable to future product changes?

TO: Josh Martin

FROM: Lee Sanford   *LS*

DATE: January 5, 19--

SUBJECT: STRATEGIES FOR EVALUATING COLLECTION PROCEDURES

Accounts receivable continue to grow. Because this rising delinquency rate is approaching an alarming level, I believe we must evaluate our current procedures to identify a viable solution. Therefore, please begin a full-scale evaluation of the collection process immediately. Specifically, you might begin by

1. Scheduling a meeting with the sales staff to discuss our current credit limits and our methods of granting credit. Based on this input, make the necessary changes.

2. Evaluating the effectiveness of the procedures used to collect past-due accounts. Could you revise the collection letters so that they appeal more effectively to the needs of specific customers? Should we consider modifying the time intervals between collection notices?

As you evaluate the collection process, call me if you need additional input. I look forward to seeing the results of the plans you initiate.

FIGURE 6-7   Improved message builds a strong relationship.

Before coming to corporate headquarters, the controller managed one of these plants and still knows many of the management team and workers at the plant. The executive must explain the exact nature of his or her bias to superiors so they can determine whether the controller should be removed from the committee to protect the usefulness of the recommendation. Chapters 16-18 will guide you in learning to write objective, well-documented reports.

6. *Are graphics carefully designed to avoid distorting facts and relationships?* For example, is it ethical for a company to overstate an insignificant change in unit sales by using a graph with inappropriate scales (see the graph on the left in Figure 6-8) or to use confusing graphic styles to hide negative information *deliberately*? The graph on the right portrays the data accurately because the scale begins at zero. Chapter 16 presents the principles of using graphics to enhance the readability of information.

> **THINK IT OVER**
> Turn to Figure 16-10 to see how a graph can be dramatic but confusing if standard-size symbols are not used to represent amounts.

If you are committed to using effective writing principles to promote ethically acceptable actions, you are now ready to begin mastering the principles of effective business communication presented in the remaining chapters in this text.

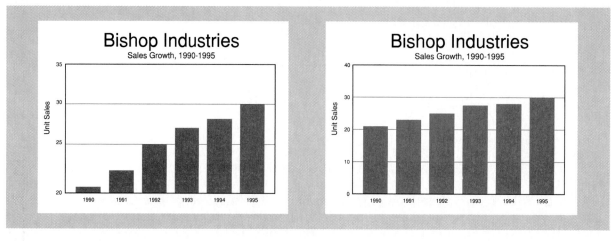

FIGURE 6-8   Distorted (left graph) and accurate (right graph) depiction of data.

SUMMARY

1 **Ethics refers to the principles of right and wrong that guide us in making decisions that affect others.** Our basic values are developed through our formative years as the result of the influence of significant individuals (parents, teachers, school, and religious institutions). Throughout life, we adjust our basic value system. We may make ethical decisions that reinforce our basic values of integrity or make small compromises that eventually erode our basic values.

2 **Understanding the major causes of unethical behavior in the workplace will make you sensitive to pressures to compromise your values.** Common causes of unethical behavior in the workplace include emphasis on profits, misplaced corporate loyalty, obsession with personal ambition, expectation of not getting caught, unethical tone set by top management, uncertainty about whether an action is wrong, and unwillingness to take an ethical stand.

3 **A framework for making an ethical decision and for supporting that decision in a written or oral message will aid you in analyzing ethical dilemmas from multiple perspectives.** The ethical framework involves (1) considering the legal implications of the decision, (2) referring to company or professional codes of ethics for direction, (3) using ethical theories and principles to determine an ethical course of action, and (4) communicating the ethical decision to appropriate individuals effectively.

4 **Guidelines to help ensure that you are communicating responsibly and ethically include** stating information truthfully, expressing ideas clearly, stating unpleasant ideas tactfully, eliminating any embellishments or exaggerations, supporting viewpoints with objective facts from credible sources, and designing graphics that do not distort facts. Enhanced ability to analyze ethical dilemmas and to express ideas clearly and tactfully will increase your chances for success in the business world.

REFERENCES

Ames: Smuggling was easy. (1994, May 21). *The Starkville Daily News,* p. 5.

Bates, L. D. (1990). Making the right choices. *Tomorrow's Business Leader, 22* (2), 17-19.

Beauchamp, T. L., & Bowie, N. E. (Eds.). (1979). *Ethical theory and business.* Englewood Cliffs, NJ: Prentice-Hall.

Crawley, J. W. (1994, July 26). It was a big deal for Stac, Microsoft after a $120 million suit: David and

Goliath forge software industry alliance. *The San Diego Union-Tribune*, p. C-1.

Donaldson, T. (1994, February 13). Business must mind its morals. *The New York Times*, p. 11.

Freeman, R. E., & Gilbert, D. R. (1988*). Corporate strategy and the search for ethics*. Englewood Cliffs, NJ: Prentice-Hall.

Gaines, T. J. (1994, April 1). Resumes becoming more fiction than fact. *San Bernardino County Sun*.

Grisham, J. (1991). *The firm*. New York: Dell Publishing.

Mathison, D. L. (1988). Business ethics cases and decision models: A call for relevancy in the classroom. *Journal of Business Ethics, 10* (7), 781.

Maynard, M. (1993, May 27). GM says ex-manager has stolen its future. *USA Today*, p. 1a.

Miller, R. L. (1990). *Economic issues for consumers*. St. Paul: West Publishing.

Oliverio, M. E. (1990). Tone at the top among early entrepreneurs. *Management Accounting, 72* (2), 19.

Reinemund, S. S. (1992). Today's ethics and tomorrow's work place. *Business Forum, 17* (2), 6-9.

Ross, W. D. (1930). *The right and the good*. Oxford, England: Hackett Publishing.

Slayton, M. (1980). *Common sense & everyday ethics*. Washington, DC: Ethics Resource Center.

Slayton, M. (1991, May-June). Perspectives. *Ethics Journal*. Washington, DC: Ethics Resource Center.

Stac and Microsoft seeking injunctions on one another. (1994, March 26). *The New York Times*, p. 39.

Traub, J. (1988, July 24). Into the mouths of babes. *New York Times Magazine*, p. 27 II.

Note: Selected portions of this chapter were extracted with permission from Spencer, B. A., & Lehman, C. M. (1990). Analyzing ethical issues: Essential ingredient in the business communication course. *Bulletin of the Association of Business Communication, 53* (3), 7-16.

REVIEW QUESTIONS

1. How does the text define ethics? Define ethics in your own words.
2. List several examples of unethical conduct by a business organization or its employees.
3. Why is it important for college students to gain skill in dealing with ethical issues?
4. Discuss the factors that contribute to a person's ability to make an ethical decision.
5. What are the most common causes of unethical behavior in the workplace?
6. Is it acceptable to make small compromises in ethical conduct? Explain.
7. Provide personal and workplace examples of pressure placed on individuals to compromise ethical principles.
8. What are the three decision points in the ethical framework?
9. What three factors must be considered before an alternative passes the legality decision point?
10. What are resource groups? How do they affect the analysis of an ethical issue?
11. What is a code of ethics? What purpose does it serve?
12. What are the advantages of comprehensive ethics awareness programs?
13. Briefly describe the major premises of (a) the utilitarian theory and (b) the doctrine of *prima facie* duties.
14. List four benefits gained from communicating ethical decisions effectively.
15. What are the six guidelines to ensure that your message is being communicated responsibly and ethically?

EXERCISES

1. Complete each of the THINK IT OVER activities that your instructor assigns.
2. Discuss the ethical principle(s) or systems that you think would be helpful to you in determining whether an issue is ethical. Do not limit your analysis to the principles and systems presented in the chapter.
3. Read *The Power of Ethical Management* by Kenneth Blanchard and Norman Vincent Peale, a short, engaging story about a sales manager's attempt to make an ethical decision. Write a brief report summarizing the ethical principles presented in this book.

4. Discuss an ethical issue that you have faced. Consider your experiences in school, employment, organizations, and so on. How did you deal with the issue? What insights have you gained from this experience? What have you learned from reading this chapter that could have aided you in handling this issue more effectively?

5. Discuss one of the ethical issues (personal or workplace) presented in this chapter. Use the framework presented in this chapter to analyze the situation. Based on your analysis, what decision would you have made? Justify your answer.

6. Locate in a current newspaper or magazine an example of an illegal act by a business organization or its employee(s). Choose an incident as closely related as possible to your intended profession. Prepare a written summary of the article.

7. Locate in a current newspaper or magazine an example of an unethical (not illegal) behavior by a business organization or its employee(s). Choose an incident as closely related as possible to your intended profession.
   a. Prepare a written summary of the article.
   b. Use the framework presented in this chapter to analyze the case of unethical behavior. Based on your analysis, what decision would you have made? Justify your answer.

8. Locate the code of ethics for your intended profession. Outline the major responsibilities placed on its practitioners. What procedures does the code of ethics provide to assist practitioners in resolving ethical issues?

9. Identify possible interactions and their legal implications that a business organization has with various resource groups: employees, owners, customers, suppliers, creditors, government, and society. Interactions with employees are provided below as a guide.

Resource Group	Interaction	Legal Implications
Employees	Equal opportunity discrimination/ sexual harassment	Civil Rights Act of 1964 and subsequent amendments, company policy
	Workplace safety	OSHA laws, labor contracts, company policy
	Benefits	Labor contracts, company policy
	Employee recommendations	Libel and slander laws, company policy

10. Analyze the graphics in newspapers, magazines, or annual reports. Locate at least one graphic that depicts facts and relationships truthfully and one that distorts facts (incorrect scale or graphic type, excessive use of graphic styles). Be prepared to justify your analysis; redesign the graphic at the direction of your instructor.

E-MAIL APPLICATION

More people are gaining access to e-mail as a communication avenue. As with other new communication channels, technology often advances faster than the organization's ability to develop adequate procedures for using it. Write a company policy that applies to acceptable use of e-mail. Address such issues as message security, company monitoring of messages, appropriate message content, etc. Send your policy over e-mail to the instructor. Word it as though it is going out to all company personnel.

CASES FOR ANALYSIS

MANAGEMENT/Ethics   `GMAT`

Case 1.   Is Hiring the Homeless to Purchase Tickets Ethical? You are a junior partner in a small ticket brokerage firm in Omaha, Nebraska. The purpose of your company is to purchase tickets to popular concerts and sporting events that will be resold. Your typical market is upper-level executives and other professionals who do not have time to stand in long lines to purchase their own tickets.

The concert promoter allows each individual to purchase only four tickets to a particular event. In the past, you hired students to stand in line to purchase tickets. Even paying minimum wage, you found this practice to be far too expensive to maintain adequate profits. You soon realized that some other, less-expensive method must be identified to secure the tickets.

Several weeks ago you hired a homeless person to stand in line. While he was waiting in line, you gave him two meals (pizza for lunch and chicken for dinner). In return for the four tickets, you paid him $50. Quite pleased with this experiment, you hired more homeless people to purchase tickets. They seemed to like the food and the money, and your profits rose steadily.

You thought everything was going well until yesterday, when you received a telephone call from one of the record stores where tickets are sold. The store manager was upset about two things. First, loyal customers were complaining that they have stood in line for hours, only to be told that all tickets had been sold. Second, the manager complained that these individuals camping out in front of the store may damage the store's image. One particularly irate customer voiced displeasure with having to wait in line with "shabby-looking people with unwashed hair."

Today the morning paper contained a very brash article questioning the ethics of your practice. With paper in hand and very disturbed, Carmen Morgan, the senior partner, rushes into your office. Having already read the article, you quickly say, "Honestly, this negative publicity came as a real surprise to me. I believed that we were not only serving our customers but were also helping the homeless—giving them two meals and money they otherwise would not have had."

Regaining her usual calm disposition, your partner asks you to analyze this practice more thoroughly, and you agree to provide a written report of your analysis. Starting your analysis, you ask yourself these questions: Are you really helping the homeless, or are you taking advantage of their predicament? Are you hurting anyone? Should you continue to hire the homeless to buy tickets? If so, should you change your procedures?

Required:

1. Use the ethical framework in Figure 6-1 to analyze the case. Based on your analysis, what decision would you make? Consider the answers to the following critical-thinking questions:
   a. What are the relevant facts?
   b. What are the ethical issues raised by the decision to employ the homeless in this manner?
   c. Who are the stakeholders affected by this decision?
   d. What legal/contractual considerations must be addressed?
   e. Does a code of ethics provide guidance for reaching a decision?
   f. What are the costs and benefits imposed by each alternative upon each stakeholder?
   g. What are the brokerage firm's obligations to each stakeholder?
   h. What should the ticket brokerage firm do?
2. Outline the major points in your recommendation to your partner.
3. Compose a memorandum to your partner if your instructor requires you to do so.

FINANCE/Ethics   `GMAT`

Case 2.   Should Management Compensation Be Restricted? Over the past two years, the salaries and bonuses of top management at Golden Value Stores have increased over 50 percent—an increase consistent with management compensation levels of similar companies. Much of this increase resulted from management's achieving a variety of non-income-related goals such as the number of retail outlets opened during the year. During the same period, however, Golden Value Stores stock and company earnings have increased at an annual rate of four percent, and dividends have increased only seven percent.

A stockholder has submitted a proposal to eliminate all management bonuses if the company does not achieve a ten-percent growth rate. You are an assistant manager of a stock mutual fund that owns 100,000 shares of Golden Value stock. You have been asked to determine how the mutual fund should cast its votes on the proposal.

1. Use the ethical framework in Figure 6-1 to analyze the situation. Based on your analysis, what decision would you make?
2. Outline the major points of your answer to the fund manager.
3. Compose a memorandum to the fund manager if your instructor requires it.

MANAGEMENT/Ethics   GMAT

Case 3.   Is Reducing Quality to Cut Costs Ethical? Haynes-McReynolds Industries, a major supplier of engine parts for a major airplane manufacturer, has developed a new production process. This process reduces the cost of production by 11 percent. The new product meets company, governmental, and customer safety standards; but the risk of failure is greater than using the present, more costly production method. If part failure occurs, an engine will shut down during flight.

Required:
1. Use the ethical framework in Figure 6-1 to analyze the situation. Based on your analysis, what decision would you make? Outline the major points of your answer to the company president.
2. As vice president of production, you adamantly opposed implementing the new production process. However, you have been instructed to initiate the more efficient process. Should your memo to the production supervisor include the issues involved in this ethical decision? Or should you provide only the details needed for the supervisor to implement the plan? Outline the major points of your answer to the production supervisor.
3. Compose a memorandum to the president and a memorandum to the production supervisor if your instructor requires them.

MANAGEMENT/Ethics   GMAT

Case 4.   Is an Ethical Issue Involved in Replacing Humans with Machines? Lolley Corporation currently employs five workers to produce Part W-132.

The engineering department has identified a robotic machine that can produce the same quantity and quality of parts and would reduce annual production costs by $15,000. The five employees would be terminated if the machine were placed in service. Last year Bradford earned $9.6 million, or $3 a share (3.2 million shares). As vice president of production, you must submit a recommendation to the company president.

Required:
1. Use the framework presented in this chapter to analyze the situation. Based on your analysis, what decision would you make?
2. Outline the major points of your recommendation to the company president.
3. Compose a memorandum to the president if your instructor requires you to do so.

CROSS DISCIPLINARY/Ethics   GMAT

Case 5.   Is the Proposed Action Ethical? Select an ethical dilemma from the following descriptions of the "Cases for Analysis" at the ends of Chapters 9-12. Turn to the appropriate case and read the complete case problem.

- Chapter 9, Case 1. Is it ethical to accept a boat captain's offer to make an "unapproved charter" that is sure to secure the accounts of several sizable investment clients?
- Chapter 9, Case 3. Should products produced with less-than-adequate materials be recalled?
- Chapter 11, Case 2. Is it ethical for a company to donate bottled water to military troops stationed overseas—or is it shrewd public relations?
- Chapter 12, Case 3. Is it ethical to overlook a vendor's error to your advantage?

Required:
1. Use the ethical framework in Figure 6-1 to analyze the situation. Based on your analysis, what decision would you make?
2. Outline the major points of your decision to the intended audience.
3. Compose a letter or memorandum to the appropriate audiences if your instructor requires you to do so.

PART 3

THE WRITING

PROCESS

CHAPTER 7

ORGANIZING AND COMPOSING

MESSAGES

OBJECTIVES

When you have completed Chapter 7, you will be able to

1 Identify the purpose of the message and the appropriate channel.

2 Envision the audience so you can adapt messages to the audience.

3 Apply techniques for adapting messages to the audience.

4 Recognize the importance of organizing a message before writing the first draft.

5 Select the appropriate outline (deductive or inductive) for developing messages by identifying the central idea and the likely receiver reaction.

6 Apply techniques for developing effective sentences and for developing unified and coherent paragraphs.

When American speed skater Dan Jansen stepped up to receive his gold medal at the 1994 winter Olympics in Lillehammer, Norway, the moment marked the culmination of years of hard work, perseverance, and practice. Jansen had qualified for his first Olympics in 1984, but he did not bring home any medals that year. By the time he reached Calgary in 1988, he was recognized as world champion in the 500-meter race. A medal seemed definite; he had worked hard and his pre-Olympic performance was virtually unsurpassed. However, devastating personal events ruled out a victory in Calgary. His sister Jane died of leukemia hours before his first event, and Jansen suffered heartbreaking falls in both the 500- and 1000-meter races.

Despite his sense of loss over his sister's death, followed by his ego-crushing performance at Calgary, Jansen continued to train and prepare for the 1992 Olympics in Albertville, France. His determination prompted an outpouring of support from his family and well-wishers the world over. However, his amazing fortitude and hard work did not lead to gold in Albertville either. Sports fans worldwide wondered if Jansen would continue his quest or whether he would allow the series of bad circumstances and poor performance to force his retirement from the sport. But Jansen had already shown that giving up was not an option.

In Lillehammer in 1994, the crowds supported Jansen as he took the ice. Sports commentators speculated about his performance and rolled footage of his previous disasters. However, Jansen's determination and back-breaking work paid off this time, and he was finally able to don a gold medal and skate around the arena as an undisputed world champion speed skater.

When athletes like Jansen first envision their goals, they work hard to master the basics of their sport. In much the same way, managers and employees who strive for success must first master the basics of written and oral communication. Building good communication skills is like acquiring athletic skills: to succeed in either field, you must first establish a goal and then possess the desire to achieve it. Then you must work hard, often repeating and practicing fundamental tasks over and over. You must persevere to overcome obstacles and not succumb to failure and mediocrity until you reach your goals and reap the rewards.

DETERMINING THE PURPOSE AND CHANNEL

Before beginning to compose the first draft of a message, you must first think about the reason for writing the message. Is the purpose to get information, to answer a question, to accept an offer, to deny a request, to seek support for a product or idea? If a message were condensed into a one-sentence telegram, that sentence would be the purpose for writing or the **central idea** of the message. Later you will learn that the central idea is used to determine the appropriate organization pattern for achieving the results you desire.

The major purpose of many business messages is to have the receiver understand a body of information and concentrate on the logical presentation of the content. Messages *to inform* are used to convey the vast amounts of information needed to complete the day-to-day operations of the business—explain instructions to employees, announce meetings and procedures, acknowledge orders, accept contracts for services, etc. Some messages are intended *to persuade*—to influence or change the attitudes or actions of the receiver. These messages might include letters promoting a product or service and seeking support for ideas and worthy causes presented to supervisors, stockholders,

LEARNING OBJECTIVE 1

What is the central idea of a message?

The major purpose of most business messages is to *inform* or *persuade*.

customers/clients, and others. You will learn to compose messages written for each of these purposes.

Selecting an appropriate channel of communication increases the likelihood that the receiver will understand and accept your message. Recall the three typical communication channels discussed in Chapter 1. For example, a written document (letter/memo, e-mail, or voice mail message) is appropriate for routine or pleasant information. Complex information may require a written document and follow up with a face-to-face meeting. A face-to-face meeting is appropriate for sending unpleasant or highly emotional messages that may be subject to misinterpretation. E-mail is especially effective when sending the same message to many people and communicating with people in different time zones but should *never* be used to send confidential information because the security of e-mail is low. E-mailing or leaving a voice mail message eliminates time-consuming games of telephone tag. Detailed messages enable the receiver to reply with timely answers to your questions.

THINK IT OVER
What is the appropriate channel for (a) telling a customer damaged merchandise will be replaced, (b) notifying a sales rep his or her job has been eliminated because of reorganization, or (c) informing sales reps of annual bonuses?

ENVISIONING THE AUDIENCE

LEARNING OBJECTIVE 2

Buy a gift that fits the recipient; design a message that fits the recipient.

Getting a strong mental picture of your receiver helps you tailor the message to the needs of a *specific* audience.

A good writer has a strong mental picture of the audience. To help you envision the audience, first focus on relevant information you know about the receiver. The more familiar you are with the receiver, the easier this task will be. When communicating with an individual, you immediately bring to mind a clear picture of the receiver—his or her physical appearance, background (education, occupation, religion, culture), values, opinions, preferences, and so on. Most important, your knowledge of the receiver's reaction in similar, previous experiences will aid you in anticipating how this receiver is likely to react in the current situation. Add to your mental picture by thoughtfully considering all you know about the receiver and how this information might affect the content and style of your final message.

To help you tailor your message to fit your audience, consider the following major areas:

THINK IT OVER
What other considerations might affect the message you write?

1. *Age.* A letter answering an elementary-school student's request for information from your company would not be worded like a letter answering a similar request from an adult.
2. *Economic level.* A banker's collection letter to a prompt-paying customer is not likely to be the same form letter sent to clients who have fallen behind on their payments for small loans.
3. *Educational/occupational background.* The technical jargon and acronyms used in a financial proposal sent to bank loan officers may be inappropriate in a proposal sent to a group of private investors. Similarly, a message to the chief executive officer of a major corporation may differ in style and content from a message to a stockholder.
4. *Culture.* The vast cultural differences between people (language, expressions, customs, values, religions) increase the complexity of the communication process. A memorandum containing typical American expressions such as "The projections are *way off base*, and the prices are *out of our ballpark*" would likely confuse a manager from a different culture. Thinking and learning patterns also vary among cultures. For example, clarity is important to North American readers; whereas, Japanese readers value beauty and "flow"

COMMUNICATION MENTOR

Writing from your own point of view is easier but not effective. Your message may make perfect sense to you, but your customer may be confused. Thus, the best business writing is reader-focused. Ask yourself—what does my reader need to know? How can I most effectively and clearly convey the information to my reader? Get a picture of the reader in your mind and concentrate on it as you plan your communication.

H. Devon Graham, Jr.
Southwest Regional Managing Partner
Arthur Andersen & Co.

(Dennett, 1988). North Americans expect a user's manual to contain an overview and then a step-by-step tutorial; however, Japanese readers are "frightened off by seeing the big picture right way. They prefer to be introduced to the parts one at a time before encountering the whole" (Amemiya and Aizu, 1985, p. 7).

5. *Rapport*. A sensitive letter written to a long-time client may differ significantly from a letter written to a newly acquired client. The rapport created by previous dealings with this client aids understanding in this new situation.

6. *Expectations*. Because accountants, doctors, and lawyers are expected to meet high standards, a letter from one of these professionals containing errors in grammar or spelling would likely cause a receiver to question the credibility of the source.

7. *Needs of the receiver*. Just as successful sales personnel begin by identifying the needs of the prospective buyer, an effective manager attempts to understand the receiver's frame of reference as a basis for organizing the message and developing the content.

You may find that envisioning an audience you know well is often such an unconscious action that you may not even recognize that you are doing it. On the other hand, envisioning those you do not know well requires additional effort before you are prepared to adapt the message to your audience.

ADAPTING THE MESSAGE TO THE AUDIENCE

After you have envisioned your audience, you are ready to adapt your message to fit the specific needs of your audience. Adaptations include assuming an empathetic attitude, focusing on the receiver's point of view, using bias-free language, avoiding statements that destroy goodwill, and projecting a positive, tactful tone.

LEARNING OBJECTIVE 3

Assume an Empathetic Attitude

Empathy is an attitude that enables a person to identify another's frame of reference (knowledge, feelings, and emotions) and to project or communicate

THINK IT OVER
Define empathy in your own words.

understanding back to the person (or animal). The phrases "walking a day in your moccasins" or "putting myself in your shoes" imply that empathy requires you to experience another person's situation firsthand. Sharing an experience does make empathy easier. For example, a person who has recovered from a life-threatening disease can more easily understand the emotions and feelings of a person who has just received a similar diagnosis. The power of empathy is central to the success of self-help groups such as Narcotics Anonymous and Mothers Against Drunk Drivers (MADD), and many cancer support groups.

Fortunately, relying on firsthand experience is not necessary to be able to provide genuine empathy. In situations when you cannot "walk in another's shoes," you can empathize by mentally projecting how you believe you would feel if that situation had happened to you. To illustrate this mental projection, Jess Lair once said, "Empathy is your pain in my heart" (Moody, 1987, p. 155).

How can being in touch with someone's feelings assist in business-related situations? First, trying to understand the situation from another's point of view makes sense. Your receivers will appreciate your attempting to understand their feelings; that is, your being in touch with them. The outcome may be mutual trust, which can greatly improve communication and people's feelings about you, your ideas, and themselves (as shown in the discussion of the Johari Window in Chapter 1). In other words, empathy is an excellent way to establish rapport and credibility and to build long-lasting personal and business relationships.

> **Empathy helps you *anticipate* the receiver's reaction to your message.**

Second, seeing a situation or problem from the receiver's perspective not only will permit you to address the receiver's needs and concerns but will also enable you to anticipate the receiver's possible reaction to the message. For example, from your knowledge of yourself and from your experiences with others, you can predict (with reasonable accuracy) receivers' reactions to various types of messages. To illustrate, ask yourself these questions:

- Would I react favorably to a message saying my request is being granted?
- Would I experience a feeling of disappointment upon learning that my request has been refused?
- Would I be pleased when an apparently sincere message praises me for a job well done?
- Would I experience some disappointment when a memo reveals that my promised pay increase is being postponed?

> **THINK IT OVER**
> Empathy is critical when communicating across cultures. In groups, generate a list of phrases and nonverbal expressions a person from another culture might not understand.

Now, reread the questions as though you were another person. Because you know *your* answers, can you predict *others'* answers with some degree of accuracy? Such predictions are possible because of commonality in human behavior. Of course, each individual is unique; but each has much in common with others. Otherwise, psychology, psychiatry, and sociology would not have survived as disciplines. Asking yourself how you would react if you were in the other person's position *before* you write a message greatly simplifies the task of organizing your message. Your knowledge of the receiver's likely reaction enables you to select relevant content, to determine the appropriate sequence of ideas, and to write in a suitable style.

> **The corporate concierge at PepsiCo makes employees' lives "a little easier" by arranging for theater tickets, picking up a birthday cake, hiring someone to wait in an employee's home for a repair or delivery person, and other similar requests (Lawlor, 1994).**

In today's competitive environment, no company can afford to alienate talented workers, and empathy is aiding companies in creating environments supportive of the needs of diverse groups. For instance, recent efforts to involve workers in continuous improvement teams provide management opportunities to see production through the eyes of the worker, the person closest to the operation, and give the worker an opportunity to be heard and appreciated. Because of increased foreign competition, companies must learn to use empathy to understand people who may not speak the same language; do not understand the culture's jargon, expressions, or nonverbal language; practice a different religion and customs; support a different political system; and apply entirely different management practices.

To illustrate empathy for the needs of dual-career and single-parent homes, some companies are introducing flexible work schedules, strong family-benefit policies, extended leaves for parents of newborns, assistance with child- and eldercare, and reductions in travel and relocations. More companies are offering employee services such as work/family seminars on various topics, tutoring for children, free shuttles for long-distance commuters, and on-site services (e.g., fitness center, repair service, pharmacy, subsidized cafeteria with take-out dinners). These companies believe that helping employees manage their personal lives will increase productivity (Lawlor, 1994).

Consider the use (or lack) of empathy in each of the following workplace examples:

THINK IT OVER
Locate articles describing companies' efforts to stay in touch with and meet employee concerns. Share personal experiences from your own workplace.

THINK IT OVER
In small groups, discuss situations you have experienced where you believe empathy (or lack of) affected communication.

Sample Message

Example 1: Hurriedly as the store closed on Thursday evening, the store manager told sales clerks:

Oh, by the way, it's time for our annual inventory. I want you here Sunday at 7 a.m. sharp and plan to stay until . . . And one other thing. Don't bother embarrassing yourself by giving me some flimsy excuse for not being able to work. I don't want to hear it. If I don't have this job done by Monday morning, the district manager will have my head. End of conversation.

Example 2: An excerpt from a letter sent to Mr. Adam Ritchey:

Dear Mr. Ritchie:

The desktop publishing software and the laser printer that you expressed an interest in is now available in our local stores. Both can be demonstrated at you convience. Please call your local sales representative to schedule a appointment. I remain

Respectfully yours,

Clint M. Taite

Clint M. Taite
District Manager

Problem Analysis

Overuse of the pronoun I emphasizes the manager's self-centered attitude. Tactless, intimidating, and overly demanding tone eliminates the possibility of feedback. Insistence on one-way communication and the timing of the message highlight no consideration for individual needs (arrangements for child- or eldercare and other extenuating circumstances).

The misspelling of the receiver's name and the grammar errors are unforgivable; the misspellings confirm incompetence (or carelessness) and disrespect for the receiver (What other reason could explain this second-rate work?). The outdated closing reduces the writer's credibility further. Although the writer is purporting expertise in a technological field, the communication does not reflect modern conventions.

The writer does not anticipate the receiver's need for the sales representative's name and telephone number; omission of these important facts communicates unconcern for the receiver.

Example 3: A U.S. manager's instructions to a new employee from an Asian culture:

Please get to work right away on <u>inputting</u> the financial data for the Smyth proposal. Oh, I need you to get this work out <u>ASAP</u>. Because this proposal is just a <u>draft</u>, why don't you just plan to give me a <u>quick-and-dirty</u> job. You can clean it up after we <u>massage the stats</u> and get final <u>blessings</u> from the <u>top dog</u>. Do you have any questions?

Can you imagine the confusion and intimidation caused by the acronyms and expressions peculiar to the U.S. environment? The final open-ended question indicates that the writer does not understand the importance of saving face to a person from an Asian culture. Deep cultural influences prevent this employee from asking questions that might indicate lack of understanding.

Focus on the Receiver's Point of View

"You attitude" increases clarity and builds relationships.

Ideas are more interesting and appealing if they are expressed from the receiver's viewpoint. Thus, develop a "you attitude," which involves thinking in terms of the other person's interests and trying to see a problem from the other's point of view. A letter or memo reflecting a "you attitude" sends a direct signal of sincere concern for the receiver's needs and interest.

You (appropriately used) conveys to receivers a feeling that messages are specifically for *them*. However, if the first-person pronoun *I* is used frequently, the sender may impress others as being self-centered—always talking about self. *I* used as the subject receives significant emphasis. Compare the following examples of writer-centered and receiver-centered statements:

THINK IT OVER
Write a sentence expressing an idea from your point of view; then rewrite it from the receiver's point of view.

I- or Writer-Centered	Receiver-Centered
<u>I</u> want to take this opportunity to offer <u>my</u> congratulations on your recent promotion to regional manager.	Congratulations on <u>your</u> recent promotion to regional manager.
<u>We</u> have two laser printers compatible with your software.	<u>Your</u> software is compatible with two of our high-quality laser printers.
<u>I</u> am interested in ordering. . . .	Please send me. . . .
<u>We</u> allow a 2-percent discount to customers who pay their total invoices within ten days.	Customers who pay within ten days may deduct 2 percent from their total invoice. (<u>You</u> could be the subject in a letter to a customer.)

To cultivate a "you attitude," concentrate on the following questions:

- Does the message address the receiver's major needs and concerns?
- Would the receiver feel this message is receiver-centered? Is the receiver kept clearly in the picture?
- Will the receiver perceive the ideas to be fair, logical, and ethical?
- Are ideas expressed clearly and concisely (to avoid lost time, money, and possible embarrassment caused when messages are misunderstood)?
- Does the message serve as a vehicle for developing positive business relationships—even when the message is negative? For example, are *please,*

COMMUNICATION MENTOR

A turn-off in any type of written correspondence is use of the word *I* and its sister words *me* and *us*. Try to eliminate these words from your vocabulary to prevent an *us* vs. *them* attitude.

Terence E. McSweeney
Director of Communications
PGA of America

thank you, and other courtesies used when appropriate? Are ideas stated tactfully and positively and in a manner that preserves the receiver's self-worth and cultivates future business?

- Is the message sent promptly to indicate courtesy?
- Does the message reflect the high standards of a business professional: quality paper, accurate formatting, printing quality, and absence of misspellings and grammatical errors?

Concentrating on these points will boost the receiver's confidence in the writer's competence and will communicate nonverbally that the receiver is valued enough to merit the writer's best effort. For people who have practiced courtesy and consideration since childhood, the "you attitude" is easy to incorporate into a written message.

Use Bias-Free Language

In today's competitive workplace, a writer or a speaker cannot afford the risk of sending an insensitive message. In addition, managers in today's highly competitive, diverse workforce cannot afford to alienate employees and customers. Therefore, select words carefully to eliminate any trace of insensitivity regarding gender, race or ethnic group, religion, age, or disability.

AVOID GENDER BIAS
Pay special attention to the pronouns "him" and "his" in the following sentences:

When your accountant completes year-end financial statements, ask <u>him</u> to send a copy to the loan officer.

The human resources manager must evaluate <u>his</u> employees' performance at least twice a year.

When the gender of a noun ("accountant" in the first sentence and "manager" in the second) has not been revealed, do not use a masculine pronoun. Although this usage was once standard and accepted, it can be considered offensive today. The receiver's attention may be diverted from the message to the writer's stereotypical attitudes and insensitivity. *Avoid using the pronoun he when referring to a group of people that may include women.*

THINK IT OVER
What gender-bias references that stereotype occupations have you heard or read about recently?

A teacher must complete in-service training to update <u>her</u> certification.

If a secretary is to advance in today's business environment, <u>she</u> must develop excellent computer skills.

The writers of these sentences are communicating an insensitive message between the lines that "only females serve in certain professions." *Avoid referring to males and females in stereotyped roles and occupations.*

Sensitive writers make sure that their writing is gender-neutral. Computer writing-analysis software highlights gender-biased references. Once it is identified, gender-biased language can be corrected in a variety of ways:

How can you avoid gender-biased language?

1. Avoid using a pronoun.
     Not: When your auditor arrives, <u>he</u> is to go. . . .
   Instead: Upon arrival, <u>your auditor</u> is to go. . . .
2. Repeat the noun.
     Not: . . . the courtesy of your guide. Ask <u>him</u> to. . . .
   Instead: . . . the courtesy of <u>your guide</u>. Ask the guide to. . . .
3. Use a plural noun.
     Not: If a supervisor needs assistance, <u>he</u> can . . . .
   Instead: If supervisors need assistance, <u>they</u> can . . . .
   (Because "they" can refer to men only, women only, or both, using "they" avoids implying that supervisors can be men only.)
4. Use pronouns from both genders.
     Not: Just call the manager. <u>He</u> will in turn . . . .
   Instead: Just call the manager. <u>He</u> or <u>she</u> will in turn . . . .

Occasional use of "he or she" may not be particularly distracting, but repeated use can take attention away from the message.

Although the English language has a common-gender plural pronoun (*they*), it does not have such a pronoun in the singular (except for *it*, which is hardly appropriate for referring to people, and *one*, the use of which is seldom advisable). *Avoid using masculine pronouns that may be considered offensive.*

Can you identify possible gender bias in the following sentences?

The <u>fireman</u> worked tirelessly to free the child trapped in the well.

The <u>businessman</u> travels approximately four months a year.

Substituting "firefighter" for "fireman" and "executive" (or a specific job title such as "insurance agent") for "businessman" is a simple way to eliminate gender bias in these sentences. Many occupational titles have been changed to reflect genuine sensitivity to gender:

THINK IT OVER
Can you add to these examples of alternatives to gender-biased terms?

Gender-Biased	Gender-Free
businessman	executive, manager, businessperson
career woman	professional
foreman	supervisor
stock boy	stock clerk
bag boy	courtesy clerk
working mother	working parent

Avoid designating an occupation by gender. For example, why include "female" in "A female doctor is opening a hematology clinic next month"? The doctor's profession, not the gender, is the point of the message. Similarly, avoid using the *-ess* ending to differentiate genders in an occupation:

Gender-Biased	Gender-Free
steward or stewardess	flight attendant
waiter or waitress	server, waitperson
hostess	host
authoress	author
poetess	poet

Could receivers perceive the expressions used in the following sentences to be insensitive or biased?

Preparing the company's annual report is a <u>man-sized</u> task.

Charles Morrow is the best <u>man</u> for the job.

This estimate of the <u>manpower</u> needed to install this information system is quite conservative.

In the first sentence, substituting "enormous" or "immense" for "man-sized" accurately describes the magnitude of the task without running the risk of offending the receiver. Similarly, "best man" would be better as "best person," and "manpower" would be better as "number of workers." *Avoid commonly used expressions in which "man" represents all humanity, such as "Man does not live by bread alone," and stereotypical characteristics, such as "manhours," "man and wife," "man-made goods," and "work of four strong men."*

AVOID RACE AND ETHNIC GROUP, AGE, RELIGION, AND DISABILITY BIAS

Changes in the demographics of the workforce are requiring managers to design bias-free messages in terms of race and ethnic group, age, religion, and disability. In fact, companies are investing in diversity workshops designed to raise awareness of racial and gender bias and to seek ways to change.

The guidelines for writing gender-sensitive messages also apply to writing messages sensitive to race and ethnic group, age, religion, and disability: *Avoid emphasizing age, ethnic group, religion, or disability when these factors are not relevant; avoid referring to these groups in stereotypical ways.* Can you identify the insensitivities in the following examples?

> Avoid language that reflects bias for race and ethnic group, age, religion, and disability.

Alfonso Perez, the <u>Spanish</u> clerk in the Quality Control Division, immediately identified the discrepancy in the raw materials.

Keith's <u>Irish</u> temper flared today when we learned of the new production quotas.

The <u>black</u> mayor of Aberdeen has announced his bid for reelection.

The <u>Jewish</u> account executive has designed a creative point-of-sale display for the Pearson campaign.

Kyle Hunt, the <u>55-year-old</u> president of Garvy-Wheaton Bank, has resigned to accept a position with another company.

> **THINK IT OVER**
> As indicated in the example, the Irish and redheads often are stereotyped as having hot tempers. What are other offensive stereotypes?

References to race or ethnic group in the first three sentences are irrelevant, just as gender is immaterial in the earlier example, "The female doctor. . . ." Eliminating the president's age will not alter the meaning of the last sentence.

Does either of the following sentences communicate a hidden negative message?

<u>Blind</u> employees will receive company memorandums by voice mail.

The new elevator is for the exclusive use of <u>handicapped</u> employees and should not be used by <u>normal</u> employees.

THINK IT OVER
What is "people first" language? Write an example.

When communicating about people with disabilities, use the "people first" language supported by Tyler (1990): Refer to the person first and the disability second. The emphasis is appropriately focused on the person's ability rather than on the disability. Avoid words with negative or judgmental connotations such as *handicap, unfortunate, afflicted,* and *victim.* When describing people without disabilities, use the word *typical* rather than *normal*; otherwise, you may inadvertently imply that people with disabilities are abnormal. Consider these more sensitive revisions:

<u>Employees with vision impairments</u> will receive company memorandums by voice mail.

The new elevator is for the exclusive use of <u>employees who have disabilities</u>.

To communicate that you are responsive to the differences of others, you must make a conscious effort to use bias-free (nondiscriminatory) language. Taking even a remote chance of offending someone is too great a risk. Using bias-free language permits the receiver to focus on your message rather than to raise serious questions about your sensitivity. Your concerted efforts to be caring and sensitive will yield tangible results: increased clarity and strong, lasting relationships—both measuring sticks for effective communication.

Avoid Statements that Destroy Goodwill

The writer's attitude toward the message and the receiver is communicated through the tone of the message.

Tone is the way a statement sounds. The tone of a message conveys the writer's or speaker's attitude toward the message and the receiver. Chances for achieving good human relations are diminished when the tone of a message is condescending, overly euphemistic or flattering, demeaning, or presumptuous.

ELIMINATE CONDESCENSION

Condescending words seem to connote that the communicator is temporarily coming down from a level of superiority to join the receiver on a level of inferiority. Note these examples:

As a retired editor of best sellers, I could assist you in editing your PTA newsletter.

With my Ph.D. and your GED, we should be able to work out a suitable set of bylaws for the new club.

Such reminders of inequality seriously hamper communication. *Avoid use of condescending words.*

COMMUNICATION MENTOR

Fewer and fewer people purposefully use biased language, yet old habits die hard. Be determined to be a sensitive communicator who doesn't burden messages with offensive language. You'll find bias-free communicating will quickly become second nature.

Cynthia Pharr
President & CEO
C. Pharr Marketing Communications

Think before you speak. If you believe you have been insensitive, be careful not to make the issue bigger by your explanation. I once heard a seminar speaker use the phrase "as clear as black and white." Then, thinking that she might have offended members of the audience, she spent 15 minutes nervously explaining the terminology. This behavior only exaggerated a statement that likely would have been ignored.

Shirley F. Olson
Vice President & Chief Financial Officer
J. J. Ferguson Sand and Gravel/Prestress/Precast

USE EUPHEMISMS CAUTIOUSLY

A **euphemism** is a term that makes an unpleasant idea seem better than it really is. For example, the idea of picking up neighborhood garbage does not sound especially inviting. Someone who does such work is often referred to as a *sanitation worker*. This term has a more pleasant connotation than *garbage collector*. Business writers prefer the euphemistic terms in the right column to the negative terms in the left column:

Negative Tone	Euphemistic Tone
died	passed away
aged or elderly	senior citizen
secretaries	office support staff
bagger	courtesy clerk
soldiers killed by their own forces	friendly casualties
Complaint Department	Customer Service
Repair Department	Maintenance Department
Inspection Department	Quality Control

THINK IT OVER
Add two more examples of euphemisms to this list.

Generally, you can recognize such expressions for what they are—unpleasant ideas presented with a little sugar coating. Knowing that the sender was simply trying to be polite and positive, you are more likely to react favorably than unfavorably. Yet, you should avoid euphemisms with excess sugar coating or those that appear to be deliberate sarcasm. For example, to refer to a janitor

Using euphemisms to ridicule or cause the receiver to misconstrue the meaning is *unethical*.

THINK IT OVER
Is *diametrically challenged* an acceptable euphemism for describing someone over-weight? *pre-owned* for used cars? *tax enhancements* for tax increases? *friendly casualties* for soldiers killed by our own weapons? Can you add others?

as a *maintenance engineer* is to risk conveying a negative metacommunication such as "I wish this janitor held a more respectable position, but I did the best I could by making it sound good." To the receiver (and to the janitor), just plain *janitor* would sound better. *Use euphemisms when the purpose is to present unpleasant thoughts politely and positively; avoid them when they will be taken as excessive or sarcastic.*

AVOID A FLATTERING TONE

Compliments (words of deserved praise) normally elicit favorable reactions. They can increase a receiver's receptivity to subsequent statements. Yet even compliments can do more harm than good if paid at the wrong time, in the wrong setting, in the presence of the wrong people, or for a suspicious motive.

Insincere compliments are detrimental to good communication.

Flattery (words of *un*deserved praise) may be accepted gracefully, but the net result is almost always negative. Although flattery *can* be accepted as a sincere compliment, the recipient is more likely to interpret undeserved praise as an attempt to curry favor. Suspicion of motive makes effective communication less likely. *Give sincere compliments judiciously; avoid flattery.*

AVOID DEMEANING EXPRESSIONS

Read the following pairs of sentences. Which sentence seems more appropriate and why?

The <u>pencil pushers</u> (or <u>bean counters</u>) require that all requisitions be approved by the inventory manager.

The <u>accountants</u> require that all requisitions be approved by the inventory manager.

Coach Roberts intends to concentrate on recruiting <u>skilled players</u> this season.

Coach Roberts intends to concentrate on recruiting <u>quarterbacks, running backs, and receivers</u> this season.

Be sure the <u>turtles</u> understand the importance of meeting next week's deadline.

Be sure the <u>management trainees</u> understand the importance of meeting next week's deadline.

THINK IT OVER
In groups, generate a list of demeaning expressions for each career field represented in the group and those used in companies with which members have experience.

In each of the preceding pairs, the first sentence can be taken as contempt for an occupation or a specific job. Like words that attack races or nationalities, words that ridicule occupations work against a writer's purpose. An expression that is designed to make an idea seem negative or disrespectful (sometimes called a *dysphemism*) is a demeaning expression. Many demeaning expressions are common across regions and perhaps even cultures. Some demeaning expressions belong to a particular company. For example, "turtles" in the last pair of sentences was coined in one firm to mock first-year employees for the slow pace at which they completed their work. Because such expressions divert attention from the real message to emotional problems that have little to do with the message, *avoid demeaning expressions.*

USE CONNOTATIVE TONE CAUTIOUSLY

Human relations can suffer when connotative words are inadvertently used instead of **denotative words**. The denotative meaning of a word is the literal meaning that most people assign to it. The **connotative meaning** is the literal meaning plus an extra message that reveals the speaker's or writer's qualitative judgment. Here is an example:

Denotative Meaning	Connotative Meaning
Another <u>employee forum</u> has been scheduled for tomorrow.	Another <u>gripe session</u> has been scheduled for tomorrow.

The second message contains a denotative meaning and an additional message: The writer has a bias for or against employee forums. The connotation may needlessly introduce thoughts about whether employee forums are beneficial. While thus occupied, the receiver may not pay sufficient attention to the statements that follow.

Note the commonality between connotations and metacommunications. Both involve messages that are implied. In the preceding examples, the connotations seem to be more harmful than helpful. At times, however, connotations can be helpful:

Denotative Meaning	Connotative but Positive Meaning
<u>Research and Development</u> has developed yet another outstanding production process.	Our <u>corporate think tank</u> has developed another outstanding production process.
John's likable personality <u>is beneficial</u> when he negotiates labor contracts.	John's likable personality <u>has made him a miracle worker</u> when he negotiates labor contracts.

Compared with denotative words, connotative words invite a wider range of interpretation. Words that elicit a positive reaction from one person could elicit a negative reaction from another.

The appropriateness of connotations varies with the audience to which they are addressed and the context in which they appear. For example, referring to a car as a "foreign job" might be received differently by a group of teenagers and a group of senior citizens. The expression is less appropriate in a research report than in a popular magazine.

In business writing *rely mainly on denotative words or connotative words that will elicit a favorable reaction*. By considering the audience, the context, and the timing, you can usually avoid connotative words that elicit unfavorable reactions.

AVOID STATEMENTS OF SURPRISE, DOUBT, AND JUDGMENT

Phrases that reveal a writer's surprise about a receiver's behavior can cause problems in human relations. Why are the following sentences risky?

I am surprised that you did not accept.

I just cannot understand your attitude.

"I am surprised" risks conveying something like "I am accustomed to normal behavior. Yours is abnormal and therefore bad or totally unjustified." "I cannot understand" takes the same risks. Such expressions are particularly

> **THINK IT OVER**
> Is an extra message conveyed in "Have you read the *latest commandment from above*?" How might you rewrite the sentence using the literal meaning? Label the two sentences *denotative* or *connotative*.

> What would "I'm surprised your idea was approved" connote?

offensive to receivers because they seem to place them in a position of recognized inferiority.

Similarly, expressions that reveal judgment of recipients' emotional state are very risky. "I am so sorry you are upset" may be intended as a heart-felt apology, but the "I am sorry" can be completely overshadowed by "you are upset." This statement could mean, "Your conduct is such that I recognize your lack of self-control. Because of your condition, you could not be thinking rationally." *Avoid expressions of surprise, doubt, and judgment when they would be interpreted as insults.*

Could "Sorry to upset you" add to (instead of soothe) irritation?

AVOID STATEMENTS OF CERTAINTY

Read the following pairs of sentences, paying attention to the underscored phrases. Which sentence, the first or the second, is better?

> I am sure you will agree that the instructions are clear.
> Re-examine the instructions to see whether they are clear.
>
> I know you will understand the importance of completing the designs by Friday.
> The designs must be completed by Friday if we are going to meet the final deadline.

In each pair, the writer of the first sentence seems to be making a declaration of certainty when certainty is hardly possible. If through prior discussion the writer *can* be sure of agreement, the first sentence is unnecessary. If the writer really *knows* the designs have been completed, the receiver is probably already aware of the idea contained in the sentence. When the phrases "I know" and "I am sure" *cannot* be true, the writer conveys a lack of empathy and respect for the receiver. If the writer stretches the truth in this way often enough, the receiver may question whether other statements are accurate or exaggerated too.

The expression "as you know" is to be avoided for the same reasons: receivers either already know that they know and the words are unnecessary, or the words are simply inaccurate. *Avoid expressions of certainty when certainty is hardly possible.*

THINK IT OVER
What is your reaction when "As you know" precedes an idea you don't know? an idea you already know?

Project a Positive, Tactful Tone

Being adept at communicating negative information will give you the confidence you need to handle sensitive situations in a positive, constructive manner. You will find that stating unpleasant ideas tactfully and positively preserves the receiver's self-worth and builds future relationships. To reduce the sting of an unpleasant thought,

To promote goodwill, learn how to "whisper" rather than "shout" bad news.

1. *State ideas using positive language.* Be cheerful and optimistic. In the following pairs of sentences, note the difference in tone between the first and second example.

Negative Tone	Positive Tone
Don't forget to submit your time and expense report by noon on Friday.	Remember to submit your time and expense report by noon on Friday.

FIGURE 7-1
Use words with positive tone to build goodwill.

Negative Tone	Positive Tone
We <u>cannot</u> ship your order until you send us full specifications.	You will receive your order as soon as you send us full specifications.
Our new electronic mail system <u>will not</u> be installed by the first of the year.	Our new electronic mail system will be installed by February 1.
You <u>neglected</u> to indicate the specifications for Part No. 332-3.	Please send the complete specifications for Part No. 332-3 so we can complete your order quickly.

Each sentence in the left column contains a negative word or phrase—"don't," "cannot," "will not," and "neglected." In each pair, both sentences are sufficiently clear; but the positive words in the sentence in the right column make the message more diplomatic. The sentences in the right column sound more pleasing and do a better job of promoting human relations. For good human relations, *rely mainly on positive words—words that speak of what can be done instead of what cannot be done, of the pleasant instead of the unpleasant.*

Positive words are *normally* preferred, but sometimes negative words are more effective in achieving the dual goals of *clarity* and positive *human relations.* For example, addition of negative words can sharpen a contrast (and thus increase clarity):

Use an oil-based paint for this purpose; <u>do not use</u> latex.

Manuscripts are to be printed; handwritten material is <u>not</u> acceptable.

When pleasant, positive words have not brought desired results, negative words may be justified. For example, a supervisor may have used positive words to instruct an accounts payable clerk to verify that the unit price on the invoice matches the unit price on the purchase order. Discovering later that the clerk is not verifying the invoices correctly, the supervisor may use negative words such as "*No*, that's the *wrong* way," demonstrate once more, and explain. If the clerk continues to complete the task incorrectly, the supervisor may feel justified in using even stronger negative words. The clerk may need the emotional jolt that negative words can provide. *When the purpose is to sharpen contrast or when positive words have not evoked the desired reaction, use negative words.*

Saturn managers' skill at conveying bad news turned a potentially disastrous situation into a "public relations coup." Faced with telling loyal Saturn customers that their cars were being recalled to repair a production defect, managers carefully planned a strategy to emphasize something positive to minimize customers' disappointment. Dealers across the U.S. invited customers to an informal get-together complete with hot dogs and refreshments while the thirty-minute repairs were made. Satisfied Saturn owners enjoyed the "party" and thousands more flocked to the recent Saturn Homecoming.

2. *Avoid using second person when stating negative ideas.* The following sentences use the second-person pronoun. In which sentence is "you" less advisable?

<u>You</u> keyed a perfect copy.

<u>You</u> made numerous mistakes on this page.

Should you use second person to present a negative idea?

The first sentence contains a positive idea. The person to whom the sentence is addressed can hardly resent being associated with perfection. The second sentence contains a negative idea. The person will likely become sensitive about the mistake when he or she is directly associated with it. If the speaker's desire is to be diplomatic (at least to be no more negative than necessary), the second sentence could be revised to avoid the use of second person: "This page contains numerous mistakes." For better human relations, *avoid second person for presenting negative ideas*. Use second person for presenting pleasant ideas. However, use of second person with negative ideas *is* an acceptable technique on the rare occasions when the purpose is to jolt the receiver by emphasizing a negative.

Normally, use passive voice to subordinate negative ideas.

3. *Use passive voice to convey negative ideas. Presenting an unpleasant thought emphatically (as active verbs do) makes human relations difficult.* Compare the tone of the following negative thoughts written in active and passive voices:

Active Voice	Passive Voice
<u>Armando</u> failed to proofread this bid proposal carefully.	The bid proposal was not proofread carefully.
<u>Armando</u> completed the job two months behind schedule.	The job was completed two months behind schedule.

Because the subject of each active sentence is the doer, the sentences are emphatic. Because the idea is negative, Armando probably would appreciate being taken out of the picture. The passive voice sentences place more emphasis on the job than on who failed to complete it. When passive voice is used, the sentences retain the essential ideas, but the ideas seem less irritating. *For negative ideas, use passive voice.*

Just as emphasis on negatives hinders human relations, emphasis on positives promotes human relations. Which sentence makes the positive idea more vivid?

Why is passive voice preferred for conveying a negative idea?

Passive Voice

The job was completed ahead of time.

Active Voice

Armando completed the job ahead of schedule.

Because "Armando" is the subject of the active voice sentence, the receiver can easily envision the action. Pleasant thoughts deserve emphasis. *For presenting positive ideas, use active voice.* Active and passive voice are discussed in greater detail in the "Writing Powerful Sentences" section later in this chapter.

4. *Use the subjunctive mood.* Sometimes, the tone of a message can be improved if the writer switches to the subjunctive mood. Subjunctive sentences employ such conditional expressions as *I wish, as if, could, would, might,* and *wish.* **Subjunctive sentences** speak of a wish, necessity, doubt, or conditions contrary to fact. Which of the following sentences seem more diplomatic?

Negative Tone

I cannot approve your transfer to our overseas operation.

I am unable to accept your invitation to speak at the November meeting.

I cannot accept the recommendation of the site-selection committee.

Positive Tone

If positions <u>were</u> available in our overseas operation, I <u>would</u> approve your transfer.

I <u>could</u> accept your invitation to speak at the November meeting if I <u>were</u> to miss the annual stockholders' meeting.

I <u>wish</u> I <u>could</u> accept the recommendation of the site-selection committee.

THINK IT OVER
In groups, write another pair of sentences to add to this list.

In all three pairs, a negative idea is involved; but the sentence in the right column transmits the negative idea in positive language. Positive language is more diplomatic. The revised sentences also include a reason. Because a reason is included, the negative idea seems less objectionable; and tone is thus improved.

Tone is important, but clarity is even more important. The revised sentence in each of the preceding pairs sufficiently *implies* the unpleasant idea without stating it directly. If for any reason a writer suspects the implication is not sufficiently strong, a direct statement in negative terms is preferable. *For tactful presentation of an unpleasant thought, consider stating it in the subjunctive mood.*

What benefit do you gain from using subjunctive mood to convey a negative idea? What is a possible drawback?

THINK IT OVER
Using a balanced approach (positives and negatives) furnishes vital feedback and an incentive to improve.

5. *Include a pleasant statement in the same sentence.* Consider the tone of the following sentences:

Negative Tone	Positive Tone
Your personal ratings in communication ability and interpersonal skills were satisfactory.	Your personal ratings in communication ability and interpersonal skills were satisfactory, but <u>your rating in technical competence was excellent.</u>
Because of increased taxes and insurance, you are obligated to increase your monthly payments to $50.	Because of increased taxes and insurance, your monthly payments will increase by $50; however, <u>your home has increased in value at the monthly rate of $150.</u>

What are five techniques for de-emphasizing negative ideas?

For improved tone, place a positive idea in the same sentence with a negative idea.

ORGANIZING THE MESSAGE

THINK IT OVER
Can you recall the five guidelines for communicating ethically and responsibly in Chapter 6? Take a moment to review them.

After you have identified the specific ways you must adapt the message to your specific audience, you are ready to organize your message. In a discussion of writing, the word **organize** means "the act of dividing a topic into parts and arranging them in an appropriate sequence." Before undertaking this process, you must be convinced that the message is the *right* message—that it is complete, accurate, fair, reasonable, ethical, and logical. If it doesn't meet these standards, it should not be sent. Good organization and good writing cannot be expected to compensate for a bad decision. Before you outline, review the framework for making ethical decisions and the guidelines for communicating responsibly presented in Chapter 6.

If you organize and write simultaneously, the task seems hopelessly complicated. Writing is much easier if questions about the organization of the message are answered first: What is the purpose of the message, what is the receiver's likely reaction, and should the message begin with the main point? Once these decisions have been made, the writer can concentrate on expressing ideas effectively.

Outline to Benefit Writer and Receiver

Outlining involves identifying the major and minor ideas and arranging them in the right sequence.

When a topic is divided into parts, one part will be recognized as a central idea and the others as minor ideas (details). The process of identifying these ideas and arranging them in the right sequence is known as **outlining**. Outlining *before* writing provides numerous benefits:

What does the *writer* gain from taking time to outline before writing?

- Encourages brevity and accuracy. (Reduces the chance of leaving out an essential idea or including an unessential idea.)
- Permits concentration on one phase at a time. (Having focused separately on (a) the ideas that need to be included, (b) the distinction between major and minor ideas, and (c) the sequence of ideas, the writer is now prepared for total concentration on the next problem—expressing.)
- Saves time in writing or dictating. (With questions about which ideas to include and their proper sequence already answered, little time is lost in moving from one point to the next.)

For the architect or city planner, organization is essential; without it, buildings are constructed with poor materials or are missing vital components. Writers need organization as well to ensure that their ideas are presented clearly and logically, increasing the likelihood that the receiver will react positively to their messages.

- Provides a psychological lift. (The feeling of success gained in preparing the outline increases confidence that the next step—writing—will be successful, too.)
- Facilitates emphasis and de-emphasis. (Although each sentence makes its contribution to the message, some sentences need to stand out more vividly in the receiver's mind than others. An effective outline ensures that important points will appear in emphatic positions.)

The preceding benefits derived from outlining are writer oriented. Because a message has been well outlined, receivers benefit, too:

- The message is more concise and accurate.
- Relationships among ideas are easier to distinguish and remember.
- Reaction to the message and its writer is more likely to be positive.

Receiver reaction to a message is strongly influenced by the sequence in which ideas are presented. A beginning sentence or an ending sentence is in an emphatic position. (Other emphasis techniques are explained later in this chapter.) Throughout this text, you will see that outlining (organizing) is important.

How does outlining benefit the *receiver*?

Sequence Ideas to Achieve Desired Goals

LEARNING OBJECTIVE 5

When planning your writing or dictating, you should strive for an outline that will serve the writer in much the same way a blueprint serves a builder or itinerary serves a traveler. When the goal is to produce a map or blueprint, thought precedes action. The same is true of outlining. Before listing the first point of an outline, you should answer the following questions in this order:

An outline serves a writer as a blueprint serves a builder and an itinerary serves a traveler.

1. What will be the central idea of the message?
2. What will be the most likely receiver reaction to the message?
3. In view of the predicted receiver reaction, should the central idea be listed *first* in the outline; or should it be listed as one of the *last* items?

What three questions must you answer before preparing an outline?

To answer the first question, think about the *reason* you are writing—the first step in the writing process. What is your purpose—extend a job offer, decline an invitation, seek support for an innovative project? The purpose is the central idea of your message. You might think of it as a message condensed into a one-sentence telegram.

To answer the second question (predicted receiver reaction), ask, "If I were the one receiving the message I am preparing to send, what would *my* reaction be?" Because you would react with pleasure to good news and displeasure to bad news, you can reasonably assume a receiver's reaction would be similar. Recall the twin goals of a communicator: clarity and effective human relations. By considering anticipated receiver reaction, a writer builds goodwill with the receiver. As shown in Figure 7-2, almost every letter will fit into one of four categories of anticipated receiver reaction: (1) pleasure, (2) displeasure, (3) interest but neither pleasure nor displeasure, or (4) no interest.

After a message (letter, memorandum, report, or speech) has been classified into one of the preceding categories, the next question is "Should the central idea be placed in the beginning sentence?" If so, present the message deductively; if not, present the message inductively.

When messages begin with the major idea, the sequence of ideas is called **deductive**. When messages withhold the major idea until accompanying details and explanations have been presented, the sequence is called **inductive**.

Consider the receiver to determine whether to use the inductive or deductive sequence. If a receiver might be antagonized by the main idea in a deductive message, antagonism can be avoided by leading up to the main idea (making the message inductive). If a writer wants to encourage receiver involvement (to generate a little concern about where the details are leading), the inductive approach is recommended. Inductive organization can be especially effective if the main idea confirms the conclusion the receiver has drawn from the preceding details—a cause is worthy of support, an applicant should be interviewed for a job, a product/service should be selected, etc. As you write letters and memorandums

Can you identify each of the four receiver reactions by reading the nonverbal expressions of the four managers in Figure 7-2?

The *deductive* sequence begins with the main idea; the *inductive* sequence begins with the explanation and details.

When do you use the deductive and inductive sequences?

FIGURE 7-2
Four receiver reactions.

C O M M U N I C A T I O N   M E N T O R

Written communication is required in any corporation. While a meeting can be a good communications tool, written correspondence is more effective—and permanent.

Terence E. McSweeney
Director of Communications
PGA of America

in Chapters 9-12, you will comprehend the benefits of using the appropriate outline for each receiver reaction:

Write Deductively (main idea first)	Write Inductively (details first)
When the message will *please* the receiver	When the message will *displease* the receiver
When the message is *routine* (will neither please nor displease)	When the receiver *may not be interested* (will need to be persuaded)

THINK IT OVER
Would you use the deductive or the inductive approach to (a) accept an invitation to speak, (b) deny credit to a customer, and (c) commend an employee for exemplary performance?

Minor ideas should be arranged in a systematic sequence.

For determining the sequence of minor ideas that accompany the major idea, the following bases for paragraph sequence are common:

1. *Time.* When reporting on a series of events or a process, paragraphs proceed from the first step through the last step.
2. *Space.* If a report is about geographic areas, paragraphs can proceed from one area to the next until all areas have been discussed.
3. *Familiarity.* If a topic is complicated, the report can begin with a point that is known or easy to understand and proceed to progressively more difficult points.
4. *Importance.* In analytical reports in which major decision-making factors are presented, the factors can be presented in order of most important to least important, or vice versa.
5. *Value.* If a report involves major factors with monetary values, paragraphs can proceed from those with greatest values to those with least values, or vice versa.

Although the principal focus is on writing, the same sequence-of-idea patterns are recommended for *oral* communication. These patterns are applicable in memorandums, e-mail, and reports as well as in letters.

WRITING THE FIRST DRAFT

Once you have determined whether the message should be presented deductively (main idea first) or inductively (explanation and details first) and planned the logical sequence of minor points, you are ready to begin composing the message.

COMMUNICATION IN ACTION

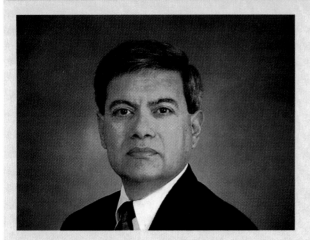

R. D. Saenz, Business Consultant

According to the Department of Labor, proficiency in verbal and written business communication skills is considered a new "key basic" in the workplace today. According to R. D. Saenz, the accounting profession is no exception. A consultant with a degree in accounting, Saenz spent nearly 11 years at Price Waterhouse, one of the top six accounting firms in the U.S. Having also been employed nine years in private industry, he knows that a college degree or advanced professional certification alone no longer meets basic required skills in the workplace.

While working as audit senior manager at Price Waterhouse, Saenz was directly involved in employee professional development. His duties involved more than developing employees technically in accounting. He worked with all facets of formal evaluation, which involved written and verbal communication. He took note of strengths and weaknesses of supervisory employees. He worked with the "cream-of-the-crop" employees who had degrees from prestigious universities. Based on the employees' backgrounds, levels of intelligence, and levels of achievement, he was sometimes appalled at their lack of ability to communicate through writing skills. He notes, "Grammatical errors quickly detract from the credibility of the writer. Errors cast a cloud over that individual's ability or competence."

One way Saenz developed employees professionally was by focusing intently on clear writing. He responded to those who needed help with writing skills. When employees explained an exception to a policy, drafted a memo about procedures, or explained a resolution, Saenz responded to their writing. If a written report were done incorrectly, he provided positive comments on why it was wrong. His comments were light hearted but professional with an appropriate tone. He set high standards for his employees and tried to communicate his knowledge of clear, concise, correct writing to them.

Saenz acquired his interest in using words effectively at an early age. Reading by the time he was four years old, he read material advanced for his age. As a youth, he liked the precision of how words can be used and naturally gravitated toward the appropriate use of words. He said, "I'm a fanatic about parallel construction. From how many people have you heard that statement?"

Still a voracious reader, Saenz finds many common connecting chords between communication and his consulting work. Saenz believes that effective word use is fundamental to the workplace. He knows that verbal and written skills of preciseness, simplicity, parallelism, and tone must be "second nature" to an accountant. Without these skills, employees simply will not succeed. The workplace of today has changed, he notes. "Employees must have more than the technical aptitude of accounting. They must also have proficiency in oral and written communication skills."

Applying What You Have Learned

1. Why does Saenz consider proficiency in oral and written communication skills basic to the accounting profession today?

2. Saenz commented that "grammatical errors quickly detract from the credibility of the writer." How might the credibility of a writer be "detracted" by grammatical errors?

3. Assume that you are an employee for a large accounting firm. Your duties include careful consideration of any employee's written work that leaves your office. Following Saenz's example, discuss some considerations to keep in mind when commenting about another employee's writing.

Normally, writing rapidly (with intent to rewrite certain portions if necessary) is better than slow, deliberate writing (with intent to avoid any need for rewriting portions). The latter approach can be time consuming and frustrating. Thinking of one way to express an idea, discarding it either before or after it is written, waiting for new inspiration, stopping to read and reread preceding sentences—these time-consuming habits can reduce the quality of the finished work.

Recall your own writing experiences. Which was more pleasant for you: (1) the time spent writing a sentence or (2) the time spent between sentences? Because the time spent between sentences can be unproductive or frustrating, that time should be reduced or eliminated. For most people, writing rapidly with the intent to rewrite certain portions if necessary is the better approach by far.

Experienced writers believe that there is no such thing as good writing, but there is such a thing as a good rewriting. If you are composing at the computer, you can quickly and easily revise your first draft on the computer screen. Electronic spellchecks available with word-processing software and writing-analysis software aid in locating spelling, typographical, and grammatical errors. Systematic revision procedures (to be covered in Chapter 8) will help you produce error-free documents that reflect positively on your company and yourself.

THINK IT OVER
In groups, discuss which of these writing methods works most effectively for each of you. What habits hinder your success or enjoyment of writing? How can you overcome them?

Author Dorothy Parker once said of her own writing, "I can't write five words that I change seven" (Charlton, 1985).

Writing Powerful Sentences

LEARNING OBJECTIVE 6

Well-written sentences will help the receiver understand the message clearly and react favorably to the writer or speaker. The following principles affect the clarity and human relations of your message: (1) use correct sentence structure, (2) rely on active voice, and (3) emphasize important points.

USE CORRECT SENTENCE STRUCTURE
The following discussion identifies problems and techniques business writers encounter frequently. For a complete review of sentences, study Appendix B or consult an English handbook.

All sentences have at least two parts: *subject* and *verb*.

Subject	Verb
Sally	transferred.
The recession	continued.

In addition to a subject and a verb, a sentence may have additional words to complete the meaning. These words are called **complements**:

Subject	Verb	Complement
Sid	transferred	overseas.
Chien	transferred	to our Hong Kong office.

Observe from the preceding examples that a complement may be expressed in one word (the first sentence) or more than one word (the second).

A group of words that is not a complete sentence is called a **phrase** or a **clause**. A phrase does not include a subject and a verb; a clause does. In the following sentences, the phrases are underlined:

One <u>of the workers</u> was absent.

The people <u>in that room</u> have voted.

The electrician fell <u>while replacing the socket</u>.

In each of the following clauses, the subject is underlined once and the verb is underlined twice:

As the <u>president</u> <u><u>reported</u></u> this morning . . .

If <u>construction</u> <u><u>is begun</u></u> soon...

Clauses are divided into two categories: *dependent* and *independent*. A **dependent clause** does not convey a complete thought. The preceding illustrations are dependent. An **independent clause** conveys a complete thought; it could be a complete sentence if presented alone:

Could a dependent clause serve as a complete sentence?

Dependent Clause	Independent Clause
As the president reported this morning,	sales increased in May.

Dependent Clause	Independent Clause
If construction is begun soon,	the job can be completed by the end of the year.

The independent clause "sales increased in May" can be stated as a separate sentence. The dependent clause "As the president reported this morning" does not convey a complete thought and should not be presented without the remainder of the sentence. When a **sentence fragment** (a portion of a sentence) is presented as a separate sentence, receivers become confused and distracted.

Sentences fall into four categories: simple, compound, complex, and compound-complex.

The four sentence types are used to add variety and to place emphasis where needed. Can you classify sentences by type?

Simple:

Independent Clause

The union has gone on strike.

Compound:

Independent Clause | Independent Clause

The union has gone on strike, and all manufacturing lines have stopped production.

Complex:

Dependent Clause | Independent Clause

Because contract terms cannot be reached, the union has gone on strike.

Compound-complex:

Dependent Clause | Independent Clause

Because contract terms cannot be reached, the union has gone

Independent Clause

on strike; but a settlement is expected at the end of the week.

In the preceding examples, note the use of punctuation to separate one clause from another. When no punctuation or coordinate conjunction appears between the clauses, the result is a **run-on sentence** or **fused sentence**. Another problem is the **comma splice**, in which the clauses are joined only with a comma instead of a comma and coordinate conjunction or a semicolon.

Review these punctuation rules carefully. Writing run-on sentences and comma splices could reflect quite negatively on your ability.

Run-On or Fused Sentence	Corrected Sentence
New forms have been ordered they should be delivered next Friday.	New forms have been ordered. They should be delivered next Friday.
	New forms have been ordered, and they should be delivered next Friday.
	New forms have been ordered; they should be delivered next Friday.
	The new forms, which were ordered last week, should be delivered next Friday.

Comma Splice	Corrected Sentence
The number of questions has been reduced from 15 to 5, the task will require 25 percent less time.	Because the number of questions has been reduced from 15 to 5, the task will require 25 percent less time.

RELY ON ACTIVE VOICE

Writers normally use active voice more heavily than passive voice because active voice conveys ideas more vividly. In sentences in which the subject is the *doer* of action, the verbs are called **active**. In sentences in which the subject is the *receiver* of action, the verbs are called **passive.**

In the following example, the sentence in the left column uses passive voice; the right, active voice:

Try to write in active voice most of the time. Using active voice suggests to the receiver that you are action-oriented and decisive.

Passive Voice	Active Voice
<u>Reports</u> are transferred electronically from remote locations to the home office.	Our <u>sales reps</u> transfer reports electronically from remote locations to the home office.

The active sentence invites the receiver to see the sales reps using a computer to complete a report. The passive sentence draws attention to a report. Using active voice makes the subject the actor, which makes the idea easier to understand. Sentences written using passive voice give receivers a less-distinct picture. In the passive sentence, the receiver becomes aware that something was done to the reports, but it does not reveal who did it.

Even when a passive sentence contains additional words to reveal the doer, the imagery is less distinct than it would be if the sentence were active:

Reports compiled by our sales representatives are transferred electronically from remote locations to the home office.

"Joan plays tennis" is active voice because Joan is performing the action. "The tennis game is being played by Joan" is passive voice because the action is being done to Joan.

THINK IT OVER
Write several active and passive voice sentences and note the difference in the vividness of the sentences.

"Reports" gets the most attention because it is the subject. The sentence seems to let a receiver know the *result* of action before revealing the doer; therefore, the sentence is less emphatic.

Although active voice conveys ideas more vividly, passive voice is useful

1. In concealing the doer ("The reports have been compiled").
2. In placing more emphasis on *what* was done and what it was *done to* than on *who did* it ("The reports have been compiled by our sales representatives").
3. In subordinating an unpleasant thought ("The Shipping Department has not been notified of this delay" rather than "You have not notified the Shipping Department of this delay.") Review the previous discussion of using passive voice to de-emphasize negative ideas on pages 188-189.

EMPHASIZE IMPORTANT IDEAS

A landscape artist wants some features in a picture to stand out boldly and others to get little attention. A musician sounds some notes loudly and others softly. Likewise, a writer or speaker wants some ideas to be *emphasized* and others to be *de-emphasized*. Normally, pleasant and important ideas should be emphasized; unpleasant and insignificant ideas should be de-emphasized. Emphasis techniques include sentence structure, repetition, words that label, position, space, format, and punctuation.

SENTENCE STRUCTURE.   Like clarity, emphasis is influenced by sentence structure. Which sentence places more emphasis on the idea of Gene's taking a job?

Gene took a job in insurance.

Gene took a job in insurance, but he really preferred a job in accounting.

The first sentence has one independent clause. Because no other idea competes with it for attention, its idea is emphasized. *For emphasis, place an idea in a simple sentence.*

Which of the following sentences places more emphasis on the idea of Gene's taking a job?

Gene took a job in insurance, but he really preferred a job in accounting.
Although he took a job in insurance, Gene really preferred a job in accounting.

Note that the first sentence is compound; the second, complex. In the first sentence, the idea of taking a job is in an independent clause. Because an independent clause makes sense if the rest of the sentence is omitted, an independent clause is more emphatic than a dependent clause. In the second sentence, the idea of taking a job is in a dependent clause. By itself, the clause would not make complete sense. Compared with the independent clause that follows ("Gene really preferred . . ."), the idea in the dependent clause is de-emphasized. *For emphasis, place an idea in an independent clause; for de-emphasis, place an idea in a dependent clause.*

REPETITION.   Which sentence places more emphasis on the idea of *success?*

The project was successful because of. . .

The project was successful; this success is attributed to . . .

In the second sentence a form of "success" is repeated. *To emphasize a word, let it appear more than once in a sentence.*

WORDS THAT LABEL.   Another way to emphasize or de-emphasize an idea is to include words that label it:

> But most important of all . . .
> A less significant aspect was . . .

For emphasis or de-emphasis, use words that label ideas as significant or insignificant.

POSITION.   In each pair, which sentence places more emphasis on the words *success* and *failure?*

> The project was a <u>success</u>; without your efforts, it would have been a <u>failure</u>.
> Your efforts contributed to the <u>success</u> of the project; otherwise, <u>failure</u> would have been the result.
>
> <u>Success</u> resulted from your efforts; <u>failure</u> would have resulted without them.
> The project was <u>successful</u> because of your efforts; without them, <u>failure</u> would have been the result.

In the first sentence, "success" and "failure" appear as the *last* words in their clauses. In the third sentence, "success" and "failure" appear as the *first* words in their clauses. For attention, words that appear first compete only with words that follow; words that appear last compete only with words that precede.

In paragraphs, the first and last words are in particularly emphatic positions. An idea that deserves emphasis can be placed in either position, but an idea that does not deserve emphasis can be placed in the middle of a long paragraph. The word *I*, which is frequently overused in messages, is especially noticeable if it appears as the first word. *I* is more noticeable if it appears as the first word in *every* paragraph. *However* is to be avoided as the first word in a paragraph if the preceding paragraph is neutral or positive. This word implies that the next idea will be negative. Unless the purpose is to place emphasis on negatives, such words as *denied, rejected*, and *disappointed* should not appear as the last words in a paragraph.

Likewise, the central idea of a talk or a report appears in the introduction (the beginning) and the conclusion (the end). Good transition sentences synthesize ideas at the end of each major division. *To emphasize a word or an idea, position it first or last in a sentence, clause, paragraph, or composition (letter, memo, e-mail, report, or speech).*

SPACE.   The various divisions of a report or speech are not expected to be of equal length, but an extraordinary amount of space devoted to a topic attaches special significance to that topic. Similarly, a topic that gets an exceedingly small amount of space is de-emphasized.

THINK IT OVER
What hidden message (metacommunication) is communicated by a message in which all paragraphs begin with *I*?

Where are the emphatic positions in sentences, paragraphs, compositions, and speeches?

FORMAT.   In the following sentences, the ideas are the same; but the emphasis is different:

> The personnel problems have been narrowed into three categories: absenteeism, tardiness, and pilferage.

> The personnel problems have been narrowed into three categories: (1) absenteeism, (2) tardiness, and (3) pilferage.

What is the effect of placing a number before each unit in a series?

In the second sentence, words preceded by numbers get special attention. Numbers or words are easier to locate when the page is reviewed. If the preceding and following sentences on a page contain no numbers, words with numbers take on special significance. The significance can be magnified even further:

> The personnel problems have been narrowed into three categories:
> * Absenteeism
> * Tardiness
> * Pilferage

The preceding example is *tabulated*; that is, the units of a series are placed in a column and may be indented (instead of being placed side by side). Because each unit in the series is on a line by itself (where it does not have to compete for attention) and because the arrangement consumes more space on the page, a tabulated series attracts attention. The items may be preceded by numbers, letters, asterisks, or various types of bullets (•, □, ✔ , ♦ , and so on), depending on the software being used. *To emphasize units in a series, place a number, letter, or bullet before each element; tabulate the series for further emphasis.*

When other ideas are in paragraph form, tabulated ideas are emphatic.

In paragraphs, sentences can be numbered and tabulated with the same effect. For example, a long report could close with a concluding paragraph that restates four supporting reasons for a conclusion. The reasons can be emphasized by

* Placing each reason on a separate indented line.
* Beginning each line (reason) with a number, letter, or bullet.
* Adding extra space (about one blank line) between each reason.

In the following example, note that the paragraph in the right column places increased emphasis on the reasons:

Less Emphasis on Reasons	**More Emphasis on Reasons**
For our needs, then, the most appropriate in-service training method is computerized instruction. This training is least expensive, allows employees to remain at their own workstations while improving their skills, affords constant awareness of progress, and lets employees progress at their own rates.	Computerized instruction is the most appropriate in-service training method because it • Is least expensive. • Allows employees to remain at their own workstations while improving their skills. • Affords constant awareness of progress. • Lets employees progress at their own rates.

Within paragraphs, emphasize a sentence by placing it first or last or by assigning it a number or bullet in a tabulated series.

Ideas that appear in headings get more attention than ideas that do not. Ideas that appear in subheadings are less emphatic than ideas that appear in major headings—a factor that should be taken into account at the outline stage. **Talking headings** (headings that reveal the conclusions reached in the following discussion) are more emphatic than general topic headings. For example, "Costs Are Prohibitive" is more emphatic than "Cost Factors."

Ideas presented in graphs, charts, tables, or pictures are emphatic. Some ideas are presented more clearly in such devices, and the contrast in appearance is appealing. You will gain proficiency in displaying complex information in appropriate graphics in Chapter 16.

PUNCTUATION.   Careful writers use punctuation marks for emphasis and de-emphasis, particularly when sentences contain appositives. An **appositive** is a word that purposefully repeats or explains a preceding word. After reading each of the following sentences, try to decide whether the appositive (leadership) is emphasized or de-emphasized.

Companies are seeking job applicants with a specific skill (leadership).

Companies are seeking job applicants with a specific skill, leadership.

Companies are seeking job applicants with a specific skill—leadership.

Companies are seeking job applicants with a specific skill: leadership.

Parentheses label an idea as parenthetical; it could be left out. An idea that could be omitted is not thought of as particularly important. Use of parentheses is like saying "The skill is not especially important, but just in case it is of interest, here it is." The comma in the second sentence implies neither emphasis nor de-emphasis. "Specific skill" and "leadership" are of about equal importance. The dash in the third sentence is considered a strong mark of punctuation; it is longer and stronger than a comma. In oral presentations, a word preceded by a long pause gets special emphasis. Likewise, a dash attaches special emphasis to an appositive. The colon in the last sentence serves the same purpose as the dash. A colon is a strong mark of punctuation that serves to magnify the appositive. *For appositives, use parentheses for de-emphasis, a comma for neutral emphasis, and a dash or colon for emphasis.*

> Describe four ways to punctuate an appositive and the emphasis provided by each mark.

> **THINK IT OVER**
> Complete Exercises 16-25 to check your understanding of emphasis.

Developing Coherent Paragraphs

Well-constructed sentences are combined into paragraphs that discuss a portion of the topic being discussed. To write effective paragraphs, you must learn to develop deductive or inductive paragraphs consistently, link ideas to achieve coherence, keep paragraphs unified, and vary sentence and paragraph length.

POSITION THE TOPIC SENTENCE APPROPRIATELY

Typically, paragraphs contain one sentence that identifies the portion of the topic being discussed and presents the central idea. That sentence is commonly called a **topic sentence**. For example, consider a pamphlet written to a company that has purchased a cellular phone. The overall topic is how to get satisfactory performance from the machine. One portion of that topic is assembly. Sentences that list the steps can appear as one paragraph, perhaps with steps numbered as follows:

"To assemble your new answering machine, take the following steps:
1.   Insert . . .
2.   Press . . . ."

Another portion (paragraph) discusses operation; another, service. Within each paragraph, one sentence serves a special function.

A topic sentence may be placed at the *beginning* or *end* of a paragraph.

If a paragraph is inductive, might a receiver know the content of the topic sentence before reading it?

In this illustration, the paragraphs are **deductive**; that is, the topic sentence *precedes* details. When topic sentences *follow* details, the paragraphs are called **inductive paragraphs**. As discussed previously, the receiver's likely reaction (pleased, displeased, interested, not initially interested) to the main idea aids in determining the appropriate sequence.

When the subject matter is complicated and the details are numerous, paragraphs sometimes begin with a main idea, follow with details, and end with a summarizing sentence. But the main idea may not be in the first sentence; the idea may need a preliminary statement. Receivers appreciate consistency in the placement of topic sentences. Once they catch on to the writer's pattern, they know where to look for main ideas.

These suggestions seldom apply to the first and last sentences of letters. Such sentences frequently appear as single-sentence paragraphs. But for reports and long paragraphs of letters, *strive for paragraphs that are consistently deductive or consistently inductive.* Regardless of which is selected, topic sentences are clearly linked with details that precede or follow.

LINK IDEAS TO ACHIEVE COHERENCE

Careful writers use coherence techniques to keep receivers from experiencing abrupt changes in thought. Although the word **coherence** is used sometimes to mean "clarity" or "understandability," it is used throughout this text to mean "cohesion." If writing or speaking is coherent, the sentences stick together; and each sentence is in some way linked to the preceding sentences. *Avoid abrupt changes in thought, and link each sentence to a preceding sentence.*

The following techniques for linking sentences are common:

What techniques are useful for achieving coherence?

1. Repeat a word that was used in the preceding sentence. The second sentence in the following example is an obvious continuation of the idea presented in the preceding sentence.

   . . . to take responsibility for the decision. This responsibility can be shared . . .

2. Use a pronoun that represents a noun used in the preceding sentence. Because "it" means "responsibility," the second sentence is linked directly with the first.

   . . . to take this responsibility. It can be shared. . . .

3. Use such connecting words as *however, therefore, yet, nevertheless, consequently, also, in addition,* and so on. "However" implies "We're continuing with the same topic, just moving into a contrasting phase."

> **. . . to take this responsibility. However, few are willing to . . .**

Remember, though, that good techniques can be *over*used. Unnecessary connectors are space consuming and distracting. Usually they can be spotted (and crossed out) in proofreading.

Just as sentences within a paragraph must link, paragraphs within a document must also link. Unless a writer (or speaker) is careful, the move from one major topic to the next will seem abrupt. A good transition sentence can bridge the gap between the two topics by summing up the preceding topic and leading a receiver to expect the next topic:

> **Cost factors, then, seemed prohibitive until efficiency factors were investigated.**

This sentence could serve as a transition between the "Cost" division heading and the "Efficiency" division heading. Because a transition sentence comes at the end of one segment and before the next, it emphasizes the central idea of the preceding segment and confirms the relationship of the two segments.

Transition sentences are very helpful if properly used, but they can be overused. For most reports, transition sentences before major headings are sufficient. Normally, transition sentences before subheadings are unnecessary. Having encountered the previous subheading only a few lines back, a receiver should readily see its relationship to the upcoming subheading. In addition, transition sentences typically summarize, and the discussion under a subheading of a report is seldom long enough to merit summarization. *Place transition sentences before major headings.*

KEEP PARAGRAPHS UNIFIED

Receivers expect the first paragraph of a message to introduce a topic, additional paragraphs to discuss it, and a final paragraph to tie them together. The in-between paragraphs should be arranged in a systematic sequence, and the end must be linked easily to some word or idea presented in the beginning. The effect of a message that is *not* unified is like that of an incomplete circle or a picture with one element obviously missing.

A letter or report with unity covers its topic adequately but will not include extraneous material. The letter or report will have a beginning sentence appropriate for the expected receiver reaction, paragraphs that present the bulk of the message, and an ending sentence that is an appropriate closing for the message presented. If the sequence is logical, coherence is easy to achieve.

A report with unity begins with an introduction that identifies the topic, reveals the thesis, and previews upcoming points. The introduction may also include some background, sources of information, and the method of treating data. Between the beginning and the ending, a unified report will have paragraphs arranged in a systematic sequence. A summary or conclusion brings all major points together.

> **THINK IT OVER**
> Which is more likely to contain transition sentences: a *letter* or a *report?*

Are transition sentences needed between *sub*topics?

What is unity?

VARY SENTENCE AND PARAGRAPH LENGTH

Short, average-length sentences are easy to read and preferred for communicating clearly. However, keeping *all* sentences short is undesirable because the message may sound monotonous, unrealistic, or elementary. A two-word sentence is acceptable; so is a 60-word sentence—if it is clear. Just as sentences should vary in length, they should also vary in structure. Some complex or compound sentences should be included with simple sentences. You will learn more about the relationship between sentence length and readability in Chapter 8.

Generally, limit paragraphs to eight to ten lines.

Variety is just as desirable in paragraph length as it is in sentence length. A paragraph can be from one line in length to a dozen lines or more. However, just as average sentence length should be kept fairly short, average paragraph length also should be kept short.

Paragraphs in business letters or memos are typically shorter than paragraphs in business reports. First and last paragraphs are normally short (one to four lines), and other paragraphs are normally no longer than six lines. A short first paragraph makes a letter or memo look more inviting to read than a long first paragraph. A short last paragraph enables a writer to emphasize parting thoughts.

What is the advantage of writing short first paragraphs in letters?

In business reports, the space between paragraphs is a welcome resting spot. Long paragraphs are difficult to read and make a page appear unattractive. Paragraph length will vary depending on the complexity of the subject matter. However, as a general rule paragraphs should be no longer than eight to ten lines. This length usually allows enough space to include a topic sentence and three or four supporting statements. If the topic cannot be discussed in this space, divide the topic into additional paragraphs.

To illustrate the effect large sections of unbroken text has on the overall appeal of a document, examine the memos in Figure 7-3 that contain identical information. Without question, the memo with the short, easy-to-read paragraphs is more inviting to read than the memo with the one bulky paragraph. Generally, *strive for short paragraphs, but vary their lengths.*

Should consistency be sacrificed to achieve variety?

Although variety is a desirable quality, it should not be achieved at the expense of consistency. Using *I* in one part of a letter and then without explanation switching to *we* is inadvisable. Using the past tense in one sentence and the present tense in another sentence creates variety at the expense of consistency—unless the shift is required to indicate actual changes in time. Unnecessary changes from active to passive voice (or vice versa) and from third to second person (or vice versa) are also discouraged.

Bulky Text   **Broken Text**

TO: All Employees

FROM: Sid Hewlette, Manager *SH*

DATE: December 15, 19--

SUBJECT: EXTRA VACATION DAY

The board of directors has approved
one additional vacation day for every
employee. This decision is our way of
expressing gratitude for the most
productive and profitable year in the
history of Barger Corporation. With the
approval of your department head, you
may select any day between January 2
and June 30. This day of vacation is in
addition to year-end bonuses you will
receive soon. Thank you for all you
have done to make the year successful,
and best wishes for a healthy and happy
new year.

TO: All Employees

FROM: Sid Hewlette, Manager *SH*

DATE: December 15, 19--

SUBJECT: EXTRA VACATION DAY

The board of directors has approved
one additional vacation day for every
employee.

This decision is our way of expressing
gratitude for the most productive and
profitable year in the history of Barger
Corporation. With the approval of your
department head, you may select any day
between January 2 and June 30. This day
of vacation is in addition to year-end
bonuses you will receive soon.

Thank you for all you have done to make
the year successful, and best wishes for a
healthy and happy new year.

FIGURE 7-3   Bulky vs. broken text. What hidden message is conveyed?

SUMMARY

1 **Writing is a systematic process that begins
by your determining the purpose of the
message (central idea) and identifying how the
central idea will likely affect the receiver.** In view
of its effect on the reader, you can determine the
appropriate channel for sending a particular message
(face-to-face, telephone, letter/memo, e-mail, voice
mail, or fax).

2 **Envisioning your audience (having a strong
mental picture of your audience) is the second step in the writing process.** Before you com-

pose the first draft, consider all you know about the
receiver including age, economic level, educational/
occupational background, culture, existing relationship, expectations, and his/her needs.

3 **The insights you gain from seeking to understand your receiver will allow you to adapt
the message to fit the receiver's needs.** You will
assume an empathetic attitude, focus on the receiver's
point of view rather than your own, use bias-free
language, avoid statements that destroy goodwill, and
project a positive, tactful tone.

4 Writing is easier if you outline the message first; that is, identify the ideas and the appropriate sequence. Outlining encourages brevity and accuracy, permits concentration on one phase at a time, saves time writing, increases confidence to complete the task, and facilitates appropriate emphasis of ideas. From a reader's point of view, well-organized messages are easier to understand and promote a more positive attitude toward the writer.

5 A part of the outlining process is deciding whether the message should be deductive (main idea first) or inductive (explanations and details first). When the receiver is expected to be pleased by the message, the main idea is presented first and details follow. Likewise, when the message is routine and not likely to arouse a feeling of pleasure or displeasure, the main idea is presented first.

When the receiver can be expected to be displeased or not initially interested, explanations and details precede the main idea.

6 Well-written sentences and unified and coherent paragraphs will help the receiver understand the message clearly and respond favorably. To write powerful sentences, use correct sentence structure, rely on active voice, and emphasize important points. To write effective paragraphs, develop deductive or inductive paragraphs consistently, link ideas to achieve coherence, keep paragraphs unified, and vary sentence and paragraph length.

Refer to the "Check Your Writing" checklist to review the guidelines for writing a first draft of the message that should be easily understood and positively received.

CHECK YOUR WRITING

FOCUS ON THE RECEIVER'S POINT OF VIEW
☐ Present ideas from the receiver's point of view; this "you attitude" conveys a feeling that the message is specifically for the receiver.

BIAS-FREE LANGUAGE
☐ Do not use the pronoun *he* when referring to a group of people that may include women.
☐ Avoid referring to males and females in sterotyped roles and occupations.
☐ Avoid expressions that reflect stereotypical characteristics.
☐ Avoid using gender-biased occupational titles or differentiating genders in an occupation.
☐ Avoid referring to group (race and ethnic group, age, religion, and disability) in stereotypical and insensitive ways.
☐ Do not emphasize race and ethnic group, age, religion, or disability when these factors are not relevant.

STATEMENTS THAT DAMAGE GOODWILL
☐ Avoid using condescending words.
☐ Use euphemisms when the purpose is to present unpleasant thoughts politely and positively.

☐ Avoid using euphemisms when they will be taken as excessive or sarcastic.
☐ Give sincere compliments.
☐ Avoid using flattery.
☐ Avoid using demeaning expressions.
☐ Rely mainly on denotative words or connotative words that will elicit a favorable reaction.
☐ Avoid expressing surprise, doubt, and judgment when they would be interpreted as insults.
☐ Avoid expressing certainty when certainty is hardly possible.

POSITIVE, TACTFUL TONE
☐ Rely mainly on positive words that speak of what can be done instead of what cannot be done, of the pleasant instead of the unpleasant. When the purpose is to sharpen contrast or when positive words have not evoked the desired reaction, use negative words.
☐ Use second person and active voice to emphasize a pleasant idea. For better human relations, avoid using second person for presenting negative ideas. Instead,

use third person and passive voice to de-emphasize the unpleasant thought.

☐ Consider stating an unpleasant thought in the subjunctive mood.

POWERFUL SENTENCES

☐ Use correct structure when writing simple, compound, complex, and compound-complex sentences. Avoid run-on sentences and comma splices.

☐ Use active voice to present important points or to present pleasant ideas and passive verbs to present less-significant points or to present unpleasant ideas.

☐ Emphasize important ideas:
  ☐ Place an idea in a simple sentence.
  ☐ Place an idea in an independent clause; for de-emphasis, place an idea in a dependent clause.
  ☐ Use an important word more than once in a sentence.
  ☐ Place an important idea first or last in a sentence, paragraph, or document.
  ☐ Precede each unit in a series by a number, a letter, or a bullet; for stronger emphasis, tabulate.

☐ Use parentheses for de-emphasis, a comma for neutral emphasis, and a dash or colon for emphasizing appositives.

☐ Use words that label ideas as significant or insignificant.

☐ Use headings, graphics, and additional space to emphasize important ideas.

COHERENT PARAGRAPHS

☐ Write deductively if a message will likely please or at least not displease. If a message will likely displease or if understanding the major idea is dependent on prior explanations, write inductively.

☐ Strive for paragraphs that are consistently deductive or consistently inductive.

☐ Make sure compositions form a unit with an obvious beginning, middle, and ending and that in-between paragraphs are arranged in a systematic sequence.

☐ Avoid abrupt changes in thought, and link each sentence to a preceding sentence. Place transition sentences before major headings.

☐ Vary sentence and paragraph length to emphasize important ideas. Limit paragraphs to eight to ten lines to maximize comprehension.

REFERENCES

Amemiya, H., & Aizu, I. (1985, October 7). Defining a good Japanese user manual. *Intercom* (Society for Technical Communication newsletter), *33*, p. 7. In Subbiah, M. (1992). Adding a new dimension to the teaching of audience analysis: Cultural awareness. *IEEE, 35* (1), 14-17.

Carnegie, D. (1964). *How to win friends and influence people.* New York: Simon & Schuster.

Charlton, J. (Ed.) (1985). *The writer's quotation book.* Stamford, CT: Ray Freeman and Company.

Dennett, J. T. (1988). Not to say is better than to say: How rhetorical structure reflects cultural context in Japanese-English technical writing. *IEEE Trans.*

Professional Communication, 31 (3), 116-119. In Subbiah, M. (1992). Adding a new dimension to the teaching of audience analysis: Cultural awareness. *IEEE, 35* (1), 14-17.

Lawlor, J. (1994, April 21). More firms offer services for employees. *USA Today*, p. B1-2.

Moody, P. G. (1987*). Skills for the electronic world—reach a little higher.* Cincinnati: South-Western Publishing Co.

Tyler, L. (1990). Communicating about people with disabilities: Does the language we use make a difference? *Bulletin of the Association of Business Communication, 53* (3), 65-67.

REVIEW QUESTIONS

1. What analogy is used to describe the purpose of a message? What are the major purposes of many business messages?
2. Why is selecting an appropriate communication channel important to the overall effectiveness of the message? Provide two examples.
3. How does envisioning the audience affect the message? What factors about the audience should you consider?
4. Define empathy.
5. List two ways empathy assists in business-related situations. Give two specific examples, personal experiences if possible.
6. Under what conditions would a euphemism be detrimental?
7. Under what conditions would connotative words be acceptable?
8. If a client or customer is obviously upset, what is wrong with your saying, "I'm sorry you are upset"?
9. What are the disadvantages of using expressions such as "*I* know you will want to . . ." and "*I am sure* you have . . ."?
10. Which is better for presenting a pleasant idea: (a) active voice or (b) passive voice? Explain.
11. What is the advantage of using a subjunctive mood for stating a negative idea?
12. When is negative language appropriate?
13. When is passive voice preferred over active voice?
14. Which provides more emphasis for an idea:
    a. A simple sentence or a complex sentence?
    b. An independent clause or a dependent clause?
    c. Parentheses or dashes?
    d. Tabulated arrangement or paragraph arrangement?
15. For a word that deserves emphasis, which position in a sentence is better? (a) Use the word as the first or last word in the sentence or (b) Place the word in the middle of the sentence.
16. Does tabulation assist in achieving emphasis? Explain.
17. What are the primary benefits of outlining before you write? How does the receiver benefit?
18. What questions should be answered before a writer decides whether to write deductively or inductively?
19. What is the distinction between deductive and inductive writing? Under what circumstances should each approach be used?
20. Is writing rapidly with intent to revise or writing slowly and deliberately more effective? Explain.
21. List some techniques for achieving coherence (a) within paragraphs and (b) among major sections of a composition.
22. Should paragraphs be uniform in length? Explain.
23. When a report stops abruptly without a "wrap-up" paragraph, which principle has been violated: (a) unity or (b) coherence?
24. What are the advantages of including transition sentences in a long report?
25. Complete each of the THINK IT OVER activities your instructor assigns.

EXERCISES

Each of the following sentences illustrates a weakness discussed in Chapter 7. (a) Using terminology presented in the chapter, identify the weakness. (b) Rewrite the sentence to eliminate the weakness. The following example illustrates the type of answer expected:

Example: You failed to sign the agreement.
Answers: a. Uses second person and active voice to convey a negative idea.
          b. The agreement must be signed.

1. Each accountant must submit his time and expense report by the 15th of each month.
2. That contractor has jewed many homebuilders by skimping on insulation and using substandard materials.
3. Kristi Delacruz, our new Puerto Rican sales rep, completed her management training in Austin.
4. Only disabled customers may use the motorized shopping carts.
5. It has been quite some time since I did this type of work, but I can help you for a while.
6. The senator's vote for the bill containing revenue enhancements does not violate her campaign pledge.
7. The computer hackers completed the network system conversion several days ahead of schedule.
8. The corporate watchdogs are planning a visit next week.
9. I am sure you will understand our reasons for refusal.
10. We realize that you are upset, but the fee is due on May 10.
11. The manager failed to sign the second copy of the engagement letter.
12. The corrected order cannot be sent until March 5.
13. You did not revise the report to include the latest sales projections for Model XL-31.
14. The consultant recommended a new marketing strategy it works much better than the strategy we formerly used.
15. This innovative advertisement was designed by J. D. McKay.

Application of Emphasis Techniques

Decide for each pair of sentences *which* one is preferred. *Why* is it preferred?

16. In which sentence does "credit" receive more emphasis?
    a. On June 7, we applied for credit.
    b. We applied for credit on June 7.
17. In which sentence does the idea of denial receive more emphasis?
    a. Although our application for credit was denied, we were encouraged to make cash purchases.
    b. Our application for credit was denied, but we were encouraged to make cash purchases.
18. Which sentence is more emphatic?
    a. Gene hit a home run in the ninth inning.
    b. A home run was hit in the ninth inning.
19. Which sentence is more emphatic?
    a. Congratulations on your recent honor.
    b. Congratulations on your receipt of the "outstanding student" award.
20. Which sentence is less emphatic?
    a. We appreciate your letting us know about your condition.
    b. We appreciate your letting us know about your migraine headaches, your shingles, and your broken thumb.
21. Which sentence places less emphasis on the negative?
    a. I will not help you with your presentation.
    b. I wish I could help you with your presentation.
22. Which sentence places more emphasis on "excuses"?
    a. We are not allowed to make one thing, excuses.
    b. We are not allowed to make one thing—excuses.
    c. We are not allowed to make one thing (excuses).
23. Which sentence is more emphatic?
    a. Miriam is expected to complete the projections tomorrow.
    b. The projections are expected to be completed tomorrow.
24. Which sentence is more emphatic?
    a. The market survey will be distributed on or before May 8.
    b. Distribution of the market survey is to be on or before May 8.
25. Which sentence places more emphasis on the units in the series?
    a. The firm has three needs: money, materials, and management.
    b. The firm has three needs: (1) money, (2) materials, and (3) management.

E-MAIL APPLICATION

Emoticons are icons created by keying combinations of symbols to produce "sideways" faces. These icons can be used to add humor to e-mail messages and to provide a lightened mood. Some examples of emoticons follow:

; .)	winking	% - (	confused
: - *	a kiss	:' - (	crying
: - b	sticking out tongue	8 -)	glasses
: - 0	shocked	: -)	smiling
= | : -	honest Abe	: - |	apathy
| - 0	asleep	: - ()	blabber mouth

Using selected emoticons, send a message that includes some "encoded" portions to a designated student in your class. Ask the student to reply with the interpretation.

CHAPTER 8

REVISING AND

PROOFREADING MESSAGES

OBJECTIVES

When you have completed Chapter 8, you will be able to

1 Edit and rewrite messages for vividness, clarity, and conciseness.

2 Identify factors affecting readability and revise messages to improve readability.

3 Revise and proofread a message for organization, content, style, mechanics, format, and layout.

Revising occupies much of a writer's time. Any manuscript—even a simple letter or memo—must be read and changed accordingly. Many times forgoing the editing or proofreading is tempting, but disaster often results from carelessness. The least that could happen might be a humorous misspelling on an internal memorandum. Although sometimes those little mistakes are amusing, incidents do occur that cause entire companies to suffer, either through negative perception by the public or actual dollars lost. For example, on May 10, 1993, Continental Airlines advertised in the *Boston Herald* one-way flights from Boston to Los Angeles for $48. Apparently, editors and copywriters from both Continental and the *Boston Herald* failed to catch the error; the advertisement should have read $148. *Advertising Age* reported that Continental's loss could be up to $4 million because approximately 20,000 round-trip tickets were sold at the advertised price, causing Continental to lose over $200 per ticket (Schmit, 1993).

Continental's mistake is only one example of how it pays—literally—to check and double check one's writing. Remember, writing *is* revising. Get accustomed to the idea that what you write will be changed. Learn to proofread your own work carefully and objectively; don't rely solely on your computer to catch mistakes. Finally, take advantage of grammar handbooks, dictionaries, and thesauruses. Like your speech or clothing, your writing is a reflection of you. It can cause you to appear sloppy, insensitive, or even ignorant—or it can prove that you are intelligent, resourceful, and careful. What will your writing say about you?

EDITING AND REWRITING

LEARNING OBJECTIVE 1

An owner of a successful public relations firm reported that clients seldom return work for revisions. The staff revises the document as many as five or six times to be certain that the material is written effectively and is grammatically correct before it is submitted to the client. This business executive and countless others have learned the invaluable lesson that poorly written business letters and reports reflect negatively on the reputation of the company. Errors distract the receiver from the message itself and thereby reduce the effectiveness of the document and reflect negatively on the person who writes it. The writer is responsible for checking each document for accuracy before sending it.

The writing principles presented in this chapter will help you revise your messages for vividness, clarity, conciseness, and readability. As a preliminary check to see how much you already know, complete the following Self-check. The sentences may also violate principles presented in Chapter 7 (receiver's point of view, bias-free language, statements that destroy goodwill, and positive tone).

CREATING VIVID IMAGES

To add energy and impact to your writing, paint vivid mental images that receivers will find exciting and will remember.

To help the receiver understand your message easily, carefully select words that paint intense, colorful word pictures. Creating clear mental images adds energy and imagination to your message, which tends to increase the overall impact of your message. To create vivid images, use specific words, select concrete nouns, eliminate clichés, and choose descriptive adjectives and adverbs.

SELF-CHECK

Cover the answers in the right column with a sheet of paper. Identify the error(s) in the words used in each sentence in the left column. Slide the cover sheet down and read the answer. Do your revisions agree with the answers given? The numbers in parentheses following the correct sentences refer to pages in the text where the writing principles are discussed.

EXAMPLE:

Send one of the gofers to pick up that report from the Tenth Street office.	Uses demeaning tone ("Gofers"). "Send one of the trainees (or assistants)" would not ridicule the person's position in the company. (184)
1. I am sure you will agree that the seminar was exceptional.	Uses unjustified expression of certainty. If the writer can be sure, the idea probably is known already and need not be stated. If the writer cannot be sure, the statement is not true. (185)
2. You neglected to specify your desired delivery date.	Uses second person and active voice to convey a negative idea. "Neglected" has a negative connotation. "Please inform us of your desired delivery date" explains what the reader must do to correct the situation. (186)
3. The top sales proposal was compiled by Maria.	Uses passive sentence, which places attention on the sales proposal. To place more emphasis on Maria's excellent work, use active voice: "Maria compiled the top sales proposal." (188)
4. An assessment of the problem was made by the production manager.	Uses an abstract noun as the subject and passive voice to convey an idea that does not need to be de-emphasized. "The production manager assessed the problem" is better. (214)
5. The *Communication Dispatch* is a very expensive magazine that will keep you updated on the latest communication technology.	Because of its vagueness, receivers will interpret "very expensive" differently. To convey a precise message, write "For $30 a year, the *Communication Dispatch* will . . ." (214)
6. Enclosed please find our latest price list.	"Enclosed please find" is a worn expression that implies something is hidden. "Refer to the enclosed price list for prices on our high-quality exercise equipment" is more effective. (215)
7. Remove the circular file from the path of perambulation.	The complex, formal words are confusing and may damage goodwill. "Remove the wastebasket from the aisle" is more effective. (219)
8. Hanging from a tree, the children saw a monkey.	The participial phrase dangles; that is, it isn't attached to the correct noun. As written, the sentence literally means that the children are hanging from a tree. "The children saw a monkey hanging from a tree" conveys the meaning the writer intended. (221)
9. There are four likely reasons for the drop in sales.	The sentence begins with an expletive (the meaningless word "there"). Better writing presents the noun first: "Four logical reasons for the drop in sales are . . ." (223)
10. I endorsed your check and deposited it.	The sentence conveys an idea that can be implied. "I deposited your check" is clear. (226)

This manager is aware that her writing skills, like her appearance, clothing, and speech, are a reflection of her proficiency as a professional. Your writing skills can prove that you are intelligent, careful, and resourceful; or they can portray you as inconsistent, insensitive, or ignorant.

Use Specific Words

Normally, specific words serve business writers better than general words. Specific words are more vivid:

General	Specific
Congratulations on your <u>recent honor</u>.	Congratulations on being named <u>employee of the month</u>.
Please submit the completed report <u>as soon as possible</u>.	Please submit the completed report by <u>March 15</u>.
Sales <u>skyrocketed</u> this month.	Sales <u>increased 10 percent</u> this month.

Sometimes, however, general words serve better than specific words:

General	Specific
Thank you for the explanation of your <u>financial status</u>.	Thank you for writing me about your <u>problems with creditors and the possibility of filing for bankruptcy</u>.
Frank told me about <u>what happened last week</u>.	Frank told me about <u>the tragedy in your family</u>.

When are general words preferred?

    In getting along with others, writers find general statements useful; they can keep negative ideas from getting more emphasis than they deserve. In addition, writers who don't have specific information or for some reason don't want to divulge it use general words. *For vivid business communication, use specific words.*

Select Concrete Nouns

Pay special attention to the underscored words in each pair of sentences. Which do you prefer, the first sentence or the second?

<u>Confirmation</u> of the date will be received from the president.

The <u>president</u> will confirm the date.

Excessive <u>travel</u> was listed by employees as their primary reason for resigning.

<u>Employees</u> listed excessive travel as their primary reason for resigning.

The first sentence in each pair uses an abstract noun as the subject; the second sentence uses a concrete noun as the subject. The subject is the main "actor" in a sentence. Therefore, the more vivid the subject is, the better. The abstract nouns "confirmation" and "travel" are hard to envision. Because the reader can easily envision "president" and "employees," the meaning of the second sentence in each pair comes through more clearly. Using an abstract noun as a sentence subject is certainly not an error. In fact, when an idea needs to be included but does not need emphasis, using an abstract noun as the subject may be desirable. Usually, however, writers and speakers will convey clearer messages if they *use concrete nouns as subjects.*

Eliminate Clichés + The old language of business.

Phrases that have become overused are called **clichés**. In each sentence, which phrase is well worn?

> **What is a cliché? How do clichés affect the effectiveness of a message?**

Pursuant to your request, the physical inventory was scheduled for May 3.

Please send a reply at your earliest convenience.

Enclosed please find a copy of my transcript.

"Pursuant to your request," "at your earliest convenience," and "enclosed please find" have been used so much that they no longer appear original. Now, look at the same sentences without the clichés:

<u>As you requested</u>, the physical inventory was scheduled for May 3.

Please send a reply by <u>Friday, November 5</u>.

<u>The enclosed transcript</u> should answer most of your questions.

Clichés can make reading monotonous and can make the writer or speaker seem like a copier. On the other hand, less frequently used words capture the reader's attention because they are original, fresh, and interesting.

Clichés present a more serious problem. Consider the following scenario:

> **What hidden message (metacommunication) might clichés convey?**

Kenneth is standing in line at a discount store. As the two shoppers in front of Kenneth prepare to leave, the cashier says, "Thanks for shopping with us today; please come again." After Kenneth pays for his merchandise, the cashier uses the same line. Because Kenneth knows the line has been used before, he may not consider the statement genuine. The cashier has used an expression that can be stated without thinking and possibly without meaning.

THINK IT OVER
In groups, generate a list of clichés used by friends, instructors, or co-workers. Discuss how you feel when these expressions are used frequently.

A worn expression can convey such messages as: "You are not special" or "For you, I won't bother to think; the phrases I use in talking with others are surely good enough for you."

Clichés are common in business communications, as the following examples show:

Clichés	Alternative Explanation
at an early date, in the near future	The expression is vague. Be specific. *Soon* is an improvement. Giving the exact date is more helpful.
at this time, at this writing, at this point in time	The expression means *now*, so why not say *now*? It is shorter and less overused. Furthermore, the words may imply (without the writer's intent) that *another* time is being considered.
attached please find, please find enclosed, you will find	These expressions seem to imply that something has been hidden or that locating it may be difficult. In addition, they usually tell what is known already—that the letter accompanies other material. References to enclosures can be made in sentences that also say something else, such as "Refer to page 7 of the enclosed folder to see the basic steps of operation."
I have your letter, your letter has been given to me for reply, we are in receipt of your letter, this letter is for the purpose of, this will acknowledge receipt of, I am writing to	These words are usually just space fillers that delay the real message. Omit them and get right to the point.
permit me to say, may I take this opportunity to say, take the liberty	Asking permission to make a statement is not necessary. Besides, asking permission and then immediately proceeding without it may imply that you are rude or are saying something that should not be said.
pursuant to your request, referring to your request, in reference to your letter	These expressions often appear at the beginning of letters. Receivers recognize them as coming from a person who says the same thing at the beginning of all letters. Referring to previous correspondence is more effective when done in an indirect manner. Instead of saying, "Pursuant to your January 21 request for a catalog, we are sending it to you today," say, "The catalog you requested on January 21 was mailed today."
please contact me if you have any further questions	If this expression says exactly what is meant and if the receiver has not encountered it frequently before, its use is not especially objectionable. However, it does have these disadvantages: (1) It implies doubt about whether other questions have been answered adequately, (2) it is especially out of place if the preceding discussion has not been about *questions*, and (3) it may encourage needless correspondence.

thanking you in advance	This presumptuous expression seems to say, "I know you will do as I have asked you to do. After you do it, I will be grateful." To express gratitude for expected or requested action, "I would appreciate your (action)" or "If you will (action), I would be grateful" are less worn and less objectionable phrases.
trusting you will, trusting this is, we hope, we trust, I hope, I trust	Not only are these expressions overused, they introduce the unpleasant idea of doubt as well. If you say, "I trust this is the information you wanted," you are suggesting your doubts; and the receiver may also begin to doubt. The expression should be omitted in most cases.
wish to, would like to	These words may convey *no* meaning, or they may convey the *wrong* meaning. "We wish to say that we have considered the idea" probably means "We have considered the idea." "We would like to recommend Mr. Clark" may be taken to mean either "We recommend Mr. Clark" or "Recommending Mr. Clark would be a pleasure, *if we could*."

The following list contains many other expressions that have become clichés:

above ("if the *above* is")	in regard to/relative to
along this line	in the event that
as a matter of fact	kindly (as in "kindly complete")
as the case may be	meet with your approval
as yet we have not heard from you	party (as in "another party wants")
at all times	please be advised that
claim, complaint	previous/prior to
due to the fact that	same (as in "have cashed same")
for your information	under separate cover
in accordance with	we regret to inform
in due course	would say
in terms of	

From a writer's or speaker's point of view, some of the preceding phrases are convenient; they can be used easily and quickly. However, to avoid monotony, to keep from seeming to have no originality, and to avoid possible human relations problems, *avoid clichés*.

THINK IT OVER
Identify expressions that have become clichés to you. Work to use them less frequently.

Choose Descriptive Adjectives and Adverbs

Compared with nouns and verbs, adjectives play a less-significant role in a sentence and present fewer problems in usage. However, adjectives and adverbs can arouse skepticism or resentment if they are used without care.

C O M M U N I C A T I O N   M E N T O R

The business world is full of people who can think and people who can communicate. We need to develop more people who can do both. Learning to think in our writing is difficult but important. To be able to organize our thoughts and communicate them to others is a worthwhile goal for all of us. It involves knowledge of vocabulary and grammar, organization skills, and conciseness. Communicating effectively does not mean writing or speaking volumes; it means conciseness and clarity.

The mission of the Financial Accounting Standards Board (FASB) is to establish and improve standards of financial accounting and reporting for the guidance and education of the public, including issuers, auditors, and users of financial information. Decisions about the allocation of resources rely heavily on credible, concise, and understandable financial information. Everything the FASB publishes is geared toward making financial information *clearer to read* and *easier to understand*.

Dennis R. Beresford, Chairman
Financial Accounting Standards Board

OVERLY STRONG ADJECTIVES AND ADVERBS

Using overly strong adjectives and adverbs may damage your credibility.

One common problem is the use of adjectives that are too strong or used too frequently:

Adjective	Adverb
Sales have been <u>fantastic</u>.	Our prices are <u>ridiculously</u> low.
Mr. Jones presented a <u>ridiculous</u> plan.	Our forecasts have been <u>fantastically</u> accurate.

Use of such adjectives and adverbs can cause a receiver to wonder about a sender's objectivity. A person who wants to report a highly satisfactory sales program should avoid "fantastic" and, instead, give details. Even though a plan may be worthy of ridicule, a person who comments on it is better off to point out areas needing improvement. By labeling a plan "ridiculous," a writer or speaker might risk being considered biased or overly negative. Communication is normally more effective if writers and speakers *avoid using adjectives and adverbs that are used too frequently by others, are overly strong, or are overly negative*.

SUPERLATIVES

What is a superlative?

Messages are sometimes influenced negatively by another form of adjective or adverb—the superlative. The **superlative** is the form of the adjective or adverb that compares the thing modified with two or more other things. Note the following superlatives:

Adjective	Adverb
This dryer is the <u>best</u> one on the market.	Yuan keys <u>fastest</u>.
The factory has the <u>worst</u> odor imaginable.	This item sells <u>best</u>.

Superlatives are very useful words. Frequently, the extreme unit in a series needs to be identified—the *highest* or *lowest* score, the *latest* news, the *most* qualified applicant. When superlatives are totally unsupported or unsupportable, however, their use is questionable. Furnishing proof that no other dryer is up to the standards of this one would be extremely difficult. Proving that one odor is the worst imaginable is practically impossible. Knowing that such statements are exaggerations, the receiver may not believe them at all. In fact, someone who has used a superlative to transmit an *unbelievable* idea may not be believed when offering support for a *believable* idea. For the sake of credibility, *use only supported or supportable superlatives.*

When are superlatives appropriate?

WRITING CLEARLY

Effective messages provide the receiver clear, specific information that can be understood easily. Read each sentence carefully to identify any sentence you believe could be misinterpreted or interpreted more than one way depending on the receiver's point of reference. Clarifying unclear sentences saves time and money for the receiver and writer and leads to strong relationships.

Choose Simple, Informal Words

The degree of formality in writing is dictated by the nature of the message and the backgrounds of the receivers. The writing in dissertations, theses, legal documents, and high-level government documents is expected to be formal. Business memorandums, e-mail messages, letters, and reports are expected to be informal. Business writers prefer the informal words from the left column rather than the formal words from the right column:

The objective of business writing is to express, not to impress. Why?

Formal Words	Informal Words
terminate	end
procure	get
remunerate	pay
corroborate	support
utilize	use
elucidate	explain

Using difficult, formal language may confuse and intimidate the receiver.

Can you clarify this message: "Management has become cognizant of the necessity for the elimination of undesirable vegetation surrounding the periphery of our facility" (McKenna, 1990)?

Simple, informal words, compared with formal words, are readily understood, easier to spell, require less time in keyboarding and less space on a page, and are less likely to draw attention away from the idea being expressed. If a receiver stops to question the writer's motive for using words similar to those in the left column, the impact of the message may be seriously diminished. Likewise, the impact would be diminished if the receiver stopped to question a writer's use of simple, informal words. That distraction is unlikely, however, if the message contains good ideas that are well organized and well supported. Under these conditions, simple words enable a receiver to get the message clearly and quickly.

Using words that have more than two or three syllables when they are the most appropriate is acceptable. However, you should avoid regular use of a

THINK IT OVER Have you ever felt intimidated when you read a textbook filled with words you could not understand?

Use simple words to convey clear meaning.

THINK IT OVER
Revise the dialogue in the cartoon above to eliminate the manager's confusion.

long, infrequently used word when a simpler, more common word has the same meaning. Professionals in some fields often use specialized terminology, often referred to as **jargon**, when communicating with colleagues in the same field. In this case, the audience is likely to understand the words, and using the jargon saves time. However, when communicating with people outside the field, professionals should select simple, common words to convey messages.

Why build a good vocabulary?

You should build your vocabulary so that you can use just the right word for expressing an idea and can understand what others have written. Just remember the purpose of business messages is not to advertise a knowledge of infrequently used words but to transmit a clear and tactful message. For the informal writing practiced in business, *use simple words instead of more complicated words that have the same meaning.*

Eliminate Misplaced Elements

Placing words, phrases, or clauses in the wrong position can confuse the receiver, as you can see in the following example:

We have taken the check to the bank, <u>which was unsigned</u>.

The sentence is confusing (or amusing) because it seems to imply that the bank was unsigned. That impression is given because the "which" clause is placed closer to "bank" than to "check." Similarly, the following sentences have very different meanings:

Place words, phrases, or clauses near the words they modify.

Confusing	Clear
The three-year budgets are being returned to the strategic planning committee, which have some serious defects. *(Does the committee have serious defects?)*	The three-year budgets, which have some serious defects, are being returned to the committee.

COMMUNICATION   MENTOR

Too many writers go to great lengths to "write right." In their attempts to sound learned, they muddy the message beyond comprehension. The best writing closely imitates speech. It is to the point. It uses familiar words and is interesting, and its sentences are short enough to follow. In other words, the message communicates.

Cynthia Pharr
President & CEO
C. Pharr Marketing Communications

Confusing	Clear
Susan displayed the financial ratios to upper-level managers on the screen. *(Are the managers displayed on the screen?)*	Susan explained to upper-level managers the financial ratios displayed on the screen.

Eliminate Dangling Modifiers

The following sentences illustrate a very common (and sometimes very serious) type of error. What causes the confusion?

While making a presentation, a surge of electricity caused the projector bulb to blow.

To create that bar chart, the information must be keyed into the spreadsheet file.

Although tired, the feasibility report had to be completed.

Re-examine the three sentences. Each begins with a modifier that precedes the independent (main) clause in the sentence. These modifiers speak of action without revealing who the doer is. "While making a presentation" does not reveal who is making the presentation. "To create that bar chart" does not indicate who is preparing the chart. "Although tired" does not indicate who is tired.

Because "surge of electricity" appears immediately after the idea of making the presentation, the surge seems to be making the presentation—not exactly the meaning the writer intends. The other sentences are also illogical: information does not create a bar chart, and a feasibility report isn't tired.

When a sentence begins with a modifier that does not reveal who the doer is, the subject of the independent clause gets credit for the action regardless of whether the credit is justified. These modifiers include

- Participial phrases (*while making a presentation*).
- Infinitive phrases (*to create that bar chart*).
- Elliptical clauses in which the subject and perhaps the verb are understood (*although tired*).

To "dangle" is to "hang loosely." A phrase dangles if it is not clearly attached to the appropriate noun or pronoun.

Dangling modifiers do not convey the true meaning the writer intends. The meaning may be illogical and perhaps even humorous (e.g., children rather than a monkey hanging from a tree in the sentence in the Self-check).

Such sentences can be corrected in two ways:

1. Change the subject of the independent clause to a word that properly defines or describes:

Dangling	Revised
While making a presentation, a surge of electricity caused the projector bulb to blow.	While making a presentation, Thomas was interrupted when a surge of electricity caused the projector bulb to blow.
To create that bar chart, the information must be keyed into a spreadsheet file.	To create that bar chart, you must key the information into a spreadsheet file.
Although tired, the feasibility report had to be completed.	Although tired, Sonia had to complete the feasibility report.

2. Recast the dangling modifier as a dependent clause:

Dangling	Revised
While making a presentation, a surge of electricity caused the projector bulb to blow.	While Thomas was making a presentation, a surge of electricity caused the projector bulb to blow.
To create that bar chart, the information must be keyed into a spreadsheet file.	If you want to create a bar chart from this information, you must key it into a spreadsheet file.
Although tired, the feasibility report had to be completed.	Although she was tired, Sonia had to complete the feasibility report.

In the revised sentences, the intended meaning is much easier to understand. Because the subject of each independent clause is placed close to the action described in each modifier, the receiver is certain who is performing the action.

Dangling modifiers occur most often when the modifier precedes the independent clause, as illustrated in the preceding examples. Dangling modifiers may fall at the end of the sentence, as well:

THINK IT OVER
Correct the following dangling modifier in both of the ways described: "The underfunding of the pension plan was detected while preparing the annual budget."

Dangling	Revised
Stan had a car wreck rushing to an important job interview.	Rushing to an important job interview, Stan had a car wreck.
The committee's selection was quite simple after considering the system's fast processing speed.	The selection was quite simple after the committee considered the system's fast processing speed.

Dangling modifiers are misleading because the introductory modifier is not properly positioned near the doer. The subject of an independent clause is presumed to be the doer of any action mentioned in a modifier that precedes it. *When the introductory modifier identifies action without revealing the doer, present the doer immediately after the modifier or recast the sentence so that the dangling modifier is a complete clause.*

Recast Expletive Beginnings

By definition, an **expletive** is a meaningless word. Expletive beginnings are not considered grammatical errors but are seldom advisable. Usually any sentence that begins with *there is, there are,* or *it is* can be improved.

What is an expletive? Why should you avoid using expletives?

Poor	Improved
There is a major problem with next year's budget.	Next year's budget has a major problem.
There are many complicated provisions within the new tax law.	The new tax law has many complicated provisions.
It is encouraging to note that sales have increased this month.	This month's increased sales are encouraging.

Although each of the preceding original sentences does have a word ("there" or "it") that precedes the verb ("is" or "are"), the subject is vague. Only after having read the entire sentence do you encounter the true subject. The revisions use fewer words in the more conventional subject-verb-complement pattern. *Avoid expletive beginnings.*

In some cases, the word *it* can serve as a first word when the antecedent is in a preceding sentence. An **antecedent** is a noun or pronoun to which another pronoun ("it") refers. To what word does "it" refer in the following sentence?

. . . of this document. It is being revised. . . .

"Document" is the antecedent of "it." Used in this manner, the pronoun "it" can serve well as a coherence technique to link ideas.

THINK IT OVER
Eliminate the expletive in "It is important to evaluate your effectiveness each time you communicate."

THINK IT OVER
Should "it" be eliminated in "The production team has completed its mission statement; it has been submitted for the presi-dent's review?" Explain.

Express Ideas in Parallel Form

In the following pairs of sentences, the ideas are the same. Which is stated better and why?

We have three stated goals: to increase production, to expand our market, and recruiting skilled workers.

We have three stated goals: to increase production, to expand our market, and to recruit skilled workers.

Mark received a superior rating in completing required paperwork, interacting with co-workers and customers, and the way he conducted himself in staff meetings.

Mark received a superior rating in completing required paperwork, interacting with co-workers and customers, and presenting his ideas in staff meetings.

Re-examine the first sentence in each pair. Because one of the three elements is presented in a form different from the others, that element does not belong—it is not parallel. The variation in construction weakens the emphasis given to each phrase in the series. The inconsistency may also distract the receiver's attention from the message.

In each pair, the second sentence is better. It presents similar phrases in a similar way grammatically:

We have three stated goals: ||| to increase production,
                            ||| to expand our market,
                        and ||| to recruit skilled workers.

Mark received a superior rating in ||| completing required paperwork,
                                    ||| interacting with co-workers,
                                and ||| presenting his ideas in staff meetings.

Can you identify the parallel elements in the following sentences?

They invested in stocks and bonds, and considered mutual funds.

She illustrated her lecture with graphs, charts, and slides, and presented a skit.

In both pairs, two independent clauses are the parallel elements. The subject "they" in the first pair and "she" in the second pair must be repeated so that each parallel item has the same sentence elements (subject, verb, and others). In the second sentence, "graphs," "charts," and "slides" are also parallel items—three nouns connected with *and*.

        || They invested in stocks,
    and || they considered mutual funds.

        || She illustrated her lecture with graphs, charts,
        || and slides;
    and || she presented a skit.

What is parallel construction and why is it important?

When ideas appear together for a certain purpose, they should have commonality in grammar. If one of the ideas is presented in a different way grammatically, it appears to be out of place. Commonality in grammatical presentation is called **parallel construction**. ◀

THINK IT OVER
What items within a resume would require careful attention to parallel construction?

The principle of parallel construction applies not only to elements in a series that appear in a sentence but also to major units in an outline, to subunits that appear under a major unit, and to headings that appear in documents. If one major heading is a complete sentence, all other major headings should be complete sentences. If one subheading is a question, all other subheadings under that division should be questions.

A concise message is not necessarily short but is written in as few words as possible.

WRITING CONCISELY

Concise messages are essential if today's information workers are to continue to process volumes of information. Some executives have reported that they read memos that are two paragraphs long but may only skim or discard longer ones. Of course, this survival technique has serious drawbacks: A vital message may be misinterpreted or never read. Learning to write concisely—to say in three words rather than ten—will mark you as a highly effective communicator. Abraham Lincoln's two-minute Gettysburg Address is a premier example. Mark Twain alluded to the *skill* needed to write concisely when he said, "I would have written a shorter book if I had had time."

Concise messages save time and money for both the writer and the receiver. The receiver's attention is directed toward the important details and is not distracted by excessive words and details. To prepare a concise message, *include only those details that the receiver needs; and state these details in the fewest possible words.*

The following techniques will help you learn to write in the fewest words possible:

1. *Eliminate redundancies.* A **redundancy** is a phrase in which one word unnecessarily repeats an idea contained in an accompanying word. In each sentence, which phrase contains a redundancy?

> *Does use of a certain word three times in a paragraph constitute redundancy?*

The accident report was full and complete.
The two twins are exactly identical.
A team meeting has been scheduled for 3 p.m. this afternoon.

Because "full" and "complete" convey the same meaning, both words are not needed. Because twins are understood to be two individuals, only "twins" is needed. "Exactly" and "identical" have the same meaning; "exactly" is not needed. Deleting "this afternoon" or revising the sentence to read "three o'clock this afternoon" would eliminate the redundancies "p.m." and "afternoon."

Use the words in the right column instead of the redundancies in the left column:

> **THINK IT OVER**
> In groups, generate a list of redundancies you have heard your friends, instructors, or co-workers use. List redundancies you use and list ways to avoid them in writing and speaking.

Redundant	Not Redundant
basic fundamentals	basics *or* fundamentals
end result	result
exact same	same
full and complete	full *or* complete
honest truth	truth
important essentials	essentials
looking forward to the future	looking forward
necessary requirement	requirement
other alternative	alternative
past history	history
personal opinion	opinion
true facts	facts or truth
serious danger	danger
severe crisis	crisis
whether or not	whether

Redundancy is unaccept-
able, but repetition can be
very useful.

Redundancy is not to be confused with repetition. In a sentence or paragraph, you may need to use a certain word again. Repetition serves a purpose and *is not* an error. Redundancy serves no purpose and *is* an error. *Avoid redundancies;* they waste words and risk distracting from the idea presented.

2. *Use active voice to reduce the number of words.* Passive voice typically adds unnecessary words such as prepositional phrases. Compare the sentence length in each of these examples:

Passive Voice	Active Voice
The user documentation was written by the systems analyst.	The systems analyst wrote the user documentation.
The loan approval procedures for new business ventures were revised by the commercial loan officer.	The commercial loan officer revised the loan approval procedures for new business ventures.

3. *Review the main purpose of your writing and identify the details that the reader needs to understand the message and to take necessary action.* More information is not necessarily better information. You may be so involved and perhaps so enthusiastic about your message that you believe the receiver needs to know everything that you know. Or perhaps you just do not take the time to empathize with your receiver by identifying the relevant details.

4. *Eliminate clichés that are often wordy and not necessary to understand the message.* For example, "Thank you for your letter," "I am writing to," and "May I take this opportunity" only delay the major purpose of the message.

5. *Do not restate ideas that are sufficiently implied.* For example,

THINK IT OVER
How much would an admissions clerk at a college need to know about you to send you information about a graduate program in business?

She <u>went to the bank</u> and made the daily deposit.

She <u>took the executive grammar course</u> and passed it.

<u>This is in response to your letter of June 25.</u>

In each case, the underlined idea can be implied without affecting the meaning. Now examine the same sentences written more concisely:

THINK IT OVER
Generate a list of statements that you commonly use or hear that could be implied easily; e.g., open your book and turn to page 50. . . .

She made the daily bank deposit.

She passed the executive grammar course.

Yes, I will be delighted to speak at the May meeting of the Boardtown Civic Club.

Notice how the following sentences are improved when implied ideas are eliminated:

Wordy	Concise
The auditor <u>reviewed the figures</u> and concluded that they are accurate.	The auditor <u>concluded</u> that the figures are accurate.
The editor <u>checked the manuscript</u> and found three grammatical errors.	The editor <u>found</u> three grammatical errors in the manuscript.

6. *Shorten sentences by using suffixes or prefixes, making changes in word form, or substituting precise words for phrases.* Note the differences in the following examples:

Wordy	Concise
She was a manager <u>who was courteous to others</u>.	She was a <u>courteous</u> manager.
He waited <u>in an impatient manner</u>.	He waited <u>impatiently</u>.
. . . the financial analysis <u>that they had not finished</u>	. . . the <u>unfinished</u> financial analysis
. . . the solution <u>that we could debate about the longest</u>.	. . . the most <u>debatable</u> solution.
The production manager disregards methods considered <u>to be of no use</u>.	The production manager disregards methods considered <u>useless</u>.
. . . sales representatives <u>with high energy levels</u>.	. . . <u>energetic</u> sales representatives.
. . . <u>arranged in alphabetic order</u>.	. . . <u>arranged alphabetically</u>.

The expressions on the right provide useful techniques for saving space and being concise. However, the examples in the left column are not grammatically incorrect or forbidden from use. In fact, sometimes their use provides just the right *emphasis*.

7. *Use a compound adjective to help reduce the number of words required to express an idea.*

Wordy	Concise
He wrote a report that was <u>up to the minute</u>.	He wrote an <u>up-to-the-minute</u> report.
Sid Hall, <u>who holds the highest rank</u> at Hooper Enterprises, is . . .	Sid Hall, <u>the highest-ranking official</u> at Hooper Enterprises, is . . .
His policy of <u>going slowly</u> was well received.	His <u>go-slow</u> policy was well received.

By using the compound adjective, you can reduce the number of words required to express your ideas and thus save the reader a little time.

IMPROVING READABILITY

Even though sentences are arranged in a logical sequence and are written coherently, the receiver may find reading the sentences difficult. Two factors contribute to the readability of a message: (1) length of the sentences and (2) difficulty of the words.

In an effort to determine the school grade level at which a passage is written, Robert Gunning (1968) developed a readability formula. This formula yields the approximate grade level a person would need to understand the material. For example, a grade level of 10 means a person needs to be able to read at the

LEARNING OBJECTIVE 2

What two factors affect the readability of a message?

The Fog Index is the approximate grade level needed to understand written material.

tenth-grade level to understand the material. Gunning referred to this formula as the *Fog Index*.

Grammar and style software programs such as *Grammatik* automatically calculate the grade level of the writing. These programs eliminate the laborious task of counting and calculating a readability index. If the readability level is considered inappropriate (too high or too low) for the audience, the writer must understand the two factors that affect readability: Short sentences and short words are easier to read. With this knowledge, the writer can input necessary revisions, recalculate the readability index, and repeat the process until the reading level is appropriate for the audience.

To compute a Fog Index:

THINK IT OVER
Study the formula carefully. Can you see how sentence length and percentage of difficult words affect the formula?

1. Select a passage of 100 words or more.
2. Find the *average sentence length* by dividing the number of words in the passage by the number of sentences. Count compound sentences as two sentences.
3. Find the percentage of *difficult* words. A *difficult* word is defined as a word with three syllables or more. Words are not to be counted as difficult if they (1) are compound words made from smaller words such as *however* or *understand;* (2) are proper nouns; or (3) are verbs that became three syllables by addition of *-ed* or *-es* such as *imposes* or *defended*. Determine the percentage of difficult words by dividing the number of words in the passage into the number of difficult words and multiplying the resulting figure by 100.
4. Add the average sentence length and the percentage of difficult words.
5. Multiply the resulting figure by 0.4 to arrive at the reading grade level of the passage. The following passage illustrates the manual calculation of the Fog Index. Sentences are numbered, and difficult words are underscored.

¹Each <u>successive</u> <u>development</u> has changed <u>society</u>. ²Early writings freed oral <u>societies</u> from <u>limitations</u> of time and space. ³Their <u>legacies</u> were transmitted in writing; ⁴therefore, <u>anthropologists</u> and <u>historians</u> have not had to rely on <u>hieroglyphs</u>, <u>pottery</u>, <u>utensils</u>, and <u>religious</u> <u>artifacts</u> to study our recent past. ⁵However, the world was <u>essentially</u> <u>illiterate</u> until the <u>development</u> of printing. ⁶Printing made <u>literature</u> <u>available</u> to other than the <u>religious</u> elite. ⁷Printing <u>multiplied</u> the <u>dimensions</u> of <u>communication</u>; ⁸those who weren't <u>literate</u> were <u>encouraged</u> to become so.

⁹High-speed printing and <u>inexpensive</u> newspress paper overcame all <u>previous</u> <u>limitations</u> and led to mass <u>communication</u>. ¹⁰With the advent of the <u>telegraph</u>, <u>telephone</u>, <u>radio</u>, and <u>television</u>, the world became a smaller place and instant <u>communication</u> commonplace. ¹¹What a milestone we achieved when millions of Americans (plus millions throughout the world) saw and heard Neil Armstrong begin his walk on the moon.

The passage contains 141 words in 11 sentences (two of the nine sentences are compound) and 34 *difficult* words. "Transmitted" is not a difficult word because it is a verb that became three syllables by adding *-ed*. "However," "overcame," and "commonplace" are not difficult words because they are made from two separate words compounded into one. "Americans" is not a difficult word because it is a familiar proper noun.

To compute the readability index:

1. Compute the average sentence length: $(141 \div 11)$ 12.80
2. Compute the percentage of difficult words: $(34 \div 41 \times 100)$ <u>24.10</u>
3. Add average sentence length and percentage of
   difficult words: $(12.8 + 24.1)$ 36.90
4. Multiply the resulting figure by 0.4: (36.9×0.4) 14.76

The Fog Index (reading grade level) of this passage is between 14 and 15.

The desirable Fog Index for most business writing is in the eight-to-eleventh-grade range. A writer need not be overly concerned if the index is a little over 11 or under 8. Trying to write at the exact grade level of the receiver is inadvisable. The writer may not know the exact grade level, and even those who have earned advanced degrees appreciate writing they can read and understand quickly and easily.

A major word of caution is needed. Writing a passage with a readability index appropriate for the audience does not guarantee that the message will be understood. Numerous factors affect whether a message is communicated effectively. Chapter 1 explained how breakdowns in communication occur at all stages in the communication process. For example, the readability may be appropriate for the audience. However, the words used may not convey the precise meaning needed for understanding, gender-biased words may create barriers to understanding, unique expressions may not be understood by a reader in a different field or from a different background, and so on. Calculating the readability index, however, provides the writer valuable feedback about the average length of the sentences and the difficulty of the words. *For quick, easy reading (and listening), use small words and short sentences.*

PROCEDURES FOR REVISING AND PROOFREADING

Although errors in writing and mechanics may seem isolated and trivial to you, these mistakes can damage your credibility. Receivers of messages that contain mistakes are much less likely to take you and your ideas seriously than if you had taken special care to proofread carefully.

If you are composing at a computer, you can input revisions quickly and easily. The electronic spellcheck available with word-processing software is helpful in locating spelling and typographical errors but cannot be relied on to detect all errors. The software, for example, cannot distinguish between the use of *principle* for *principal* or determine whether a number should be written as a word or appear as a numeral.

Writing-analysis programs can help you locate grammatical errors as well as improve your style—the way you express ideas. Typically, these programs require writers to (1) compose the document at the keyboard, (2) instruct the program to analyze the writing, (3) study the writing analysis (which includes a readability index), and (4) revise the text incorporating valid suggestions only. For example, the computer may critique the sentence "Authorization of this procedure is recommended . . ." in this way: "Sentence begins with a long, abstract noun and uses passive voice. In rewriting, try 'Authorize' and active voice." Because these suggestions are valid, the writer can quickly input the changes and improve the style of the sentence. On the other hand, the writer would reject the suggestion to rewrite a sentence using active voice if the intention were to use passive voice to de-emphasize negative information.

What Fog Index is recommended for most business writing?

What purpose does calculating a readability index serve?

LEARNING OBJECTIVE 3

THINK IT OVER
In groups, discuss errors you have seen in company marquees, displays, or correspondence. Bring copies to share with the class if possible. Did these errors affect your attitude toward the company?

THINK IT OVER
Use your library's databases to locate examples of errors that caused as much damage as Continental's keying error discussed in the chapter opening. Share with the class.

How can writing-analysis software improve your writing?

If you have not used
writing-analysis software,
determine if this software
is available in your com-
puter lab and begin learning to use the software to
analyze your writing.

Figure 8-1 illustrates the feedback you might receive if you analyzed a document using *Grammatik*. By allowing *Grammatik* to critique this document, you are able to correct an error in pronoun usage and to confirm the correct use of a commonly misused word. *Grammatik* provides definitions of *principle* and *principal* and allows the writer to select the appropriate word. Because *principle* is correct in this context, you would select "Ignore Phrase" from the commands at the bottom of the screen. Among the stylistic errors that *Grammatik* detects are wordy sentences, passive voice, jargon, and gender-biased language. After reviewing the entire document, *Grammatik* displays a document summary showing a readability index, average sentence and paragraph length, and other useful statistics.

You must understand basic
writing principles to
benefit from computer-
generated writing
critiques.

Using computer software to critique writing can be extremely valuable if the writer recognizes that (1) the software is a tool to improve style and (2) the writer may overrule the computer's advice to achieve specific objectives. Those who are familiar with the principles of writing will benefit most from writing-analysis programs. For example, how helpful would the preceding suggestion be if the writer

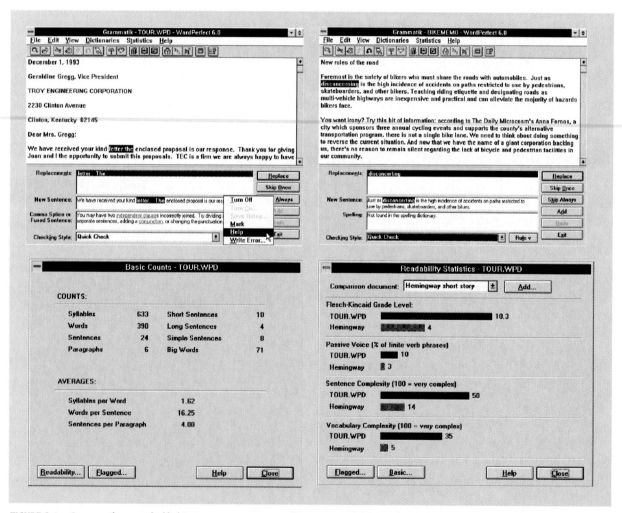

FIGURE 8-1   *Grammatik screens highlighting a run-on sentence, spelling error, readability index, and other statistics.*

When NASA scientists and engineers prepare a shuttle for launch, an elaborate system of checks and procedures must be followed. Attention is given to the minutest detail; seemingly inconsequential irregularities can spell disaster. Likewise, you should follow standard procedures when reviewing documents for content, organization, mechanics, and format, so that errors, no matter how slight, will not keep you "grounded."

does not understand what an abstract noun or passive voice is? Obviously, a writer who has an effective style will spend less time revising and will be more likely to understand and benefit from the computer's suggestions.

Following systematic revision procedures will help writers produce error-free documents that reflect positively on the company and themselves. These procedures require proofreading several times for a specific purpose each time. Writers using computers also should proofread using the electronic spellcheck and save the corrections in case the document is needed again. Because errors on the screen are sometimes difficult to locate, proofreading a printed page is essential. Regardless of the method you use to produce the document, the finished product should be free of errors in (1) content, organization, and style; (2) mechanics; and (3) format and layout.

Edit for Content, Organization, and Style

Proofread the document first to locate errors in content, organization, and style. Ask yourself these questions:

1. Is all information complete? Have I included all the details the receiver needs to understand the message and to take necessary action?
2. Is the information accurate? Have I checked the accuracy of any calculations, dates, names, addresses, and numbers?
3. Does the message treat the receiver honestly and ethically?
4. Is the main idea presented appropriately based on the receiver's likely reaction to the main idea (deductive or inductive organization)?
5. Are supporting ideas presented in a logical order?
6. Is the message clear? Will the receiver interpret the information correctly?
7. Is the message concise and written at an appropriate level for the receiver?
8. Does the message reflect a considerate, caring attitude? Is the message primarily focused on the receiver's needs?

THINK IT OVER
Key the letter in the proofreading application in the end-of-chapter exercises (or some other document) and evaluate its effectiveness using a writing-analysis program. What were the major weaknesses?

A spellcheck does not free you from the responsibility of carefully proofreading each document.

Take a few minutes to review the standard proofreaders' marks listed in Appendix A. Then use them consistently so you can quickly mark revisions and others (supervisors or co-writers) can understand your revisions easily.

COMMUNICATION   MENTOR

Preparing a message free of grammatical and typographical errors is imperative. However, the writer's most important function is to assure that the reader fully understands the message.

Two of the most common barriers to clear writing are pseudosophisticated language and technical jargon. Some people mistakenly believe that their letters or reports will be considered more important if they are filled with long words and complicated phrases. Instead, writers should strive for clarity. The same can be said of those who rely heavily on technical jargon, including acronyms.

One of the easiest ways to avoid these pitfalls is to ask people unfamiliar with your work to review what you've written. Listen to their comments, and simplify the portions of the document that are confusing. The time spent editing and rewriting saves even more time—and confusion—in the long run.

Hugh B. Jacks
President and Owner
Potential Enterprises & Adventure Safaris

Edit for Mechanics

Proofread a second time to locate the following mechanical errors:

Is proofreading one time adequate if your goal is to prepare error-free messages?

1. Typographical, grammatical, capitalization, and punctuation errors.
2. Incomplete sentences.
3. Omitted and repeated words.
4. Word substitutions (*your* and *you*) and words that sound alike (*there* for *their*).

Proofread a third time *reading from right to left* to check again for any typographical or spelling errors. Reading in reverse requires reading slowly and concentrating deliberately on the text. Proofread carefully for potentially damaging errors that an electronic spellcheck cannot detect.

Edit for Format and Layout

Assume that you have been asked to explain to a co-worker a systematic way for proofreading company correspondence. What steps would you describe?

Follow these steps to be certain the document adheres to conventional business formats:

1. Study the conventional business formats in Appendix A. Compare your document with the illustrations shown in Appendix A and make any revisions. Are all standard parts of the document included and presented in an acceptable format? Does the message begin on the correct line? Should the right margin be justified or jagged?
2. Proofread letter parts, including the date line, letter address, salutation, subject line, and closing lines. Research indicates that many errors appear in the opening sections of letters because writers typically begin proofreading at the first paragraph.
3. Be sure that all necessary special letter parts (mailing notation, attention line, subject line, enclosure, copy and mailing notations, second-page heading, and the writer's address for a personal business letter) are included.
4. Check to be sure that numbered items are in correct order; inserting and deleting text may have changed the order of these items.
5. Consider whether the text has the visual impact you desire. Could you increase the readability of long, uninterrupted blocks of texts by using enumerated or indented lists, headings, or different typestyles (boldface, underlines, italics, or shadow type)?

Could you increase the overall appeal by including graphics or using different fonts of various sizes and shapes? Could you partition the text into logical, easy-to-read sections by using graphic lines, boxes, and borders?

6. Be certain that the document is signed or initialed (depending on the document).

7. Print the document on high-quality bond paper. The envelope and second-page paper (if needed) should match the letterhead. The printing should read in the same direction as the watermark (the design imprinted on high-quality paper).

The letter in Figure 8-2 has been revised for (1) content, organization, and style; (2) mechanics; and (3) format and layout. Changes are noted using proofreaders' marks, a standard, simplified way to show where changes or corrections need to be made. The detailed explanation will help you understand how the revisions improve the quality of the final draft. To aid you in editing your own documents, review the proofreaders' marks in Figure A-1 in Appendix A.

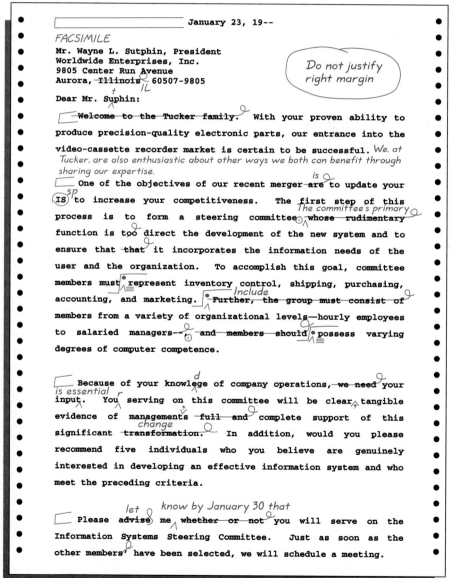

FIGURE 8-2   Rough-draft of a letter (excerpt).

ORGANIZATION, CONTENT, AND STYLE

Eliminate clichés: "Welcome to Tucker" and "Please advise me."

Insert a smooth transition from the opening paragraph into ¶2.

Spell out "IS" to ensure understanding.

Break long sentence in ¶2 into two shorter sentences to increase readability.

Use simple words to increase clarity: Replace "rudimentary" and "transformation."

Eliminate redundancies: "full and complete" and "whether or not."

Write from the receiver's viewpoint: "Your input is essential."

Write specific, action-oriented ending: "by January 30."

ERRORS UNDETECTED BY SPELLCHECK

Verify spelling of receiver's name, "Sutphin."

Correct word substitutions: "too" for "to" and "you" for "your."

Omit repeated word: "that."

MECHANICS

Spell "knowledge" correctly.

Use a singular verb when "one" is the subject.

Use a possessive pronoun before gerund: "your serving."

Place comma between coordinate adjectives: "clear, tangible."

Use an apostrophe to show possession: "management's."

Omit apostrophe after plural noun: "members."

FORMAT AND LAYOUT

Begin all lines at the left margin in block letter style.

Insert mailing notation: "FACSIMILE."

Format criteria in a bulleted list for emphasis.

Use jagged right margin for improved appearance.

Center letter vertically on high-quality letterhead.

COMMUNICATION IN ACTION

Cynthia Pharr, C. Pharr Marketing Communications

Receiving attention from a respected national newspaper presents a challenge for most business organizations, even when the news is positive. When negative comments are printed, however, the challenge can become daunting. Any financial analyst's comments in the national media about the book value of a company's stock can have a tremendous impact on the price of the stock.

Cynthia Pharr, president and CEO of C. Pharr Marketing Communications, recently faced a challenge in her role of handling public relations for a large corporation. *The Wall Street Journal* printed an article in which a financial analyst made negative comments about the stock price of Showbiz Pizza Time, Inc., a restaurant company for which Cynthia Pharr serves on the Board of Directors. Well-written responses to such analysts can "turn that analyst around" and potentially change his or her attitude toward a company.

In the newspaper article, the analyst had "turned up his nose" at Showbiz's stock because he was not enamored with the concept of the restaurant and believed "they have rubber pizza." Rebuttal letters to such negative comments often include numbers and harsh logic, focusing on economic reasons in an attempt to change the financial analyst's thinking. Instead, Pharr chose a lighter theme, more in line with the company's fun-loving slogan, "Where a Kid Can Be a Kid!"

Her letter to the financial analyst was written from Chuck E. Cheese, Showbiz's large rat icon. Chuck E. Cheese wrote, "You say we serve rubber pizza. The enclosed sample of rubber pizza is definitely not what we serve. Please be our guest at Showbiz and see what we're really serving."

Because the analyst also criticized Showbiz as a "kind of faddy thing," Pharr enclosed a photograph of one of her children as a toddler. Chuck E. Cheese identified the toddler as a fan for over ten years and wrote, "This young man thought we were pretty neat in the early 80s, and he's all grown up now. When you come to see us, you won't see the same kid running around, and thank goodness—he's too big for the rides! However, you will see lots of little guys who think we're pretty special."

The letter ended with a comment about getting re-acquainted and being friends and mentioned two free passes to Showbiz Pizza that were enclosed. The analyst's points were rebutted but in a fun-loving style.

Applying What You Have Learned

1. Why was the lighter theme of Pharr's letter to the financial analyst appropriate for a rebuttal?
2. Assume that you are the financial analyst. What impact do you believe the letter and its enclosures would have on you?

SUMMARY

1 Errors in word usage and style (the way ideas are expressed) can result in lost meaning, lost time, distraction, and concern about the writer's or speaker's background. Writing-analysis programs are available; however, they are most helpful to those who know the basics.

Techniques that will enable you to write messages that can be easily understood and positively received are summarized in the "Check Your Writing" checklist. These techniques include creating vivid images, writing clearly, and writing concisely.

2 The readability of a message is affected by the length of the sentences and the difficulty of the words. Therefore, for quick, easy reading,

use simple words and short sentences. A readability index (grade level for reader to understand the material) of eighth-to-eleventh grade range is appropriate for most business writing. Writing a message with a readability index appropriate for an audience does not guarantee understanding but does provide valuable feedback on the average length of the sentences and the difficulty of the words.

3 Be willing to revise a document as many times as necessary to be certain that it conveys the message effectively and is error free. Follow systematic procedures for proofreading for content, organization, and style; mechanics; and format and layout.

CHECK YOUR WRITING

VIVID WRITING
- ☐ Use specific words.
- ☐ Choose concrete nouns as subjects of sentences to achieve clear, emphatic writing.
- ☐ Avoid using clichés.
- ☐ Avoid using adjectives and adverbs that are used too frequently or are overly negative.
- ☐ Use only supported or supportable superlatives to maintain credibility.

CLARITY
- ☐ Use simple words for informal business writing instead of using more complicated words that have the same meaning.
- ☐ Place a word, a phrase, or a clause near the word it describes.
- ☐ Avoid dangling modifiers. When the introductory phrase identifies action without revealing the doer, present the doer immediately after the phrase.
- ☐ Avoid using expletive beginnings.
- ☐ Present multiple units in the same way grammatically—parallel construction.

CONCISENESS
- ☐ Do not use redundancies—unnecessary repetition of an idea.
- ☐ Avoid unnecessary details; omit ideas that can be implied.
- ☐ Shorten wordy sentences by using suffixes or prefixes, making changes in word form, or substituting precise words for phrases.

READABILITY
- ☐ Use simple words and short sentences for quick, easy reading (and listening).
- ☐ Strive for short paragraphs but vary their lengths.
- ☐ Emphasize a sentence by placing it first or last within a paragraph or by assigning it a number in a tabulated series.

SYSTEMATIC PROOFREADING
- ☐ Proofread for content, organization, and style; mechanics; and format and layout.

REFERENCES

Gunning, R. (1968). *The technique of clear writing.* New York: McGraw Hill.

McKenna, J. F. (1990, March 19). Tales from the circular file. *Industry Week*, p. 38.

Schmit, J. (1993, May 25). Continental's $4 million typo. *USA Today*, p. 1B.

REVIEW QUESTIONS

1. Normally, concrete nouns serve well as sentence subjects. Under what condition would abstract nouns serve better?
2. What are the disadvantages of using clichés?
3. When is the use of superlatives detrimental?
4. When would difficult, technical terms or formal writing be justified?
5. List two disadvantages of beginning sentences with expletives.
6. Discuss five ways to prepare a concise message.
7. If the objective in revising a report is to reduce the readability level from 16 to 12, what editorial changes would you make?
8. Provide a brief argument for editing and revising business correspondence carefully.
9. Discuss the limitations of an electronic spellcheck. Can it be relied on for proofreading?
10. Who is more likely to benefit from a writing-analysis program, the person who (a) is very familiar with the basics of grammar or (b) knows little about the basics of grammar? Explain.
11. Outline the systematic steps for proofreading.
12. Complete each of the THINK IT OVER activities your instructor assigns.

EXERCISES

Each of the following sentences illustrates a weakness discussed in Chapter 8. (a) Using terminology presented in the chapter, identify the weakness. (b) Rewrite the sentence to eliminate the weakness. The example illustrates the type of answer expected:

Example: You did not record a personal greeting on your voice mail.

Answers: a. Uses second person and active voice to convey a negative idea.
        b. Please record a personal greeting on your voice mail.

1. Our market share plummeted to new lows last year.
2. A revision of the report is necessary.
3. Recommendations from the site-selection committee will be presented at the next staff meeting.
4. This is written to acknowledge receipt of your letter.
5. The plant manager has dictated utopian production quotas.
6. Our cafeteria serves the best coffee in the world.
7. We conclusively consolidated our endeavors to revoke the capitulation in earnings.
8. Your report is being read by the department supervisor, which was received today.
9. Until unanimously convinced, a verdict was not reached.
10. My tax forms were completed and mailed before March 15.
11. The basic fundamentals are outlined in the manual.
12. I am writing in response to your recent claim letter.
13. Lin developed a design that was loaded with creativity.
14. There is a meeting scheduled on May 15.
15. Our main personnel problems are absenteeism, apathy, and the lowering of employee morale.

PROOFREADING APPLICATION

Use proofreaders' marks to correct errors in spelling, grammar, word usage, punctuation, numbers, abbreviations, and formatting of the following business letter. You should find approximately 15 errors. Do not revise a sentence and state its idea in an entirely different way.

February 28, 19--

McMahan Manufacturing
2376 Tillotson Avenue
New Orleans, Louisiana 70183-2376

Ladies and Gentlemen,

Congradulations on being selected to attend the two day seminar on effective listening. The seminar will be held in Atlanta, Georgia on March 15. These five guidelines for effective listening should be helpful as you begin to analyze your own listening skills.

1.   Learn to block out distractions that interfere with effective listening.

2.   Take notes on the material to reinforce you memory.

3.   Become sincrely interested in what the speaker is saying, this procedure will help you retain information.

3.   Listen to the entire message before responding to be certain that you here everything.

4.   Listen with an open mind, otherwise, you may miss key points.

5.   Identify your weaknesses in listening and work to improve them.

We are eager for you to this professional development seminar. When you return please be sure to share this valuable information with others at McMahon.

Leigh Kuykendall
Consultant

E-MAIL APPLICATION

Your instructor will send you an e-mail message containing the letter in the previous proofreading application. Import the letter into the word-processing software you are using. Use the redline feature to mark insertions and use the strikeout feature to mark any deletions so that you can quickly verify the accuracy of work when the corrections are provided.

Developing effective training programs for organizations (skill development and employee awareness programs) involves thorough planning, articulate writing and editing, and meticulous proofreading.

The planning process involves (1) identifying the audience, the purpose and the outcome expected by the client, selecting the appropriate media (written, video, computer interactive) for presenting the message and (2) identifying and *understanding* the message to be communicated.

After considering these crucial issues, the writer(s) develops a first draft using the style, language, tone, and approach that is appropriate for the audience and the specific content to be communicated. Finally, the writer(s) and others are involved in editing for accuracy, consistency in style among collaborative writers, format, and mechanics.

Discussion Questions

1. According to Jim Amatulli, what information must a writer identify before writing the first draft of a document?
2. Describe the process involved in identifying the content of the message and organizing it effectively.
3. What process is used to control for consistency, accuracy, and effectiveness of the message when several writers work collaboratively on a project?
4. Describe the (a) editing process and (b) the two proofreading methods used at Amatulli.
5. How have electronic spellcheckers affected the writing of Jim Amatulli? What *two* cautions does he offer about the reliability of electronic spellchecks?
6. Study carefully the writing project Jo Huntington described. (1) Identify the audience, the purpose and intended outcome, and the media combination selected; (2) describe the content of the message and the specific approach used to present the message; and (3) discuss how collaborative writing enhanced this project.
7. What does Jim Amatulli mean when he describes the objective and subjective nature of communication?

Applications

As a senior writer in a business communications consulting firm, your task is to *plan* a message that will increase the membership of a student organization of your choice or increase involvement in a community organization such as the United Way, Scouts, etc. Your preliminary planning involves providing answers to the following questions:

1. Who is the audience? What is the purpose and intended outcome of the message?
2. What medium or media combination (written document, video, interactive computer program) is appropriate for communicating the message?
3. What steps will you take to identify the content of the message and ensure that you understand the exact message to be communicated?
4. What approach (e.g., language and style) is appropriate for communicating this message effectively?

PART 4

COMMUNICATING THROUGH LETTERS, MEMORANDUMS, AND E-MAIL MESSAGES

CHAPTER 9

WRITING ABOUT THE

PLEASANT AND THE ROUTINE

OBJECTIVES

When you have completed Chapter 9, you will be able to

1 List the steps in the deductive outline and identify the advantages of using it to convey good news or routine information.

2 Write letters presenting claims and making adjustments.

3 Compose letters making and responding favorably to routine requests.

4 Compose letters requesting credit information and credit and letters providing credit information and extending credit.

5 Write letters making orders and responding favorably to order letters.

6 Prepare memorandums and e-mail messages that convey good news or routine information.

Much of the Florida Gulf Coast is dotted with typical beach towns—strips of fast-food restaurants, miniature golf courses, amusement parks, and night clubs. These are not the things that long-term residents or prospective home buyers want to see every day. In response to the desire for a quiet town on the Gulf Coast, developer Robert Davis envisioned the town of Seaside. Seaside would be a town planned for its residents. Architects Andres Duany and Elizabeth Plater-Zyberk designed the development, which has a pleasing array of shops and businesses along with homes for residents of all ages. It has a definite center with plenty of public space. An efficient system of interconnecting streets makes Seaside pedestrian-friendly. Many of the houses and buildings are designed in the Victorian style of the 19th century, generating a feeling of nostalgia and creating the atmosphere of a typical small town. Seaside is a winner because of its ingenuity in design and development (Gerloff, 1994).

Had the developer not had empathy for those in the market for a home away from the typical tourist environment and had less visionary and thorough architects managed the design, Seaside may have never come about. However, because of Davis' knowledge of his potential clients' needs and desires and the carefully researched and planned designs of Duany and Plater-Zyberk, the community is a success. Your success as a writer involves similar skills. You must know your audience and have empathy, the awareness of how the receiver may react. In addition, careful organization ensures that your message will be understood and received in the most effective way.

BUSINESS LETTERS

You can organize business messages either deductively or inductively depending on your prediction of the receiver's reaction to your main idea. However, learning to organize business messages according to the appropriate outline will improve your chances of writing a document that elicits the response or action you desire.

In Chapter 9, you will learn to write letters that convey ideas that a receiver likely will find *pleasing* or *routine*. Messages that convey pleasant messages are referred to as **good-news** messages. Messages that are of interest to the reader but are not likely to generate an emotional reaction are referred to as **routine** messages.

Good-news or routine messages follow a **deductive sequence**–the message begins with the main idea. To present good-news and routine information deductively, begin with the major idea, followed by supporting details as depicted in Figure 9-1. In both outlines, the third point (closing thought) may be

LEARNING OBJECTIVE 1

Do you remember the four reader reactions discussed in Chapter 7? This chapter addresses messages written when the receiver likely will be *pleased* (good-news) or *interested* (routine).

THINK IT OVER
Generally, when should you begin a message with the main idea? Turn back to Chapter 7 if necessary.

Good-News Message	Routine Message
• States the pleasant idea.	• States the main idea.
• Provides details or explanations.	• Provides details or explanations.
• Reminds receiver of the good news or includes a future-oriented closing thought.	• Reminds receiver of the main idea or includes a future-oriented closing thought.

FIGURE 9-1   Deductive pattern used in good-news and routine messages.

U. S. businesspeople tend to use deductive (direct) style for letters and memos far more than do their counterparts in other parts of the world. In the Orient, for example, businesspeople use an indirect pattern even for good-news and neutral messages. Can you name other cultures that shun the "get-straight-to-the-point" approach embraced by U.S. executives?

What are the advantages of the deductive pattern for good-news and routine letters?

Write the steps in the deductive outline recommended for good-news and routine messages in your notebook.

THINK IT OVER
According to the outline, will all good-news and routine letters have three paragraphs? Explain.

THINK IT OVER
What do you recall from Chapter 7 about the general length of paragraphs in business letters?

omitted without seriously impairing effectiveness; however, including it unifies the message and avoids abruptness.

The deductive pattern has several advantages:

1. The first sentence is easy to write. After writing it, the details follow easily.
2. The first sentence is likely to attract attention because it gets the attention it deserves in this emphatic position.
3. Encountering good news in the first sentence puts receivers in a pleasant frame of mind, and they are receptive to the details that follow.
4. The arrangement may save receivers some time. Once they get the important idea, they can move rapidly through the supporting details.

Ineffective and effective applications of the deductive outline are illustrated in sample letters in this chapter. The Ø symbol is placed over *poor* examples of writing for easy identification. When you see this familiar symbol (Ø), remember that you are about to read an example of what you should *not* do.

Typically, a rather poorly organized and poorly written example is followed by a well-organized and well-written example. Some sentences or sections of each letter are numbered and correspond to the numbers in the commentary beside the letter. The detailed comments will help you see how principles are applied or violated. The commentary on poor examples explains why certain techniques should be avoided. The commentary on well-written examples demonstrates ways to avoid certain types of mistakes. The well-written examples are designed to illustrate the application of principles discussed in Chapters 7, 8, and 9. They are not intended as models of exact words, phrases, or sentences that should appear in letters you write. At the conclusion of this chapter, you should be able to apply the principles you have learned and create your own well-written letters and memorandums.

To assist you in recognizing standard business formats, many of the examples in Chapter 9 are positioned correctly on letterhead and are formatted with appropriate letter parts. Study Appendix A, which provides a detailed explanation and illustrations of the standard formats and layout of business letters and memorandums. When you are confident you understand this information, return to this chapter to review the sample good-news and routine letters and memorandums.

THINK IT OVER
In groups, turn to Appendix A and discuss the two punctuation styles and the three letter formats. How do writers sign letters? Identify each standard and special letter part and the correct position and spacing of each part. Locate the two-letter postal abbreviations in Figure A-12.

Routine Claims

A **claim letter** is a request for an adjustment. When writers ask for something to which they think they are entitled (such as a refund, replacement, exchange, or payment for damages), the letter is called a *claim letter*.

LEARNING OBJECTIVE 2

CLAIM LETTER

Requests for adjustments can be divided into two groups: **routine claims** and **persuasive claims**. Persuasive claims, which are discussed in Chapter 11, assume that a request will be granted only after explanations and persuasive arguments have been presented. Routine claims (possibly because of guarantees, warranties, or other contractual conditions) assume that a request will be granted quickly and willingly, without persuasion. Because you expect routine claims to be granted willingly, a forceful, accusatory tone is inappropriate.

When the claim is routine, the deductive outline will contain the following points:

Should a routine claim letter *begin* with the main idea?

1. Request action in the first sentence.
2. Explain the details supporting the request for action.
3. Close with an expression of appreciation for taking the action requested.

The letter in Figure 9-2 is written **inductively**—the details are presented before the main idea. Surely the programmer intended to write the in-program documentation; otherwise, the contract would not have been signed. Because a mistake is obvious, the programmer would not need to be persuaded. Because she can expect the programmer to correct the problem, the MIS manager can ask for the adjustment *before* providing an explanation.

[1] Begins with details, delaying the answer to the receiver's request; is writer-oriented.

[2] Uses a forceful tone to convey a fact that the receiver already knows.

[3, 4] Continues with more details about the problem presented with no empathy for receiver; uses second person and negative language, which emphasize the writer's blame.

[5] Presents a reason for making the upcoming request; misspells "maintenance."

[6] States the main point (claim) that should have been presented in the first paragraph; continues forceful tone that will likely damage human relations.

[1] We at MetaTech contracted with you to write the new marketing analysis program for our chemical engineering subsidiary, ChemiCo, Inc. [2] The contract required you to create the source code and write user *and* operator documentation.

[3] However, once we looked at the program, we realized you had failed to provide us with in-program documentation that would enable us to maintain the program efficiently. [4] No other company has failed to supply us with this information.

[5] We would like for our people to be able to maintain the program instead of calling you repeatedly to do routine maintenance work. [6] Please modify the program to the agreed upon specifications and fulfill your contract with us.

FIGURE 9-2 Poor example of a routine claim letter.

The writer is confident that her routine request for an adjustment will be granted. Therefore, in the revision (Figure 9-3) she simply states the request (in the first sentence) and follows with the details without showing anger, disgust, suspicion, or disappointment. Beginning with the major point gives it the emphasis it deserves.

FAVORABLE RESPONSE TO A CLAIM LETTER

Businesses *want* their customers to write when merchandise or service is not satisfactory. They want to learn of ways in which goods and services can be improved, and they want their customers to receive value for the money they

METATECH Inc.
2150 River Road
Las Cruces, NM 88004-8319
(505) 555-9450 Fax: (505) 555-1583

June 5, 19--

Mr. Zahid Ahmed
Sales Manager
Precision Computer Services
900 Oakland Terrace
El Paso, TX 79910-4156

Dear Mr. Ahmed:

¹ Please include in-program documentation with the marketing analysis software you created for us.

² Our data processing personnel regularly modify application programs to meet the constantly changing information needs of our business. ³ The application programmers will need in-program documentation to understand how the program code relates to the system documentation you have provided to us. ⁴ Other application programs we have purchased from you were equipped with this information.

⁵ The user and operator documentation appear to be well done; thus, we plan to begin training our staff immediately.

Sincerely,

Linda A. Reynolds
Linda A. Reynolds
MIS Manager

mle

FIGURE 9-3   Good example of a routine claim letter.

spend. With considerable confidence, they can assume that writers of claim letters think their claims are valid. By responding fairly to legitimate requests in **adjustment letters,** businesses can gain a reputation for standing behind their goods and services. A loyal customer may become even more loyal after a business has demonstrated its integrity.

An adjustment letter is a response to a claim letter.

Because the subject of an adjustment letter is related to the goods or services provided, the letter can serve easily and efficiently as a low-pressure sales letter. With only a little extra space, the letter can include resale or sales promotional material. **Resale** is a term referring to a discussion of goods or services already bought. It reminds customers and clients that they made a good choice in selecting a firm with which to do business, or it reminds them of the good qualities of their purchase. **Sales promotional material** refers to statements made about related merchandise or service. For example, a letter about a company's wallpaper might also mention its paint. Mentioning the paint is using sales promotional material. Subtle sales messages that are included in adjustment letters have a good chance of being read, but direct sales letters may not be read at all.

Include a sales message in an adjustment letter. *Resale* and *sales promotional material* are terms that refer to this message. Write definitions to these terms in your notebook.

When the response to a claim letter is favorable, present ideas in the following deductive sequence:

1. Reveal the good news in the first sentence.
2. Explain the circumstances.
3. Close on a pleasant, forward-looking note.

Although the word *grant* is acceptable when talking about claims, its use in adjustment letters is discouraged. An expression such as "Your claim is being granted" unnecessarily implies that the writer is in a position of power.

Is using the word *grant* in an adjustment acceptable? Explain.

THINK IT OVER
In groups, write a sentence-by-sentence analysis of Figure 9-4.

Ordinarily, a response to a written message is also a written message. Sometimes, people write letters to confirm ideas they have already discussed on the telephone. Consider the written reply to the claim about missing in-program documentation in Figure 9-4. How would this letter affect MetaTech's impression of the computer company's commitment to stand behind its application programs?

Eager to learn if (and when) she will receive the in-program documentation, the MIS manager will resent having to read through the obvious facts in the first three sentences. The vague explanation with no specific assurance that the documentation has been shipped may anger the MIS manager further. Finally, the last paragraph sheds considerable doubt on the integrity of the entire program.

Notice the deductive outline and the explanation in the good example in Figure 9-5. The writer knows that the MIS manager will be pleased the in-program documentation will be sent with only a brief delay. Therefore, he gives the

Thank you for your letter of June 5. It has been referred to me for reply.

We have studied your contract and talked to the programmers about your complaint. We just don't know how it could have happened, but the in-program documentation was not shipped with the rest of the program.

Thank you for calling this matter to our attention, and we certainly hope the new program and documentation meet your needs.

FIGURE 9-4   Poor example of a favorable response to a routine claim letter.

PRECISION COMPUTER SERVICES
900 Oakland Terrace   El Paso, TX 79910-4156
(505) 555-0800   Fax - (505) 555-2300

June 10, 19--

Ms. Linda A. Reynolds
MIS Manager
MetaTech, Inc.
2150 River Road
Las Cruces, NM 88004-8319

Dear Ms. Reynolds

1 The revised source code with the proper in-program documentation should be shipped to you within three weeks.

2 Thank you for bringing this situation to our attention so quickly while the programmers are still able to remember the program logic and write the documentation easily. 3 Although your program was subjected to our normal operating quality control review, a separate review of program documentation was omitted inadvertently.

4 Our programmers enjoy the opportunity of sharing new coding techniques with other computer professionals. 5 Please call us at 555-0800 if your application programmers would like to spend a few hours touring our facilities and talking shop with our programmers.

Sincerely

Zahid Ahmed

Zahid Ahmed

---

1 Begins with the good news (main idea) for deserved emphasis; assures receiver that action is being taken already.

2 Expresses appreciation for being informed about the omission.

3 Presents explanation and assures company the in-program documentation meets company's rigorous standards.

4, 5 Attempts to regain possible lost goodwill by offering specialized training.

Illustrates open punctuation. Colon after the salutation and comma after the complimentary close are omitted.

THINK IT OVER
Identify the sales message in Figure 9-5. Does the letter contain resale, sales promotional material, or both?

FIGURE 9-5   *Good example of a favorable response to a routine claim letter.*

receiver this good news in the first sentence. The details and closing sentence follow naturally and easily showing no reluctance for correcting the problem.

Routine Request Letters

LEARNING OBJECTIVE 3

Notice how routine requests and favorable responses to them use the same sequence-of-ideas pattern. Compared with persuasive requests (discussed in Chapter 11), routine requests are shorter.

ROUTINE REQUESTS

Most businesspeople write letters requesting information about people, prices, products, and services. Because the request is a door opener for future business, receivers accept it optimistically. At the same time, they arrive at an opinion about the writer based on the quality of the letter. The following points presented in a deductive outline can serve as a guide for preparing effective requests that are expected to be fulfilled.

1. Make the major request in the first sentence.
2. Follow the major request with the details that will make the request clear. If possible, use tabulations for added emphasis.
3. Close with a forward look to the receiver's next step.

Figure 9-6 is a vague request letter. Figure 9-7 is the same request handled more efficiently.

Note that the good example (Figure 9-7) starts with a direct request for specific information. Then as much detail as necessary is presented to enable the receiver to answer specifically. The good letter ends confidently with appreciation for the action requested. The letter is short; but because it conveys enough information and has a tone of politeness, it is long enough.

FAVORABLE RESPONSE TO A ROUTINE REQUEST

The letter in Figure 9-8 responds favorably to a request. However, it conveys the decision without much enthusiasm.

With a little planning and consideration for the executive transferring overseas, the letter in Figure 9-9 could have been written just as quickly. Note the specific answers to the receiver's questions and the helpful, sincere tone.

FAVORABLE RESPONSE TO A FAVOR

Occasionally, as a business professional, you will be asked special favors. You may receive invitations to speak at various civic or education groups, spearhead fundraising and other service projects, or offer your expertise in other sundry ways. If you say "yes," you might as well say it enthusiastically. Sending an unplanned, stereotyped acceptance suggests that the contribution will be similar.

In the letter in Figure 9-10, the TV production manager of a local public relations firm graciously accepts an invitation to emcee an awards banquet for the Chamber of Commerce. His polite request for specific information assures

> **THINK IT OVER**
> Why extend a request or favor in the first sentence?

---

[1] For the past five years, I have worked as a staff engineer in the Environmental Group at Newsom. [2] Yesterday, I received news of my impending transfer to Paris, France, to work in our plant location there.

[3] I am writing you to ask if you have any advice to help me make my transition to the Paris operation—my first overseas assignment. [4] Because you have been working in the Paris office for the past ten years, I felt you would already know the ropes and could be a great help.

[5] Any advice you can provide would be greatly appreciated.

FIGURE 9-6   Poor example of a routine request.

[1, 2] Delays request (the main idea of the letter).

[3] Presents the request vaguely. [4] Contains an expression, "know the ropes," that may be difficult to interpret if the receiver is from a culture other than the U.S.

[5] Closes with a superficial statement.

Newsom Engineering Consultants
9800 South Spartan Road
Harrisburg, PA 17105-9800
(717) **555-9042**
Fax - (717) **555-3811**

November 3, 19--

[1] Ms. Kim Sorrels, Project Manager
Newsom Engineering Consultants
89, rue de Penthievre
75008 Paris
FRANCE

[2] Dear Ms. Sorrels:

[3] Would you please assist me as I begin plans to transfer to the Environmental Group in the Paris operation—my first overseas assignment? [4] Because you have been working in this overseas location for several years, you may be able to give me some ideas on the following items:

[5] 1. Can you suggest a strategy to help me optimize my purchase of francs, especially during the transition period?

[6] 2. What degree of proficiency should I have in the French language? If I must speak French fluently, how can I manage until I learn the language?

[7] 3. Can you suggest any books or other resources that will prepare my family and me for living abroad?

[8] I will arrive on May 26 to begin work on June 2. [9] Even though my transfer is six months away, my family and I wish to make our transition as smooth as possible. [10] Consequently, receiving this information from you will help us achieve that goal.

Sincerely,

Marcus Psenka

Marcus Psenka
Staff Engineer

Side notes (left margin):

[1] Illustrates the format of a French address; *rue* is the French word for street.

[2] Uses traditional U.S. salutation because the recipient is North American. *Monsieur* or *Madame* is an appropriate courtesy title when addressing a French man or woman, respectively. In French, *Dear* is used only when the recipient is known well.

[3, 4] States request plainly.

[5-7] Asks specific questions; uses enumeration for emphasis.

[8-10] Expresses appreciation and alludes to action.

THINK IT OVER

1. Identify the main idea and the details in Figure 9-6. Jot them down in the correct, deductive sequence. Compare your outline with Figure 9-7.

2. Comment on the value of "I am writing" in Sentence 3.

3. What could you say other than "know the ropes" that an international audience would understand?

4. How do the numbers enhance the content and appearance of Figure 9-7?

5. What genuine, original idea could you develop in the last paragraph?

FIGURE 9-7   Good example of a routine request.

1 I read your request hurriedly and hopefully my response will provide the logistics for your transition to the Paris operation.

2 The exchange rate fluctuates rapidly; I'd say you will need at least $5,000 for starting expenses. 3 Your other questions are difficult to answer; you'll just have to work them out when you get here. 4 I will introduce you to some of the staff here and help you find your way around on the first day, but after that you're on your own.

5 May we in the Paris office take this opportunity to welcome you to the overseas operation. We look forward to your arrival on June 2.

1 Focuses on writer; tone suggests lack of interest in helping; is vague; uses overly complex word.

2-4 Includes details that are not specific or helpful; not directly related to the questions asked.

5 Is wordy and unconvincing because of the negative tone.

FIGURE 9-8   Poor example of a favorable response to a routine request.

THINK IT OVER
Is the letter in Figure 9-8 written deductively? What are the major weaknesses? How would you revise the letter to convince the expatriate you want to help? Compare your ideas with Figure 9-9.

Newsom Engineering Consultants
89, rue de Penthièvre
75008 Paris
FRANCE
14 555-08-33   Fax 14 555-78-56

November 7, 19--

Mr. Marcus Psenka, Staff Engineer
Newsom Engineering Consultants
9800 South Spartan Road
Harrisburg, PA 17105-9800

Dear Mr. Psenka:

1 Congratulations on your transfer to the Paris office. I am happy that we will be working together and am pleased to answer your questions.

2 • The franc has been declining against the U.S. dollar steadily for several weeks, and economists are predicting that this trend will continue. Therefore, I suggest you immediately purchase the francs you will need for the first several months. You can easily keep in touch with the fluctuating exchange rates by reviewing the "Money Rates" section of *The Wall Street Journal* each day.

3 • English is used most often in the office. Becoming familiar with the French culture, customs, and economy will be beneficial. Several guidebooks are available from the director of International Operations at the home office. I recommend that you read these books thoroughly and share them with your wife and children, too.

4 • Jason O'Lenick has just left the Paris office to work in the Houston office. He would be able to answer many of your questions. You can reach him at (403) 555-1393.

5 Please fax me your travel plans, and I will make arrangements to meet you at the airport and help you get settled in your new home.

Sincerely,

Kim Sorrels

Kim Sorrels
Project Manager

1 Shows sincere interest in the request and the person.

2, 3 Provides specific answers and guidelines; uses bullets to highlight answers.

4 Provides additional helpful information.

5 Includes a specific offer that helps communicate genuine interest in the person and his transition.

THINK IT OVER
Knowing that international mail is slow and that Marcus needs a quick response, Kim decides to fax her letter. What special notation should she add to the letter in Figure 9-9? Consult Appendix A.

FIGURE 9-9   Good example of a favorable response to a routine request.

Edwards & Patton Public Relations
139 Northbend Road
Bakersfield, CA 93307-0139
(805) 555-3000   Fax - (805) 555-1490

July 11, 19--

Ms. Jeanne Saunders, President
Chamber of Commerce
3156 North Center Street
Bakersfield, CA 93302-3156

Dear Jeanne:

¹ Yes, I will be honored to emcee the annual Chamber of Commerce banquet beginning at 6 p.m. on August 25 in the City Auditorium.

² The format you described with a brief motivational speech followed by the service award presentations is an excellent change for this year's program. ³ As soon as you have secured the speaker, please send me a detailed profile so that I can prepare an appropriate introduction. ⁴ A brief description of each award and the person presenting it would help me plan smooth transitions between each award. ⁵ Please send a tentative copy of the program when it is complete.

⁶ Jeanne, I am eager to help the Chamber of Commerce celebrate another banner year on August 25. Let me know if I can help in any other way as plans develop.

Sincerely,

Erik

⁸ Erik Arnett, Director

¹ Accepts immediately; therefore, the receiver is relieved no one else will have to be asked. Confirms the time, date, and place.

² Uses a *you* attitude to confirm the change in the format.

³⁻⁵ Outlines specific requests to ensure a highly organized, professional affair.

⁶ Uses the receiver's name to personalize the letter and involve the reader.

⁷ Closes by restating enthusiasm and commitment for the project.

⁸ Signs first name only because he knows the reader well.

The right margin is not justified to improve comprehension and convey the idea the letter was not methodically generated by a computer.

FIGURE 9-10   Good example of a favorable response to an invitation.

THINK IT OVER
Give several examples of Erik's efforts to show empathy for the reader in his acceptance letter in Figure 9-10. Why does he sign his first name only?

the Chamber director that this busy manager is committed to doing an outstanding job as emcee. His closing remarks reinforce the enthusiasm evident throughout the letter.

If responses to invitations were frequent, the preceding letter could be stored on secondary storage (disk or hard drive) of a computer, retrieved, and revised to respond to the next invitation. Individualized form letters produced using computer-based technology enable businesses to communicate quickly and efficiently with clients or customers.

FORM LETTERS FOR ROUTINE RESPONSES

Form letters are a fast and efficient way of transmitting frequently recurring messages to which receiver reaction is likely favorable or neutral. Inputting the customer's name and address and other variables (information that differs for each receiver) personalizes each letter to meet the needs of its receiver. Refer to Figure 5-5 to understand how the mail-merge feature of word-processing software automates the production of form letters.

To personalize letters even further, companies may use form paragraphs that have been stored in separate files on secondary storage (disk or hard drive). Perhaps as many as five versions of a paragraph related to a typical request are available for use in a routine request letter. The originator selects the appropriate paragraph according to the receiver's request. After assembling the selected files on the computer screen, the originator inputs any variables (name and address). A copy of the personalized letter is printed on letterhead and sent to the receiver.

Organizations that serve a multitude of people with a mission of providing economical service (governmental agencies, public utilities) use forms similar to the form in the following example. To communicate a routine message, a support staff member simply places a check mark beside the message that applies. The company's letterhead usually appears at the top of the form and a general salutation such as "Dear Customer" is used.

> Form letters can save time and money but must be written carefully to avoid sounding cold and impersonal.

☐ The late charge has been waived because it resulted from circumstances beyond your control.

☐ The late charge appears to be valid; please add the amount to your next monthly payment.

☑ A late charge of $_25_ has been waived; however, an unpaid late charge of $_25_ remains on your account. Please add the amount to your next monthly payment.

Routine Letters About Credit

Normally, credit information is requested and transmitted electronically from the national credit reporting agencies to companies requesting credit references. However, when companies choose to request information directly from other businesses, individual credit requests and responses must be written.

LEARNING OBJECTIVE 4

REQUEST FOR INFORMATION

If a response to a company's request for credit information is likely to be favorable, present the following points in a deductive outline:

1. Identify the request and name the applicant in the opening sentence or in a subject line.
2. Assure the receiver that the reply will be kept confidential.
3. Detail the information requested. Use a tabulated-form layout to make the reply easy.
4. End courteously. Offer the same assistance to the receiver.

Printed forms on which the names of the reference and the applicant can be supplied increase efficiency. Another desirable arrangement, shown in the following excerpt of a credit request, is to include fill-in items within the letter.

> THINK IT OVER
> Look at the routine letter with inside address keyed in all caps with no punctuation in the "Envelopes" section of Appendix A. Why is this format recommended? When is it appropriate?

> Form letters are an efficient way to obtain credit information.

COMMUNICATION IN ACTION

Barbara Barrett, Jackson Zoo

When Barbara Barrett's letter for support from the state legislator went all the way to the Mississippi governor's desk, little did she realize the high profile status her routine request would receive. She was pleased to have the publicity for the Jackson Zoo, but she didn't anticipate the governor's readership. Although her letter received a favorable response, she realized the importance such mailings can have.

As zoo director, Barrett corresponds regularly with legislators, media personnel, and friends of the zoo. Much of her correspondence is in the form of routine letters, which are designed to cultivate friendships. These letters reach various audiences all through the state. Each year, for instance, she writes all Mississippi television stations to thank them for their support of the zoo. With the letter, she includes free passes to the zoo for the station's staff. Similarly, when Barrett corresponds with legislators each year, she thanks them for their support and sends them free family passes.

Before corresponding with legislators, Barrett asks, "What would this person want out of his or her relationship with the zoo?" She attempts to assess what legislators want from the sponsorship and how they would benefit by contributing to the zoo. If a senator or representative visits the zoo, Barrett wants "the stage to be set" so that the experience will be a good one. Her letters help her to reach this goal. She knows that the easiest legislators to contact are those who have brought their children or grandchildren to the zoo. She believes no one can remember the zoo without relating it to his or her own experiences.

Attempting to assess readers' needs and prepare them for a visit to the zoo is no easy task. Through her experience, however, Barrett has learned how to write in a fresh way that communicates clearly. First and foremost, she believes, her message must be clear, precise, and easily understood by the reader. In a busy legislator's office, her letter may be read only once or simply scanned. To receive the attention it needs, the letter must be clear and short. She says, "Three short letters that are read is better than one long letter that is not read."

Next, she starts every letter with a simple thank you. If she addresses a legislator, she begins with "Thank you for your involvement this past weekend." By saying thanks at first, she believes her letter makes a positive impact on the reader. Because a letter from the zoo can be less formal than similar correspondence from other non-profit organizations, she occasionally uses humor to gain interest. Barrett tells of a sponsor who donated $10,000 for a Koala exhibit. When thanking the sponsor for the contribution, she stated, "Many visitors have related to us that this was perhaps their first and only opportunity to meet Koala bears face-to-face." This humorous statement helped stimulate the sponsor to feel positive about the zoo and about the contribution that was made.

Barrett's routine letters "pave the way" with visitors by cultivating goodwill and personal contact. Visitors to the Jackson Zoo are prepared to have a good time. Many visitors come with families, sharing precious leisure time with each other. Barrett believes families have very little time to share together. Because more mothers are working outside the home, families visit the zoo to share some wholesome time together. Barrett's business communication skills are evidently working. The Jackson Zoo has succeeded in its goal of offering excellent family interactive experiences that are fun.

Applying What You Have Learned

1. Discuss how Barrett's letters prepare legislators and other visitors for a fun visit to the zoo.
2. What questions did Barrett mentally answer before writing her letter to legislators?
3. Assume that you work as the assistant director for the Jackson Zoo and will correspond with the Honorable Mary L. Jackson, Mississippi State Senate, Capitol Building, P.O. Box 1018, Jackson, MS 39215-1018. Senator Jackson visited the zoo last weekend with her family, having used free family passes you sent her in previous correspondence. Compose a routine letter of support to Senator Jackson, acknowledging her visit to the zoo with her family. Use brevity and conciseness, realizing you will have only a few moments to communicate your message.

The information can be provided and the letter returned with a minimum of cost or effort. Also, note this credit request was made by the credit applicant and not the prospective creditor. Consequently, the credit reference is assured that the request is legitimate and that the applicant wishes to have credit information provided.

> Please provide credit information to Seacoast Distributors. This information will facilitate our purchasing products on account.
>
> Please complete the blanks that follow. Your reply will be held in strict confidence. Return the completed letter to Seacoast Distributors in the addressed, stamped envelope.
>
> Time sold on credit _____   Credit limit _____
>
> Balance due _____   Past due _____
>
> Remarks _____
>
> Authorized signature _____
>
> We appreciate your help in obtaining credit from this new vendor. Please drop by the Cafe to enjoy our delicious menu additions.

RESPONSE TO A REQUEST FOR INFORMATION

Replies to requests for credit information usually are very simple—just fill in the blanks and return the letter. If the request does not include a form, follow a deductive plan in writing the reply: the major idea followed by supporting details.

> *Discuss the legal implications of credit information letters.*

In credit information letters, writers have an ethical and legal obligation to themselves, the credit applicant, and the business extending credit. You must be able to document any statement you make in order to defend yourself against a defamation charge. Thus, good advice is to stick with facts; omit any opinions. "I'm sure he will pay promptly" is an opinion that should be omitted but include the documentable fact that "His payments are always prompt." Can you safely say a customer *is* a good credit risk when all you know is that he/she *had* a good credit record when he/she purchased from you?

REQUEST FOR CREDIT

When people or businesses want to begin buying on credit and assume credit will be willingly extended, they can place their request in the first sentence and follow with details. This approach is recommended only when the writer's supporting financial statements are assumed sufficient to merit a "yes" response. The credit request in Figure 9-11 follows the deductive plan effectively.

FAVORABLE RESPONSE TO A REQUEST FOR CREDIT

A timely response is preferable for any business document, but especially important when communicating about credit. The Equal Credit Opportunity Act (ECOA) requires that a credit applicant be notified of the credit decision within 30 days of the receipt of the request or application. You will learn more about other legal implications related to credit when we discuss credit denials in Chapter 10.

> *What legal requirements apply to letters extending credit?*

Effective "yes" replies to requests for credit should include the following points in the deductive outline:

Wellness Connection
5800 Catlett Street   Ocean City, MD 21842-5800   410 555-4910

June 3, 19--

Image Athletic Clothing, Inc.
740 Morgan Avenue
Springfield, MA 01101-0740

REQUEST FOR CREDIT AND SHIPMENT OF FIRST ORDER

[1] Will you please fill the enclosed order on a credit basis? [2] We are eager to offer your popular line of athletic clothing to our customers.

[3] Established in 1974, we are the largest indoor athletic facility in Ocean City. [4] Our club offers members the most diversified selection of recreational activities available locally—from aerobics and racquetball to a health-food cafe.

[5] The enclosed financial statements indicate that we purchase on account regularly from other vendors. [6] Credit references can be provided. [7] If you need additional information, please write to me.

[8] Many of our customers have been asking us to stock your line; therefore, we expect to place a similar order every six weeks.

Chi Wang
Chi Wang
Manager

[9] Enclosures

Notes in left margin:

[1, 2] States the major idea and shows interest in the company.

[3, 4] Gives background information about the company.

[5-7] Provides details needed for credit to be extended.

[8] Closes with a look to the future.

[9] Uses an enclosure notation to alert the reader information is enclosed.

Uses simplified block format, which eliminates the need for an impersonal salutation for a letter addressed to a company.

FIGURE 9-11   *Good example of a request for credit.*

1. Begin by saying credit terms have been arranged; or if an order has been placed, begin by telling of the shipment of goods, thereby implying the credit has been extended.
2. Indicate the foundation upon which the credit extension is based.
3. Present and explain the credit terms.
4. Include some resale or sales promotional material.
5. End with a confident look toward future business.

Firms receive so many requests for credit that the costs of individualized letters are prohibitive; therefore, most favorable replies to credit requests are form letters. To personalize the letter, however, the writer merges the loan applicant's

COMMUNICATION MENTOR

The Russian language is extremely formal, and often a number of different words can be used to convey a general meaning. To ensure that the exact meaning is conveyed to the reader, a professional staff member proficient in both Russian and English reviews much of our Russian correspondence. Detailed and significant messages and documents such as proposals and reports translated from English are reviewed carefully for possible language barriers.

Larry E. Wilson, Managing Partner
Arthur Andersen, Moscow

name, address, amount of loan, and terms into the computer file containing the form letter information. Typically, form messages read something like this:

Dear [TITLE] [LAST NAME]

We are pleased to extend credit privileges to you. Temporarily, you may purchase up to **[CREDIT LIMIT]** worth of merchandise on time. Our credit terms are **[TERMS]**. We welcome you as a credit customer of our expanding organization.

Although such form messages are effective for informing the customer that credit is being extended, they do little to promote sales and goodwill. Whether to say "yes" by form letter or by individualized letter is a problem that each credit manager must settle individually. If the list of credit customers is relatively short and few names are being added, individualized letters may be practical. A credit manager may choose to use individualized letters if the workload in the department is such that letters can be sent without overworking or adding personnel.

You have learned to discuss the shipment and extend credit in the first sentence, use resale and sales promotional material, and write as if you expect future orders. You should discuss the basis for your decision to extend credit to prevent collection problems that may arise later. Indicating that you are extending credit on the basis of an applicant's prompt-paying habits with present creditors encourages continuation of those habits with you. You recognize a reputation and challenge the purchaser to live up to it. If financial situations become difficult, the purchaser will probably remember the compliment and try to pay you first.

Why discuss the basis for extending credit? credit terms?

Unless customers know exactly when payments are expected (credit terms), they may not make them on time. Unless they know exactly what the discount terms are, they may take unauthorized discounts. Furthermore, taking time to discuss terms in detail suggests that terms are important and that you expect them to be followed. These principles are applied in Figure 9-12.

Although the letter in Figure 9-12 was written to a dealer, the same principles apply when writing to a consumer. Each one should be addressed in terms of individual interests. Dealers are concerned about markup, marketability, and display; consumers are concerned about price, appearance, and durability. Consumers may require a more detailed explanation of credit terms.

The letter in Figure 9-12 performed a dual function: it said "yes" to an application for credit and "Yes, we are filling your order." Because of its importance, the credit aspect was emphasized more than the acknowledgment of the order. In

Advanced Electronics Corporation
3019 Milam Road Lansing, MI 48909-3019
Telephone: (517) 555-1089 Fax: (517) 555-1123

October 15, 19--

[1] Attention Order Department
[2] Washington Technologies
MC2397 Succ. A
Montreal, Que.
H3C 2J7 CANADA

Ladies and Gentlemen:

[3] Ten VISIONZ video cameras were shipped by Fastgo Air Express and should arrive in time for your Winter Fest.

[4] Because of your favorable current credit rating, we are sending the shipment subject to the usual credit terms, 2/10, n/30. [5] By paying this invoice within ten days, you save $150.

[6] The VISIONZ camera is known for its 8:1, fl .4 power zoom lens and 2-lux light sensitivity—features that will allow your customers to take high-quality pictures with a minimum of light. [7] The display inside the viewer will give your customers additional helpful information.

[8] Because many of your customers may be interested in a higher zoom, we strongly suggest that at least one of your display models be equipped with the telephoto adapter for the VISIONZ. [9] Please refer to the enclosed folder for the brochure explaining this economical enhancement to a quality video camera.

Sincerely,

Cara L. Fontenot
Credit Manager

Enclosure

FIGURE 9-12 Good example of a favorable response to a credit request.

[1,2] Illustrates correct Canadian address. Uses attention line in letter addressed to a company to assure efficient delivery. Could use simplified format to avoid impersonal salutation.

[3] Presents good news. Indicates that the writer has some consideration for the problems of a dealer. Implies the credit extension.

[4] Recognizes the dealer for earning the credit privilege. Gives a reason for the credit extension; it was not extended arbitrarily. Introduces the credit terms. Addressed to a dealer, the letter does not need to explain what "2/10, n/30" means.

[5] Encourages taking advantage of the discount in terms of profits for the dealer.

[6,7] Presents resale.

[8,9] Looks confidently forward to future orders.

other cases (in which the order is for cash or the credit terms are already clearly understood), the primary purpose of writing may be to acknowledge an order.

Routine Letters About Orders

LEARNING OBJECTIVE 5

Like routine letters about credit, routine letters about orders put the main idea in the first sentence. Details are usually tabulated, especially when more than one item is ordered.

ORDER LETTER

Order letters create one-half of a contract. They constitute the offer portion of a contract that is fulfilled when the shipper sends the goods, thereby creating the acceptance part of the contract. In large companies, the normal procedure is to use purchase order forms for ordering. Most consumers buying from direct marketing companies use the order forms enclosed with catalogs.

As a customer, making sure your order letter or form is complete with every detail is most important. If you sell by mail, you will want to design the form so that customers can complete it easily and accurately.

In today's technological environment, calling an 800 number to place an order, mailing, faxing order forms, and placing an order via an online catalog are common ways of initiating the acquisition process. However, writing an order letter is still necessary if the vendor does not provide an order blank or the customer has not established credit with the vendor. Some orders may be too complex to be communicated by telephone, and order blanks are not available. For example, calling an 800 number to order a copy of a leading software program is a simple matter. However, consider the entrepreneur ordering everything needed to build and operate a driving range; the vendor provides a beautiful four-color catalog but *no* order form. Wanting to be absolutely certain that the order is filled accurately so the grand opening is not delayed while waiting for critical items to be returned and reshipped, this entrepreneur wisely wrote the order letter shown in Figure 9-13.

Order letters include the following points in a deductive outline:

1. Use order language in the first sentence. Say, "Please ship," "Please send," or some other suitable statement that assures the seller of the desire to buy. Avoid indefinite statements like "I'm interested" or "I'd like to."
2. Detail carefully the items ordered. Be specific by mentioning catalog numbers, prices, colors, sizes, and all other information that will enable the seller to fill the order promptly and without the need for further correspondence.
3. Include a payment plan and shipping instructions. Remember that the shipper is free to ship by the normal method in the absence of specific instructions from the buyer. Tell when, where, and how the order is to be shipped.
4. Close the letter with a confident expectation of delivery.

> When is writing an order letter preferable to calling an 800 number, completing an order blank, or placing an order via an online catalog?

> List two possible interpretations of "I would like to order. . . ."

Please ship the following items, listed in your current catalog:

Item	Stock No.	Qty.	Unit Price	Total Price
Lighting system	A-931	1	$4,875	$4,875
Tee mats	T-137	8	200	1,600
Range balls	R-861	300 dz	6	1,800
Range pails	R-318	30	5	150
Ball picker	B-590	1	995	995
Men's club	ML-33	15	24	360
Ladies' club	LL-14	10	24	240
Juniors' club	JL-76	15	22	330
TOTAL				$10,350

Please charge this order to my account number 32067 and ship by Federal Express.

FIGURE 9-13   Good example of an order letter (excerpt).

Companies send acknowl-
edgments to encourage
future orders.

THINK IT OVER
Bring to class examples of
letters of acknowledgments
received from merchandise you
have ordered or used by companies for which you work. Be
prepared to discuss the efficiency and communication
effectiveness of each example.

FIGURE 9-14
*Good example of a computer-
generated sales order.*

FAVORABLE RESPONSE TO AN ORDER LETTER

When customers place an order for merchandise, they expect to get exactly what they ordered as quickly as possible. Most orders can be acknowledged by shipping the order; no letter is necessary. For initial orders and for orders that cannot be filled quickly and precisely, companies send **acknowledgment letters**, a document that indicates the order has been received and is being processed. Typically, acknowledgment letters are preprinted letters or a copy of the sales order because sending individualized letters is not cost effective and will not reach the customer in a timely manner. The example of a computer-generated sales order shown in Figure 9-14 illustrates that these forms are impersonal. However, customers appreciate the company's acknowledging the order and giving them an idea of when the order will arrive.

Central Golf Supply Company, Inc.
9033 Valley Hill Road / Chicago, IL 60607-9033

SALES ORDER
No. 9726

SOLD TO:
REESE SPORTING GOODS
4900 NORTH MAIN STREET
ASHEBORO, NC 27203-4900

SHIP TO:
SAME

DATE	SHIP VIA	SHIP DATE	TERMS
10/14/--	FREIGHT EX.	11/20/--	N/30

PURCHASE ORDER NO.	ORDER DATE	SALESPERSON	CUSTOMER NO.
LETTER	10/1/--		32067

QTY ORDERED	QTY SHIPPED	QTY BO	ITEM NO.	DESCRIPTION	UNIT PRICE	EXTENDED PRICE
1	1		A-931	Lighting system	$4,875.00	$ 4,875.00
8	8		T-137	Tee mats	200.00	1,600.00
300 dz	300 dz		R-861	Range balls	6.00	1,800.00
30	30		R-318	Range pail	5.00	150.00
1	1		B-590	Ball picker	995.00	995.00
15	15		ML-33	Men's club	24.00	360.00
10	10		LL-14	Ladies' club	24.00	240.00
15	15		JL-76	Juniors' club	22.00	330.00

*Thank You
For Your Business.*

SUBTOTAL	$10,350.00
FREIGHT	52.35
TAX	724.50
TOTAL	$11,126.85

Nonroutine orders require individualized acknowledgment letters. Although initial orders can be acknowledged through form letters, the letters are more effective if individually written. When well written, these letters not only acknowledge the order but also create customer goodwill and encourage the customer to place additional orders. Because saying "yes" is easy, you may develop the habit of using clichés and selecting words that make your letters sound as cold and mechanical as the letter in Figure 9-15.

When are *form acknowledgments* inappropriate?

[1] Thank you for your order, which we really appreciate. [2] We sincerely welcome you to our ever-growing list of satisfied customers.

[3] We were delighted to send you 30 CS 382 computer systems. [4] They were shipped by express today.

[5] We are sure you will find our company a good one to deal with and that our computer systems are of the finest quality.

[6] Please find our latest price list enclosed. [7] Thank you for your patronage.

FIGURE 9-15   *Poor example of a favorable response to an order letter.*

[1, 2] Begins with clichés saying what has been said already to thousands of customers.

[3] Sounds exaggerated and thus insincere.

[4] Presents main idea that should have been presented earlier.

[5] Includes unsupportable statement of certainty.

[6,7] Closes with more clichés.

Is this letter effective enough to create customer goodwill or generate future orders? Let's see how the same letter sounds when it confirms shipment of goods in the first sentence, includes concrete resale on the product and company, and eliminates business jargon (see Figure 9-16).

A major purpose of the acknowledgment letter is to encourage future orders. An effective technique to achieve this goal is to state that the merchandise was sent, include resale, and imply that future orders will be handled in the same manner. Don't expect to encourage future business by just filling the page with words like *welcome* and *gratitude*. They are overused words, and many people whose merchandise and services are poor overwork them. Appropriate action implies both gratitude *and* welcome. When conveying these qualities in writing, make sure you are sincere and original.

If a company is truly grateful for clients' patronage, why not say, "Thank you for your patronage" as the last sentence in all letters to clients?

MEMORANDUMS AND E-MAIL MESSAGES

Because letters go to people outside a business and memorandums (commonly referred to as memos) and e-mail messages go to people within a business, their formats are different. A memo needs no return address, inside address, salutation, or complimentary closing. Instead, a typical memo and e-mail message presents (on separate lines) (1) the name of the person *to* whom the message is addressed, (2) the name of the person *from* whom the message comes, (3) the *date*, and (4) the *subject*. When a memo is addressed to more than one person, all their names appear on the "TO" line. If the list is long, a common practice is to write "Distribution" on the "TO" line. Then, beneath the last line of the memo, write the word *Distribution* and follow it with an alphabetized list of the names. In addition to simplifying interoffice mailing and reference, alphabetizing eliminates the risk of having someone on the list wonder whether names appear in order of importance.

As discussed in Chapter 5, sending a single message to multiple receivers simultaneously is a distinct advantage of e-mail. The writer simply inputs one or more addresses (often separated by commas) or creates distribution lists (address macros) for groups of people with whom he or she corresponds frequently.

LEARNING OBJECTIVE 6

THINK IT OVER
To which audience are memorandums and e-mail messages directed?

THINK IT OVER
If you have not learned to create a distribution list for sending e-mail to multiple readers, locate the commands or ask someone to help you learn this time-saving feature. Complete the e-mail application at the end of the chapter.

Advanced Electronics Corporation
3019 Milam Road   Lansing, MI 48909-3019
Telephone: (517) 555-1089 · Fax: (517) 555-1123

May 3, 19--

Blanco Electronics
DX3926 Succ. B
Toronto, Ont.
M5E 157 CANADA

PURCHASE ORDER NO. 37490

[1] Thirty CS 382 computer systems were shipped to your store by Fastgo Air Express today.

[2] Each unit has been customized according to your specifications. These modifications include **one CD-ROM disk drive, one 3 1/2" disk drive, math co-processor, and memory expansion card to facilitate future memory needs.**

[3] With these distinctive features, these computers will provide your customers with leading-edge technology. [4]The flexibility of this system will allow your customers to take advantage of software innovations quickly and efficiently.

[5] With the custom features of these CS 382s, your customers can work optimally at the office. [6] The NB-1 is available now. [7] This notebook computer has the power your customers will need for work they take home or to other remote locations. [8]Its easy-to-use trackball and backlit liquid crystal display have made the NB-1 a popular portable.

[9] To make this preferred portable technology available to your customers, review the enclosed specifications and complete the enclosed order form. [10]Your order will be shipped immediately.

Vann R. Hamm

Vann R. Hamm
Sales Manager

[11] Enclosures

FIGURE 9-16   Good example of a favorable response to an order letter.

The marginal notes alongside the figure read:

[1] Implies sufficiently that the order has been received and filled. Refers to specific merchandise shipped and reveals method of shipment.

[2] Confirms the specific modifications for this customer order.

[3, 4] Points out specific qualities of the merchandise (uses resale).

[5-8] Mentions related merchandise (uses sales promotional material).

[9, 10] Refers to enclosures without using an entire sentence. Implies additional orders are expected.

[11] Uses an enclosure notation to alert reader that other information is included.

Uses simplified block format to avoid impersonal salutation.

What three guidelines make e-mail messages easier to read?

THINK IT OVER
How important are grammatical correctness and careful proofreading in e-mail messages?

When sending a message to a group for which a distribution list has been created, the writer must input only the address assigned to the desired distribution; some systems allow you to select the desired distribution from a list appearing on the screen. With quick, easy commands, a writer can send an e-mail message to individuals other than the recipient (synonymous with the copy notation used in printed messages) or forward incoming e-mail messages to individuals who might be interested in or need to be informed of the content of the message. Before continuing, you may wish to reread the "Electronic Mail" and "Guidelines for Communicating Electronically" sections of Chapter 5. Pay careful attention to the basic e-mail style guidelines that makes e-mail easier to read.

COMMUNICATION MENTOR

Use proper grammar in electronic mail. Your notes could be forwarded to many people whom you have not met, and these notes could make your first impressions on them.

Sajan K. Thomas
Vice President
Prudential Institutional Investors

Principles of writing (see Chapters 7 and 8) that apply to business letters also apply to memos and e-mail messages. An exception is the use of technical jargon, which is more likely to be useful in memorandums and e-mail messages. Because people doing similar work are almost sure to know the technical terms associated with it, jargon will be understood, will not be taken as an attempt to impress, and will save time. For the same reasons, acronyms, abbreviations, and shortened forms, such as *info, rep, demo*, and *stat*, are more useful in memos and e-mail messages than in letters.

Principles of organizing that apply to letters also apply to memos and e-mail messages. In both, empathy is the basis for deciding whether to proceed deductively or inductively. In addition, memos may use other bases for determining the sequence of ideas; for example, time (reporting events in the order in which they happened), order of importance, and geography.

Graphics are appropriate whenever they strengthen your efforts to communicate, regardless of the medium—letter, report, or memo. Tables, graphs, charts, and pictures may be either integrated into the content of the memo or attached as supporting material. You will learn techniques for preparing effective graphics in Chapter 16. Tabulation and enumeration are also useful in memorandums.

The **subject line** (1) tells the receiver what the following message is about and (2) sets the stage for the receiver to understand the message. The following suggestions should be helpful in preparing subject lines:

1. Make the subject line as long as necessary. If, for example, your subject is the report of a meeting, "Report of Meeting" is a poor subject line. "Report of June 10 Meeting on Relocation of Dublin Plant" is a better subject line. In addition to aiding understanding, subject lines provide information helpful to records clerks.

2. Think of the five Ws to give you some clues for good subject lines: *Who, What, When, Where*, and *Why*. Key words help in the development of good subject lines.

3. Repeat the subject in the body of the memorandum. Opening sentences should not include wording such as "This is . . ." and "The above-mentioned subject . . ." The body of the memorandum should be a complete thought and should not rely on the subject line for elaboration. A good opening sentence might be a repetition of most of the subject line. Even if the subject line were omitted, the memorandum would still be clear, logical, and complete.

4. Keyboard the subject line in all capital letters if additional emphasis is desired.

What one principle of writing used in business letters *does not* apply to memos and e-mail messages?

THINK IT OVER
Generate a list of technical jargon, acronyms, and abbreviations that people in your field will readily understand but may be foreign to those outside the field.

THINK IT OVER
Is including graphics in memos and e-mail messages necessary? Has technology affected the use of graphics within business documents? (Refer to Chapter 5 if necessary.)

Like a title to a report, the subject line gives the reader the gist of the message, which aids in understanding the message.

What suggestions could you offer for writing an effective subject line?

Where does the main idea appear in memos and e-mail messages?

THINK IT OVER
In groups, turn to the "Memorandums" section of Appendix A and discuss the two memorandum formats and differences between letters and memos. How do writers sign memorandums?

Write a memorandum deductively when it contains good news or neutral information. Write inductively when a memorandum contains bad news or is intended to persuade. (Inductive memos are discussed in greater detail in Chapters 10 and 11.)

Examples of memorandums in Chapter 9 are formatted according to standard business formats for memos. Study carefully the detailed explanation and illustrations of standard formats (formal and simplified) and layout of memorandums in Appendix A. When you are confident you understand this information, return to this chapter to review the examples.

Good-News Memorandums

The memorandum in Figure 9-17 conveys good news. As a good-news message, this memo presents the main idea in the first sentence.

Routine Memorandums

The memo is the most frequently used method of communicating standard operating procedures and other instructions, changes related to personnel, and other matters for which a written record is needed.

Managers who have shunned letter writing for long-distance telephone calls are now writing again thanks to the ease and power of e-mail (Verity, 1994).

MEMORANDUMS OUTLINING PROCEDURES OR GIVING INSTRUCTIONS

Instructions to employees must be conveyed clearly and accurately to facilitate the day-to-day operations of business and to prevent negative feelings that occur when mistakes are made and work must be redone. Managers must take special care in writing standard operating procedures to ensure that all employees complete the procedure accurately and consistently.

What steps should you take to ensure that procedures and instructions can be understood and followed consistently?

Before writing instructions, walk through each step to understand it and to locate potential trouble spots. Then attempt to determine how much employees already know about the process and to anticipate any questions or problems. Then, as you write instructions that require more than a few simple steps, follow these guidelines:

BURKE
INDUSTRIAL
109 Conway Drive   Dothan, AL 36301-0109   205 555 9000   Fax 205 555 3487

TO: All Full-Time Employees

FROM: Gary L. Mayfield, President & CEO   G.L.M.

DATE: April 5, 19--

[1] SUBJECT: MATCHING FUNDS PROGRAM APPROVED

[2] The stockholders have approved the union's petition for the corporation to implement a matching funds program for contributions you make to institutions of higher learning.

[3] We are pleased the stockholders have expressed such strong support of your commitment to higher education. [4] You may recall the original petition limited annual contributions to $100 a person. [5] However, the plan approved by the stockholders raised the annual contributions limit to $250 a person.

[6] Beginning May 1 you may submit requests for Burke Industrial to match your contributions to any institution of higher learning you choose. [7] Simply obtain the appropriate form from the Human Resources Department. [8] Then complete the form and return it with your canceled check written to the educational institution.

[9] Thank you for your keen interest in this program. [10] With your generous giving and the matching funds, we at Burke Industrial can make a significant contribution to providing quality education.

cep

[1] Gets attention by placing good news in the subject line.

[2] Includes good news in emphatic first-sentence position.

[3-5] Follows with an explanation.

[6-8] Continues with details for submitting request.

[9, 10] Closes on a pleasant note.

FIGURE 9-17   Good example of a good-news memorandum.

1. Begin each step with an action statement to create a vivid picture of the employee completing the task. Using an action verb and the understood subject *you* is more vivid than a sentence written in passive voice. For example, a loan officer attempting to learn new procedures for evaluating new venture loans can understand "*identify* assets available to collateralize the loan" more easily than "assets available to collateralize the loan should be identified."

2. Itemize each step on a separate line to add emphasis and to simplify reading. Number each step to indicate that the procedures should be completed in a particular order. If the order is not important, use bullets (•, ◆, ■ , *) to draw attention to each step.

Inadequate or mishandled information can damage employee morale. Communicate to solve problems and create a better working environment. Employees who are well-informed are less likely to suffer stress, be absent, or have job complications. Managers are rewarded with trust and honesty generated by open communication.

3. Consider preparing a flow chart depicting the procedures if the clarity of the procedure merits the cost of preparing such a sophisticated chart. Take a look at Figure 16-12, which simplifies the steps involved in processing a telephone order in an effort to minimize errors.
4. Complete the procedure by following your instructions step by step. Correct any errors you locate.
5. Ask a colleague or employee to walk through the procedures to locate ambiguous statements, omissions of relevant information, and other errors and to anticipate potential problems.

THINK IT OVER
To expand your employees' use of e-mail, write a memo to "all employees" including instructions for attaching a word-processing file to an e-mail message. Follow the guidelines carefully, including asking someone to evaluate your steps.

Consider the seemingly simple task of telling employees what to do if a newly installed badge reader will not record their time when they report to work. The human resources director might quickly respond, "No need for written instructions; just tell the employees to get to work and then get them a new badge." The process of writing step-by-step procedures might alert the manager to the potential abuses that could result from issuing a new badge without obtaining the supposedly damaged card. In addition, ambiguous and inconsistent verbal instructions (developed in the midst of the chaos) could result in an inaccurate payroll. A chaotic environment and suspicion about whether management is giving them proper credit for hours worked could cause employees to mistrust management and lower morale. Having anticipated these potential problems and worked through the procedures carefully, the discerning manager wrote the instructions in Figure 9-18.

THINK IT OVER
Sending messages to a group of people at the same time is a distinct advantage to e-mail. What are other messages that could be damaging to employee morale if some employees received the message before others?

MEMORANDUMS ABOUT PERSONNEL CHANGES

An introductory memorandum distributed on or before a newly hired person's first day on the job assists in getting the new relationship off to a good start. Before the grapevine could generate rumors, a prudent human resources manager quickly sent all employees the e-mail message in Figure 9-19 confirming an employee's resignation and at the same time soliciting support in the interim.

TO: Line Supervisors

FROM: David Pruitt, Human Resources Manager *D.P.*

DATE: January 3, 19--

SUBJECT: PROCEDURES FOR REPLACING DAMAGED BADGE READERS

[1] Our recent transition from a punch clock to badge readers to record employees' time has run smoothly. [2] However, we anticipate the possibility of defective badge readers, especially as they become worn over time.

[3] To ensure the accuracy of the payroll, please instruct your employees to follow these procedures in the event the reader does not read their badges:

[4] 1. Complete a copy of Form PR-17 (copy attached).

[5] 2. Attach the damaged badge to the completed Form PR-17.

[6] 3. Give the card to Gena Kaminski in the Payroll Office by 10 a.m. She will prepare a new badge and send it to you with Form PR-17 by the end of the day.

[7] 4. Distribute the new badge to the employee. Instruct the employee *not* to use the new badge today but to report his/her departing time directly to you.

[8] 5. Record the employee's departing time on Form PR-17 and return it to Gena in the Payroll Office.

[9] Attachment

[1,2] Introduces the main idea.

[3] Introduces the upcoming list of steps.

[4-8] Begins each sequential step with an action verb (subject "you" understood) to help supervisors visualize themselves completing the procedures. Enumerates each step to direct attention to each step. Uses numbers rather than bullets to emphasize that each step must be completed in sequence.

[9] Adds attachment notation to alert reader that something other than the memo is included.

THINK IT OVER
Why are the procedures numbered in Figure 9-18? Would bullets be just as effective?

FIGURE 9-18   Good example of a memorandum outlining procedures.

MEMORANDUM WRITTEN "TO THE FILE"

When information needs to be converted into written form and filed for future reference, the record may be made in memo form (Figure 9-20). Writing the information in the memo will assist the writer in remembering and using the information.

Summaries of disciplinary actions taken can also be written as a memo and placed in an employee's personnel file. These memos serve as important documentation in the event of litigation—legally defensible evidence of action taken. More importantly, these confidential records can remind the supervisor of specific weaknesses in performance that employees may need help in overcoming.

What is the purpose of a "to the file" memo?

Refer to Figure A-8 in Appendix A. The headings divide the content into two logical divisions (advertising and sales staff), which increases the readability.

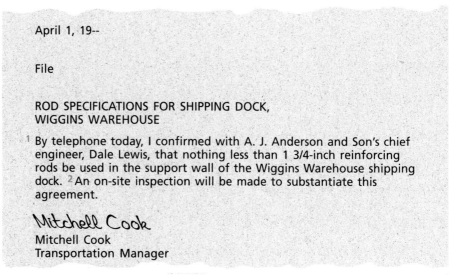

Mail - [APPOINTMENT OF STEPHEN WHITE, COMMUNICATIONS SPECIALIST]

File   Edit   View   Mail   Window   Help

Compose   Reply   Reply All   Forward   Move   Delete   Previous   Next

Send   Check Names   Attach   Options   Address

To: All Sales Personnel

FROM: Brad Graham, Vice President of Operations

DATE: April 1, 19--

[1] I'm pleased to announce the appointment of Stephen White as communication specialist in the corporate communications department. [2] He will fill the position vacated by Kenneth Furniss and will begin work on May 6.

[3] Steve comes to us from Gynco Industries where he was in charge of mass media relations. [4] His duties with us will include long-range planning and liaison with our ad agency, Smith and Moore. [5] He has degrees in public relations and marketing.

[6] Steve merits your full support. [7] We wish him much success and extend a sincere welcome to our organization.

1 message   3:54PM

Sidebar notes (left margin):

[1] Begins with major idea.

[2] Refers to the one being replaced and gives a general idea of the new employee's duties. Includes starting date.

[3-5] Provides relative background and duties. Uses "Steve" to suggest Mr. White's probable preference. Reveals previous duties and education to add to the new employee's initial credibility.

[6,7] Encourages present employees to be cooperative and seeks to make Steve feel welcome.

FIGURE 9-19   Good example of an e-mail message about personnel changes.

Lengthy memorandums may be divided into logical sections. Using headings to denote the divisions will alert the receiver to the information that is ahead and make the information easier to comprehend.

Before writing a pleasant or routine message, study carefully the overall suggestions in the "General Writing Guidelines" on page 269. Then, study the specific suggestions in the "Check Your Writing" checklist that follows the chapter summary. After you have written a rough draft, compare your work with the "Check Your Writing" checklist and make any revisions.

April 1, 19--

File

ROD SPECIFICATIONS FOR SHIPPING DOCK, WIGGINS WAREHOUSE

[1] By telephone today, I confirmed with A. J. Anderson and Son's chief engineer, Dale Lewis, that nothing less than 1 3/4-inch reinforcing rods be used in the support wall of the Wiggins Warehouse shipping dock. [2] An on-site inspection will be made to substantiate this agreement.

Mitchell Cook
Mitchell Cook
Transportation Manager

Sidebar notes (left margin):

[1] Records details that may be needed when the subject is discussed later.

[2] Includes additional information that affects future plans.

Illustrates the simplified memo, a time-saving format for such a routine memorandum.

FIGURE 9-20   Good example of a "to the file" memorandum (excerpt).

COMMUNICATION   MENTOR

I encourage written documentation of each significant event relating to client matters. This documentation should present significant issues in a concise, understandable manner that can be distributed to each "need-to-know" person on the team.

Larry E. Wilson, Managing Partner
Arthur Andersen, Moscow

SUMMARY

1   When the receiver can be expected to be pleased by the message, the main idea is presented first and details follow. Likewise, when the message is *routine* and not likely to arouse a feeling of pleasure or displeasure, the main idea is presented first (as illustrated in the letters, memorandums, and e-mail messages in this chapter). The deductive approach is appropriate for routine claim letters, routine requests, routine letters about credit and about orders, and favorable responses.

2   A routine claim requests the adjustment in the first sentence because you assume the company will make the adjustment without persuasion. Continue with an explanation of the problem to support the request and an expression of appreciation for taking the action. An adjustment letter extends the adjustment in the first sentence and explains the circumstances related to correcting the problem. The closing may include sales promotional material or other futuristic comments indicating your confidence that the customer will continue doing business with a company that has a reputation for fairness.

3   A routine request begins with the major request, includes details that will clarify the request, and alludes to the receiver's response. A response to a routine request provides the information requested, provides necessary details, and closes with a personal, courteous ending.

4   A letter requesting credit information begins with the request, outlines the informa-tion needed, and ends courteously. When providing credit information, give only verifiable facts to avoid possible litigation. A request for credit begins with the request, provides details needed to extend the credit, and closes by showing appreciation. A letter extending credit begins by extending credit, indicates the basis for the decision, explains credit terms, and may include resale. The closing may include sales promotional material or other futuristic comments. Credit extension letters must adhere to legal guidelines related to credit.

5   An order letter authorizes the purchase, includes detailed information about the items ordered, specifies payment and delivery plans, and closes with confidence the delivery will be made. Form or computer-generated acknowledgment letters assure customers that orders will be filled quickly. An individualized acknowledgment that confirms shipment and includes resale on the product and the company generates goodwill and future business.

6   Memorandums and e-mail messages are sent to receivers inside the organization. Acceptable memo and e-mail formats are less formal than business letter formats. Providing a descriptive subject line aids the receiver in understanding these internal messages. The deductive approach is also appropriate for memos and e-mail messages that contain good news as the central idea and convey such nonemotional information as noncontroversial changes in policies and procedures, instructions, personnel changes, and written records of information included in a "to the file" memo.

7 **The writing principles that apply to letters also apply to memos and e-mail messages.** Both are written informally; but memorandums normally make extensive use of jargon, abbreviations, acronyms, and graphics. E-mail messages are especially useful for sending a single message to multiple receivers. Despite the perceived informality and temporary nature of e-mail messages, writers should give the same meticulous attention to accuracy and grammatical correctness of these electronic documents as they do to printed documents.

✓ CHECK YOUR WRITING

PLEASANT AND ROUTINE MESSAGES

CONTENT
- ☐ Major idea is clearly identified.
- ☐ Supporting detail is sufficient.
- ☐ Facts or figures are accurate.
- ☐ Message is ethical and abides by any legal requirements.

ORGANIZATION
- ☐ Major idea is in the first sentence.
- ☐ Supporting details are presented in a logical sequence.
- ☐ Final paragraph is courteous and indicates a continuing relationship with the receiver; may include sales promotional material.

STYLE
- ☐ Words will be readily understood.
- ☐ Syntax is acceptable.
- ☐ Sentences are relatively short.
- ☐ Variety appears in sentence length and structure.
- ☐ Significant words are in emphatic positions.
- ☐ Significant or positive thoughts are stated in simple sentences or in independent clauses.
- ☐ Active voice predominates.
- ☐ First person is used sparingly or not at all.
- ☐ Ideas cohere (changes in thought are not abrupt).
- ☐ Expression is original (sentences are not copied directly from the definition of the problem or from sample letters in text; clichés are avoided).

MECHANICS
- ☐ Keyboarding, spelling, grammar, and punctuation are perfect.
- ☐ Paragraphs are relatively short.

LETTERS
- ☐ Letter style is acceptable (block, modified block, or simplified).
- ☐ Letter is balanced on the page.
- ☐ Letter parts are in appropriate vertical and horizontal position.
- ☐ Return address (if plain paper is used)
- ☐ Dateline
- ☐ Letter address
- ☐ Salutation (if needed for letter style used)
- ☐ Subject line (if needed)
- ☐ Complimentary close (if needed for letter style used)
- ☐ Keyboarded name (and title)
- ☐ Letter is signed legibly
- ☐ Reference initials (if needed)
- ☐ Enclosure notation (if needed)
- ☐ Other special letter parts (if needed)

MEMORANDUMS
- ☐ *TO, FROM, DATE,* and *SUBJECT* information is included.
- ☐ Side margins are consistent.
- ☐ Courtesy titles are omitted on TO and FROM lines.
- ☐ Lines are single-spaced; blank space appears between paragraphs; paragraphs are not indented.
- ☐ Tabulated sentences are indented for emphasis (if appropriate for letter style used).
- ☐ Handwritten initials are placed by the name on the FROM line or signed in the space provided in the simplified format.

GENERAL WRITING GUIDELINES

When composing letters and memorandums for the exercises, applications, and cases in this and all remaining chapters, proceed in the following manner:

1. Study Chapter 9 before composing letters and memorandums. Look for principles that can be applied, not for expressions or sentences to paraphrase or use in your message.
2. Study the writing problem until you understand the facts.
3. Assume that you are the person facing the writing problem.
4. Anticipate the receiver reaction and prepare an outline for your message.
5. Compose rapidly without looking at the definition of the problem and without looking at sample letters from the text. A sentence written to *define* a letter-writing problem may not be appropriate in a letter designed to *solve* the problem. Concentrate on planning and expressing ideas to achieve clarity and to promote good human relations.
6. Refer to the definition of the problem for names, addresses, and amounts before keying the message. The receiver's name and address appears at the end of each exercise. Unless otherwise instructed, key your name as the sender.
7. Exercise discretion by identifying the information the receiver actually needs to respond to your message. Consider the confidentiality of the information revealed.
8. Consider the legal and ethical implications of your message. If necessary, investigate the problem to identify possible legal requirements for the message you are writing. Using the principles and ethical theories that parallel your moral system, select an ethical action and write the appropriate message.
9. Reread your message carefully to assure that you have expressed ideas clearly, stated unpleasant ideas tactfully and positively, included complete and accurate information, supported your ideas with objective facts, avoided embellishing or exaggerating the facts, and designed graphics to clarify the facts.
10. Review carefully the placement of the standard parts of the letter, the acceptable business formats, the two punctuation types, and the special letter parts required in particular situations. Unless otherwise instructed, key the letter or memo according to the formatting instructions provided in Appendix A. Study two-letter postal abbreviations, word-division rules, abbreviation rules, keyboarding rules (e.g., number of spaces after punctuation), and proofreaders' marks in Appendix A.
11. Refer to the "Check Your Writing" checklist at the end of the chapter before handing in an assignment. By comparing your message with the list, you will (1) gain confidence that your message meets high standards and (2) identify any changes that need to be made.

Thoughtful use of the checklist can improve your grade on an assignment as well as indelibly stamp in your mind the four qualities that your writing should have:

- The *right* ideas with sufficient support (content).
- The best *sequence* of ideas for clear understanding and human relations (organization).
- The most appropriate ways to *express* ideas in words and sentences (style).
- High *standards* in putting words on paper—keyboarding, spelling, and punctuating (mechanics).

REFERENCES

Gerloff, R. (1994, May-June). The new urbanism takes hold. *Utne Reader*, pp. 28-30.

Verity, J. W. (1994). The information revolution: How digital technology is changing the way we work and live. *Business Week*, 1994 Special Issue, pp. 10–18.

REVIEW QUESTIONS

1. List the steps in the deductive outline recommended for good-news and routine messages. Is this outline recommended for written messages applicable to oral messages?
2. What is a claim letter? Distinguish between the two major types of claim letters.
3. List the outline recommended when the claim is routine.
4. What term is used to label responses to claim letters?
5. What is the difference between resale and sales-promotional material? Provide an example of each.
6. List the outline recommended when the response to a claim letter is favorable.
7. When is the word *grant* appropriate when communicating about claim letters? Suggest an appropriate substitution.
8. List the major weaknesses in the poor example of a favorable response to a routine claim letter in Figure 9-4.
9. List the outline recommended for a routine request.
10. Discuss several ways form letters can be used to respond to routine requests effectively.
11. List the outline recommended when the response to a request for credit information is likely to be favorable.
12. Provide suggestions for writing a legally defensible credit information letter.
13. Why is the simplified block letter format an excellent choice for a letter addressed to a company?
14. List the outline recommended when the response to a request for credit is likely to be favorable.
15. Why should you discuss the foundation upon which you based your decision to extend credit in the letter extending credit? credit terms?
16. Provide examples of circumstances when an order letter would be written. Discuss the organization and content of order letters.
17. Give two reasons why sending individualized letters of acknowledgment is not recommended. Describe the procedure typically used by companies to acknowledge orders. Describe a situation when sending an individualized letter of acknowledgment would be appropriate and explain why.
18. Who is the audience to whom memos and e-mail messages are addressed? Do principles of organizing applied in the writing of letters also apply in the writing of memos and e-mail messages? Explain.
19. What is a distinct advantage of e-mail messages? Discuss the general procedures required to accomplish this task. List the guidelines for writing effective e-mail messages.
20. Are business jargon, acronyms, shortened words, and graphics useful in memos and e-mail messages? Why?
21. What purpose does the subject line of a memo or e-mail message serve? Provide suggestions for writing an effective subject line.
22. Provide guidelines for writing instructions that can be understood and followed consistently.
23. How do enumerations (bullets or numbered lists) affect the effectiveness of a message explaining a procedure or giving instructions? When should numbers versus bullets be used to mark each step?
24. What is a "to the file" memo? Provide circumstances when it should be used.
25. Must memorandums and e-mail messages be formatted as a continuous group of single-spaced paragraphs, or can they contain headings to denote logical divisions in the content? Explain.

EXERCISES

1. Complete each of the THINK IT OVER activities your instructor assigns.
2. Find an example of both a well-written and a poorly written good-news letter or memorandum. Analyze the strengths and weaknesses of each document. Be prepared to discuss them in class.
3. Analyze the effectiveness of the following sentences from a good-news message:
   a. After much deliberation, my office decided to approve your transfer to Moscow.
   b. The outstanding color graphics and charts were prepared and faxed to us by Prentiss Anderson, one of our staff accountants.
   c. We offer you the position effective November 1 provided you return these forms by October 12.
   d. The convention agenda was prepared by the girls in the office.
   e. Enclosed please find a stamped, addressed envelope for returning the completed credit application.
4. Analyze the effectiveness of the following opening sentences for a good-news message:
   a. This letter is in response to your application for credit dated June 30; your application has now been received.
   b. Our company prides itself on its customer relations department; therefore, we have decided to return your payment for the merchandise in question.
   c. We are sure you will enjoy the requested introductory software package, even though it has been made obsolete by our latest line of programs.
   d. Although we have decided to grant your credit request, we caution you (along with all of our customers) to use your credit wisely.
   e. I am writing this memo to tell you that the controller, Peter Johnson, said that each department's final budget must be submitted by June 1.

5. Prepare a deductive outline to accept the following invitation. You need to know the exact time the dinner will begin. Does a reception precede the dinner as it did two years ago? The earliest you can arrive is 6:30 p.m. The title of your speech will be "Total Quality Management: Empowering People to Succeed."

September 3, 19--

Mr. W. H. Venezia
P. O. Box 3783
Philadelphia, PA 19105-3783

Dear Mr. Venezia:

You can be extremely helpful to the members of the Lakewood Civic Club. Our annual inter-chapter meeting with three chapters in nearby cities will be held on October 17 at 6 p.m.

We are excited at the prospect of having you speak on a current topic of your choice as you did two years ago. You can enjoy good fellowship, a great audience, an excellent dinner, and a $200 honorarium.

Please let me know that you will accept the invitation by October 1. Please let us have a title for your talk to use in the program and in our correspondence to the guest chapters.

Sincerely,

Jeanne Bradford

Mrs. Jeanne Bradford
Program Chair

6. Analyze the following letter. Pinpoint its strengths and weaknesses and then revise the letter.

June 21, 19--

Raymond J. Chung, Manager
Aspen State Bank
P. O. Drawer 3919
Springfield, IL 62703-3919

Dear Mr. Chung

This letter is in reply to your questions concerning the deductibility of your educational expenses. We have researched this tax question carefully.

According to Section 162 of the Internal Revenue Code, educational expenses (college tuition, books, supplies, etc.) are not deductible for a person who is acquiring skills to begin a new career. However, you explained that your employer is requiring you to take international business and computer applications courses to enhance your ability to work in your present field. Consequently, your educational expenses are deductible.

We look forward to working with you in the future.

Sincerely,

Sandra Marin

Sandra Marin, CPA

E-MAIL APPLICATION

Create an address macro (distribution list) containing the e-mail addresses of five classmates and the instructor. Then compose a memo explaining how to study effectively for a business communication exam. Send the message to the macro address recipients.

APPLICATIONS

ACCOUNTING

1. **Requesting Adjustment for Billing Error.** When Jose Moya, the accounts payable clerk at Metal Fabricators, Inc., paid the November 10 invoice to Newton Plastics on November 15, he deducted the 2-percent discount given when customers pay total invoices within 10 days (credit terms are 2/10; n/30). Today, Jose received a statement from Newton Plastics requesting payment for $159.30, the amount of the 2-percent discount.

   Required: As Jose Moya, the accounts payable clerk, write a letter of explanation to Newton Plastics Corp., 800 New Light Road, Appleton, WI 54911-2703. Mention the documents Jose will include to verify the company's right to the discount.

MANAGEMENT

2. **Customized Drinking Cups Are Wrong Size.** Athletic concessions at Carver College placed an order for 50,000 twenty-ounce plastic cups at 15 cents each from Custom Plastics Products. Each cup was to be imprinted with the college's mascot and this year's basketball slogan, "Soaring to New Heights." The concessions manager noticed, when inspecting the order, that the vendor had sent 16-ounce cups and not the 20-ounce cups that were ordered. Because concession items must be priced in 50-cent intervals to expedite service time, the regular drink price of $1.50 cannot be adjusted to reflect the reduced quantity. After serious consideration, the manager decided that selling the 16-ounce drink for the same price would be inadvisable. Basketball season starts in only two weeks; therefore, the manager must act quickly.

   Required: As the concessions manager, write the vendor explaining the error in the shipment and asking that the order be filled correctly and quickly. Address the letter to Custom Plastics Products, 1200 Ridgewood Road, Springfield, MO 65808-1200.

Marketing

3. **Correct-Size Cups Are on the Way.** The claims manager at Custom Plastics Products was con-

cerned about the error made in the plastic cups for Carver College (Application 2). Working at peak levels for the past three weeks, the workers made a simple but rather costly mistake. However, the immediate problem is to give this order a priority rating and get it out to Carver College, a long-standing customer, in time for the first basketball game.

Required: Write the concessions manager at Carver College explaining the mistake and apologizing for the inconvenience. Assure the manager that the correct order will arrive on time and ask the manager to return the 16-ounce cups at the company's expense. Address the letter to Russell Hollister, Carver College, Athletic Department, P. O. Drawer 2193, Topeka, KS 66601-2193.

MANAGEMENT

4. **Order Does Not Meet Minimum Standards: Routine Claim.** As standard procedure, the quality-control department at Chenney Manufacturing, Inc., tested a randomly selected sample of an order of 10,000 ASTM A 325 connection pad bolts received from Purvis Metals Corporation. Because these bolts connect the ends of the frame to the rafter of the company's prefabricated storage buildings, the reliability of the bolts is critical. To meet minimum standards, the connection pad bolts (34" by 212") must withstand 40,100 pounds of pressure per square inch. Of the 78 bolts tested, 5 bolts stripped; thus, the number of defective bolts exceeded the required 99-percent confidence level. Therefore, the entire shipment must be rejected and returned.

Required: As the manager of the shipping department, return the shipment. Mention the sales invoice (#73-31-3444) you are including to identify the order. Address the letter to Purvis Metals Corporation, 1985 Northland Road, Chattanooga, TN 37401-1985.

MANAGEMENT

5. **Acknowledging an Error in an Order.** As soon as Purvis Metals Corporation received the letter from the shipping department manager (Applica-

tion 4), the quality-control manager began investigating the problem. Finally, the manager discovered that the problem was quite simple: The order was inadvertently filled with bolts of a lesser quality than those ordered.

Required: Write the shipping department manager at Chenney Manufacturing explaining the mistake and apologizing for the inconvenience. Because Chenney Manufacturing is a long-time customer, you must attempt to regain the goodwill that has been lost. Address the letter to Chenney Manufacturing, Inc., 8900 Blackburn Road, Windsor, NC 27983-8900.

ACCOUNTING

6. **Routine Request for Accommodations During an Annual Audit.** Gibbs and Zager, CPAs, is preparing for its annual financial audit of Salina Processors, Inc. The staff will work in the client's office for three weeks beginning March 1. To facilitate an efficient and cost-effective audit, you as the audit manager plan to write to the controller at Salina requesting specific arrangements. The four accountants will need adequate work space during the three-week audit. A guided tour of the production facilities should be planned for the first day of the visit. For the first time, you are recommending that the client arrange to have bills for the accountants' hotel accommodations sent directly to Salina. This procedure will save the client the 10 percent added to the audit fee to cover the cost of processing these charges.

Required: As the audit manager, write a letter to Kendall Ellis, the controller, outlining these specific arrangements. Gosa Processors, Inc., 9334 Tower Building, Wichita, KS 67202-9334.

CONSUMER

7. **Request for Product Information.** A recent publication contains a picture of a product in which you have a special interest. If you had appropriate answers to certain questions, you might order the product.

Required: Write a letter to the manufacturer. Ask at least three questions. Consider using enumerations to emphasize the questions. For example, number the questions or precede them with bullets (∗, □, ◆, ✓, etc.). Indent the questions five spaces from both margins if you format the letter in modified block format.

FINANCE/Legal

8. **Credit Approval for Construction Engineer.** A construction engineer's credit application at Home Building & Supply has been approved. Initially, the engineer's credit limit is $100,000. As her construction projects expand, the limit can be raised if necessary. Home Building & Supply has prepared a pamphlet that gives details of the credit terms.

Required: As an official of the firm, write a letter conveying the good news. Call the engineer's attention to the enclosed credit-terms pamphlet. (Assume the pamphlet has been prepared already.) Ms. Connie S. Powell, Room 347 Irish Hall, Southstate University, Woodland, NE 68451-9731.

FINANCE/Legal

9. **Credit Information Needed to Approve Line of Credit.** Burns Construction has requested a line of credit for building materials from your company, Thompson Building Supply.

Required: As the building supply manager, write a letter requesting Burns's credit records from its credit reference, Mobile Brickyard. The letter should adhere to all legal guidelines relating to credit requests. Mobile Brickyard, 1279 McKnight Road, Mobile, AL 36609-1279.

MANAGEMENT

10. **Order for Staff/Alumni Reception.** Frank McPherson, administrative assistant to the partner in charge, is responsible for planning the annual staff/alumni reception for Brooks and Lincoln, a regional accounting firm. Arrangements already have been made to hold this annual event at the Epley Resort, one of the city's preferred hotels, on Saturday, June 27, from 7 to 9 p.m. During Frank's initial tour of the facility, the restaurant manager gave him a complete menu including prices and asked that he place his order by May 30. He also reminded Frank to add to the order 7 percent sales tax and 17 percent service charge on all food and beverages.

After reviewing the menu and consulting several others at the office, Frank decided to place an order for the following items: 1 assorted international cheese tray with fruits and crackers at $125, 1 display of fresh garden vegetables served with assorted dips at $75, 1 iced jumbo gulf shrimp tray with cocktail sauce at $160, 1 baked Virginia ham tray with rolls and condiments (approximately 80 portions) at $150, 1 assorted gourmet cookie and candy tray at $50, 6 pounds of fancy mixed nuts at $14 per pound, 8 gallons of fruit punch at $18 per gallon, 1 gallon of regular coffee at $22.50, and 1 gallon of decaffeinated coffee at $22.50.

Required: Write the order letter that Frank McPherson sends to the Epley Resort, 1083 Central Avenue, Winter Haven, FL 32789-1003.

COMMUNITY SERVICE

11. **Accepting an Invitation to Perform a Civic Duty.** You have been employed for several years in your career field. Today you were asked to assist in an activity sponsored by a civic organization in your area. Depending on your interest and expertise, provide the exact nature of this activity. For example, a financial planner might have been asked to discuss mutual funds at a monthly meeting; an accountant, to prepare tax returns as a service project for senior citizens; and a computer programmer, to assist an organization in automating its membership records.

Required: Accept the request and include any details needed to make arrangements for your participation in this activity.

FINANCE

12. **Time to Diversify Stock Portfolio.** In your position as a financial planner, you developed a long-term investment strategy for Paul Caufield. This strategy called for 50 percent of Mr. Caufield's account to be invested in New York Stock Exchange securities. As a result of increases in stock prices, the client's stock holdings now comprise 60 percent of his account. Thus, you must recommend that he sell stock amounting to at least 10 percent of his account. Using your knowledge of the stock market, identify the stocks you believe Mr. Caufield should sell and justify your decision. He owns $20,000 of IBM, $10,000 of Wal-Mart, and $20,000 of Microsoft. (You may assume the client owns other stock if you wish.)

Required: As the financial planner, communicate your recommendation to Mr. Caufield. You might encourage him to call for an appointment if he wishes further consultation about his investment portfolio.

MARKETING/International

13. **Successful Sales Campaign: Letter to Parent Company.** You are the senior marketing consultant for an international computer company with offices in Finland, England, France, and Japan. Six months ago you initiated a new sales campaign for promoting your medical office software in the Finnish market. The resulting measures of success have included increases in sales, in percentage of orders and personal calls resulting from receipt of demonstration disks, and in percentage of sales calls resulting in an order.

Required: Write a letter to the head of the U.S. office stating the good news and including specific details about the effectiveness of this campaign. Address the letter to Ryan Vasek, Systems, Inc., 705 Westbrook Street, Evansville, IN 47711-7711.

REAL ESTATE/Technology

14. **Video Presentations Expedite Real Estate Showings.** Richardson Development Corporation is completing final stages of its prototype of a technological advance in the real estate business. Within the next two years, prospective buyers can view video presentations of available homes. At last, you, the marketing manager, have been given approval to begin initial promotion of this product. Because this technology will greatly affect the manner in which real estate transactions are conducted (video presentations in the office rather than endless hours transporting buyers from site to site), you realize that the first stage of promotion is educating realtors. In other words, your purpose is not to sell; instead, your purpose is to introduce the new technology, discuss its capabilities (benefits to realtor, buyer, and seller), and encourage realtors to consider this technology as they make long-range plans, especially in terms of computer capabilities.

Required: As the marketing manager, write a form letter to area realtors. Address the sample letter to Ms. Shannon Ware, Broker-Owner, South

Realty Company, 9837 22nd Avenue North, Champlin, MN 55316-9837.

HUMAN RESOURCES MANAGEMENT

15. **Request for Intern Approved.** Margaret Cobb, a senior account executive in a public relations firm, sent the following request to the firm's chief executive officer:

The University of Springfield public relations program has asked us to participate in its internship program. The program is designed to provide its juniors at least 150 hours of on-the-job experience over a 10-week period.

The upcoming Nicholson's campaign would provide a meaningful experience to an intern. In addition, the intern's contributions would help us meet the hopelessly tight deadlines inherent in a national ad campaign.

Let me have your answer by July 5 so I can initiate the interview process and have the intern on board when we begin preliminary planning for the Nicholson campaign.

Required: As the chief executive officer, write a memo to Margaret Cobb approving the firm's participation in the internship program and authorizing her to coordinate the selection of the intern and work assignments. Provide instructions related to compensation (salary/fringe benefits) and any other information you believe is pertinent. (You may submit the memo in e-mail format if your instructor asks you to do so.)

HUMAN RESOURCES MANAGEMENT

16. **Controlling Health Care Costs.** Erskine Industries reduces its health care benefit costs by using a self-insured medical plan. The company pays the health care bills of each employee directly to the health care provider rather than paying an insurance premium to an insurance company. In an effort to control these costs, Erskine undertook a plan to increase the level of preventive health care. The plan included classes in smoking cessation, drug and alcohol rehabilitation, and physical fitness. The company constructed a walking track and began paying employees' membership in one of the city's exercise clubs. Now, two years after the program was initiated, the company is seeing a decline of 8 percent in the monthly medical costs.

Required: Write a memo to all employees informing them of the program's success and praising them for their commitment to the various programs.

HUMAN RESOURCES MANAGEMENT

17. **Reaping Benefits of Total Quality Management Program.** Several years ago Maxwell Corporation initiated a total quality management program to improve the quality of the recliners it manufactures. Finally, the company is reaping the payoffs of this program: increased market share, sales, and profits. Because of employee satisfaction, the workforce is stable; absenteeism is no longer a problem, and employee turnover is almost nonexistent. To express appreciation for the employees' sustained effort, the board of directors has approved an extra day of vacation. The vacation day may be taken between January 2 and June 30 of the next year.

Required: Write this good-news memo to the employees as director of human resources.

MANAGEMENT/Technology

18. **Memorandum Announcing Major Change in Operations.** On March 1, 19--, the board of directors approved the expenditure of resources to convert to optical scanners to track the flow of production through the plant. After extensive research (including information from a quality circle of employees directly involved in the work flow), the vice president of information systems ordered the appropriate hardware. All equipment needed for the conversion has arrived. The vice president of information systems anticipates that approximately one month will be needed to install and test the equipment. To facilitate a smooth transition, the supervisors must begin to prepare the employees for the conversion.

Required:
1. Consider the appropriate strategy (procedures) for informing employees of a major change in day-to-day operations. Consult academic and practitioner journals for information related to employee resistance to change.
2. Write the memo to the supervisors.

HUMAN RESOURCES MANAGEMENT

19. **New Insurance Carrier Announced.** You are the director of human resources for Intertech, a computer manufacturer employing 1,300 people. You have changed insurance carriers recently (from Sharp & Rankin to Foster Insurance Company) to take advantage of lower premiums without reducing coverage. Foster Insurance Co. will bill Intertech for its portion of the insurance premium on a quarterly rather than a monthly basis. In return for the reduced premium, Intertech will assume responsibility of verifying the validity of the policyholders and dependents. Unlike the previous carrier, Foster requires pre-approval for nonemergency hospitalization; a brochure explaining detailed procedures will be distributed to each policyholder. With the new plan, the annual deductible is reduced from $500 to $250 annually (for the policyholder and each dependent).

Required:

1. Decide what information should be included in the memorandum informing employees of the change of insurance carrier. Consider whether an e-mail message would be an appropriate channel for this message.
2. Compose a memo or e-mail message to all employees.

HUMAN RESOURCES MANAGEMENT

20. **Memo Announcing Earthquake Preparedness Plan.** Recently, earthquake tremors have been jarring your community. As personnel manager for Dorney & Associates, located in the high-rise Aldridge Building, you decide to communicate your company's earthquake preparedness plan to all employees. A documentary on public television offered several procedures on how to react during an earthquake. The following suggestions were included in the program: (1) Elevators should not be used. (2) Fire alarms or sprinkler systems may activate and startle people. (3) Earthquakes do not kill; buildings do. (4) If outside, open areas are safer than areas near wires, signs, buildings, or trees. (5) People in offices should drop to the floor, take cover under desks, and ride out the tremor. (6) If no desks or tables are near, people should seek cover against an interior wall. (7) Windows, glass doors, tall furniture, and hanging objects should be avoided.

Required:

1. Consider the content of the memorandum. Which of the suggestions provided are pertinent to your company? Can you provide other suggestions? Consult professional literature related to earthquake preparedness to support your decision.
2. Write the memo to employees communicating your company's earthquake preparedness plan.

CASES FOR ANALYSIS

FINANCE/Ethics · GMAT

Case 1. Analyzing an Ethical Situation: A Sound Decision or a Clever Way Out? In an effort to secure a large investment account, Eastman, Inc., has decided to host a weekend boating expedition for a select group of prospective clients.

Today you received the following electronic message from your supervisor:

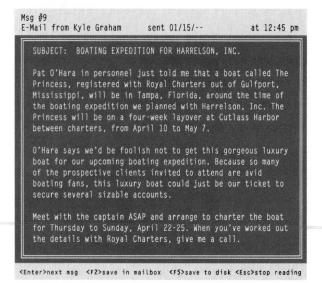

```
Msg #9
E-Mail from Kyle Graham     sent 01/15/--          at 12:45 pm

SUBJECT:  BOATING EXPEDITION FOR HARRELSON, INC.

Pat O'Hara in personnel just told me that a boat called The
Princess, registered with Royal Charters out of Gulfport,
Mississippi, will be in Tampa, Florida, around the time of
the boating expedition we planned with Harrelson, Inc. The
Princess will be on a four-week layover at Cutlass Harbor
between charters, from April 10 to May 7.

O'Hara says we'd be foolish not to get this gorgeous luxury
boat for our upcoming boating expedition. Because so many
of the prospective clients invited to attend are avid
boating fans, this luxury boat could just be our ticket to
secure several sizable accounts.

Meet with the captain ASAP and arrange to charter the boat
for Thursday to Sunday, April 22-25. When you've worked out
the details with Royal Charters, give me a call.
```
```
<Enter>next msg  <F2>save in mailbox  <F5>save to disk <Esc>stop reading
```

When you reached the captain, he explained that the owner does not usually allow unscheduled charters. After you convinced him of the importance of chartering *The Princess* for this expedition, the captain offered to let you charter the boat for $1,000 a day (normal rate is $2,000). He assured you he would submit the money to the owner and explain the situation when he returned to the home port.

Required:
1. Decide whether it is ethical to accept the captain's offer. Consider these points:
   a. What are the relevant facts?
   b. What are the ethical issues raised by the decision to charter the boat under these circumstances?
   c. Who (which stockholders) will be affected by this decision?
   d. What are the costs and benefits imposed by each alternative on each person listed in Step c?
   e. What are the firm's obligations to each person listed in Step c?
   f. What should you as the firm's representative do?
2. Based on your decision, write *one* of the following documents:
   a. Write to the captain accepting the offer to charter the boat, confirming the $1,000 rate, and providing details about the dates. Decide whether any other information should be included to ensure that the captain fulfills his side of this verbal contract. Address the letter to Doug Perez, 234 Sandy Beach Road, Tampa, FL 33602-2098.
   b. Having decided to refuse the captain's offer, write a letter to the owner requesting a special charter. Based on your ethical analysis, decide whether to mention the captain's offer. Address the letter to David Crenshaw, Royal Charters, 4029 Beach Drive, Gulfport, MS 39507-0234.
   c. Do any other options exist? If so, write the letter or memo to the appropriate person.
3. Awaiting a reply from the owner or the captain (depending on the decision made in Step 2), write a memo to your supervisor (Martin Sinclair) informing him of your action and including your analysis of this ethical situation.

MANAGEMENT/Interpersonal

Case 2. Communicating Concern for Employees. At this week's staff meeting, several of the managers commented that employee morale was quite low and that employees were producing at suboptimal rates. The controller quickly interjected that the financial condition of the company would not permit raises or additional fringe benefits.

At this point you jumped in: "The answer to this situation is clearly not wages and fringe benefits. I am convinced that these employees need to feel as if the company cares about them as individuals, as members of a team. Other companies have been very successful in developing methods to communicate their concern for employees, and they have reaped the benefits in terms of increased employee morale and productivity."

Because of your interest in and apparent knowledge of employee motivation, you were asked to research the situation and recommend action.

Required:

1. Create a specific scenario. For example, select a particular business, identify the specific employee group involved, and generally describe the work environment of the group.

2. Identify something that management can do to symbolize concern for this group of employees. Review the research related to employee motivation (e.g., management and human resources management textbooks and academic journals in the management field). Read current practitioners' journals to determine what ideas other companies have implemented successfully.

3. Write a memo to your supervisor (Jennifer Williams) convincing her to implement your idea. Use your research to provide evidence that the idea is theoretically sound or that it has been successful in another company (whichever is appropriate). Provide specific information about the benefits to be gained and the costs of implementation.

4. Assume that your supervisor has enthusiastically supported your idea (memo written in Step 3); the idea was theoretically sound, and she felt the company could only gain. For your supervisor's signature, write a memo to the employees telling them about the idea. Consider whether your description of the idea to the employees will be different from the description to your supervisor and incorporate any changes in your message.

MANAGEMENT/Ethics   `GMAT`

Case 3.   Is Providing Possibly Faulty Swing Sets Unethical? For the last six months, you have been responsible for inspecting and approving the quality of swing sets (Model 2353) before they are shipped to customers. One afternoon as you were reviewing past records, you noted a change in the product specifications and were curious about the reason for this change. Discussing this issue with the production manager, you learned that later product research indicated that the original metal used was not heavy enough.

You are concerned because you know that at least 10,000 of these swing sets are still in use. You contend that if the reinforcement bars break while a child is swinging, an accident could occur. The production manager says, "Even our new swing sets will eventually break. It's been over two years and we haven't had any complaints yet. The problem's been solved; why bring it up now? It will not only cost money to recall the product but would damage our image." The production manager advises you not to bring the issue up again; otherwise, you may not be considered a team player.

Required:

1. Decide whether it is ethical to allow the swing sets that do not meet company standards to remain in use. Consider these points:
   a. What are the relevant facts?
   b. What are the ethical issues raised by the decision whether to recall the swing sets?
   c. Who (which stakeholders) will be affected by this decision?
   d. What are the costs and benefits imposed by each alternative on each person listed in Step c?
   e. What are the company's obligations to each person listed in Step c?
   f. What should you as the company's representative do?

2. Based on your decision, write *one* of the following documents:
   a. Write a letter to the vice president of production advocating recall of these products. Include complete justification for your decision.
   b. Write a memo to the production manager stating that you have reconsidered your thoughts on the swing sets and believe the sets should not be recalled. Include complete justification for your decision.
   c. Do any other options exist? If so, write a letter or memo to the appropriate individual.

CHAPTER 10

OBJECTIVES

When you have completed Chapter 10, you will be able to

 1 List the steps in the inductive outline and identify the advantages of using it to convey bad news.

 2 Write letters denying adjustments.

 3 Write letters refusing to complete an order.

 4 Write letters refusing a favor.

 5 Compose letters denying credit.

 6 Prepare memorandums and e-mail messages that convey bad news.

 7 List ways to handle special problems about the unpleasant.

The work environment in the 1990s has been anything but "business as usual," and forecasters predict continued uncertainty. As many large corporations come to terms with global economic changes, managers and CEOs realize that the days of lifetime employment with a single company are gone.

In 1993, Boeing, one of the largest aerospace companies in the world, announced its plans to cut 28,000 jobs over 18 months. Because approximately 100,000 people work at the company's main facility and corporate headquarters in Seattle, Washington, the entire Puget Sound area looks to Boeing as a major source of revenue and economic growth. The area is so economically defined by the aerospace giant that the two local newspapers have reporters assigned solely to Boeing. Therefore, Boeing managers and public relations staff had a two-fold mission before the bad news broke: first to tell employees, then to handle the media.

Boeing's 12,000 managers were selected as primary communicators. They received the information the day before the public release and announced the cutbacks at the start of the 7 a.m. shift, notifying the press at 11 a.m. Policies of open dialogue between managers and employees had created a sense of community, and most employees were prepared for the announcement. In addition, Boeing used a number of communication tools and formats to keep the lines of communication open, including a weekly company-wide newspaper, division/group newsletters, a video, and frequent e-mail messages.

As a result of Boeing's professional handling of this situation, employees and managers maintained good relations, and public opinion of Boeing remained positive (Major, 1993). Although most managers are rarely faced with such an overwhelming task, these practices can be applied on a smaller scale. Employers have to turn down job applicants and refuse employees' requests for promotion and requests for other changes in their jobs or work procedures. Companies must tell employees and customers of unpopular changes; banks often refuse loans. Accountants must refuse audit engagements if a conflict of interest exists. Individuals and employees must alert companies of mistakes made in completing an order or handling an account. Finally, everyone (individuals and companies) at some point must refuse a request for a favor.

You have already learned the importance of keeping the lines of communication open between management and employees. When you must communicate bad news, inform employees in a timely and honest manner. Use your empathy skills; be sensitive to your employees' needs and feelings. Finally, if the press must be notified, always share the news with employees first. Although communicating bad news is never pleasant, honesty and tactful, empathetic communication make the job easier and reduce tension.

COMMUNICATING THE BAD NEWS

LEARNING OBJECTIVE 1

How does empathy assist in conveying unpleasant news?

As illustrated in the Boeing example, knowing how to communicate bad news as delicately and clearly as possible is an essential business skill. A skillful manager will attempt to say "no" in such a way that the reader or listener supports the decision and is willing to continue a positive relationship with the company. To do this successfully, the manager must first have *empathy*; she or he must try to understand how the recipient of the unpleasant news will feel. If you are sending the information in a letter, you must first think how you would ap-

Coping with bad news is never fun. When the Buffalo Bills earned the dubious title as the team to suffer the most Super Bowl defeats, team managers rushed in to shore up morale through communication. The management of the team goes into the record books as an example of a well-organized, motivated group that refuses to give up. Instead of despairing over their losses, they bounce back by taking responsibility, acknowledging their strengths, recognizing their losses, determining where they failed, and then acting on what they learn (Schroer, 1993).

proach the news if the recipient were there to receive it in person. A letter is much less likely to be "cold" if you use empathy in addition to tact and effective writing skills.

Perhaps your personal response to a claim or a request, for example, would be much different from the tactful response needed to soothe negative feelings and ensure a harmonious relationship with the customer. Your response may be especially different when you doubt whether the request is legitimate or when you do not have the time required to write an effective bad-news letter. When this conflict exists, keep in mind that you are writing the letter on behalf of your company and that your response is a direct reflection on the company's image.

The importance of effective bad-news communication is illustrated by the story of a man who carried in his coat pocket a job-refusal letter he had received from a company some time past. Frequently he would show this superbly written letter to others and comment, "I'd accept a job from this company any day because this letter made me feel *good* about myself even though the company couldn't hire me." Obviously, this letter was not an impersonal form letter, nor was it written in haste without genuine *empathy* for the receiver's feelings.

THINK IT OVER
Can you relay similar incidents when you felt good or bad about a person or company who gave you unpleasant news? Contrast the approach used in both cases.

Sequence of Ideas

Just as good news is accompanied with details, bad news is accompanied with supporting details (reasons, explanations). If the bad news is presented in the first sentence, the reaction is likely to be negative: "They never gave me a fair chance," "That's unfair," "This just can't be." Having made a value judgment on reading the first sentence, receivers are naturally reluctant to change their minds before the last sentence—even though the intervening sentences present a valid basis for doing so. Having been disappointed by the idea contained in the first sentence, receivers are tempted to concentrate on *refuting* (instead of *understanding*) supporting details.

What is the reader's natural reaction if the bad news is placed in the first sentence?

From the writer's point of view, details that support a refusal are very important. If the supporting details are understood and believed, the message may be readily accepted and good business relationships preserved. Because the reasons behind the bad news are so important, the writer needs to organize the message in such a way as to emphasize the reasons.

COMMUNICATION   MENTOR

Communicating "with disagreement" is one of the most difficult tasks you will face. A few "do's" and "don'ts" you will find helpful follow:

Do maintain an open mind—even on points of disagreement.

Do demonstrate respect for the opposition. You dislike the ideas, not the person presenting them.

Do listen to your opposition.

Do read body language.

Don't become emotional.

Don't prepare your response when you should be listening.

Don't become focused on your choice of words.

Don't engage in cross-talk; cross-listening is the key.

Remember you are looking for a *positive outcome, not a body count.*

Shirley F. Olson
Vice President & Chief Financial Officer
J. J. Ferguson Sand and Gravel/Prestress/Precast

The chances of getting the receiver to understand the reasons are much better *before* the bad news is presented than *after* the bad news is presented. If the bad news precedes the reasons (1) the message might be discarded before this important portion is even read, or (2) the disappointment experienced upon reading the bad news might interfere with the receiver's ability to comprehend or accept the supporting explanation.

The writer can simplify the process by using the four-step outline shown in Figure 10-1. These four steps are applied in letters and memorandums illustrated in the pages that follow.

STEP 1: INTRODUCTORY PARAGRAPH

The introductory paragraph in the bad-news or refusal letter should (1) let the receiver know what the letter is about (without stating the obvious) and (2) serve as a transition into the discussion of reasons (without revealing the bad news or leading the receiver to expect good news). If these objectives can be accomplished in one sentence, that sentence can be the first paragraph.

Why is the explanation for the refusal so important? Where should it appear in the outline?

If the bad news precedes the reasons, in what two ways might the receiver react?

Write the steps in the inductive approach recommended for bad-news messages in your notebook.

What does the first paragraph seek to accomplish?

BAD-NEWS MESSAGE

- Begins with the neutral idea that leads to the reason for the refusal.

- Presents the facts, analysis, and reasons for the refusal.

- States the refusal using positive tone and de-emphasis techniques.

- Closes with an idea that shifts emphasis away from the refusal.

FIGURE 10-1   Inductive sequence-of-ideas pattern used in unpleasant messages.

Form letters have earned a negative connotation because of their tendency to be insensitive and impersonal. However, you can effectively personalize a form letter to keep your reader from feeling like another "address."

STEP 2: FACTS, ANALYSIS, AND REASONS

People who are refused want to know why. To them (and to the person doing the refusing) the reasons are vital; they must be transmitted and received. A well-written first paragraph should transition the receiver smoothly into a logical, but concise, discussion of the reason for the refusal. By the time a receiver has finished reading the explanation, the upcoming statement of refusal may be foreseen and accepted as valid.

STEP 3: REFUSAL STATEMENT

The refusal statement should be in the same paragraph as the reasons. It should not be placed in a paragraph by itself; this arrangement would place too much emphasis on the bad news. Because the preceding explanation is tactful and seems valid, the sentence that states the bad news may arouse little or no resentment. If the writing were strictly inductive, the refusal statement would be last. Placing a statement of refusal (or bad news) in the last sentence or paragraph, however, would have the effect of placing too much emphasis on it. Preferably, *reasons* (instead of bad news) should remain uppermost in the receiver's mind. Placing bad news last would make the ending seem cold and abrupt.

Why not save the bad news for the final sentence?

Offering a **counterproposal**—alternative to the action requested—will assist in preserving future relationships with the receiver. Because it states what you *can* do, including a counterproposal may eliminate the need to state the refusal directly. The counterproposal can follow a refusal stated in a tactful, sensitive manner.

A counterproposal convinces the reader you really do want to help.

STEP 4: CLOSING PARAGRAPH

A closing paragraph that is about some aspect of the topic other than the bad news itself helps in several ways. It assists in (1) de-emphasizing the unpleasant part of the message, (2) conveying some useful information that should logically follow (instead of precede) bad news, (3) showing that the writer has a positive attitude, and (4) adding a unifying quality to the message.

What does the final paragraph seek to accomplish?

Although the preceding outline has four points, a bad-news letter may or may not have four paragraphs. More than one paragraph may be necessary for conveying supporting reasons. In the illustrations in this chapter (as well as examples in Appendix A), note that first and final paragraphs are seldom longer than two sentences. In fact, one-sentence paragraphs (as beginnings) look more inviting to read.

The inductive sequence of ideas has the following advantages:

THINK IT OVER
How does sequence affect the way you expect a reader to react to a bad-news letter?

- It sufficiently identifies the subject of the letter without first turning the receiver off.
- It presents the reasons *before* the refusal, where they are more likely to be understood.
- It emphasizes the reasons by letting them precede the refusal.
- It avoids a negative reaction. By the time the reasons are read, they seem sensible, and the refusal is foreseen. Because it is expected, the statement of refusal does not come as a shock.
- It de-emphasizes the refusal by closing on a neutral or pleasant note. By showing a willingness to cooperate in some other way, the writer conveys a desire to be helpful.

Which is less desirable: an impatient or an angry reader? What can you do to minimize the delay in reaching the bad news? (Refer to Chapter 7 if necessary.)

You may speculate that receivers may become impatient when a letter is inductive. Concise, well-written explanations are not likely to make receivers impatient. They relate to the receiver's problem, present information not already known, and help the receiver understand. However, if receivers become impatient while reading well-written explanations, that impatience is less damaging to understanding than would be the anger or disgust that often results from encountering bad news in the first sentence.

When would a deductive presentation of bad news be appropriate? Can you provide examples?

Normally, the writer's purpose is to convey a clear message and retain the recipient's goodwill; thus, the inductive outline is appropriate. In the rare circumstances in which a choice must be made between the two, clarity is the better choice. When the deductive approach will serve a writer's purpose better, it should be used. For example, if you submit a clear and tactful refusal and the receiver resubmits the request, a deductive presentation may be justified in the second refusal. Apparently, the refusal needs the emphasis provided by a deductive outline. Placing a refusal in the first sentence can be justified when one or more of the following circumstances exists:

THINK IT OVER
You are responding to a third request from the same customer for a product you no longer carry. Would the inductive outline be appropriate? Explain.

1. The letter is the second response to a repeated request.
2. A very small, insignificant matter is involved.
3. A request is obviously ridiculous, immoral, unethical, illegal, or dangerous.
4. A writer's intent is to "shake" the receiver.
5. A writer-reader relationship is so close and long-standing that satisfactory human relations can be taken for granted.
6. The writer *wants* to demonstrate authority.

In most writing situations, the preceding circumstances do not exist. When they do, a writer's goals may be accomplished by stating bad news in the first sentence.

Style

In messages that convey bad news, three stylistic qualities merit special attention: emphasis techniques, positive language, and implication.

COMMUNICATION MENTOR

Open and close any letter or memo on a positive note even if doing so requires some creative writing. The receiver's tolerance level for negative news seems to increase when the bad news is sandwiched between some positive elements.

Terence E. McSweeney
Director of Communications
PGA of America

A principle of human relations is "Emphasize the positive; de-emphasize the negative." For a review of *emphasis techniques*, see Chapter 7. The outline recommended for bad-news messages de-emphasizes the statement of bad news; in other words, it subordinates the bad news by putting it in a less important position. Likewise, stylistic techniques work toward the same goal: subordinating bad news by placing it in the dependent clause, using passive voice, expressing in general terms, and using abstract nouns or things (instead of the person written to) as the subject of a sentence. Although a refusal (bad news) needs to be clear, subordination of it allows the reasoning for the refusal to get deserved emphasis.

Positive language accents the good instead of the bad, the pleasant instead of the unpleasant, what can be done instead of what cannot be done. Compared with a negative idea presented in negative terms, a negative idea presented in positive terms is more likely to be accepted. When you are tempted to use the following terms, search instead for words or ideas that sound more positive:

> **How do you subordinate bad news?** Turn to Chapter 7 ("Emphasize Important Ideas" and "Project a Positive, Tactful Tone" sections). Make a list of each technique presented and provide your own example of each one.

chagrined	failure	lied	overlooked
complaint	ignorant	misinformed	regrettable
disappointed	ignored	mistake	ridiculous
disgusted	inexcusable	neglect	underhanded
disregard	insinuation	nonsense	upset
error	irresponsible	obnoxious	wrong

> **Think of some other words that could be added to this list and the list of positive words that follow.**

To businesspeople who conscientiously practice empathy, such terms may not even come to mind when communicating the unpleasant. Words in the preceding list evoke negative feelings that contrast sharply with the positive feelings evoked by words such as

accurate	cordial	freedom	pretty
approval	correct	generous	productive
assist	durable	gratitude	prosper
cheerful	energetic	happy	recommendation
commend	enthusiasm	health	respect
concise	fragrance	peace	true

To increase the number of pleasant-sounding words in your writing, practice thinking positively. Strive to see the good in situations and in others. Will Rogers professed to being able to see some good in every person he met.

Implication is often an effective way of transmitting an unpleasant idea; that is, the idea is not expressed, yet the receiver understands. For example, during the noon hour one employee says to another, "Will you go with me to see this afternoon's baseball game?" "No, I won't" communicates a negative response, but it seems unnecessarily direct and harsh. The same message (invitation is rejected) can be clearly stated in an *indirect way* (by implication):

Must refusals be stated directly?

Indirect	Implication
I wish I could.	Other responsibilities forbid, but the recipient would like to accept.
I must get my work done.	By revealing the necessity of working instead, the worker conveys the "no" answer.
If I watched baseball this afternoon, I'd be transferred tomorrow.	By stating an unacceptable consequence of acceptance, the worker conveys the idea of nonacceptance.
I'm a football fan.	By indicating a preference for another sport, the worker conveys nonacceptance.

THINK IT OVER
Which of these sentences illustrate use of the subjunctive mood? Refer to Appendix B to learn more about subjunctive mood.

THINK IT OVER
Write a sentence that implies bad news. Contrast that sentence to a direct statement of bad news.

By implying the "no" answer, the foregoing responses (1) use positive language, (2) convey reasons or at least a positive attitude, and (3) seem more respectful. These implication techniques (as well as emphasis/de-emphasis, positive language, and inductive sequence) are illustrated in the letters that follow.

SAYING "NO" TO AN ADJUSTMENT REQUEST

LEARNING OBJECTIVE 2

Assume a financial planner receives the following query from a client about a statement.

> Please correct my statement that explains my stock holdings with the Stitson Fund. On the day I purchased the shares, you used the per-share amount in the second column of the financial section of the paper. The statement now shows my shares valued using the amount in the first column. Because I could find no explanation for the discrepancy, I assume an error has been made.

The client recently purchased 100 shares of a front-end mutual fund at $50.00 a share. The fund immediately deducted $2.50 per share as its front-end fee. Thus, the client's investment is worth only $47.50 per share. The client's inquiry shows a lack of understanding of the concept of front-end mutual funds or the buy and sell share prices reported in the newspaper. Despite the financial planner's exasperation at the client's lack of knowledge, the response must be more tactful than that illustrated in Figure 10-2.

In the revised letter in Figure 10-3, note that the first sentence reveals the subject matter of the letter and leads into a presentation of reasons. Reasons precede the refusal, the statement of refusal is de-emphasized, and the final sentence is about something other than the refusal.

THINK IT OVER
1. Identify the main idea and the details in Figure 10-2. Jot them down in the correct inductive sequence. Compare your outline with Figure 10-3.
2. Identify words/phrases that contribute to the negative tone. Refer to "Adapting the Message to the Audience" in Chapter 7 if necessary.

> ¹ Your letter questioning your investment statement has been received. ² I am sorry but we cannot adjust your statement as you requested. ³ Clearly, the statement is correct.
>
> ⁴ In our discussions prior to the stock purchase, I clearly explained that you would be required to pay us a front-end fee to manage your account.
>
> ⁵ I am sure you can understand my position in this matter. ⁶ Thank you for doing business with us; and if you have any further questions, do not hesitate to call or write.

FIGURE 10-2   Poor example of a "no" response to an adjustment request.

1,2 Begins with an idea (receipt of the request) that could be implied. Apologizing for a justified decision is not necessary. Refusing in the first sentence emphasizes the refusal.

3 Offers explanation that may not receive the emphasis it deserves, especially if reaction to the first sentence has been "They're totally unfair."

4 Presents an explanation too brief and too technical to be understood. Patronizing tone may intimidate the receiver.

5 Uses a cliché that may undermine the decision.

6 Uses another cliché. The words may seem polite but insincere. May lead to unnecessary correspondence if taken literally.

Adjustment letters that say "no" follow a general sequence of ideas: (1) Begin with a neutral or factual sentence that leads to the reasons behind the "no" answer, (2) present the reasons and explanations, (3) present the refusal in an unemphatic manner, and (4) close with an off-the-subject thought. Naturally, the ending should be related to the letter or to the business relationship, but it should not be specifically about the refusal. Although the same pattern is followed in order, favor, and credit refusals, those letters are sufficiently different to make a discussion of each helpful.

SAYING "NO" TO AN ORDER FOR MERCHANDISE

For various reasons, you may not be able to send merchandise that people have ordered.

LEARNING OBJECTIVE 3

1. You may be able to send it, but there will be a waiting period. (At such times, you would acknowledge the order and write a letter saying "Yes, you will receive the . . . by . . . ")
2. You may not sell directly to consumers. (You would tell the customer where to buy the merchandise.)
3. You may not have what the customer ordered, but you have something that will serve his or her needs better. (You would wait to fill the order until you have made the customer understand that you have something better.)

Why might you refuse to fill an order?

For orders that cannot be filled, the inductive approach recommended for all "no" letters is preferred. The following request must be refused because the manufacturer does not sell directly to consumers:

Please send an OpticScan II laser printer. According to the fall catalog, the model number is 07-433-33. I don't have a price list; please send the printer COD.

If a manufacturer received many similar requests, they would very likely be answered by form letter. However, form letters do not have to be as cold and indifferent as the letter in Figure 10-4.

Harrison & Pearson, LTD, CPAs
7601 Faulkner Building, Suite 350
Billings, MT 59101-7601
(406) 555-3400   Fax (406) 555-6874

January 21, 19--

Mr. Michael Cecola
986 Brookdale Avenue
Laurel, MS 39440-8976

Dear Michael

[1] Thank you for taking such a keen interest in your investment. [2] We appreciate your allowing us to help you clarify your recent investment statement.

[3] Mutual funds use a variety of methods to offset the fund's administrative costs. [4] The Stitson Fund is a front-end load fund, meaning that investors pay a fee only at the time they invest funds. [5] Other mutual funds deduct administrative costs from the annual investment income credited to the account; others are rear-end load funds, deducting a percentage when funds are withdrawn. [6] We believe that front-end mutual funds will provide you with the best return on your investment.

[7] The amount columns in the newspaper report the sell and buy prices for the mutual fund. [8] You purchased your shares for the $50 buy price reported in the second column. [9] The amount in the first column, the sell amount, will be used when your shares are ultimately sold. [10] The Stitson Fund uses this sell price on its statements to report the current value of your investment.

[11] Michael, I'm planning a luncheon meeting on January 30 for anyone interested in learning more about mutual funds and other investment strategies for beginning investors. [12] Please plan to come.

Sincerely

Jennifer D. George

Jennifer D. George
Certified Financial Planner

dmr

FIGURE 10-3   Good example of a "no" response to an adjustment request.

Margin notes:

1,2 Reveals the subject matter of the letter and leads to the explanation.

3-6 Presents a clear explanation of the fees charged for managing the investment. Explains technical terms so the reader can understand.

7-10 Continues to help the reader understand how to interpret the statement without sounding demeaning. Implies the refusal because the explanation indicates that the stock value is correct as shown on the statement.

11,12 Shifts emphasis away from the refusal and looks confidently to future business.

Uses open punctuation; the colon after the salutation and the comma after the complimentary close are omitted.

The general plan of the revised letter in Figure 10-5 is to make customers' desire for the merchandise so strong that they will be willing to wait for it and to purchase it through conventional merchandising outlets.

If the merchandise involved in the letter in Figure 10-5 were expensive or if orders sent directly to the manufacturer were rare, sending a form letter would not be appropriate. Both form letters and individual letters can benefit from the application of the following suggestions:

1. Imply receipt of the order and confirm the customer's good choice of merchandise.

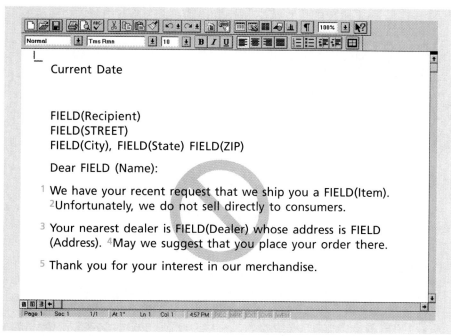

Sidebar notes:

[1] Begins with "we," which places focus on writer; could have implied receipt of the order.

[2] Presents distribution through dealers as unfortunate rather than presenting advantages.

[3] Gives the exact name and address of a local dealer, which is commendable.

[4] Misses a chance for resale.

[5] Closes with a superficial statement.

Merge function inserts variables for each customer in the bracketed positions; each personalized letter is printed on letterhead and signed.

Letter content:

Current Date

FIELD(Recipient)
FIELD(STREET)
FIELD(City), FIELD(State) FIELD(ZIP)

Dear FIELD (Name):

[1] We have your recent request that we ship you a FIELD(Item). [2] Unfortunately, we do not sell directly to consumers.

[3] Your nearest dealer is FIELD(Dealer) whose address is FIELD (Address). [4] May we suggest that you place your order there.

[5] Thank you for your interest in our merchandise.

FIGURE 10-4   Poor example of "no" response to an order—company does not sell directly to consumers.

2. Use resale—favorable statements about the product ordered—to make the customer willing to reorder through the proper channel.
3. Give reasons why sales are through dealers. Suggest or spell out how advantageously customers can buy through a dealer.
4. Use positive language to explain that the order is not being filled.

Sometimes, customers order one item when they can more profitably use another. Consider the contractor who has ordered light bulbs that are inappropriate for the intended use. Filling the order as submitted would be a mistake, and the customer is likely to be dissatisfied.

Although the form letter in Figure 10-6 may achieve the desired results (convince the recipient that the type of light bulb ordered is not the type needed), sound writing principles are applied more effectively in the letter in Figure 10-7.

The resale and the sales promotional material in the good example did not cost anything as far as supplies and postage are concerned—the company had to write anyway. The receiver is almost sure to read this material—something that cannot be said of the many sales messages that are instantly discarded.

When people say "no" in a letter, they usually do so because they think "no" is the better answer for all concerned. They can see how recipients will ultimately benefit from the refusal. If a letter is based on a sound decision, and if it has been well written, recipients will probably recognize that the senders did them a favor by saying "no."

SAYING "NO" TO A REQUEST FOR A FAVOR

When a request for a favor must be denied, the same reasons-before-refusal pattern is recommended. To ensure positive relationships, the recipient of a request for a favor may offer a *counterproposal*—an alternative to the action

THINK IT OVER
What format changes would be necessary if the letter in Figure 10-4 had been directed to the attention of the purchasing agent? Turn to Appendix A ("Special Letter Parts") for the answer.

THINK IT OVER
What is an advantage of including sales promotional material in an order refusal?

What is a counterproposal? How does including one improve the effectiveness of a bad-news letter?

LEARNING OBJECTIVE 4

¹ Introduces the subject and leads to an explanation.

² Provides resale on the item ordered.

³ Begins the explanation.

⁴ Reveals—in positive language—that sales are not made directly to consumers. Lets the reader see an advantage in the manufacturer's not selling to consumers directly.

⁵ Closes by providing needed information.

Advanced Electronics Corporation
3019 Milam Road   Lansing, MI 48909-3019
Telephone: (517) 555-1089   Fax: (517) 555-1123

June 21, 19--

Mr. Pat Stennett
Schmidt Music Center
400 West Fifth Avenue
Wausau, WI 54401-0400

Dear Mr. Stennett:

¹ When we first began marketing the OpticScan II laser printer, we wanted to provide laser printer capabilities suitable for businesses of all sizes.

² Now available with ten scalable fonts, the OpticScan II will allow you to choose exactly the right style for any layout. ³ As manufacturers, we devote all our time to enhancing our current products and to developing innovative new products. ⁴ Because we concentrate solely on these efforts (and leave selling and advertising to retailers), we have been able to develop products that meet the ever-changing technological needs of today's businesses.

⁵ To see our new OpticScan II printer in operation, visit your nearest OpticScan retailer—Moore Suppliers, 1000 Forest Hill, Wausau, WI 54401-0400.

Sincerely,

Gloria Espino

Gloria Espino
Sales Manager

FIGURE 10-5   *Good example of a "no" response to an order—company does not sell directly to consumers.*

---

¹ Presents information that could have been implied; focuses on writer.

² Reveals the refusal before the explanation. "However" indicates that negatives follow.

³ Provides no reasons; repetitive and vague.

⁴ Implies lack of expertise on part of customer.

⁵ Provides a disadvantage but no benefits for making the substitution; uses "in the long run," a cliché.

⁶ Presents needed information, but the idea of "holding" the order seems negative. "Hear from you" is worn and implies oral communication.

THINK IT OVER
How do you think the reader would respond to Figure 10-6? What changes would improve the response?

SUBJECT: Purchase Order No. 430-9831-7

¹ We received your order for 400 incandescent light bulbs (Stock No. 71731). ² However, we need to explain why this particular bulb is inappropriate.

³ The incandescent bulb is not appropriate for your intended use. ⁴ We have another product better suited to your purposes. May we have your permission to substitute halogen bulbs? ⁵ Although these bulbs are more expensive, we feel the benefits will far outweigh the costs in the long run.

⁶ Your order will be held until we hear from you.

FIGURE 10-6   *Poor example of a "no" response to an order—merchandise does not meet customer's needs.*

Worldwide Electronics Incorporated
55 NORTH PARK ROAD   SAN ANTONIO, TX 78207-2963   (903) 555-6731, FAX (903) 555-1305

November 9, 19--

Ms. Lacy Cochran
Cochran Construction Co.
1900 Water Valley Road
Lincoln, NE 68501-1900

1 Re: Purchase Order No. 47061

Dear Ms. Cochran:

2 The incandescent bulb you ordered has been proven to be 10 percent brighter than others of its type and is ideal for occasional use for short intervals.

3 According to our sales representative, Jeff Cox, you plan to install the bulbs in the parking lot lights of the new Clover Mall. 4 Because these bulbs will burn all night for security reasons, the halogen bulb designed for heavy-duty, long-term use is better suited for your needs.

5 The longer life of the halogen will more than compensate for the larger initial investment required. 6 You will also benefit from the convenience and cost efficiency of replacing bulbs less frequently.
7 Refer to the enclosed pamphlet for additional details about the performance of the halogen bulb (Stock No. S9-13).

8 To authorize us to ship the long-lasting halogen bulb, simply check the appropriate square on the enclosed card and return in the enclosed envelope with your payment for the additional cost.

Sincerely,

Richard L Godinez

Richard L. Godinez
Sales Manager

9 Enclosures

FIGURE 10-7 Good example of a "no" response to an order—merchandise ordered does not meet customer's needs.

1 Uses a reference line to direct reader to source documents.

2 Acknowledges order but is noncommittal about shipment. Includes resale on the contractor's choice, which leads to the explanation.

3, 4 Continues with explanation by providing specific details about this receiver's needs.

5, 6 Reveals a disadvantage of the alternative, but de-emphasizes it by putting it in a sentence that states primary advantages (sales promotional material).

7 Includes an enclosure to present more details and to reinforce ideas in the letter.

8 Seeks permission to ship a more appropriate bulb. Makes response easy. The card might include a line for canceling the order, but letter does not discuss this option.

9 Includes enclosure notation to alert reader that other information is enclosed.

THINK IT OVER
When do you use a reference line rather than a subject line? Turn to Appendix A ("Special Letter Parts") for the answer.

requested. In the letter in Figure 10-8, the writer explains why the company cannot lend an executive to direct a major community effort and recommends a member of the company's senior executive corps as a counterproposal.

The preceding letters—all of which are *responses* to prior correspondence—use the same principles of sequence and style that are recommended for letters that *initiate* communication about unpleasant topics. The same principles apply whether the communication is a letter or a memorandum.

Hanneman Industries
2700 Ridgeway, Cambridge, MA 02139-2700
(617) 555-8630 Fax: (617) 555-7961

March 18, 19--

Mr. Gordon Schwin
Peterson Foundation
9835 Crosland Building
Cambridge, MA 02140-9835

Dear Gordon

1 You are to be commended for your commitment to create an endowment for the Kirkland Homeless Shelter. 2 This much-needed project will aid the hundreds of homeless and increase the community's awareness of the needs of this sector of our population.

3 The success of this project depends on a good project director. 4 The organizational, leadership, and public relations activities you described demand an individual with upper-level managerial experience.

5 During the last year, Hanneman has decentralized its organization, reducing the number of upper-level managers to the minimal level needed. 6 Although our current personnel shortage prevents us from lending you an executive, we do want to support your worthy project.

7 Maralee Graves in our senior executive corps directed a similar short-term project, Homes for Humanity. 8 She organized the campaign, solicited area coordinators, and managed publicity. 9 If you can benefit from her services, call her at 555-8630, extension 791.

10 Sincerely

Kathryn

Kathryn Hare
President

1,2 Introduces the subject without revealing whether the answer will be "yes" or "no."

3-5 Gives reasons.

6 Subordinates the refusal by placing it in the dependent clause of a complex sentence. Alludes to help in another form.

7-9 Closes on a positive note by offering a counterproposal. Summarizing the executive's responsibilities and providing her telephone number increases the genuineness of the offer.

10 Signs first name only because the writer knows the receiver well.

FIGURE 10-8   Good example of a "no" response for a favor, including counterproposal.

SAYING "NO" TO A CREDIT REQUEST

LEARNING OBJECTIVE 5

Maintaining goodwill when writing a credit refusal is especially critical because this customer may be an outstanding credit risk in the future.

Once you have evaluated a request for credit and have decided "no" is the better answer, your primary writing problem is to say "no" so tactfully that you keep the business relationship on a cash basis. When requests for credit are accompanied with an order, your credit refusals may serve as acknowledgment letters. Of course, every business letter is directly or indirectly a sales letter. Prospective customers will be disappointed when they cannot buy on a credit basis. However, if you keep them sold on your goods and services, they may prefer to buy from you on a cash basis instead of seeking credit privileges elsewhere.

COMMUNICATION   MENTOR

You and your company often will be judged only on the basis of your letter because the recipient may never see you. Choose your words carefully. If you must say no to a request, begin positively by mentioning how you have enjoyed the working relationship. Then deliver the bad news, emphasizing why; e.g., credit has been refused because of a poor pay record. End on a positive note such as with an offer to continue business on a cash basis. A poorly written letter can be worse then an unsatisfactory oral response because the receiver has the "document on file."

Shirley F. Olson
Vice President & Chief Financial Officer
J. J. Ferguson Sand and Gravel/Prestress/Precast

When the credit investigation shows that applicants are poor credit risks, too many credit writers no longer regard them as possible customers. They write to them in a cold, matter-of-fact manner. They do not consider that such applicants may still be interested in doing business on a cash basis and may qualify for credit later.

In credit refusals, as in other types of refusals, the major portion of the message should be an explanation for the refusal. You cannot expect your receiver to agree that your "no" answer is the right answer unless you give the reasons behind it. Naturally, those who send you credit information will expect you to keep it confidential. If you give the reasons without using the names of those from whom you obtained your information, you are not violating confidence. You are passing along the truth as a justification for your business decision.

Both writers and readers benefit from the explanation of the reasons behind the refusal. For writers, the explanation helps to establish fair-mindedness; it shows that the decision was not arbitrary. For receivers, the explanation not only presents the truth to which they are entitled, it also has guidance value. From it they learn to adjust habits and, as a result, qualify for credit purchases later.

Because of the legal implications involved in refusing credit, a legal counsel should review your credit refusal letters to ensure that they comply with laws related to fair credit practices. For example, the Equal Credit Opportunity Act (ECOA) requires that the credit applicant be notified of the credit decision within 30 calendar days. Applicants who are denied credit must be informed of the reasons for the refusal. When the decision is based on information obtained from a consumer reporting agency (as opposed to financial statements or other information provided by the applicant), the credit denial may include the name, address, and telephone number of the agency and remind applicants that the Fair Credit Reporting Act provides them the right to know the nature of the information in their credit file. Credit denials may also include a standard statement that the ECOA prohibits creditors from discriminating against credit applicants on the basis of a number of protected characteristics (race, color, religion, national origin, sex, marital status, age).

To avoid litigation, some companies choose to omit the explanation from the credit denial and invite the applicant to call or come in to discuss the reasons. Alternately, they may suggest that the receiver obtain further information

> What is a good counter-proposal in a letter that refuses credit? Can you think of others?

> Why is a poorly *written* refusal worse than an unsatisfactory *oral* one?

> Why discuss reasons for a credit refusal?

> What are some of the legal implications involved in refusing credit?

from the credit reporting agency whose name, address, and telephone number are provided.

Assume that a retailer of electronic devices has placed an initial order and requested credit privileges. After examining financial statements that were enclosed, the wholesaler decides the request should be denied. Review the letter in Figure 10-9 to identify techniques used to refuse credit while preserving relations with this customer—who may very well have money in the near future.

The credit refusal in Figure 10-9 provides an explanation for the refusal and offers a 1-percent discount for goods purchased on a cash basis. No information about a credit reporting agency is necessary because the applicant provided all

Why include resale in a credit refusal?

[1] Implies receipt of the order and uses resale to confirm applicant's good choice of product.

[2] Leads to explanation by implying approval of one of the applicant's practices (supplying most recently developed items).

[3] Leads to discussion of another practice that is the basis for the refusal.

[4] Provides further detail.

[5] Continues with the explanation.

[6] Uses positive language to express the refusal. Recommends discount cash purchases—a counterproposal to the refusal.

[7] Looks confidently to the future and reminds the applicant of the commendable practice discussed in the second sentence.

[8] Encourages subsequent application and thus implies continued business is expected.

[9] Reminds of the desired action—the counterproposal.

[10] Closes with sales promotional material. Uses "timely" as a reminder of the applicant's commendable business practice and as a technique for developing unity.

Worldwide Electronics Incorporated
55 NORTH PARK ROAD   SAN ANTONIO, TX 78207-2963   (903) 555-6731, FAX (903) 555-1305

May 16, 19--

Mr. Kelly Beavers
Purchasing Agent
Locke Office Supply
1600 Main Street
Lorain, OH 44052-1600

Dear Mr. Beavers:

[1] The items listed in your order of May 6 have been selling very rapidly in recent weeks. [2] Supplying customers' demands for the latest in electronic technology is sound business practice.

[3] Another sound practice is careful control of indebtedness, according to specialists in accounting and finance. [4] Their formula for control is to maintain at least a 2-to-1 ratio of current assets to current liabilities. [5] Experience has taught us that, for the benefit of all concerned, credit should be available only to purchasers who meet that ratio. [6] Because your ratio is approximately 1 1/4 to 1, you are encouraged to make cash purchases and take advantage of a 1-percent discount.

[7] By continuing to supply your customers with timely merchandise, you should be able to improve the ratio. [8] Then, we would welcome an opportunity to review your credit application. [9] Use the enclosed envelope to send us your check for $1,487.53 to cover your current order, and your order will be shipped promptly.

[10] Other timely items (such as the most recent in video games) are shown in the enclosed folder.

Sincerely,

Murray L. Wagner
Murray L. Wagner
Credit Manager

mpl
Enclosures

FIGURE 10-9   Good example of a "no" response to a credit request.

COMMUNICATION IN ACTION

Shirley F. Olson, J. J. Ferguson Sand & Gravel/ Prestress/Precast

Establishing empathy and goodwill with customers helps managers and employees build long-term interpersonal relationships in the workplace. For those who handle credit requests, empathy and goodwill become more important when saying "no" to a credit request. Nowhere is this fact more evident than in the residential and commercial construction industry.

J. J. Ferguson, a sand and gravel/prestress/precast company, has been in operation 53 years and is one of the oldest construction industries in the South. To keep J. J. Ferguson successful, Shirley Olson, vice president and chief financial officer, must at times say no to credit requests for residential or commercial development. Olson and her father have developed a unique father-and-daughter business in economically volatile times.

Whether the credit request involves large, state government contracts or small orders of merchandise, Olson is very careful about how she delivers bad news. She explains that a customer who is a poor credit risk today may be a good credit risk six to twelve months from now. "The construction business is very volatile," she says, "and an individual who does $5,000 a month in business today may do $50,000 a month in two years." The future of her company depends on keeping goodwill with those customers.

To illustrate her point, she cites a recent example. One long-term customer, who at one time had been a good credit risk, had extended his credit beyond the company's limits. When the customer

requested additional credit, Olson had to say "no." In doing so, she explains, "I want to keep his business but just not extend him credit." However, she manages to maintain empathy and goodwill when facing this difficult challenge of saying "no" to an established, long-term customer.

When first facing this challenge, Olson explained to the customer how much she appreciated his business over the years. Olson recognized the fact that he had stayed with J. J. Ferguson and with his own company during some tough times. She stated she had extended his credit 90 days further than with other customers.

Because of the volume of his business, she had extended his credit several times. She explained she wanted to keep his business but could not extend it any further. She stated, "As soon as you can reduce terms to 60 days, let's talk again. We'll get back on a credit basis. Until then, stay with us." Finally, Olson communicated that as soon as she received money from him, she would extend credit again. "Extending credit for 60 days in the construction industry is typical," she says, "since most people do not get money for 60 days to pay against their own credit."

Olson's empathy and goodwill with this customer show the importance of building long-term relationships. Those relationships have helped provide the long-term business for J. J. Ferguson to grow into a successful company employing 250-325 personnel during peak seasonal business.

Applying What You Have Learned
1. What impact did empathy have on the organization and style of Olson's message when denying credit?
2. Assume that you work for J. J. Ferguson and must correspond with Mr. Jim Read, Read Construction Co., 203 Woolbright Road, Whitehall, OH 43213-2987. A longstanding customer of six years with an excellent credit rating, Mr. Read has requested additional credit of $30,000 for July. Assume further that Mr. Read had extended his credit beyond the company limit of 60 days and was given an additional 30 days' extension. Write a letter saying "no" to his credit request.

the information on which the decision was based. It makes no apology for action taken that would only cause the applicant to speculate that the decision was arbitrary.

Including resale is helpful in a credit refusal letter for four reasons: (1) It might cause credit applicants to prefer your brand, perhaps being willing to buy it even on a cash basis; (2) it suggests that the writer is trying to be helpful; (3) it makes the writing easier—negative thoughts are easier to de-emphasize when cushioned with resale material, and you seem confident of future cash purchases; and (4) it can confirm the credit applicant's judgment (suggesting the applicant made a good choice of merchandise is giving an indirect compliment).

WRITING BAD-NEWS MEMORANDUMS AND E-MAIL MESSAGES

LEARNING OBJECTIVE 6

THINK IT OVER
To calm employee anxiety during a recent crisis, Northwest Airlines carried company news online every day and published a newsletter twice a month.

Use an online database to locate an article about another company's success or failure in handling a similar crisis (e.g., Blue Cross/Blue Shield scandal over its financial management, charges that hypodermic needles had been found in Pepsi cans). Share with the class or in groups.

Well-written memorandums can build employee support for unpleasant circumstances.

THINK IT OVER
What *one* change in Figure 10-10 would help alter employees' support for the relocation?

Being able to initiate messages that convey bad news is as important as responding "no" to messages from customers/clients and others outside the company. Employees are seeking *honest* answers from management about slumping profits, massive layoffs as a result of downsizing, and major changes in their organizations. Companies are reengineering to improve quality, job performance, and advancement prospects and to overcome scandals by management and other issues. Managers who can communicate negative information in a sensitive, honest, and timely way are successful in calming employees' fears and doubts and in building positive employee relations. Effective managers recognize that morale, like customer goodwill, is fragile—easily damaged and difficult to repair.

Consider the company president who wrote the following message (Figure 10-10) to communicate to employees a relocation of the company's manufacturing facility. After sending the following e-mail message, the president should

```
Msg #9
E-Mail from Paul Marshall      sent 09/14/19--          at 8:45 am

  TO:      All Employees
  FROM:    Paul Marshall, President
  DATE:    September 14, 19--
  SUBJECT: COMPANY WILL RELOCATE MARCH 5.

  Effective March 5, 19--, we will relocate our plant facility to
  Griffin, Georgia. Approved by the Board of Directors at its last
  meeting, this relocation will enable the company to reduce its
  operating expenses by 15 percent.

  All employees wishing to relocate should notify their supervisors
  by the end of next week. If you have any questions, please do not
  hesitate to call.


  <Enter> next msg    <F2> save in mailbox    <F5> save to disk    <Esc> stop reading
```

FIGURE 10-10   Poor example of a bad-news e-mail message.

not be surprised to learn that employees are resisting the relocation. In fact, many perceive the company to be an enemy uprooting defenseless families from their homes simply for financial gain.

In the revision (Figure 10-11), the president anticipates the employees' natural resistance to this stunning announcement; therefore, he presents the explanations *before* the bad news. The revision focuses on the benefits employees can gain from the move, which should generate more support for the move and trust in management than the original blunt statement that a decision had been made for the benefit of the company. Care was used in writing a subject line that introduced the subject of the message without revealing the bad news. Retaining the original subject line "Company Will Relocate March 5," would defeat the

THINK IT OVER
Do you think bad news should be sent via e-mail?

Memorandums that convey bad news are written inductively also.

TO: All Employees

FROM: Paul Marshall, President   P.M.

DATE: September 14, 19--

[1] SUBJECT: PROPOSED PLAN FOR INCREASING MANUFACTURING CAPACITY

[2] As we have projected, our present production facilities will soon be unable to meet the increased demand for our product. [3] Therefore, for several years we have been studying whether to expand our current manufacturing facility or relocate to another site.

[4] High property taxes and transportation costs increases every year are compelling reasons to consider alternative sites. [5] Likewise, attracting new talent into this high-cost metro area has become more difficult each year. [6] In fact, both of our newly hired unit supervisors are commuting over one hour just to obtain affordable housing.

[7] Although relocating could provide a long-term economic benefit to the company, moving out of New York City could enhance the quality of life for us all. [8] In a suburban city, we could enjoy day-to-day living in a relaxed, small-town environment with all the benefits of a large city only a short drive away. [9] These two factors alone have convinced us that moving the manufacturing facility to Griffin, Georgia, a city of 70,000 located fifty miles southeast of Atlanta, would benefit the company and its employees.

[10] All employees wishing to relocate may resume their duties at the same salary structure. [11] Your supervisor will explain the logistics of the move at your unit's next meeting. [12] Now let us all work together for a smooth transition to many challenging opportunities awaiting in Griffin.

[1] Uses a subject line to introduce the topic but not does not reveal bad news.

[2, 3] Uses buffer to introduce the topic and lead into reasons.

[4-8] Presents benefits the company and employees will gain from relocating.

[9] Presents the bad news while reminding receiver of the benefits.

[10] Assures employees that no one's job is in jeopardy.

[11] Anticipates questions about the logistics of the move.

[12] Ends with positive appeal as a technique for developing unity.

FIGURE 10-11   Good example of a bad-news memorandum.

purpose of the inductive outline developed in the revision. Sending a printed memorandum is a more effective channel for communicating such sensitive information than the efficient e-mail message.

HANDLING SPECIAL PROBLEMS ABOUT THE UNPLEASANT

You will likely find writing the first paragraph, the statement of bad news, and the last paragraph of inductive messages challenging.

First Paragraph

The introductory paragraph of a bad-news letter should let the receiver know the topic of the letter without saying the obvious. It should build a transition into the discussion of reasons without revealing the bad news or leading a receiver to expect good news. The following introductory sentences reveal the subject of the letter, but they have weaknesses:

Subject	Weaknesses
I am writing in response to your letter requesting . . .	The letter is obviously a response; omission of this idea would shorten the message. An *I* beginning signals that the letter may be writer centered.
Your letter of the 14th has been given to me for reply.	The fact that a person other than the original writer is responding is obvious and not important.
I can understand how you felt when you were asked to pay an extra $54.	Having requested a refund, a receiver may be led to expect it. This overly empathetic statement may lead the reader to expect a refund. When a preceding statement has implied that an affirmative decision will follow, a negative decision is all the more disappointing.
Although the refund requested in your letter of May 1 cannot be approved, . . .	Immediate emotional reaction may cause the letter to be put aside at this point, or it may interfere with understanding the explanations that follow.
Your request for an adjustment has been considered. However, . . .	The statement is neutral; does not reveal whether the answer is "yes" or "no." Such a beginning has about the same effect as an outright "no" beginning.

The transitional word *however* immediately signals a change in thought—bad news is imminent in this case.

THINK IT OVER
Critique the first paragraph of the letter in Exercise 6 (end-of-chapter activities). Suggest an idea that would be a natural transition to the discussion of the reasons.

The following introductory paragraphs (1) identify the subject of the message and (2) serve as a transition into the discussion of reasons for a denial. (To illustrate transition/cohesion, the first words of the second paragraph are also presented.)

Subject and Transition	Description
The double-indemnity feature of your policy has two provisions. In each, the words are "natural causes" and "accidental." "Natural causes" are defined as . . .	To a policyholder who has submitted a double-indemnity claim, the topic of the letter is recognized immediately. "In each" relates the second sentence to the first; "natural causes" provides the transition from the introductory paragraph to the second paragraph, which begins the explanations.
Your application was reviewed separately by two loan officers. Each officer considered . . .	To a potential borrower who has applied for a loan, the subject of the letter is quickly established. Use of "officer" in the second paragraph is a coherence technique—an idea introduced in the first sentence is continued in the second. In the second paragraph, discussion of the officers' reviews will satisfy an expectation aroused in the first sentence.
After your request for permission to pick up leftover potatoes, we reviewed our experiences of recent years. Last year, two incidents . . .	An office of a food-for-the-hungry mission would immediately recognize the request that the mission be allowed to enter a grower's field and harvest potatoes left by the mechanical pickers. Note that repetition of "year" ties the second paragraph to the first and that the second paragraph intends to present details of the "experiences" mentioned in the introductory paragraph.

The preceding effective introductory paragraphs introduce a discussion without stating bad news or leading the receiver to expect good news. Additional ideas can be incorporated into effective beginning paragraphs:

THINK IT OVER
What are six ways to begin a bad-news message? Which of these ideas are developed in the good examples in this chapter?

1. *A compliment.* A letter denying a customer's request could begin by recognizing that customer's promptness in making payments.
2. *A point of agreement.* If the letter being answered makes a statement with which you can agree, a sentence that reveals agreement could get the letter off to a positive discussion of other points.
3. *Some good news.* When a letter contains a request that must be refused and another that is being answered favorably, beginning with the favorable answer can be effective.
4. *Resale.* If the subject of correspondence is a product that was purchased, a refusal could begin with some favorable statement about the product.
5. *A review.* Refusal of a current request could be introduced by referring to the initial transaction or by reviewing certain circumstances that preceded the transaction.

6. *Gratitude.* Although an unjustified request may have been made, the receiver may have done or said something for which you are grateful. An expression of gratitude could be used as a positive beginning.

Bad-News Sentence

In a sense, a paragraph that presents the reasoning behind a refusal at least partially conveys the refusal before it is stated directly or indirectly. Yet, one sentence needs to convey (directly or by implication) the conclusion to which the preceding details have been leading. The most important considerations are *positive language* and *emphasis.*

Do not place the refusal in a simple sentence. Avoid using active voice and first person.

Your request is therefore being denied.

or

We are therefore denying your request.

Being negative, the idea is not pleasant. Stated in negative terms, the idea is still less pleasant. Both sentences seem to heighten abrasiveness through use of emphasis techniques. The simple sentences are emphatic. "Denied" stands out vividly in the first sentence because it is the last word. The second sentence is in first person and active voice, which are emphatic.

THINK IT OVER
Could approving the $1,500 credit suffice without stating directly that the $3,000 has been denied?

The preceding figures do not justify raising your credit limit to $3,000 as you requested, by they do justify raising the limit to $1,500.

The sentence uses negative language, but places the negative idea in a long, two-clause sentence that includes a positive idea.

Implication is a helpful technique to use to soften the impact of a negative idea. The following sentences illustrate commendable techniques for *implying* a refusal:

THINK IT OVER
Can you relate to the value of balancing negative feedback with a few positives when your performance on the job or in class is being critiqued? How does the balanced approach affect your feeling toward the sender and the task at hand? Give examples.

Although the Bell Road property was selected as the building site, nearness to the railroad was considered a plus for the Hampton property. *[Statement made to the owner of Hampton.]*

Reveals what was *not* done by stating what *was* done. Note also the passive construction and the complex sentence, both of which de-emphasize. "Bell Road property was selected"—the bad news—appears in the dependent clause, which is less emphatic than an independent clause. Inclusion of a positive (nearness to the railroad) assists in de-emphasizing the negative.

If the price were $15,000, the contract would have been accepted.

States a condition under which the answer would have been "yes" instead of "no." Note use of the subjunctive words "if" and "would."

By accepting the arrangement, the ABC Company would have tripled its insurance costs.

States the obviously unacceptable results of complying with a request.

Last Paragraph

After presenting valid reasons and a tactful refusal, the closing paragraph should include useful information and demonstrate empathy. It cannot do so by including statements such as these:

We trust this explanation is satisfactory.	Could be taken as a confession of doubt about the validity of the decision.	*All these statements undermine the decision and may cause the reader to question whether the decision may be arbitrary.*
We hope you will understand our position.	May imply doubt about the receiver's ability to understand. Use of "position" seems to heighten controversy; positions are expected to be defended.	
We are sorry to disappoint you.	Risks a negative retort: "If it made you feel so bad, why did you do it?" Can be interpreted as an apology for the action taken. If a decision merits an apology, its validity is questionable.	
Thank you for your interest.	This well-worn statement is often used thoughtlessly. Some refusals are addressed to people who have apparently *not* been interested enough to listen, read, or remember; otherwise, they would not have made the requests. For them, the sentence is inappropriate. For others, it may seem shallow and superficial.	
When we can be of further help, please do not hesitate to call or write.	This sentence is well worn and negative. *Further* help may seem especially inappropriate to someone who has just read a denial. The writer may see the *explanations* as helpful, but the receiver may think the *denial* is being labeled as "helpful."	

The final paragraph is usually shorter than the preceding explanatory paragraphs. Sometimes, a one-sentence closing is enough; other messages may require two or three sentences. The final sentence should seem like an *appropriate* closing; that is, it will bring a unifying quality to the whole message. Repetition of a word (or reference to some positive idea) that appears early in the letter serves this purpose well. Restatement of the refusal (or direct reference to it) would only serve to emphasize it. Possibilities for the final sentence include reference to some pleasant aspect of the preceding discussion, resale, sales promotional material, an alternative solution to the receiver's problem, some future aspect of the business relationship, or an expression of willingness to assist in some *other* way. Consider the following closures that use the preceding suggestions:

Why is the last paragraph often shorter than the sentences containing the reasons?

Should a reference to the refusal be included in the final paragraph?

COMMUNICATION   MENTOR

When communicating to a bank's Board of Directors after a recently completed regulatory activity, I begin with a positive aspect of the examination—maybe earnings increased slightly or management has taken adequate actions to correct previously noted regulatory concerns. My discussion of the concerns includes suggestions on how the Board can correct them. This practice is usually well received by my audience.

Gabriel Swan
Federal Bank Examiner

THINK IT OVER
List ways for using the last paragraph to add unity to the letter. Turn to Chapter 7 ("Developing Coherent Paragraphs") to review the concept of unity.

Your addition of the home mortgage rider to your policy last year was certainly a wise decision.

Refers to something pleasant from the preceding discussion. "Home mortgage" and other provisions had been mentioned in the early part of a letter to a client who was refused a double-indemnity settlement.

According to a recent survey, a four-headed VCR produces sound qualities that are far superior; it was an ideal choice.

Uses resale, a reminder that his four-headed VCR has a superior feature. The request for without-cost repair had been denied.

Mini-sized compacts and adapters are now available; see the enclosed folder.

Includes sales promotional material. Request for without-cost repair had been denied.

Our representative will show you some samples during next week's sales call.

Looks to a future event. The samples had been proposed as a possible solution to the receiver's problem.

If you would like to see the orientation film we show to management trainees, you would be most welcome.

Seeks to show a good attitude by offering to do something else. The receiver had been refused permission to interview certain employees on the job.

THINK IT OVER
Recall an incident where you received or communicated a disappointing message. Did the sender apply the principles presented in this chapter? Can you suggest ways the message could have been improved?

The principles that apply to writing bad-news letters, memorandums, and e-mail messages also apply to oral messages that convey bad news. Before writing a bad-news message, study carefully the overall suggestions in the "General Writing Guidelines" in Chapter 9, page 269. Then, study the specific suggestions in the "Check Your Writing" checklist that follows the chapter summary in Chapter 10. Compare your work with this checklist again after you have written a rough draft and make any revisions.

SUMMARY

1 When the receiver can be expected to be *displeased* by the message, the reasons for the refusal are presented before the main idea. The inductive approach is appropriate for letters denying adjustments, refusing orders, refusing a favor, denying credit, and memorandums and e-mail messages conveying bad news.

The steps in the inductive outline include (1) introducing the topic with a neutral idea that sets the stage for the explanation; (2) presenting a concise, logical explanation for the refusal; (3) implying or stating the refusal using positive language; and (4) closing with a positive, courteous ending that shifts the focus away from the bad news.

2 A letter denying an adjustment begins with a neutral or factual sentence that leads to the reason for the refusal. The opening sentence might include resale to reaffirm the reader's confidence in your merchandise or services. Next, present the explanation for the refusal and then the refusal in a positive, nonemphatic manner. Close with a positive thought such as sales promotional material that indicates you expect to do business with the customer again.

3 A letter refusing to complete an order implies receipt of the order and uses resale to reaffirm the customer's confidence in the merchandise. Continue with reasons for selling the merchandise through dealers and benefits to the customer. Close with information needed for customer to reorder through the proper channel.

5 Credit refusal letters must comply with laws related to fair credit practices and should be reviewed carefully by legal counsel. Begin the letter by implying receipt of an order and using resale that could convince the applicant to buy your merchandise on a cash basis when he or she learns later that credit has been denied. You may provide an explanation for the refusal and encourage the customer to apply for credit later or offer a discount on cash purchases. Your legal counsel may require that you omit the explanation and invite the applicant to call or come in to discuss the reasons or to obtain more information from the credit reporting agency whose name, address, and telephone number you provide in the letter.

6 Memorandums and e-mail messages conveying bad news are written inductively. Being able to communicate negative information to employees in a sensitive, honest, and timely manner is a powerful way to build positive employee relations.

7 Writing the first paragraph, bad-news sentence, and last paragraph of a bad-news letter present special problems:

First Sentence: The first paragraph of a bad-news letter should identify the subject of the message without stating the obvious and serve as a transition into the explanation. Effective beginning paragraphs might include a compliment, a point of agreement, good news, resale, a review of circumstances related to the message, or an expression of gratitude.

Bad-News Sentence: When writing the bad-news sentence, avoid overly negative words and statements that automatically set up barriers to your message. Instead, use positive techniques such as stating what you can do rather than what you cannot do, including a positive fact in the same sentence with the negative idea, or offering a counterproposal to minimize the receiver's disappointment.

Use the subjunctive mood or imply the bad news if you believe the reader will understand your refusal clearly. If you must state the bad news directly, avoid using a simple sentence for the refusal unless your intention is to emphasize the "no." Place the negative message in the dependent clause of a complex sentence to deemphasize the negative.

Last Paragraph: The closing paragraph should demonstrate empathy but should not include statements that may cause the reader to question the fairness of your decision. Do not mention the refusal in the final paragraph. Instead, end with an idea that brings a positive, unifying quality to the letter; e.g., referring to a pleasant idea mentioned earlier in the letter, resale, sales promotional material, or a counterproposal.

CHECK YOUR WRITING

UNPLEASANT MESSAGES

CONTENT

- ☐ Major idea is clearly identified.
- ☐ Supporting detail is sufficient.
- ☐ Facts or figures are accurate.
- ☐ Message is ethical and abides by legal requirements.

ORGANIZATION

- ☐ First sentence introduces the general subject
  - ☐ without stating the bad news.
  - ☐ without leading a receiver to expect good news.
  - ☐ without making such an obvious statement as "I am replying to your letter" or "Your letter has been received."
- ☐ Details or explanations precede bad news.
- ☐ Main idea (unpleasant idea) emerges from preceding discussion.
- ☐ Closing sentences are about something positive (an alternative, resale, or sales promotion).

STYLE

- ☐ Words will be readily understood.
- ☐ Sentences are relatively short.
- ☐ Sentences vary in length and structure.
- ☐ Principal idea (the unpleasant idea or the refusal) is sufficiently clear.
- ☐ Some techniques of subordination are used to keep the bad news from emerging with unnecessary vividness. For example, bad news
  - ☐ appears in a dependent clause.
  - ☐ is stated in passive voice.
  - ☐ is revealed through indirect statement.
  - ☐ is revealed through the use of subjunctive mood.
- ☐ First person is used sparingly or not at all.
- ☐ Ideas cohere (changes in thought are not abrupt).
- ☐ Expression is original (sentences are not copied directly from the definition of the problem or from sample letters in the text); clichés are omitted.

MECHANICS

- ☐ Keyboarding, spelling, grammar, and punctuation are perfect.
- ☐ Paragraphs are relatively short.

LETTERS

- ☐ Letter style is acceptable (block, modified block, or simplified).
- ☐ Letter is balanced on the page.
- ☐ Letter parts are in appropriate vertical and horizontal position.
  - ☐ Return address (if plain paper is used)
  - ☐ Dateline
  - ☐ Letter address
  - ☐ Salutation (if needed)
  - ☐ Subject line (if needed)
  - ☐ Complimentary close (if needed)
  - ☐ Letter is signed legibly.
  - ☐ Keyboarded name (and title)
  - ☐ Reference initials (if needed)
  - ☐ Enclosure notation (if needed)
  - ☐ Other special letter parts (if needed)

MEMORANDUMS

- ☐ *TO, FROM, DATE,* and *SUBJECT* lines completed.
- ☐ Side margins are consistent.
- ☐ Courtesy titles are omitted in *TO* and *FROM* lines.
- ☐ Lines are single-spaced; blank space appears between paragraphs; paragraphs are not indented.
- ☐ Tabulated items are indented for emphasis (if appropriate \letter style used).
- ☐ Handwritten initials are placed by name on the *FROM* line (or signed in the space provided in the simplified format).

REFERENCES

Major, M. J. (1993, December). Candor helps Boeing handle massive layoffs. *Public Relations Journal*, pp. 20-21.

Schroer, Judith. (1994, February 3). Bowled-over Bills tackle morale issue. *USA Today*, p. 5B.

REVIEW QUESTIONS

1. List the four points that would appear in an outline for a letter that conveys bad news. (List them in the best sequence.)
2. What two functions do the first paragraph serve? Does "I am responding to your letter of the 25th" accomplish both of these functions? Explain.
3. One disadvantage of stating a refusal in the first sentence is that the reader may stop reading at that point. State another disadvantage.
4. What would be the disadvantage of waiting until the last sentence to convey bad news?
5. What objectives should the final paragraph accomplish? Is placing the refusal statement in a paragraph by itself acceptable?
6. List some conditions under which a writer would be justified in stating bad news in the first sentence.
7. How can writers reduce the risk that readers will become impatient while reading explanations that precede bad news?
8. Explain how the inductive outline de-emphasizes the bad news.
9. Prepare a list of techniques for de-emphasizing a refusal. List each technique for projecting a positive tone and de-emphasizing negative ideas discussed in Chapter 7 ("Project a Positive, Tactful Tone" and "Emphasize Important Ideas" sections). Provide an example of your own for each technique.
10. Which will make a refusal stand out more vividly in a reader's mind: (a) a direct statement or (b) implication? Compose a sentence conveying bad news in both ways: directly and by implication.
11. List the outline recommended when an adjustment must be refused.
12. In which part of a refusal letter would resale and sales promotional material be most appropriate?
13. List the outline recommended when refusing to send merchandise inappropriate for the customer's needs.
14. What is a counterproposal? How does it assist in achieving the human relations goal of business communication?
15. Discuss the legal implications involved in writing credit refusals.
16. Discuss why using the inductive approach for writing memorandums and e-mail messages is important.
17. List six recommended ideas for introducing the bad news in the first paragraph. Which of these ideas is used for each of the good examples in this chapter?
18. Should the closing sentence apologize for action taken? Explain.
19. Should a writer strive to achieve unity by referring to the statement of refusal in the last paragraph? Explain.
20. Study each of the good examples in the chapter and compile a list of the approaches used to close the letter/memo in a positive way.

EXERCISES

1. Complete each of the THINK IT OVER activities your instructor assigns.
2. Locate an example of both a well-written and a poorly written bad-news letter or memorandum. Analyze the strengths and weaknesses of each document. Be prepared to discuss in class.
3. Team up with a classmate to defend the use of the inductive or the deductive outline for bad-news messages. Consider whether your argument would vary if you were communicating with people of other cultures or other specific audiences. Consult the business literature to provide realistic examples and viewpoints that may strengthen your position.
4. Analyze the effectiveness of the following opening sentences in a bad-news message:
   a. Company policy does not allow me to approve the proposed transaction.
   b. Tommy MacDougal received the promotion; you did not.
   c. Our departmental award went to Charles Henning; you were our first runner-up.
   d. We cannot grant you a refund. However, if you will agree to pay the shipping costs, we will send replacements for your defective spinning reels.
   e. This letter is in response to your complaint of April 9.
5. Revise the following sentences to ensure positive tone:
   a. We cannot accept an application sent after May 9.
   b. Employees cannot smoke in the main office.
   c. I am sorry, but we cannot be responsible for the service charges on your car; the damage occurred at the dealership, not our factory.
   d. Your request for transfer to Kyoto, Japan, has been denied.
   e. We cannot accept this poorly organized report.
6. Analyze the following letter. Identify its strengths and weaknesses and rewrite the letter.

8677 Southbend Road
Ashland, KY 41101-8677
April 6, 19--

Ms. Gayle Doerr
8280 Thornapple Road
Ashland, KY 41101-8230

Dear Gayle:

I am pleased and honored to have been asked to serve as president of the Ashland Jaycees for the coming year.

However, I regret to inform you that I cannot serve in this important position. Last year, obligations kept me from attending seven of the twenty-five meetings. Unfortunately, commitments for the coming year are even greater than last year. The position of president requires a tremendous amount of attention—much more than I can give at this particular time.

Once again, I appreciate the confidence you have placed in me but am sorry that my plans preclude my serving as president this year. I look forward to participating in this year's activities and am especially eager to chair the Goodwill Marathon project again this year.

Sincerely,

Clark P. Nawara

Clark P. Nawara

E-MAIL APPLICATION

As president of Cenco Enterprises, compose a memo to your staff explaining that a customary end-of-year employee bonus will not be possible due to declining sales. Be careful to justify your decision while not alarming the recipients. E-mail the memo to your instructor.

APPLICATIONS

MARKETING

1. **Wallpaper Cannot Be Returned**. Arlene Collins ordered six double rolls of an expensive wallpaper design to redecorate her living room. Using the store sample, she carefully matched paint to one of the predominant colors in the wallpaper and had a professional paint the ceiling while she waited delivery on the wallpaper. Now she insists that the tint in the wallpaper she ordered is significantly different from the sample she saw in the wallpaper book. The tint definitely does not match her newly painted ceiling. The interior designer from whom she purchased the wallpaper refuses to make an adjustment; therefore, Ms. Collins has written the manufacturer requesting a complete refund.

   Required: As the claims manager for the wallpaper manufacturer, write Ms. Collins refusing the adjustment. Explain that uncontrollable differences in the dyeing process for each run of wallpaper produced result in slight variations in the tint of each run, including the samples in the wallpaper books. For example, you might explain that customers ordering additional rolls of the same wallpaper pattern are shipped rolls manufactured in the same run, which ensures that the tint is identical to the paper shipped in the original order. Ms. Collins' address is 34 South Clanton Street, Lincoln, NE 68501-8730. As you plan the message, consider the following issues:

   1. How can you use the opening paragraph to establish a connection with Ms. Collins? How can you show your empathy for her concerns?
   2. How technical should your explanation about the variations occurring in the manufacturing process be? Can you think of an analogy that would illustrate how variations occur in other situations; e.g., cooking, sewing, building?
   3. Can you suggest solutions to her problem; e.g., resources who might identify ways to use the wallpaper?

4. Consider how you will generate goodwill in the final paragraph. Would offering a discount on a subsequent order reinforce your concern or undermine the legitimacy of your refusal?

MARKETING

2. **Caterer Must Charge for Additional Guests**. PartyTime Limited recently catered an annual staff/alumni banquet for SRM Industries. Unfortunately, when reporting the number of attendees, SRM's function organizer did not consider the number of alumni who would bring guests. Soon after the guests began to arrive, PartyTime's staff recognized the problem and began improvising to accommodate 25 additional guests. Only a few people were aware of the confusion, and the food was served just a few minutes late. The head of accounting at SRM has refused to pay the charges for the additional guests. She insists that SRM agreed to pay the contracted rate provided in writing prior to the banquet.

   Required: As manager of PartyTime Limited, write the head of accounting refusing to allow her to deduct the charges for the additional service. Remind her that the additional charge includes only the cost of providing the food for the extra guests and not the labor involved in these last-minute preparations. Address your letter to Tandi McRae, Accounting and Budget, SRM Industries, 7821 South Third Street, Conway, AR 72032-7839.

BANKING

3. **Borrowers Cannot Open Up a Locked-in Interest Rate**. When they completed a mortgage application on June 7, Bart and Kathy Harris "locked in" on an 8-percent mortgage loan. When they closed on the house on June 27 (legally bought the house), the prevailing rates were lower than the 8 percent they locked in. Thus, they have requested that the bank lower the interest rate; that is, to open up the locked-in interest rate.

The bank must refuse to lower the rate. The lock-in protects the borrower from rising interest rates while the mortgage application is processed. A lock-in is *not* a guarantee that a borrower will get lower rates should interest rates drop.

Required: As the loan officer, write the Harrises explaining that the bank cannot lower their interest rate. The address is 103 Pinebrook Lane, Bowling Green, KY 42101-0876.

MANAGEMENT

4. **Restocking Fee To Be Paid on Returned Merchandise.** Snowcap Limited, a tourist shop located near a popular ski resort, purchased its stock of skis from Downhill Manufacturing. At the end of the season, Snowcap's owner, Kim Flaunt, returned the unsold skis and requested a full refund of $2,435. Downhill Manufacturing charges a 15-percent restocking fee for returned merchandise; this policy is printed clearly on the inside cover of its catalog and in bold print at the bottom of the order form. Operators explain this charge to customers placing orders on the company's 800 number.

Required: As the credit manager at Downhill Manufacturing, write Kim Flaunt, enclosing the refund check and explaining the deduction for the 15-percent restocking fee. The address is 905 Southhaven Street, Boise, ID 83707-7313.

MANAGEMENT

5. **Policy Covers Material Value Only.** Continental Movers, a small moving company in Iowa, transported Jeff and Toni Bailey's belongings to Davenport. An oil painting that had belonged to Mr. Bailey's great-grandmother was torn in transit. When completing the required insurance claim forms, the Baileys requested payment of $10,000, which they considered to be the value of this heirloom. However, the insurance policy covers only the material cost ($250). Before the Baileys' possessions were moved, one of Continental's representatives carefully explained the policy to the Baileys, and they signed the policy stating that they understood its stipulations.

Required: As claims manager at Continental Movers, write an appropriate letter to Mr. and Mrs. Jeff Bailey, 873 North Spruce Lane, Davenport, IA 52802-8510.

MANAGEMENT

6. **Dry Sprinkler System Is More Appropriate for Cold Climates.** As the owner of Greiner Plumbing Contractors, you have reviewed the specifications for a new clubhouse at the Edgewood Golf Club. You are concerned that the plans include a traditional wet sprinkler system that carries water in the pipes to be used in case of fire. If exposed to subfreezing temperatures over extended periods, the water in the pipes will freeze and then break, causing water damage to the structure. This freezing problem has caused unnecessary damages to several of your previous contracts; therefore, you now recommend installation of a dry sprinkler system. In this system, the pipes contain pressurized air that opens a valve for sprinkler action when the fire is detected. Because the dry system is less conventional and more expensive than the wet system, few architects are including the dry systems in their blueprints.

The client has three options: (1) authorize the architect to redesign the blueprint to include the dry system, (2) instruct you to install the wet system with a heat source in the attic to be used during subfreezing temperatures, or (3) arrange for another contractor to install the wet system (without the heat source). You are convinced that any dissatisfaction resulting from the unnecessary damages caused by broken pipes will more adversely affect your company than sacrificing the contract.

Required: Write the letter explaining the need for the dry system and presenting the three options. Mention a brochure that you are including that explains and illustrates the dry system. Address the letter to Mr. Stephen Shook, Manager, Edgewood Golf Club, 957 Edgewood Boulevard, Springfield, IL 62701-3498.

ACCOUNTING

7. **Interim Audit Must Be Rescheduled.** The auditors from Laird & Associates are due to arrive Monday to begin the interim audit of FTE Enterprises. As FTE's controller, you just learned today (Wednesday) that a group of business

executives from Moscow will arrive on Monday to examine your accounting information systems. Previously you had agreed to assist this group in implementing similar accounting strategies in their country whenever they could arrange to be in Milwaukee. Because the visitation involves not only you but the entire MIS Department and several employees in the Accounting Department, you must arrange for the interim audit to be rescheduled.

As you plan your message, consider the following issues:

1. What method would be most effective for transmitting this timely message? The postponement is more than a mere inconvenience because staff assignments are made several months in advance.
2. How can you organize your reasons for the postponement? Could a deductive outline be used effectively in this situation?
3. What could you do to make the rescheduling process easier to generate goodwill in the closing words?

Required: Depending on your answers to these questions, complete one of the following activities: (a) write a letter to Tom Delancy, Laird & Associates, 411 McDowell Road, Charleston, IN 47111-0411 (include any necessary mailing notations) or (b) outline what you will say if you telephoned Tom personally to explain the situation.

COMMUNITY SERVICE

8. **Sorry, But You Did Not Make the Team.** Your job as loan manager of a local bank requires a great deal of writing, but today's project could prove to be one of your most challenging yet. For the first time, you are coaching a Little League baseball team for 12-year-old boys. Last night you completed tryouts and promised the players they would be notified of the results within a couple of days. As you left the field, one of the veteran coaches handed you the following form letter most coaches mail to players who do not make the team.

April 25, 19--

Dear Player:

Thank you for trying out for the 12-year-old competitive baseball team. However, I am sorry to inform you that you did not make it this year.

I hope your plans are to continue with baseball whether it be Little League or some other team.

Sincerely,

Ron Sims   Gene Rankin

Ron Sims and Gene Rankin

You appreciate the coach's willingness to help, but you believe this insensitive letter may damage these young boys' self-esteem and squelch their enthusiasm for baseball.

Required: Revise the form letter to the youths who did not make your team. You may want to customize the letter to provide specific reasons for a player's not making the team and suggest ways to improve his game. Address a sample letter to a fictitious player.

MANAGEMENT/Public Sector

9. **Decision to Relocate Corporate Headquarters Is Final.** Recently the board of directors of Regal Discount Stores decided to relocate its corporate headquarters from New York City to one of the city's suburbs. The mayor of New York City, James Flynn, has written the board urging it to reconsider its decision to relocate. Despite the individual members' personal preference to keep the headquarters in the city, the board agreed that the decision to relocate was in the best interest of the company. The following factors led to the decision: (1) The lower tax rates in the suburbs would provide an economic advantage. (2) The company's salary structure is affected by the direct and indirect costs of commuting required of employees who live in the suburbs. (3) During the past few years, the company has had difficulty recruiting managerial talent, who prefer living in the suburbs. (4) Several major competitors are already located in the suburbs.

Required: As chairman of the board, write a letter to the mayor refusing his request. Address it to James Flynn, Mayor of New York City, New York, NY 10001-7600. Consult a reference manual to identify the appropriate courtesy title and salutation for this public official.

ADVERTISING

10. **Parent Company Refuses to Continue Support of Not-for-Profit Program.** ChemCon Engineering, a family-owned business, has underwritten an adult literacy program on public television for the past five years. The owners and the public relations director believe that the financial support of this worthwhile project has been a favorable public relations tool. Recently, ChemCon was bought out by Petrol Corp. When approached by the television program director to renew financial commitment to the literacy program, the new president refused. The president is not opposed to efforts to increase adult literacy; however, top management at Petrol sees little, if any, merit in sponsoring public television programs. Therefore, no advertising dollars are channeled into projects such as this one.

Required: As the public relations director, write the letter to the television station refusing to contribute to the program. Address it to Lisa Aultman, Program Director, WRMW Television, P.O. Drawer 93001, Salem, OR 97301-8461.

COMMUNITY SERVICE/Public Sector

11. **All Bids Are Over Architect's Estimate.** The City of Rochester had solicited bid proposals from contractors to build a community recreational center including an indoor pool, basketball court, racquetball court, weight-lifting room, aerobics room, and snack bar. As chair of the Building Committee, you are disappointed to learn that the lowest bid from the ten contractors submitting proposals was $20,500 higher than the amount estimated by the architects. You immediately begin to think of possible solutions to this problem: Eliminating the weight-lifting room would save $30,000, yet you quickly remember the majority of the community is supportive of the new recreational center. With this level of support, perhaps initiating another fund-raising drive to raise the additional money would be feasible.

Required:
1. Write a letter to Mary Sinn, City Administrator, informing her that all bids are over the architect's estimate and present your suggestions for continuing the project. Advise that a meeting of the City Council be called; the low-bid contractor and architect would be present to discuss the proposed alternatives.
2. Write a form letter to the contractors submitting the bids for the recreational center. Inform them that all bids were above the architect's estimate; therefore, you will modify the blueprints and request revised bids at that time. Address the sample letter to Dunn/Malcolm Construction, 9831 Downing Street, Minneapolis, MN 55440-9831.

MIS

12. **Price Reductions in Computer Industry Are Inevitable.** As a sales rep for Reese Computer Systems, you recently sold Mitchell Savings and Loan a local area network to replace its current obsolete system. A week later, the client asked you to delay installation of the system to allow the MIS Department ample time to finalize preparations for the system. Since the sale, the price of this system has dropped 15 percent. Stan Martin, the MIS manager at Mitchell, learned of the price reduction and has requested a similar reduction in the cost of its system. Unfortunately, you had already purchased the hardware when the client asked for the delay and did not benefit from a manufacturer's price reduction.

Required: Write the refusal to Stan Martin, Mitchell Savings and Loan, 8324 Randall Street, Cheyenne, WY 82009-8324.

ACCOUNTING

13. **Unable to Speak at Seminar.** For several years, you as a civic-minded accountant have conducted seminars on investments for various organizations. This year, the Beta Alpha Psi chapter at the local university has asked you to assist with the annual VITA (Voluntary Income Tax Assistance) program. Specifically, the group wishes you to devote two evenings to assist the accounting students as they complete income tax returns. The dates selected are during the last two weeks in March—a particularly

inconvenient time for you. You need every moment that month if you are to satisfy the needs of your clients.

Required: Write a letter refusing the request. Dr. Marion Collier, Accounting Department, Central State College, P.O. Drawer 419, Oakwood, IA 63981-0532.

FINANCE/Legal

14. **New Credit Policies Affect Real Estate Loans Adversely.** Robbins Construction Corp. has requested $14 million from Colonial National Bank to build a 200,000-square-foot shopping center. Three major chains (department store, discount store, and electronics/video outlet)—adequate anchors for this size center—have already signed leases, and 80 percent of the remaining space has been leased. Robbins has presented budgets showing how the income from this center can service the loan, and the development itself is offered as collateral for the loan.

    Under previous lending guidelines, the bank could approve a real estate loan if it had reasonable assurance that the borrower could repay the loan from either the income from operations or the sale of the development. Because of the current decline in the economy, however, lending guidelines for real estate loans have become stricter. The borrower must now provide assurance that the loan can be repaid from sources other than the development itself, typically the income or assets of other businesses or personal investments. Thus, these new guidelines are designed to ensure payment of the loan regardless of the success or failure of the proposed development.

    Required: As the loan manager, write a letter to Julian Robbins refusing to approve the loan. P.O. Box 9408, Eau Claire, WI 54703-9408.

FINANCE/Legal

15. **Customer Credit Too Risky to Obtain Loan.** You are the director of loans at Wheaton State Bank in Cleveland, Ohio. You receive a letter from John Curro, who applied for a loan to buy a stereo system. You denied his loan because his credit history revealed that he had three credit cards charged to the maximum with two months'

payments overdue. In his letter, Mr. Nelson quoted the Ohio discrimination laws that require all creditors to make credit equally available to all credit-worthy customers.

Required: Write to John Curro restating reasons for denying credit and pointing out that the law emphasized equal access to credit-worthy customers. His address is 910 Miller Court, Cleveland, OH 44101-8600.

FINANCE/Legal

16. **Loan Denied for Poor Credit Customer.** Having decided to build an addition to their home, Rodney and Amy Latham made an application for a $15,000 loan from a personal finance company. A report from a consumer reporting agency revealed a consistent record of slow payment. On more than one occasion, they paid only after forceful attempts at collection.

    Required: As manager of the local branch of the finance company, write a refusal letter. Provide the name, address, and telephone number of the consumer reporting agency (you supply) and invite the Lathams to come in to discuss the refusal. Rodney and Amy Latham, P.O. Box 432, Baxter, WI 54321-5590.

HUMAN RESOURCES MANAGEMENT

17. **Company Downsizing Announced.** As director of human resources at Vaughn & Merrill, an architectural firm, you must notify employees that the firm will be downsized. All departments will be reduced by at least 20 percent; many of the employees will also be asked to assume duties not included in their original job description. For example, upper-level personnel will complete additional support-staff responsibilities, and architects will oversee all phases of a project such as preparing bids, developing budgets, and supervising work crews. The company is still considering issues such as severance pay, continuation of benefits, and outplacement services.

    As you plan this message to all employees, consider the following issues:

    1. Should you write generally about the downsizing plan or provide specific details wherever possible?

2. What can you include to ease employees' fears and tensions about their futures? What information can you supply to convey the idea that the company is not their enemy in this situation?

3. Should you convey this sensitive issue in a memo to all employees? in a meeting of all employees? face-to-face with department supervisors?

Required: Incorporating the ideas you have generated, write either (a) a memo notifying all employees of the downsizing plan, (b) a memo to all employees announcing an important meeting *and* on a separate page write an outline of the talk you will give at the meeting, or (c) a memo to supervisors instructing them to notify their employees of the plan. Include suggestions for managing the tensions created by the negative information.

HUMAN RESOURCES MANAGEMENT

18. **Back to the Road for Sales Reps.** You are the sales manager for a national pharmaceutical company. Several years ago, in an effort to cut costs, your company required sales reps to make sales contacts primarily by telephone and fax machine rather than one-to-one sales calls with doctors who were often too busy to meet with the rep. Utilizing communication technology allowed the company to reduce the sales staff and excessive travel costs. Morale of the sales force has increased because reps prefer working in the office. You believe, however, the company's recent decline in sales is a result of this policy. Research shows that the success rate of telephone/fax contacts is 50 percent compared to an 85 percent success rate with personal contacts. An informal survey of the company's current customers indicated that they prefer talking with the sales rep in person, especially when considering a new drug. Thus, management has accepted your recommendation that the sales force begin making personal sales calls three days a week to maintain relations with existing clients and to acquire new customers.

Required: Write a memo to the sales force informing them of this change.

MANAGEMENT/Legal   GMAT

19. **To Fire or Not to Fire.** You are the controller for a regional mail-order catalog company with outlets in the Northeast. You have received a call from a customer, Penny Benjamin, who has not received her merchandise although the $564 check has been returned with her bank statement. Upon investigating this situation, you learn that similar complaints have been received over the past year. Using a variety of auditing procedures, you suspect that Will Mallory, the mailroom clerk, has cashed the checks. When you call Will in to discuss the matter, he confessed to the thefts, explaining that he spent the money to support a gambling habit. Over the past year, he had stolen a total of $20,590.

As the controller, you must write a memo to your supervisor telling her about the embezzlement and recommending appropriate action. You are honestly confused about which of the following options you should recommend:

a. Terminate Will's employment and write off the loss.
b. Terminate Will's employment and initiate a civil lawsuit in an attempt to recover the money.
c. Terminate Will's employment and file criminal charges of embezzlement.
d. Retain Will in his current position with the agreement he will pay back the embezzled funds in installments.
e. Retain Will but transfer him to a position with no access to cash and require him to pay back the embezzled funds in installments.

As you think about these options, consider the following issues:

• Will has fully cooperated with your investigation, providing documentation and aiding you in pinpointing the exact amount embezzled. He seems repentant not because he has been caught but because he has hurt the company and understands he has broken the law. He insists that he intended to pay the money back as soon as he could. Should his attitude influence your decision?
• Many mail-order companies have recently been in the media for various fraud cases;

this negative coverage has damaged your company's image. Could this fact affect your decision?

- Is recovering the money critical? Is ensuring that Will faces the consequences of his actions critical?

Required: Write a memo to your supervisor, Jill Ainsworth, explaining the embezzlement and presenting your recommended action with logical justification.

HUMAN RESOURCES MANAGEMENT

20. **Written Disciplinary Action Required.** Functioning as the controller for the regional mail-order catalog company, you have decided to retain the employee who embezzled $20,590 from your company but transfer him to the Maintenance Department where he will have no access to cash (Application 19). You conducted a formal disciplinary conference with Will to present your decision and to notify him of his transfer.

Required: Write a memo to Will's file about this issue. The memo will briefly explain the fraudulent activity, the action you have taken with justification, and a brief summary of statements make during the disciplinary conference.

CASES FOR ANALYSIS

MANAGEMENT/Interpersonal

Case 1.   Plant Will Close for Two Weeks. Economic troubles have hit the Janata Forge Machinists Plant. Many employees have been laid off, and the grapevine has begun to promote rumors that additional employees will be laid off and that the company is going bankrupt. Communication related to the initial layoffs was poor and reactive. Top management is convinced that communication between employer and employees must be improved if the company is to survive this economic downturn.

As plant manager, you must announce to employees that the plant will close for two weeks at Christmas. Workers will be paid only 50 percent of their salaries for the two weeks the plant is closed.

Required:

1. To minimize employee fear and inaccurate rumors, research ways to communicate this negative information. Follow these suggestions: Review the research related to communication crises, specifically employer-employee relations (e.g., public relations textbooks and academic journals in the communication field); and read current practitioners' journals to learn what approaches other companies have taken to improve communication with employees when the company is facing financial difficulty.

2. As the plant manager, use your research to write a memorandum informing employees of their reduced work schedule during Christmas.

3. As the plant manager, write a memorandum to the president (Mark Rackley) providing general guidelines for improved employer-employee relations during a financial crisis. Include complete and accurate documentation of your sources. Your intention is that Mr. Rackley will distribute this memorandum (or the information within it) so that other managers can benefit from your research.

MANAGEMENT

Case 2.   Minimizing the Negative Publicity Associated with Product Recalls. Recently a new employee in quality control learned that the product description of the company's swing set (Model 2352) was modified because the metal used in the swing sets was not strong enough. Reinforcement bars could break under the weight of children swinging from them. When confronted, the production manager said there was no need to recall the 10,000 swings made from the inferior metal and insisted that the employee not mention the issue again.

After careful analysis of this difficult ethical dilemma, the employee wrote a memorandum to you, the vice president of production, advocating recall of these dangerous swing sets. You are convinced that the swing sets should be recalled despite the negative publicity that will follow. This situation is new to you; you've never been faced with communicating about a crisis situation. You must carefully consider the strategy you should take. You are certain of one thing; you have two equally important purposes: (1) You must disclose necessary information about the problem with the swing sets as honestly as you can and (2) at the same time, maintain the customer's confidence in the company's products and in its integrity.

Required:
1. Identify the important guidelines for communicating crisis information. Follow these suggestions: Review the research related to crisis communication (e.g., public relations textbooks and academic journals in the communication field), read current practitioners' journals to learn what approaches other companies have taken (e.g., product tampering, oil spills, and toxic waste contamination), and/or interview a public relations director of a company in your area or a public relations professor.
2. Based on your knowledge, write a recall letter to be sent to customers owning the swing sets. Inform customers of what you believe to be the appropriate restitution (repayment) for the defective product. Address the sample letter to Mrs. Jean O'Toole, 1278 Webster Boulevard, Omaha, NE 68101-8100.

ACCOUNTING/Ethics/Legal   `GMAT`

Case 3.   An Accountant's Knowledge of a Fraudulent Tax Return: What Action Is Legal? Is It Ethical?
As a tax accountant in a large accounting firm, you prepared Bradley Ford's tax return last year. The return indicated that Mr. Ford was due a small tax refund; his business reported less net income than in the prior year. Now, more than a year later, Mr. Ford has asked your assistance in preparing a business plan to secure a loan. Immediately you notice that last year's income statement shows twice the net income of the income statement you used to prepare the tax return. When you question Mr. Ford about the discrepancy, his evasive response assures you that the understatement of net income for tax purposes was intentional.

Required:
1. Write a letter to Mr. Ford asking him to authorize you to file an amended tax return. The amended return will require your client to pay additional taxes, interest, and penalties. Address the letter to Bradley Ford, 3300 Parkway Drive, Fresno, CA 91316-3300.
2. Assume that the client refuses to authorize you to amend the tax return. Complete the following research to assist in making an informed response:
   a. Identify what action the IRS requires of tax preparers upon learning that a filed tax return was fraudulent. Consult tax references such as the circulars published by the Internal Revenue Service.
   b. Determine what action the Code of Ethics of the American Institute of Certified Public Accountants (AICPA) indicates is appropriate for a certified public accountant to take in this circumstance. For this information, refer to tax references such as the *Statements on Responsibilities in Tax Practice*.
3. After analyzing the research completed in Step 2, write a memo to the tax partner communicating your analysis of the situation and the action you propose that the firm take. List the sources of information to increase the credibility of your position.
4. The tax partner was impressed with your meticulous research and documentation and has approved your decision in the Ford case. The partner has authorized you to prepare a letter to the client communicating the firm's action. Prepare the letter for the partner's signature; include your reference initials in all capital letters to identify the originator of the message in the event clarification is needed. Address the letter to Bradley Ford, 3300 Parkway Drive, Fresno, CA 91316-3300.

CHAPTER 11

WRITING TO

PERSUADE

OBJECTIVES

When you have completed Chapter 11, you will be
able to

1 Develop effective outlines and appeals for messages that persuade.

2 Write effective sales messages and persuasive
requests (claim, favor, information requests, and
persuasion within organizations) that are persuasive, but ethical.

3 Write collection letters at various stages of the
collection process.

Laura is a manager for a large national firm. She enjoys her career and thrives on the challenge of performing at her peak while raising her two children. However, last year, she began showing signs of burnout. Managing her career and finding time to care for the children without feeling exhausted most of the time had become increasingly difficult. While skimming a business publication one day, she noticed an article about telecommuting—a plan that enables employees to work from home on certain days with the assistance of a computer with a modem and facsimile machine. Intrigued, Laura continued to research the plan. She discovered that telecommuting offers several advantages for both employees and companies. Telecommuting, Laura concluded, is what she needed to do.

Of course, she needed to obtain permission from her supervisor to begin telecommuting, so she developed a plan. First, Laura made a list of her job duties. Of these, she listed the ones she could perform at home. Then she made a list of the benefits of telecommuting, emphasizing in particular how the company would benefit. She anticipated possible objections to her plan and developed responses for those protests. Finally, she drafted a proposal in the form of a letter to her supervisor, including the information she had organized. She even included copies of her research materials for support.

After some minor negotiating, Laura was allowed to begin telecommuting on a temporary basis while management evaluated its efficiency. Now she is a permanent telecommuter and plans to maintain this schedule until her children are older. She is more productive because of reduced stress and fewer interruptions, and the company is benefiting from this increased productivity (Dumas, 1994).

Laura may have been one more burnout statistic had it not been for her initiative and, most importantly, her excellent writing skills. Effective persuasive writing is a crucial skill to have. Without it, many goals may be postponed or never reached; but, these skills can be learned, like any other. All it takes is practice.

PERSUASION STRATEGIES

LEARNING OBJECTIVE 1

THINK IT OVER
In small groups, generate a list of persuasive messages you received recently.

THINK IT OVER
What types of persuasive messages have you written previously? Did you feel prepared to write them effectively?

The previous telecommuting example illustrates persuasion at work. **Persuasion** is the art of influencing others to accept your point of view. It is not an attempt to trap someone into taking action favorable to the writer. Instead, it is an honest, organized presentation of information upon which a person may choose to act. In all occupations and professions, rich rewards await those who can use well-informed and well-prepared presentations to persuade others to accept their ideas or buy their products, services, or ideas.

How do you learn to persuade others through written communication? Have you ever written a cover letter, filled out an application for a job, or written an essay for college entry or a scholarship? If so, you already have experience with this type of writing.

For persuasion to be effective, you must understand your product, service, or idea; know your audience; anticipate the arguments that may come from the audience; and have a rational and logical response to those arguments. Remember, persuasion need not be a hard sell; it can simply be a way of getting a client or your supervisor to say "yes." Although many of the examples and discussions in this chapter concentrate on selling *products and services*, similar principles apply to selling an *idea, your organization*, and *your own abilities*.

Plan Before You Write

Success in *writing* is directly related to success in preliminary *thinking*. If the right questions have been asked and answered, the writing will be easier and the message will be more persuasive. You might ask

- Who are the people to whom the message is directed, and what are their wants and needs?
- What are the strong features (points) of the product, service, or idea?
- How is the product or service different from its competition? How is the proposed idea superior to other viable alternatives?
- What specific action is wanted?
- Which writing principles will be especially helpful?

Preliminary planning is vital.

KNOW THE PRODUCT, SERVICE, OR IDEA

You cannot be satisfied with knowing the product, service, or idea in a general way; you need details. Get your information by (1) reading all available literature; (2) using the product and watching others use it; (3) comparing the product, service, or idea with others; (4) conducting tests and experiments; and (5) soliciting reports from users.

Before you write, you need concrete answers to such questions as these:

- What will the product, service, or idea do for the receiver(s)?
- What are its superior features (e.g., design and quality or receiver-benefit)?
- What is the cost to the receiver?

What questions must be answered before writing a persuasive message?

Similar questions must be answered about other viable alternatives or competing products. Of particular importance is the question, "What is the major difference?" People are inclined to choose an item (or alternative) that has some distinct advantage. For example, some people may choose a brand of bread because it is high in fiber and contains no cholesterol; still others may choose bread because it is wrapped in two-layer paper.

Why is the major difference so important?

KNOW THE RECEIVER

Is a persuasive message to be written and addressed to an individual or to a group? If it is addressed to a group, what characteristics do the members have in

Envision yourself as the person receiving the message.

common? What are their common goals, their occupational levels, their educational status? To what extent have their needs and wants been satisfied? (See the discussion of Maslow's needs hierarchy in Chapter 1.)

Some people may respond favorably to appeals to physiological, security, and safety needs (to save time and money, to be comfortable, to be healthy, or to avoid danger). People with such needs would be impressed with a discussion of such benefits as convenience, durability, efficiency, or serviceability. Others may respond favorably to appeals to their social, ego, and self-actualizing needs (to be loved, entertained, remembered, popular, praised, appreciated, or respected). Consider the varying appeals used in a memo to employees and to supervisors seeking support of telecommuting. The memo to employees would appeal to the need for greater flexibility and reduced stress. Appeals directed at supervisors would focus on increased productivity and morale, reduced costs (office space), and compliance with the Clean Air Act (federal law requiring companies to find ways to get employees off the road to reduce air pollution and traffic congestion).

IDENTIFY THE DESIRED ACTION

What do you want the receiver to do? Complete an order form and enclose a personal check? Return a card requesting a representative to call? Write for more information? Approve your request to allow you to telecommute two days a week? Whatever the desired action, you need to have a clear definition of it before beginning to compose the message.

Apply Sound Writing Principles

The principles of unity, coherence, and emphasis are just as important in persuasive messages as in other messages. In addition, some other principles seem to be especially helpful in persuasive messages:

1. *Use concrete nouns and active verbs.* Concrete nouns and active verbs help receivers see the product, service, or idea and its benefits more vividly than do abstract nouns and passive verbs.
2. *Use specific language.* General words seem to imply subjectivity unless they are well supported with specifics. Specific language is space consuming (saying that something is "great" is less space consuming than telling what makes it so); therefore, persuasive messages are usually longer than other messages. Still, persuasive messages need to be concise; they should say what needs to be said without wasting words.
3. *Let receivers have the spotlight.* If receivers are made the subject of some of the sentences, if they can visualize themselves with the product in their hands, if they can get the feel of using it for enjoyment or to solve problems, the chances of creating a desire are increased.
4. *Be certain your persuasive message presents the facts honestly, truthfully, and objectively.* Overzealous sales representatives or imaginative writers can use language skillfully to create less-than-accurate perceptions in the minds of receivers. However, legal guidelines related to advertising provide clear guidance for misrepresentation of products or services. If you exaggerate or mislead in a letter and use the U.S. Postal Service to deliver the letter, you can be charged with the federal offense of mail fraud. Penalties can include significant fines and imprisonment.

What is an "appeal"?

THINK IT OVER
Consider a decision to telecommute. What appeals would be appropriate to persuade supervisors and employees?

Decide what action you want the receiver to take before you write.

THINK IT OVER
Turn to Chapter 7 for a quick review of coherence ("Developing Coherent Paragraphs") and emphasis ("Emphasize Important Ideas").

Why are persuasive messages usually longer than other messages?

You are selling the benefits gained, not the product, service, or idea.

What are ethical and legal implications of persuasive messages?

Before you can write an effective sales letter, you must know as much as possible about the product you are trying to sell. You must also be aware of the readers' needs and any doubts or questions they may have about your product.

Critique your persuasive messages to make certain you can substantiate all claims made about your product or service. Using concrete evidence and objective language will help you create an accurate representation of your product, service, or idea (and the competition if mentioned). Honestly ask yourself if you embellished or exaggerated any point. Have you deliberately omitted, distorted, or hidden important information that does not support your argument so that the receiver completely misses it? Recall the investment manager's letter to an investor reporting that the client's stock portfolio has experienced 24-percent growth but omits the fact that the stock market as a whole has increased 32 percent in the same period (Chapter 6). The investor may miss this important comparison as the manager intended and may lose faith in the manager's credibility. Businesses have learned that unethical behavior, such as overstating the capabilities of a product or service (promising more than can be delivered), is not good for business in the long run. Use the effective persuasion techniques you will learn in this chapter only if your motive is genuine—not to exploit the receiver.

THINK IT OVER
Is inflating your resume similar to embellishing a sales letter? What might be the effects?

5. *Stress a central selling point or appeal.* Few products, services, or ideas have everything. A thorough analysis will ordinarily reveal some feature that is different from the features of competing products or some benefit not provided by other viable alternatives. This point of difference can be developed into a theme that is woven throughout the entire letter. Or, instead of using a point of difference as a central selling point, a writer may choose to stress one of the major satisfactions derived from using the item or doing as asked (approving a claim or responding favorably to a request). A central selling point (*theme*) should be introduced early in the message and should be reinforced throughout the remainder of the message.

What is the central selling point? Why is it important?

6. *Use an inductive outline.* About ninety years ago, Sherwin Cody (1906, pp. 122-126) summarized the persuasive process into four basic steps called *AIDA*.

The steps have been varied somewhat and have had different labels, but the fundamentals remain relatively unchanged. The AIDA steps for selling are

What are the four steps in the selling procedure?

A Get the receiver's *attention*.
I Introduce the product, service, or idea and arouse *interest* in it.
D Create *desire* by presenting convincing evidence of the value of the product, service, or idea.
A Encourage *action*.

Should a persuasive message have four paragraphs—one for each point of the outline?

A sales letter written following these steps is inductive. The main idea, which is the request for action, appears in the *last* paragraph after presenting the details—convincing reasons for the receiver to comply with the request.

Each step is essential, but the steps do not necessarily require equal amounts of space. Good persuasive writing does not require separate sentences and paragraphs for each phase of a letter—(a) getting attention; (b) introducing the product, service, or idea; (c) giving evidence; and (d) stimulating action. Points (a) and (b) *could* appear in the same sentence, and Point (c) could require many paragraphs. Blend the steps in the four-step outline to prepare effective and persuasive (1) sales letters; (2) claims, favors, and information requests; (3) requests within organizations; and (4) collection letters.

SALES LETTERS

LEARNING OBJECTIVE 2

Why are unsolicited sales letters more difficult to write than solicited sales letters?

The four-point outline is appropriate for an **unsolicited sales letter**, a letter written to someone who has not requested it. A **solicited sales letter** has been requested by a potential buyer or supporter; e.g., a letter written to answer this interested person's question. Someone who has invited a persuasive message has given some attention to the product, service, or idea already; an attention-getting sentence is hardly essential. However, such a sentence is essential when the receiver is not known to have expressed an interest previously. The very first sentence, then, is deliberately designed to make a receiver put aside other thoughts and concentrate on the rest of the message.

First Paragraph: An Attention-Getter

The first sentence should arouse desire to read the sentences that follow.

Various techniques have been successful in convincing receivers to put aside whatever they are doing or thinking about and consider an unsolicited sales letter. Some commonly used attention-getting devices include

- **A personal experience:** *When a doctor gives you instructions, how often have you thought, "I wish you had time to explain" or "I wish I knew more about medical matters."*
- **A solution to a problem (outstanding feature/benefit):** *Imagine creating a customized multimedia presentation that . . . .*
- **A startling announcement:** *More teens die as a result of suicide each month than die in auto accidents in the same time period.*
- **A what-if opening:** *What if I told you there is a saving plan that will enable you to retire three years earlier?*

- **A question:** *Why should you invest in a company that has lost money for six straight years?*
- **A story:** *Here's a typical day of a manager who uses Wilson Enterprises Voice Mail.*
- **A proverb or quote from a famous person:** *P. T. Barnum supposedly said, "There's a sucker born every minute." At Northland Candy Factory, we make the saying come true!*
- **A split sentence:** *Picture . . .*

   your audience's enthusiastic response to eye-catching graphics and colorful visuals to support your major points.

Other attention-getters include an analogy, a gift, an offer or a bargain, or a comment on an enclosed product sample. Regardless of the attention-getting technique you choose for any letter, you should ask some pertinent questions: (1) Is the attention-getter related to the product, service, or idea and its virtues? (2) Does the first sentence introduce a central selling feature? (3) Is the attention-getter addressed to the receiver's needs? (4) Does the attention-getter sound interesting? (5) Is the attention-getter original? (6) Is the first paragraph short?

THINK IT OVER
As a group, use one of the techniques presented to write a creative attention-getter for a product, service, or idea of your choice. Brainstorm in groups to generate a number of ideas.

START WITH THE PRODUCT, SERVICE, OR IDEA

The beginning sentence must suggest a relationship between the receiver and the product, service, or idea. It must pave the way for the remainder of the sales letter. The sentences that follow the first sentence should grow naturally from it. (See the discussion of coherence in Chapter 7.) If receivers do not see the relationship between the first sentences and the sales appeal, they may react negatively to the whole message—they may think they have been tricked into reading.

Ordinarily, you will have no difficulty in thinking of some way to get attention. The main problem, however, is getting attention in an appropriate manner. Is the following attention-getter related to the product and its virtues?

If the attention-getter does not relate to the product, service, or idea, the receiver may feel misled.

> Would you like to be the chief executive officer of one of America's largest companies?
>
> As CEO of Barkley Enterprises, you can launch new products, invest in third-world countries, or arrange billion dollar buyouts. Barkley Enterprises is one of several companies at your command in the new computer software game developed by Creative Diversions Software.

When the first sentence exaggerates or seems to mislead, the receiver may not read the remaining sentences.

The beginning sentence is emphatic because it is short and it is a question. However, it suggests that the remainder of the letter will be about obtaining a top management position, which it is not. All three sentences combined suggest that the writer is using high-pressure techniques. The computer software game has relevant virtues; one of them could have been emphasized by placing it in the first sentence.

FOCUS ON A CENTRAL SELLING FEATURE

Almost every product, service, or idea will in some respects be superior to its competition. If it is not, such factors as favorable price, fast delivery, or superior service may be used as the primary appeal. This primary appeal (central selling

Select a major feature of the product or a primary user benefit; emphasize it throughout the message.

point) must be emphasized, and one of the most effective ways to emphasize a point is by position in the letter. An outstanding feature mentioned in the middle of a letter may go unnoticed, but it will stand out if mentioned in the first sentence. Note how the following sentence introduces the central selling feature and leads naturally into the sentences that follow:

A complete collection of Salvador Dali prints—only at the PosterShop!

You can select complete sets of prints by Doré and Monet, as well as Dali, at the PosterShop, the only fine arts poster dealer with this comprehensive selection of works of art by the "masters." PosterShop will also frame these prints professionally so you can display them in your home as proudly as you would the originals.

ADDRESS THE RECEIVER'S NEEDS

Few people will buy just because doing so will solve a problem for someone else. How would a student react to the following sales opening?

After years of effort and expense, we have developed an electronic dictionary.

With the emphasis on the seller and the seller's problems, the sentence is not particularly appealing. Revised, the beginning paragraph is changed to focus on a problem the receiver has:

Relate the topic to something relevant and important to the receiver.

Your first draft is complete. Time is short and your spelling must be perfect. You can use Right-Spell (an electronic dictionary) to meet your term paper deadline.

Empathy—an important factor in all communication—is especially important in persuasive communication. Before and during writing, think in terms of receiver interests.

USE AN ORIGINAL APPROACH

An original story or anecdote is a more effective attention-getter than one the receiver likely has heard already.

All the preceding attention-getting devices (and others, too) are useful. You can use any of them without plagiarizing. For example, beginning a sales letter with an anecdote is all right, but you should not use one with which many people are already familiar. The following personal story grabs the receiver's attention and leads into a presentation of the new features available with *WordPerfect 6.0* [1] (Nelson, 1993, p. 37):

I step into my favorite restaurant, and the waiters all dive for cover. Only the restaurant owner has the guts to take my order—as if she really needs to ask. "I'll have the usual," I say. "Give me . . . the *All You Can Eat Buffet*." For the next two hours, I stuff myself. I indulge at the salad bar and I gorge at the taco bar. As much as I consume, though, I haven't tried everything—I just don't have room.

In many ways, WordPerfect 6.0 is like that gigantic buffet. The new WP is packed with powerful, useful features. . . .

1 WordPerfect 6.0 is a registered trademark of WordPerfect Corporation.

Good sales writing often reveals in the first sentence how a product, service, or idea can solve a receiver's problem. However, when mentioning the feature, do not use the same peculiar combination of words other people are known to use. That is a bad sales technique; it is also poor composition. People like to read something new and fresh; it gets their attention and interest. Writers should enjoy creating something new.

KEEP PARAGRAPHS SHORT

The spaces between paragraphs serve three purposes: (1) To show the dividing place between ideas, (2) to improve appearance, and (3) to provide convenient resting places for the eyes. What is your psychological reaction to a fifteen-line paragraph? Doesn't reading it seem an arduous physical and mental chore?

A receiver is encouraged to take that first step if it is a short one. If possible, hold the first and last paragraph to three or fewer lines. A one-line paragraph (even a very short line) is very acceptable. You can use paragraphs less than one sentence long! Put four or five words on the first line and complete the sentence in a new paragraph. Be careful to include key attention-getting words that either introduce the product, service, or idea or lead to its introduction. Take another look at Figure 7-2 to contrast the readability and appeal of a document with short paragraphs and one with unbroken, bulky text.

Introducing the Product, Service, or Idea

A persuasive message is certainly off to a good start if the first sentences cause the receiver to think, "Here's a solution to one of my problems," "Here's something I need," or "Here's something I want."

You may lead the receiver to such a thought by introducing the product, service, or idea in the very first sentence. If you do, you have succeeded in both getting attention and arousing interest in one sentence. If your introduction of the product, service, or idea is to be effective, you need affirmative answers to the following questions: (1) Is the introduction cohesive? (2) Is the introduction action centered? (3) Does the introduction stress a central selling point?

BE COHESIVE

If the attention-getter does not introduce the product, service, or idea, it should lead naturally to the introduction. One sentence should grow naturally from another. Note the abrupt change in thought in the following example:

> Employees appreciate a company providing a safe work environment.
>
> The Markham Human Resources Association has been conducting a survey for the last six months. Their primary aim is to improve the safety of office work environments.

The last words of the first sentence—"safe work environment"—are related to "safety of office work environments"—the last words of the last sentence. However, no word or phrase in the first sentence is readily identified with the words of the second sentence. The abrupt change in thought is confusing. The writer may have sought diligently for an attention-getter; this one, however, is not particularly related to the sales message that follows. Has the relationship between the two sentences been improved in the second example?

What are the purposes of paragraphs?

Today's TV generation does not want to read long sections of unbroken text.

Should the first paragraph be the longest?

THINK IT OVER
Bring several sales letters to class and in groups evaluate each attention-getter on the five elements presented.

Notice how this approach would blend Points a and b in the four-point outline.

Let one sentence lead smoothly to the next.

Employees appreciate a company's providing a safe work environment.

That's one thing the Markham Human Resources Association learned from its six-month survey of the safety of the office work environment. For added protection from radiation emissions, more companies are purchasing LogicTech's low-radiation computer monitors . . . .

The second sentence is tied to the first by the word "that's." The "safety" of the second sentence refers to the "protection" of the third. The LogicTech low-radiation monitor is introduced as a means of providing a safe work environment.

BE ACTION ORIENTED

If you want to introduce a product, service, or idea in an interesting way, you need to do more than bring it into the view of the receiver and begin describing it. Remember, active voice is more emphatic than passive voice. Action is eye catching—it holds attention and interest more readily than description. Remember, too, that *people* are expected to act and *things* to be acted upon.

In some sentences, use the *receiver* as the subject.

Place the product, service, or idea in your receivers' hands and talk about their using it or benefiting from accepting your idea. They will get a clearer picture when reading about something happening than when reading a product description. Also, the picture becomes all the more vivid when the receiver is the hero of the story—the person taking the action. If you put receivers to work using your product, service, or idea to solve problems, they will be the subject of most of your sentences.

THINK IT OVER
Turn to Figures 11-1 and 11-2. Is the receiver or product or idea the subject of most of the sentences? What benefits will the receiver receive from buying the pager and sponsoring the swim team?

However, a small amount of product description is necessary and natural. Too many sales writers overdo it, though, as in the following excerpt:

The ClassicForm treadmill is powered by a five-horsepower motor. The patented electronic control system features a digital display screen with variable speed and pause controls.

See how each sentence has a *thing* as the subject. You are looking at a still picture. Now, let a *person* be the subject and watch that person do something with the treadmill.

As you step on the ClassicForm treadmill to begin your workout, you will immediately enjoy the smooth, even movement. No more jarring starts and stops of other treadmills. That's because our unique electronic control center puts *you* in total control of your workout. All you have to do is press the ON button to start accelerating to your desired speed, which you can easily monitor on the clear digital display. Getting tired? Just press COAST to reduce the speed. Need to stop for a moment? Press the PAUSE button to bring your treadmill to a gradual stop. The strength of the five-horsepower motor will provide you this smooth, even movement for years to come.

Let receivers see the *benefit* they derive from using the product.

In a sense, you do not sell products, services, or ideas—you sell what they will do. You sell the pleasure people derive from the use of a product, service, or idea. Logically, then, you have to write more about that use than about the product, service, or idea.

STRESS THE CENTRAL SELLING POINT

If the attention-getter does not introduce a distinctive feature, it should lead to
it. You can stress important points by position in the letter and by space allocated to the point. As soon as receivers visualize the product, service, or idea,
they need to have attention called to its outstanding features; the features are
therefore emphasized because they are mentioned first. If you want to devote
much space to the outstanding features, introduce them early. Note how the
attention-getter introduces the distinctive selling feature (ease of operation) and
how the following sentences keep the receivers' eyes focused on that feature:

When should the central
selling point be intro-
duced?

> If you know how to write a check and record it in your checkbook, then you
> can operate Easy Accounting. It's that <u>easy to use</u>. Just click the check icon to
> display a blank check. Use the number keys to enter the amount of the check
> and Easy Accounting fills in the word version of the amount. Doesn't that
> sound <u>easy</u>?
>
> Now click at the category box and <u>conveniently</u> view a complete listing of your
> accounts. Move the arrow to the account of your choice and click. The account is
> written on the check and posted to your records <u>automatically</u>.

By stressing one point, you do not limit the message to that point. For
example, while *ease of operation* is being stressed, other features are mentioned.
A good film presents a star who is seen throughout most of the film; a good term
paper presents a central idea that is supported throughout; a school yearbook
develops a theme—a sales letter should stress a central selling point.

Does stressing one point
mean excluding other
points?

Convince the Receivers with Evidence

After you have made an interesting introduction to your product, service, or
idea, present enough supporting evidence to satisfy your receivers' needs.

EMPHASIZE THE CENTRAL SELLING POINT

Keep one or two main features uppermost in the receivers' minds. When presenting evidence, choose evidence that supports this feature(s). For example, using
appearance as an outstanding selling feature of compact cars while presenting
abundant evidence to show economy of operation would be inconsistent.

USE CONCRETE LANGUAGE

Few people will believe general statements without supporting factual evidence.
Saying a certain machine or method is efficient is not enough. You must say *how
you know* it is efficient and present some data to illustrate *how* efficient. Saying
a piece of furniture is durable is not enough. Durability exists in varying degrees. You must present information that shows what makes it durable and also
define *how* durable.

Why should you avoid
unsupported generalities?

The convincing-evidence portion of the sales letter needs to include all the
information about the product, service, or idea. You can establish durability, for
example, by presenting information about the manufacturing process, the quality of the raw materials, or the skill of the workers:

Why are facts and figures
important in the evidence
section?

> KCC Publishing's Garnet Classics will last your child a lifetime—pages bound
> in durable gold-embossed hardback, treated with special protectants to
> retard paper aging, and machine-sewn (not glued) for long-lasting quality.

The 100-percent cotton fiber paper can withstand years of turning the pages. The joy of reading can last for years as your children explore the world of classic literature with KCC's Garnet Classics.

Discussing the results of research increases the receiver's credibility in your message.

Presenting research evidence to support your statements is another way to increase your chances of convincing receivers to buy:

We asked 50 night-shift sawmill workers to wear Wilkers Steel-Toe Boots to work for one month. Fifty others wore Shilling boots for the same period of time. At the end of the month, we examined each pair of boots for wear. Twenty-five pairs of the Shilling boots had at least part of a sole missing, compared with only six pairs of the Wilkers boots. Another ten Shilling steel-toe tips were loose, compared with three on the Wilkers boots.

Relating the experiment takes more space and time, but it is well worth the effort. Experimental facts are much more convincing than general remarks about superior durability and appearance.

Evidence presented must not only *be* authentic; it must *sound* authentic, too. Facts and figures help. Talking about pages treated with special protectants to retard aging and machine-sewn pages suggests the writer is well informed. These facts increase receiver confidence. Facts and figures are even more impressive if the receiver can get some kind of internal verification of their accuracy. For example, the following paragraph presents figures and gives their derivation:

We insulated 30 houses in Buffalo last year. Before installing the insulation, we asked each homeowner to tell us the total fuel bill for the four coldest months—November, December, January, and February. The average cost was $408, or $102 a month. After installation, we discovered the fuel bill for the same four-month period was $296, or $74 a month—a saving of $28 a month, or 25 percent.

THINK IT OVER
Have you experienced this information overload? Share your experiences with the class or in groups.

Do not go overboard and inundate your receivers with an abundance of facts or technical data that will bore, frustrate, or alienate them. Never make your receivers feel ignorant by trying to impress them with facts and figures they may not understand.

BE OBJECTIVE

What are some signs of subjectivity?

Use language people will believe. Specific, concrete language makes letters sound authentic. Unsupported superlatives, exaggerations, flowery statements, unsupported claims, incomplete comparisons, and remarks suggesting certainty all make letters sound like high-pressure sales talk. Just one such sentence can destroy confidence in the whole letter. Examine the following statements to see whether they give convincing evidence. Would they make a receiver want to buy? Or do they merely remind the receiver of someone's desire to sell?

Might an unsupported superlative in one sentence reduce confidence in subsequent statements?

This antibiotic is the best on the market today. It represents the very latest in biochemical research.

The way to tell which antibiotic is best is to gather information about all antibiotics marketed and then choose the one with superior characteristics. You know the writer is likely to have a bias in favor of the particular drug being sold. However, you do not know whether the writer actually spent time researching other antibiotics or whether the writer would know how to evaluate this information. You certainly do not know whether the writer knows enough about biochemical research to say truthfully what the very latest is.

> **Gardeners are turning handsprings in their excitement over our new weed killer!**

Really? Doesn't that statement seem preposterous? If you do not believe in the handsprings, can you believe in the weed killer?

> **Stretch those tired limbs out on one of our luscious water beds. It's like floating on a gentle dreamcloud on a warm, sunny afternoon. Ah, what soothing relaxation!**

Adjectives in every sentence suggest subjectivity. Even though some people may be persuaded by such writing, many will see it as an attempt to trick them.

Note the incomplete comparison in the following example:

> **SunBlock provides you better protection from the sun's dangerous ultraviolet rays.**

With which sunscreens are SunBlock being compared? All *other* sunscreens? With *most* other sunscreens? With *one* unnamed brand? With *a few other* brands? Unless an additional sentence identifies the other elements in the comparison, you do not know. Too often, the writer of such a sentence hopes the receiver will assume the comparison is with *all* others. Written with that intent, the incomplete comparison is *unethical*. Likewise, statements of certainty are often inaccurate or misleading:

> **We are sure you will want a full-year's subscription to *Personal Investor's Digest*; but even if you don't, this first issue is yours to keep.**

Can the writer be sure? "If you don't" conveys a connotation that the writer is *not* sure.

INTERPRET THE EVIDENCE

Naturally, your receivers will be less familiar with the product, service, or idea and its uses than you will be. Not only do you have an obligation to give information, you should interpret it if necessary. Point out how the information will benefit the receiver. For example,

> **Although more expensive to construct, conventional foundations virtually eliminate soil-movement problems and the resulting structural damage.**

Some prospects may not fully comprehend what "conventional" means for them. To make the most of this feature, clearly interpret *why* a conventional foundation is superior to a traditional slab foundation. The economic factor

---

THINK IT OVER
Could receivers perceive this subjective writing to be an attempt to trick them into buying? Is that ethical?

Can incomplete comparisons be misleading?

Why should you interpret statements?

should not have been introduced until the meaning of a conventional foundation had been fully explained. The following revision interprets this feature:

> Traditional slab foundations are *one* solid 8-inch-thick piece of concrete poured on the soil surface. In contrast, the walls of a conventional foundation are several feet thick, and the floor of the structure is supported by a series of columns connected to the exterior walls with steel-reinforced concrete. If soil movement results in less support under any section of the foundation, the thick walls of the conventional foundation evenly distribute the weight throughout the wall, preventing any structure damage.

The following excerpt from a sales letter used a compact disc as the subject of the sentence. Note how it states a cold figure without interpretation:

> This compact disc (CD-ROM) can store 600 megabytes of information.

Now see how interpretation makes the letter more convincing:

> This compact disc (CD-ROM) can store 600 megabytes of information. With this capacity, you have enough space to store a complete set of encyclopedias and 15 minutes of informative videos.

The revision shows what the figure means in terms of receiver benefits and makes use of a valuable interpretative technique—the comparison. You can often make a point more convincing by comparing something unfamiliar with something familiar. Most people are familiar with the amount of information contained in an encyclopedia, so they can now visualize the storage capacity of the CD-ROM. Comparison can also be used to interpret prices. Advertisers frequently compare the cost of sponsoring a child in a third-world country to the price of a fast-food lunch. An insurance representative might write this sentence:

> The annual premium for this 20-year, limited-payment policy is $219, or 60 cents a day—about the cost of a cup of coffee.

BE CAREFUL WHEN YOU TALK ABOUT PRICE

Most sales letters should mention price. They should either state the price or say something to assure the receiver that the price is not unreasonable. Logically, price should be introduced late in the letter—after most of the advantages have been discussed. Few people want to part with their money until they have been shown how they can benefit by doing so.

People are inclined to react negatively to price. They may think it is too high, even when it is actually low. Some ways to overcome price resistance:

1. Introduce price only after presenting the product, service, or idea and its virtues.
2. Keep price talk out of the first and last paragraphs—unless, of course, price is the distinctive feature.
3. Use figures to illustrate how enough money can be saved to pay for the expenditure. (For example, say that a $60 turbo-vent that saved $10 a month on summer electric bills would save approximately $60 in two, 3-month summers and that the vent would last for many summers.)
4. State price in terms of small units. (Twelve dollars a month seems like less than $144 a year.)

Let receivers see the relationship of features and benefits.

T H I N K   I T   O V E R
Be prepared to interpret a technical concept in your field to a potential customer/client (e.g., finance majors might interpret tax-deferred annuities in terms of the needs of a specific target audience). Alternatively, you could interpret a feature of a product.

Why should you introduce price late in a letter?

if you can aford this,   # you can afford this.

$3.99 a day   ## $1.67 a day

This advertisement for Jennifer Convertibles compares the cost of a relatively expensive piece of furniture with the cost of a typical fast-food lunch. Presenting the price in small units is one effective technique for de-emphasizing the price.

5. Invite comparison of like products, services, or ideas with similar features.
6. Use facts and figures to illustrate that the price is reasonable.
7. Mention price in a complex or compound sentence that relates or summarizes the virtues of the product, service, or idea. In the sentence in which price is mentioned, remind receivers of what they get in return. The positive aspects (satisfaction from using the product, service, or idea) should be put beside the negative aspects (giving up money). With convincing evidence, the positive features should remain uppermost in a receiver's mind; therefore, the emphasis is taken off the negative features. Note the following illustrations:

> Small enough to fit in the palm of your hand and big enough to record a three-hour lecture, the voice-activated Minicord sells for $70 during March.

> For a $48 yearly subscription fee, Medisearch brings you a monthly digest of recent medical research that is written in nontechnical language.

> Purigard saves the average pool owner about $10 in chemicals each month; thus, the $150 unit completely pays for itself in 15 months.

Why state price in a long compound or complex sentence?

8. Place the figure representing price in a position other than the first or last word of a sentence. (See the preceding illustrations.) First and last words are emphatic; but, unless it is the central selling point, price should be subordinated.

KNOW HOW AND WHEN TO USE
ENCLOSURES, TESTIMONIALS, AND GUARANTEES

Ordinarily, an enclosure is less significant than the letter itself. A letter should make the receiver want to read the enclosure. Thus, the preferred technique is to refer to the enclosure late in the letter, after the major portion of the evidence has been given. Because receivers have already seen the enclosure, avoid calling attention to it by saying "Enclosed you will find" or "We have enclosed a brochure." An enclosure is easily referred to in a sentence that is not a cliché and says something else:

Why avoid introducing the enclosure in the first paragraph?

> The enclosed annual report will help you understand the types of information provided to small- and medium-sized companies by Lincoln Business Data, Inc.

Archbishop Desmond Tutu helped direct worldwide attention to the problem of apartheid in South Africa, and he attracted a large group of supporters. However, he also faced a great deal of opposition to his ideas. When you are trying to convince others to adopt your ideas and you know your receiver is hostile toward them, you must be diplomatic and persuasive, which calls for the inductive approach.

THINK IT OVER
Using these guidelines, write a sentence referring to a resume included with an application letter for a job.

If a product, service, or idea is really beneficial, some people are likely to report their satisfaction. If they do not write voluntarily, you can invite their comments through questionnaires or by attaching cards to the merchandise. Users are urged to fill out the cards after they have used the merchandise for a certain time. One way to convince prospective customers that they will like the product, service, or idea is to give them concrete evidence that other people like it. Tell what others have said (with permission, of course) about the usefulness of your product, service, or idea.

Offering guarantees and free trials can *convince* the receiver to buy.

Guarantees and free trials convey both negative and positive connotations. By revealing willingness to refund money or exchange an unsatisfactory unit if necessary, a writer confesses a negative: the purchase could be regretted or refused. However, the positive connotations are stronger than the negatives: the seller has a definite plan for ensuring that buyers get value for money spent. In addition, the seller exhibits willingness for the buyer to check a product, service, or idea personally and compare it with others. The seller also implies confidence that a free trial will result in a purchase and that the product will meet standards set in the guarantee. If terms of a guarantee are long or complex, they can be included in an enclosure.

Last Paragraph: Motivating the Receiver to Action

Regardless of the kind of evidence provided, give it for the purpose of motivating action. If preceding paragraphs have been unconvincing, a well-written final paragraph has little chance of success.

What are some characteristics of the action ending?

Your chances of getting action are increased if you (1) state the specific action wanted, (2) allude to the reward for taking action in the same sentence in which action is encouraged, (3) present the action as being easy to take, (4) provide some stimulus to quick action, and (5) ask confidently.

MENTION THE SPECIFIC ACTION YOU WANT

Unless specific instructions are included, such general instructions as "let us hear from you," "take action on the matter," and "make a response" are ineffective. Whether the receiver is to fill out an order blank and return it with a check, place a telephone call, or return an enclosed card, define the desired action in specific terms.

ALLUDE TO THE REWARD FOR TAKING ACTION

For both psychological and logical reasons, receivers are encouraged to act if they are reminded of the reward for acting. A well-written sales letter mentions a distinctive selling feature (the reward for using our product or service or accepting our idea). This feature should be introduced early—perhaps in the first sentence—and stressed in the following paragraphs. Because the distinctive selling feature is the main idea to present, assure that it sticks in the receiver's mind. Work it into your parting words, where it will be emphasized.

Why allude to the reward for taking action?

A central selling feature is a thread of continuity running through every paragraph. To end without a final reference to the selling feature (theme) would be like ending a speech without summarizing remarks.

PRESENT ACTION AS BEING EASY TO TAKE

People naturally hesitate to attempt something that is difficult or time consuming. Instead of asking receivers to fill in their names and addresses on order forms or return cards and envelopes, do that work for them. If action is easy or consumes little time, receivers may act immediately; otherwise, they may procrastinate.

What is one way to reduce the likelihood of procrastination?

PROVIDE A STIMULUS FOR QUICK ACTION

The longer the receiver waits to take action on your proposal, the persuasive evidence will be harder to remember, and the receiver will be less likely to act. Therefore, you prefer for the receiver to act quickly. Reference to the central selling point (assuming it has been well received) helps to stimulate action. Here are some commonly used appeals for getting quick action:

Buy while present prices are still in effect.

Buy while the present supply lasts.

Buy before the holidays (Father's Day, the end of the season, etc.).

Buy now while a rebate is being offered.

Buy quickly to get product benefits quickly.

Prospects will not necessarily act because you tell them to act. The following expressions seem to shout *too* loudly for action:

Act today.	Do it now.	Don't delay.
Hurry, hurry, hurry.	Why wait?	Don't wait another minute.

ASK CONFIDENTLY FOR ACTION

Persuasive writers who have a good product, service, or idea and have presented evidence well have a right to feel confident. Instead of "*If* you want to save time in cleaning, fill in and return . . . ," writers can demonstrate confidence in favorable action by stating, "To save time in cleaning, fill in and return . . . ." Statements suggesting lack of confidence, such as "If you agree . . ." and "I *hope* you will . . . ," should be avoided. (Recall the discussion of doubtful expressions in Chapter 7: "I hope you will" also connotes, "In view of my weak presentation, I recognize that you *may not*.") Between the lines, such thoughts convey, "I have some doubts about my product or my selling ability." If such doubts exist in the mind of the writer, they will be generated in the mind of the receiver.

Why avoid *hope* and *if* statements in the action ending?

For good appearance and proper emphasis, the last paragraph should be relatively short. Yet, the last paragraph has a lot to do: It must suggest the specific action wanted, refer to the distinctive selling feature, present action as

What ideas should appear in the final paragraph?

being easy to take, encourage quick action, and ask confidently. Observe how the following closing paragraph attempts to accomplish these tasks:

[1] The ease of operations makes TMC's new productivity software an asset for any busy executive. [2] The ease of ordering is just as attractive. [3] From a touch-tone telephone, simply dial 1-800-555-8341. [4] Then input the five-digit number printed in the top right corner of the attached card. [5] Your name and address will be entered automatically into our system, an expedient way to get your productivity software to you within five working days along with a bill for payment. [6] Those who order by August 12 will also receive 10 high-density memory disks free with their order.

[1] Final reference to the central selling point.

[2-5] Makes action easy; defines definite action.

[6] Stimulus to quick action.

The following version is an improvement because it places the central selling point in the last line:

From a touch-tone telephone, simply dial 1-800-555-8341. Then input the five-digit number printed in the top right corner of the attached card. Your name and address will be entered automatically into our system, an expedient way to get your productivity software to you within five working days along with a bill for payment. Those who order by August 12 will also receive 10 high-density memory disks free with their order. TMC's new productivity software is as easy to use as it is to order!

Figures 11-1 and 11-2 illustrate the principles discussed in the preceding pages. Typically, sales letters are longer than letters that present routine information or convey good news. Specific details (essential in getting action) are space consuming.

The letters in Figures 11-1 and 11-2 illustrate *unsolicited sales letters*, one for a product and the other for an idea. The same principles apply in writing a *solicited sales letter*, with one exception: Because the solicited sales letter is a response to a request for information, an attention-getter is not essential.

Some sales letters have no attention-getters.

PERSUASIVE REQUESTS

The preceding discussion of sales letters assumed the product, service, or idea was sufficiently worthy to reward the receiver for taking action. The discussion of persuasive requests assumes requests are reasonable—that compliance is *justified* when the request is for an adjustment, that compliance will (in some way) be *rewarded* when the request is for a favor.

Common types of persuasive requests are claim letters and letters that request special favors and information. Although their purpose is to get favorable action, the letters invite action only after attempting to arouse a desire to take action and providing a logical argument to overcome any resistance anticipated from the receiver.

Worldwide Electronics Incorporated
55 NORTH PARK ROAD   SAN ANTONIO, TX 78207-2963   (903) 555-6731, FAX (903) 555-1305

April 30, 19--

Dr. Dale Stanton
2900 Medical Plaza
Wichita Falls, TX 76307-2900

Dear Dr. Stanton:

¹ If you need an afternoon swinging a golf club, but you are worried you will miss an important call, you need the ProCall pager.

² To make sure you will be able to catch that important call wherever you are, ProSystems is introducing the ProCall pager. ³ Wherever you go, you carry it with you. ⁴ When people need to reach you, they simply call ProCall's 800 number and key in your code. ⁵ Within seconds, our nationwide satellite system relays the message to your ProCall pager—and you never miss a call.

⁶ The ProCall system reaches you almost anywhere in the United States and weighs less (2.5 ounces) than a golf ball driving down the fairway. ⁷ The ProCall pager keeps you on top of your game and in touch with your important calls for only $30 a month (about a dollar a day).

⁸ To receive your ProCall pager, just initial the enclosed card. ⁹ Mail the card before June 1 and receive your first month of service free.

Sincerely,

R. Gaylon Yates

R. Gaylon Yates
Sales Manager

Enclosure

---

¹ Seeks to gain attention by introducing an experience the receiver has probably had. Presents "important call" as central selling point.

² Introduces the product as a solution to a problem. Uses "important call" to achieve transition from the preceding sentence and to reinforce the central selling point.

³ Begins presentation of evidence. Uses a pronoun for coherence. Uses receiver as subject of an active-voice sentence.

⁴, ⁵ Shows how easy it is to solve the problem—the reason to buy.

⁶ Continues presentation of the evidence. Uses active voice.

⁷ Presents price in a sentence that reinforces the primary reward for paying that price.

⁸, ⁹ Associates action with reward for taking action, identifies specific action desired, makes action easy, and rewards quick action.

FIGURE 11-1   Good example of a letter promoting a product.

Making a Claim

Claim letters are often routine because the basis for the claim is a guarantee or some other assurance that an adjustment will be made without need of persuasion. However, when an immediate remedy is doubtful, persuasion is necessary. In a typical large business, the claim letter is passed on to the claims adjuster for response.

Often, any reasonable claim will be adjusted to the customer's satisfaction. Therefore, venting strong displeasure in the claim letter is of little value. It can alienate the claims adjuster—the one person from whom cooperation is sought. Remember, adjusters are human beings, too. They may have had little or nothing

Use the four-point AIDA outline for persuasive requests.

What is the difference between a persuasive claim and the routine claim letters discussed in Chapter 9?

Starkville Swim Association
Starkville, MS 39759-6723

[1] Includes writer's return address with letterhead because this organization does not have a company office with an address and telephone number.

[2, 3] Begins with a compliment.

[4, 5] Introduces competitive swimming as a worthwhile community effort similar to baseball—something the receiver already supports.

[6, 7] Continues to build interest by showing benefits youth gain from competitive swimming, still using baseball as a parallel.

[8-10] Summarizes problems that hinder youths' participation in swimming.

[1] 763 North Wiggins Street
Starkville, MS 39759-3417
October 25, 19--

Ms. Lisa Perkins, Manager
Belview Office Supply Company
89 Chadwick Lane
Starkville, MS 39759-9543

Dear Ms. Perkins:

[2] You are to be commended for sponsoring a Starkville Little League baseball team each year. [3] Your investment keeps registration fees in reach of each family in our community and helps develop character in our community's youth.

[4] Many youth in our community do not participate in baseball. However, some of these youth have special talents that lend themselves to different sports. [5] Specifically, many youth who have difficulty competing in the traditional sports of football, basketball, and baseball often find they can excel in swimming.

[6] Of the nearly 1,000 youth who have joined the Starkville Swim Association (SSA) during the past ten years, 50 of these athletes have received college athletic scholarships. [7] More importantly, all of these youth have learned the important lessons of hard work, teamwork, and personal commitment—the same lessons learned through participation in our baseball program.

[8] Unlike other sports that rely on volunteer coaches, national association guidelines mandate that swim coaches have competitive swimming experience and special safety training. [9] Swimming associations rarely find these qualifications in parent volunteers. [10] The increasing

FIGURE 11-2   Good example of a letter promoting an idea, page 1.

Research shows that "complainers" are more likely to continue to do business with a company than those who do not complain. Businesses that know how to resolve claims effectively will retain 95 percent of the "complainers" as repeat customers (Bell, 1994).

to do with the manufacture and sale of the product or direct delivery of the service. They did not create the need for the claim letter.

From the point of view of the claims adjuster, claims should be welcomed. Only a small percentage of claims are from unethical individuals; the great bulk are from people who believe they have a legitimate complaint. The way in which the adjuster handles the claim determines, to a large extent, the goodwill of the company. For the adjuster, granting a claim is much easier than refusing it. Because saying "no" is one of the most difficult writing tasks, the writer of a persuasive claim letter has an advantage over the adjuster.

Ms. Lisa Perkins
Page 2
October 28, 19--

cost of a full-time coach and pool rental fees are making the annual
registration fee prohibitive to many families.

[11] The Starkville Swim Association invites you to become one of ten
corporate sponsors of the swim team. [12] Your sponsorship of $500
would help offset these rising costs and maintain the current annual
registration fee of $100 so that more youth could take advantage of
the abundant benefits of swimming.

[13] Sponsoring the Starkville Fins (our team name) would also benefit
Belview Office Supply. [14] Your sponsorship will entitle you to display
your company logo on all SSA publications. [15] In addition, your logo
would be displayed on the back of t-shirts worn by each swimmer.

[16] Can we count on you to help our city's youth enjoy the experience of
competitive swimming? [17] Call me at 555-1345 to reserve your place
as one of the team's sponsors.

Sincerely,

David M. Hilton

David M. Hilton
President

[11, 12] Includes the request
with an appeal to the
receiver's known commit-
ment to supporting the
community's youth.

[13-15] Discusses the direct
benefits the company can
gain.

[16, 17] States the specific
action to be taken and
again alludes to the
benefit to the youth.

FIGURE 11-2   Good example of a letter promoting an idea, page 2.

Like sales letters, persuasive claim letters should use an inductive sequence.
Unlike routine claim letters, persuasive claims do not begin by asking for an
adjustment. The poor example in Figure 11-3 uses a deductive sequence.

Please reimburse us $1,250 for services not rendered at our recent
meeting at your resort.

We paid $5 more per room than the rates at a comparable hotel so
our guests could work out in the exercise room shown in your
brochure. However, our members were unable to use the equipment
because the exercise room was actually located four blocks from the
hotel at a local health club.

We hope you will see fit to refund $5 for each of the 250 rooms we
rented because we were not told of the location and chose the hotel
on the basis of the incorrect information.

FIGURE 11-3   Poor example of a persuasive claim.

THINK IT OVER
What appeal might be developed to convince the receiver to
make the adjustment? Compare
your ideas with Figure 11-4.

Two major changes would improve this letter: (1) writing inductively (to reduce the chance of a negative reaction in the first sentence) and (2) stressing an appeal throughout the letter (to emphasize an incentive for taking favorable action). In a persuasive claim letter, an *appeal* serves the same purpose that a *central selling feature* does in a sales letter. Both serve as a theme; both remind the receiver of a benefit that accrues from doing as asked. Note the application of these techniques in the revision in Figure 11-4.

Knowledge of effective claim writing should never be used as a means of taking advantage of someone. Hiding an unjustifiable claim under a cloak of untrue statements is difficult and strictly unethical. Adjusters are fair-minded people who will give the benefit of the doubt, but they will not satisfy an unhappy customer simply to avoid a problem.

Making untrue statements to elicit a favorable claim is *unethical*.

June 5, 19--

Mr. Albert Michaela
Seaside Regency Resort
1465 Beachfront Vista
Sarasota, FL 34230-1465

Dear Mr. Michaela:

[1] Seaside Regency and our company, Seafood Delights, are much alike: We both give customers a taste of life on the seashore and emphasize total customer well-being. [2] Both of us are providing aesthetic pleasure and physical fitness—Seafood Delights with healthy menu choices, Seaside Regency with an exercise room for resort guests.

[3] This compatibility with our values is one of the reasons we chose your resort for our recent Annual Beach Get-Away, a meeting of our franchisees and corporate leaders. [4] Eager for our franchisees (our guests) to use the exercise room pictured in your brochure to unwind after a full day of meetings and other events, we selected your resort over other comparable ones even though we would be charged an additional fee for the exercise room.

[5] Obviously, our guests were disappointed when they learned that the exercise room was not in the resort but actually located at a health club four blocks away. [6] A tight schedule of meetings and frequent dinner events limited the time our guests had available for commuting to the health club for a workout. [7] Many did not feel safe leaving the resort late in the evening, the only block of time long enough for a workout.

[8] Because your resort advertised the availability of a fully equipped exercise room without explaining it was located in a health club outside the resort, our guests were deprived of physical fitness opportunities available at comparable hotels. [9] In addition, Seafood Delights was billed an additional $5 per room for this *unused* service.

[1] Seeks attention by discussing goals common to receiver.

[2] Reveals the subject of the letter (the exercise room) and continues the central appeal—commitment to guests' physical fitness needs.

[3] Includes a further reminder of the central appeal.

[4] Provides needed details.

[5-7] Continues with needed details.

[8, 9] Presents reasoning that leads to the request for a refund and a subtle reminder of the central appeal.

[10] Connects the request with the resort's commitment to serve guest's physical fitness needs.

FIGURE 11-4   Good example of a persuasive claim, page 1.

Mr. Albert Michaela
Page 2
June 5, 19--

10 For these reasons, please refund us $5 for each of the 250 rooms we
rented, confirming your commitment to customer service—aesthetic
and physical fitness.

Sincerely,

Wanda R. Goldman

Wanda R. Goldman
Human Resources Manager

slc

FIGURE 11-4   Good example of a persuasive claim, page 2.

Asking a Favor

Occasionally, everyone has to ask someone else for a special favor—action for which there is not much reward, time, or inclination. For example, suppose a professional association wants to host its annual fund-raiser dinner at an exclusive country club. The program chair of the association must write a letter to the club's general manager requesting permission to use the club. Will a deductive letter be successful?

When a deductive approach is used in a persuasive situation, chances of getting cooperation are minimal. For example, what might be a probable reaction to the following beginning sentence?

Please send me, without charge, your $350 multimedia learning package on office safety.

If the first sentence gets a negative reaction, a decision to refuse may be made instantly. Having thought "no," the receiver may not read the rest of the letter or may hold stubbornly to that decision in spite of a well-written persuasive argument that follows the opening sentence. Note that the letter in Figure 11-5 asks the favor *before* presenting any benefit for doing so.

The letter illustrated in Figure 11-6 uses an inductive approach. Note the extent to which it applies principles discussed earlier. As this letter shows, if the preceding paragraphs adequately emphasize a receiver's reward for complying, the final paragraph need not shout loudly for action.

1 The Long Beach Medical Association (LBMA) will hold its annual dinner/dance on Saturday, November 5.

2 We would very much like to have this event at Crystal Stream from 7 p.m. on that evening. 3 We expect several hundred guests to attend.

4 Will you let me know as soon as possible if we may hold the dance at Crystal Stream?

FIGURE 11-5   Poor example of a persuasive request (asking for a favor).

What are some common errors in asking favors?

How might the receiver react to a persuasive letter written deductively?

Even when the reward for taking action is small or intangible, point it out.

1 Begins with an announcement that may be of little interest to the receiver.

2 Asks the favor before letting the person see any reason for accepting.

3 Does not include important information such as the type of dance, food, and number involved; overuses the pronoun *we* throughout letter.

4 Sounds somewhat doubtful.

LONG BEACH MEDICAL ASSOCIATION
7800 NORTH WASCO AVENUE, LONG BEACH, CA 90801-7800
(714) 555-8900   Fax - (714) 555-7619

March 23, 19--

Mr. Jose Fuentes
General Manager
Crystal Stream
P.O. Box 2383
Long Beach, CA 90810-2393

Dear Mr. Fuentes:

1-3 Begins on a point that is related and of interest to the receiver.

[1] The opening of Crystal Stream was a landmark event. [2] People all over the city are applauding your signature golf course designed to challenge golfers of all skill levels. [3] The beautiful Williamsburg-style clubhouse and exquisite homes complement our upscale, growing community.

4 Reveals membership's enthusiasm for holding the dinner/dance at the club and presents benefits that help to increase the receiver's enthusiasm for the proposal.

[4] Because of the intense community interest in your facility, the Long Beach Medical Association (LBMA) believes Crystal Stream is the perfect location for its annual charity dinner/dance for the Kids for Life Foundation. [5] Last year this foundation defrayed medical expenses for five children from our community who suffer from muscular dystrophy. [6] We are confident that holding this event at Crystal Stream would increase participation in this worthy community event by at least 25 percent.

5, 6 Provides additional benefits for saying yes.

7, 8 Provides additional benefits for saying yes.

[7] Many LBMA members are interested in memberships in Crystal Stream. [8] While participating in this community event, these members would have an ideal chance to learn more about the recreational and social opportunities of the exclusive Crystal Stream.

9-11 Provides details that will be useful if the receiver accepts.

[9] This black-tie dinner/dance is scheduled for November 5, from 7 p.m. to 1 a.m. [10] Typically 400 guests have attended; however, at least 500 members are expected if the event were held at Crystal Stream. [11] A definite number can be confirmed two weeks prior to the event.

12, 13 Seeks specific action.

THINK IT OVER
Can you readily identify the benefits Crystal Stream derives from allowing the LBMA to use its facility by reading Figure 11-6? What outline was used for this persuasive request?

Mr. Jose Fuentes
Page 2
March 23, 19--

[12] Please send a confirmation by May 1 that Crystal Stream will be the site for this year's dinner/dance. [13] Then we can finalize the details and promote this sure-to-be spectacular event at Crystal Stream.

Sincerely,

Lorene M. Swoope

Lorene M. Swoope, M.D.
Program Chair

FIGURE 11-6   Good example of a persuasive request (asking for a favor).

COMMUNICATION MENTOR

Let's say you are preparing a memo to your supervisor; you're hoping for approval of a cost-saving project you want to spearhead. Something fairly similar to it had been tried years ago; it failed miserably, embarrassing your supervisor and the department manager. You *know* that seeking approval is an uphill battle, but you believe in yourself and the project. What tone should this sensitive memo take?

The temptation may be to position your project point-for-point in contrast to the old one, pounding on the relative merits of yours in an effort to convey its superiority.

Resist this temptation as you would a term paper over spring break. Never directly mention the other project in your memo. Memories of its failure may be keen, and direct comparisons will be counterproductive to the objectivity you want to elicit in your receivers. Rather, emphasize the strength of your plan by stressing features that are designed to avoid known pitfalls.

Your supervisor and the department manager will get the message, and you will get your project. The moral to take away from all of this: don't stand on the grave of a bad idea to sell a new one.

James F. Hurley
Executive Vice President
California Federal Bank

Requesting Information

Requests for information are common in business. Information for research reports frequently is obtained by questionnaire. Validity and reliability of results are strongly influenced by the percentage of return. If a letter inviting respondents to complete a questionnaire is written carelessly, responses may be insufficient. Analyze the effectiveness of the request in Figure 11-7.

1 Please complete the enclosed questionnaire and return it to me in the envelope provided. 2 I dislike having to impose on the valuable time of a busy executive such as you, but in order for me to complete the research for my thesis at the university, I must seek first-hand information from business leaders.

3 The study deals with the attitudes of purchasing agents toward vendor gratuities. 4 As I believe you know, gifts from sellers to executives who do the buying for companies pose a problem of great concern. 5 The questionnaire seeks information about practices in your firm and about your own opinions.

6 Responses will be kept confidential, of course. 7 Please return the questionnaire to me by May 1.

FIGURE 11-7   Poor example of a request for information.

1 Invites action without having first given any incentive.

2 Puts writer and receiver on different levels by suggesting humility. Use of "impose" could serve as a reminder that the request is an imposition and therefore should be denied.

3 Reveals the nature of the research—a point that should have been introduced earlier.

4 Risks alienation by introducing doubts about the receiver's knowledge.

5, 6 Lets the receiver know what to expect but needs to include some incentive for responding.

7 Uses an action ending, but it seems a little demanding, especially when no incentive has been introduced.

The most serious weaknesses of the letter in Figure 11-7 are asking too quickly for action and providing no incentive for action. Sometimes the reward for taking action is very small and indirect, but the letter needs to make these benefits evident. Note the reward in the revision of the letter in Figure 11-8 (it appeals to the higher order of needs discussed by Maslow).

Persuading Within Organizations

Persuasive memorandums are longer because of the extra space needed for developing an appeal. When preparing to write the memorandum in Figure

[1] Provides return address because plain paper is used.

[2] Seeks attention by establishing the letter as a document related to the receiver's work—a timely topic.

[3] Calls attention to the importance of the topic the receiver may have sought to solve.

[4] Leads to an introduction of the questionnaire as a way to find answers.

[5] Introduces the questionnaire.

[6] Reminds of the reward for taking action. Professional managers who now have (or already had) an interest in the problem would see the sharing of results as a positive. Thus, they would be more inclined to say "yes" when the specific request is made.

[7] Makes the request for action in a complex sentence that contains a positive idea.

[8] Presents some needed assurance that request will require little time.

[9] Mentions a deadline in a sentence that reminds of the reward for complying.

[10] Expresses gratitude, alludes to the reward for participating, and adds unity by using the words "vendors" and "gratuities" that tie in with the first paragraph.

[11] Includes enclosure notation.

[1] 32 Cedar Court
Augusta, GA 31902-1910
March 1, 19--

Mr. Travis Kinsey
Purchasing Agent
City National Bank
2500 Center Street
Augusta, GA 31902-2500

Dear Mr. Kinsey:

[2] What if vendors continue making more and larger gifts to purchasing agents? [3] For ethical and economic reasons, this question is of vital importance to purchasing agents. [4] Yet, it has not been answered in the literature, and recent purchasing journals have emphatically called for answers based on research.

[5] For my master's thesis on purchasing behavior, I am seeking opinions from selected purchasing managers. [6] Results will be shared with participants soon after the data are interpreted.

[7] To ensure that the study is complete and authoritative, please participate by completing the enclosed questionnaire and returning it to me in the envelope provided. [8] Your answers, which can be indicated quickly by making check marks, will be confidential and reported only as part of group data. [9] To send a report of the findings to you and other participating managers before school ends in early June, I need to receive the enclosed forms by May 1.

[10] I appreciate your help and am eager to share with you a summary of what I learn about vendors and gratuities.

Sincerely,

Carmen L. Rankin

Carmen L. Rankin

[11] Enclosures

FIGURE 11-8   Good example of a request for information.

11-9, the store manager recalls a past attempt to computerize perpetual inventory that failed miserably. At that time, most employees could be easily categorized as computer illiterate; they required extensive training and were resistant to any effort to computerize. The company finally abandoned the computerization effort when the computer system could not be upgraded to handle higher inventory levels.

Anticipating the managing partner's resistance, the store manager decides to write the memorandum inductively. Thus, the subject line does not reveal *how* the manager proposes to improve the efficiency of maintaining inventory counts. To increase his chances of gaining approval, the store manager heeded the

Why are routine requests shorter than persuasive requests?

Use inductive approach to overcome resistance.

THINK IT OVER
What two problems did the manager *anticipate* the partner would have with the new system? Were these problems addressed with a logical, convincing explanation?

Crafts Galore

397 Peachway Drive, Knoxville, TN 37901-0397
(615) 555-9200   Fax - (615) 555-3909

TO: Josh Griffith, Managing Partner

FROM: Yang Lin, Store Manager   *YL*

DATE: September 20, 19--

[1] SUBJECT: Proposal to Improve the Efficiency
                  of Maintaining Inventory Counts

[2] One of our competitive advantages is the wide variety of materials we offer crafts enthusiasts in our city. [3] However, our manual system has become inadequate for maintaining this large inventory.

[4] A computerized perpetual inventory would eliminate the need to close the store two days in each major season to count stock and update our records. [5] This system would also provide management with timely and accurate information about inventory levels.

[6] Our employees have been using computers for other applications (word processing and general ledger) for several months; therefore, I would anticipate little resistance to this type of change in daily operations. [7] In fact, several inventory clerks have suggested getting perpetual inventory on the computer already. [8] This prior computer training would likely reduce the cost of implementing this computerized system significantly.

[9] Unlike older computer equipment, today's hardware is designed to be flexible. [10] No longer must new computers be purchased to take advantage of new technologies. [11] For example, more powerful microprocessors can be inserted directly into this system. [12] Thus, as our business grows and technology changes, we would be able to upgrade this system to meet our changing demands.

[13] Take a look at the attached brochure describing the exact specifications and the cost of a perpetual inventory system. [14] After you have considered this change, please call so we can discuss this critical enhancement to our efficient delivery of products to our customers.

Attachment

[1] Gives the purpose of the memo without revealing the specific request.

[2, 3] Links a company strength that leads logically to the problem; does not reveal the actual request.

[4, 5] Builds interest by providing specific benefits of the computerized system.

[6-12] Reduces resistance by discussing changes that will alleviate prior problems experienced with a computerized system; does not refer to past failures directly.

[13] Refers to enclosure after presenting evidence.

[14] Alludes to benefits and closes with a specific action to be taken.

FIGURE 11-9   Good example of a persuasive memorandum.

previous advice from your mentor, James F. Hurley; he stressed the features designed to avoid known pitfalls (computer literacy of employees and obsolescence of computer systems) but did not mention the past failure.

Often employees must make persuasive requests of their supervisors. For example, they may recommend a change in a procedure, acquisition of equipment or a particular software, or attendance of a training program to improve their ability to complete a job function. They may justify a promotion or job reclassification or recommendation. The buyer writing the persuasive memorandum in Figure 11-10 opens with a straightforward statement about the problem

1, 2 Opens with discussion of problem and the telecommuting proposal.

3-5 Outlines duties that can be completed more efficiently away from the office. Recommends specific changes in meetings in an effort to address resistance to the proposal.

6-8 Alludes to the benefits of telecommuting.

9, 10 Closes with specific action to be taken next.

TO: Sandie McClintock, Gifts Marketing Director
FROM: Laura Nobles, Buyer, Gift Department   L. N.
DATE: November 16, 19--
SUBJECT: Enhancing Productivity Through Telecommuting

1 Since the announcement in last week's meeting that we must identify ways to reduce the number of daily commuters, I've considered several possible options. 2 I believe telecommuting could not only reduce my number of commutes but increase my productivity as well.

3 One component of my job is conducting research and compiling marketing reports; e.g., weekly product line sales and inventory reports, competitors' new catalog analyses, and suppliers' new product reports. 4 Preparing these reports efficiently requires a day of uninterrupted time. 5 With my current work schedule and with sales representatives randomly calling for marketing advice throughout each day, I am pressured to get these reports prepared in time for Friday's marketing managers' meeting.

6 Telecommuting on Wednesdays would allow me to concentrate on preparing these reports and coordinate product ordering and marketing strategies without distractions. 7 On Thursday morning, we could discuss the sales reports and marketing plans before Friday's meeting. 8 This plan still allows sales representatives to contact me four days each week.

9 Can we meet to discuss the benefits of my telecommuting during our Monday meeting? 10 By then I should know how soon I could get the equipment and software needed to equip a home office to process information and to communicate with appropriate personnel effectively.

FIGURE 11-10   Good example of a persuasive memorandum.

and her telecommuting proposal because compliance with the Clean Air Act was the subject of a staff meeting. Her thorough analysis of duties that could be efficiently completed away from the office provided convincing evidence that telecommuting is a feasible recommendation. The specific changes she suggests in scheduling required meetings, and the progress report on equipping a home office aids her in counteracting any resistance to her proposal. Her call to discuss the proposal at the next meeting is clear and specific and reminds the supervisor of the benefits of the proposal.

COLLECTION LETTERS

As in other persuasive messages, the primary purpose of a collection letter is to get action (payment). A secondary goal is to maintain a customer's goodwill.

Collection letters are generally written inductively (exceptions are discussed later in this chapter); but they are shorter than other letters. Normally, customers know that they owe (no need to devote space to informing them); and they expect to be asked for payment (no need for an attention-getter and no need for an apology). If a letter is short, its main point (pay is expected) stands out vividly. Compared with a long letter, a short letter has a greater chance of being read in its entirety. In a long letter, the main point might be in the skipped-over portion or may have to compete for attention with minor points.

Collection letters are often written by specialists; however, understanding the characteristics of a good collection series and the various stages in the series will enable you to help design an effective collection plan. To avoid litigation, you must research applicable laws (e.g., number of calls about a debt and the times at which calls can be made, value-laden language that may be perceived to be libelous, etc.).

Characteristics of a Collection Series

Knowing that slow-to-pay customers may not respond to the first attempts at collection, businesses that use collection letters normally use a *series* (if the first letter does not bring a response, a second letter is sent, then a third, and so on). An effective series of collection letters incorporates the following characteristics: timeliness, regularity, understanding, and increasing urgency.

1. *Timeliness.* A collection writer should not put off sending a letter. The longer debtors are given to pay, the longer they will usually take. Most people react favorably to deadlines. Deadlines stick in our minds and provide the motivation to act. Effective collection efforts should be made promptly, and they should encourage payment by certain dates.
2. *Regularity.* Never let the obligation out of the debtor's mind. Although you cannot send a collection letter every day, you can base the time lapse between letters on your previous experience with debtors and on a knowledge of the overall effectiveness of your collection practices. A regular system for mailings impresses on debtors the efficiency of collection practices.
3. *Understanding.* Understanding involves adaptability and skill in human relations. The collection series must be adaptable to the nature of the debtor. Good-pay risks should probably be given more time to pay than debtors with poor-pay reputations. You should recognize that many debtors have very good reasons for not having paid on time. They should be given every opportunity to meet their obligations or to explain why they are unable to do so.

What two purposes must be achieved through collection letters?

Compare and contrast collection letters with other persuasive messages.

What are the legal implications of collection letters?

What are the four characteristics of an effective collection series?

Understanding also influences the regularity of the collection series. Letters should not be sent so close together that the debtor will not have a chance to pay before the next letter arrives. No one likes to receive a collection letter after the bill has been paid. Some collection letters paradoxically accuse the debtor of trying to avoid payment and then end with a sentence that says, "If you have already paid, please ignore this letter." This notation is appropriate on friendly, printed reminders only.

4. *Increasing urgency.* Increase urgency in the letter tone as the seriousness of the delinquency increases. Adverbs can add urgency to collection language. Instead of being *important*, a problem has become *extremely important*. Words and phrases such as *must, compelled*, and *no other alternative* are important in the later collection stages.

Most collection authorities classify the letters in the series according to the names that describe the seriousness of the problem. These classes are called the stages in the *collection series.*

Stages in the Collection Series

The number of letters in a collection series varies with the collection philosophy of the company and the nature of the debtor. Companies send as many letters as necessary to collect the money or until collection is hopeless and must be attempted through legal action. The following stages are used: (1) reminder, (2) inquiry, (3) appeal, (4) strong appeal or urgency, and (5) ultimatum. Figure 11-11 illustrates the steps in a typical collection series.

REMINDER

Are letters typically written at the reminder stage? Explain.

What is the major goal of the reminder stage? What procedures do companies often use at this stage?

Many people will pay promptly when they receive a bill. Shortly after the due date, a simple reminder will usually bring in most of the remaining accounts. The reminder is typically a duplicate of the original statement with a rubber-stamped notation saying "second notice," "past due," or "please remit." To send a collection letter at this stage would be risky for goodwill. The assumption is that the obligation has been overlooked and will be paid when the reminder is received. Very often, companies will use two or three reminders before moving to the letter-writing stage. Remember, letters cost money. They should be used only when a company is reasonably sure collection is going to be difficult.

Colored gummed stickers may be attached to the statement for their attention-getting qualities. Some companies send reminders automatically generated by computers at specified intervals (for example, 30, 45, and 60 days past due). Other companies send a copy of the original statement produced on colored paper or stamped "second request." The aim at the reminder stage is to make sure the receiver recognizes the reminder element. This step should be accomplished as though the reminder were a routine procedure (which it is); the debtor should not feel singled out for special attention. For that reason, avoid initialed handwritten reminders at this stage.

INQUIRY

What is the major goal of the inquiry stage?

After sending the normal number of reminders without success, companies resort to letters. To increase efficiency, many organizations use form letters that may be initiated automatically by the computer or by a collector. In either case, the form letters are personalized by inserting the debtor's name and address, salutation, amount owed, and date payment is due.

COMMUNICATION IN ACTION

Mike Mills, American Woodmark

Persuading company executives to accept new ways of doing business presents a challenge for many senior managers. As a transportation manager for American Woodmark Corporation, Mike Mills is responsible for moving his company from the "dark ages" of transportation to new technologies in distribution. He serves as a change agent in American Woodmark, "scanning" the business environment and recommending improvements in the distribution of their products, including kitchen cabinets for residential homes. Implementing changes through persuasive communication is an important part of Mills's work at American Woodmark.

Working in a company that employs 2,500 personnel and recorded sales of $171 million in 1993, Mills manages the physical distribution of one of three regional assembly distribution facilities, directly supervising about 30 personnel. Persuasive communication commonly occurs in a company this size in proposals, reports, and internal memorandums. When submitting persuasive proposals, Mills follows a persuasive process of defining the problem, outlining objectives, selecting alternatives, and choosing a solution. He also includes cost estimates, time for implementation, and schedule of payback for the company. He once proposed a new computer system and projected it would result in $120,000 annualized savings. After the system was installed, American Woodmark conducted a 28-workday analysis of the system's effectiveness and found that it actually saved $130,000 annually, a very accurate prediction indeed.

Such successful change comes about as a result of persuasive communication and hard work.

Recently, Mills developed a transportation change and submitted it through a written proposal. At the time, American Woodmark's trucks were delivering products directly to builders in the Baltimore/Washington area. Mills proposed instead that a third party or outside carrier deliver the products to builders. However, some company executives, including his supervisor, were uncomfortable with this proposed change. They raised quality control issues and discussed customer service problems. Mills knew he faced a tough sell. In his proposal, he asserted, "We may lose some control, but from a cost standpoint and improved service standpoint, it is an overall good move for the company as long as we manage the third-party relationship."

Mills based his presentation to his supervisor on statistics and numbers. "My supervisor is a numbers person, so I adapt to his style," Mills remarked. "I support my cost analysis with as many facts and figures as I can." The persuasion worked. Mills's supervisor approved the outside carrier. In an analysis conducted several months later, the change proved cost effective for the company. Mills commented, "When you're asked to be a change agent and suggest a major change, you must ensure that the change proves beneficial." The third-party carrier saved the company money, and quality customer service was maintained. To Mills's credit, persuasion and business communication go hand-in-hand, creating success for him at American Woodmark.

Applying What You Have Learned

1. Mills used facts and figures as evidence in the outside carrier proposal. Give an example of a different proposal in which using evidence other than numbers or statistics would be appropriate.

2. Assume that you are a transportation manager at American Woodmark. After preliminary research and analysis, you develop a plan for a Home Delivery Program in which products are delivered directly to residential homes. Normally, American Woodmark uses commercial stores such as The Home Depot to reach its customers. This new program is innovative and will begin on a trial basis in Milwaukee, Wisconsin. Write a memorandum to your supervisor, Cyndi Johnson, convincing her to approve a pilot test of this new distribution system.

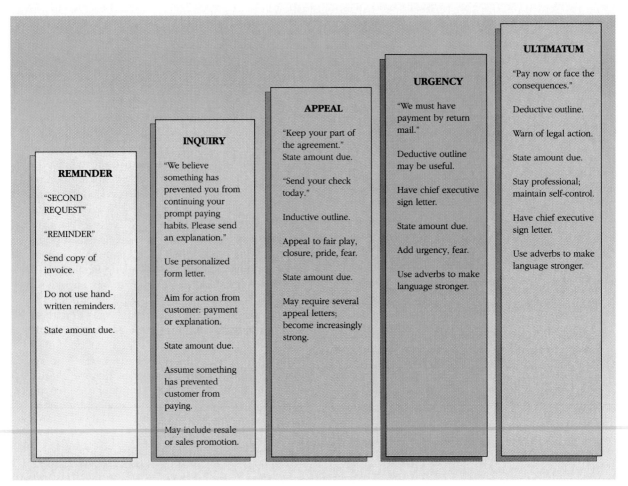

FIGURE 11-11　Stages in the collection-letter series.

In all letters at the inquiry stage, the assumption must be that something has prevented the debtor from paying. The aim is to get some action from the customer in the form of either a check or an explanation. Follow these guidelines in writing effective inquiry letters:

1. Because reminders have failed to bring payment, something is wrong.
2. Action on the part of the debtor is necessary. Either a payment or an explanation is expected.
3. With empathy, think and write positively.
4. Make it easy for the debtor to reply, but do not provide excuses for nonpayment.

The inquiry should not provide an excuse for nonpayment or mention that the customer had merely overlooked paying. Inexperienced collectors often violate these two important principles. Inquiry letters often ask whether something is wrong with the goods purchased or service provided. If people are attempting to avoid payment as long as possible, they will be glad to tell you something was wrong with your product or service.

One letter of helpful inquiry is sufficient because additional letters may give the debtor the idea you will continue to wait. You must increase urgency by reducing the proportion of helpful talk as you proceed from one stage to the

Would providing an excuse be an attempt to show empathy for the receiver's situation?

next. Helpful talk can be used in the appeal and ultimatum stages, but it should not predominate as in the inquiry stage.

APPEAL

By writing a short letter restricted to one appeal, a collection writer (1) increases the chances that the entire letter will be read, (2) places emphasis on the appeal used, and (3) reserves something new to say if an additional letter is needed. Typically, collection letters use appeals selected from the following list:

- *Fair play.* Collectors often appeal to the debtor's sense of cooperation, loyalty, and honesty. For example: "The mutual contract we entered into was based on two things. The first was our ability to make delivery as agreed. The second was your ability to pay as agreed. We kept our part of the agreement, and the only way to complete the agreement is for you to send a check for $156 today."
- *Closure.* According to the closure principle in Gestalt psychology, people gain satisfaction from concluding that which they have begun; that is, from taking the final step—paying—in a business transaction. For example: "Send your check for $156 today so that we can mark your account 'Paid in Full.'"
- *Fear.* Collectors know that many people fear loss of credit privilege, loss of possessions, and the possibility of litigation. For example, "So that you can continue to offer your customers the quality merchandise they demand, you must safeguard your good credit report. To do so, please send your check for $156 today."

An "appeal" letter should be short and should develop *one* appeal. Why?

What is the major goal of an appeal?

Each of the preceding appeals can be used to help a customer see the advantage of paying. Certain appeals—a threat of physical violence and a statement of intent to destroy a credit reputation (by telling friends, relatives, employers, and others)—are illegal. Creditors are normally within legal limits when they provide facts about an account to firms or individuals entitled to receive such information. Appeals to fear, being negative, should be used only after more positive appeals have been given a chance to solve the collection problem.

Describe appeals that are illegal.

For those debtors who have ignored the notices, reminders, and inquiries, the collection writer must select the appeal most suitable for the individual case and determine the best method of developing that appeal. The delinquent customer whose account has reached this stage must be persuaded to pay. Follow these two guidelines for the appeal letter(s):

1. Keep in mind the personal nature of the appeal. It is written for one person or for one company. Personalize the letter by calling the receiver by name if the use of the name falls naturally into place as you compose.
2. Write the letter from the receiver's point of view. You should not plead your own poverty as a reason why payment should be made. Instead, select an appropriate appeal and drive it home. Concentrate on one appeal. Multiple-appeal letters do not provide time or space to develop a single appeal properly.

Appeals in this stage intimidate only slightly, if at all. They suggest that the debtor might lose some tangible possession or be forced to become involved in a distasteful credit or legal entanglement. Typically, fear appeals are reserved for the strong-appeal or ultimatum letters.

STRONG APPEAL OR URGENCY

What is the major goal of the strong appeal or urgency stage? What procedures do companies often use at this stage?

The strong-appeal letter emphasizes urgency. It says, in effect, "We must have the payment by return mail." By developing the basic appeals and insisting on payment for the debtor's own good, the writer adds urgency. Partial payments may be satisfactory, offers to accept time notes may be made, or full payment may be demanded. Comments about the cost of a lawsuit are common in urgency letters. Although implications about the loss of credit or possessions may be used, the best psychology is to let the receiver know you are still willing to square things without undue embarrassment. To emphasize the crucial status of the delinquency, the strong-appeal or urgency letter may be signed by a top executive rather than by a member of the collection staff.

The appeal stages, both mild and strong, must of necessity involve human sensitivity, perhaps more than in any other communications issue. The deftness with which the writer handles the collection problem determines which customers are retained for the company. At the same time, the account has reached a crucial stage at which the assumption is that the customer will pay only after a persuasive challenge.

To develop the strong appeal from the mild appeal, follow these suggestions:

1. Change the appeal from one of challenging the debtor's *retention* of a favorable credit rating, a good reputation, or a prized possession to one of definitely implying that a debtor is about to *lose* something of value or *face a distasteful dilemma*.
2. Decrease the persuasive tone. Become more demanding.
3. Instead of discussing why the debtor *does not* pay, talk about why the debtor *must* pay.
4. Offer the debtor a choice between two or more things, none of which enables the debtor to get off the hook.
5. Let the debtor know clearly that the weight of evidence and the legal aspects definitely favor you and not the debtor.
6. Consider using the deductive approach.

Recall from Chapter 10 that sometimes bad news is appropriately placed in the first sentence. Late in the collection series, nothing (including the inductive approach) has worked. At this stage, the creditor may be justified in "shaking" the debtor or demonstrating some authority. Someone who has waited unusually long to pay a debt may respond to unusual treatment. By beginning with a direct request for payment or setting a time by which payment must be made, a deductive letter could get results when preceding inductive letters have failed. The action beginning is very emphatic. If it shocks a debtor into payment, good. If it does not, little is lost by trying the deductive approach.

ULTIMATUM

What is the major goal of the ultimatum stage?

When strong appeals fail to do their work, the collection writer must take the only remaining course of action: a letter that says, "You must pay now of your own volition or we will use every possible legal means to enforce collection." The debtor must pay or face the consequences. Whatever recourse you have to final collection must be mentioned in the letter. You must make the most of the fact that you will use the courts, a collection agency, or an attorney to enforce collection. Unfortunately, accounts that have reached this stage may be as costly to the lender as they are to the borrower. Furthermore, if payment is not made, you are sure to lose the customer. If payment is made, you would probably be hesitant about extending further credit to the customer.

Despite this dilemma, your letter should not use language that will make you susceptible to legal action by the customer. Keep your self-control, show some patience, and stay above the name-calling level. Any effort you can make to retain goodwill is worthwhile. Above all, avoid preaching because debtors who get to this stage do not react favorably to advice about how they should have acted. The ultimatum letter in Figure 11-12 shows that the tone has changed from "must pay" to "now or else."

Note how the ultimatum letter reviews the sequence of events, past and future, to indicate the seriousness of the matter. At this late stage, deductive writing is an option. To emphasize the ultimatum, the letter could have used the third paragraph as the beginning paragraph. If the ultimatum letter does not result in collection, the only recourse is to tell the debtor you are taking the steps promised. The account is no longer in your hands.

Before writing a persuasive message, study carefully the overall suggestions in the "General Writing Guidelines" in Chapter 9, page 269. Then, study the specific suggestions in the "Check Your Writing" checklist that follows the chapter summary. Compare your work with this checklist again after you have written a rough draft and make any revisions.

SUMMARY

1 The purpose of a persuasive message is to influence others to take a particular action or to accept your point of view. Effective persuasion involves understanding the product, service, or idea you are promoting; knowing your audience; presenting convincing evidence; and having a rational response to anticipated resistance to your arguments.

Persuasive messages should be presented in the inductive sequence using the AIDA steps for selling: Get the receiver's attention, introduce the product or request, give evidence the receiver gains by buying or complying, and encourage action. Effective persuasive letters build on a central selling point interwoven throughout the message. The receivers, rather than the product, serve as the subject of many of the sentences. Therefore, receivers can envision themselves using the product, contracting for the service, or complying with a request.

2 A persuasive request such as a claim letter, a letter that requests special favors and information, and memos that present recommendations or changes are written inductively. They are organized around a primary appeal and are longer than a typical routine message because you must provide convincing evidence of receiver benefit.

3 Collection letters are written to get payment and to maintain a customer's goodwill. A collection letter is shorter than other persuasive requests because debtors already know that they owe money. A five-stage series of letters can be written to obtain payment. The stages in a collection series are (1) reminder, (2) inquiry, (3) appeal, (4) strong appeal, and (5) ultimatum. Each letter becomes increasingly urgent and presents *one* appeal. If no response results, the next letter presents a different appeal.

DIVERSIFIED HEALTH SERVICES
8900 HOSPITAL ROAD, CINCINNATI, OH 45227-2076
PHONE: (513) 555-8756   FAX: (513) 555-9103

May 20, 19--

Mr. Chris Alexander, Office Manager
Kraker Internal Medicine Associates
210 Medical Arts Pavilion, Suite A
Cincinnati, OH 45227-2076

Dear Mr. Alexander

When we agreed some three months ago to ship medical supplies
and equipment, you agreed that you would pay the $1,265 within
30 days. Yet the 30 days have gone by, then 60. Now more than 90
days have elapsed.

Because our overdue notices and letters have gone unanswered, our
patience is exhausted; however, our interest in you and in your
welfare is not. Your name will be submitted as "nonpay" unless we
receive your check for $1,265 by May 27. The effect of a bad report
could restrict your ability to purchase medical supplies and equipment on credit. In addition, our legal department would be forced
to bring suit for collection.

We have every right to enforce legal collection. You have until
May 27 to retain your good record and to avoid legal embarrassment.

Sincerely

Victor Romero

Victor Romero
President

klr

FIGURE 11-12   Good example of an ultimatum.

REFERENCES

Bell, J. D. (1994). Motivate, educate, and add realism to business communication using the claim
letter. *Business Education Forum, 48* (2), 42-43.

Cody, S. (1906). *Success in letter writing: Business and
social.* Chicago: A. C. McClurg.

Dumas, L. S. (1994, June). Home work: The
telecommuting option. *Working Mother,* pp. 22-26.

Nelson, E. (1993). WordPerfect 6.0: 10 new things it
does for you. *WordPerfect Magazine, 5* (7), 36-38,
40, 42-43.

CHECK YOUR WRITING

SALES LETTERS

CONTENT
- ☐ Writer is convinced that the product or service is worthy of consideration.
- ☐ Letter includes sufficient evidence of usefulness to the purchaser.
- ☐ Price is revealed (in the letter or an enclosure).
- ☐ Central selling point is apparent.
- ☐ Specific action desired is identified.
- ☐ Message is ethical and abides by legal requirements.

ORGANIZATION
- ☐ Sequence of ideas is inductive.
- ☐ First sentence is a good attention-getter.
- ☐ Central selling point is introduced in the first two or three sentences and reinforced through the rest of the letter.
- ☐ Price is introduced only after receiver benefits have been presented.
- ☐ Price (what the receiver gives) is associated directly with reward (what the receiver gets).
- ☐ Final paragraph mentions (a) the specific action desired, (b) the receiver's reward for taking the action, (c) an inducement for taking action quickly, and (d) the action as being easy to take.

STYLE
- ☐ Language is objective.
- ☐ Active verbs predominate.
- ☐ Concrete nouns predominate.
- ☐ Sentences are relatively short.
- ☐ Sentences vary in length and structure.
- ☐ Significant words are in emphatic positions.
- ☐ Ideas cohere; changes in thought are not abrupt.
- ☐ Through synonyms or direct repetition, the central selling point is frequently called to the receiver's attention.
- ☐ Expression is original (sentences are not copied directly from the definition of the problem or from sample letters in the text; clichés are omitted).

- ☐ Unity is achieved by including in the final paragraph a key word or idea (central selling point) that was introduced in the first paragraph.

MECHANICS
- ☐ Letter parts are in appropriate positions; acceptable format is used.
- ☐ First and last paragraphs are short (no more than two or three lines).
- ☐ All paragraphs are relatively short.
- ☐ "Enclosure" is keyed if a brochure or pamphlet is to be enclosed.
- ☐ Keyboarding, spelling, and punctuation are perfect.

PERSUASIVE REQUESTS

CONTENT
- ☐ Writer is convinced that the idea is valid, that the proposal has merit.
- ☐ Receiver will benefit, and the way or ways in which the receiver will benefit are pointed out.
- ☐ A primary appeal (central selling feature) is incorporated.
- ☐ The specific action desired is identified.

ORGANIZATION
- ☐ Sequence of ideas is inductive.
- ☐ First sentence gets attention and reveals the subject of the message.
- ☐ The major appeal is introduced in the first two or three sentences and reinforced throughout the rest of the message.
- ☐ Receiver benefits are pointed out.
- ☐ Desired action is associated with the receiver's reward for taking action.
- ☐ Final paragraph includes a reference to the specific action desired and the primary appeal. The paragraph emphasizes the ease of taking action and (if appropriate) includes a stimulus for quick action.

STYLE

- ☐ Language is objective and positive.
- ☐ Active verbs and concrete nouns predominate.
- ☐ Sentences are relatively short but vary in length and structure.
- ☐ Significant words are in emphatic positions.
- ☐ Ideas cohere; changes in thought are not abrupt.
- ☐ Primary appeal is frequently called to the receiver's attention through synonyms or repetition of a word.
- ☐ Expression is original (sentences are not copied directly from the definition of the problem or from sample letters in the text; clichés are omitted).
- ☐ Unity is achieved by including in the final paragraph a key word or idea (the primary appeal) that was used in the first paragraph.

MECHANICS

- ☐ Letter parts are in appropriate position; acceptable format is used. In memorandums, the *TO, FROM, DATE,* and *SUBJECT* lines are properly completed.
- ☐ In memorandums, courtesy titles are omitted in the *TO* and *FROM* lines.
- ☐ Paragraphs are relatively short but vary in length.
- ☐ "Enclosure" is keyed on the letter/memo if a document other than the letter/memo is to be enclosed.
- ☐ Keyboarding, spelling, and punctuation are perfect.

COLLECTION LETTERS

CONTENT

- ☐ Inquiry letter simply asks for explanation, may include resale or sales promotion, states amount due.
- ☐ Each appeal letter is limited to one appeal.
- ☐ Each appeal letter is a little more forceful than the preceding one.
- ☐ Each appeal letter states amount due.

- ☐ Urgency letter is signed by a higher official than the one who signed the appeal letters, reveals seriousness of delay, and states amount due.
- ☐ Ultimatum letter leaves the way open for payment by a certain date and time; states amount due.
- ☐ Compared with other persuasive letters, a collection letter is relatively short.

ORGANIZATION

- ☐ Sequence of ideas is inductive; ultimatum letter may use deductive sequence.
- ☐ Inquiry leads up to request for explanation.
- ☐ Appeal letter reveals in the first sentence that letter is about the debt, introduces one receiver benefit (appeal) for paying, requests payment, and mentions exact amount due.
- ☐ Urgency letter (from a higher official) reveals that letter is about the account, gives a brief summary of the attempts to collect, urges payment, and states exact amount due.
- ☐ Ultimatum letter sets a date by which payment is expected and states action that will be taken if payment is not received; states exact amount due.

STYLE

- ☐ Verbs are active; nouns are concrete.
- ☐ Appropriate words at the appeals stage include *mutual, fair, cooperative,* and *agreed.*
- ☐ Adverbs are used to make language stronger at the urgency and ultimatum stages (e.g., *very* important, *extremely* critical).

MECHANICS

- ☐ Letter parts are in appropriate positions; acceptable format is used.
- ☐ Letters, though short, are balanced on the page.
- ☐ Keyboarding, spelling, and punctuation are perfect.

REVIEW QUESTIONS

1. Summarize the types of information you should gather as you plan a persuasive message.
2. List the writing principles that are important in writing an effective persuasive message.
3. What are the legal and ethical implications of persuasive messages?
4. Define "central selling feature." When should it be introduced and included in a persuasive message?
5. List the four steps in the outline recommended for persuasive messages.
6. What are the characteristics of a good attention-getter? List five techniques for getting receivers' attention.
7. Why are sales letters normally longer than routine letters? Should the first and last paragraph be shortest or longest?
8. Under what condition would the use of superlatives be acceptable in persuasive messages?
9. In persuasive messages, why are incomplete comparisons to be avoided? Compose a sentence that includes an incomplete comparison; rewrite, completing the comparison.
10. Summarize the effective techniques for convincing the receiver that your product, service, or idea has value.
11. List effective techniques for presenting the price.
12. List the characteristics of an effective action ending.
13. What is the principal difference between a persuasive claim and a routine claim?
14. What is meant by an "appeal" in a persuasive letter?
15. What outline is recommended for a persuasive request?
16. Which should receive more emphasis in a persuasive request: (a) the action desired or (b) the reward for taking action?
17. What would be the disadvantage of including "If you agree, please . . . " and "I hope you will be able to . . . " in the paragraph that asks for action?
18. In a letter that introduces a long questionnaire and encourages the receiver to complete and return, should the writing be persuasive? Explain.
19. Ideally, should a persuasive request for action be stated in a simple sentence? Explain.
20. Why are collection letters normally shorter than other persuasive letters?
21. Give one example of how computers are being used to simplify the collection process.
22. Should an inquiry letter ask whether merchandise and service have been satisfactory? Explain.
23. In a collection series, how many letters should include a request for reasons for the delay in payment?
24. At the appeals stage in a collection series, how many appeals should each letter have?
25. Which would have greater justification for use of negative terms: (a) an inquiry letter or (b) an ultimatum letter? Explain.

EXERCISES

1. Complete each of the THINK IT OVER activities your instructor assigns.
2. Select an unsolicited sales letter you (or a friend) received. List (a) the principles it applies and (b) the principles it violates. Rewrite the letter, retaining its strengths and correcting its weaknesses.
3. Clip a picture of an advertised product from a newspaper or magazine. Using the principles presented in this chapter, write an unsolicited sales letter. Attach the picture to the letter. Make sure your letter has a central selling point and presents evidence to convince the receiver to buy.
4. Analyze the effectiveness of each sentence as the opening for a persuasive message:
   a. Don't you want to make the world a better place? Instead of worrying about the starving in Africa, let's take care of our own—donate canned food to the local Homeless Haven in time for the holidays!
   b. John F. Kennedy said, "Ask not what your country can do for you; ask what you can do for your country." One of the best ways to support American capitalism is to let Carville Consultants make your business better.

c. You haven't lived until you've owned a Multi-Sound Compact Disc Storage Chest!

d. For an investment of $550, you can own the best high-pressure washer on the market from Sims, Inc.

e. The enclosed folder shows our latest prices on lead glass windows.

f. This new policy I am proposing will revolutionize our sales figures within three months. (request)

g. I am requesting to be promoted to regional sales manager because I have a proven track record of turning around sales revenues within two months. (request)

h. The merchandise you sent Maxwell Corporation on September 3 is defective, and we refuse to pay for it. (claim)

5. Analyze the effectiveness of the convincing evidence included in the following sentences in a persuasive request:

a. Reorganizing the loan department will help us serve our clients better and cut costs.

b. I know you are extremely busy, but we would really like to have you come speak to us on effective investing.

c. Southside Recycling has four regional offices in each county in Texas with headquarters in Dallas. Our professional staff consists of 15 members at each location.

d. You wonder if you can get quality education at our school and still save money? Dollar for dollar, tuition and fees at Carlton State give you the best education value for your money.

6. Analyze the following letter. Pinpoint its strengths and weaknesses and then revise the letter

November 5th, 19--

Kendall L. Perrigan
901 Summerland Road
Lake City, FL 32055-9019

Dear Sir,

I thank you for your inquiry regarding our schooner, The Mary Ann. Please find the enclosed information which I hope you will find interesting.

The Mary Ann is a 103 year-old gaffed rugged wooden schooner currently able to accomodate 32 passengers. Early next season we will be increasing our capacity to 49 passengers. The Mary Ann is 89 feet long and weighs approximately 60 gross tons.

Our rates for the 19-- season were $300 per hour for a minimum of three hours. There will be a price increase next year but it will be minimal.

Although the 19-- season is over, we are currently taking reservations for next season which will commence during April 19--. Please consider advance booking with us if you are at all interested in that special day as each year we have to turn away so many people who request a particular time and day. We do offer discounts to customers who are able to make reservations and pay in full before March 31st, 19--.

Should you have any questions or like to view our unique, historic sailing vessel then please do not hesitate to contact me.

Yours sincerely,

Glenda Hoover

Glenda Hoover
Office Manager

E-MAIL APPLICATION

Identify a situation in your work, educational experience, or school and community organizations that requires persuasion. How are you uniquely qualified for a scholarship, award, internship, admission into graduate school or honorary organization, or election to an officer position in a student or community organization? How could a change in a procedure improve the quality and efficiency of your work? How could a particular software, training program, or equipment improve your ability to complete a job function? Why should you be promoted or your present job reclassified to a level of higher responsibility?

Send your instructor an e-mail message describing the exact nature of your persuasive situation and asking approval for this topic. After receiving your instructor's approval, write the persuasive message to the appropriate person, convincing him or her to accept your idea or take the action you have recommended. Obtain the facts and figures necessary to present your argument, identify the benefits the receiver will derive from complying, anticipate the arguments that may come from the receiver, and have a rational and logical response to those arguments. Indicate the exact action you wish to be taken.

APPLICATIONS

MARKETING

1. **Promoting a Home Security System.** As the local sales manager for Southern Alarms Systems, you are preparing a sales letter to send to prospective customers; you plan to target the letter primarily to families with small children. Your system, Security Plus, can identify as many as 16 different protected zones—doors, windows, smoke and motion detectors and others, allowing flexibility in the protection customers desire. For example, customers can engage all protected zones when away from home. However, when in the house, customers can secure the doors and windows but disengage the motion detectors for free movement around the house. A variety of sensors put in selected places in the home send a clear signal whenever there is a problem, pinpointing the exact location of the problem (e.g., a motion sensor reports the exact hallway or protects silverware cases or other valuable items). In the event of intrusion or fire, the alarm goes off (special sound if a fire has been detected), and the system's computer dials Security Plus which may, in turn, dial the police dispatcher with a report. To facilitate entering the protected house, a "delay" can be programmed on one door, allowing customers 30 seconds to disarm the system before the alarm goes off; the system beeps to remind the customer to turn off the system when he or she enters this door. At night when everyone has entered the house, the customer can disengage the "delay" so that the alarm would sound immediately if a problem were detected at any door or window.

One-touch commands are used to control the system from a command panel mounted on the wall or free standing on a desk; the back-lighted keypad makes it easy to give commands in a dim room. One-touch keys can be programmed for special uses (to instruct the system to sound a signal when a certain door is opened to alert parents that a toddler has left the house). The command panel displays important information about the status of the home's protection. Levels of protection include perimeter instant (doors and windows; alarm sounds instantly), perimeter delay (doors and windows; 30-second delay on one door), and all instant (doors and windows, interior motion detectors, and other zones; instant alarm). The *User's Guide* that comes with the system contains complete operating instructions. Available in bright brass or stainless steel, the command center compliments any decor. As an incentive to purchase, you plan to offer the first six months' service contract ($15 a month) for free. Customers should call your toll-free number to arrange for a personal sales call.

Required: Write a letter providing a letter address for a fictitious customer.

FINANCE/HUMAN RESOURCES MANAGEMENT

2. **Persuading Employees to Enhance Financial Planning.** Several years ago your non-profit company ran a campaign to sign up employees for 403(b) plans. Section 403(b) of the Internal Revenue Code allows employees to invest up to 25 percent of their gross wages in tax-deferred annuities. Contributions to the annuities are not taxed until funds are withdrawn upon retirement. Unfortunately, a recent report from your human resources department indicates that only 22 percent of your employees have taken advantage of this plan. Based on your conversations with several employees, you believe that many employees do not understand the benefits of the plan.

   Required: As director of human resources, write a memo to all employees persuading them to attend a meeting to gain additional information about this financial planning strategy.

MARKETING

3. **Promoting a Product of Your Choice.** Select a product that you own, assume that you are its distributor, and write a sales letter addressed to customers who are your age. Regardless of whether you select an item as expensive as a car or as inexpensive as a small pocket calculator, choose a product on which you are "sold." You have pride in it, you have benefited greatly from its use, you are well informed about it, and you could heartily recommend it to others. You may assume an accompanying picture, folder, or pamphlet is included with the letter.

   Required: Write a sales letter providing an inside address for a fictitious customer.

MARKETING/International

4. **Earning a Finder's Fee for Exceptional British Stamps.** A client who wishes to start for his son a collection of high-quality European stamps has asked you, a dealer in European stamps, to locate them. You have located a solid page of 100 stamps issued 10 years ago to commemorate British statesman Winston Churchill. This page is in-

tact; no rows have been removed. Your own investigation has authenticated the dyes and inks on the stamps; you have also inspected the glue on the back and found no flaws. In short, the stamps are in mint condition. The owner paid 50 British pounds for the entire sheet and wishes to sell it for 200 pounds. You feel that the stamps are a very good buy for a beginning collector.

   Required:
   1. Locate the currency exchange rate so that you can give your client the price in U.S. dollars. Add 10 percent to the price for a finder's fee.
   2. Write a sales letter to Glenn Marshall, 1103 Commerce Street, Denton, TX 76205-2955.

MARKETING

5. **Securing a Radio Advertisement to Promote a Grand Opening.** You are the sales manager for WLOX, a radio station that specializes in classic rock—the music of the 60s to now—the favorite tunes of the 25-40 age group. Your research shows that your regular broadcast audience consists of 9,900 households in suburban Seattle. The average household in this area consists of 3.7 people.

   A deli-style restaurant is scheduled to open within your broadcast area during the next month. You feel that your audience demographics fit well into the deli's marketing niche. A well-placed spot aired during "drive time" (7:30 to 8:30 a.m. and 4:00 to 6:00 p.m.) could attract customers to the deli for lunch and dinner. You plan to recommend that the owner purchase forty 30-second spots to be run during the week of the deli's grand opening. You sell 30-second spots for $150 each.

   Required: Write a letter to Carmen Costello, Ole Tyme Deli, 1405 McKee Boulevard, Tacoma, WA 98413-1405.

REAL ESTATE

6. **Exposing Potential Members to Resort Property and Privileges.** As the public relations director of Crystal Stream, an upscale residential/recreational development in Sacramento, California, one of your major responsibilities is to secure memberships. You believe people must be given an opportunity to experience Crystal Stream firsthand; that is, to see your signature golf course and to dine in your luxurious Williamsburg-style

clubhouse. You intend to write a letter to prospects and include a certificate to be redeemed for 18 free holes of golf and a delicious appetizer and beverage in your dining room. Prospects will be instructed to call the pro shop to schedule a tee time. Accompanying the letter and certificate will be a four-color brochure that tells the history of the 712-acre development and includes pictures of the clubhouse, dining and meeting rooms, pool, and exercise rooms. The brochure also includes a detailed map of the course.

Required: Write a persuasive letter to Mr. and Mrs. David R. Denson, 373 Joline Avenue, Sacramento, CA 95813-0373.

GENERAL

7. **Party Time: Special Request.** The letter shown in Figure 11-6 is a persuasive request from the Long Beach Medical Association requesting permission to hold a charity event at Crystal Stream (description of the resort appears in Application 6). As social chairperson of your fraternity or sorority, you are certain Crystal Stream is the perfect place to hold your annual spring formal. Crystal Stream is a very exclusive club; consequently, its management may be reluctant to grant your request. Perhaps they have heard stories from other clubs about fraternity/sorority groups holding wild parties on their grounds that resulted in thousands of dollars' worth of damage to the property.

Required:

1. Consider specific reasons why your fraternity/sorority should be allowed to use the club. What essential details should you provide about the dance?
2. Write a letter persuading management to allow you to hold the party at Crystal Stream. Refer to Figure 11-6 for the address.

MANAGEMENT

8. **Beauty Lies in the Eyes of the Beholder.** Down-Home Barbeque, a restaurant chain in the South, routinely seeks weathered wood and antique pieces to create a rustic decor in its family restaurants. While driving his son's friend home from a scout meeting, the manager of the Mena store noticed a large, run-down building several yards to one side of a small, immaculate farmhouse.

When he inquired about the building, the owner, Mrs. Cox, reported that she and her husband had used it for storing canned goods and farm tools over the fifty years they had owned the farm. She commented, "I know it doesn't look like much, but I've never had the heart to tear it down. It's full of so many memories. But that's not all—the legend is it was once a general store, a real hub of activity in its time."

Immediately the manager reports to the owner that this "lucky find" could provide a majority of the items the company will need to build the new restaurant planned for Mountain View and to refurbish the Jackson store (weathered lumber, cross-cut saws, corn shellers, pump handles, washboards, various old dishes and much more). However, convincing Mrs. Cox to sell this building—this family landmark and perhaps county legend—would require an empathetic appeal.

Required: Write a letter persuading Mrs. Cox to allow you to purchase the building and its contents for use in your restaurants. Louise Cox, 976 Thompson Road, Mena, AR 71953-0976.

COMMUNITY SERVICE/Ethics

9. **Volunteer Must Complete Commitment.** HomeBuilders, a not-for-profit organization that builds low-mortgage houses for needy families, recently initiated its annual fund-raising drive. Tom McHann, the manager of McHann Electronic Service, was among numerous business executives who volunteered to solicit pledges from 50 area businesses. These volunteers agreed to submit pledges weekly and to complete the drive by May 15. With the deadline only two weeks away, Tom has turned in only five pledge cards. Most of the other volunteers have completed at least 80 percent of their solicitations.

Required: Write a letter to Tom persuading him to call on the remaining 45 businesses and to submit the pledges by the deadline. Tom's address is 1239 McDowell Road, Indianapolis, IN 46206-1239.

PUBLIC RELATIONS

10. **Advertising Inconsistent with Company Philosophy.** Since the turn of the century, Williams

Department Store has been the most influential business in your home town. The Williams family have been pillars of the community, taking leadership roles in church, civic, and economic development activities. The current company president, Patrick Williams, is especially active in an agency that works with drug rehabilitation.

Having returned home as the company's new data processing manager, you are puzzled that the company is advertising during a weekly television program that regularly displays parental discretion notices. The show frequently shows drug use in a way that would be enticing to children. You believe advertising on this show is inconsistent with the company's long-standing corporate culture and may hurt the company's reputation.

Required: Write a memo to the company president that will persuade the president to discontinue the advertisements on the television show (specify program) that carries parental discretion notices.

FINANCE

11. **Using Effective Persuasion Techniques to Prevent a Hostile Takeover.** Winton-Pearson, Inc., is attempting a hostile takeover of Carroll Industry by offering to buy stock at $55 when the current level is $40. As the chief executive officer of Carroll, you hope to prevent this takeover by communicating to the stockholders the benefits of not selling at the higher price. Two years ago, Carroll Industry renegotiated its contract with union workers. That action positioned the company at a cost disadvantage to its competitors, thus reducing corporate profits. You have learned through reliable sources that your major competitors will renegotiate their union contracts within the year. Consequently, they will face the same increases in employee wages; and their current advantage will be dissipated. Management is confident that Carroll will quickly reap the benefits of taking the initiative and renegotiating labor contracts two years ago.

Required: Write a letter to the stockholders persuading them not to sell their stock; you are the chief executive officer of Carroll. Address the letter to Mrs. Helen Munson, 8311 Desert Lane, Tucson, AZ 85702-8311.

MANAGEMENT/Public Sector

12. **Proposed Tax Hike: Persuasive Campaign.** A special election has been scheduled for a referendum on a 2-percent tax on prepared food and beverages. The tax has been proposed by the Tucson City Planning Board (the municipal government) as a means of providing public funding for the newly formed Tucson Development Council (TDC). Officials estimate the tax will produce approximately $900,000 in revenues. According to the bill, half the funds would be used to fund the TDC, which will handle all local economic developmental projects. Twenty-five percent would be used by the Visitors and Convention Council for the development of tourism within the county, and 25 percent would be used to construct a welcome center. As president of the Tucson Chamber of Commerce, you are convinced that economic development, especially increased tourism, will benefit the entire community. Bringing more people to Tucson will create jobs and income for the people here. You have obtained current membership lists of the area civic clubs.

Required: Compose a form letter to be sent to members of the other civic clubs persuading them to support the tax. Address the letter to Alex Davies, 104 Duggar Acres, Tucson, AZ 85702-0104.

MANAGEMENT

13. **Music Video Missing Creative Symbolism.** After negotiating with a number of video producers, the rock group Thunderbolt contracted with Harrelson Producers to direct and produce the band's first music video. Thunderbolt was extremely impressed with the clips from other music videos that Harrelson presented as examples of its work. All these videos were heavy with graphic symbolism and creative shots of the musicians. The producer assured the band members they would be allowed to critique the first draft of the video; the $100,000 fee would be payable when the final video was delivered. When the first draft arrived, Thunderbolt and its general manager eagerly began to critique the tape. Their almost-uncontrollable excitement quickly vanished. Unlike the clips they had reviewed, at least half of this videotape depicted the band singing in a live-concert format. The video included little symbolism, dancing, or any shots of the band in any format other than live-concert.

Required: Write a persuasive letter outlining the specific changes you, as Thunderbolt's general manager, believe are necessary for the video to meet the specifications upon which you agreed. Address the letter to Harrelson Producers, 3674 Elmhurst Avenue, Los Angeles, CA 90052-3674.

CONSUMER

14. **Equipment Malfunction Justifies an Exchange.** Six months ago you bought what was considered a top-of-the-line VCR from an electronics franchise in your town. After one week of use, it malfunctioned. Because it had a two-year warranty, you returned it to the dealer for repair. One week later you took it home, and it broke again. After six months of continually returning the malfunctioning VCR for repair, you feel you deserve a new VCR. The local dealer will not give you a new machine, so you decide to write to the manufacturer.

Required: Write a persuasive letter explaining that you feel justified in asking for a new VCR because yours has been in the repair shop more than it has been available for use. Address the letter to Televideo, 580 West Lakes Blvd., Milwaukee, WI 53202-0580. (You may adapt this case to an actual problem you have experienced for which you would have written a persuasive claim.)

HOTEL MANAGEMENT

15. **Disappointing Services: Request for Adjustment.** For his fifth wedding anniversary, Todd Gray decided to take his wife to one of New York City's top luxury hotels for a weekend. Although the price seemed to be very high ($295 per night), Todd felt that he had made a perfect choice for their fifth anniversary. However, the hotel did not live up to the couple's expectations. The service was slow and impersonal, the staff was unfriendly, and the room left much to be desired. Both Todd and his wife thought they could have had a more pleasant stay at a mid-level hotel.

Required:

1. Consider these points: Do you believe that Todd is justified in asking for a full refund? What reasons support his justification? If the refund is not justifiable, what reasonable adjustment should he request?

2. Write a letter to the hotel asking for the adjustment you, as Todd Gray, feel is justified. Address the letter to James Parker, Manager, Anderson House, 708 East 26th Street, New York City, NY 10001-1708.

COMMUNITY SERVICE

16. **Securing Volunteer Services for Service Organization.** You are responsible for finding a suitable person to perform a special activity for a service organization to which you belong. Using your own interests and creativity, specify the exact nature of this activity. For example, you might ask a financial planner to discuss mutual funds at a monthly meeting; an accountant to prepare tax returns for senior citizens; or a computer programmer to assist in automating membership records. Assume that the individual must be convinced to respond favorably because of circumstances that you specify (e.g., too busy, not a member of your organization, no previous experience in such civic activities, etc.).

Required: Write a letter to the person of your choice inviting him/her to assist in the activity you specified. Include any details needed to make arrangements for his/her participation in this activity.

MANAGEMENT/Technology

17. **Investigating Online Connections Important for Company Productivity.** You have read extensively about the information superhighway and the benefits small companies are gaining from online services and Internet connections. You are convinced that your company could operate more productively and perhaps do more business if you "got on line." Although most of the managers you have talked with about the feasibility of going online seem interested, none has the expertise needed to initiate the startup. You noticed an ad for a three-day seminar entitled "Making Online Services Work for You," and decide that this intensive training would provide the knowledge needed to develop a strategic plan for the company to take advantage of this new technology.

Required: Write a persuasive memo to the president requesting approval for you, as the assistant accountant, to attend the seminar at company expense. Attach a copy of an article that outlines the value of "being wired" and provides specific examples of companies' innovative use of online technology.

MANAGEMENT/Technology

18. **Persuading a Manager to Start a FaxFood Line.** Gordon's Deli is filled to capacity during the lunch hour because of its convenient location in the center of the downtown business district and its reputation for delicious specialty foods. Employed as a summer employee, daily you watch small groups of office workers stand impatiently checking their watches as they wait for a table; other groups leave as soon as they see the long lines. While waiting for a table, numerous customers have told you they prefer your wide selection of healthy food choices over the other fast-food restaurants in the area. Often they cannot leave the office for lunch because of pressing deadlines and are forced to skip lunch or eat snacks from a vending machine. No space is available for expanding the dining room to shorten the waiting line. However, you believe customers who are eating on the run would react favorably to what you are calling a FaxFood Line: Customers would fax their orders with delivery to their office guaranteed within a half hour. You realize that not all your menu items can be delivered effectively, and you cannot afford to deliver "small" orders. Other resistance includes the logistics of receiving and confirming orders especially for those ordering as a group from the same office but who want individual totals.

Required:

1. Write a memo to persuade the manager to introduce the FaxFood Line. Mention you are attaching a draft of a sales letter promoting the new service to downtown office workers and the forms (see Step 3) needed to expedite your plan. (You do not have to design the forms unless directed by your instructor.)
2. Write a sales letter promoting this new service to downtown office workers. (Provide your own name for the service if you wish.)
3. Design an order form for the FaxFood Line and the confirmation form you will send after the order is received. Use your own creativity to generate a list of menu items or select them from the menu of your favorite deli.

MIS/Technology/Ethics/Legal

19. **Convincing Employees to Follow Computer Security Policy.** When you read about the most recent incident of computer abuse (a student used a friend's e-mail address and password to send a threatening e-mail message to the President of the United States) you knew you had to do a better job of enforcing the company's computer security policy. You are especially concerned that few employees seem to understand that e-mail is not confidential, the necessity of writing "good" passwords and changing them often, and following logout procedures when leaving a terminal, and possibly others.

Required: Write a memo, as MIS manager, to all employees persuading them to adhere to these computer security measures. Review Chapter 5 and obtain any other facts needed to help employees recognize the benefits they can gain from complying.

COLLECTION/Legal

20. **Collecting an Overdue Payment.** When Stan Watson was campaigning for election as county sheriff, he had $1,500 worth of signs printed. He paid $1,000, and the printing shop agreed to accept the remaining $500 after the election. After losing the election, Stan paid $100—the first of what were to be five monthly payments. Two weeks have passed since his second payment was due, but no check has arrived.

Required: Write the letters requested by your instructor:

a. Write an inquiry letter to Stan Watson, P.O. Box 121, your city.
b. A month has passed and Stan has paid nothing. He now needs to pay $200. Write an appeal letter.
c. Two weeks ago you sent the appeal letter to Stan, and he has not yet responded. Write another letter with a different appeal.
d. Two weeks after sending the second appeal to Stan, you have received no response. Write another letter with a stronger appeal.
e. Two weeks after sending the final appeal letter, write Stan an ultimatum.

CASES FOR ANALYSIS

MARKETING/Legal

Case 1.   Determining the Legal Implications of Using a Person's Photograph in an Advertisement. During local television news coverage of a blues festival, the reporter and the camera crew shot some footage of a family of six (including four small children) arriving at the festival in a minivan. Your car dealership sells minivans of the same make, and you want to use the footage in your television commercials. The television station agrees to let you use its footage and gives you the name and address of the family involved.

Required:

1. Because you have never used pictures acquired in this way, the dealership owner (Anthony Coffin) wants you to research the legal guidelines for using a person's photograph. He has several concerns: What information must be included in the letter to meet these legal guidelines? How specific must you be in describing the use of the pictures? Should you offer to pay the family a fee for these pictures?

2. Write a memo to your supervisor providing the results of the research you conducted in Step 1. Include complete and accurate documentation of your sources. This memo will serve as a record of your efforts to ensure legality on this issue.

3. Write the letter to the family asking permission to use the photograph in your ad campaign and including the pertinent information identified in Step 1. Address the letter to Mr. and Mrs. Curtis Alford, 4211 Main Street, Memphis, TN 38115-4211.

MARKETING/Ethics   `GMAT`

Case 2.   Charitable Contributions or Shrewd Public Relations? As the president of a bottled water company, you have been looking constantly for a way to promote your product. The United States has just sent hundreds of troops to a foreign country to defend it against a possible military attack. Because soldiers will need plenty of water in this dry climate, you see this situation as a possible solution to your sales problem.

Required:

1. Write a persuasive letter to military officials asking them to purchase your bottled water for the

military troops in this foreign country. Address the letter to the Procurement Department, use the simplified block format that omits the salutation, and sign your name as the president.

2. Assume that the military officials refused to offer your company a contract to supply bottled water to the military troops. Your marketing/public relations department has proposed that the company donate 500,000 bottles of water to the military. Decide whether it is ethical to donate the bottled water. Consider these points:
   a. What are the relevant facts?
   b. What are the ethical issues raised by the decision to donate the bottled water?
   c. Who (which stakeholders) will be affected by this decision?
   d. What are the costs and benefits imposed by each alternative on each person listed in Step c?
   e. What are the company's obligations to each person listed in Step c?
   f. What should you as the company's representative do?

3. Based on your decision, complete *one* of the following activities:
   a. Write a letter to the president voicing your dissenting opinion, as a stockholder, on the donation of the water. Address the letter to Michael Stevens, Sparkling Springs Water Company, 2731 North Lake Street, Chicago, IL 60607-2731.
   b. Write a news release, as the public relations director, stating that your company has decided to donate 500,000 bottles of water to the military.
   c. Do any other options exist? If so, write a letter, memo, or other document to the appropriate individual.

MARKETING/Technology

Case 3.   Developing Support for a Worthy Community Effort. As a member of a local civic group, you are organizing an annual community project to provide holiday gifts to underprivileged children. Today, one of the members of the committee gave you a draft of a letter soliciting support for the project. After reading the letter, you have two major concerns: (1) The basic principles of persuasive writing have not been applied; therefore, you are not certain how effectively the letter will be in drawing support for your worthy project. (2) You feel a more attractive, creative layout would increase the impact of the content. You received the following draft:

November 29, 19--

Mrs. Evelyn Floyd
9655 Tenth Street
Cambridge, MA 02140-9655

Dear Mrs. Floyd

The Thirteenth Annual Holiday Store will be held in the lobby of the Main Street Fire Station on Dec. 6, 7, and 8 from 3:00 to 6:00 p.m. New toys will be given to the parents of approximately 400 underprivileged children at this time.

If you can HELP any or all of the following afternoons, we will need YOU to help set up and operate the store. We need volunteers on the afternoon of Dec. 6, 7, and 8 to set up the store and work as clerks and gift wrappers. We need you to please sign your name below, indicating the date you will be able to help.

Name _____
Phone _____
Date & Time Available _____

Also, contributions to The Holiday Store are needed and will be greatly appreciated.

Please return this form to either Mari Cooper, 3771 Abilene Street, Cambridge, MA 02140-3771 (555-1043) or Frances Kuhnle, 101 Mangrove Drive, Boston, MA 02184-0101 (555-9031). THANK YOU!

Sincerely

Teresa Huddleston
Teresa Huddleston

Required:

1. Revise the letter incorporating the principles of effective persuasion.
2. Use desktop publishing capabilities available to you to design a creative, attention-getting layout, including a letterhead, for this document. Provide a fictitious name and address for the civic club. Use the page-design layout principles in Chapter 5 as a guide.

Discussion Questions

1. Cynthia Pharr likens the sales letter to a personal sales call. Explain how the two activities are similar.
2. Michael Fleming puts forth the idea that practicing conciseness shows concern for your receiver/audience. Explain this concept.
3. What constitutes an effective opening for a sales letter? Give examples of techniques that may attract the receiver's attention. What should the writer guard against in structuring the opening?
4. Explain the concept of being receiver-oriented. How is this idea applied in persuasive messages?
5. How do surface characteristics, such as the envelope and stationery, affect the receivers' responses to a persuasive letter?

Preparing effective persuasive communication requires a carefully tuned set of skills. First, the writer must understand the needs and motivations of the intended audience and how to make the product, service, or idea appealing. Second, the writer must be able to predict and overcome any reason the receiver may have for rejecting the message, so as to assure the desired outcome. Third, the writer must be convincing, yet courteous; persuasive, yet polite.

Whether selling products, services, or ideas, a business' success or failure often rests on its employees' strengths of persuasion.

Application

You must construct an effective persuasive message to persuade your audience to support a product, service, or idea of your choice (e.g., the idea your instructor approved in the e-mail application in the end-of-chapter activities). Remember to include (1) an effective opening; (2) a concise, on-target discussion of your product; (3) convincing evidence that your product, service, or idea will meet the receivers' needs, including a logical argument to overcome any resistance you anticipate; and (4) a courteous, effective call for action.

CHAPTER 12

WRITING SPECIAL

LETTERS

OBJECTIVES

When you have completed Chapter 12, you will
be able to

1 Write messages that congratulate, acknowledge congratulations, thank you, welcome, wish farewell, and invite.

2 Compose seasonal messages that extend appreciation.

3 Compose a condolence and an apology.

4 Write an effective news release.

5 Write letters that identify situations that deserve commendation and those that need improvement.

Can you remember a time when someone praised you for work you did? Everyone knows the good feeling when receiving recognition and appreciation for one's efforts. It can even spark increased enthusiasm and creativity.

One example of a company that puts praise into practice is DowElanco in Indianapolis, Indiana. Every month the company has a "Praise/Victory" luncheon to acknowledge the accomplishments of the approximately thirty workers in the division. Peter Paradiso, Business Services Manager of Customer Services at DowElanco, says that the luncheon started when one employee in the department went from desk to desk gathering "praises" from everyone. She created a newsletter based on these "praises" and organized a luncheon to celebrate. Now the event is sanctioned and organized by management.

Most of the time the luncheon is potluck with each employee bringing an item to share. Sometimes, however, the event takes a humorous turn. Mr. Paradiso recalls one instance when the luncheon became an Italian cooking contest when he offered to make lasagna, and his Italian supervisor challenged the lasagna with homemade meatballs. Clearly, the luncheon is a successful activity that all employees enjoy. It shows how the management is willing to take the time to praise employees for work well done, which leads to increased morale, worker satisfaction, and productivity.

The "Praise/Victory" luncheons offer an opportunity to praise employees orally. For some circumstances, however, the manager will want to put the message in writing—a permanent and tangible sign of the manager's praise. Empathetic managers take advantage of occasions to write **goodwill messages**—letters, memorandums, and e-mail messages that build strong, lasting relationships among employees as well as clients, customers, and various other groups. They send genuine goodwill messages promptly, and they make sure they follow the rules of professional protocol precisely.

CONGRATULATIONS

LEARNING OBJECTIVE 1

Letters of congratulations normally require an answer.

How many times a year do you overlook an opportunity to congratulate someone?

THINK IT OVER
In groups, debate the benefits of handwritten or keyboarded notes written by managers. What is your preference?

Sending congratulatory messages provides an excellent way for managers to build goodwill. Because the subject matter of congratulatory letters is positive, they are easy (and enjoyable) to write. Normally, they should receive a response.

Writing Congratulations

How often do you read about the election, promotion, or other significant achievement of a colleague or acquaintance and think that a note or telephone call of congratulations would be in order—only to procrastinate until it is too late? The successful executive takes advantage of the situation to build goodwill for the company and for herself or himself. Some executives accomplish this goodwill gesture by using a note card. Although handwritten messages are acceptable, keyboarded ones permit more to be said; and busy managers can prepare them more efficiently. The thoughtfulness of sending letters of congratulations is genuinely appreciated. When your letter is the only one the person receives, it really stands out.

In addition to promotions and elections, such events as births, weddings, and engagements call for acknowledgment. Because your message will please the receiver, (1) begin with the congratulations—your reason for writing, (2) tell how you learned about the event or accomplishment, and (3) close with a warm, courteous statement. The following excerpt from a short e-mail message extends congratulations for a promotion:

> **Please accept my warmest congratulations and best wishes for your success. I just read of your promotion to sales division head in the monthly newsletter.**

When a colleague wins an award or is elected to office, a congratulatory note is a lift for both the one who sends it and the one who receives it. The following example illustrates this congratulatory message:

> **Congratulations on your receipt of the Jaycees Community Contribution Award. The entire community and I recognize your commitment to serving the people in our community. Best wishes.**

People do not get too old or too successful to feel good when their contributions are recognized by others.

For an engagement, the letter may take a warm and enthusiastic tone, as in the following example:

> **Congratulations. I just heard of your engagement and wish you and Sachi every happiness. She has always impressed me as a warm and friendly person. Best wishes to both of you in your life together.**

Note the friendliness displayed in letters of congratulations. Because they are usually sent to friends and acquaintances, congratulatory messages and acknowledgments are casual, warm, and sometimes witty. You should not delay your message until it is too late to take advantage of the immediacy of the accomplishment.

To accomplish its goodwill objective, a letter of congratulations must be sent as soon as possible.

Replying to Congratulations

In almost all cases, letters of congratulations should be answered. An acknowledgment might take the following form:

> **Thank you for your good wishes concerning my promotion. I look forward to working more closely with you in the future. Thanks again for the note.**

Some replies take a tongue-in-cheek tone, particularly when the promotion is to a rather high-pressure position:

> **Many thanks for your nice words about my promotion and for the good wishes. I'll remember your confidence during some of those sure-to-be-trying days!**
>
> **The job is going to be demanding, especially during this transition time. However, I'm going to give it my all. Your thoughtfulness will definitely help ease the burden. Again, I truly appreciate your support.**

Letting a congratulatory message go unanswered is somewhat like failing to say "You're welcome" when someone has said "Thank you." Of course, the message and words used to convey it are important; but the act of responding conveys a positive metacommunication. Impact is reduced, though, if the tone implies self-confessed unworthiness or egotism:

Failing to acknowledge congratulatory messages is compared to what other action?

The response is no place for showing humility or feeding the ego.

Writing congratulatory messages to employees shows that you value their work and that you are pleased with their performance. The employees' likely response is a more positive attitude toward their jobs and motivation to set and work to meet challenging goals.

I'm not sure I have the qualities you mentioned.	Unworthiness
Others were more deserving than I.	Unworthiness
Thanks for your note about my receiving the Realtor of the Month award and for recognizing my energy, sincerity, and expertise.	Ego

THANK-YOU MESSAGES

Should thank-yous be handwritten or key-boarded?

Thank-yous should begin with an expression of thanks (the reason you are writing).

Following the receipt of a gift, attendance as a guest, an interview, or any of the great variety of circumstances in which a follow-up letter of thanks might be desirable, a thoughtful person will take the time to send a written message. As with all other special-letter situations, your message should be written deductively and reflect your sincere feelings of gratitude. When couples have been guests, one person usually sends the thank-you message for both. The message should be informal; a simple handwritten note is sufficient. When written in a business office to respond to a business situation, the message may be keyed on letterhead. Here's a message of thanks for a weekend visit. Rather than the routine, thank-you-for-a-lovely-weekend thought, the letter includes something specific that the writer enjoyed:

What is included to make this letter sound sincere and not like a form letter that could be sent for numerous circumstances?

Ray and I thoroughly enjoyed our excursion this weekend on Lake Douglas. Since we moved here from Savannah, sailing has become a rare pleasure for us. You were kind to invite us. Thanks again for a delightful time.

A thank-you note covering a business situation might be sent electronically. Note the example in Figure 12-1 (1) begins with a statement of thanks; (2) is specific about that which is appreciated, which reflects a sincere feeling of gratitude; and (3) closes with a warm statement.

In many cases, thanks could be conveyed as well by telephone calls. However, notes seem much more thoughtful.

All gifts received should be acknowledged by a thank-you note. Identify the gift, tell why you like it, and describe how you will use it:

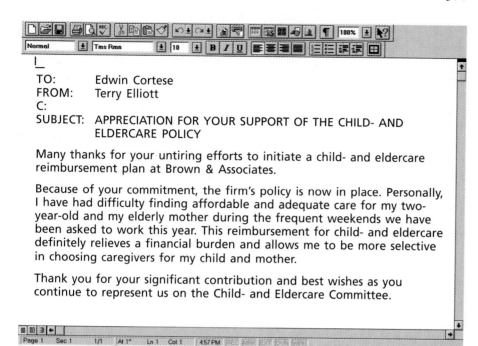

TO: Edwin Cortese
FROM: Terry Elliott
C:
SUBJECT: APPRECIATION FOR YOUR SUPPORT OF THE CHILD- AND
             ELDERCARE POLICY

Many thanks for your untiring efforts to initiate a child- and eldercare reimbursement plan at Brown & Associates.

Because of your commitment, the firm's policy is now in place. Personally, I have had difficulty finding affordable and adequate care for my two-year-old and my elderly mother during the frequent weekends we have been asked to work this year. This reimbursement for child- and eldercare definitely relieves a financial burden and allows me to be more selective in choosing caregivers for my child and mother.

Thank you for your significant contribution and best wishes as you continue to represent us on the Child- and Eldercare Committee.

FIGURE 12-1   Good example of a thank-you memo sent electronically.

THINK IT OVER
Where is the main idea positioned in Figure 12-1? What other favorable characteristics do you see?

After conducting an in-service seminar for you, I was pleasantly surprised to receive the desk calendar. The convenience of being able to plan my week at a glance is an unexpected byproduct of my work with Syntex. Thanks for your kindness and for this useful gift.

What points should be included in a thank-you letter for a gift?

Such letters are easy to write, and they require little time. Yet, too many people put them off until later. The letter is postponed until tomorrow, then tomorrow, and is never sent.

Procrastination robs you of an important chance to build goodwill.

WELCOMES AND FAREWELLS

For most new employees, the first day on a job is trying—new tasks, new responsibilities, and new people. When introduced, many will extend an *oral* welcome. Those who bother to drop a *written* welcome into the mail box or send an e-mail message will make a special impact:

Why *write* a message welcoming a new employee?

Welcome to the Accounting Department!

George has planned a thorough orientation for your first day. Afterwards, if you have any questions about our facilities or procedures, just stop by Room 121. As soon as schedules permit, let's have lunch together. Best wishes for a long and happy tenure with us.

Positive as the impact of the *words* may be, the *thoughtfulness* demonstrated by taking time to write may have an even greater impact.

For those who are leaving a job, many colleagues and friends will say some things that will make the departing employee feel good; but not many will

Will a *written* farewell have a strong impact?

bother to *write*. The written message is likely to have a stronger impact; it may be kept or shared with family members. To identify ideas that might be included, reflect on experiences with the departing person. Brief reference to special interests, skills, accomplishments, or mutual problems may be appropriate. One who has demonstrated an appreciation for humor may enjoy a touch of it. In any case, the message ought to be brief, sincere, and personal:

> I will miss you, but I am glad to see you get the professional advancement you have earned.
>
> You leave an unmatched reputation for efficiency, punctuality, and integrity. But give me a little time; I'll find someone who can match your skills at backgammon during the lunch hour.
>
> Best wishes for success and happiness on the new job.

What to say in farewell letters (as well as other letters discussed in Chapter 12) is important. For most people, though, *taking time to write* them is the major challenge.

INVITATIONS

Informal invitations are similar to a business letter. What is executive stationery?

Like most other special letters, invitations are written in the deductive pattern and are relatively short. Responses to invitations should be handled similarly. An informal invitation resembles a business letter. When sent from a business office, the letter is sometimes keyboarded on executive stationery, which is smaller than the regular business letterhead. Wording should be conversational, as though the writer were extending the invitation orally. The letter in Figure 12-2 is an example.

When should invitations be acknowledged?

All invitations should be acknowledged promptly. Often formal invitations include "RSVP" and a telephone number. The RSVP notation informs invited guests that the host is expecting an immediate telephone reply to facilitate plans for the event. "Regrets only" requires a reply only if the invited guest cannot attend. When a telephone RSVP is not mentioned, either a keyboarded or a handwritten reply is satisfactory and should use the same conversational style as used in the invitation.

What is the meaning of RSVP?

Although many formal invitations are handwritten, especially for smaller groups, formal invitations generally are printed and follow formats found in etiquette books. Replies to formal invitations follow a pattern similar to the invitation. Although formal etiquette calls for handwritten replies to invitations, business protocol permits use of keyed messages. Refer to formal etiquette books for specific formats for writing formal invitations and replies.

SEASONAL MESSAGES

LEARNING OBJECTIVE 2

What are seasonal messages? Why do companies write them?

Many businesses send messages to their clients, customers, or employees at certain times of the year: Thanksgiving, religious holidays, birthdays, the beginning of a new concert season, the anniversary of the opening of an active account, and so on. The intent is to demonstrate goodwill through an expression of good wishes or appreciation. Such messages remind recipients that they

STAGGERS WHOLESALERS
3130 Lone Oak Drive
Hartford, CT 06101-3130
(203) 555-9700 Fax (203) 555-8765

June 15, 19--

Ms. Susan Ainsworth
903 Peach Orchard Lane
Waterbury, CT 06701-8723

Dear Ms. Ainsworth:

You are invited to be our guest at the Moorcliff Resort for our annual Dealers' Convention Banquet. It will be held at the River Oak Banquet Room on Saturday, July 10.

The evening will begin with a reception at seven o'clock, followed by dinner, a speaker, and the awards presentation. For the first time this year, an award will be presented to the dealer with the largest percentage of new accounts acquired during the dealer's second year with Staggers Wholesalers.

Please let us at Staggers know by July 5 whether you will attend. I will be eager to see you there.

Sincerely yours,

Keith R. Staggers

Keith R. Staggers
President

FIGURE 12-2   Good example of an informal invitation.

are important to the business and that they are remembered at a special time. For that reason, sales material (even very low-pressure sales messages) should not be included. It would reduce the impact of the primary message. Thinking they had been trapped into reading a sales pitch, readers might be resentful.

Seasonal messages may be stored in the computer, retrieved, and sent on letterhead with the recipient's address and a salutation. More frequently, they are mass produced and written as though they were addressed to members of a group, as the following example illustrates:

Resist the urge to include a sales message in a seasonal message.

December 30, 19--

All Employees

Bridges appreciates your efforts this past year. Thanks to you, every goal has been reached or exceeded. As a token, a gift certificate will be included in your next pay envelope.

May your holiday season be an enjoyable one.

Rodney W. Wagner

Rodney W. Wagner
President

To a valued customer, the following letter would be encouraging:

One year ago today, you opened an account with us. Thank you for buying your building materials from us during the past year. Your promptness in paying has certainly been noticed, and we want you to know it has been appreciated.

Compared with the goodwill generated by such letters, the cost is likely to be small.

CONDOLENCES

Are informal cards acceptable for condolences? Are keyboarded notes acceptable?

A letter of sympathy to the family of a friend or business associate who has died should be written promptly. However, the sympathy message presents a difficult writing problem; and these messages are often put off until too late or are not sent at all. One way to solve the problem, although a little impersonal, is to send an informal card, which may be purchased in a stationery shop, and include a short handwritten message: "Deepest Sympathy" or "Deeply saddened by your loss. Sympathy to you and your family." Although etiquette now allows keyboarded messages to be sent when the deceased is a business associate, a handwritten message provides a much more personal tone than does any other kind.

Write the recommended outline for a condolence in your notebook.

The simplest plan for such messages is to (1) start with a statement of sympathy, (2) follow with sentences about mutual experiences or relationships, and (3) close with some words of comfort and affection. The letter in Figure 12-3 is to the mother of a deceased acquaintance.

When a close relative (spouse, son, daughter, mother, or father) of a close friend dies, write the friend a letter of sympathy. Printed sympathy cards may also be used; but, in general, the closer the relationship, the greater the need for a personal written message of condolence.

APOLOGIES

What is the best way to handle apologies?

The best way to handle an apology is to avoid the need for it. Sometimes, though, events do not turn out as planned, and it is your fault. Looking back, your conduct is regrettable, or some circumstance has prevented you from doing your best. In such cases, apologies are in order—for your own peace of mind and for good future relationships with an offended person.

Whether to apologize face to face, over the telephone, or in writing is a personal matter. The nature of the business, custom, seriousness of the infraction,

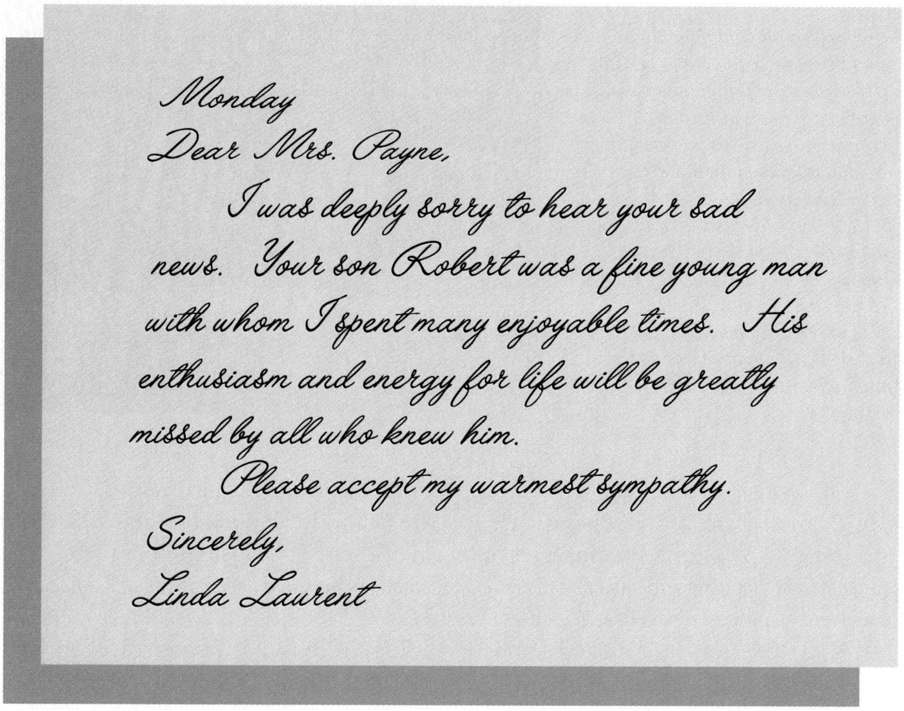

Monday
Dear Mrs. Payne,
I was deeply sorry to hear your sad news. Your son Robert was a fine young man with whom I spent many enjoyable times. His enthusiasm and energy for life will be greatly missed by all who knew him.
Please accept my warmest sympathy.
Sincerely,
Linda Laurent

FIGURE 12-3   Good example of a handwritten condolence.

personalities, and other factors are considerations. Regardless of the channel selected, the principles are the same: (1) Be sincere, (2) be direct, and (3) be brief.

When apologizing, people who have made mistakes are inclined to condemn themselves too severely or describe the mistake too vividly, as illustrated in the following apology:

> I would like to apologize for two inexcusable errors I made in introducing you at yesterday's luncheon.
>
> Looking at the tape this morning, I watched in horror as I pronounced your name as "Peabody" instead of "Peaberry" and stated your alma mater as "Northwest" instead of "Northwestern." Please forgive me for making these terrible blunders.

Mr. Peaberry probably had noticed the errors in pronunciation but quickly dismissed them as rather common human errors, but suppose he *had* been irritated by them. Labeling them as inexcusable and using "horror" in talking about them (along with actual restatement of the incorrect words) would reinforce his irritation. That reinforcement would work against the purpose of the apology. The revision that follows is better. The writer apologizes directly and uses general terms to avoid reinforcing the unpleasantness of the mispronunciations.

> Please accept my apology for the way I pronounced two words when introducing you at yesterday's luncheon, your name and your alma mater's name!
>
> You deserved—and I wanted you to have—a memorable introduction. My tongue could have cooperated better, but it always has positive things to say when your name is mentioned.

What three words describe an effective apology?

Should general or specific words be used in an apology? Why?

THINK IT OVER
Should the apology (main idea) appear in the final sentence?

The best way to handle apologies is to avoid getting into situations where you will need to make them. Dateline NBC made a serious mistake when a truck was rigged with explosive material to demonstrate a defect in the manufacture of the trucks that made them prone to explode on impact. Angry reactions from the automaker forced an investigation and an embarrassing apology from the show and the network. When you must apologize, remember to be sincere, direct, and brief; avoid justifications and overly strong descriptions.

Beyond apologizing, *do* something to make amends—if you can.

THINK IT OVER
Using an online database, locate articles discussing at least two examples of public apologies made by companies or individuals (e.g., McDonalds' printing sacred Koran scriptures on Happy Meal bags, Milli Vanilli's lip-syncing an award-winning album, etc.). Be prepared to discuss how each apology was handled. What improvements can you recommend?

1 Begins inductively.

2 Uses negative language. Emphasizes "vulgar language" by placing it at the end of a short paragraph.

3 Uses negative language. Some details of the reprimand could make the statement more convincing.

4 Apologizes a second time. Emphasizes the word "apology" (and its negative connotations) by placing it at the end of the last sentence.

Of course, an apology without appropriate action is of little value. (Meeting Mr. Peaberry again and saying, "Hello, Mr. Peabody" would be fatal.) Without stooping to pick up a classmate's books, an apology for causing them to fall is of little value. Again, empathy is the key: People who have the right attitude have the best chance of finding the right words.

Sometimes, an unsolicited letter of apology removes a barrier or even preserves a business relationship. For example, at the home office of a major firm, a client's representative parked in a space designated for officers only. Before reaching the entrance, the representative was stopped by a security officer who asked that the car be moved to the visitor's lot. According to the vice president of finance (who happened to observe the incident), the security officer was obviously angry and used vulgar language in asking that the car be moved. Cheerfully, the representative returned to the car and drove away (perhaps with the intent of terminating the business relationship).

Immediately, the VP wrote an apology to the representative. By apologizing quickly, the VP may have avoided the necessity of responding to a strongly worded letter reporting the incident. Unfortunately, the letter (Figure 12-4) focuses on negatives and could make the matter worse. The revision (Figure 12-5) is more direct, more positive, and more detailed.

> 1 In the parking lot this morning, I overheard the discussion between you and the security officer. 2 For him and for our firm, I apologize for his vulgar language.
>
> 3 He has been reprimanded, and we assure you that his conduct is regrettable. 4 Please accept our apology.

FIGURE 12-4   Poor example of an apology.

NEWS RELEASES

LEARNING OBJECTIVE 4

A **news release** contains information that a company wishes to communicate to the media—newspapers, magazines, radio, and television. To ensure that the media will find your news release appealing to its audience, include these points:

905 South Nottingham Road
Knoxville, TN 37901-0905
(615) 555-8760 Fax (615) 555-1207

December 5, 19--

Mr. David Patel
South-Central Electronics
895 South Ferry Road
Knoxville, TN 37939-3109

Dear Mr. Patel:

1 Please accept my apology for the manner in which our security officer spoke to you this morning. 2He had been instructed to keep certain parking spaces open for company officers, but he should have remembered his obligation to be courteous and helpful.

3 The chief of security has already assigned the officer to (a) restudy the security manual and (b) attend the human relations seminars now required of all newly hired employees. 4When you call at our offices again, you can expect efficiency and courtesy, which have been our goals for the past twelve years.

Sincerely,

Gilda R. Montgomery

Gilda R. Montgomery
Vice President of Finance

wlk

1 Emphasizes the apology by placing it in the first sentence. Reveals the purpose of the letter. "Manner" of speaking is more positive than "vulgar language."

2 Confirms the officer's right to ask that the car be moved but (through the subjunctive mood and positive words) disapproves of officer's methods.

3 Reports measures taken to avoid repetition of such incidents. By reporting something that has been *done*, the letter strengthens credibility of the apology statement.

4 Closes with a positive look to future transactions.

FIGURE 12-5   Good example of an apology.

1. Write deductively with concern for brevity and clarity.
2. Give sufficient information (thinking of *who, what, when, where, why,* and *how* will help to ensure good coverage).
3. Include the preferred date on which the message is to appear.
4. Include the name of the contact person—the company official responsible for the release.
5. Use company letterhead (individuals should include a return address and telephone and fax numbers).

The example in Figure 12-6 illustrates these points.

THINK IT OVER
What is the main idea Figure 12-6? Where does it appear? Locate the other items that should appear in a news release.

```
                    McCARTHY BUILDERS
                    9631 Davidson Line Road
                    Meridian, MS 39301-1812
                (601) 555-1300  Fax (601) 555-1143

CONTACT:  Vince Wilford, Vice President
          McCarthy Builders
          (601) 555-1300

FOR IMMEDIATE RELEASE—March 15, 19--


              McCARTHY TO BUILD NEW SUBDIVISION

     Meridian, Miss.—On June 1, McCarthy Builders will begin con-
struction of new homes on a 40-acre tract at the northeast corner of
Bell and Ray roads.
     The project, expected to be completed in about two years, will
feature stucco walls and tile roofs. The four different floor plans
range in size from 2,000 to 3,000 square feet.
     According to Vince Wilford, vice president of McCarthy, models
should be ready for viewing in early September.

                            # # #
```

FIGURE 12-6   *Good example of a news release.*

Why begin news releases with the main idea?

Knowing that brevity is important to the media, you need to be very conscious of it, too. If a release has to be shortened, the media may eliminate the most important portion (to the submitter). If the telephone number appears on the release sheet, the news media may take time to call about possible deletions or ask for more information.

COMMENDATIONS AND CONSTRUCTIVE CRITICISMS

LEARNING OBJECTIVE 5

Even though evaluation is not your intent, you can hardly escape noticing when the attitudes and performances of others are especially good or especially bad. For those who deserve high marks, letters can encourage; for those who deserve low marks, letters can alert.

COMMUNICATION   MENTOR

The greatest praise any of us as individuals can receive is the unsolicited and unexpected. Conveying this praise to others, even in the smallest way, can take you a long way in helping to achieve support for your personal and professional goals.

Terence E. McSweeney
Director of Communications
PGA of America

Commendations

Letters that recognize positive qualities or performances are especially effective. People usually are not reluctant to say, "Thank you," "A great performance," "You have certainly helped me," and so on. Yet, because people seldom bother to *write* them, such messages are especially meaningful—even treasured. Compared with those who merely *say* nice things, people who take time to *write* them are more likely to be perceived as sincere.

Why are written *compliments so effective?*

Although a letter of commendation is intended to recognize, reward, and encourage the receiver, it also benefits the sender. Contributing to another's happiness, paying tribute to one who deserves it, encouraging that which is commendable—such feelings can contribute to the sender's own sense of well-being and worth. Such positive thinking can have a salutary influence on the sender's own attitude and performance.

In an intangible way, how do letters of commendation benefit their writers?

Some of the potential value (to sender and receiver) is lost if a letter is mechanical, such as the following example:

> Your speech to our Business Breakfast Club was very much appreciated. You are an excellent speaker, and you have good ideas. Thank you.

To a speaker who has worked hard preparing and who has not been paid, such a letter may have *some* value. After all, the sender cared enough to write. Yet, such a letter could have been sent to any speaker, even if its writer had slept through the entire speech. A note closed with *sincerely* does not necessarily make the ideas seem sincere. Because the following good example is more specific, it is more meaningful:

Should a letter that commends be couched in general terms?

> This past week I have found myself applying some of the time management principles discussed at the seminar you conducted last week for the Society of Real Estate Appraisers.
>
> Prioritizing my tasks really helped me keep my perspective; and when I performed the time analysis, I easily identified some areas I can manage more effectively.
>
> Thank you for an informative and useful seminar.

The revision does not sound so much like a form letter. At least its writer was aware of the main points made and had already applied the information.

A different approach—a letter of commendation to the speaker's employer—could result in a tangible reward as well, as shown in Figure 12-7. With such letters addressed to an employer, an employee's chances for promotion are increased.

Why write to an employer *about an employee who has gone beyond the call of duty?*

THINK IT OVER
What is the purpose of the copy notation (used in Figure 12-7)? Turn to Appendix A ("Special Letter Parts") to answer this question.

**Society of
Real Estate
Appraisers** 763 Collins Ave., Lansing, MI 48909-0763
(517) 555-9073 Fax (517) 555-9108

November 30, 19--

Mr. L. Nathan Jefferson
Jefferson Electronics
1903 Front Street
Oshkosh, WI 54901-1903

Dear Mr. Jefferson:

Daniel Hatton, human resources manager for your firm, gave a very interesting and useful seminar at last week's meeting of the Society of Real Estate Appraisers.

In a well-organized and interesting presentation, he offered several time management techniques that have worked very well for me. I observed the intense interest of the other members of the audience and the willingness of many of them to voice their positive reactions to his comments on how disorganization causes stress. His seminar was very well received by this group.

Possibly, Mr. Hatton told you that he led a seminar for our group; I wanted you know that he gave an outstanding presentation—totally consistent with the competence one sees in your employees.

Sincerely,

Michael L. Sims

Michael L. Sims
Vice President

c Mr. Daniel Hatton

FIGURE 12-7   Good example of a commendation letter sent to an employer.

Such letters should be written for the purpose of commending deserving people; they should not be written for the purpose of possible self-gain. Sometimes, however, those who take time to write such letters receive some unexpected benefits.

As an undergraduate student, Henry Kissinger wrote a letter of appreciation to a Prussian general who had spoken at his university. Touched by such thoughtfulness, the general invited Mr. Kissinger to dinner. Concluding that the young man had unusually keen insights into international affairs, the general was instrumental in getting Kissinger admitted to graduate study.

Although generous praise is seldom objectionable, a letter or memo of commendation may not fully achieve its purpose if it reaches the point of exaggeration or uses language that is hardly believable. The message in Figure 12-8 is an example.

Is self-gain a legitimate motive for writing a letter that commends?

THINK IT OVER
In groups, discuss strokes or written commendations you have sent or received. How did the action affect the sender and receiver? What changes would you recommend after reading this chapter?

The marketing consultants the New York office sent to us here in Texas were by far the best and most informed marketing executives we have ever worked with.

Because they helped us identify our primary weakness, we are confident that the Dallas office should exceed our sales quotas during the coming fiscal period. Unlike many other consultants sent to us from the home office, this team was eager to learn to think like Texans.

Once again, thank you for sending us this brilliant team.

FIGURE 12-8   Poor example of a commendation.

In the writer's mind, the statements may be true; but in the reader's mind, they may seem unbelievable. Because the language is strong and the statements are not supported, the letter could arouse thoughts about how bad other consultants were; or it could arouse questions about the writer's motives. The vice president would probably be more impressed with the letter in Figure 12-9.

Although the message does not use strong language, it conveys a stronger compliment than the previous message. Without the words "best" and "brilliant," it reveals *why* the staff's reaction was favorable.

The net effects of this letter are positive: (1) The writer feels good for having passed on a deserved compliment, (2) management gains some assurance that the consulting team's efforts are effective, (3) the team about whom the letter was written is encouraged to continue an effective technique, and (4) other divisions may have an increased likelihood of exposure to similar high-quality consulting.

Constructive Criticisms

A person who has had a bad experience as a result of another person's conduct may be reluctant to write about that experience. Suppose, for example, the consultants in the preceding illustration had been ineffective. Before writing about the problem, a manager would recognize the following risks: (1) being stereotyped as a complainer, (2) being associated with negative thoughts and thus thought of in negative terms, or (3) appearing to challenge one of management's prior decisions (choice of the consultants). Yet such risks may be worth taking because of the benefits: (1) The writer gets a feeling of having exercised a responsibility, (2) management learns of changes that need to be made, (3) the team about whom the letter is written modifies techniques and is thus more successful, and (4) other divisions may be exposed to consultants who are more effective.

Are exaggerations advisable?

Does strong language strengthen a compliment?

Who benefits from a commendation letter sent to the subject's employer?

Why are people hesitant about writing letters that point out negatives?

When another person has made or is making mistakes, what can be gained by writing a letter?

COMMUNICATION   MENTOR

We strongly believe that our Russian staff must know that we care about them and are aware of their accomplishments. This knowledge builds teamwork and boosts confidence. Communicating praise is also quite a departure from the "Soviet" way and must be handled delicately, especially when commendations are distributed widely. We must always be fair without showing favoritism. Commendation letters should be brief and extremely upbeat.

Larry E. Wilson, Managing Partner
Arthur Andersen, Moscow

COLUMBUS STEEL CORPORATION   2500 Lincoln Green Road, Austin, TX 78710-2500
(512) 555-9000   Fax (512) 555-6573

January 25, 19--

Mr. Stephen B. Agacer
Vice President of Marketing
Burnham-Weber Industries
1590 Avenue of the Patriots
New York, NY 10002-1590

Dear Mr. Agacer

Recently, the New York office sent an outstanding team of marketing consultants to assist us in identifying methods of increasing our
market share in the Southwest sales region.

The consultants listened intently as our managers helped them
understand the peculiarities of the Southwest market. All members
of the team functioned like professionals, asking probing questions
and quietly observing our methods without placing undue pressure
on our staff. Their courteous and helpful manner created an open
line of communication that led to a successful two weeks of work.
They left us with an accurate knowledge of our strengths and
weaknesses and several new strategies for promoting our products.

After incorporating these new strategies, the Austin office should
be able to meet its sales quotas during the coming fiscal period.
Thank you for sending this capable team.

Sincerely

Gene Chappell

Gene Chappell
Vice President of Sales

FIGURE 12-9   Good example of a commendation.

Are letters that seek revenge advisable?

In the decision to write about negatives, the primary consideration is intent. If the intent is to hurt or to get even, the message should not be written. Including false information would be *unethical* and *illegal*. To avoid litigation charges, include only specific facts you can verify and avoid opinions about the person's character or ability. The guidelines for writing legally defensible employee recommendations apply to this letter (see "Negative Recommendations" in Chapter 14.)

In a written message that contains negative information about a person's performance, evaluative words (your opinion) are discouraged. Instead of presenting facts, the message in Figure 12-10 judges.

> Our recent sessions with the home-office marketing consultants here in Texas were a complete waste of time.
>
> The consultants knew nothing about our problems in the Southwest and refused to listen to us explain the specific needs of our markets. For these reasons, the consulting effort yielded no useful information.

FIGURE 12-10   Poor example of a constructive criticism letter.

THINK IT OVER
How do you write a legally defensible negative evaluation of a person's performance? Refer to Chapter 14 ("Negative Recommendations") to answer this question.

In the writer's mind, the first sentence may be fair and accurate; but in the mind of the reader, "complete waste of time" may seem overly harsh. The phrase may convey the tone of a habitual fault-finder. Without details, the charges made in the second sentence lack force. If "complete waste of time" strikes the receiver as an exaggeration, the whole message loses impact. Overall, the letter is short, general, and negative. By comparison, the revision in Figure 12-11 is long, specific, and positive.

Because one person took the time to write a letter, many could benefit. Although not always easy or pleasant, writing about negatives can be thought of as a civic responsibility. For example, a person who returns from a long stay at a major hotel might, upon returning home, write a letter to the management commending certain employees. If the stay had not been pleasant and weaknesses in hotel operation had been detected, a tactful letter pointing out the negatives would probably be appreciated. Future guests could benefit from the effort of that one person.

THINK IT OVER
In groups, discuss letters presenting negative qualities you have sent or received. To whom was the letter addressed? Was the intent genuine? What changes would you recommend after reading this chapter?

Whether negative evaluations are presented in writing or in conversation, the same principles apply: have a positive intent, be factual, use positive language, and leave judgment to the recipient.

Why should you avoid use of judgmental terms?

Before writing a special letter, study carefully the overall suggestions in the "General Writing Guidelines" in Chapter 9, page 269. Then, study the specific suggestions in the "Check Your Writing" checklist that follows the chapter summary. After you have written a rough draft, compare your work with the "Check Your Writing" checklist and make any revisions.

Folk wisdom says that one bad apple can spoil the whole bunch. In some cases, an employee's poor performance can affect an entire group. When you have to discuss someone's negative qualities, do so to facilitate cooperation or generate improvement, not to "get even." Keep the criticism constructive, not personal.

COLUMBUS STEEL CORPORATION   2500 Lincoln Green Road, Austin, TX 78710-2500
(512) 555-9000 . Fax (512) 555-6573

January 25, 19--

Mr. Stephen B. Agacer
Vice President of Marketing
Burnham-Weber Industries
1590 Avenue of the Patriots
New York, NY 10002-1590

Dear Mr. Agacer:

¹ A team of New York-based marketing consultants has just left our office. ²They spent two weeks attempting to pinpoint weaknesses in our marketing strategies.

³ Gaining insights from successful approaches used in other divisions of the company is an excellent idea; however, several aspects of this team's performance need to be called to your attention:

⁴ 1. During their stay, the consultants seemed less interested in analyzing our problems and more concerned with instructing us in the strategies they have used in the Northeast. Although excellent in theory, many of these ideas are not applicable to our particular target market. When we attempted to provide essential information about our market, the team refused to listen.

⁵ 2. From the day they arrived, the team members clearly communicated their status as the experts. On one occasion, our marketing manager intervened to explain his perspective of a specific problem. The head consultant immediately reminded him that if we could have done the job ourselves, we wouldn't have asked

Mr. Stephen B. Agacer
Page 2
January 25, 19--

for this team's help. Other similar situations occurred. Consequently, their attitude of superiority soon created a formidable barrier to communication, which obviously restricted the effectiveness of their efforts.

⁶ The marketing department appreciates your efforts to help us identify ways to improve our marketing efforts. ⁷In the spirit of helpfulness, I am passing this confidential information to you.

Sincerely,

Gene Chappell

Gene Chappell
Vice President of Sales

Margin annotations:

1, 2 Introduces a discussion of the consulting project at the Austin office.

3 Tries to convey fair-mindedness and establish credibility by acknowledging good points in a letter that discusses bad points.

4 Presents a statement of fact without labeling it in negative terms. Judgment is left to the reader.

5 Includes a verifiable statement. If such conduct is deplorable, outrageous, or insulting, the reader will be aware of it without the writer's use of such terms.

6 Ends on a pleasant note that seeks to add credibility to the preceding negatives.

7 Uses "confidential" as a safeguard; the information is intended for professional use only, not designed to hurt and not to be thought of as gossip.

FIGURE 12-11   Good example of a constructive criticism letter.

COMMUNICATION IN ACTION

Honorable Ronnie Musgrove
Mississippi State Senator

When Mississippi state senator Ronnie Musgrove receives a letter from one of his constituents, he assumes the letter must be important. Senator Musgrove, who was elected in 1987 to the 52-member senate, believes the issues about which constituents write genuinely affect them. Although only a small percentage of his 50,000 constituents write him, each letter he receives may represent a larger issue, affecting a broad spectrum of people. Because he responds to genuine concerns, his written correspondence is an important part of his contact with the public.

As chair of the Senate Education Committee, Senator Musgrove received a request from a woman concerned about Mississippi's state health insurance plan for public school teachers. Hoping to receive some assistance on a family matter, the woman wrote Senator Musgrove about an error an insurance administrator made in handling her mother's claim. Because Senator Musgrove's committee decisions directly affect over 60 percent of the state's budget, including teachers' health insurance plans, he was familiar with her concern.

Responding in writing, Senator Musgrove began by expressing genuine empathy toward her concern, stating that he would promptly address the issue. "Writing skills become extremely important in these contacts," he said. "I must understand the situation before drawing conclusions, and I must communicate clearly and concisely to the person involved." He concluded his letter with a statement of the specific action he planned to take. "These special letters are important," he adds. "They are a reflection of my office and the type of senator that I am."

Many constituents write because of problems with state agencies with which they believe a state official can help. "In this case, if the insurance administrator has interpreted the policy correctly, I will consider other action to help my constituent. Legislative action may be needed." As a result of his efforts, Senator Musgrove clarified a vaguely worded policy and directed the woman toward an equitable solution with her deductible. "I believe I am helping people when I can respond effectively to their requests," he stated. "My letter achieved its purpose, and I helped a constituent."

Applying What You Have Learned

1. When Senator Musgrove receives a letter from a constituent, what is the importance of a written response expressing genuine concern and interest in the issue the constituent raised?

2. Assume that you work as an aide in Senator Musgrove's office. A constituent, who is an educator working for a public school, had written the senator objecting to the handling of her insurance claim. The educator explained that she lost a portion of her deductible during a change in insurance administrators. The senator asked you to draft a letter for him, expressing his concern for her loss and explaining that the issue will be addressed. Draft a letter to Jolene Forrest, 250 Hampton Circle, Jackson, MS 39288-0250.

SUMMARY

1 Empathetic managers do not overlook occasions to write messages that create goodwill among employees as well as clients, customers, and others. They send genuine messages promptly, and they follow the rules of professional protocol precisely. Putting the message in writing provides a permanent record of the recognition that can be kept, shared with family, or used to document excellence during the performance appraisal process.

Congratulatory messages and acknowledgments, thank-yous, welcomes, and farewells should be written immediately to take advantage of the immediacy of the situation. These letters are written deductively and are relatively short. Although they may be handwritten, most are keyboarded for the sake of efficiency and to provide additional space for a complete message.

Thank-you letters expressing appreciation of a kindness or special assistance reflect sincere feelings of gratitude. Express appreciation for a specific item to create a sincere, warm tone. A thank-you note for a gift identifies the gift, tells why you liked it, and describes how you will use it.

Informal invitations have the conversational tone of a business letter and may appear on executive stationery. All invitations should be acknowledged promptly following the provisions indicated in the RSVP. Refer to social protocol books for sending and acknowledging formal invitations.

2 Seasonal messages are sent to clients, customers, and employees at certain times of the year to express appreciation. These goodwill messages should not include sales promotional material.

3 Condolences start with a statement of sympathy, followed by sentences about mutual experiences or relationships, and close with some words of comfort or affection. A handwritten note will convey the personal tone more effectively than a printed card or keyboarded letter.

Avoid the need for an apology; however, write one when you believe you have not done your best. State the apology *once* at the beginning of the message, avoid making excuses and overly strong descriptions of the mistake, and be brief.

4 A news release contains information a company communicates to the media. Include the following points in an effective news release: (1) begin with the main idea, (2) sequence other information in order of importance to ensure that a version shortened by the media will include the most important information, (3) give sufficient information (who, what, when, where, why, and how), (4) include a preferred date for the message to appear, and (5) include a contact person who could provide additional information.

5 Commendation letters highlight exceptional performance but avoid exaggerations and strong, unsupported statements that the reader may not believe. The motive for writing letters providing constructive criticism should be to help—not to get even. The letter includes verifiable facts and omits evaluative words, allowing the reader to make logical judgments based on facts.

CHECK YOUR WRITING

To check your writing of a message in one of the special-letters categories, first check the points listed under *special letters*. Then check the points listed under the category you are interested in. For example, check a letter of apology against the qualities listed under *special letters* and the three listed under *apologies*.

SPECIAL LETTERS
- ☐ Are direct, brief, and sincere.
- ☐ Use an acceptable format.
- ☐ Achieve correctness in grammar, spelling, punctuation, and keyboarding.

CONGRATULATORY LETTERS
- ☐ Begin by stating the congratulations.
- ☐ Refer to the event in specific terms to convey a sincere tone.
- ☐ Are mailed immediately after the event.

RESPONSES TO CONGRATULATORY LETTERS
- ☐ Begin by acknowledging receipt of a congratulatory letter.
- ☐ Accept praise graciously; are not egotistical.

THANK-YOUS
- ☐ Begin with a statement of thanks.
- ☐ Are specific about that which is appreciated.
- ☐ Reflect a sincere feeling of gratitude.

WELCOMES AND FAREWELLS
- ☐ Convey an attitude of friendliness and willingness to help with adjustment to a new job.
- ☐ Are tailor-made to the individual—a reference to a common experience, special skills and interests, accomplishments, or mutual problems.

INVITATIONS
- ☐ Informal invitations have a conversational tone.
- ☐ Invitations with RSVP notations require immediate replies.
- ☐ Formal invitations and replies to them follow standard formats found in formal etiquette books.

SEASONAL MESSAGES
- ☐ Are written to build goodwill and should not include sales promotional material.

CONDOLENCES
- ☐ Begin with a statement of condolence.
- ☐ Refer to mutual experiences or relationships.
- ☐ Close with words of comfort or affection.

APOLOGIES
- ☐ Include the apology only once in the message.
- ☐ Should not be overly self-critical.
- ☐ Should not describe a mistake too vividly.
- ☐ Include a possible solution to the situation, if possible.

NEWS RELEASES
- ☐ Begin with the main idea.
- ☐ Sequence other information in order of importance in the event an editor cuts from the bottom up.
- ☐ Give sufficient information (*who, what, when, where, why*, and *how*) that will appeal to the specific audience.
- ☐ Follow standard format for a news release.

COMMENDATIONS AND CONSTRUCTIVE CRITICISMS
- ☐ Are written for the right purpose.
- ☐ Are deductive if they are commendations, inductive if they are constructive criticisms.
- ☐ Are factual (not judgmental) if they contain negative information.

REVIEW QUESTIONS

1. What benefits are obtained from writing congratulations? What types of events should managers acknowledge?

2. When expressing congratulations, which is more likely to have a strong impact: (a) an interoffice telephone call or (b) a memorandum or e-mail message?

3. Present an argument for and against handwriting or keyboarding notes written by managers.

4. Should congratulatory messages be acknowledged? List two common pitfalls in writing these responses.

5. For most letters in the "special" category, which is preferred: (a) deductive presentation or (b) inductive presentation?

6. List the outline recommended for a thank-you letter for a gift.

7. Compare and contrast an informal invitation to an invitation formatted as a business letter.

8. Why should sales messages be omitted from seasonal messages?

9. Describe the appropriate points to include in a farewell message.

10. When expressing condolence, what determines whether to send a printed card or a personalized letter?

11. List the outline recommended for a condolence.

12. Which is better for writing news releases: (a) deductive sequence or (b) inductive sequence? Explain.

13. Discuss the major points for writing effective news releases.

14. How are writers rewarded for the time they spend in writing letters of commendation?

15. What are the disadvantages of using superlatives and other strong adjectives and adverbs in a letter that commends someone for a job well done?

16. By writing a letter or memorandum that reports someone's failure to do a job well, what risks does a writer take?

17. When reporting someone's failure to do a job well, why should judgmental terms be avoided? What other advice would you offer for writing this sensitive letter?

18. When the purpose of a message is to apologize, should it begin and end with the apology? Explain.

19. Which is the better expression? (a) "Please accept my apology for . . ." or (b) "I would like to apologize for . . ." Why?

20. Should a writer use strong adjectives to describe the mistake for which an apology is presented? Explain.

EXERCISES

1. Complete each of the THINK IT OVER activities your instructor assigns.

2. In groups of three or four members, discuss the advantages and disadvantages of handwriting goodwill messages, keyboarding them, or sending commercial greeting cards. Initiate a formal discussion. Consult the business and business protocol (social etiquette) literature to support your views.

3. In groups of three or four members, discuss the role of special messages in achieving the goals of an organization. Consult business literature to support your views.

4. Analyze the effectiveness of the following sentences for special messages:

   a. I would like to say congratulations on your recent honor.

   b. Even though my schedule was disrupted, thanks again for inviting me to your home.

   c. I just heard the supervisor finally gave you that promotion.

   d. The presentation at the dealer's meeting by Jason Embry was one of the worst I have ever attended.

   e. Christine Focisi can come and lead another seminar for us any day!

   f. I am so sorry for the irresponsible way I handled your recent request.

   g. As a long-standing partner in Magner & Carroll Sales, I always enjoy welcoming our new sales staff to the company.

5. Analyze the following letter. Identify the strengths and weaknesses and then rewrite the letter

December 2, 19--

Keith Ballard, Supervisor,
High-Cotton Pants Section

QUALITY PERFORMANCE AT MAYNARD ENTERPRISES

Being a sewing-machine operator in our plant is a very demanding job. Boredom and fatigue often cause errors and cut-rate products.

However, last month in your section, all the high-cotton pants met our quality standards. We commend you on this achievement. Thank you for making Maynard products better than ever!

Brian Anderson

Brian Anderson
Production Manager

rta

E-MAIL APPLICATION

 Send an e-mail message to your instructor addressing the preferred channel(s) to use for each of the following messages. Justify your decision. Choose between a mail letter or memo, faxed letter or memo, handwritten note, e-mail message, telephone call, or face-to-face meeting.

Message Type

Notice of employee dismissal

Thanks for a job well done on a special project

Employee performance appraisal

Condolence message

Congratulations on marriage

Apology for problem incurred in handling a transaction

APPLICATIONS

MANAGEMENT/International

1. **Congratulations on Completion of Spanish Course**. You are the president of a fashion design firm. You have heard through the grapevine that Dennis Pierce, one of your firm's sales representatives, has just completed an intensive course in conversational Spanish. Your company has recently expanded to sell your clothing overseas, and you feel that his skill will enable him to be an excellent sales representative to potential customers in Spain.

Required:
1. Write a memorandum of congratulations (or e-mail message if your instructor requires), as Stephanie Royston, to Dennis Pierce.
2. Write a memorandum (or e-mail message if your instructor requires), as Dennis Pierce, to Stephanie Royston in response to the memorandum of congratulations.

MANAGEMENT

2. **Praise to Well-Deserving Employees**. As president of Wolcott Discount Stores, you have very much appreciated your employees' conduct during the peak sales season. With huge crowds attending, the days seemed hectic. Many employees worked overtime in the evenings and on weekends. No accidents occurred, very few customers complained, and sales were much larger than anticipated.

Required: Now that the heavy work season is over, write a memorandum to all employees expressing your appreciation.

MANAGEMENT

3. **A Job Well Done**. You are the committee chairperson responsible for finding a suitable person to perform a special activity for a service organization to which you belong. Using your own interests and creativity, you specified the exact nature of this activity. For example, you could have asked a financial planner to discuss mutual funds at a monthly meeting; an accountant, to prepare tax returns as a service for senior citizens; or a computer programmer, to assist in automating membership records. This person agreed to perform the service you requested and completed the task in an exemplary fashion. You have received complimentary comments from the officers, members, and other individuals served by the project (provide specifics).

Required: Write a memorandum (or e-mail message) to this individual. Commend the volunteer for a job well done.

MANAGEMENT/Ethical

4. **Response to Commendation for High Ethical Standards**. As a sales representative for a fashion design firm, you have recently learned that one of your firm's designers has been "stealing" designs from another company. You brought this fact to the attention of the director of the design team, who ignored the problem. Finally, you explained the situation to the vice president. Yesterday, you received an electronic message from the president commending you on your high ethical standards and your persistence in pursuing the issue regardless of the personal consequences.

Required: Write a memorandum in response to the president, Terrence Downes.

MARKETING/International

5. **Help from Overseas: Letter of Appreciation**. Sheila Leigh lost her luggage in flight to a two-week international marketing seminar in Germany. To make matters worse, as she was leaving the airport to go to the hotel, she left her traveler's checks in the taxi. Immediately, Sheila called her German liaison contact, Anna Herpfer, who offered to handle the red tape. By the first day of the seminar, Anna had given Sheila replacement traveler's checks and had assured Sheila that the airline would deliver the luggage in two days. During the overseas stay, Anna was unfailingly courteous and polite.

Required: Write the thank-you letter to Anna Herpfer, Bahnhofstr. 9, 7000 Weinstadt 2, Germany.

EDUCATION/Public Sector

6. **A Political Stand for Education: Letter of Appreciation.** On an education reform bill, your local representative to the U.S. House of Representatives made an impressive speech to the House concerning the need for improvements in funding for public education. The representative's words were quoted on national television. The bill in question eventually died in committee, but you appreciate the representative's taking a stand on this issue.

   Required: Write a letter to your representative expressing your appreciation and encouragement. Research needed to write this letter includes (1) locating the name and address of your representative and (2) consulting a reference manual to identify the appropriate courtesy title for this public official.

CAREER DEVELOPMENT

7. **Writing a Letter of Deserved Thanks.** Donald Keller, human resources director for a local firm, was invited to talk to your class about resume writing. Trying to incorporate his suggestions, you prepared a resume and submitted it to your college's career-services division. In subsequent interviews, you have been highly commended for having prepared an outstanding resume.

   Required: Write a letter of appreciation to Mr. Keller, Southside Manufacturing, Inc., 189 South 29th Avenue, Portland, ME 04101-1897.

SMALL BUSINESS

8. **Thank-you for Business Referrals.** You own a photography studio and serve a small clientele, taking class pictures for area schools and ad pictures for small businesses. Leonard Tomlinson, a photographer who worked for you several months ago, recommended you to a couple to take pictures for their wedding. The couple, Angela and Michael Nelson, were so impressed with your work that they have recommended you enthusiastically to several other couples seeking a photographer for their weddings.

   Required: Write Leonard a letter of appreciation for his original referral. His address is 12 Main Boulevard, Dowingtown, PA 19335-8100.

CAREER DEVELOPMENT

9. **Letter of Appreciation for Assistance in Job Placement.** You graduated from college with a double major in marketing and fine arts and accepted a job with Heartbeats, a regional greeting card company. During your four-year stay, you worked closely with both the artists and the sales personnel in marketing several new lines of cards. However, an illness in your family has required you to relocate to another state. The senior manager at Heartbeats was instrumental in helping you gain a similar position with a national greeting card company.

   Required: Write the manager a letter of appreciation. Victoria Sanchez, 715 McAdams Avenue, Thomasville, NC 27360-8601. Use plain paper and provide a fictitious return address.

EDUCATION

10. **Welcome New Members.** Write a letter of welcome to be sent to new members of a business organization for which you serve as vice president of membership. Supply necessary details about an upcoming meeting or a brief description of the organization's activities for the semester.

    Required: Address the letter to Sam Wilkins, P. O. Box 1937, at your college.

PUBLIC RELATIONS

11. **Welcome to the Club: A Public Relations Tool.** As a member of Boleware and Forde Advertising in Pueblo, you and your co-workers are encouraged to join civic clubs in the community to increase the company's visibility. Your membership in the Pueblo Civic Club has enabled you to get to know many of the businesspeople coming to the city, and you are confident that these informal contacts have led to the acquisition of many of your advertising clients. Ray Schwartz, the owner of the new delicatessen on Clematis Drive, sat next to you at the meeting this week.

    Required: Write a personal letter welcoming Ray to the club and the city. Ray Schwartz, Goodtime Deli, 117 Clematis Drive, Pueblo, CO 81002-0117.

FINANCE

12. **Farewell and Thanks For** . . .   You have worked for Rhodes and Richter Brokerage Firm for seven years. When you entered the Wall Street company just out of college, your manager, Kent LaRoi, became a mentor to you, helping you adjust to the firm's corporate culture. He often gave you constructive criticism and generous "pats on the back" when they were deserved. You were especially appreciative of a powerful commendation letter he sent to your supervisor after your work led to the acquisition of a prominent client. Kent is retiring after 25 years of service to the company.

    Required: Write a farewell letter to Kent. His address is 112 Southaven Street, Brooklyn, NY 11223-0112.

HUMAN RELATIONS

13. **Apology for Missed Meeting.** You missed yesterday's meeting of the Planning Committee; your report on tax considerations for the proposed site for the construction of an apartment complex was on the agenda. Your flight from Denver was over an hour late departing because of heavy fog. Hoping for clearance to take off at any time, airline attendants would not allow you to leave the plane to telephone to explain your delay.

    Required: Write an apology to Larry Pruitt, the chair of the Planning Committee.

MANAGEMENT

14. **An Expression of Sympathy.** A friend with whom you had worked closely as a fellow officer in a community organization died in an automobile accident.

    Required: Write a letter of condolence to the friend's spouse (or closest relative).

PUBLIC RELATIONS

15. **Employee Promotion: News Release.** You are a manager in a furniture factory in Minneapolis. Your company recently began sending news releases of events within the company to the *Minneapolis Daily Dispatch*. The past three releases, concerning a sales drive, a local community service award, and a special event recently sponsored by the company were reduced to minor items in a news-brief column in the weekly "Money" section. The next article you plan to submit announces Sonja Garcia's recent promotion from production manager to vice president of product research and development.

    Required: Write a news release to send to the *Dispatch*, carefully avoiding overt attempts to "sell" the company through the release.

EDUCATION

16. **To a Professor: A Job Well Done.** The semester is almost over. One of your professors taught an outstanding course.

    Required: Write a letter to that professor's department head. Your purpose is to commend a deserving person.

MANAGEMENT

17. **Excellent Performance Commended.** Ferdenez Public Relations participates in an internship program with Mesa State University. Typically, the company accepts three students majoring in public relations, advertising, and commercial art to complete a one-semester internship. Depending on the student's major, an account executive is assigned to coordinate and to evaluate the intern's work. After the student has completed the internship, the account executive writes an evaluation letter, which serves as one criterion for assigning a grade for the internship.

    This semester you worked closely with Amanda Sorrell, a commercial art major. Her workplace demeanor was excellent; she was always eager to begin one challenging assignment after another. Unlike interns you have supervised in the past, she did not use her inexperience as an excuse for mistakes (which were few). She was eager to learn, asked intelligent questions, and had a creative sense of layout and design. Janine's, an upscale clothing store and a major account, sent a letter complimenting the firm for the newspaper advertisements it prepared for Janine's spring fashion show. Amanda was responsible for a number of the creative ideas developed in this ad campaign and completed a significant portion of the work.

Required: As the account executive supervising Amanda's internship, write a letter evaluating Amanda's performance. Send the letter to Tara Warren, Associate Professor, Communications Department, Mesa State University, P.O. Drawer CO, Flagstaff, AZ 86001-2801.

JOURNALISM/Interpersonal

18. **Blowing the Whistle: A Positive Evaluation.** As publisher of a large metropolitan daily newspaper in Kansas City, you bear final responsibility for the financial health of the publication. Recently, Wayne Ricard, one of your advertising representatives, reported (with evidence) several instances over a one-year period in which the advertising manager intentionally failed to enter advertising revenues on the computer. Because Wayne was willing to come forward with his concerns and with concrete evidence, management was able to initiate a full criminal investigation. The missing money was found invested with LRC Lenders (a recently failed savings and loan in your city) in the ad manager's name; the advertising manager was convicted of embezzlement and fraud.

Required: Write a memorandum of commendation to Wayne for his part in the investigation.

EDUCATION

19. **An Attempt to Help Others: Constructive Criticism.** Your semester will be concluding two weeks from now. One of your professors (use a fictitious name) has been exceedingly ineffective.

You want to help the department, students who may be in that professor's class later, and the professor.

Required: Write a letter to the professor's department head reporting objective, specific information about the professor's performance.

ACCOUNTING/Interpersonal

20. **Shortcomings in Professional Behavior Overshadow Strong Technical Skills: Constructive Criticism.** Impressed with Audrey Seneca's excellent scholastic record and high scores on the CPA exam, Wadsworth & Associates, a leading accounting firm, hired the new college graduate. Audrey has been working on site for one of Wadsworth's major audit clients for the past few weeks. You are the controller at Wadsworth and have made the following observations about Audrey's general appearance and demeanor. Because Audrey is very easy going, she often extends her casual attitude to her relations with clients, dressing too informally and blurring the distinctions between business and personal relationships. Audrey does faultless work; she actually takes her work quite seriously.

Required: Write a letter to the audit manager. Your intent is to alert Wadsworth of Audrey's shortcomings so that steps can be taken to help Audrey modify her actions. Address the letter to Jay McKinley, Audit Manager, Wadsworth & Associates, 609 Elliot Building, East Brunswick, NJ 08816-1834.

CASES FOR ANALYSIS

MANAGEMENT/International

Case 1.   Promoting International Understanding Rather than Reacting to Problems. Hariri Oil is an offshore drilling company that has extensive dealings with oil concerns in Mexico. One afternoon the senior partner received a disturbing call from Alberto Rodriguez, a business associate at Fuentes Oil. Rodriguez was very upset and puzzled by the behavior of Robert Smith, one of Hariri's production supervisors in Mexico City. Rodriguez had scheduled an appointment with Smith at 11:30 a.m. When Rodriguez arrived at 12:10, Smith had already gone to lunch. Very frustrated, Rodriguez returned to Smith's office at 2 p.m. (normal afternoon reopening in Mexico), but Smith didn't have time to discuss the matter and referred Rodriguez to the secretary to schedule another appointment.

Very disturbed, the partner called Robert Smith for his side of the story. Smith said, "I assumed that

Rodriguez was not planning to keep his appointment; otherwise, he would have called to explain that he had been detained but was on his way." Smith did not perceive his treatment of Rodriguez later that day as cold and unconcerned.

The partner realizes that Smith has not been in Mexico long enough to appreciate the importance Mexicans place on personal relationships and the relative casualness with which Mexicans regard time. However, because Smith's behavior has created ill will for Hariri, an apology must be written.

Required:

1. As the partner, write a letter of apology to Rodriguez. Address the letter to Alberto Rodriguez, Paseo Kulkulkan, 77500 Cancun, Q.R., Mexico.

2. As the partner, write a memorandum to the U.S. managers who have been working in Mexico less than one year. Your purpose is to highlight major differences in culture and business practices between Mexico and the United States. Send a copy to Ana Maria Silva, Director, International Assignments Division, in the home office. Conduct necessary research to prepare accurate, useful, and well-documented information. Provide a separate references page so that employees can locate your sources for additional study if needed. Refer to the references page as an attachment to the memorandum. Use in-text parenthetical citations (author, year) within the memorandum. *Keep in mind that you are attempting to solve a particular problem for a specific audience. You are not writing a general term paper on intercultural differences.*

3. Write a cover letter to accompany the copy of the memorandum being sent to Ms. Silva. Explain the negative fallout being felt because U.S. managers are not prepared for assuming assignments overseas and encourage her to initiate efforts to alleviate this difficulty for future employees. Address the letter to Anna Maria Silva, Hariri Oil, 8633 Franklin Avenue, San Bernardino, CA 92403-8633.

MANAGEMENT/Public Sector

Case 2. Gaining Support for a Plastics Recycling Plant. You are a member of the city council in Monroeville, a small town in rural Alabama. The mayor has asked you to chair a task force to evaluate the feasibility of building a plastics recycling plant in the city. Carpet yarn, fiberfill for parkas, floor tiles,

wastebaskets, and "plastic lumber" for park furniture and decks are just a few of the materials that can be produced by recycling plastic containers and other plastic items. After completing extensive research including a tour of an existing plant and a meeting with the city's officials, you wholeheartedly support the plant in Monroeville. To determine the community's feelings, you have talked with a number of community leaders as well as individuals selected at random. For the most part, people are uninformed about the significant benefits gained from recycling, some are apathetic to the need to preserve our environment, and a few prominent business leaders are adamantly opposed to building the recycling plant. Write the following letters as chair of the Environmental Preservation Task Force:

Required:

1. Write a letter to the mayor recommending that the plastics recycling plant be built in Monroeville. Support your decision with justifiable reasons. Your letter should contain the pros and cons of the decision. Address the letter to Lee M. Penkoff, Mayor's Office, City Hall, Monroeville, AL 36460-9648. Be sure to include an appropriate salutation for this public official.

2. Assume that the mayor has approved the construction of the recycling plant and has begun accepting bids from construction companies. Because of your intense interest and expertise in environmental concerns, the mayor has asked you to launch a public awareness campaign. Your purpose is not only to gain support for the plastics recycling plant but also to educate the public about the benefits of recycling. Complete *one* of the following activities:

   a. Write a letter to the community leaders of Monroeville soliciting their support of the plastics recycling plant. Although this message is similar to the letter sent to the mayor, consider changes in the information included and the emphasis appropriate for this particular audience. Attempt to anticipate the public's reactions to the message. Include in the letter address: Community Leaders of Monroeville, Monroeville, AL 36460-6732. Use an appropriate salutation for a letter addressed to a group, or use the simplified block format.

   b. Write a news release announcing the opening of the recycling plant and outlining the benefits it will bring to the community. Address it to the editor of *The Clarion*, P.O. Box 189-BC, Monroeville, AL 36460-6330. Because you do not know the editor's name, use the simplified block format.

c. Develop a brochure to be included in the letter to community leaders (Step 2a) and distributed by other means throughout the community. The brochure will focus on the benefits to be gained from recycling, particularly the many available uses of recycled plastics. If desktop publishing capabilities are available, design a creative, appealing layout for the brochure.

ACCOUNTING/Ethics   GMAT

Case 3.   Is Overlooking a Vendor's Error to Your Advantage Ethical? Douglas is responsible for checking the accuracy of invoices received from suppliers for purchases of inventory. A supplier recently shipped the company $5,000 worth of merchandise but neglected to include the merchandise on the invoice. Immediately, Douglas requested a revised invoice from the supplier. Learning of this request, Douglas's supervisor severely reprimanded him for not overlooking the vendor's error, thus costing the company $5,000.

Functioning as plant manager, you hear nothing of this conversation from Douglas or his supervisor. However, several comments filtering through the grapevine convince you that you must take appropriate action.

Required:

1. Decide whether it is ethical to overlook the erroneous billing. Consider these points:
   a. What are the relevant facts?
   b. What are the ethical issues raised by the decision whether to mention the erroneous billing?
   c. Who (which stakeholders) will be affected by this decision?
   d. What are the costs and benefits imposed by each alternative on each person listed in Step c?
   e. What are the company's obligations to each person listed in Step c?
   f. What should you as the company's representative do?

2. Based on your decision, complete *one* of the following activities:
   a. Write a memorandum (or e-mail message if your instructor requires) to Douglas commending him for his ethical behavior. State that this document will be placed in his personnel file for use in future performance appraisals.
   b. You feel it is ethical to overlook the vendor's mistake. Write a persuasive memorandum to Douglas explaining that overlooking similar errors in the future would be in his "best interest."
   c. Do any other options exist? If so, write a letter or memorandum to the appropriate individual.

3. Write a memorandum to Douglas' supervisor, Scott Lindsay, explaining the action that you took regarding Douglas' behavior. The action taken in Step 2 will affect the content and set the tone for this memo.

PART 5

COMMUNICATING ABOUT

WORK AND JOBS

CHAPTER 13

PREPARING RESUMES AND

APPLICATION LETTERS

OBJECTIVES
When you have completed Chapter 13, you will be able to

1 Complete systematic self-, career, and job analyses.

2 Prepare an effective chronological, functional, or combination chronological and functional resume.

3 Locate information about employers' needs for workers.

4 Write an application letter that effectively introduces an accompanying resume.

José will soon graduate from a major university with a bachelor's degree in management. He is concerned about job opportunities, and with good reason. Currently, jobs are in a buyer's market—employers daily sift through thousands of resumes, a large number from experienced workers who are looking for jobs due to corporate downsizing (Clegg, 1994). In addition, José will be competing with other recent graduates for entry-level positions, which have become scarce. A recent survey by Workplace America revealed that executive recruiters received a record 1.6 million resumes in the past year, although they had only 11,900 positions open (Salwen, 1994). José knows that the competition is fierce, but he also knows he is intelligent, hard-working, and has good communication skills. In fact, his writing skills may be the deciding factor in whether he will get a job or be just another applicant.

José is now taking the first concrete step toward securing employment: writing his resume. Throughout his college years, he has had the foresight to enlist in activities and programs that will be to his future advantage, such as internships in his field, summer jobs relating to his career, and extracurricular activities like sports and social organizations that illustrate his well-integrated talents and interests. He has also achieved a respectable GPA. After he drafts a resume accentuating his strengths and abilities, he spends a little extra time on its physical appearance: He varies bold and regular type, uses headings that are eye-catching and easy to read, and prints the resume on high-quality paper in a tasteful color. Finally, before he sends it anywhere, he proofreads it carefully several times. He knows that even a keying error may characterize him as sloppy or indicate to a potential employer he does not have adequate written communication skills. José plans to send his resume to several different companies. Although he knows he may not get an interview, at least he knows he is in the competition, and his resume won't work against him.

Your resume and accompanying application letter may be the most important documents you will write at this time in your life. A good resume can mean employment, success, and, with those things, happiness and a sense of self-worth. However, a mediocre or flawed resume and application letter are only a waste of your time, the prospective employer's time, and good paper.

Before you write your resume, take some time to know yourself and your goals, strengths, and weaknesses. Then study the many different formats in this chapter before deciding on one. Finally, never underestimate the importance of good grammar and accurate spelling and punctuation. Proofread carefully several times. Remember, your resume is what represents you to employers.

SETTING GOALS AND PLANNING

For many years, a financial counselor conducted seminars for people who had very high economic aspirations. He asked participants to ponder the question, "How rich do I want to be?" He asked each person to write that figure on a small card, place it in his or her wallet, and look at it each night and morning. Two things were vital to his success: He set a goal, and he developed a plan for reaching it. The daily reminders of the goal increased the likelihood of attaining it.

LEARNING OBJECTIVE 1

Have you set *your* career goals? Do you have a plan for reaching them?

Goal setting does for individuals what management by objectives does for businesses. Setting goals forces people to consider these questions: What is to be accomplished? How is it best accomplished? How is progress measured? Are decisions congruent with goals? Important as such questions are, they sometimes do not get the attention they deserve. Many college seniors have confided to advisers, "I'm scared. About all I've ever done is go to school. Now I'll have to earn a living. How do I find a suitable job?"

Life's happiness is directly related to life's work.

Because the answer to that question can mean the difference between a pleasant life and an unpleasant one, it deserves careful attention. A suitable job provides satisfaction at all of Maslow's needs levels, from basic economic to self-actualizing needs. During your working lifetime, you will spend about one-third of your nonsleeping time on the job (and probably much additional time thinking about your work). The right job for you will not be drudgery; the work itself will be satisfying. It will give you a sense of well-being; you can see its positive impact on others. The satisfaction derived from work has a positive influence on enjoyment of nonworking hours.

Research and analyze before choosing a career.

Students often devote too little time and thought to career decisions, or they unnecessarily postpone making career decisions. Of the many courses required to achieve your degree, how much time is devoted to one course? (Think of the daily reading assignments, doing research, preparing for tests, writing a term paper, and so on.) Are you willing to spend that much time gathering, recording, and analyzing information that will lead to a satisfying career? Would you be willing to start putting together a notebook of information that would guide you to the best career?

Just as finding the right career is important for you, finding the right employees is important for the employer. Before they can offer you a job, employers need information about you—in writing. Your **resume** is the written document that provides a basis for judgment about your capabilities on the job. In preparing this vital document, your major concerns should be (1) gathering essential information, (2) planning the resume, and (3) constructing the resume.

GETTING ESSENTIAL INFORMATION

Why make a *written* record of career information? Recall from the discussion of sales letters that knowing the product, service, or idea is a prerequisite to writing. Likewise, knowing yourself is a prerequisite for preparing a resume. Although reading and thinking are beneficial, they are not enough. Career-related information should be written in a personal career notebook. Just as an accountant uses a spreadsheet when preparing a profit-and-loss statement and a balance sheet, job seekers can use a career notebook in preparing a resume. Keeping such a notebook (1) encourages the gathering of pertinent information, (2) makes review and summary easy, and (3) assists in analysis. Putting thoughts on paper helps in clarifying, remembering, and analyzing information.

Self-Analysis

Preparing a thorough, neat notebook will help you write a winning resume and interview effectively.

To be able to sell yourself in a resume, you must first identify your qualifications, focusing primarily on your capabilities that meet the employer's needs. Answering the questions in Figure 13-1 is a good way to begin your self-analysis. Write the questions (double- or triple-spaced) in your career notebook or key them into a computer file.

CAREER NOTEBOOK

Self-Analysis Questions

The kind of person I am

1. Do I have a high level of aspiration?
2. Do I communicate well?
3. Am I dependable?
4. Am I energetic?
5. Am I free of personal habits that would interfere with my work?
6. Am I financially independent?
7. Am I a leader?
8. Am I people oriented (or would I like to work alone)?
9. Am I self-confident (without being egotistical)?
10. Do I spend time wisely?

My aptitudes (results of psychological tests)

1. Do I have a high quantitative aptitude?
2. Do I have a high verbal aptitude (written and oral)?
3. Do I have a high aptitude for learning foreign languages?
4. Do I have a high mechanical aptitude?
5. Do I have a high aptitude for problem solving?

My achievements

1. What is my overall grade-point average?
2. What is the grade-point average in my major?
3. In which courses have I excelled?
4. Which courses have been most difficult?
5. Have I done well in problem-solving courses?

6. What have been my achievements in extracurricular activities, in jobs I have held, or in volunteer work?

My interests

1. What are my favorite academic interests (the courses I liked best, not necessarily the ones in which I made the best grade)?
2. Which professional magazines or journals are most appealing?
3. What type of books or magazines do I read for pleasure?
4. To which campus and off-campus organizations do I belong?
5. How do I prefer to spend leisure time?
6. Do I like to travel?

My education

1. What is my declared major in college, and when do I expect to graduate?
2. What special training have I received—cooperative education, internships, related workshops, and seminars?
3. What special skills do I possess—foreign languages, computer competency?

My experience

1. What summertime jobs have I held?
2. What part-time jobs have I held?
3. What full-time jobs have I held?

FIGURE 13-1   Self-analysis questions.

THINK IT OVER
Check your library or college bookstore for other sources of career information.

After preparing these questions (and others you may want to add) for your notebook, write your answer below each question. Thoughtful answers to such questions will almost certainly point out some strengths (about which you can feel good) and some weaknesses (which you can begin to correct). The thinking required to answer the questions is excellent preparation for writing a resume. Having written thoughtful answers to these questions, you will have a good chance of providing ready answers for questions asked during an employment interview.

Career Analysis

THINK IT OVER
Prepare the self-analysis section
of your career notebook, using
Figure 13-1 as a guide.

The same technique—asking and answering questions—is helpful in career analysis. Try to answer the questions in Figure 13-2.

To locate answers to the career-analysis questions, refer to the following sources. These and other books are available in school or community libraries and in many college and university career service centers.

* Bolles, R. N. (1990). *What color is your parachute? A practical manual for job hunters and career changers.* Berkeley, CA: Ten Speed Press.
* *Career opportunities.* Chicago, IL: J.G. Ferguson (published monthly).
* Bureau of Employment Security, U.S. Department of Labor. (1991). *Dictionary of occupational titles.* Washington, DC: U.S. Government Printing Office.

*FIGURE 13-2
Career-analysis questions.*

CAREER NOTEBOOK

Career-Analysis Questions

Type of career (such as accounting, finance, distribution, sales, etc.)
1. Which aptitudes (quantitative, verbal, mechanical) would be most beneficial?
2. Is the occupation considered a "pressure" occupation?
3. Do significant health hazards exist?
4. Is relocation or frequent travel expected?
5. Is the field crowded, or is it short of workers?

Preparation
1. What are the academic requirements (degree, major)?
2. What are the professional requirements (certificates)?
3. Are continuing education or training programs expected and available?
4. What experiences are considered prerequisite?

Rewards
1. What is the standard salary of beginning workers?
2. Do significant opportunities for advancement in salary and responsibility exist?
3. What are the fringe benefits?
4. What are the intangible rewards?

Future of the field
1. Is the field expected to expand or contract?
2. Will the field be strongly influenced by changes in technology?
3. Is competition in the field increasing?
4. Will changes in political administrations or governmental regulation have a significant impact on the field?

- Bureau of Labor Statistics, U.S. Department of Labor. *Occupational outlook handbook.* Washington, DC: U.S. Government Printing Office (published yearly).
- Powell, C.R. (1990). *Career planning today.* (2nd ed.). Dubuque, IA: Kendall-Hunt.

After writing answers to the career-oriented questions in your notebook, you almost certainly will have either an increased enthusiasm for your chosen career or a feeling that you should consider other careers. Either way, the effort has been worthwhile. Once you have selected the right field for your career, you can begin to examine a specific job in that field.

Job Analysis

Most college graduates with little or no experience expect to take what is commonly known as an *entry-level position.* Many businesses provide training or orientation programs for newly hired employees. Before preparing a resume, students need to ask and answer the questions in Figure 13-3.

THINK IT OVER
Get into groups with others majoring in your field and brainstorm about the answers to the specific questions in Figures 13-2 and 13-3. Conduct necessary research to complete the career and job analyses on your own.

FIGURE 13-3
Job-analysis questions.

CAREER NOTEBOOK

Job-Analysis Questions

1. What are the specific duties and responsibilities? (Good sources: the firm's personnel office, local public and private employment offices, the college or university's career services office, and the *Dictionary of Occupational Titles.*)

2. Do my personal characteristics seem compatible with the specified duties and responsibilities? Aptitudes? Interests? Others—dependability, leadership, aspirations, desire to work alone or with others, size of company, fast-paced vs. conservative environment, dress code, interest in product/service firm offers, willingness to relocate or travel (specify where—country overseas, size of city)?

3. Does my education satisfy requirements for the position (degrees earned or in progress, cooperative education, internships, special training programs, directly related courses)? Would I be willing to continue my education?

4. Are my experiences directly related to the job's specified duties and responsibilities? (List related summer jobs, part-time jobs, or full-time jobs. If experience is scant, what aspects of the academic program, school-related activities, volunteer work, or other jobs are related to the job in which you are interested?)

Interview with a Career Person

THINK IT OVER
Interview a career person in
your field, using the questions
in Figure 13-4 as a guide.

Before making the decision to embark on a certain career, you can profit greatly from interviewing someone who is already pursuing it. The interview is to your advantage, regardless of whether it increases your enthusiasm or reveals that the career is definitely not for you. For maximum benefit, prepare a set of questions such as those listed in Figure 13-4.

Company/Job Profile

Prepare a company/job
profile for the company/
job in which you expect to
be interviewing.

Completing the self-, career, and job analyses has allowed you to collect a great deal of information. The next step is to compile this information in a format that will allow you to compare your qualifications with the company and job requirements—to determine whether a match between you and the potential job is possible. Insert another page in your career notebook for this comparison of the company and job requirements with your qualifications and needs.

A company/job profile for an entry-level audit accountant in an international public accounting firm is shown in Figure 13-5. After completing the two columns, an individual can easily identify the exact areas in which company/job requirements and qualifications and needs do not match. Basic qualifications and salary and advancement expectations seem very compatible; the major differences are in work surroundings, amount of travel and overtime, and communication (oral and interpersonal) skills. By identifying the relative importance of these areas, the individual can decide whether pursuing a job in an international public accounting firm would be wise. Would he/she be willing to seek assistance in refining communication skills? Would he/she be willing to learn to work effectively in groups? How important are limited overtime and fewer travel requirements? Could he/she adapt to working in temporary locations without a desk of his/her own?

FIGURE 13-4
Job-analysis questions: Interview
with a career person.

CAREER NOTEBOOK

Job Analysis—Interview with a Career Person

1. When did you become interested in this field?

2. What do you see as an ideal preparation for entry?

3. What was your first job in this field?

4. Do reasonable opportunities for advancement exist?

5. Does the field have potential for growth?

6. What tasks do you perform on a typical day?

7. What do you like best about your career?

8. What do you dislike?

9. What is your advice to someone who is considering entry into this field?

CAREER NOTEBOOK

Comparison of Job Requirements with Qualifications: International Accounting Firm—Entry-Level Audit Staff

	Company/Job Requirements	My Qualifications and Needs
Education:	Bachelor's degree in accountancy with 3.5 or higher GPA.	Will receive B.S. degree with 3.8 GPA.
Certification:	CPA preferred; expected within three years.	Committed to earning CPA within two years.
General knowledge:	Broad understanding of all business areas (marketing, finance, management, information systems, etc.); history; world cultures; economic, political, and social systems; and ethical theories.	Undergraduate curriculum provided courses in each area.
Intellectual skills:	Highly analytical; ability to solve diverse and unstructured problems for many unfamiliar settings (represent clients in various businesses); meticulous attention to detail.	Excelled in quantitative courses; performed well in preparing cases requiring creative solutions to problems without clear-cut answers.
Computer skills:	Proficiency in spreadsheet, word processing, and disk operating system; knowledgeable of general ledger and data management programs.	Proficient in the operation of *Windows, Quattro Pro, Word Perfect for Windows* and familiar with leading general ledger programs and *Paradox.*
Communication:	Secure and transfer information easily; present and defend views formally and informally in writing or orally.	Proficient in written communication; attempting to overcome fear of speaking before groups; often reluctant to defend ideas if I encounter resistance.
Interpersonal skills:	Work efficiently in groups of diverse members to accomplish a task (e.g., with other members of the audit staff assigned to each audit and with the client); must withstand and resolve conflict (with peers and clients).	Prefer working independently; have had poor experiences completing class group projects.
Management skills:	Organize and delegate tasks; motivate and develop other people.	Part-time work and leadership roles in student groups provided opportunities to refine these management skills.
Work enviornment:	Work primarily on location at the client's office with temporary work sites (conference table, work room); may share a desk with other staff when days spent in the office rotate.	Must feel in control of my own work space; a desk organized for my sole use is important.

FIGURE 13-5   Comparison of company and job requirements with qualifications.

Psychometric profile:	Can work on numerous audits simultaneously, to shift gears from one project to another readily, to organize work to meet tight and often coinciding deadlines, and to meet any unexpected requirements; willing to revise work until it meets the high standards set by an international accounting firm.	Prefer to complete one project before moving to another; difficult to manage more than one major activity at once; often take criticism personally.
Ethical standards:	Must abide by the AICPA Code of Professional Conduct.	High moral standards as result of family background; willing to abide by code of ethics that upholds the high standards of the profession.
Salary range:	$30,000-$35,000 annually.	$28,000-$34,000 annually.
Travel:	Approximately 25%.	No more than 10%.
Overtime:	Average 15 hours per month; peaks between February 1 and April 1.	Limited overtime desired.
Career path:	Well-defined path; typically promoted from staff accountant to audit senior after 3 years; from audit senior to manager after 6 years; eligible for partner after 10 years.	Well-defined career path with frequent changes in responsibilities.
Prestige level:	High.	Medium to high prestige desired.

FIGURE 13-5, continued   *Comparison of company and job requirements with qualifications.*

Did you know that most entry-level employees are seeking a second job within six months?

You will probably never find the job and the organization that will satisfy *all* your needs and meet *all* your requirements. Some factors will be more important to you than others. The benefits gained from this analysis will far outweigh the time and energy spent in gathering valid information about a company and job requirements and in evaluating your qualifications and needs. This analysis may prevent you from becoming one of the increasing number of entry-level workers who are looking for another job after only six months because their qualifications and needs were not compatible with the company and job requirements.

What purpose does a resume serve?

With your self-, career-, and job analyses recorded in your career notebook, you can quickly review information as necessary. Use the notebook for other job-related information, too. Add pertinent questions and answers to the lists you have made; occasionally review and update your lists. Reserve some pages for clippings of career- and job-related information. Record addresses and telephone numbers of firms for which you would consider working, employers and supervisors for whom you have worked (along with specific dates on which employment began and ended), and references. Include a copy of a transcript or a list of courses taken. Record notes taken during interviews.

Recording answers in your career notebook should have helped you (1) identify your qualifications as they relate to an employer's needs, (2) ensure that you have selected the right career, and (3) compare your qualifications with the duties and responsibilities of the job you are seeking. Because you have a record of this analysis in your career notebook, you can easily review this information to identify the information that should be included on your resume.

PLANNING YOUR RESUME

A job announcement that appeared in several midwestern newspapers described a career opportunity for someone with two years' sales experience to sell medical equipment to hospitals. John W. applied. He was well qualified and had sold medical equipment before. He knew the territory, was willing to relocate, and had a proven track record of successful selling—but he was not invited to an interview. The same was true of Mary M., Bill T., and countless others. Of the nearly 200 people who applied for the position, fewer than a dozen were selected for interviews. This true story, told by Barnum (1987) in "Writing Resumes That Sell," occurs every day. Without a resume that sells your qualifications in terms of the employer's needs, you will never have an opportunity to sell yourself at an interview.

Because an employer typically spends two minutes or less reading a resume (Holley, Higgins, & Speights, 1988), you have very little time to explain why you are the best person for the job. You must selectively choose *what* to say, *how to say* it, and *how to arrange* it on the page so that it can be read quickly but thoroughly. A concise, informative, easy-to-read summary of your relevant qualifications will not only get you an interview but also will tell the employer that you possess the straightforward communication skills demanded in today's information-intensive society.

The standard information found in a winning resume includes

- Identification.
- Objective—job (or type of work) being sought.
- Summary of achievements (optional).
- Qualifications (primarily your education and experience).
- Personal information (included only if it is related to the job duties and/or strengthens the resume).
- References (often just a statement that references are available; however, references can be listed under certain circumstances).

Examples of resumes are provided in this chapter (Figures 13-8 to 13-12) to illustrate these standard resume parts and various resume formats. No *one* universal resume works effectively in today's job market. The format, content, and style of your resume depend on your specific qualifications, the job field (conservative or creative), and the individual personality you wish to portray. In fact, you will likely develop different resumes for slightly different job objectives. The information you include on each resume will be based on your assessment of whether the receiver will want or need the information, your personal preference, and moral judgment.

The goal of the resume is to get an interview, so ask yourself this question: "Does including this information increase my chances of getting an interview?" If the answer is "yes," include the information; if the answer is "no," omit the information and use the space to develop your qualifications.

When selecting information to be included, honestly ask yourself, "Does this information present my qualifications honestly and ethically, or does it inflate my qualifications to increase my chances of getting the job?" If you have the

LEARNING OBJECTIVE 2

How will preparing a career notebook facilitate your job search?

How much time do you need to explain why you should be hired?

What *three* decisions must you make when planning and writing a winning resume?

What information is included in an effective resume?

THINK IT OVER
What is your reaction to "I'll just use the format and style my friend used on her resume; she got a job with it"?

What is the goal of a resume? What information should you include in a resume?

Murphy's Law No. 2

The *one* little exaggeration on your resumé is the one they check!

C86-4 The Drawing Board™ Box 660429 Dallas, Texas © Wheeler Group, Inc., 1985

slightest inclination that including a piece of information will inflate your quali-fications, omit it. This action allows you to uphold high ethical values.

What are the consequences of providing false informa-tion on a resume?

What are the consequences of inflating your qualifications? First, the inter-viewer may uncover your "exaggeration" when verifying the information on a resume and can legally terminate your employment. Interviewers can tell numerous stories of applicants who claimed to have received degrees from schools they never attended, worked for nonexistent companies, or worked for compa-nies that have no knowledge of the applicant. Second, if your employer becomes aware that you secured a job in an unethical manner, you probably will lose your employer's trust. This lack of trust may prevent you from advancing in the company. Third, if you are hired based on false qualifications, you may find yourself unable to perform the duties of a job for which you are not qualified.

Identification

Be certain the interviewer can reach you by mail or telephone during regular office hours.

Your objective is to provide information that will allow the interviewer to reach you. Include your name, current address, and telephone number. To ensure that the interviewer can quickly locate this information, center it on the page. Most word-processing programs and printers allow you to increase the size of this and other information for added emphasis.

Answering machine greet-ings should be courteous, clear, and professional. Avoid music, jokes, and clever remarks.

You may also include a permanent address (parents' address) if you are interviewing when classes are not in session. If you are rarely at home during typical office hours (the time the interviewer is likely to call), provide a tele-phone number where messages can be left. Explain to those taking messages that prospective employers may be calling; therefore, their accuracy in taking messages and the impression they make while taking the message could affect your job search. Evaluate the personal message on your answering machine to be certain that it portrays you as a person serious about securing a job.

Olympic athletes know that a split second or a fraction of an inch often determines who wins. Today's job market is almost that competitive. Even a minor error can mean the difference between employment and joblessness.

Job and/or Career Objective

Following the "Identification" section, state your job/career objective—the job you want. Interviewers can see immediately whether the job you are seeking matches the one they have to offer. Therefore, a good job/career objective must be specific enough to be meaningful yet general enough to apply to a variety of jobs. The following example illustrates a general objective that has been revised to describe a specific job:

What are the characteristics of a good job objective?

THINK IT OVER
Write a career/job objective for a position you wish to pursue; e.g., full- or part-time job, or an internship. Is the objective it specific enough to be meaningful?

General Objective	Specific Objective
A position that offers both a challenge and a good opportunity for growth.	To secure an entry-level position in sales, leading to sales management.
A responsible position with a progressive organization that provides the opportunity for managerial development and growth commensurate with ability and attitudes.	To enter the management training program of a progressive firm that provides opportunities for advancement.

Some experts argue that a statement of your job or career objective may limit your job opportunities. Your objective should be obvious from your qualifications, they say. In general, however, making your objective clear at the beginning assures the interviewer that you have a definite career goal.

Summary of Achievements

In the "Summary of Achievements" section, summarize your major qualifications. By reading the career objective and a summary statement about your achievements, interviewers know *what* you want (whether your interests match theirs) and *why* the employer would want to hire you. A recent survey revealed

What purpose does a summary statement serve?

Including a summary
statement can set your
resume apart from com-
petitors who do not real-
ize that employers would
like to see this section.

that hiring officials consider summary statements an important item to include on a resume; yet few job applicants include summary statements (Griffin and Anderson, 1994).

To be certain that you highlight qualifications, write the "Summary of Achievements" section after you have written the entire resume. Barnum's (1987) three methods for summarizing qualifications are illustrated in the following examples:

Separate Objective and Qualifications

OBJECTIVE: To secure an entry-level position in international sales, leading to sales management.

SUMMARY OF ACHIEVEMENTS: Bachelor of Science in Marketing including three semesters of cooperative education experience with a large retail store and three international business courses (one completed abroad); proficiency in Spanish and French; effective team worker and communicator.

Combine Objective with Qualifications in One Section

OBJECTIVE: To secure a position in sales, leading to sales management. International sales/marketing executive with three years' successful experience in sales, marketing, advertising, and contract negotiation with international suppliers.

Link Objective and Summary in One Section

OBJECTIVE: Position as a sales representative where demonstrated commission selling and hard work bring rewards.

Accomplishments:
- Three years' straight-commission sales.
- Average of $35,000-$55,000 a year in commissioned earnings.
- Consistent success in development and growth of territories.

Information in the resume
must support the sum-
mary statement presented
in the opening section.

The "Summary of Achievements" section is optional. Some experts argue that this section is not beneficial unless your background is unusually varied. If you include a summary statement, be certain that the remainder of the resume supports the statement; otherwise, you may be eliminated from consideration ("Write a Resume that Works," 1990).

Qualifications

Information gained from
self-, career, and job
analyses will aid you in
dividing this section into
appropriate divisions.

The "Qualifications" section varies depending on the information identified in the self-, career, and job analyses. This information is used to divide the qualifications into appropriate parts, choose appropriate labels for them, and arrange them in the best sequence. Usually, qualifications stem from your education and work experience (words that appear as headings in some resumes). Arrange these categories depending on which you perceive as more impressive to the employer, with the more impressive category appearing first. For example, education is usually the chief qualification of a recent college graduate; therefore, education appears first. However, a sales representative with related work experience might list experience first, particularly if the educational background is inadequate for the job sought.

EDUCATION

Beginning with the most recent, list the degree, major, school, and graduation date. Include a blank line between schools so that the employer can see them at a glance. Using empathy for the interviewer's needs, determine the order for this information and follow that order consistently for each school attended. For example, the interviewer would probably want to know first whether you have the appropriate degree, then the institution, and so on. Recent or near college graduates should omit high school activities because that information is "old news." However, include high school activities if they provide a pertinent dimension to your qualifications. For example, having attended high school abroad is a definite advantage to an applicant seeking employment in an international firm. In addition, high school accomplishments may be relevant for freshmen or sophomores seeking cooperative education assignments, scholarships, or part-time jobs. Of course, this information will be replaced with college activities when the resume is revised for subsequent jobs or other uses.

Include overall and major grade-point averages if they are B or better—but be prepared to discuss any omissions during an interview. Honors and achievements that relate directly to education can be incorporated in this section or included in a separate section. Examples include scholarships, appearance on academic lists, and initiation into honor societies. If honors and achievements are included in the "Education" section, be sure to include plenty of white space or to use bullets to highlight these points (see Figures 13-8 and 13-10).

The "Education" section could also include a list of equipment operated and special skills and abilities such as foreign language and computer competency. A list of courses typically required in your field is unnecessary and occupies valuable space. However, you should include any courses, workshops, or educational experiences that are not usual requirements. Examples include internships, cooperative education semesters, "shadowing," "over-the-shoulder" experiences, and study abroad.

Should you include information about high school? Explain.

Include GPA only if it strengthens your qualifications.

THINK IT OVER
Jot on paper any educational experiences you have had other than degrees earned.

WORK EXPERIENCE

The "Work Experience" section provides information about your employment history. For each job held, list the job title, company name, dates of employment, primary responsibilities, and key accomplishments. The jobs may be listed in reverse chronological order (beginning with the most recent) or in order of job relatedness. Begin with the job that most obviously relates to the job being sought if you have gaps in your work history, if the job you are seeking is very different from the job you currently hold, or if you are just entering the job market and have little if any related work experience.

Arrange the order and format of information about each job (dates, job title, company, description, and accomplishments) so that the most important information is emphasized—but be sure all job information is formatted consistently. An applicant who has held numerous jobs in a short time should "bury" dates of employment within the text rather than surround them with white space. If the job relates directly to the job being sought, you might give the job title prominence by listing it first or surrounding it with white space.

Omit *obvious* job duties. The job title provides basic information about what you did. By stressing what you accomplished on the job, you will set

When should you list jobs with the most job-related experience first?

THINK IT OVER
Review Chapter 7 ("Emphasize Important Ideas") and generate a list of other techniques that you could use to control the emphasis of ideas on a resume.

Accomplishments neatly
bulleted so interviewers
can readily locate them
"glitter like diamonds."

What is the advantage of
using subject-understood
sentences and action verbs
as first words?

THINK IT OVER

Describe the value you gained
from one job experience that
can be transferred to the job
being sought. Use action verbs
and an understood subject.
Compare your example with
Figure 13-6.

yourself apart from other applicants who simply list a job description; and you
will provide deeper insight into your ambition, capability, and personality. Recall instances when your personal involvement played a key role in the success
of a project. Perhaps you uncovered a wasteful, labor-intensive procedure that
was resolved through your innovation, or you bridged a gap in a communication breakdown. These instances neatly bulleted (see Figure 13-10) under the
company name and job title "glitter like diamonds" (Charles, 1988).

Because interviewers spend such a short time reading resumes, the style
must be direct and simple. Therefore, a resume should use crisp phrases to help
employers see the value of the applicant's education and experiences. To save
space and to emphasize what you have accomplished, use these stylistic techniques: omit pronouns referring to yourself (*I, me, my*), use subject-understood
sentences, begin sentences with action verbs, and select adjectives carefully, as
shown in Figure 13-6.

Instead of	Use
I had responsibility for development of new territory.	Developed new territory.
My duties included designing computer systems and writing user documentation manuals.	Developed computer programs to monitor accounting systems including carefully written documentation manuals that enabled users to operate these sophisticated systems effectively.
I was the store manager and supervised eight employees.	Managed operations of store with sales volume of $1,000,000 and supervised eight employees.
My sales consistently exceeded sales quota.	Earned average of $35,000-$55,000 a year in commissioned earnings. Received service award for exceeding sales quota two of three years employed.
I was a member of the Student Council, Society for the Advancement of Management, Phi Kappa Phi, and Chi Omega Social Sorority.	Developed effective interpersonal skills through involvement in student organizations such as the Student Council . . .

FIGURE 13-6   Use an action verb in a subject-understood sentence.

Because employers are looking for people who will *work*, action verbs are
especially appropriate. In the subject-understood sentences in the right column
of Figure 13-6, using action words as first words provides emphasis. The following list contains action verbs that are useful in resumes:

accomplished	computed	expanded	organized	scheduled
achieved	controlled	implemented	planned	sold
administered	counseled	increased	prepared	studied
analyzed	created	initiated	presented	supported
assisted	developed	invented	proposed	wrote
compiled	drafted	maintained	recruited	
completed	established	managed	researched	

To give the employer a vivid picture of you as a productive employee, you may find some of the following adjectives helpful as you describe your work experience:

adaptable	consistent	forceful	productive	sincere
analytical	dependable	independent	reliable	systematic
conscientious	efficient	objective	resourceful	tactful

To avoid a tone of egotism, do not use too many adjectives or adverbs that seem overly strong. Plan to do some careful editing after writing your first draft.

HONORS AND ACTIVITIES

Make a trial list of any other information that qualifies you for the job. Divide the list into appropriate divisions and then select an appropriate label. Your heading might be "Honors and Activities" unless you listed honors and achievements in the "Education" section. You might include a section for "Activities," "Leadership Activities," or "Memberships" depending on the items listed. You might also include a separate section on "Military Service," "Civic Activities," "Volunteer Work," or "Interests." If you have only a few items under each category, use a more general term and combine the lists. If your list is lengthy, divide it into more than one category; interviewers prefer "bite-size" pieces because they are easier to read and can be remembered more readily.

Resist the urge to include everything you have ever done; keep in mind that every item you add distracts from other information. Consider summarizing information that is relevant but does not merit several separate lines; for example, "Involved in art, drama, and choral groups." To decide whether to include certain information, ask these questions: How closely related is it to the job being sought? Does it provide job-related information that has not been presented elsewhere?

THINK IT OVER
The title of this section varies depending on the items listed within the section. What sections will you include on your resume?

Ask yourself: Does the information relate to the job being sought?

Personal Information

Because a resume should contain primarily information that is relevant to an applicant's experience and qualifications, personal information (not related to the job) must be carefully selected. The space could be used more effectively to include more about your qualifications or to add more white space. Personal information is commonly placed at the end of a resume just above the "References" section because it is less important than qualifications (education and experience).

Under the 1964 Civil Rights Act and Americans with Disabilities Act (ADA) (and subsequent amendments), employers cannot make hiring decisions based on gender, religion, age, marital status, disability, or national origin. Employers prefer that this information be omitted from a resume because questions could be raised about whether the information had been used in the hiring decision. Employers prefer that a photograph not accompany a resume because a photograph provides information about gender, age, and national origin.

Such personal information as height, weight, and color of hair and eyes is not normally worthy of inclusion. Reveal ethnic background or disability only if doing so is to your advantage. For example, certain businesses may be actively seeking employees in certain ethnic groups; that is, the ethnic background is a legitimate part of the job description. For such a business, ethnic information is useful and appreciated.

Instead of including unrelated personal information, develop your qualifications or leave more white space to increase appeal and readability.

What types of personal information must you omit?

Would you reveal that you do not smoke or are affiliated with a particular religious or civic group?

If personal information (other than the information covered by employment legislation) strengthens the resume, you may include it. Major categories include interests, hobbies, avocations, and willingness to relocate. For example, an applicant for a religious or political organization may benefit from revealing affiliation with such an organization. For the person who really wants a smoke-free work environment, "nonsmoker" on the resume may restrict the number of interviews with employers who condone smoking and increase the number of interviews with employers who do not.

THINK IT OVER
What criteria will help you select the personal information to be included on a resume? List the items you will include on your resume.

In making a decision about whether to include certain personal information, consider these three criteria: (1) How closely is it related to the job being sought? (2) Does it portray me as a well-rounded, happy individual off the job? (3) Is it controversial?

If not included under some other heading in the resume, the following items are possibilities for inclusion under the "Personal Information" heading: oral and written communication skills, computer competency, foreign- or computer-language skills, military service, community service, scholastic honors, job-related hobbies, and professional association memberships. Favorite sports may be included, but be cautious. To an employer who plays golf regularly, your enthusiasm for it may be a plus. To one who does not, it could be a small but eliminating factor. Listing a sport that is stereotyped as dangerous or overly time consuming is risky.

References

A list of references (people who have agreed to supply information about you when requested) may be included. Listing names, addresses, and telephone numbers of people who can provide information about you adds credibility to the resume. Employers, former employers, teachers, and former teachers are good possibilities. Friends, relatives, and neighbors are not (because of their bias in your favor).

THINK IT OVER
If you have not done so already, visit your career services center and learn about the services they provide.

In some businesses, interviews often are conducted *before* references are contacted. Therefore, instead of supplying a list of references on the resume, an applicant can include the statement, "References will be supplied on request."

Applicants may also include a statement such as "For references . . . " or "For additional information . . . " and give the address of the career services center of their college or university. As a service to graduates, the career services center will mail to prospective employers a complete employment portfolio including recommendation letters collected from your references.

If references are not listed on a resume, a list of references can be provided after a successful interview. By withholding references until they are requested, an applicant may avoid unnecessary or untimely requests being sent to the present employer. The interview gives an applicant a chance to assess the desirability of the job. Until then, the applicant may not want the present employer to receive inquiries (which may be interpreted as dissatisfaction with the present job). In addition, withholding references until after the interview and until the applicant is certain about his or her interest in the job is a courtesy to the references. Even the most enthusiastic references may become apathetic after providing recommendations to endless interviewers. For this same reason, applicants should communicate with references if a job search continues longer than is expected. A letter of thanks and an update on the job search will assure references that their efforts are appreciated. Refer to Chapter 14 for guidelines for communicating with references.

What are the advantages and disadvantages of including a list of references?

On a separate page, place the word REFERENCES and your name, address, and telephone number in a visible position and balance the list (name, address, and telephone number) attractively on the page. Use paper of the same size, color, weight, and texture as your resume. When asked for references at the end of a successful interview, you can immediately provide the references page to the interviewer. If you need additional time to consider the interview, you can mail the references page within a day or so. Whether it is handed to the interviewer personally or mailed, the references page professionally complements your resume. Furthermore, you have impressed the interviewer with your promptness in completing this task—a positive indicator that you will handle other duties similarly. An example of a references page is shown in Figure 13-9.

Your resume will need to meet high standards of content. All parts are important, but the most important portion is the one that covers your qualifications. If they seem compatible with job requirements, you have a good message to present. Confident that you have a good message, you are now ready to put it on paper—to construct a resume that will impress an employer favorably.

Always ask your references for permission to list their names as references before you put them on your resume or give them to an interviewer.

In what ways should the references page complement the resume?

What hidden message do you send when you promptly submit a list of references in person or by mail?

CONSTRUCTING A RESUME

Instead of constructing a resume to suit *you*, try to make one that you think will suit the person who will read it. The acceptable resumes illustrated later in this chapter are not intended to restrict your own creativity. Your goal is to produce a resume that will emphasize the compatibility of your qualifications and the prospective employer's job requirements using effective organization, style, and mechanics.

Use empathy; the resume is designed to impress the *employer*.

Selecting the Organizational Plan

The general organization of all resumes is fairly standard: identification (name, address, and telephone number), job objectives, qualifications, personal information, and references. The primary organizational challenge is in dividing the qualifications section into parts, choosing labels for them, and arranging them in the best sequence. Reviewing your self-, career-, and job-analysis data, you will recognize that your qualifications stem mainly from your education and your experience. Your task is to decide how to present these two categories of qualifications. Resumes usually are organized in one of three ways: reverse chronological order (most recent activity listed first), functional order (most important activity listed first), or a combination of chronological and functional orders. To determine which organizational plan to use, make trial outlines using each one.

CHRONOLOGICAL RESUME

The **chronological resume** is the traditional organization format for resumes. Two headings normally appear in the portion that presents qualifications: "Education" and "Experience." Which one should appear first? Decide which one you think is more impressive to the employer, and put that one first. Within each section, the most recent information is presented first (reverse chronological order). Reverse chronological order is easier to use and is more common than functional order; however, it is not always more effective.

THINK IT OVER
Five years after graduation, which would probably appear first on a resume: (a) "Education" or (b) "Experience"?

COMMUNICATION MENTOR

Be straightforward. Resumes should be complete, yet to the point. Too often, attempts to create unique resumes backfire and do more harm than good. Including a concise recap of your course of study is important, as is listing significant work experience gained while in school. Don't underestimate the importance of referencing personal interests. Employers consider hobbies and leisure-time activities to get a sense of the individual behind the statistics.

Cynthia Pharr
President & CEO
C. Pharr Marketing Communications

THINK IT OVER
If you had little or no related experience, which resume plan would probably be better: (a) chronological or (b) functional? Explain.

Why list the experience most closely related to the job sought first?

The chronological resume is an especially effective format for applicants who have progressed up a clearly defined career ladder and want to move up another rung. The format is less effective for applicants who have gaps in their work histories, are seeking jobs different from the job currently held, or are just entering the job market with little or no experience (Baxter, 1987; "Write a Resume that Works," 1990).

If you choose the chronological format, look at the two headings from the employer's point of view and reverse their positions if doing so is to your advantage. Under the "Experience" division, jobs are listed in reverse order. Assuming you have progressed typically, your latest job is likely to be more closely related to the job being sought than the first job held. Placing the latest or current job first will give it the emphasis it deserves. Include beginning and ending dates for each job. Listing jobs in chronological order is not a requirement. If listing jobs in order of their *relatedness* to the job sought or the *value of experience provided* is to your advantage, deviate from the time-oriented sequence. Begin with the job that will make the best impression.

You completed these analyses when you prepared your career notebook.

How does a functional resume report experience and education?

FUNCTIONAL RESUME

In a **functional resume**, points of primary interest to employers—transferable skills—appear in major headings. These headings highlight what an applicant can do for the employer—functions that can be performed well. Under each heading, an applicant could draw from educational and/or work-related experience to provide supporting evidence.

A functional resume requires a complete analysis of self, career, and the job sought. Suppose, for example, that a person seeking a job as an assistant hospital administrator wants to emphasize qualifications by placing them in major headings. From the hospital's advertisement of the job and from accumulated job-appraisal information, an applicant sees this job as both an administrative and a public relations job. The job requires skill in communicating and knowledge of accounting and finance. Thus, headings in the qualifications portion of the resume could be (1) "Administration," (2) "Public Relations," (3) "Communication," and (4) "Budgeting." Under "Public Relations," for example, an applicant could reveal that a public relations course was taken at State University, from which a degree is to be conferred in June, and that a sales job at ABC Store provided abundant opportunity to apply principles learned. With other head-

COMMUNICATION IN ACTION

Julie Thompson Stovall
Merck & Company, Inc.

Having earned a marketing degree and acquired background courses in the medical field, university graduate Julie Thompson Stovall sought employment with a large pharmaceutical company. She knew competition for positions in large corporations was intense, but she was surprised when she learned 50,000 applicants had applied for 350 positions in Merck & Company, Inc., a large pharmaceutical company based in Pennsylvania. Competition was evidently fierce. What would give her credentials a competitive edge over other applicants?

"I learned that good resumes set you apart from other applicants," Stovall said. "Most importantly, the resume should be tailored to the position for which you are applying." Stovall tailored her resume to the pharmaceutical company. Placed strategically in a summary of qualifications at the beginning of her resume, she listed her pre-med courses before the education section. This science background, coupled with her marketing degree, carefully matched a position with Merck and caught the attention of the interviewer.

Her strategy worked. Stovall is now employed as a pharmaceutical specialist for Merck & Company, Inc., successfully representing three pharmaceutical products. Calling on physicians and pharmacists at hospitals, she has wide latitude and independence in her time. Stovall relates, "Merck was looking for someone who could manage time well, work independently, and maintain self-motivation. I put on my resume that I had financed 100% of my college education to show a work ethic, independence, and motivation."

Stovall's approach is typical of a more general, important point in writing resumes. Stovall states, "Put things you want to talk about at the top of the resume; by doing so, the employer will focus on these things. This emphasis will help you in the interview process." Thus, the applicant can talk about important or comfortable things in the interview. When giving her educational background, Stovall also included her 3.5 grade-point average. She knows many corporations require at least a 3.0 grade-point average, although exceptions are sometimes made. She cautions against including a low average because the applicant may draw unnecessary attention to his or her grades. "You want to emphasize your strong points and focus on the right things. The interviewer can ask about GPA later. Besides, the 3.0 criterion is flexible with many employers."

Stovall believes other points helped give her resume a competitive edge. She listed her involvement in numerous groups and organizations toward the end of her resume. "By holding office in some of these organizations, I showed leadership qualities." Stovall states, "Merely attending class is easy. Show that you are willing to get involved, even if you do so during your last semester in college. Corporations look for involvement. By getting involved, you show you can balance activities and manage time." By including memberships and offices held, she believes her resume caught the interest of Merck. Her approach certainly proved successful for her.

Applying What You Have Learned

1. Select from the organizational plans discussed in Chapter 13 the one you think Stovall followed when writing her resume. Explain your choice.
2. Assume that you were applying for a position in a large medical corporation. What job analysis questions would you ask yourself before you prepared your resume?

ings receiving similar treatment, the qualifications portion reveals the significant aspects of education and experience.

Should major headings be presented in alphabetical order?

Order of importance is probably the best sequence for functional headings. If you have prepared an accurate job analysis and self-analysis, the selected headings will highlight points of special interest to the employer. Glancing at headings only, an employer could see that you have the qualities needed for success on the job. By carefully selecting headings, you reveal knowledge of the requisites for success on that job.

What do the headings in the functional resume emphasize? What important question do they answer?

Having done the thinking required for preparing a functional resume, you are well prepared for a question that is commonly asked in interviews: "What can you do for us?" The answer is revealed in your major headings. They emphasize the functions you can perform and the special qualifications you have to offer.

If you consider yourself well qualified, a functional resume is worth considering. If your education or experience is scant, a functional resume may be best for you. Using "Education" and "Experience" as headings (as in a chronological resume) works against your purpose if you have little to report under the headings; the format would emphasize the absence of education or experience.

When is a functional resume recommended?

COMBINATION CHRONOLOGICAL AND FUNCTIONAL RESUME

The **combination chronological and functional resume** *combines* features of chronological and functional resumes. This format can give quick assurance that educational and experience requirements are met and still use other headings that emphasize qualifications. For example, the "Qualifications" section could have headings such as these:

Education	List the degree, major, school, and graduation date.
Experience	Briefly list jobs held currently and previously.
Administration Public Relations Communication Budgeting	Give details drawn from education and/or experience.

Functional headings vary for different jobs. In fact, two people applying for the same job would likely choose different headings or list similar headings in a distinctive sequence. Select headings that are appropriate for you and that the employer will see as directly related to the job.

When planning the resume, take note of specific job requirements. They are good possibilities for functional headings. For example, for a job that requires bonding, "Top Security Clearance" gets deserved attention as a heading. Each of the following conditions, if it applies to the job sought, could be the basis for a heading: the work is in small groups, the work requires much overtime in certain seasons, travel is frequent, overseas assignments are a possibility, adaptability to rapid changes is desirable, ability to take criticism is essential, long and detailed reports are required, or lateral transfers can be expected. Choosing appropriate headings is a critical decision in resume preparation.

THINK IT OVER
Look at your company/job profile and list possible headings that would highlight the job requirements.

Enhancing the Layout

Can poor mechanics counteract superior content, organization, and style? Explain.

Because first impressions are so powerful, the arrangement of a resume on the page is just as important as the content. If the page is arranged unattractively, is unappealing, or is in poor taste, the message may never be read. Errors in keyboarding, spelling, and punctuation may be taken as evidence of a poor academic background, lack of respect for the employer, carelessness, or haste. Many interviewers believe that a resume is an example of an applicant's best work. Hence, they believe that a person who submits a sloppily prepared resume will probably do the same type of work if hired. With this thought in mind, strive for perfection; give *110 percent* of your effort to this important task—one that could open the door to the job you really want.

As in writing other difficult documents, prepare a rough draft as quickly as you can and then revise as many times as needed to prepare an effective resume that sells you. After you are confident with the resume, ask at least two other people to check it for you. Carefully select people who are knowledgeable about resume preparation and the job you are seeking and can suggest ways to present your qualifications more effectively. After you have incorporated those changes, ask a skillful proofreader to review the document.

THINK IT OVER
Write several rough drafts and ask at least two people for advice and proofreading.

Knowing that you will prepare two or more drafts before finally producing the final resume, you should plan to produce it using word-processing software. You can easily revise the stored file, and you can experiment with various formats to determine which one will highlight your strengths most effectively. To make a good first impression, consider the formatting and layout guidelines in Figure 13-7.

For most students, a resume can be arranged on one page. As students gain experience, additional pages are needed. Some employers insist that the "best" length for a resume is one page. A one-page resume that includes irrelevant information is too long. A two-page resume that omits relevant information is too short.

Unless directed to submit a one-page resume, present your qualifications *in as few words as possible* even if that requires more than one page.

A person with few qualifications applying for a lower-level job may be able to present all relevant information effectively on one page. A person with a great deal of experience applying for a higher-level job would struggle to include all relevant information on one page. The resume probably would appear dense and complicated because of narrow margins and large blocks of run-on text (multiple lines with no space to break them). This crowded resume reformatted onto two pages would have high initial impact. This easy-to-read format would simplify the interviewer's task of identifying an applicant's qualifications, and busy interviewers would appreciate the effort. As you gain significant experience, you may need two or more pages to format an informative, easy-to-read resume.

Examples of Resumes

The resumes illustrated in Figures 13-8, 13-10, 13-11, and 13-12 demonstrate the organizational, formatting, and layout principles discussed so far. Figure 13-9 is an example of a references page.

FINDING PROSPECTIVE EMPLOYERS

The career notebook is especially helpful for organizing information about job opportunities. Under the name, address, and telephone number of each employer who has a job in which you have an interest, leave some space for recording additional data. Record the date of each job call you make and receive (along with what you learned from the call), the date of each returned call, the name of the person who called, the date you sent a resume, and so on. By listing each

LEARNING OBJECTIVE 3

Why alphabetize your list of prospective employers?

CAREER NOTEBOOK

Design Enhancements for Resumes

- *Print the resume on standard-size (8¹/₂" by 11") paper.* Because an application letter will accompany a resume, use the large (No. 10) envelope. You may want to consider using a mailing envelope large enough to accommodate the resume and letter unfolded. Unfolded on the reader's desk, the resume and letter may get favorable attention.

- *Use high-quality paper, preferably 24-pound, 100-percent cotton fiber paper.* Select a neutral color—white, buff, or gray. Be certain that the watermark is positioned so that it can be read across the sheet in the same direction as the printing.

- *Print the resume with clear, sharp type that will reproduce well.* Electronic typewriters and letter-quality printers (*not* dot matrix) are acceptable. Preferably, use a laser printer to take advantage of the increased print quality. Use various sizes and styles of types to enhance your resume; however, limit the number of type styles and sizes so the page is not overwhelming and confusing. Keep the resume clean and simple to read.

    Laser printers and word-processing software with desktop publishing capability are readily available today, and your competitors will be exploiting these tools to make an outstanding first impression. Consequently, you will find the time and expense involved in gaining access to this equipment a necessity, not a luxury. The resume examples in this chapter illustrate graphic enhancements made using word-processing software.

- *Balance the resume attractively on the page with approximately equal margins.* Use generous white space so the resume looks uncluttered and easy to read.

- *Use headings to partition major divisions.* These divisions will help the interviewer locate pertinent information easily and quickly.

- *Use an outline format when possible to list* activities and events on separate lines. Include bullets (•, ◆) to emphasize multiple points.

- *Use special print effects for emphasis.* Choose from indentation, underlining, capitalization, font changes (size and appearance), and graphic lines and borders to enhance the style, readability, and overall impact.

- *Be consistent throughout the resume.* For example, if you double-space before the first heading and key it in bold print with all capital letters, key all headings in the same way. Select the order for presenting information about education and work experience; then be consistent with each school and job. Consistently include the information listed under each school or job unless you have a specific reason for omitting it; e.g., a grade-point average below B.

- *Include your name and a page number at the top of the second and successive pages of a resume.* With each new page, the interviewer is exposed to your name once again. If the pages of the resume are separated, they can be collated again if each page is identified.

- *Consider adding a statement of your creativity and originality.* However, be certain that your creativity will not be construed as gimmicky and consequently distract from the content of the resume. For example, preparing a highly effective resume layout including borders, lines, and graphics communicates creativity as well as proficiency in use of computer-based technology. Demonstrating creativity is particularly useful for creative fields such as advertising, public relations, and graphic design and in fields in which computer competency is required.

FIGURE 13-7   Resume format and layout guidelines.

KAREN E. LOLLEY
980 Cambridge Road
Bangor, ME 04401-8572
(207) 555-6543

CAREER OBJECTIVE	To obtain a management position in the information systems division of a major corporation. Emphasis in developing applications.
SUMMARY OF QUALIFICATIONS	Bachelor's degree in management information systems, proficient in operation of MS-DOS, Windows, and Unix systems and major applications software. Applied computer knowledge while completing cooperative education requirements with a leading company. Willing to relocate.
EDUCATION	B.B.A. MANAGEMENT INFORMATION SYSTEMS, Leonard University, June, 1996. Grade-point average: 3.6 (4.0 scale). Financed 80 percent of education with scholarships and part-time work. Environments: MS-DOS, Windows, and Unix Languages: COBOL, BASIC, and Pascal Application Software: *dBase V, Word for Windows, Excel,* and *PowerPoint*
RELATED EXPERIENCE	***Management Assistant****, Cooperative Education Program, Central Computer Services, Boston, Massachusetts, January, 1995 to May, 1995. • Provided technical support to end users for hardware and software approved by the company. • Applied knowledge of languages and application software in realistic MIS environment and assisted in the installation of a local area network. • Developed interpersonal skills while interacting with computer users.
VOLUNTEER WORK	Served as unpaid assistant at Lindsey Hospital, 15 hours a week, Summers 1991 to 1994. Acquired valuable work habits—dependability, time management, and human relations.
HONORS AND ACTIVITIES	Dean's Scholar (3.6 GPA or higher) President, Data Processing and Management Association
REFERENCES	Available on request.

Annotations:

The centered format and larger type size emphasize the identification section.

Two-column format allows interviewer to locate specific sections easily. Larger type size is used for headings.

The statements of goals and qualifications reveals what type of work is sought and why the employer would want to hire Karen.

Educational strengths include high GPA (B or better) and a list of specific computer competencies.

Action verbs vividly portray work experience.

Listing voluntary work indicates a service attitude and people-oriented experiences.

References will be provided after a successful interview.

FIGURE 13-8   Chronological resume with volunteer work and honors and activities in separate sections.

prospective employer on a separate sheet and alphabetizing the sheets, you can find a name quickly and respond effectively to a returned telephone call.

Information about career and job opportunities is available from many different sources, including networks, career services centers, employers' offices, employment agencies and contractors, help-wanted ads, libraries, and professional organizations.

Networks

The majority of job openings are never advertised. Therefore, developing a network of contacts may be the most valuable source of information about jobs.

Prepared at the same time
as the resume, the refer-
ences can be provided
immediately following a
successful interview.
Paper (color, texture, and
size) and print type match
the resume.

References include two
former employers and a
professor. The list does
not include friends,
relatives, or clergy.

Each reference includes
courtesy title, full name,
company affiliation,
address, and telephone
number (where person can
be reached during regular
office hours).

References are balanced
attractively on the page.

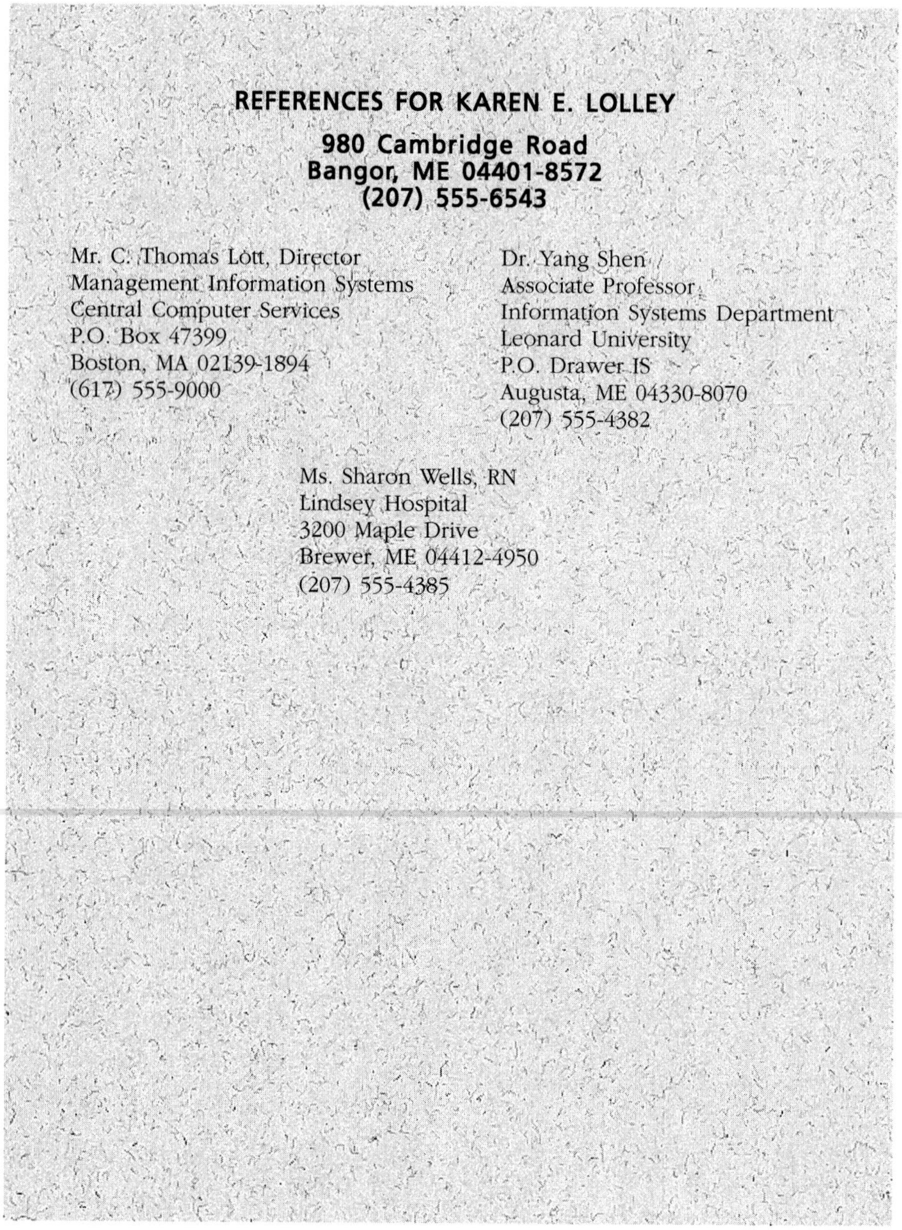

REFERENCES FOR KAREN E. LOLLEY

980 Cambridge Road
Bangor, ME 04401-8572
(207) 555-6543

Mr. C. Thomas Lott, Director
Management Information Systems
Central Computer Services
P.O. Box 47399
Boston, MA 02139-1894
(617) 555-9000

Dr. Yang Shen
Associate Professor
Information Systems Department
Leonard University
P.O. Drawer IS
Augusta, ME 04330-8070
(207) 555-4382

Ms. Sharon Wells, RN
Lindsey Hospital
3200 Maple Drive
Brewer, ME 04412-4950
(207) 555-4385

FIGURE 13-9   References.

Your network may include current and past employers, guest speakers in your
classes or at student organization meetings, business contacts you met while in-
terning or participating in shadowing or over-the-shoulder experiences, and so
on. Let these individuals know the type of job you are seeking and ask their
advice for finding employment in today's competitive market.

Career Services Centers

THINK IT OVER
Take the time now to register
with your career services center.

Do not wait until your last semester to learn about the services provided by your
school's career services center. It may be listed under such names as "Career
Services Department," "Career Services Division," or "Placement Center."

RICHARD M. SCHMIDT

School Address

P.O. Box 390
Rockland College
Wilmington, DE 19735-7189
(302) 555-6753

Permanent Address

735 South McClean Avenue
Smyrna, DE 19977-3905
(302) 555-9247

Richard provides a school and permanent address to ensure that the interviewer can reach him during school holidays.

CAREER OBJECTIVES

Immediate: To enter a management-trainee program.

Eventual: To specialize in human resources management in an international operation.

Richard applies for entrance into a trainee program he knows is available.

SUMMARY OF QUALIFICATIONS

B.S., management with a concentration in human resources management; have gained managerial experience, communication, and interpersonal skills through part-time employment; am proficient in primary software applications; speak Spanish and exposed to other cultures through extensive travel and interaction with international students.

Qualifications briefly summarize why the employer should hire Richard.

MANAGEMENT-ORIENTED EDUCATION

Bachelor of Science, Rockland College, Wilmington, Delaware. To be conferred on May 1, 1996.

Major: MANAGEMENT, with a concentration in human resources. Related courses: International Management, International Communication, Spanish (three semesters), and computer applications courses.

Grade-Point Average: Major: 3.8; overall 3.7 (based on 4.0 scale).

Honors: Beta Gamma Sigma (business honorary society).
Recipient of Robert L. Parvin Academic Scholarship (ACT score above 30).
Listed on the Dean's or President's List for seven semesters (GPA 3.6 or better).

Subdividing the "Education" section emphasizes major points and increases readability (eliminates large sections of run-on text).

Academic honors are integrated within the "Education" section and provide evidence of Richard's ability to succeed. Other activities could be included in a separate section following "Experience."

FIGURE 13-10 Chronological resume with honors and achievements integrated in the "Education" section.

Typically, the center has a browsing room loaded with career information and job-announcement bulletins. Career counseling is usually available. Through the center, students can schedule on-campus interviews with company recruiters who make regular visits to the campus.

The career services center can be especially helpful to students who are looking for a job. Students complete a form, giving information about academic major, progress toward a degree, graduation date, career goals, and so on. Students then ask three to five people (professors, employers, or others who could provide valid information) to send letters of recommendation to the center. The form and letters are reproduced for sending to prospective employers when requested. With this arrangement, a reference submits only one letter of recom-

The career services center can provide an employer with several *letters of recommendation in response to* one *call.*

Heading clearly identifies
the second page of
Richard's resume.

Richard M. Schmidt   **Page 2**

MANAGEMENT-RELATED EXPERIENCE

Freemont Inn   **Desk Manager**
Smyrna, Delaware   **Summers 1994 to present**

Make room reservations, register guests, keep computerized records, and
supervise bellhops and desk clerks.

Bullets highlight accomplishments stated in brief phrases beginning with action verbs.

- Promoted from desk clerk to desk manager after one year.
- Developed effective interpersonal skills through continuous interactions
  with guests and supervision of 12 employees.
- Gained computer competency and refined organizational skills.
- Initiated employee participation program; implemented several more
  efficient procedures as a result of ideas submitted.

Rockland College   **Residence Hall Assistant**
Wilmington, Louisiana   **August 1993 to present**

Supervise 72 male residents from at least six different countries; enforce
college regulations; provide individual and group counseling for academic
and personal problems; prepare work schedules and handle payroll for 5
resident assistants and 13 desk assistants.

- Developed effective communication skills while counseling residents;
  learned the value of empathetic listening and seeing ideas from the
  other person's perspective—skills relevant to quality employee training.
- Designed computer-based work scheduling program that was adopted
  for use by all other residence hall directors.

Horizontal lines partition
the resume into logical
divisions and simplify the
interviewer's task of locating each major division.

PERSONAL INFORMATION

Only personal information
that strengthens the
resume is included.

Developed cultural awareness through extensive travel throughout Europe
and Mexico. Have a strong interest in physical fitness; exercise regularly—
swim, jog, and play tennis. Certified as CPR and lifeguard instructor for
the American Red Cross. Willing to relocate.

ADDITIONAL INFORMATION

Because the Career
Services Center will
provide recommendations
from Richard's references,
references are not listed;
the space is used to
develop other qualifications.

Letters from references and a transcript are available from Career Services
Center, Rockland College, P.O. Box 3000, Wilmington, DE 19735-3000,
(302) 555-2390.

FIGURE 13-10, continued
Chronological resume with honors and achievements integrated within "Education" sections.

mendation; but it can be sent to many different employers. By making one call
to the career services center, a prospective employer can get three or more
recommendations plus additional data. In addition, the career services center
provides on-campus interviews, workshops on resume writing and interviewing
skills, and other job-search skills.

Employers' Offices

Employers who have not advertised their employment needs may respond favorably to a telephoned or personal inquiry. The receptionist may be able to

MONICA GONZALEZ
895 Yorkshire Road
Corpus Christi, TX 78469-7310
(512) 555-6743

OBJECTIVE	To acquire a position in retail clothing sales with possible advancement to sales management.
SALES-ORIENTED	Have had a strong interest in sales and fashion since childhood; began designing and making clothes at age 14. Have had three years' part-time experience in fast foods. Currently, a senior majoring in marketing at West State College. Subscribe to *Retail Selling*. Graduate in May, 1996.
PUBLIC RELATIONS SKILLS	Learned tactfulness when taking and filling orders in the fast-food business (Bayside Deli, part-time from August 1992 to May 1995). Commended by manager for diplomacy with patrons and staff. Earned an A in Interpersonal Communication and will take Public Relations next year. Gained experience coping with various personality types while volunteering as a counselor at Camp Seminole for three summers.
RECORDKEEPING SKILLS	Used cash register and balanced receipts against records each day at Bayside Deli. Now taking two classes (accounting and computer science) that emphasize keeping records electronically.
DEPENDABILITY	Report regularly and promptly when scheduled for work. Have never been late for work in three years. Attend classes regularly. Open, close, and take cash to bank.
LEARNING CAPACITY	Commended for learning work procedures quickly. On the Dean's List for the last two semesters. Achieved 3.6 grade-point average (on a 4.0 scale) in major courses to date.
REFERENCES	Available upon request.

Centered format and larger type size emphasize the identification section.

Horizontal line adds interest and partitions the identification section from the evidence that follows.

Two-column format allows interviewer to locate specific sections easily. Bold typeface and all-capitals are consistently used to display headings.

Headings emphasize qualities the applicant offers as a solution to the employer's problem. A quick look at the headings suggests that Monica knows important requisites for success in sales.

In the material under each heading, Monica draws from education and/or experience for support.

FIGURE 13-11   Functional resume.

provide useful information, direct you to someone with whom you can talk, or set up an appointment.

Employment Agencies and Contractors

Telephone directories list city, county, state, and federal employment agencies that provide free or inexpensive services. Some agencies offer a recorded answering service; by dialing and listening, callers can get information about job opportunities and the procedure for using the agency's services. Fees charged by private agencies are paid by either the employee or the employer. This fee

How can employment contractors help in finding a job?

RICHARD M. SCHMIDT

School Address

Rockland College
P.O. Box 390
Wilmington, DE 19735-7189
(302) 555-6753
Messages: (302) 555-8312

Permanent Address

735 South McClean Avenue
Smyrna, DE 19977-3905
(302) 555-9247

CAREER OBJECTIVE	To enter a management-trainee program and later specialize in human resources management.
MANAGERIAL EDUCATION	To earn B.S. degree in MANAGEMENT with concentration in human resources management, May 1, 1996. Grade-point average to date: major 3.8 and overall 3.7 (on a 4.0 scale).

Achievements: Initiated into Beta Gamma Sigma (business honorary society) and Phi Kappa Phi (top 10% of junior and senior class); received Robert L. Parvin Academic Scholarship (ACT score above 30); listed on the Dean's or President's List for seven semesters (GPA 3.6 or better).

MANAGERIAL EXPERIENCE

Desk manager, Freemont Inn in Smyrna.
- Worked part-time since May, 1994.
- Supervise bellhops, reserve rooms, register guests, and keep computerized records.

Residence hall director, Rockland College, August, 1993, to present.
- Supervise 72 male residents.
- Enforce college regulations.
- Provide individual and group counseling to residents having academic and personal problems.
- Prepare work schedules and handle payroll for 5 resident assistants and 13 desk assistants.

This telephone number is necessary because Richard is away from his telephone during regular office hours and does not have an answering machine.

"Education" and "Experience" are traditional headings on a chronological resume.

FIGURE 13-12   Combination chronological and functional resume.

usually is based on the first month's salary and must be paid within a few months. Some agencies specialize in finding high-level executives or specialists for major firms. Employment "contractors" specialize in providing temporary employees. Instead of helping you find a permanent job, a contractor may be able to use your services on a temporary basis until you find a full-time job.

Help-Wanted Ads

Remember that many good jobs are not advertised in help-wanted ads.

Responses to advertised positions should be made as quickly as possible after the ad is circulated. If your resume is received early and is impressive, you could get a favorable response before other applications are received.

Richard M. Schmidt   **Page 2**

COMMUNICATION SKILLS   Developed effective communication skills while counseling residents; learned the value of empathetic listening and seeing ideas from the other person's perspective—skills relevant to quality employee training. Developed effective interpersonal skills through continuous interactions with hotel guests and supervision of 12 employees. Wrote memos, letters, business reports, and term papers and gave oral presentations in business courses.

ACCEPT CRITICISM   Benefited from criticism of written materials and from critiques of oral presentations. Sensitive at first, came to recognize criticism as intent to help. Improved oral presentations after self-criticisms of taped presentations. Appreciate the need for tact in giving constructive criticism.

COMPUTER LITERATE   Elected to take three computer courses in addition to the two required for management majors. The most recently studied software programs (*WordPerfect* and *PageMaker*) are especially useful in producing effective reports. Applied basic computer skills and learned software programs specific to hotel management while working for Freemont Inn. Designed computer-based work scheduling program that was adopted for use by all other residence hall directors.

REFERENCES   Letters from references and a transcript are available from Career Services Center, Rockland College, P.O. Box CS, Wilmington, DE 19735-3000, (302) 555-2390.

Other headings are commonly placed on a functional resume. Headings that emphasize the skills vital to success in a trainee program were identified through self- and career analysis (including an interview with a successful manager who had completed a management training program).

All major divisions have one common denominator; each is a factor in managerial success.

References could be listed if Richard is confident he wants to work for this company and believes providing them will strengthen his resume.

FIGURE 13-12, *continued   Combination chronological and functional resume.*

If an ad invites response to a box number without giving a name, be cautious. The employer could be legitimate but does not want present employees to know about the ad or does not want applicants to telephone or drop by the premises. However, you have a right to be suspicious of someone who wants to remain obscure while learning everything you reveal in your resume.

Online Databases and Printed Sources

The Internet and commercial online services provide instant access to numerous job listings and a wealth of resources for interviewing and job searching. Dolan and Schumacher's (1994) provides the top U.S. sources for an online job search and the following advice for taking advantage of this new age of job searching. Identify and subscribe to the specific directories or user groups that likely will post job announcements in your field. Send an electronic resume, followed by a printed copy to the job opening you retrieve from an online source. Be sure your resume adheres to any special format requirements for posting resumes online. Search relevant online sources such as gopher to identify names and e-mail addresses of contacts (friends/colleagues) at the company, background information about the company, and other job-search resources. Initiate an e-mail conversation with a contact at the company to learn more about the job and to create rapport with the target company.

The following printed sources are useful in identifying firms in need of employees:

Annual reports from major firms
Black Enterprise (annual June issue)
Career, The Annual Guide to Business Opportunities
College Placement Council (CPC) Manual
Company newsletters
Directory of American Firms Operating in Foreign Countries
Dun and Bradstreet's *Million Dollar Directory*
Encyclopedia of Careers and Vocational Guidance
Engineering Index
Forbes (Annual Directory Issue published May 15)
Fortune
Moody's *Manuals*
Science Research Associates' Occupational Briefs
Standard and Poor's *Register of Corporations, Directors, and Executives*
Trade or professional journals
United States Civil Service Commission job listings
The Wall Street Journal
National Business Employment Weekly

Professional Organizations

Officers of professional organizations, through their contacts with members, are sometimes good sources of information about job opportunities. Much job information is exchanged at meetings of professional associations. In response to help-wanted and position-wanted columns in journals of some professional organizations, interviews are sometimes arranged and conducted at hotels or schools in which the organization holds its annual meeting.

In addition to the professional growth that comes from membership in professional organizations, active participation is a good way to learn about job opportunities. Visiting lecturers sometimes provide job information. In addition, employers are favorably impressed when club membership is listed on the resume. They are even more impressed if the applicant is (or has been) an officer in the organization (implied leadership, community commitment, willingness to exert effort without tangible reward, social acceptance, or high level of aspiration). By joining and actively participating in professional, social, and honorary

COMMUNICATION MENTOR

An application letter should communicate your desire to obtain a position with a company and what you think you can "bring to the table" for that company. The letter should be formal but contain some personal item that will help the prospective employer identify you more readily.

Another technique is to add a short one- or two-page biography to the employment package. This document will enable a prospective employer to learn more about you from your perspective.

Terence E. McSweeney
Director of Communications
PGA of America

organizations for their majors, college students increase their opportunities to develop rapport with peers and professors. One of the benefits is sharing job information.

A student who expects to graduate in May should begin the search for prospective employers months beforehand. Waiting too long to begin and then hurrying through the job-search process could be detrimental to future employment.

APPLICATION LETTERS

When employers invite you to send a resume, they expect you to include an **application letter**. The two go together. A resume summarizes information related to the job's requirements and the applicant's qualifications. An application letter (1) seeks to arouse interest in the resume, (2) introduces it, and (3) interprets it in terms of employer benefits. One of its functions is to introduce, so the application letter is placed on top of the resume, where it will be seen first.

Because it seeks to arouse interest and to point out employer benefits, the application letter is persuasive and, thus, written inductively. It is designed to convince an employer that qualifications are adequate just as a sales letter is designed to convince a buyer that a product will satisfy a need. Like sales letters, application letters are either solicited or unsolicited. Job advertisements *solicit* applications. Unsolicited application letters have greater need for attention-getters; otherwise, solicited and unsolicited application letters are based on the same principles.

Unsolicited application letters are sometimes referred to as "prospecting" letters. The same basic letter (perhaps with slight modifications) can be sent to many prospective employers. By sending unsolicited letters, (1) you increase the possibility of finding employers who have employment needs, (2) you compete with fewer applicants than you would if letters were solicited, and (3) you may alert employers to needs not previously identified. Impressed by the qualities described in an unsolicited application letter, an employer could create a job. The writer of an unsolicited application letter has demonstrated initiative, a

LEARNING OBJECTIVE 4

What is the purpose of an application letter?

What does an application letter have in common with a *sales* letter?

What are the advantages and disadvantages of sending "prospecting" application letters?

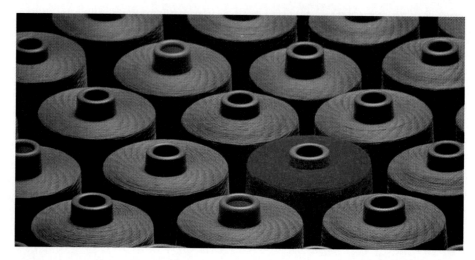

When you write your application letter, be sure that the letter is a reflection of your personality and not a copy of a standard application letter. You want your letter to stand apart and identify you as a unique individual.

quality most employers appreciate. However, sending unsolicited letters has some disadvantages: (1) Because the employer's specific needs are not known, the opening paragraph is likely to be more general than the opening paragraph in unsolicited letters; and (2) depending on the ratio of responses to letters sent, the process could be expensive.

The job application letter is one of the most important letters you will ever write.

Because satisfaction derived from work plays a major role in life's total enjoyment and because the decision to interview is based primarily on reaction to the application letter and resume, these documents may be among the most important you will ever write. Even after an interview, the application letter and resume could receive further scrutiny and turn out to be deciding factors in your favor.

A cartoon depicted an employer holding an application letter with an applicant sitting across the desk. The dialogue read, "I wish I could interview the person who wrote this letter." Study sample applications but write a letter that reflects your personality.

They represent *you*. They should be different from any other person's. Copying or paraphrasing someone else's resume or application letter is a serious mistake, but you can benefit from studying letters in which others have applied or violated principles. In evaluating application letters written by others (and in thinking about your *own* letter to be written later), keep in mind the criteria by which any writing can be evaluated.

Organization

Write the outline recommended for an application letter in your notebook.

As a persuasive letter, an application letter uses the same sequence of parts as a sales letter:

Sales Letter	Application Letter
Gets attention	Gets attention
Introduces product/service	Introduces qualifications
Presents evidence	Presents evidence
Encourages action	Encourages action

THINK IT OVER
What central appeal could you develop to convince an employer to hire you? How might you introduce it in the attention-getting paragraph?

Like a well-written sales letter, a well-written application letter uses a central selling feature as a theme. The central selling feature is introduced in the first or second paragraph and stressed in paragraphs that follow. Two to four paragraphs are normally sufficient for supporting evidence. Consider order of importance as a basis for their sequence, with the most significant aspects of your preparation coming first.

A persuasive letter is designed to get action, which in this case is to get the reader to (1) read the resume and (2) invite you to an interview. Preferably, reference to the resume comes near the end of the letter. If you refer to it in the first or second paragraph, readers may wonder whether they are expected to put the letter aside at that point and look at the resume. Because your purpose in writing is to get an interview, the final paragraph is the logical place for making reference to it. Now that your message is complete, the next move is the reader's. The organizational decision about where to *place* reference to the interview is easy; deciding what ideas to include and how to *express* them is more challenging.

What is the desired action in an application letter?

Should the first paragraph introduce the resume?

Content

If content is satisfactory, the letter will contain the *right ideas*; that is, the *message* will be appropriate. Do you think the following letter is effective?

> To Whom It May Concern:
>
> Wishing to be considered for an entry-level accounting position in your tax department, I submit the enclosed resume.
>
> After you have studied it, I shall appreciate your calling me to set up an interview.

The letter identifies the job sought, introduces the resume, and encourages action—but what is missing? Does it attempt to arouse the manager's interest? Does it lead the manager to expect something positive in the resume? Does it include anything that might cause the manager to think, "I'm eager to see *this applicant's* resume"?

LENGTH

Did you recognize the preceding letter as being too short to serve well as a sales letter? Remember, persuasive messages have to be long enough to give supporting evidence. Some human resources managers favor short application letters, pointing out that only a few seconds can be spared for reading each letter. A short letter that is *read*, they argue, will do an applicant more good than a long one that is merely *skimmed*. They see brevity as a virtue that can be demonstrated in an application letter.

Employers are very busy. Is that a valid argument for keeping application letters short?

Other human resource managers favor longer letters. They point out that good employees are hard to find and that longer letters provide (1) more information and (2) more opportunity to evaluate. If the first lines arouse interest, employers will thoroughly and eagerly read additional paragraphs if doing so will possibly help resolve an employment problem.

By making paragraphs long enough to include interpretation of experiences on the present or previous job, you can give an employer some confidence that you are well prepared for your next job. For example, the following excerpt from an applicant whose only work experience was at a fast-food restaurant is short and general:

> For three months last summer, I worked at Bayside Deli. Evaluations of my work were superior. While the assistant manager was on vacation, I supervised a crew of five on the evening shift.

As the only reference to the Bayside Deli experience, the paragraph does convey one employer's apparent satisfaction with performance. Superior evaluations and some supervisory responsibility are evidence of that satisfaction, but added details and interpretation could make the message more convincing:

> In my summer job at Bayside Deli, I learned the value of listening carefully when taking orders, making change quickly and accurately, offering suggestions when customers seemed hesitant, and keeping a cheerful attitude. Supervising a crew of five while the assistant manager was on vacation, I appreciated the importance of fairness and diplomacy in working with other employees.

THINK IT OVER
To be convincing, include details. Refer to Chapter 11 and list other techniques for making evidence convincing to the reader. Which do you think you can use in your application letter?

Answer the employer's question: "What can you bring to the table?" by describing what you *learned* on a previous job.

Apparently, the applicant's experience has been meaningful. It called attention to qualities that managers like to see in employees: willingness to listen, speed, accuracy, concern for clients or customers, a positive attitude, fairness, and tact. As a *learning* experience, the Bayside Deli job has taught or reinforced some principles that the employer will see can be transferred to the job being sought.

For graduating students entering the world of full-time work for the first time, their educational backgrounds usually are more impressive than their work histories. They can benefit from interpreting their educational experiences as meaningful, job-related experiences. An applicant for acceptance into an auditor's trainee program should do more than merely report having taken auditing theory and practice:

Write about school as a *learning* experience that can be transferred to the job sought.

> In my auditing theory and practice class, I could see specific application of principles encountered in my human relations and psychology classes. Questions about leadership and motivation seemed to recur throughout the course: What really motivates executives? Why are auditors feared at many levels? How can those fears be overcome? How can egos be salvaged? "Consider the human element" was a frequent admonition. That element was the focus of my term paper, "The Auditor as a Psychologist."

To be convincing, be specific, but *original*.

Because the preceding paragraph included questions discussed in a class, do not assume that your application letter should do likewise. Or because this paragraph gives the title of a term paper, do not assume the same technique is a must for your letter. The techniques illustrated are commendable because they help to portray the educational experience as meaningful and related to the job sought. Recognizing that auditors must be tactful (a point on which the person reading the letter will surely agree), the applicant included some details of a class. That technique is a basic in persuasion: Do not just say a product or idea is good; say what makes it good. Do not just say that a certain educational or work experience was beneficial; say what made it so.

Your letter is approaching a desirable length if it succeeds in arousing interest and helps the reader see ways in which your services would be beneficial. One page is usually enough, especially for graduates entering the job market. Yet if circumstances seem to justify a longer letter, two- or three-page letters are acceptable.

SOURCE OF JOB INFORMATION

Sometimes, referring to your source of job information may be to your advantage. For example, if a person well known in a large business spoke to your class and indicated a need for employees in a certain category, revealing that person's name in the first paragraph could serve as an attention-getter. Or referring to the newspaper or magazine in which a job was advertised is an easy way to identify the job sought. A reference is easy to include in a beginning sentence.

Sometimes, using the name of a person the employer knows is a good way to begin.

KNOWLEDGE OF EMPLOYER'S ACTIVITIES

A thorough job search may have identified current trends in the industry you are entering. The company to which you are applying may have had a recent stock split, announced the upcoming opening of a new branch, or introduced a new product. Sentences that *imply* your knowledge of such matters may make a favorable impression. They show that you really are interested in the field, read widely, do more than you are required to do, gather information before making decisions, and so on.

Be informed, but do not sound like a private detective.

KNOWLEDGE OF JOB REQUIREMENTS

Such statements as "The requirements of this job are . . ." or "I understand that this job requires . . ." are seldom necessary. Your knowledge of job requirements is usually assumed. They need not be stated directly (doing so takes up space and repeats what is known already). If a certain job is known to place special emphasis on certain requirements, however, your awareness of that emphasis could be a point in your favor. For example, a certain accounting job requires frequent and complicated written reports. Instead of writing, "I understand the job requires frequent reports" (which is already known), you could refer to writing experiences you have had or your preference for work that requires writing (if that is true). Your understanding is revealed without a direct statement.

THINK IT OVER
What tone is reflected if you state job requirements directly (review Chapter 7)? How can you reveal knowledge of job requirements without stating them directly?

Some ads for employment force respondents to include certain information: "Must provide own transportation and be willing to travel. Give educational background, work experience, and salary expected." These points must be discussed in the responding letter. Preferably, the question of salary is left until the interview; but if an ad requests a statement about it, the letter should include that statement. You may give a minimum figure or range, indicate willingness to accept a figure that is customary for work of that type, or indicate a preference for discussing salary at the interview.

Unless an ad requests a statement on salary, an application letter should not mention it. Like the price of a product in a sales letter, salary in an application letter is a negative. Do not emphasize what you want from the company (money); instead emphasize what you can contribute to it. Until after the interview, neither the employer nor the applicant knows whether the two are compatible. If they are not, a discussion of salary is pointless. Like salary, the following ideas (sometimes found in application letters) should be omitted.

Should you mention salary in a prospecting application letter?

DISCUSSION OF YOUR OWN PROBLEMS

Your need to earn more income, to be closer to your work, to have more pleasant surroundings, or to gain greater advancement opportunities are of little interest to the firm. The excitement you experienced upon learning about a job opportunity is not worth mentioning. The possible implication is that, for you, jobs are really hard to find, perhaps because of your shortcomings. Use empathy and concentrate on reporting that which will meet the employer's needs.

Use empathy. Express ideas in terms of the employer's needs.

STATEMENTS OF THE OBVIOUS

"This is an application," "I read your ad," and "I am writing to apply for" are sufficiently understood without making direct statements. With the letter *and* resume in hand, a reader learns nothing from "A resume is enclosed." Already aware of job requirements and requisites for success in a certain job, managers need not be told again. Such sentences as "An auditor should be able to . . ." and "Sales personnel should avoid . . ." seem to lecture. Although they may reveal familiarity with matters important to the job, they may be resented.

CURRENT EMPLOYER'S SHORTCOMINGS

Regardless of how negatively you perceive your present employer, that perception has little to do with your prospective employer's needs. Also, if you knock your present employer, you could be perceived as someone who would do the same to the next employer.

SELF-CONDEMNING STATEMENTS

Concentrate on reporting your strengths. Surely, you would not apply for a job you thought you could not do. Just tell the aspects of your background that have prepared you for that job. Reporting failure or lack of aptitude at some other endeavor only weakens your case. Mentioning it could raise questions about your self-esteem. Instead of apologizing for some shortcoming, look for positive aspects of your education or experience. Reporting them may be to your advantage.

BOASTFUL CONNOTATIONS

Self-confidence is commendable, but overconfidence (or worse still, just plain bragging) is objectionable. Like unsupported or unsupportable superlatives in sales letters, some self-judgmental terms can do more harm than good. Instead of labeling your performance as "superior" or "excellent," give supporting facts. A manager may think of them as evidence of superiority or excellence and react favorably.

FLATTERY

If a firm is well known for its rapid expansion, currently successful advertising campaign, competitive advantage, or superior product, conveying your awareness of these positive achievements is to your advantage. On the other hand, deliberate attempts at flattery will almost surely be detected. They are more likely to be resented than appreciated. For example, referring to the employer as "*the* leader in the field," "the best in the business," or "a company with an outstanding record" is risky. If such labels are inaccurate, they will be so recognized. If they are accurate, their use is still risky. Flattery could be taken as an attempt to get a favorable decision as a reward for making a complimentary statement.

BIOGRAPHICAL DISCOURSE

In certain situations, chronology is the best order in which to arrange items. Listing jobs in the order in which they were held is one legitimate sequence, but an application letter should not sound like a history of a job seeker's life. The narrative approach is likely to emphasize the individual too much and the employer's needs too little. For organizing an application letter, chronology is seldom the best sequence.

Style

Stylistic principles that apply in other writing (especially in persuasive writing) also apply in writing application letters. Some stylistic matters as job language, clichés, and tactful action statements deserve special attention.

USE LANGUAGE USED ON THE JOB

If an application letter contains terminology commonly used by accountants, an applicant for an accounting job implies familiarity with the job and the language used. An applicant for a financial position would benefit from using acronyms such as ECOA for Equal Credit Opportunity Act, abbreviations, and other terms such as *front-end load* well known in the financial field but not altogether meaningful to others. Such language would communicate clearly, save space, and imply a financial background. The same principle applies to writing about other occupations. Use this specialized language only when you are confident your reader will understand.

> **THINK IT OVER**
> What terminology or acronyms could you include to communicate your knowledge of your field?

AVOID OVERUSED WORDS AND EXPRESSIONS

Some words that are useful in talking *about* letters of application are often used too frequently *in* them:

> Avoid using words and sentences that have been overused by other applicants.

Applicant	If the letter shows how you are suited for the job sought, you need not label yourself as an "applicant." Obviously, you are.
Application	As a page that introduces a resume and discusses your preparation for a job, your letter is obviously an application.
I	Because the letter is designed to sell your services, some use of "I" is natural and expected; but try to restrict the number of times "I" is used. Empathy for the employer will help. "I" is especially noticeable if it is the first word of consecutive paragraphs.
Interview	The word "interview" is very commonly used in the final paragraph and connotes a formal question-and-answer session. The *idea* of a face-to-face meeting can be introduced without using "interview." "Talk with you," "discuss the work," and "come to your office" are possibilities.
Opening	Meaning "an unfilled position," "opening" is readily understood; but it seems abstract, is overused, and usually unneeded.
Position	A "position" may be thought of as a title that someone *holds*; it does not necessarily apply to *work*. Compared with "job" or "work," it may sound more formal than you want.
Qualifications	Employers will recognize training, education, and experience as "qualifications" without a label. Leave the word to implication or use such words as "background," "preparation," or "record."
Vacancy	Like "opening," the word seems abstract, overused, and usually unnecessary.

Using some of the preceding words would not be an error, but they could take up space and make your letter sound like competitors' letters. The following examples illustrate overused sentences and phrases:

Consider me an applicant for the position	The letter and resume sufficiently imply desire for consideration.
I would like to apply for . . .	"Would like to" connotes desire to apply if conditions were different. Application is evident without use of "apply."
. . . to become associated with . . .	The phrase seems vague, formal, and even condescending. The goal is to get a job, not to associate with an employer.
. . . your organization [your firm, your company].	Avoid these terms or use the name of the unit instead.
. . . interview at your earliest convenience.	Avoid or find other words to express the idea.

ENCOURAGE ACTION

Because an invitation to interview is the objective of the letter, the reader needs to be motivated to extend the invitation. Encouraging action is a delicate matter. The desired action is for the reader to (1) *write a letter* or (2) *place a telephone call* inviting you to a face-to-face discussion. The choice (write or call) is best left to the employer. Asking for a written response when the employer prefers to call (or vice versa) could result in no response. The goal is to introduce the idea of action without apologizing for doing so and without being demanding or "pushy." Find *your* words for achieving it, and try to avoid some frequently made errors:

1. *Setting a date.* "May I have an appointment with you on March 14." Grateful to have any appointment at all, you are better off to let the employer set the date. The date you name could be inconvenient; or even if it is convenient for the employer, your forwardness in setting it could be resented.
2. *Giving permission to call.* "You may call me at 555-6543." By making the call sound like a privilege (may call), you could alienate the reader. Implied meaning: You are very selective about the calls you take, but the employer does qualify.
3. *Reporting capability of response.* "You can call me at 555-6543." When a number or address is given, employers are well aware that they are capable of using it (can call).
4. *Expressing doubt.* "If you agree," "I hope you will," and "should you decide" use subjunctive words in which your awareness of possible negative results is implied. By showing lack of confidence, you may reduce reader confidence.
5. *Suggesting a one-way conversation.* ". . . when I can talk to you about the job." Use of "with you" (instead of "to you") implies a two-way conversation.
6. *Sounding overconfident.* "I know you will want to set up an appointment." If the writer does not know, the statement is inaccurate; if the writer does know, it seems unnecessary and egotistical.
7. *Sounding apologetic.* "May I take some of your time" or "I know how busy you are" may seem considerate, but the hoped-for interview should be thought of as advantageous to both people involved. Apology is totally out of place in a letter that discusses ways in which the employer benefits from hiring you.

An applicant with strong qualifications need not press forcefully for action.

If the final paragraph (action closing) of your letter is preceded by paragraphs that are impressive, you need not press hard for a response. Just mentioning the idea of a future discussion is probably sufficient. Compared with the action endings of sales letters, the endings of application letters have less need for forceful statements that define specific action. Surely, an employer who has just finished reading an impressive application would know what to do about it. Forceful statements about *when* and *how* to respond are unnecessary and could arouse resentment.

As closing sentences that refer to an invitation to interview, the following sentences are free of the weaknesses pointed out in preceding illustrations. They are not intended as model sentences that should appear in *your* letter. When the time comes to write your own closing sentence, write it, analyze it carefully, and rewrite it if necessary. Because finding the right job is so important to you, you will be well rewarded for the time and thought invested. Four active closings are critiqued in the following list:

1. *"When a date and time can be arranged, I would like to talk with you."* Passively constructed, "can be arranged" does not indicate who will do the arranging. If the work of extending the invitation is performed by an assistant, the employer's part is fast and easy—just tell the assistant to schedule an interview and inform the applicant. If the employer's needs have been satisfied already or if the letter and resume are not impressive, the date and time for an interview are irrelevant; no action is requested or expected. In the independent clause, "I would like to talk with you," the meeting place and the subject of the conversation are understood.

2. *"I would appreciate an opportunity to discuss the loan officer's job with you."* Reference to action is not direct. If the opportunity arises, it will be as a result of the reader's action. Assuming that preceding sentences have not overused "I," use of first person is appropriate. Appreciation is more emphatic when expressed in first person.

3. *"With two days' notice, I could meet with you at any hour of your working day."* The indirect reference to action is not forceful. However, if the applicant has impressive qualifications, the reader will want an interview and will not need to be pushed. How the notice is given is the reader's choice. Intended to show consideration for the employer's time schedule, "at any hour" could imply an overabundance of free time or even lack of concern for completing the present employer's work. Yet, the resume will show whether the applicant now has a job. The "two days' notice" could indicate a flexible working schedule. Or the applicant may need time to arrange for a replacement while the interview is being conducted.

4. *"To discuss your employment needs and my production-scheduling experience, I would appreciate an appointment."* When and if the appointment occurs is up to the employer. For an applicant who has had significant related experience and has made that experience a central selling feature, incorporating it into the action closing adds unity and stresses the applicant's strongest qualification. To increase emphasis on the word "experience," the independent clause could be moved to the beginning of the sentence. As the last word in the final paragraph, "experience" would stand out vividly.

Mechanics

Compared with superior qualifications, physical arrangement on a page may seem insignificant. Yet, even before the letter is read, it communicates some-

> Before the letter is read, its appearance has already communicated something about the applicant.

thing about you. If it conveys a negative impression, it may not be read at all. The size, color, and quality of paper influence readers' reactions; so do margins, letter format, keyboarding, and paragraphing.

Which two special letter parts *must* be included on an application letter?

Use plain bond paper for this personal-business letter. Using your present employer's letterhead is unacceptable because you are not representing your employer. If necessary, refer to Appendix A for letter formats and standard and special letter parts. Include your street address and city, state, and ZIP code above the date. Include "Enclosure" a double space below the signature block to alert the employer that a resume is enclosed. The proper letter format is shown in the good examples of application letters in Figures 13-14 and 13-15.

What criteria will you use to select paper for an application letter? Is using your employer's letterhead for an application letter acceptable?

Paper used for the application letter, the resume, and the envelope must match in color, weight, cotton-fiber content, texture, and size. The watermark should be readable across the sheet in the same direction as the printing. Refer to the resume format and layout guidelines in Figure 13-7 for exact paper and high-quality printing requirements.

Strive for perfection.

Errors in grammar, spelling, and punctuation could imply that you pay little attention to detail, do your work hastily, have shortcomings in basic education, or lack pride or respect. Because the letter represents you and will be thought of as the best you can do, allow yourself time to do it well. Get opinions from others and make revisions where necessary.

Examples of Application Letters

This section on application letters has given you an opportunity to think *separately* about content, organization, style, and mechanics. Analyzing *entire letters* will enable you to synthesize, to understand why some practices should be avoided, and to see how principles can be applied. For each letter, (1) read each sentence carefully, (2) identify the principles you think are applied or violated, and (3) read the notation about each sentence. The thinking involved in such letter analysis will pay dividends when you later compose your own letter of application.

The letters in Figures 13-13 and 13-14 are designed to accompany the chronological resume in Figure 13-8. Many of the principles discussed in this section are violated in Figure 13-13; e.g., clichés and "I" language are used. In the revision (Figure 13-14), "I" is not entirely eliminated; but it is used less frequently. Information that appears on the resume is not directly restated; rather, ways in which educational and work experiences are directly related to the job being sought are pointed out. Look closely at the letter in Figure 13-15. Notice how the writer's qualifications correspond closely to the job requirements listed in the company/job profile of an entry-level auditor in Figure 13-5: intellectual skills, computer skills, interpersonal skills, knowledge of work environment, ethical standards, and communication skills. This applicant's research paid dividends as she was prepared to discuss those experiences important to the accounting firm.

After reading the letter of application and the accompanying resume, the employer should be able to see the connection between the applicant's experiences and the job's requirements. That connection needs to be emphasized in the letter or the resume. In Figure 13-14, the letter of application interprets experiences because its accompanying chronological resume (Figure 13-8) does not. Because the functional resume in Figure 13-11 points out the commonality of experiences and job requirements, the application letter, therefore, need not do

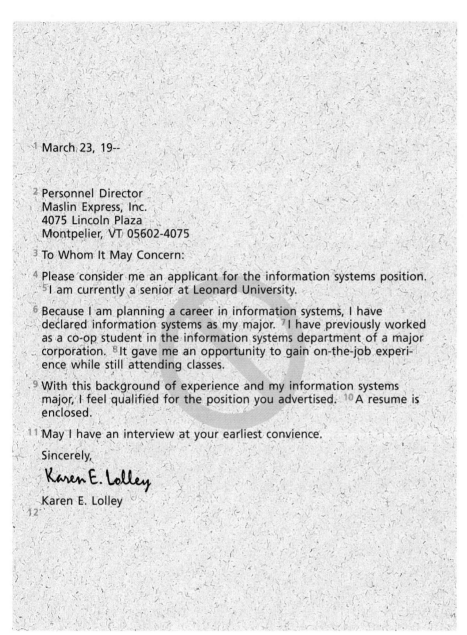

March 23, 19--

Personnel Director
Maslin Express, Inc.
4075 Lincoln Plaza
Montpelier, VT 05602-4075

To Whom It May Concern:

Please consider me an applicant for the information systems position. I am currently a senior at Leonard University.

Because I am planning a career in information systems, I have declared information systems as my major. I have previously worked as a co-op student in the information systems department of a major corporation. It gave me an opportunity to gain on-the-job experience while still attending classes.

With this background of experience and my information systems major, I feel qualified for the position you advertised. A resume is enclosed.

May I have an interview at your earliest convience.

Sincerely,

Karen E. Lolley

Karen E. Lolley

1 Omits the sender's address, needed when using plain paper.

2 Does not address the letter to a specific individual, reducing the effectiveness.

3 Uses an impersonal salutation, making the letter sound like a form letter.

4 Uses a cliché.

5 Conveys an egotistical tone by using "I" as the first word in a sentence.

6-8 Continues to use "I" in self-oriented sentences. States the obvious without relating education or experience to the job at Maslin Express.

9 Makes a commendable attempt to interpret experiences as beneficial and job related. Passes judgment on her own qualifications, which is best left to the employer.

10 Refers to the resume by stating the obvious; does not call attention to the qualifications listed on the resume.

11 Uses a cliché in the action closing. Misspells "convenience."

12 Omits the enclosure notation.

FIGURE 13-13   Poor example of an application letter to accompany a chronological resume.

so. The letter would simply identify the job applied for, give just enough highlights to generate interest in the resume, refer the reader to it, and allude to action.

In the resumes and letters illustrated, applicants have high grade-point averages. Good grades suggest willingness to work hard, ability to learn quickly, and (possibly) skill in human relations. Compared with other professions, the accounting profession is reportedly most influenced by a high grade index. The reasoning is that knowledge of accounting principles and techniques is vital, and graduates who have the highest grades will know the most. Because students with 4.0 grade-point averages are sometimes stereotyped as "bookworms" or

1 Includes sender's address because plain paper is used.

2 Addresses letter to a specific person within the company.

3 Includes a salutation to a specific addressee.

4 Identifies a specific job and introduces applicant's background.

5 Includes career idea early—to set the applicant apart from others whose interests may be less serious.

6, 7 Leads to ways skills have prepared for a job in information systems.

8, 9 Points out experiences on the previous job that could be transferred. Uses words commonly used in the field; reveals an awareness of qualities essential for success.

10 Introduces the resume. Uses an action closing without sounding pushy or apologetic. Expresses no preference for a call or a letter.

11 Includes enclosure notation to alert the employer that a resume is included.

1 980 Cambridge Road
Bangor, ME 04401-8572
March 23, 19--

2 Mr. Alex Jennings
Personnel Director
Maslin Express, Inc.
4075 Lincoln Plaza
Montpelier, VT 05602-4075

3 Dear Mr. Jennings:

4 My thorough education and related experience have prepared me for an entry-level position in information systems.

5 Earning a degree in Management Information Systems has provided me with an in-depth understanding of the field as well as an overall view of the major areas of business. 6 Upper-level courses have given me opportunities for gaining technical proficiency in structured programming, business applications software, and systems design. 7 My experience with *Clipper*, a major database management system, has involved developing applications and providing user support, including detailed documentation.

8 Working as a co-op student for Central Computer Services exposed me to the information systems operations of a major corporation and allowed me to apply knowledge and skills acquired in the classroom. 9 As part of a technical support group, I worked directly with users to solve both hardware and software problems.

10 After you have reviewed the enclosed resume, I would welcome a chance to discuss career opportunities with Maslin Express.

Sincerely,

Karen E. Lolley

Karen E. Lolley

11 Enclosure

FIGURE 13-14   *Good example of an application letter to accompany a chronological resume.*

socially insensitive, such students should present personal information that depicts them as well rounded. The resume or the application letter could—by reporting special interests, activities, and accomplishments—counter the stereotype.

Most students who have a grade-point average between 2.0 and 3.0 (on a 4.0 scale) choose not to report their grades. Employers reading resumes (most of whom are likely to be graduates themselves) are well aware that most colleges award degrees to students who have at least a 2.0 average. Applicants who

P.O. Box 2407
Nashville, TN 37202-2407
October 15, 19--

Mr. Warren Kurtz
Nicovich & Read, CPAs
1000 Plaza Court
Austin, TX 78710-1000

Dear Mr. Kurtz:

An auditing emphasis in accounting and my related job experience qualify me to function effectively as an auditor in your firm.

Because of my interest in auditing, I chose the majority of my accounting electives from the auditing course offerings. I especially enjoyed Auditing Practice. Unstructured, often ambiguous problems that require creative solutions are among my favorite assignments.

As a result of taking Accounting Information Systems and other computer courses, I am proficient in the operation of *Lotus 1-2-3, WordPerfect for Windows, Paradox,* and several general ledger and graphics programs. I gained valuable experience using this software while working for Devlin & Cole, CPAs.

My experience at Devlin & Cole, CPAs also gave me countless opportunities to interact with practicing auditors, often assisting them on site with clients. I learned to appreciate the need to work long, irregular hours; function effectively in groups; and develop positive relationships with clients and staff. My rating on the written and oral communication skills component of my performance evaluation was consistently "excellent," solid evidence of my ability to write and deliver clear, concise, and ethical messages— primarily planning memos, letters, and audit reports.

References on the enclosed resume would be glad to comment on my accounting education and experience. Please call or write so we can discuss the possibility of my joining the audit staff of Nicovich & Read.

Sincerely,

Sara Beth Christophel

Sara Beth Christophel

Enclosure

FIGURE 13-15   Good example of an application letter to accompany a chronological resume.

choose not to report their grade-point averages can, instead, emphasize note-worthy school activities, offices held, volunteer work, or part-time work.

Before writing a resume and application letter, study carefully the overall suggestions in the "General Writing Guidelines" placed before the chapter exercises in Chapter 9, page 269. Then, study the specific suggestions in the "Check Your Writing" checklist that follows the chapter summary. Compare your work with this checklist again after you have written a rough draft and make any revisions.

SUMMARY

1 **Because life's enjoyment is strongly influenced by success on the job, planning and preparing for a career are vital.** Like other important decisions, you must gather information to make wise career decisions and preferably should record it in a career notebook for easy reference. Ask questions about yourself, about a possible career, and about a specific job in the chosen field. Interview people already working at the job. Recording and analyzing this information will assist you in selecting a satisfying career and preparing an effective resume.

A resume includes identification, objective, summary of achievements, qualifications, personal information, and references. To compete favorably for a job, exploit computer technology to develop an appealing, easy-to-read design and print a high-quality copy. Like other written documents, resumes and application letters should reflect high standards of content, organization, style, and mechanics. If an employer detects errors in any of these categories, you will probably not be granted an interview.

2 **Chronological resumes use "Education" and "Experience" as headings and list experiences in reverse chronological order.** Functional resumes use qualifications the applicant possesses as headings. The combination chronological and functional resume lists education and experience and uses functional headings that emphasize qualifications. Choose the resume type you feel most effectively presents your qualifications.

3 **Names and addresses of possible employers may be obtained from networks, career services centers at schools, employers' offices, employment agencies and contractors, help-wanted ads, online databases and printed sources, and professional organizations.**

4 **An application letter accompanies a resume.** The purposes are to introduce the applicant and the resume, arouse interest in the information given on the resume, and assist an employer in seeing ways in which the applicant's services would be desirable. As such, it is a persuasive letter—beginning with an attention-getter, including a central appeal and convincing evidence, and closing with an indirect reference to the enclosed resume and desired action (invitation to an interview).

Use terminology that will be used on the job to indicate your familiarity with the field and avoid using words and expressions overused in application letters. Encourage the reader to extend an interview without apologizing or being too demanding. Leave the decision to call or write to the employer's preference. Finally, prepare the application letter, resume, and envelope on plain, high-quality bond paper. Proofread carefully to ensure your employment credentials are error-free, an example of your best work.

CHECK YOUR WRITING

RESUME

CONTENT
- ☐ Is based on self-, career, and job analyses.
- ☐ Includes qualifications compatible with job requirements.
- ☐ Includes only relevant ideas.
- ☐ Presents qualifications truthfully and honestly.

ORGANIZATION
- ☐ Headings are arranged in appropriate sequence.
- ☐ Significant ideas are in emphatic positions.
- ☐ Experiences are listed consistently, either in time sequence or in order of importance.

STYLE
- ☐ Omits personal pronouns.
- ☐ Uses action verbs.
- ☐ Uses past tense for previous jobs; present tense for present job.
- ☐ Places significant words in emphatic positions.
- ☐ Uses parallelism in listing multiple items.
- ☐ Uses positive language.
- ☐ Uses simple words (but some jargon of the field is acceptable).
- ☐ Uses correct grammar.

MECHANICS
- ☐ Is printed on high-quality (24-pound, 100-percent cotton-fiber content), neutral-colored paper.
- ☐ Is printed with clear, sharp print.
- ☐ Is balanced on the page.
- ☐ Uses ample margins even if a second page is required.
- ☐ Includes a page number on all pages except the first.
- ☐ Positions headings consistently throughout.
- ☐ Uses an outline format or bullets to emphasize multiple points.
- ☐ Uses indentation, underlining, capitalization, font changes, and graphic lines or borders to enhance overall impact.

APPLICATION LETTER

CONTENT
- ☐ Includes valid ideas (statements are true).
- ☐ Identifies the letter as an application for a certain job.
- ☐ Excludes nonessential ideas.
- ☐ Emphasizes significant qualifications.
- ☐ Makes reference to enclosed resume.
- ☐ Ends with action closing that is neither apologetic nor pushy.

ORGANIZATION
- ☐ Begins by revealing the job sought in the attention-getter.
- ☐ Presents paragraphs in most appropriate sequence (order of importance is possibly best).
- ☐ Ends with a reference to action employer is to take (call or write and extend an invitation to an interview).

STYLE
- ☐ Uses simple language (no attempt to impress with a sophisticated vocabulary; some professional jargon is justified).
- ☐ Uses relatively short sentences with sufficient variety.
- ☐ Places significant words in emphatic positions.
- ☐ Uses correct grammar.

MECHANICS
- ☐ Includes writer's address above the date.
- ☐ Includes equal side margins (approximately one inch).
- ☐ Is balanced on the page.
- ☐ Is printed on plain paper that matches the resume.
- ☐ Has relatively short first and last paragraphs; others are held to fewer than six or seven lines.
- ☐ Contains *no* keying, grammar, spelling, or punctuation errors.

REFERENCES

Barnum, C. M. (1987, September-October). Writing resumes that sell. *Management World*, pp. 10-13.

Baxter, N. (1987, Spring). Resumes, application forms, cover letters, and interviews. *Occupational Outlook Quarterly*, pp. 17-23.

Charles, P. J. (1988, September-October). Resumes without clutter. *Management World*, pp. 19-20.

Clegg, P. (1994, September 6). Jury's in: jobs scarce for law school grads. *The Sacramento Bee*, p. 1A.

Dolan, D. R., & Schumacher, J. E. (1994). Top U.S. sources for an online job search. *Database, 17*(5), 34.

Griffin, M. A., & Anderson, P. L. (1994). Resume content. *Business Education Forum, 48*(3), 11-14.

Holley, W. H., Jr., Higgins, E., & Speights, S. (1988, December). Resumes and cover letters: What do HR managers really want? *Personnel*, pp. 49-51.

Salwen, K. G. (1994, February 15). Labor letter. *The Wall Street Journal*, p. 1A.

Write a resume that works: It's simple: Custom tailor each one to the job. (1990, June). *Changing Times*, pp. 91, 93, 95.

REVIEW QUESTIONS

1. For a college student, what are the advantages of developing a career notebook? Briefly describe the types of information that should be included.
2. What are several good library sources for learning about the duties and responsibilities of a certain job?
3. What is the purpose of a resume? List the standard information included in a resume.
4. What are the consequences of inflating your qualifications on a resume?
5. What are the characteristics of a good job objective?
6. What is the purpose of the "Summary of Achievements" section? Must it be included in every resume? Explain.
7. List at least three types of information that could be included in the "Education" section. Should you include information about your high school (diploma and activities)?
8. What are the advantages of using subject-understood sentences in resumes? Action verbs? Crisp phrases? Descriptive but not overly strong adjectives? Provide one example of your own.
9. What criteria should be used for selecting information to be included on a resume—especially honors and activities?
10. What are the advantages and disadvantages of including personal information on a resume? What criteria are used to select which personal information to include, if any?
11. Under what conditions might you choose to include or not include references on a resume? Is obtaining permission from references necessary?
12. How do you provide references to prospective employers if you choose not to include a list on your resume?
13. Describe the three organization patterns of resumes and tell under what circumstances each would be effective.
14. Discuss five guidelines for formatting an attractive, highly professional resume.
15. List five sources from which prospective employers' names and addresses may be obtained.
16. Should an application letter and a resume contain the same information? Explain.
17. What outline is recommended for application letters?
18. List techniques for writing effective persuasive letters that should be applied in application letters. Refer to Chapter 11 to answer this question if necessary.
19. Why should you avoid words frequently used in application letters? List some of these words.
20. What action is sought in an application letter? What tone should you avoid in the action closing of an application letter? How does this differ from a sales letter?

EXERCISES

1. Complete each of the THINK IT OVER activities that your instructor assigns.
2. Study the following application letter. Make a list of ways in which principles discussed in this chapter are applied and violated. Then rewrite the letter, eliminating its principal weaknesses. Be prepared to discuss the letter in class.

Allen S. Gossage
105 Pear Orchard Road
Atlanta, GA 30345-2334
March 5, 19--

Ms. Kathryn D. Leverette
Powe Associates, Inc.
9800 Parkview Avenue
Birmingham, Al. 35202-6321

[1]Please consider me for the insurance position you advertized in yesterday's paper. [2]As you can see from the attached resume, I have worked for a real estate firm for the last fifteen years. [3]As you know, real estate experience is very similiar to insurance experience.

[4]An insurance man needs (above all else) dependability. [5]He needs to be accurate, courteous, and understanding. [6]He needs to be able to communicate, both orally and written. [7]I have written many letters in connection with my work in real estate. [8]Actually, I do most of the correspondence for the other people in this office. [9]As a student in college, you will observe that I have been exposed to Marshall McLuhan's theories in various courses. [10]I have observed the influence of his thinking in all the writing I do.

[11]While in school (where I compiled a 3.621 average as a business major) I took some very valuable courses in insurance. [12]Work in real estate has kept me in constant contact with insurance matters.

[13]References (and details of my qualifications) are presented in organized form on the enclosed resume which is attached for your convenience. [14]I shall look forward to the opportunity of meeting you personaly and discussing my qualifications.

Sincerely

allen S. Gossage

Allen S. Gossage

3. Study the following application letter. Make a list of ways in which the principles discussed in this chapter are applied and violated. Then rewrite the letter, eliminating its principal weaknesses. Be prepared to discuss the letter in class.

September 5, 19--

McConnell Stores, Ltd.
New Brunswick, NJ 08902-7543

Dear Sirs:

[1]Please consider me as an applicant for the buyer's position you advertized in last nights issue of the *Times Meridian*. [2]The primary advantage I would have as a buyer is my heavy educational background. [3]Among the courses I have taken are buyer behavior, retailing, marketing, public relations, and advertizing. [4]I am sure you realize the many ways in which these courses can prepare one for a career in marketing.

[5]In addition to my classes, my educational background includes work in the university bookstore, service on the school yearbook, and president of my fraternity. [6]I will be receiving my degree on May 5, 19--. [7]If you can use an energetic young man with my educational background, I will appreciate you studying the resume which you will find inclosed. [8]May I have an interview at your earliest convience. [9]So I can put my educational background to work for you.

Sincerely,

Yuan Chiang

Yuan Chiang

E-MAIL APPLICATION

 Your instructor will distribute a sample resume to the class or may ask you to exchange a rough draft of your resume with another class member. You are to critique its effectiveness using the guidelines and the examples provided in the chapter. Send an e-mail message to your instructor (or the student if you evaluated a class member's resume) giving your overall impression of the resume and specific suggestions for improving it. Printscreen to obtain a copy of your message and submit it to your instructor. Submit a copy of the resume if you critiqued a student's resume.

APPLICATIONS

CAREER DEVELOPMENT

1. **Getting Essential Information to Make a Wise Career Decision.** Prepare the career notebook described at the beginning of this chapter. At the top of separate pages, identify major sections: self-analysis, career analysis, job analysis, and interview with career person. Then, seek answers to the questions listed in each of the following categories:
   a. Self-analysis: Figure 13-1.
   b. Career analysis: Figure 13-2.
   c. Job analysis: Figure 13-3.
   d. Interview with a career person: Figure 13-4. Select a person currently working in your career field. To validate information you receive, you may wish to interview two people. A person who has worked in a particular field but is not currently involved might be more objective (for instance, an accountant in public accounting now working in private industry or teaching accounting).

CAREER DEVELOPMENT

2. **Preparing a Company/Job Profile.** Use information obtained from completing Application 1 to prepare a company/job profile for the company/job in which you expect to be interviewing. Begin a new section in your career notebook: COMPANY PROFILE FOR _____ (supply company name). Insert the completed profile in your career notebook. Using Figure 13-5 as a guide, complete these steps:
   a. Review the completed profile and note the degree of compatibility between your qualification and the company and job requirements.
   b. Compile a list of strengths and weaknesses (lack of a match between your qualifications and job requirements) as they relate to the job requirements.
   c. Consider carefully the deficiencies you must overcome before your qualifications fully match the job requirements. What are possible strategies for overcoming these deficiencies? Are any of these strategies feasible, or is overcoming these deficiencies out of your control?
   d. Analyze the final comparison and decide whether interviewing for this job would be wise.

CAREER DEVELOPMENT

3. **Preparing a Resume and an Application Letter for a Job of Your Choice.** Write a resume and an application letter for a job you would like to have. Use information compiled in Applications 1 and 2 to identify information that should be included in the resume and application letter. Make the assumption you prefer:
   a. You are applying for an immediate part-time job.
   b. You are applying for a full-time job for next summer.
   c. You are applying for a cooperative education assignment or internship.
   d. You are applying for a full-time job immediately after you graduate. Look at the list of courses you plan to take and write as though you had taken them and satisfied the requirements for a degree.

Follow the guidelines presented in this chapter for preparing a resume. As a minimum, incorporate the valid comments of at least two others competent in proofreading and resume design. Use the desktop publishing capability available to you to produce a highly effective, professional document.

CAREER DEVELOPMENT

4. **Preparing an Effective Application Letter for a Scholarship.** Assume that a $1,500 scholarship for students in your major field of study has been advertised in *Business Week*. The money comes from a national honor society in your discipline. The recipient must (a) have a B or higher grade average, (b) have more than 60 hours of college credit, (c) be free to attend a week-long, expenses-paid convention in Houston during the second week of May, and (d) write a satisfactory letter of application. Address your application letter to The Scholarship Foundation, 301 Skinner Boulevard, St. Louis, MO 63155-3038.

CASES FOR ANALYSIS

HUMAN RESOURCES MANAGEMENT

Case 1. Outplaced Workers Need Employment Advice. Baker Mortgage Corporation has just completed radical reorganization and downsizing; consequently, approximately 50 top- and middle-level managers are seeking employment. Because many of these individuals have been with your company for ten years or more, they are finding the job-search process difficult. To assist these outplaced employees in finding jobs, the board of directors voted to open an Outplacement Center; and you have been hired to direct the center. Your first action was to set up an office with telephones, area newspapers (want ads), and current articles on job searching. After interviewing a few of these individuals, you realize they need basic information about preparing job credentials (resume and application letter). Immediately, you begin to develop a handout (flyer or pamphlet) presenting concise, informative, and easy-to-follow guidelines for writing job credentials that will win an interview.

Required:

1. Conduct needed research to locate relevant, up-to-date information. Cite a number of sources to be certain that your information is objective; use appropriate documentation within the document to protect yourself and your company against plagiarism and to assist the managers in locating your references for further research. Be creative in the way you direct your reader to the bibliography you will provide.

2. Review the research to determine which information will be relevant to your particular audience. For example, giving guidelines about including high school activities or part-time work during college would be unnecessary to these veteran workers.

3. Write these relevant guidelines using the information gathered in Steps 1 and 2.

4. Use desktop publishing capabilities available to you to design a creative, attention-getting layout for this document. Refer to Chapter 5 for page-design layout principles.

HUMAN RESOURCES MANAGEMENT

Case 2.   Preparing a One-Page Resume for an Outplaced Employee. As the director of the Outplacement Center for Baker Mortgage Corporation, you help outplaced employees prepare professional resumes that reflect their abilities. Today, you are preparing a resume for Kevin Rueter, who left the following narrative of his qualifications with you. He is interested in securing a position as a senior loan officer in a major banking firm.

EMPLOYMENT INFORMATION

Kevin W. Rueter, 8901 Brookdale Road, Pueblo, CO 81002-8901.

Personal data: 38 years old, divorced, two children (John 8, Jeanne 5), 6'4" tall, in excellent health (wear glasses and hearing aid). Exercise regularly, primarily racquetball and lifting weights. Also enjoy golf.

I received a Bachelor of Science in Business at Westbrook University in May of 1978. My major was Finance and Real Estate; my overall grade-point average was 3.6. While in college, my activities included: Phi Kappa Phi, Beta Gamma Sigma, Dean's list for four semesters, recipient of the Du Bois Foundation Scholarship (awarded to outstanding finance majors), intramural football and tennis, president of the Student Association, Who's Who Among Students in American Colleges and Universities, Hall of Fame, president of the Banking and Finance Association. I graduated in the top 10 percent of a class of 100 at Blair High School in Pueblo, Colorado, in 1971.

My employment history includes the following: (1) Teller at Saguaro Bank during summers of 1972-74. I worked 20 hours a week and was promoted from Teller I to Teller III. (2) Completed a one-semester internship (gained three hours' credit toward degree) at Sunbelt Bank in Fr. Collins from September to December, 1977. Selection process was very competitive. My primary responsibilities were to assist the branch manager and approve small consumer loans. (3) Commercial Loan Officer, Baker Mortgage

Corporation from June, 1978 to November, 1995. My duties included managing a $25 million loan portfolio, making substantial credit decisions for loans averaging $800,000 each, and striving to achieve realistic lending goals. I also arranged loans for various types of clients (importers and exporters, wholesalers, and manufacturers) with tremendous sales. Completed Baker's intensive training program for commercial loan officers, which required me to pass an intermediate accounting examination before being admitted and to pass an arduous loan officer's examination when I finished.

Currently I volunteer as a Little League baseball coach (ages 6-8) and as a Boy Scout troop leader (ages 10-12).

The following individuals have agreed to provide additional information about my qualifications: (1) Paul J. Bryant, Head Teller, Saguaro Bank, 905 Courtland Drive, Pueblo, CO 81002-0905; (2) Ellyn Broome, Vice President, Sunbelt Bank, 3900 Central Avenue, Ft. Collins, CO 80521-3900; (3) James L. Hawthorne, Vice President of Commercial Loans, Baker Mortgage Corporation, 2500 North Mesquite Drive, Pueblo, CO 81002-3728; (4) Cynthia M. Buntyn, Baker Mortgage Corporation, same address as given above; (5) Rev. Joseph E. Kerns, Faith Church of Pueblo, 3710 Friar Lane, Pueblo, CO 81002-3710; and (6) Richard G. Rueter, President, Chamber of Commerce, 9310 Commerce Street, Pueblo, CO 81002-9310.

Required:

1. Review the narrative and consider answers to the following questions:
   a. What is Kevin's career objective?
   b. What information is relevant to Kevin's career objective?
   c. Has essential information been omitted? (Supply fictitious information if needed.)
   d. Which resume type do you think would present Kevin's qualifications most effectively: chronological, functional, or combination chronological and functional? Explain.
   e. Would a "Summary of Qualifications" section strengthen Kevin's resume? Explain.
   f. Should Kevin list his references on the resume

or state that a list is available? Should he prepare a separate references page? Which of the references are the most appropriate (assuming that all will provide positive recommendations)?

2. Prepare Kevin's resume (and references page if necessary) referring to the analysis prepared in Step 1 and following the guidelines presented in this chapter. Incorporate the valid comments made by at least two others competent in proofreading and resume design. Use the desktop publishing capability available to you to produce a highly effective, professional document.

CHAPTER 14

JOB INTERVIEWS, EMPLOYMENT

MESSAGES, AND PERFORMANCE

APPRAISALS

OBJECTIVES
When you have completed Chapter 14, you will
be able to

1 Explain the nature of structured, unstructured, and stress interviews.

2 Recognize the interviewer's role in the job interview process.

3 Prepare for and participate effectively in a job interview.

4 Recognize and bypass illegal interview questions.

5 Write effective letters related to employment (follow-up, thank-you, job-acceptance, job-refusal, and resignation letters, and recommendation requests) and complete application forms accurately.

6 Write positive and negative recommendations that are legally defensible.

7 Participate effectively in a performance appraisal interview.

Isako sits in the reception area of the office. She has arrived a few minutes early for her interview to allow herself time to unwind and focus on what she will say. She has hoped for an interview with this company since she met the recruiter at the campus job fair. Isako knows that the interview does not guarantee a job offer; she is competing in one of the toughest job markets in recent history. Not only are other recent graduates looking for jobs, but so are recently unemployed professionals whose jobs were axed as part of corporate downsizing.

Although she feels confident, she is a little nervous; but she relaxes when she thinks of how well-prepared she is. She not only has researched the company and knows its operations, but she has also studied the industry itself, including current issues and VIPs. In addition, she has rehearsed the interview using role play and visualization, reviewing a list of possible questions. She has reviewed her resume to be able to answer any question about it that may come up. Finally, she has chosen to wear a simple conservative business suit so that her interviewer will see her as a mature, professional candidate for the job. Isako knows that her interviewer may conduct the interview in a number of ways: formally or informally, structured or unstructured. She is prepared for any of these formats. When the interviewer walks into the reception area to greet her, she is ready with a smile and a firm handshake, certain that the interview will be a success.

Does the idea of an interview cause you anxiety as it does many people? With some preparation and practice, you can be a successful interviewer or interviewee. In addition to the obvious oral communication skills you need for these tasks, you must possess impeccable writing skills for thank-you letters, acceptance letters, rejection letters, and requests for recommendations. Lack of preparation and poor communication skills cannot be hidden in an interview situation. Interviews allow you to "sell" yourself to a prospective employer; do not let carelessness cost you an important "sell."

TYPES OF EMPLOYMENT INTERVIEWS

LEARNING OBJECTIVE 1

Depending on the goals of the interviewer, interviews may follow a formal structure or be allowed to take their own course. Both structured and unstructured interviews can be intentionally stressful—called *stress interviews*.

Structured and Computer-Assisted Interviews

In a **structured interview**, the interviewer follows a predetermined agenda, including a checklist of items or a series of questions and statements designed to elicit the necessary information or interviewee reaction. Because each applicant answers the same questions, the interviewer has comparable data to evaluate.

Computer-assisted interviews overcome typical human interviewer errors.

One type of structured interview is conducted by a computer. Companies are finding computer-assisted interviews to be a reliable and effective way to conduct preliminary job interviews. Applicants use a computer to provide answers to a list of carefully selected questions. Because expert computer systems can overcome some of the inherent problems with traditional face-to-face interviews, the overall quality of the selection process improves. Typical human interviewer errors include forgetting to ask important questions, talking too much, being reluctant to ask sensitive questions, forming unjustified negative first impressions, obtaining unreliable and illegal information that makes an applicant feel judged, and using interview data ineffectively.

Research has shown that applicants prefer computer interviews to human interviews. They respond more honestly to a computer and are less likely to provide polite, socially acceptable responses (Mitchell, 1990).

By reviewing the comprehensive report generated by the computer, the human interviewer can reliably and quickly decide whether to invite the applicant for a second interview and identify the specific information that must be obtained from the applicant during a second interview.

The computer report contains standard, reliable information about each applicant, alerts the human interviewer to any contradictory responses (e.g., applicant indicated he was terminated for absenteeism but later indicated that he thought his former employer would give him an outstanding recommendation), and highlights any potential problem areas (for example, an applicant responded that she would remain on the job less than a year). The report also generates a list of structured interview questions for the human interviewer to ask (for example, "Mary, you said you feel your former employer would rate you average. Why don't you feel it would be higher?").

What types of information does a computer-generated interview report provide?

In light of the high costs of interviewing and the importance of selecting employees matched to the job, more and more companies will be using computer-assisted interviewing to screen applicants (Mitchell, 1990). Regardless of whether the interview is face-to-face or computer assisted, you will need to provide objective, truthful evidence of your qualifications as they relate to specific job requirements.

THINK IT OVER
What are the benefits and costs of computer-assisted interviewing to the company and the applicant? Use the online database in your library to help you obtain more information to answer this question.

Unstructured Interviews

An **unstructured interview** is a freewheeling exchange and may shift from one subject to another, depending on the interests of the participants. Some experienced interviewers are able to make a structured interview seem unstructured. The goal of many unstructured interviews is to explore unknown areas in search of new ideas.

What is the goal of many unstructured interviews?

Stress Interviews

A **stress interview** is designed to place the interviewee in an anxiety-producing situation so an evaluation of the interviewee's performance under stress may be made.

In all cases, interviewees should attempt to assess the nature of the interview quickly and adjust behavior accordingly. As the following discussion of the role of the interviewer reveals, you, as an interviewee, can perform much better when you understand the interviewer's purpose.

Understanding that interviewers sometimes deliberately create anxiety to assess your ability to perform under stress should help you handle stress interviews more effectively.

JOB INTERVIEWER'S ROLE

The success of any interview depends on the communication skills of the participants and how strongly each wants to practice them. As a guide, the following four steps apply to almost all interviewing and vary with the types of interviews: (1) preparation, (2) interchange, (3) evaluation, and (4) action.

LEARNING OBJECTIVE 2

What are the four steps involved in interviewing?

Preparing for the Interview

Preparation may be the most neglected of the four steps, yet it may be the most important. Preparation involves the following elements:

1. *Purpose.* What is the purpose of the interview? What are the expected outcomes? What style is appropriate, and what atmosphere is better—relaxed or stressful?
2. *Physical arrangements.* Is the physical setup consistent with the purpose? Is privacy adequate? What distractions should be eliminated?
3. *Self-understanding.* Does the interviewer have an awareness of his or her own strengths and weaknesses, prejudices, biases, perceptions, and other possible barriers to effective communication?
4. *Understanding the other person.* What is known or should be known about the interviewee? What are her or his values, aspirations, motives, and background?

Through effective preparation, the interviewer can set the stage for whatever kind of interview is desired. If the interview is to be structured, are items to be discussed arranged in proper sequence? Will the nature of the questions elicit information-revealing responses? Will the sequence lead to a relaxed interview or to a stressful one?

When you, as a job applicant, plan for your interview, keep in mind that most personnel interviewers have probably gone through these preparatory steps. This reminder will help you determine the interview style, so you can adapt your behavior appropriately.

Meeting Face to Face—The Interchange

Does a first impression last long?

During the interview, both the interviewer and the interviewee should pay particular attention to the following factors:

1. *Rapport.* How well have you reached a common ground to establish a climate consistent with the purpose of the meeting? Does an air of mutual respect exist?
2. *Flexibility.* Can the interviewer redirect the flow of discussion when it strays from the purpose and disrupts the original plan?
3. *Two-way flow.* Are the participants engaged in two-way communication, or is one or the other turning it into a one-way situation?

THINK IT OVER
Feedback and effective listening are important communication skills in an interview. Review these sections in Chapter 1.

As either the interviewer or the interviewee, you can become far more effective than the usual participant if you develop some simple techniques for providing feedback and for clarifying issues. Listening in the classroom, for example, is relatively easy to do because you assume a listening role as your primary activity. In an interview, however, you will be both a listener and a speaker; and some of your listening time will be spent preparing what you will say when it is your turn to speak.

Interviewing as a process is much like ordinary one-to-one conversation, differing primarily in the higher degree of tension that normally goes with interviewing. Thus, you should work to make your transition from listener to speaker as smooth as possible. If you have not listened thoroughly enough to understand completely, your response to the other person will probably be inadequate. Effective, active listening involves mental concentration and good physical posture. Listening is not a passive activity as many people believe.

Questioning is one technique used by good conversationalists and interview participants to gain more information before making a complete response. Questioning can also encourage a shy person to participate more fully.

An example of a question to get more information:

Applicant: I had no idea I would be promoted so quickly.

Interviewer: What qualities do you think led to your promotion?

A question to clarify word meaning:

Applicant: Your answer is somewhat nebulous.

Interviewer: What exactly do you mean? (Hint: *nebulous* means *unclear*.)

A question to seek feelings:

Applicant: Then I was promoted to a job I didn't like.

Interviewer: How did you adjust to that?

Questions are effective forms of feedback and tend to keep the interview moving when it might otherwise fall flat. **Direct questions** can be answered easily and briefly. They ask for "yes" or "no" answers or for factual information. "Do you like to fly?" "When will you graduate?" "Have you traveled overseas?" Because they call for factual information, direct questions do not help much in encouraging the dialogue of the interview. **Indirect questions**, however, do contribute to dialogue because they call for answers that require thought on the part of the receiver. "Why do you believe accounting is the career for you?" "What experience have you had in working as part of a team or group?"

Define direct and indirect questions and give an example of each.

Questions or statements are often a form of paraphrasing—restating the content or the intent of the sender's message to check your own understanding.

Interviewers often paraphrase an applicant's answer to clarify the meaning.

Applicant: My resume shows that I was actively involved in college student groups.

Interviewer: These activities must have provided an excellent opportunity to meet people.

Applicant: Yes, these activities provided me opportunities to interact with people of all types and to develop leadership skills.

We use the techniques of questioning and paraphrasing most of the time in conversation. The thoughtful use of these techniques can contribute much to interviewing situations and to two-way communication flow.

Evaluating the Interview

Decision-making time arrives at the interview. Is the interviewer prepared to analyze alternative actions? Should the decision be made or postponed? Should the interviewee be invited for further interviews? Should the interviewee be told a letter will be sent at a later time? The interviewer should know what action to take simply because arriving at some kind of decision or outcome was considered in the preparation step. Does each of the two participants know exactly what is to be done? Has a mutual understanding been developed?

Some Interviewer Guidelines

Explaining interview procedures to the applicant will help create a nonthreatening climate.

The interviewee should be told the interviewer's guidelines because they can help both parties in the meeting. If the interviewer plans to take notes during the interview, for example, the interviewee must be forewarned. Otherwise, the interviewee might freeze when the interviewer takes notes. On the other hand, if notes are not made, the job applicant in a personnel interview might feel that he or she is not receiving fair consideration. The interviewer should introduce the note-taking idea with a statement such as: "I like to take a few notes during the interview to jog my memory later and to make sure we cover everything we should. We can also use them near the end of the interview to make sure your comments and my understanding are in agreement. Do you mind?" Following agreement, note taking will not be a barrier, particularly if the notes are not considered secret and if they are for the interviewer's use only. Leaving the notes in a visible place will help assure the interviewee. Of course, the interviewer can always add personal impressions to the notes after the interviewee leaves.

THINK IT OVER
Think about interviews in which you have participated. What techniques did the interviewer practice that eased or increased your anxiety?

The interviewer can help establish the style of the interview by proper use of voice tone and volume. A friendly tone may put the applicant at ease. A harsh, aggressive tone may frighten the applicant and result in a stressful situation. In the same way, the interviewer can set the stage for a relaxed or stressful interview simply by organizing questions. Asking the most difficult question first, for example, may throw the applicant into a frenzied state. Body posture is also an important element. By paying attention through eye contact and by appearing interested through the use of acknowledging head motions and a general body posture indicating concern, the interviewer has a better opportunity to pursue the goals of the interview.

Some of these techniques must be practiced by both participants.

These guidelines have much to do with the effectiveness of the interview, but the kinds of questions asked can determine its success or failure. Questions that can be answered with a simple "yes" or "no" don't contribute much and may leave interviewees in a position of having to stray from the subject to put themselves in a better light. Questions that ask how, what, or why provide openings for genuine discussion.

Interviewer Prohibitions

Interviewers must describe all working conditions to any job applicant. The applicant then must decide whether he or she is willing and able to meet those conditions. In addition, interviewers need to know if the applicant can do the job, is willing to do the job, and will fit in with others in the company.

What do the EEOC guidelines prohibit?

In seeking answers to these questions, interviewers sometimes ask questions that invade the applicant's privacy and that violate the Equal Employment Opportunity Commission (EEOC) and Fair Employment Practices Guidelines. These EEOC guidelines prohibit discriminatory hiring based on race, creed, color, gender, national origin, disability, and age. For example, turning down an applicant for any of the following reasons is illegal:

- Customers do not want to deal with a particular gender or ethnic group or a person with a disability.

- Co-workers might object.
- The position requires travel with members of opposite genders.
- Working hours are unusual.
- Restroom facilities are lacking.
- A lower salary is offered to other applicants of equivalent background.

Interviewers must not introduce questions or information that might lead to discriminatory hiring. Access to such information could be used as evidence against the company in the case of litigation even if the information were not used in the hiring process.

To ensure fairness, interviewers should be absolutely certain that all questions and comments are relevant to the job for which the applicant is being considered. If a question is not job related, it may not be legal; therefore, it should not be asked. Fairness of questions may vary depending on the job requirements. For example, the arrest/conviction record of a person applying for a police officer job could be highly relevant to the job; but the same information could be illegal for a person applying for a job as an engineer (Hunt & Eadie, 1987).

In general, the following subjects should not be introduced during an interview or during the small talk that precedes or follows an interview:

1. *National origin.* "You have an unusual accent; where were you born?" "What religious holidays will require you to miss work?" "What is your immigration status?"
2. *Age.* "I see you attended Central State University; what years were you there?" "Could you provide a copy of your birth certificate?"
3. *Disability.* "Do you have any problems with your eyesight or hearing?" "Can you manage a long flight of stairs?"
4. *Health.* "What is your general state of health?" "Have you ever had a major illness?" "Have you ever been treated by a psychiatrist?"
5. *Height and weight.* "Do you realize a more athletic person is usually hired for this job?"
6. *Marital status.* "Are you married?" "Who is going to watch your children if you come to work for us?" "Do you plan to have children?" "How many?" "Is your spouse employed?" "Do you realize that this job requires a great deal of travel and may require you to relocate?"
7. *Arrests/convictions.* "Have you ever been arrested other than for traffic violations? If so, explain." (Some states allow questions about convictions but not arrests.)
8. *Financial situation.* "Do you own your own home, rent, or live with your parents?" "How long have you lived at your present address?"
9. *Alcohol or drug use.* "Do you drink alcoholic beverages?" "Do you use or have you used drugs?"

James Nunan, vice president of human resources at SCICON Systems, a software company in Palo Alto, California, believes that most of today's managers ask illegal questions accidentally, not purposely (Jenks, 1988). However, in view of increasing litigation and the court's decisive stand on discriminatory hiring, interviewers must be certain they are up to date on employment law. In addition, job applicants (especially those seeking jobs in high-market-demand areas) who are well informed about employment law will not tolerate such questions.

Is obtaining discriminatory information but not using it as the basis for a hiring decision a legally defensible practice?

Avoid these illegal interview questions.

THINK IT OVER
Use the online database in your library to locate articles discussing any recent changes in employment law. Be prepared to discuss them in class.

COMMUNICATION   MENTOR

If a time-pressed business executive has granted you an interview, you should feel obligated to do enough preparatory work to make the interview meaningful. Research the industry and the history of the business. Know some of the issues facing the company or its constituents. Prepare a few questions that indicate you've done your homework.

Go to the interview with a clear view of your objective. If you are unfocused in career direction or unsure of your abilities, ask family, friends, and career counselors to help you make decisions. Using a business interview to try to set basic career direction is a waste of both your time and the interviewer's.

Cynthia Pharr
President & CEO
C. Pharr Marketing Communications

Following the guidelines discussed here will ensure that the interviewer is thoroughly prepared for the interview. No matter how casual or how formal the interview may seem to be, you can be sure that considerable effort went into planning it. Obviously, interviews can never be identical.

Participants change as a result of each interview experience, and each experience gives them greater self-confidence. Competent interviewing is one of the most satisfying and rewarding management skills.

JOB INTERVIEWEE'S ROLE

LEARNING OBJECTIVE 3

Because job searches in the '90s are intensely competitive, learning to interview effectively can mean a job offer. Estimates are that only one job offer results from 100 interviews.

Just as the interviewer proceeds through a step-by-step process, so should the interviewee. As the interviewee, you will want to engage in some pre-interview activities, prepare to perform well during the interview, and take appropriate action after the interview.

College students generally schedule on-campus interviews with representatives from various business organizations. Following the on-campus interviews, successful candidates often are invited for further interviews on the company premises. The purpose of the second interview is to give executives and administrators, other than the personnel interviewer, an opportunity to appraise the candidate. Whether on campus or on company premises, interview methods and practices apply to the situation. When the interview is with company executives, the candidate will probably encounter a wide variety of interview styles. Preliminary planning can pay rich dividends.

Preparing for the Interview

Pre-interview planning involves learning something about the company or organization, doing some studying about yourself, and making sure your appearance and mannerisms will not detract from the impression you hope to make.

STUDY THE COMPANY

Few errors are more detrimental than knowing little about the organization. No knowledge probably indicates insincerity, and the interviewer does not want to waste precious interview time providing the candidate with information that should have been gathered long before.

Companies that have publicly traded stock are required to publish annual reports. Many business school libraries have a file of annual reports and several financial service reports. Other information can be obtained from financial newspapers and electronic sources such as the Internet. Employees of the company or other students who have been interviewed may be of help to the interviewee. Some major schools have prepared videotape interviews with various company recruiters and make the tapes available to students. Preparing a guide similar to the one shown in Figure 14-1 for each company with which you interview will help you learn about each company. Place the guide in your career notebook.

Standard & Poor's Standard Corporation Descriptions is an excellent directory of large companies; *Business-to-Business Yellow Pages* lists hundreds of small companies.

CAREER NOTEBOOK

Company Information

Name. Know that *IBM* stands for *International Business Machines Corporation,* for example.

Status in the industry. Know the company's share of the market, its Fortune 500 standing if any, its sales, and its number of employees.

Latest stock market quote.

Recent news and developments. Read current business periodicals for special-feature articles on the company, its new products, and its corporate leadership.

Scope of the company. Is it local, national, or international?

Corporate officers. Know the names of the chairperson, president, and chief executive officer.

Products and services.

Job Information

Job title. Know the job titles of typical entry-level positions.

Job qualifications. Understand the specific knowledge and skills desired.

Probable salary range.

Career path of the job. Are opportunities for advancement available?

FIGURE 14-1
Interviewee's guide for studying a company.

Projecting a confident, mentally alert impression through your speech and appearance from the moment you walk into an interview is vital because most interview decisions are made in the first four minutes. Be prepared to provide <u>quick</u>, <u>intelligent</u> responses to questions about your education and experiences that required you to apply skills learned in the classroom.

STUDY YOURSELF

When you know something about the company, you will also know something about the kinds of jobs or training programs the company has to offer. Next, review your answers to the company/job profile (Figure 13-5). This systematic comparison of your qualifications and job requirements helped you identify pertinent information (strengths or special abilities) to be included in your resume. If you cannot see a relationship between you and the job or company, you will not be able to demonstrate the interest or sincerity needed to sell yourself.

THINK IT OVER
Study the company/job profile you completed in Chapter 13 and jot down three key points supporting why you are right for the job. Practice by recording them or saying them to a friend until you feel comfortable.

PLAN YOUR APPEARANCE

Many companies have "images" to maintain. Will you fit?

An employment interviewer once said that if the job applicant did not meet her *extremities* test, the interview might as well not take place. She went on to explain that the extremities were the candidate's fingernails, hair, and shoes. The fingernails had to be clean and neat, the shoes shined, or at least clean, and the hair clean and well groomed. Long hair on men met the standard, incidentally, if clean and well groomed. The interviewer felt that if the candidate did not take care of those items, the candidate could not really be serious about, or fit into, her organization. Another interviewer turned down an otherwise outstanding applicant because the applicant could not look him in the eye when he answered a question. Interviewers, like everyone else, are subject to personal perceptions and biases.

In terms of appearance, the applicant should

- Be as clean and well groomed as possible.
- Wear appropriate footwear.
- Select appropriate clothes for the interview.

For specific guidelines, read articles and books in current magazines. Talk with professors in your field, professors of professional protocol (business etiquette), personnel at the career services center, and graduates who have recently acquired jobs in your field.

Use the online database in your library to locate articles or books about dressing for an interview.

If necessary, borrow clothes from a friend. Research the company dress code—real or implied—ahead of time. If you *look* and *dress* like the people who already work at the company, the interviewer will be able to visualize your working there. Your college placement officer may be able to provide helpful hints.

PLAN YOUR TIME

One of the worst things you can do is be late for an interview. If something should happen to prevent your arriving on time, telephone an apology. Another mistake is to miss the interview entirely. Plan your time so that you will arrive early. This planning allows you to unwind and review mentally the things you plan to accomplish.

Meeting Face to Face—The Interchange

Now that you have gone through the planning stages, you are ready for the interview. Your job is to sell yourself so successfully that you are invited to proceed to the next step in the hiring process. The first step is an on-campus interview; the next step, an interview with company executives. You should not expect to receive a firm job offer in the first interview, but one may be made.

OPENING FORMALITIES

When you meet the interviewer, use the interviewer's name if you are sure you know how to pronounce it correctly. You may ask how to pronounce the name if necessary. Even if the interviewer calls you by your first name, always use the interviewer's surname unless specifically invited to do otherwise. Usually, the interviewer will initiate the handshake, although you may do so. In either case, apply a firm handshake. You do not want to leave the impression that you are weak or timid. At the same time, you do not want to overdo the firm grip and leave an impression of being overbearing. Once the introduction is over, wait for the interviewer to invite you to be seated. These common courtesies—using the correct name, applying a firm handshake, and waiting to be seated—can contribute to a favorable first impression. Use your body language to add to that impression. Sit erect and lean forward slightly to express interest. Avoid slouching, chewing gum, and fidgeting—none will help your image.

The interviewer will begin the conversation and effectively set the stage for the interview. You might expect either some nonbusiness talk or a direct opening into the business of the interview.

A positive or negative impression is created during the first four minutes of an interview; this impression often determines, albeit unconsciously, the outcome of the interview. You should be able to determine quickly whether the interview will be structured or unstructured, nonstressful or stressful.

During these early minutes, make appropriate eye contact with the interviewer and be conscious of the nonverbal messages the two of you are sending. Some professional interviewers may look out the window while you are talking, stand up and stretch, or do other things early to detect your reaction. You can usually tell whether these actions are genuine; quite probably, they are acts. Retain your composure!

A survey of employment interviewers revealed the top ten barriers to effective communication during an interview (Golen & Lynch, 1987). These barriers are listed in Figure 14-2. As you proceed to an interview, evaluate your communication skills in each of these areas and take steps to eliminate any weaknesses.

INTERVIEWING GUIDELINES

Much of the information about you will appear on your resume or company application form, already available to the interviewer. Thus, the interviewer most likely will seek to go beyond such things as your education, work experience,

Repeating the interviewer's name will help you remember it.

THINK IT OVER
Practice these opening formalities until you have perfected them.

You cannot afford to take the first few seconds of an interview to "warm up." Often, interviewers make their decisions based on the impression you make in the first *four seconds* of the interview.

Be aware of subtle differences in nonverbal communication, especially if the interviewer is from a culture other than yours. For example, a North American interviewer who sees eye contact as a sign of trust may perceive an Asian female who keeps her eyes lowered as a sign of respect to be uninterested or not listening.

FIGURE 14-2
Rank order of interview communication barriers.

Rank	Barrier
1	Tendency not to listen
2	Lack of credibility
3	Lack of interest in subject discussed
4	Hostile attitudes
5	Use of profanity
6	Poor organization of ideas
7	Resistance to change
8	Know-it-all attitude
9	Lack of trust
10	Lack of feedback

Know your resume thoroughly. It's a source for interviewer questions.

and extracurricular activities. He or she will attempt to assess your attitudes toward work and the probability of fitting you successfully into the organization.

The best way to prepare for the interview discussion is to study the company and yourself. In addition, you can prepare to answer questions such as those listed in Figure 14-3. Having thoughtfully answered such questions *before* the interview, you can give smooth and confident answers *during* the interview. Practice by having a friend ask you these difficult questions.

Do you have special training or an out-of-the-ordinary background?

Your education is your *major asset* if you are a student. You should point out its relationship to the job for which you are being considered. Even more important, the fact that you have succeeded in school indicates that you have the ability to learn. Because most companies expect you to learn something on the job, your ability to learn and thus to become productive quickly may be your greatest asset. So your most important response to the interviewer's questions may be about your ability to learn. Even lack of work experience may be an asset: You have acquired no bad work habits that you will have to unlearn!

Surveys have shown that, other than job-related skills, *communication* and *interpersonal skills* are the hardest skills to find in job candidates (Half, 1994).

Your *interpersonal skills*—getting along with others—may be an important attribute. What did you do in college that helped you get along with others? Were you a member, an officer, or president of an organization? What did you accomplish? How did others perceive you? Were you a leader? The extracurricular activities listed on your resume give an indication of these traits, but how you talk about them in your interview helps. "I started as corresponding secretary and was subsequently elected to higher office for four semesters, eventually becoming president" may be a statement that proves your leadership qualities. If at the same time your organization went on to greater heights, all the more power to you.

Can humility and confidence be combined?

Humility pays off in all interviews. If you are being interviewed by a representative of General Motors, do not suggest that you can turn the company around. A candidate for the presidency of a university was not considered further when he said he could turn the university around; the university was already successful. Incidentally, he had been president of another university for only six months and claimed he had turned that university around. Obviously, the candidate had not become familiar with the problems of the university. He had failed to take even the first step toward a successful interview: Study the company.

Get across the idea of "I like your company."

"Why do you want to work for us?" is not a difficult question to handle if you do some planning. In addition to your study of the company from the literature, you can usually locate someone who works for the company to tell you about it. You can sometimes visit a local office of the firm as well. Then you can make a

FIGURE 14-3
Frequently asked tough interview questions.

CAREER NOTEBOOK

Universal Questions for Students and Employed Job Changers

1. Tell us about yourself.
2. What are your career plans (long term and short term)? What position do you plan to have in five years?
3. What are some of the factors that led you to choose your college major? Your college/university? When did you choose your college major?
4. What courses did you like least? Best? Explain.
5. What do you know about opportunities in the field in which you are trained?
6. What do you know about our company?
7. Why do you want to work for us?
8. Why should we hire you? What qualifications do you have that make you feel that you should be hired over others?
9. What are your greatest strengths?
10. What do you consider your greatest weaknesses that we should know about?
11. What do you think are the real qualifications for this job?
12. What do you think determines a person's progress in an organization?
13. How do your qualifications compare with the job requirements?
14. Describe a time when you (a) worked well under pressure, (b) worked effectively with others, (c) organized a major project, (d) motivated and led others, (e) solved a difficult problem, and (f) accepted constructive criticism.
15. Describe something you have done that shows initiative and willingness to work.
16. How have your extracurricular activities, part-time work experience, or volunteer work prepared you for work in our company?
17. What is important to you in a job? What interests you most about this job?
18. How do you spend your spare time? What are your hobbies? What do you do to keep in good physical condition?
19. What are your salary expectations?
20. Describe the characteristics of an individual whom you especially admire.
21. Are you willing to take some psychological or drug tests before we discuss an employment offer?

Additional Questions for Employed Job Changers

22. Why do you want to leave your present job?
23. What opportunities do you have for promotion with your present employer?
24. What salary are you making and what do you hope to earn on your next job?
25. What is your opinion about your present co-workers and your supervisor?

favorable impression simply by referring to the people you have talked with about the working conditions, company achievements, and career paths. You will also show that you are strongly interested in the company and not just interviewing for practice. The interviewer not only attempts to develop an impression of you but also evaluates you in comparison with others being interviewed for the position. Your responses can indicate your sincere interest in getting a job with this company rather than just any company.

Your response to inquiries about why you should be hired will be a composite of some of the things already discussed. You have the proper education, you have proved you have the ability to learn, and you are enthusiastic about working for the company. If you really understand the job requirements, you should have little difficulty relating your skills and knowledge to the job. If the immediate job will lead to supervisory or management responsibilities later, make certain that you stress your skill in getting along with others and working successfully as part of a team.

A question about whether the company can offer you a career path is probably best answered with a question such as "I believe someone like me has a future with your company, but I would like to discuss the normal progression with the company. Can you tell me about it?" Most candidates for positions with public accounting firms are familiar with the steps from staff accountant to partner; but the steps are not so clearly defined in marketing, finance, and management paths. An open discussion can provide you with new information.

Recognize that *everyone* has a weakness. When asked about your greatest strengths and weaknesses, you can make an impression by acknowledging a weakness. To do otherwise may display a lack of humility. Avoid volunteering a weakness that will eliminate you from consideration for the job, however. An applicant for a controller's position revealed that his greatest weakness was his dislike for details. Because the controller's job requires meticulous attention to details, this applicant was immediately eliminated from consideration.

As a general rule, mention a weakness that can be perceived as a strength. For example, you may indicate that you occasionally become overcommitted to extracurricular activities, particularly if your resume shows a high level of extracurricular participation. Use this response only if you also have a strong academic record. Do not confess that your overcommitment resulted in a failure to pursue your education properly.

Your greatest strength probably is easy to identify: (1) the ability to learn, (2) the ability to work with others and to assume leadership roles, (3) the ability to organize your time in such a way that you can achieve academically while still participating in nonclass activities or work, or (4) skill in problem solving. Because the question asks for your greatest strength, you should focus on a single point rather than brag about all of your strengths.

Questions about how you spend your spare time and about how your extracurricular activities have added to your education are designed to make you elaborate on resume items. Give some thought to these items so you can appear to have broad, balanced interests rather than a single, time-consuming avocation.

What's important in a job goes beyond financial reward. Although applicants are all interested in a paycheck, any job satisfies that need—some will pay more, some less; but the paycheck is a part of the job and should not be your primary concern. Intrinsic rewards such as personal job satisfaction, the feeling of accomplishment, and making a contribution to society are things you should think about discussing in the interview. You should like what you are doing and find a challenging job that will satisfy these needs.

One of the major reasons that college graduates change jobs is lack of challenge and the resulting dislike for the job. Research has shown that most of us change jobs two or three times before finding our career occupation. So, as you

---

Focus on all levels of your experience (classes, internships, co-op semesters, student organizations, work experience) and show exactly how these experiences can be transferred to the job you are seeking.

THINK IT OVER
Do you know the typical career path in your field? Talk with a professor or professional in your field to answer this question.

THINK IT OVER
Think seriously about the weakness you could describe that could be perceived as a desirable trait. Jot down your answer to this standard interview question in your career notebook.

Develop a sincere, straightforward answer!

Focus on the satisfaction gained from contributing to a company rather than the paycheck you will receive.

COMMUNICATION MENTOR

Take care to avoid overselling yourself in job interviews. This sounds so fundamental, yet it's the mistake that can put even experienced job applicants at an immediate disadvantage.

A candidate may think, for example, that a certain high-tech company's elite profile suggests that it would expect super-intelligence in applicants. The candidate then presents herself with a finger-snapping brashness that ill-suits her real personality and looks superficial to the interviewer. Another candidate for an administrative position in a health-care organization might try to demonstrate a sense of compassion and understanding for the sick, but will seem insincere to the interviewer.

All candidates may possess the attributes they were attempting to project in the interview, but each may get the opposite reading. The point is, stick to what is natural for you in the way you act and react to the job interviewer. Don't try to paint the whole landscape of your character in one interview.

James F. Hurley
Executive Vice President
California Federal Bank

engage in the interview, look for things that will satisfy your immediate needs and lead to future challenges. Job changes usually involve hardships of some sort, and careful consideration of how the job and the company will meet your needs can prevent later problems.

HANDLING ILLEGAL INTERVIEW QUESTIONS

As an interviewee, you must decide how you will handle illegal interview questions. Will you refuse to answer and inform the interviewer that the question is improper—and risk offending or embarrassing the interviewer? Or will you answer the question knowing that it is illegal and your answer is not related to the job requirements? Obviously, the latter option is more likely to keep you in the running for the job; but you may feel that you have compromised important principles.

A third and more effective alternative is to answer the legitimate concern that probably lies behind the illegal question rather than give a direct answer or refuse to answer the illegal question (Jenks, 1988). For example, an interviewer who asks, "Do you plan to have children?" is probably concerned about how long you might remain on the job. An answer to this concern would be "I plan to pursue a career regardless of whether I decide to raise a family." The interviewer who asks, "Have you ever been arrested other than for traffic violations?" is probably concerned about employee dishonesty. An appropriate answer to this concern is "Nothing I have ever done would give you any concern that I would breach your company's trust."

If you can see no legitimate concern in a question, such as "Do you own your own home, rent, or live with your parents?" answer, "I'm not sure how that question relates to the job. Can you explain?"

LEARNING OBJECTIVE 4

THINK IT OVER
Which of these methods for answering illegal interview questions do you think would work for you?

COMMUNICATION   MENTOR

Be well prepared for an interview. Then relax and listen—*actively* listen. A question that springs from your genuine interest in and curiosity about what you're hearing will be much more impressive to an interviewer than standard, "canned" questions. Your genuine, honest response to a question you've heard correctly will be much more effective.

H. Devon Graham, Jr.
Southwest Regional Managing Partner
Arthur Andersen & Co.

ASKING QUESTIONS OF THE INTERVIEWER

A new job is like a marriage. Both the interviewer and interviewee must know as much as possible about each other before making a commitment to increase the likelihood that the relationship will be lengthy and mutually beneficial ("10 Interview Mistakes," 1990).

What hidden message is communicated by asking for information that is available in printed sources?

Should you ask about salary and benefits?

A good way to determine whether the job is right for you is to ask *pertinent* questions. Good questions show the interviewer that you have initiative and are interested in making a well-informed decision. For that reason, be certain not to say, "I don't have any questions." Focus on questions that help you gain information about the company and specifically the job that you could not learn from printed sources or persons other than the interviewer. Do not waste the interviewer's time asking questions that show you are unprepared for the interview (for example, questions about the company's scope, products/services, job requirements, new developments). Having committed a block of uninterrupted time to talk with you, the interviewer will resent this blatant lack of commitment and respect for the company. Avoid questions about salary and benefits that imply you are interested more in money than in the contribution you can make.

Weave your questions throughout the interview rather than asking all questions at the end of the interview.

To show further initiative, introduce questions throughout the interview whenever appropriate rather than waiting until you are asked whether you have questions. This approach will promote positive two-way interaction and should create a relaxed, unintimidating atmosphere. Just remember that the *interviewer* is in charge of the interview. Add your own questions to the typical interviewee questions shown in Figure 14-4.

HANDLING SALARY AND BENEFITS DISCUSSION

THINK IT OVER
Do you know the general salary range for your prospective job? Talk with a professor or professional in your field to answer this question.

For most entry-level positions, the beginning salary is fixed. However, if you have work experience, excellent scholarship records, or added maturity, you may be able to obtain a larger salary. The interviewer should initiate the salary topic. What you should know is the general range for candidates with your qualifications so that your response to a question about how much you would expect is reasonable. If your qualifications are about average for the job, you can indicate that you would expect to be paid the going rate or within the normal range. If you have added qualifications, you might say, "With my two years of work experience, I would expect to start at the upper end of the normal salary range."

CAREER NOTEBOOK

1. What is a typical day like in this job?
2. What type of people would I be working with (peers) and for (supervisors)?
3. Why do you need someone for this job (why can this job not be done by a current employee)?
4. What circumstances led to the departure of the person I would be replacing? What is the turnover rate of people in this job? (or, How many people have held this job in the past five years?)
5. To an interviewer who has worked for the company for an extended time: Why do you continue to work for this company?
6. Would you describe the initial training program for people in this position?
7. What types of ongoing employee in-service training programs do you provide?
8. How much value does your firm place on a master's degree?
9. Do you prefer to see an applicant who has gained work experience before completing a graduate degree?
10. How do you feel this field has changed in the past ten years? How do you feel it will change in the next ten years?
11. What advice do you wish you had been given when you were starting out?
12. Do you have any questions about my qualifications?
13. When can I expect to hear from you about your decision?

FIGURE 14-4
Typical questions asked by interviewees during an interview.

Should you stress opportunity over salary?

If you have other job offers, you are in a position to compare salaries, jobs, and companies. In this case, you may suggest to the interviewer that you would expect a competitive salary and that you have been offered X dollars by another firm. If salary has not been mentioned, and you really want to know about it, simply ask courteously how much the salary would be for someone with your qualifications. In any case, though, if you really believe the job offers the nonmonetary benefits you seek, do not attempt to make salary a major issue.

Normally, an interviewer will introduce the subject of benefits without your asking about them. In some cases, a discussion of total salary and "perks" (perquisites) is reserved for a follow-up interview. If nothing has been said about certain benefits, you should take the liberty of asking, particularly when an item may be especially important to you. Health care, for example, may be very important when you have children. Retirement planning, however, is less appropriate for a new graduate to discuss.

COMMUNICATION   MENTOR

Be clean, polished, and well presented when you arrive for your interview, at least 10 minutes early.

When answering questions, be brief but make sure to get your point across. Sometimes a yes or no answer will suffice. Always be upbeat, bright, cheerful, and never tired. Smile when possible, as personality counts a great deal in a job interview.

Ask questions. Asking questions about an area in which you have limited knowledge is a sure sign of intelligence. Remember, any prospective employer would probably like to hire you for life, not the next 18 months. Therefore, asking long-range questions enhances your qualifications as a good candidate for a position.

Even if it becomes apparent that you are not the person for the job or the company is not for you, be cordial, interested, and positive. Although you may not be the right candidate for Company A, you may be just the person for Company B. An interviewer recommending a job candidate to a competitor for possible hiring is not uncommon.

Terence E. McSweeney
Director of Communications
PGA of America

CLOSING THE INTERVIEW

The interviewer will provide cues indicating that the interview is completed by rising or making a comment about the next step to be taken. At that point, do not prolong the interview needlessly. Simply rise, accept the handshake, thank the interviewer for the opportunity to meet, and close by saying you look forward to hearing from the company. The neatness with which you close the interview may be almost as important as the first impression you made. Be enthusiastic. If you really want the job, you might ask for it!

Practicing for Interviews

"You've got to be as effective as a 30-second commercial," says Wilder, a consultant who coaches job hunters. This impact requires long hours of committed practice.

Use a third person as an observer and critique a videotape of a mock interview.

Sincerity is essential to presenting yourself favorably. Although most people tend to be nervous during their first interview, they gain confidence with experience. Therefore, practice and rehearse your interviewing style. Work with a friend in mock interviews, alternating roles as interviewer and interviewee. Then follow each practice interview with a constructive critique of each other's performance. A few such interviews will give you some experience and will make the first real interview more effective.

The job interview may be the most important face-to-face interaction you ever have. You will be selling yourself in competition with others. How you listen and how you talk are characteristics the interviewer will be able to measure. Your actions, your mannerisms, and your appearance will combine to give the total picture of how you come across. Added to the obvious things you have acquired from your education, experience, and activities, your interview performance can give a skilled interviewer an excellent picture of you. Practice leads to perfection, so the time you devote to preparing for the

COMMUNICATION IN ACTION

William Montes, RE\MAX of Florida, Inc.

Finding employment is a top priority for most university graduates. Whether seeking a career change or pursuing a new position, a graduate who understands the interview process may gain a position over intense competition. Knowing what an interviewer expects provides invaluable knowledge to the applicant.

William Montes understands how some applicants gain the edge over the competition. Having begun his career as a personnel assistant in 1973, Montes eventually founded his own executive recruiting firm in 1983. Montes' company specialized in finding applicants for the science and engineering disciples. With this rich background in the employment process, Montes sold his company and became Director of Marketing for RE\MAX of Florida, Inc.

An experienced interviewer, Montes knows the importance of the interviewing process in business communication. "The most important part of the interview process comes before the face-to-face interview," Montes states. "As an applicant or an interviewer, you must know the position and its qualifications from a behavioral standpoint." Montes stresses the importance of this approach. When focusing on behaviors, he looks at what a person has done in the past because it may lead him to hire that person. How important is past performance or behavior to job success? "I can predict what people will do by what they have done," Montes claims. "People have a pattern of accom-

plishments, failures, and job movement." He cautions that an applicant's past performance must be represented accurately when communicating in the interview.

Montes takes his approach a step further. Before he begins recruiting, he has a very clear idea of what a person needs to be able to do to be successful in a position. He once recruited someone for an engineering position, which was a technical position entitled Director of Quality Assurance. The company wanted someone who could evaluate the quality of the production process. From interviews with other people who worked closely with the person in that position, Montes identified certain traits and experiences the applicant should have. Consequently, when he began recruiting in the marketplace, he sought people with those traits and experiences.

What if an applicant has no work experience on which to base performance? Montes believes that new graduates must know their goals and personal strengths and separate themselves "from the pack." To separate themselves, he suggests a telephone call or an actual visit to a company. Talk with the director or person in charge of the position, he adds, and send your resume personally to that decision maker. "Your resume may be sent to human resources, but the decision maker will be impressed that you took the effort to make a personal contact," Montes states.

College work can also be an indication of job performance. An applicant can highlight such college work habits as attendance, time management, and involvement. Montes appreciates applicants who study a company, plan for an interview, and can identify personal goals and strengths. In his view, these applicants have an edge over increasingly intense interview competition. By planning and preparing, "Applicants practice good business communication," he adds.

Applying What You Have Learned

1. According to Montes, what is the most important part of the interview process?
2. What steps does Montes suggest recent graduates take when preparing for an employment interview?

COMMUNICATION MENTOR

Always follow up an interview with a thank-you note and a reminder of your interest, if applicable. Even if you have decided you would not want the position if offered, thank your interviewer for the opportunity and time given you. Recommendations can still be forthcoming through these individuals.

Terence E. McSweeney
Director of Communications
PGA of America

interview may determine the payoff by making you stand a little higher than your competition.

PREPARING OTHER EMPLOYMENT MESSAGES

LEARNING OBJECTIVE 5

Types of Employment
Messages:
  Follow-up letters
  Thank-you letters
  Application forms
  Job-acceptance letters
  Job-refusal letters
  Resignation letters
  Recommendation
    requests
  Recommendation letters

Could a follow-up letter
imply perseverance?

Preparing a winning resume and application letter is an important first step in a job search. To expedite your job search, you may need to write other employment letters: send a follow-up letter to a company that does not respond to your resume, send a thank-you letter after an interview, complete an application form, accept a job offer, reject other job offers, and communicate with references. A career change will require a carefully written resignation letter.

Follow-Up Letters

When an application letter and resume do not elicit a response, a follow-up letter may bring results. Sent a few weeks or months after the original letter, it includes a reminder that an application for a certain job is on file, presents additional education or experience accumulated, points out its relationship to the job, and closes with a reference to desired action. In addition to conveying new information, follow-up letters indicate persistence (a quality that impresses some employers). Figure 14-5 shows a good example of a follow-up letter.

Thank-You Letters

Even though you said
"thank you" at the close of
the interview, should you
write a "thank-you" letter?

After a job interview, a letter of appreciation is a professional courtesy and should be sent promptly. Even if during the interview you decided you do not want the job or you and the interviewer mutually agreed that the job is not for you, a thank-you letter is appropriate. It expresses gratitude, refers to some point discussed in the interview, and closes pleasantly. You may mention the possibility of applying again after qualifications have been improved. If you were asked to submit some statement or further information, a prompt follow-up action becomes even more important.

Write the outline for a
thank-you letter in your
notebook.

After an interview has gone well and you think a job offer is a possibility, include these ideas in the letter of appreciation: express gratitude, identify the specific job applied for, refer to some point discussed in the interview (the strength of the interview), and close by making some reference to the expected call or letter that conveys the employer's decision (see Figure 14-6).

P.O. Box 2407
Dallas, TX 79022-2407
October 23, 19--

Mr. Warren Kurtz
Nicovich & Read, CPAs
1000 Plaza Court
Austin, TX 78710-1000

Dear Mr. Kurtz:

[1] Recently I applied for an audit staff position at Nicovich & Read's and now have additional qualifications to report.

[2] The enclosed, updated resume shows that I have passed the Auditing and Practice and Law sections of the CPA exam; I will take the final section at the next sitting. [3] In addition, I have finished my last semester of cooperative education experience with Devlin & Cole, CPAs. [4] This realistic work experience has added value to my formal education and confirmed my interest in working as an auditor.

[5] Mr. Kurtz, I would welcome the opportunity to visit your office and talk more about the contributions I could make as an auditor for Nicovich & Read. Please write or call me at (512) 555-5098.

Sincerely,

Sara Beth Christophel

Sara Beth Christophel

Enclosure

[1] States main idea and clearly identifies the position being sought.

[2-4] Refers to the enclosed resume; summarizes additional qualifications.

[5] Assures employer that Sara Beth is still interested in the job.

FIGURE 14-5   *Good example of a follow-up letter.*

If a thank-you letter confirms that your enthusiasm for a job increased during the interview, the impact on the decision could be favorable. For maximum impact, send a thank-you letter as quickly as possible after an interview—the day of the interview or the following day.

The resume, application letter, and thank-you letter can be retained in a personal computer and adapted for submission to other firms when needed. Many job seekers keep a record of their efforts on a computer: dates on which letters and resumes were sent to certain firms, answers received, names of people talked with, facts conveyed, and so on. When an interviewer calls, you can retrieve and view that company's record while you are talking with the interviewer.

A tardy thank-you letter has less impact.

Is a personal computer useful in a job search?

P.O. Box 2407
Dallas, TX 79022-2407
October 23, 19--

Mr. Warren Kurtz
Nicovich & Read, CPAs
1000 Plaza Court
Austin, TX 78710-1000

Dear Mr. Kurtz:

[1] Thank you for taking the time to talk with me about the auditing position at Nicovich and Read.

[2] Our discussion of the diversity of your clients and of your plan to open an office in Mexico City was especially appealing. [3]Thus, as you recommended, I have purchased the multimedia language series and am quickly regaining the fluency in Spanish I had during high school.

[4] Mr. Kurtz, I would welcome the opportunity to work with your international clients and to be involved in an exciting and challenging new international venture. [5]I am eager to receive a call from your office next week.

Sincerely,

Sara Beth Christophel

Sara Beth Christophel

FIGURE 14-6   *Good example of a thank-you letter.*

[1] States the main idea:—appreciation for the interview and information gained.

[2, 3] Includes specific points discussed during the interview, increasing the sincerity of the letter and the likelihood the interviewer will remember the applicant.

[4, 5] Assures the employer Sara Beth is interested in the job and politely reminds the employer she is awaiting a reply.

Application Forms

A well-organized career notebook assists in giving quick, accurate information.

Before going to work on a new job, you will almost certainly complete the employer's application and employment forms. Some application forms, especially for applicants who apply for jobs with a high level of responsibility, are very long. They may actually appear to be tests in which applicants give their answers to hypothetical questions and write defenses for their answers. Increasing numbers of companies are designing employment forms to identify applicants' written communication skills. Review the guidelines in Figure 14-7 for completing application forms:

CAREER NOTEBOOK

Guidelines for Completing an Application Form

1. *Read the entire form before you begin completing it.* This procedure will prevent you from making careless mistakes caused by not understanding the form. Preparing a rough draft on a photocopy of the form is an excellent idea.

2. *Follow instructions.* If the form calls for last name first and you write your first name first, the damage could be fatal. If instructions clearly say "Print" and you write cursively instead, you could be stereotyped immediately as a bungler. When the form has multiple copies, place the form on a hard surface and put enough pressure on the pen to make the last copy clear. If instructions say, "Do not fold," honor them.

3. *Complete forms neatly.* If erasing is necessary, do it cleanly. Such techniques as marking through an original answer and squeezing another, or printing in all-capital letters in some blanks and in capital-and-lowercase letters in others may imply indecisiveness, carelessness, lack of respect, or haste. Unless instructions or circumstances forbid, key your answers for a neat, legible document.

4. *Respond to all questions.* For any questions that do not apply, write "NA" in the blank. If the form provides space for you to add additional information or make a comment, try to include something worthwhile. Competitors, especially those who habitually do no more than is required of them, will probably leave such spaces blank.

5. *Answer questions accurately.* If you have developed a career notebook (as described in Chapter 13), it will contain much information that would be called for on an employment form: transcripts of courses taken, dates of employment on other jobs, names and addresses of references, and so on. Carry it in a briefcase or portfolio and take it with you to employment offices and interviews. With a copy of your resume and application letter in the notebook, you can make sure all factual statements are consistent with statements on the form. Providing false information would be unethical and impractical. It could result in your being hired for a job you cannot do well or termination in disgrace when the misrepresentation is discovered.

6. *Keep a copy.* Save a copy of the application form for future reference. If you complete the application form before the interview, reviewing it prior to the interview could be to your advantage.

FIGURE 14-7   Guidelines for completing an application form.

Job-Acceptance Letters

A job offer may be extended either by telephone or by letter. If a job offer is extended over the telephone, request that the company send a written confirmation of the job offer. The confirmation should include the job title, salary, benefits, starting date, and anything else negotiated.

Often companies require a written acceptance of a job offer. Note the deductive sequence of the letter shown in Figure 14-8: acceptance, details, and closing (confirms the report-for-work date).

Write the outline for a job-acceptance letter in your notebook.

908 Timbercove Lane
Marion, NC 28752-1696
March 30, 19--

Ms. Virginia Sanchez
Personnel Director
Tabor Stores, Inc.
7800 Brookdale Road
Charlotte, NC 28228-7800

Dear Ms. Sanchez:

I accept your employment offer as a market analyst. Thank you for
responding so quickly after our discussion on Thursday.

As you requested, I have signed the agreement outlining the specific
details of my employment. Your copy is enclosed, and I have kept a
copy for my records.

If you should need to communicate with me before I report for work
on May 14, please call me at 555-6543.

Sincerely,

Sydney W. Williamson

Sydney W. Williamson

Enclosures

1, 2 Begins by stating the main news: job offer is being accepted.

3, 4 Continues with any necessary details.

5 Confirms the beginning employment date.

Includes sender's address because letter printed on plain paper.

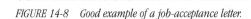

FIGURE 14-8   Good example of a job-acceptance letter.

Job-Refusal Letters

Should job-refusal letters be organized like bad-news letters? Write the outline in your notebook.

Like other messages that convey unpleasant news, job-refusal letters are written inductively: a beginning that reveals the nature of the subject, explanations that lead to a refusal, the refusal, and a pleasant ending. Of course, certain reasons (even though valid in your mind) are better left unsaid: questionable company goals or methods of operation, negative attitude of present employees, possible bankruptcy, unsatisfactory working conditions, and so on. The applicant who prefers not to be specific about the reason for turning down a job might write this explanation:

> After thoughtfully considering job offers received this week, I have decided to accept a job in the actuarial department of an insurance company.

You may want to be more specific about your reasons for refusal when you have a positive attitude toward the company or believe you may want to reapply at some later date. The letter in Figure 14-9 includes the reasons for refusal.

Should job-refusal letters include the reason for refusing the job? Explain.

THINK IT OVER
How does a letter printed on plain paper differ from a letter printed on letter-head? Refer to Appendix A to answer this question.

104 Medford Way
Davenport, IA 52802-1923
October 21, 19--

Mr. J. D. Walrath, Loan Manager
Walrath Financial Services, Ltd.
1835 Woodward Building
Des Moines, IA 50318-1835

Dear Mr. Walrath:

[1] I appreciate your spending time with me discussing the loan officer's job.

[2] Thank you for your candid comparison of my background and opportunities in finance and insurance. [3] Having received job offers in both fields, I am now convinced that a career in insurance is more consistent with my aptitudes and goals. [4] Today, I am accepting a job in the actuarial department of States Mutual.

[5] Thank you for the confidence demonstrated by the job offer. [6] When I receive reports of Walrath's continued success, I will think of the dedicated people who work for the company.

Sincerely,

Mitchell Runnels

Mitchell Runnels

[1] Begins with a neutral but related idea to buffer the bad news.

[2-4] Presents reasons that lead to the refusal diplomatically.

[5, 6] Ends letter on a positive note that anticipates future association with the company.

FIGURE 14-9   Good example of a job-refusal letter.

Resignation Letters

Resigning from a job requires you to communicate this fact appropriately. By the time you have reached the point of resignation, you will know whether your employer expects it to be in writing. You may have "given your notice" in person or written a formal resignation. Regardless of whether the resignation is given orally or in writing, show empathy for your employer by giving enough time to allow the employer time to find a replacement.

What document format is appropriate for resigna-tion letters?

The memorandum format is appropriate for a resignation because the message is communicated between people *within* a company. However, some writers prefer the letter format to convey this formal message. Hence, this message is commonly referred to as a **resignation letter**.

Why emphasize positive ideas?

Write the outline for a resignation letter in your notebook.

Thinking positively, treat a resignation letter as a bad-news letter. Because your employer has had confidence in you, has benefited from your services, and will have to seek a replacement, your impending departure *is* bad news. As such, the letter is written inductively. It calls attention to your job, gives your reasons for leaving it, conveys the resignation, and closes on a positive note (see Figure 14-10).

A resignation letter is not an appropriate instrument for telling executives how a business should be operated. Harshly worded statements could result in immediate termination or cause human relations problems during your remaining working days. Remember, too, that your supervisor may subsequently review the resignation letter just before writing a recommendation letter for you.

Your letter of resignation may not come as a complete surprise to its reader. The new employer may have already asked the old employer for a letter of recommendation.

Recommendation Letters

LEARNING OBJECTIVE 6

Usually, letters of recommendation are written in response to a request. The request may come from the applicant or from the prospective employer.

APPLICANT'S REQUEST AND THANKS FOR RECOMMENDATION

When prospective employers tell applicants to have recommendation letters sent, the normal procedure is to telephone each reference. As the applicant, you would identify the job for which you are applying, give a complete address to which the letter is to be sent, and indicate a date by which the employer needs the letter.

Do not apologize for asking someone to spend time writing about you.

In the conversation, you may need to remind the reference of a previously expressed willingness to supply employment information about you. By sharing some information about job requirements and reporting recent job-related experiences that are relevant, you may assist the reference in writing an effective letter. Indicate your gratitude, but do not apologize for making the request. (The reference has already agreed to write such a letter and will likely take pleasure in assisting a deserving person.)

What information should be included in a request for a recommendation?

Similar information is included when the request for a recommendation is made by letter, as the letter in Figure 14-11 shows.

What information should be included in a thank-you letter to a reference?

People who have applied for jobs can greatly assist their references by alerting them to imminent requests for information, especially if considerable time has elapsed since the applicant and reference have last seen each other. Enclosing a recent resume and providing any other pertinent information (for example, name change) may enable the reference to write a letter that is specific and convincing. If the job search becomes longer than anticipated, a follow-up letter to references

guyton stores 715 South Sumner St, Portland, OR 97208-3190, (503) 555-3200 Fax (503) 555-8004

TO: Brad Zumwalt, Director, Sales Personnel

FROM: Janet R. Garrigus, Manager, Women's Apparel   *J.G.*

DATE: May 5, 19--

SUBJECT: PLEASURE OF SERVING GUYTON STORES

¹ My job as manager of Women's Apparel for the last two years has been a rewarding experience. ²It has taught me much about the marketing of clothing and changing preferences in style.

³ Predicting public acceptance of certain styles has been fascinating. ⁴From the time I declared a major in fashion merchandising, I have wanted to become a buyer. ⁵Before I accepted my present job in management, that goal was discussed. ⁶Now, it is becoming a reality; I have accepted a job as buyer for Belton beginning one month from today. ⁷If satisfactory with you, I would like May 31 to be my last day as manager here.

⁸ This job has allowed me to grow professionally. ⁹Thanks to you and others, I have had the privilege of trying new ideas and selecting sales personnel who get along well with one another and with customers. ¹⁰Thank you for having confidence in me, for your positive rapport with the sales staff, and for your expressions of appreciation for my work.

¹¹ As I continue my career in fashion merchandising, I will always recall pleasant memories of my job at Guyton.

1, 2 Begins with appreciative comment about job to buffer the bad news.

3-5 Presents reasons that lead to the main idea, the resignation.

6 States the resignation.

7 Adds additional details.

8-10 Conveys genuine appreciation for the experience gained at Guyton.

11 Ends on a cordial note.

FIGURE 14-10   Good example of a resignation letter.

explaining the delay and expressing gratitude for their efforts is appropriate. Sending sincere, original thank-you letters to references after a position has been accepted is a thoughtful gesture and helps build a positive relationship with a person who may continue to be important to your career. The letter in Figure 14-12 is brief and avoids clichés and exaggerated expressions of praise but instead gives specific examples of the importance of the reference's recommendation.

EMPLOYER'S REQUEST FOR RECOMMENDATION
When businesses request information about prospective employees, use of forms is fairly standard. The forms normally allow space for responding to specific

Bullets are useful for highlighting a list of qualifications.

104 Medford Way
Davenport, IA 52802-1923
October 8, 19--

Dr. Larry Enplaincourt, Professor
Finance Department
South State College
P.O. Drawer FN
Windsor, MO 65360-1987

Dear Dr. Enplaincourt

[1] As one step in my application for a loan officer's job, States Mutual has asked me for letters of recommendation.

[2] Since receiving permission to use your name as a reference, I have completed the B.S. degree with a major in finance and real estate. [3] If a job offer is made, I would enter the loan officer trainee program and later specialize in real estate loans. [4] The enclosed resume will give you a summary of my academic and work experience as preparation for a job in the loan department.

[5] Please mail the recommendation to the following address by October 15: Mr. Lyle Richardson, Human Resources Department, States Mutual, Inc., 1835 River Bend Drive, Windsor, MO 65360-1835.

[6] I certainly appreciate your willingness to assist in my job search.

Sincerely

Mitchell Runnels

Mitchell Runnels

Enclosure

---

[1] States the main idea—request for recommendation.

[2], [3] Provides details.

[4] Refers to enclosed resume, which will aid the reference in writing the recommendation.

[5] Provides needed information.

[6] Ends with an appreciative comment.

FIGURE 14-11   Good example of a request for a recommendation.

questions, and they either provide space for respondents to express themselves or invite them to attach a letter. When the request is by letter (instead of a form), the letter needs to identify the specific type of information wanted. Numbering and tabulating assist the writer in emphasizing and the reader in responding, as is shown in the excerpt of a letter in Figure 14-13.

NEGATIVE RECOMMENDATIONS

What four options are available when you must respond negatively to a recommendation?

Almost everyone who asks permission to use your name as a reference will expect your recommendation to be favorable. For a person whom you could not favorably recommend, you have the option of (1) saying "No" when asked for permission to use your name, (2) letting the request go unanswered,

P.O. Box 2407
Dallas, TX 79022-2407
November 10, 19--

Dr. Gerald P. Wilkes
Professor of Accountancy
Southern State University
P.O. Drawer AC
San Antonio, TX 78207-4670

Dear Dr. Wilkes:

[1] Thank you so much for the letter of recommendation you prepared for my application to Nicovich & Read. [2] Today, I learned that I have been hired and will begin work next month.

[3] Because the position is in auditing, I believe your comments about my performance in your auditing and systems classes carried a great deal of weight. [4] Mr. Kurtz commented he was impressed with the wealth of evidence and examples you provided to support your statements—unlike the many general recommendations he frequently receives.

[5] Dr. Wilkes, I appreciate your helping me secure an excellent position in a highly competitive job market. [6] Thanks for the recommendation and your outstanding instruction. I look forward to talking with you about how I am faring in the "real world" when I return to campus for fall homecoming.

Sincerely,

Sara Beth Christophel

Sara Beth Christophel

[1] States the main idea—thank you for the recommendation.

[2] Informs reference of success in locating job.

[3,4] Communicates sincere appreciation of the references assistance; uses specific examples and avoids strong exaggeration.

[5,6] Restates main idea and anticipates a continued relationship; is original and sincere.

FIGURE 14-12   *Good example of a thank-you letter to a reference.*

(3) responding with an objective appraisal, or (4) responding by letter and inviting a telephone call.

Refusing permission may be difficult; but, for you, it is easier than writing a negative letter. For the applicant, your refusing to serve as a reference may be preferable to your accepting and subsequently sending a negative letter.

Failure to answer a request for information is in effect a negative response, even though the employer does not know whether you received the request. Nonresponse is legal and requires no effort; but (recognizing your responsibility to the applicant, the employer, and yourself) this option would probably be totally unacceptable to you.

THINK IT OVER
Choosing not to respond is legal, but is it ethical?

1 Begins with the request for a recommendation.

2,3 Asks for specific information; uses bullets to highlight needed information.

4 Requests other information.

5 Expresses appreciation for complying with request and provides a deadline.

1 Mr. Ming Lin has told us that you would be willing to provide information about his background for a job as a financial analyst at the Centerville State Bank.

2 Please give us your candid and confidential comments on each of the following job traits that are vital to the financial analyst's job:

3 •Dependability
• Tact (with clients and other personnel)
• Written and oral communication skills
• Knowledge of financial regulations
• Ethical standards

4 Add any other information you think would assist us in predicting his performance in this job. 5 We would appreciate your comments by June 24.

FIGURE 14-13   Good example of an employer's request for a recommendation.

Responding with an objective appraisal will give you the satisfaction of having exercised a responsibility to both applicant and employer. Because of your letter, an employer may escape some difficulty encountered after hiring an unqualified person. Your letter could spare an applicant the agony of going to work on a job that leads to failure. Figure 14-14 is an example of a well-written negative recommendation.

What is the advantage of labeling your letter "confidential" and reminding the reader that the information was requested?

The word "confidential" in a request letter implies that the response will be seen only by the person or persons who have responsibility for the hiring decision. Yet, after taking the job, the employee may have a legal right to inspect the personnel folder. Recognizing the possibility of hurt feelings, ruined friendships, and legal action, respondents are inclined to omit negatives or present them with extreme care.

What steps can you take to protect yourself against possible lawsuits?

Because of the threat of possible litigation, your letter must be written carefully so it can be defended if necessary. The following guidelines can help you write defensible recommendations:

1. *Provide only job-related information that will aid the reader in determining whether the applicant is employable.* If you are not familiar with the requirements of the job applied for, ask the requester to send you a job description. Use this document to include information that is *directly* relevant to the future job and to eliminate irrelevant information that could be defamatory.

2. *Avoid vague, general statements of the applicant's personal ability.* Instead, provide specific examples of performance and the situation in which the performance occurred. Include information such as the difficulty and complexity of the task, degree of applicant's control in the task, and the consequences of the performance, particularly rewards (Knouse, 1987).

3. *Report facts, not judgments.* For example, the number of workdays missed without prior communication with the supervisor is a verifiable fact. To label it as "a terrible record" or "irresponsible" is to pass judgment (which is best left to the reader). Avoid such defaming and judgmental words as *corrupt, crook, dishonest, hypocrite,* and *incompetent.*

4. *Include some positives, even if your overall recommendation is negative.* Conversely, including *no* more than one negative fact in a positive letter may

Gresham Grocery
1500 Nottingham Road, Denver, CO 80202-3480
303-555-1030 Fax 303-555-9807

June 5, 19--

Ms. Melanie Hillman
Store Manager
Templeton Food Center
3712 North Birch Avenue
Arvada, CO 80001-3712

Dear Ms. Hillman:

[1] MARK FULGHAM'S EMPLOYMENT RECORD

[2] Gresham Grocery provides the confidential employment information about Mark Fulgham you requested in your June 1 letter.

[3] He worked from October 1 to December 13 as a courtesy clerk in our Greenwood store. [4] He had above-average skills at packing groceries, and he seemed to have good rapport with customers.

[5] On three occasions (each on a Monday morning), he did not report to work as scheduled; and he had not given the shift supervisor any notice of his absence. [6] He left the store at Gresham Grocery's request.

[7] While he was on the job, his work was satisfactory.

Sincerely,

Margarita E. Diaz

Margarita E. Diaz
Store Manager

[1] Identifies clearly the nature of the letter in the subject line.

[2] States the main idea—request for employment information.

[3], [4] Provides specific, objective information that can be verified easily.

[5], [6] Provides additional objective information; omits opinions or value judgments. Can be easily verified.

[7] Describes Fulgham's past performance but does not project how he will perform on other jobs.

FIGURE 14-14   Good example of a negative recommendation.

make the letter appear more credible in the eyes of the reader (Knouse, 1987). Be certain to provide specific statements about the less-than-satisfactory performance and the overall context of the situation.

5. *Use an inductive sequence and stylistic techniques of de-emphasis (unless your feelings are strong and you think emphasis of the negative is justified).* Normally, the inductive sequence with de-emphasis techniques will seem considerate.

6. *Respond only to requests for specific information and indicate that your letter is written in response to a request.* Label your letter as confidential. These legal precautions indicate that your intent was not to defame but to give an honest answer to a legitimate request for information. In addition, studies show that employers prefer confidential letters rather than open letters that

When you must include negative information in a recommendation letter, be sure that you separate fact from opinion. Including only objective facts that can be supported is a foolproof safeguard against litigation and the temptation to retaliate for problems and losses caused by an employee's poor performance.

allow the applicant access to the letter. Employers perceive the letters to be a more honest evaluation of the applicant's employability (Knouse, 1987).

What is the advantage of inviting the reader to call you for information about a reference?

Responding by letter and inviting a telephone call enable a reference to avoid putting negative ideas in writing. The letter is short, positive, and easy to write, as Figure 14-15 shows. Recognizing the possibility of negatives, which the reference did not want to state in written form, the recipient might not call. In response to such a call, abide by the same precautions that apply to writing letters of recommendation.

[1] **States the main idea.**

[2] **Indicates preference to provide employment information by telephone.**

> Dear Mr. Pondel
>
> TRAVIS KELLEY'S EMPLOYMENT RECORD
>
> [1] Travis Kelley worked as a systems analyst for JEMCO from August 15, 1993, to December 30, 1995.
>
> [2] The confidential information you requested will be provided by telephone: (601) 555-5432.

FIGURE 14-15   Good example of a letter inviting a telephone call to secure negative information.

POSITIVE RECOMMENDATIONS

How could strong adjectives be detrimental?

Fortunately, most people who invite you to write a recommendation are confident you will report positive information. Because it is designed to help a deserving applicant, your message should be believable. Believability may be questioned if the letter includes unsupported superlatives and adjectives or adverbs that are overly strong.

Before requesting a recommendation, the employer has almost certainly seen the applicant's resume, application letter, and (possibly) application forms. Although the effect of your letter may be to *confirm* some of the information already submitted, do not devote all your space to *repeating* it. Instead, concentrate on presenting information the employer probably does not have. Your statements about proficiency and capacity to interact with others will be of special interest.

Regardless of whether a recommendation is for a promotion within the firm or for work in another firm, the same principles apply. For promotion within a firm, use the memorandum format, as shown in Figure 14-16.

Focus on information that the interviewer has not read already.

SOUTHLAND
National Bank

1590 Centran Avenue
Abeline, TX 79604-1590
Telephone (817) 555-9174
FAX (817) 555-3809

TO: Nancy Harris, Chair, Promotion Committee

FROM: Scott Mirandi, Chief Loan Officer *S.M.*

DATE: May 1, 19--

SUBJECT: MURRAY LAUGHLIN'S PROMOTION TO SENIOR
                LOAN OFFICER

[1] Murray Laughlin would be an ideal senior loan officer. [2] For the following reasons, I recommend his promotion:

[3] • **He is efficient.** Beginning with a $14 million loan portfolio, he now manages $25 million. In three years, the number of clients has grown from 16 to 26. Clients are astonished at the speed with which he completes paperwork.

[4] • **He stays informed.** Daily, he spends time on the financial monitor and financial journals. Because of his knowledge, he has frequently made loans that would otherwise have gone to competitors.

[5] • **He works well with the staff.** Colleagues communicate easily with him. His friendly, positive disposition contributes to our pleasant office atmosphere.

[6] • **He helps maintain Southland's public image.** Active in Kiwanis and in fundraising for the needy, he has frequent contacts with clients, prospective clients, and competitors in social situations. To me, he is an ideal person for reflecting the bank's image.

[7] A promotion would reward Murray for the part he has played in expanding our loans and would help us to keep him on our team.

1, 2 Introduces the main idea—the recommendation.

3-6 Emphasizes each reason the promotion is deserved. Each short sentence following the bullet has high impact.

7 Restates the main idea.

FIGURE 14-16   Good example of a recommendation memorandum.

Employees' organizational skills, technical knowledge, analytical skills, and *writing* and *speaking* ability are assessed at the end of each bank examination. These written evaluations form the basis for each employee's annual performance evaluation.

Gabriel Swan
Federal Bank Examiner

PERFORMANCE APPRAISALS

LEARNING OBJECTIVE 7

Are interviewing skills important after you secure a job? Explain.

Your ability to speak confidently and intelligently about your abilities will help you secure a desirable job. Effective interviewing skills will be just as valuable once you begin work. You will be involved in interviews with your supervisor for various reasons: to seek advice or information about your work and working conditions, to receive informal feedback about your progress, to receive a deserved promotion, and to discuss other personnel matters. In addition, your supervisor will conduct a performance appraisal interview to evaluate your performance. This formal interview typically occurs annually on the anniversary of your start of employment.

People need clear, direct feedback about their performance if they are to improve.

Regardless of the job, employees need clear, direct feedback about their performance if they are to improve. This feedback also allows employees to fulfill important personal needs for accomplishment and success. Despite these crucial benefits, some employers hesitate to provide such feedback; and many employees are reluctant to participate effectively in appraisal interviews. The following sections identify the communication skills critical for an open, honest discussion about an employee's performance. Understanding and refining these skills should help you prepare for a relaxed and highly effective performance appraisal process.

Guidelines for Employees

To increase your effectiveness during your performance appraisal interview, develop the following communication skills related specifically to this sensitive interview (Lehman, Taylor, & Forde, 1990):

What is the value of having two performance appraisal interviews? What is the purpose of each?

1. *Ask that your employer evaluate your performance more frequently than at the end of the evaluation period.* Learn to accept constructive criticism from your supervisor and seek evaluation of your performance on a more frequent, informal basis if your supervisor does not readily provide it.

2. *Request a more informal review of your performance near the midpoint of the evaluation period.* The sole purpose of this developmental appraisal interview is to identify specific strategies for improvement by the end of the evaluation period. At that time, your supervisor will conduct a second appraisal interview for the purpose of evaluation that will be linked to promotions, pay raises, and terminations. Human resources management research

supports two separate appraisal interviews; one interview *cannot* measure past performance and improve future performance (Novit, 1986; Schneier, Beatty, & Baird, 1986). Employers cannot function in two roles—counselors and judges—at the same time.

3. *Learn to evaluate your own performance honestly.* Then you can be actively involved in developing strategies for improvement rather than reacting to your supervisor's appraisals. In a study by Herbert Meyer (1975) in which employees in a plant rated themselves, 95 percent considered themselves among the top 50 percent in job performance. Obviously, the first step in learning effective self-evaluation techniques is to be aware of a tendency to overrate your abilities!

> Evaluating your own performance honestly is difficult, as the Meyer study clearly indicates.

List the weaknesses you perceive to be affecting job performance and try to pinpoint a reason for each of the weaknesses listed. If you are receiving frequent, informal feedback from your supervisor, this task will not be difficult. Identify a specific action that you are willing and able to take to overcome the weakness. Honestly answer these questions: Do I have any control over improving or eliminating the weakness? Am I willing to take the steps necessary? This example of a self-evaluation will help you identify your own weaknesses:

> **THINK IT OVER**
> What weaknesses do you perceive to be affecting your performance in this class? What action are you willing and able to take to overcome this weakness?

I have *no control* over completing client proposals by the deadline because the marketing staff is habitually late providing data needed for finalizing the budget. However, I am *unwilling* to work independently to solve problems needed to complete work assignments (i.e., locate answers in policy manuals and reference books); instead, I will continue to rely on co-workers and my supervisor. Finally, I *am willing* to begin following standard proofreading procedures that will increase the quality of my work (eliminate the constant keyboarding and grammatical errors that others have noticed).

4. *Review the specific actions that you are willing and able to implement and prepare an overall plan for future performance.* With a clear understanding of your own performance and a detailed plan of action, you are well prepared to participate in setting performance goals for the next evaluation period. Participating in setting your goals will help you better understand what you must do and help you build a commitment to meet the goals (Latham & Wexley, 1981).

5. *Encourage your supervisor to help you set clear, specific, measurable goals.* "I will try to do better" is a poor goal because you cannot tell whether the goal has been met. With such a vague goal, you might try harder but not hard enough to improve performance. Better goals are "I will produce all documents following standard policy and procedures," "I will meet all deadlines," or "I will not be tardy more than twice during the remainder of the period." A portion of a performance appraisal form covering engagement administration skills and relationship building and teamwork skills is shown in Figure 14-17.

> **THINK IT OVER**
> Based on your evaluation of your performance in this course, set realistic goals that will enable you to improve your performance by the end of the semester.

Guidelines for Supervisors

You will be able to perform better during the performance appraisal interview if you understand your supervisor's role. At some point in your career, you will be required to evaluate the performance of employees reporting to you. If you are

FIGURE 14-17
Engagement administration skills and relationship building and teamwork skills are critical components of KPMG Peat Marwick's performance appraisal instrument. Learning to evaluate your own performance objectively and being able to discuss your strengths and weaknesses openly with your supervisor will lead to improvements in job performance.

KMPG Peat Marwick

PERFORMANCE EVALUATION—PROFESSIONAL AUDIT STAFF

(TO BE COMPLETED FOR ASSIGNMENTS OF 80 HOURS OR MORE)

Name _____ Staff Classification _____ Total Hours _____

Engagement _____ Engagement # _____ Start Date _____ End Date _____

Is this person Above ☐   At ☐   Below ☐ his/her current staff classification on this work assignment?

Describe work _____

─────────────── EVALUATION RATINGS ───────────────

AE–Consistently Exceeds Expectation   EE–Exceeds Expection   AT–Consistently Meets Expectation   NI–Needs Improvement
NA–Not Applicable

GUIDANCE: AT – indicates performance consistently meets high quality requirements of the position and the Firm, and indicates individual is on track for advancement. All other ratings should be measured against this standard.

AE	EE	AT	NI	NA	**ENGAGEMENT ADMINISTRATION SKILLS**
☐	☐	☐	☐	☐	• Meets time deadlines while meeting quality requirements.
☐	☐	☐	☐	☐	• Recognizes and promptly advises supervisors of important budget issues.
☐	☐	☐	☐	☐	• Demonstrates good judgment and analytical ability, and uses common sense in making decisions.
☐	☐	☐	☐	☐	• Documentation is complete, legible, and well organized.
☐	☐	☐	☐	☐	• Demonstrates effective oral and written communication skills.

AE	EE	AT	NI	NA	**RELATIONSHIP BUILDING AND TEAMWORK SKILLS**
☐	☐	☐	☐	☐	• Presents a positive image of the Firm, and demonstrates poise, maturity, and self-confidence.
☐	☐	☐	☐	☐	• Is well respected and effectively develops, motivates, and supervises others.
☐	☐	☐	☐	☐	• Works as part of a team, considers feelings and perspectives of others.
☐	☐	☐	☐	☐	• Develops and maintains a strong relationship with client personnel.
☐	☐	☐	☐	☐	• Able to call on strong relationships to resolve engagement fee and technical issues, and to identify and sell new business.

working for a company with a well-defined career path, your opportunity to conduct an effective performance appraisal could occur quickly. Develop the communication skills presented in the following guidelines (Lehman & Taylor, 1991):

1. *Involve employees in the appraisal process.* They will find the process more beneficial when they are allowed to participate. Begin by building a positive, trusting relationship so that employees will be willing to disclose their weaknesses and work *with* you in developing a plan for improvement. Providing frequent, informal feedback (including praise) in a positive, constructive way is an excellent beginning.

2. *Create a warm, nonthreatening climate for the appraisal interview.* Sit in a chair facing the employee or at a round table rather than behind your desk to emphasize the counseling, participative nature of a developmental interview. If your office is pleasant and attractive, your employees are more likely to have positive feelings (Mintz, 1956).

   Begin the interview by stating its purpose. For example, "We're here today to find ways to improve your future performance—not to measure

THINK IT OVER
What can you do to create a warm, nonthreatening environment? Add to this list by locating additional readings using an online database.

your performance" would be reassuring to an employee reporting for a developmental interview.

3. *Be prepared and highly organized.* Being disorganized and unprepared communicates that you are unconcerned about the importance of the process. For the same reason, allow no interruptions during the interview. Outline definite points to be made and issues to be discussed. Complete all paperwork before the interview. Invite the employees to share their weaknesses and possible strategies for improvement.

4. *Avoid generalizations, broad statements, and opinions.* For example, do not say, "Keep up the good work," "Just keep doing what you're doing," or "If you were a little more ambitious, you would meet deadlines." The fact is that the employee is not meeting deadlines. The reason for the less-than-satisfactory performance—lack of ambition—is your opinion. In addition, this statement emphasizes personal shortcomings rather than a deficiency in job performance.

5. *Offer specific, job-related behavioral comments.* For example, say "I liked the way you handled our refusal to manage the Larkin contract." Such comments tell employees that you value their work because you have observed their actions and know exactly what they are doing.

6. *Limit the number of weaknesses discussed during the interview to two or three.* Employees will become confused and defensive if you point out too many criticisms at once. Your informal feedback in the past should have included most of the problems already. After discussing weaknesses, offer praise about specific examples of good performance so the employee leaves on a positive note.

Why limit criticism to only a few points?

7. *Involve the employee in setting realistic performance goals.* Employees who help set goals are more committed to seeing that the goals are met. However, employees need some input from you; otherwise, they may overestimate their abilities and set goals too high (a common tendency).

Following these guidelines will ensure that you are prepared for your first performance appraisal interview. Being able to communicate effectively during this important interview will pay handsome dividends. You are more likely to receive clear, specific feedback about your performance and to participate actively in setting goals for future performance. As an active participant in this process, you will better understand what is expected of you and will be more committed to meeting the goals you and your supervisor set.

What benefits will you gain from knowing how to participate actively in a performance appraisal interview?

Before you write one of the employment messages in this chapter, study carefully the overall suggestions in the "General Writing Guidelines" placed before the chapter exercises in Chapter 9, page 269. Then, study the specific suggestions in the "Check Your Writing" checklist that follows the chapter summary. Compare your work with this checklist again after you have written a rough draft and make any revisions. Use "Check Your Writing" as a checklist for an effective job interview and performance appraisal.

SUMMARY

1 Structured interviews follow a preset, highly structured format; unstructured interviews follow no standard format but explore for information. Computer-assisted interviews provide standard, reliable information on applicants during the preliminary interview stages.

2 Interviewers and interviewees have responsibilities for the success of the meeting that must be planned and practiced. Interviewers must learn to listen effectively, ask questions that elicit complete, specific responses, determine and communicate to the applicant procedures that will be followed during the interview, create a positive, nonthreatening environment, and be certain not to ask any illegal interview questions.

3 Interviewees must follow these effective interviewing practices: know basic information about the company, arrive on time dressed appropriately for the interview, present a polished first impression following appropriate protocol, be prepared to discuss key qualifications, bypass illegal questions, and ask questions that show initiative and genuine interest in the company.

4 An interviewee must recognize illegal interview questions—those that seek information that is not related to the job and is likely discriminatory. Refusing to answer an illegal question could be detrimental to your chances to secure the job, but answering the question may compromise your ethical values. An effective technique is to answer the legitimate concern behind the illegal question rather than to give a direct answer.

5 Follow these guidelines for writing effective letters related to employment:

Follow-up letters—are sent a few weeks after an applicant does not receive a response from an application. The follow-up letter includes a reminder that an application has been made, presents additional education or experience, and asks for an action (an interview).

Application forms—requere that instructions be followed carefully. Neatness, completeness, and accuracy are expected.

Job-acceptance letters—are written deductively and include the acceptance, details, and a closing that confirms the date the employee will begin work.

Job refusal letters—are written inductively. They have a neutral beginning, reasons that lead to the refusal, and a goodwill closing.

Resignation letters—confirm that termination plans are definite and usually satisfy a company's requirement that resignations be submitted in writing. Assuming resignations are usually bad news for an employer, they are written inductively, with emphasis on positive aspects of the job.

Requests for recommendations—include specific information about the job requirements and the applicant's qualifications to assist the reference in writing a convincing recommendation.

Thank-you letters to references—is a professional courtesy. A letter providing an update on the status of the job search should be sent to the reference if the job search extends longer than expected.

6 **Recommendation letters for job seekers with good qualifications are written deductively; otherwise, inductively.** Guidelines for writing legally defensible recommendations include (1) providing only job-related information; (b) avoiding vague, general statements of a personal nature; (c) reporting facts, not judgments, (d) including some positive facts to provide a balanced recommendation; and (e) providing only information that is requested, indicating your letter is written in response to a request, and labeling your letter as confidential.

7 **Effective interviewing skills are important in the performance appraisal interview, usually conducted once a year.** Employees who actively participate in an honest evaluation of their performance are more likely to receive the clear, direct feedback they need to improve their performance. Employers must create an honest, nonthreatening climate that fosters open, honest communication and offers specific, job-related statements that lead to improvement.

CHECK YOUR WRITING

INTERVIEWS

PLANNING STAGE
☐ Learn as much as you can about the job requirements, range of salary and benefits, and the interviewer.
☐ Research the company with whom you are interviewing (products/services, financial condition, growth potential).
☐ Identify the *specific* qualifications that are compatible with the job requirements and any other information you learned about the company. Be prepared to discuss them clearly and concisely.
☐ Plan your appearance—clean, well-groomed, and appropriate clothing.
☐ Plan to arrive early to communicate promptness and to prepare mentally for the interview.

OPENING FORMALITIES
☐ Greet the interviewer by name with a smile, direct eye contact, and a firm handshake.
☐ Wait for the interviewer to ask you to be seated.
☐ Sit erect and lean forward slightly to convey interest.

BODY OF THE INTERVIEW
☐ Be ready to explain how your qualifications relate to the job requirements using multiple, specific examples.
☐ Identify illegal interview questions; address the concern behind an illegal question or tactfully avoid answering the question.
☐ Ask pertinent questions that communicate intelligence and genuine interest in the company. Introduce questions throughout the interview where appropriate.
☐ Allow the interviewer to initiate a discussion of salary and benefits. Be prepared to provide a general salary range for applicants with your qualifications.

CLOSING THE INTERVIEW
☐ Watch for cues the interview is ending; rise, accept the interviewer's handshake, and communicate enthusiasm.
☐ Express appreciation for the interview and say you are eager to hear from the company.

OTHER EMPLOYMENT MESSAGES

FOLLOW-UP LETTERS
☐ Remind receiver that application is on file and applicant is interested in the job.
☐ Present additional education or experience gained since previous correspondence; do not repeat information presented earlier.
☐ Close with courteous request for an interview.

THANK-YOU LETTERS
☐ Express appreciation for the interview and mention the specific job for which the applicant has applied.
☐ Refer to a specific point discussed in the interview.
☐ Close with a reference to an expected call or letter conveying the interviewer's decision.

APPLICATION FORMS
☐ Read the entire form before completing it and follow instructions precisely.
☐ Complete the form neatly and accurately.
☐ Respond to all questions; insert N/A for questions that do not apply.
☐ Retain a copy for your records.

JOB-ACCEPTANCE LETTERS
☐ Begin by accepting the job offer; specify position.
☐ Provide necessary details.
☐ Close with a courteous ending that confirms the date employment begins.

JOB-REFUSAL LETTERS

- ☐ Begin with a neutral, related idea that leads to the explanation for the refusal.
- ☐ Present the reasons that lead to a diplomatic statement of the refusal.
- ☐ Close positively, anticipating future association with the company.

RESIGNATION LETTERS

- ☐ Begin with positive statement about the job to cushion the bad news.
- ☐ Present explanation, state the resignation, and provide any details.
- ☐ Close with an appreciative statement about experience with the company.

RECOMMENDATION REQUESTS

- ☐ Begin with the request for the recommendation.
- ☐ Provide necessary details including reference to an enclosed resume.
- ☐ End with an appreciative statement for the reference's willingness to aid in the job search.
- ☐ Require a follow-up letter explaining delays and expressing appreciation for extended job searches.

EMPLOYER'S RECOMMENDATION REQUESTS

- ☐ Begin with request for the recommendation.
- ☐ Specify type of information needed.
- ☐ End courteously with a reminder to provide the recommendation by a specified date.

NEGATIVE RECOMMENDATIONS

- ☐ Begin by stating *confidential* information *requested* by the receiver is being provided.

- ☐ Provide *specific, objective* information that can be verified; omit opinions and value judgments. Invite receiver to telephone to avoid including negative statements in writing.
- ☐ End with courteous statement.

POSITIVE RECOMMENDATIONS

- ☐ Begin with a statement of recommendation.
- ☐ Provide *specific, objective* information that the interviewer likely has not received already.
- ☐ Avoid unsupported superlatives and overly strong adjectives and adverbs that destroy credibility.
- ☐ End by restating the positive recommendation.

PERFORMANCE APPRAISALS

GUIDELINES FOR EMPLOYEES

- ☐ Request frequent, informal feedback on job performance with an informal evaluation at the midpoint of the evaluation period.
- ☐ Learn to evaluate your performance honestly and then develop a specific plan for improving performance.
- ☐ Work with your supervisor to set clear, specific, measurable goals.

GUIDELINES FOR EMPLOYERS

- ☐ Involve employees in the appraisal process, particularly in setting realistic performance goals.
- ☐ Create a warm, nonthreatening atmosphere for the appraisal interview; be prepared and highly organized.
- ☐ Avoid generalizations, broad statements, and opinions; offer specific, job-related behavioral comments about two or three weaknesses.

REFERENCES

Golen, S. P., & Lynch, D. H. (1987, Spring). The seriousness of communication barriers in the interviewer-interviewee relationship. *Delta Pi Epsilon Journal, 29* (2), 47-55.

Half, R. (1994, June). Managing your career: How can I improve my resume. *Management Accounting,* p. 12.

Hunt, G. T., & Eadie, W. F. (1987). *Interviewing: A communication approach.* New York: Holt, Rinehart and Winston.

Jenks, J. M. (1988, Spring). Tactful answers to illegal interview questions. *National Business Employment Weekly,* p. 37.

Knouse, S. B. (1987). Confidentiality and the letter of recommendation: A new approach. *Bulletin of the Association for Business Communication, 50* (3), 6-8.

Latham, G. P., & Wexley, K. N. (1981). *Increasing productivity through performance appraisal.* Reading, MA: Addison-Wesley.

Lehman, C. M., & Taylor, G. S. (1991). Participative appraisal of student performance + effective communication skills = long-run success. *Journal of Business and Technical Communication, 5* (3), 307-320.

Lehman, C. M., Taylor, G. S., & Forde, C. M. (1990). Experiential approach to performance appraisal. *Business Education Forum, 44* (5), 25-29.

McGee, K. G. (1992, May 12). How to get a good job in bad times. *Family Circle,* pp. 31, 36.

Meyer, H. H. (1975). The pay-for-performance dilemma. *Organizational Dynamics, 3* (3), 39-50.

Mintz, N. L. (1956). Effects of esthetic surroundings: II. prolonged and repeated experience in a "beautiful" and an "ugly" room. *Journal of Psychology, 41,* 247-254.

Mitchell, B. (1990). Interviewing face-to-interface. *Personnel, 67* (1), 23-25.

Novit, M. S. (1986). Performance appraisals. In *Essentials of personnel management* (2nd ed.). Englewood Cliffs, NJ: Prentice-Hall.

Schneier, C. E., Beatty, R. W., & Baird, L. (1986). How to conduct a successful performance appraisal system. *Training and Development Journal, 40* (4), 38-42.

10 Interview Mistakes That Can Cost You the Job. (1990, March). *Tomorrow's Business Leader,* p. 19.

REVIEW QUESTIONS

1. How do structured and unstructured interviews differ? How is computer-assisted interviewing being used to screen applicants?

2. How do responses to direct and indirect questions differ?

3. Compose three statements or questions that might be considered discriminatory in employment interviews.

4. List some possible sources of information about a company and three important facts you should locate.

5. What posture and body movements can the interviewee use to impress an interviewer favorably?

6. Write a brief statement discussing the potential value of your education to an employer. Add information about your work experience, involvement in student organizations, and other experience.

7. List four leading barriers to communication in employment interviews.

8. Discuss three ways an interviewee can handle illegal interview questions. What are the advantages and disadvantages of each?

9. What is a good strategy to use when you are asked about your major weakness? Provide a specific example you might use.

10. What ideas are included in a follow-up letter?

11. In a thank-you letter, what is the advantage of referring to some point discussed in the interview?

12. List some suggestions for completing employment forms.

13. Which would be written deductively: (a) an acceptance letter or (b) a refusal letter? What ideas should be included in each of these letters?

14. Describe the ideas recommended for inclusion in a resignation letter.

15. Professor Ulmer agreed to serve as one of your employment references, but you have not talked with her for two years. Today, you listed her name on an application form. Should you write to her? Explain.

16. An employee whom you fired last year has given your name as a reference. In the responding letter, would you include some positives *and* negatives? Discuss guidelines for writing a recommendation that you can legally defend.

17. Discuss the guidelines for writing a legally defensible recommendation.

18. What is the primary purpose(s) of a performance appraisal interview? Discuss important guidelines for employees being interviewed during a performance appraisal interview.

19. Discuss several important steps employers should take to ensure an effective performance appraisal interview.

20. Complete each of the THINK IT OVER activities that your instructor assigns.

E-MAIL APPLICATION

Your instructor will divide the class into groups of two. One member will send an e-mail message; the other will respond. The sender will compose an e-mail message to the other member asking for a thoughtful response to five tough interview questions. At least one of the questions should be sensitive in nature (possibly illegal or quite close). Printscreen to obtain a copy of the original message to submit to your instructor. The team member receiving the message will e-mail answers to the five questions. The instructor may ask that you reverse roles so that each of you has experience composing and answering difficult interview questions.

APPLICATIONS

CAREER DEVELOPMENT

1. **Researching a Company and Asking Questions of an Interviewer.** Form small groups and research a company of your choice. Use the information in Figure 14-1 as a guide for your research. Generate a list of ten questions to ask an interviewer from the company you researched. Write original questions that communicate initiative, intelligence, and genuine interest in the company and the job. Submit your research in a memo to your instructor.

CAREER DEVELOPMENT

2. **Preparing to Answer Interview Questions Effectively.** Turn to Figure 14-3 and write the answers to the interview questions in your career notebook; study them in preparation for an interview. As directed by your instructor, complete one or more of the following activities:
   a. Be prepared to discuss your answers in class.
   b. Divide into small groups to discuss your answers. Revise your answers, incorporating relevant feedback and being sure that the answers are truthful and reflect your individual personality.
   c. Set up a mock interview with a friend serving as the interviewer.

CAREER DEVELOPMENT

3. **Practicing a Job Interview.** Form groups of four to practice job interviews. Each person should have available a copy of his or her resume. Alternatively play the roles of interviewer and interviewee, with the two additional people serving as critical observers. Change places until all four have had an opportunity to serve as interviewer and interviewee. You may assume that the jobs being applied for are the ones for which you have selected and designed applications. Alternatively, use one of the following positions:

a. A part-time job visiting high schools to sell seniors on the idea of attending your school.
b. A full-time summer job as a management intern in a local bank.

This activity may be adapted for videotaping and review.

CAREER DEVELOPMENT

4. **Following Up on a Job.** Assume that you are offered the job (or internship) for which you have applied. Make the assumption you prefer:
   a. You applied for an immediate part-time job.
   b. You applied for a full-time job for next summer.
   c. You applied for a cooperative education assignment or internship.
   d. You applied for a full-time job immediately after your graduation. Look at the list of courses you plan to take and write as though you had taken them and satisfied the requirements for a degree.

Write a follow-up letter for the job (internship) for which you have applied. Supply an address.

CAREER DEVELOPMENT

5. **Saying Thank You for an Interview.** Assume that you were interviewed for the job for which you applied in Application 4. Write a thank-you letter to the interviewer. Supply an address.

CAREER DEVELOPMENT

6. **Accepting a Job Offer.** Write a letter of acceptance for the job (internship) for which you applied in Application 4. Supply an address.

CAREER DEVELOPMENT

7. **Refusing a Job Offer Diplomatically.** Assume that the job search identified in Application 4 was very successful; you were offered two positions. Write a letter refusing one of the job offers. Because you want to maintain a positive relationship with the company you are refusing to work for, provide specific reasons for your decision. Supply an address.

CAREER DEVELOPMENT

8. **Resigning from a Job.** Write a letter resigning from your current job. If you are not currently employed, supply fictitious information.

CAREER DEVELOPMENT

9. **Requesting a Letter of Recommendation.** Write a letter requesting a reference to provide information to prospective employers. Provide specific information about how your qualifications relate to the job requirements and enclose a resume. Supply an appropriate name and address.

CAREER DEVELOPMENT

10. **Informing a Reference of an Extended Job Search.** Your job search is taking much longer than you had hoped. Because your references have been providing recommendations for six months now, you must write expressing your gratitude and updating them on the status of your job search. If your qualifications have changed, include an updated resume. Address a letter to one of your references. Supply an appropriate name and address.

CASES FOR ANALYSIS

HUMAN RESOURCES MANAGEMENT/LEGAL

Case 1.   Discrimination Hiring Needs Must Be Watched. As a standard procedure, applicants for jobs with Carr Department Stores are interviewed by the manager and other selected employees. The home office has recently received some complaints from applicants who were not hired. True or not, the applicants have pointed out some possible violations of the Equal Employment Opportunity Commission's guidelines (which prohibit discriminatory hiring based on specified characteristics). Such topics are to be avoided in interviews, or in the "small talk" that precedes them. Direct or indirect questions about these specified characteristics (e.g., age or marital status) are not to be asked. Store managers need to review the guidelines themselves (in the *Policy and Procedures Manual* in each store manager's office) and make sure others who talk with job applicants are also familiar with the guidelines. Otherwise, Carr could be severely embarrassed.

Required: As human resources director, complete the following:
1. Research the current legal guidelines of the Equal Employment Opportunity Commission.
2. Write a memorandum addressed to the store managers urging them to adhere strictly to the guidelines, reviewing the basic guidelines, and informing them of recent changes. Cite a number of sources to be certain that your information is objective. Because of the timeliness of this problem, sources must be current. Use appropriate documentation within the memo to protect yourself and Carr against plagiarism and to assist the managers in locating your references for further research.
3. Use desktop publishing equipment available to you to prepare an attractive, appealing flyer explaining the legal guidelines. You believe an attractive flyer will have greater impact and will be a more useful reference than the memo (Step 2) that contains explanatory information. Write a memo to the store managers explaining the attached flyer.

MANAGEMENT/ETHICS/LEGAL

Case 2.   A Negative Job Recommendation: What Is the Appropriate Course of Action? As the office manager of CompuTel, a computer systems consulting firm with relatively high personnel turnover, you often receive requests to write job recommendations for past employees. Last week, you received a letter from Donald Bryant, human resources director at Advanced Softworks, Inc., stating that Miriam Tyner listed your name as a reference on her job application.

After working for three years as a software developer, Tyner resigned to accept a similar job in a competing firm. You were pleased to see her leave for a number of reasons. She was often abrasive to coworkers and clients (she frequently received complaints) and was uncooperative and self-centered. She never considered her work as a part of an overall team effort. Other than her poor human relations

skills, Tyner's job performance was outstanding; you can cite several examples of extraordinary work. She is a highly skilled programmer with a B.A. in computer engineering and an M.A. in management and information systems.

Required:
1. Decide whether you should provide a recommendation for Miriam Tyner. If so, what kind of recommendation should you write? Consider these points:
   a. What are the consequences if you ignore the request?
   b. What are the consequences of your writing a neutral recommendation (state dates of employment and job title) *or* acknowledging the request and inviting Donald Bryant to telephone you for a confidential conversation?
   c. Would you consider it ethical to write a positive recommendation, ignoring Tyner's poor human relations skills?
   d. Should you mention Tyner's poor human relations skills as well as her competence? If you include negative information, what precautions can you take as safeguards against possible legal action?
2. Based on your decision, write *one* of the following messages:
   a. Write a memo to the file stating that you are ignoring a request for a recommendation on Miriam Tyner and justifying your action.
   b. Write a recommendation letter including only the positive information. Write a brief memo to the file explaining why you chose to omit negative information.
   c. Write a letter including an objective appraisal of Tyner's performance (include positive and negative information).
   d. Write a letter responding to the request for a recommendation and inviting a telephone call to acquire confidential information. Write a dialogue of your anticipated telephone conversation with Mark Carlson.

Address the letter to Donald Bryant, Advanced Softworks, Inc., 1015 Industrial Park, Birmingham, AL 35214-1015.

Every job seeker desires to be effective in employ-ment communication. The stakes are obvious and high. Preliminary analysis of one's strengths and weaknesses and careful planning of arrangement and format are essential to the development of an effec-tive resume and application letter. In addition to plan-ning and organizing, originality is a plus, as the job seeker must somehow distinguish his or her resume from the countless others with which it competes. Success at this stage means that an interview is granted, at which time a candidate has the opportu-nity to sell him or herself to the company as well as to take a closer look at what the company has to offer.

Interviewing involves the use of numerous inter-personal communication skills, both verbal and non-verbal. The challenge of the interview is to relax, while realizing that every word, action, and response is being scrutinized. No small task!

Discussion Questions

1. Hyman Albritton suggests that a job seeker should prepare two resumes. Explain the two and tell the purpose of each.
2. List three "do's" and three "don'ts" for resume preparation.
3. What is the "call for action" John Cripe mentions as essential in the application letter?
4. What advice does Marie Mulvoy have concern-ing dress for the interview?
5. Conducting a self-awareness activity is suggested as a helpful prelude to the employment search process. What is involved? How does it benefit the job seeker?

Application

Interview a businessperson who is involved in employment interviewing. Prepare a written summary that includes answers to the following questions: (1) What strategies are used for "weeding out" re-sumes of job applicants? (2) What are five questions most commonly asked by the interviewer? (3) What is the interviewer looking for in terms of the candidate's nonverbal communication skills?

PART 6

COMMUNICATING

THROUGH REPORTS

CHAPTER 15

THE REPORT PROCESS

AND RESEARCH METHODS

OBJECTIVES

When you have completed Chapter 15, you will
be able to

1 Identify the characteristics of a report and
the various classifications of business
reports.

2 Identify the four steps in the problem-
solving process.

3 Select an appropriate secondary and/or
primary method for solving a problem.

4 Explain the purpose of sampling and two
sampling techniques.

5 Apply techniques for developing effective
questionnaires.

6 Discuss the common problems encountered in
collecting and interpreting data.

For many years Sears, Roebuck & Co. enjoyed the status of being America's leading retailer. For the past several years, however, the company's earnings have plummeted. A number of factors are responsible: increased competition, a poor public image, outdated and ineffective policies, and a lack of vision for the future. Sears Chief Executive Arthur C. Martinez, however, has shaken things up. Since he arrived in September, 1992, he has begun a massive program to overhaul the once-great retailer. He ordered the closure of 113 stores showing poor performance, halted the production of the costly catalogs, and initiated a trendy ad campaign focusing on a new, improved women's apparel line.

Last year Sears reported a net income of $752 million compared with a loss of $2.98 billion in 1993. The main reason for the turnaround, according to Martinez, is keeping up to date with suppliers and, most importantly, knowing who the customers are. Combining and researching the company's databases revealed that a majority of Sears shoppers are not men in search of hardware, but women between the ages of 25 and 50 in the market for everything from tools to clothing. Sears' new push is toward renewing its apparel lines, devoting more floor space to clothing, and changing its dowdy, staid reputation. While things seem to be on the upswing, Martinez admits the company has a long way to go. "Part of my job is to keep a vague sense of unease percolating through the entire company," he says. "The minute you say the job is done, you're dead" (Chandler, 1994, p. 102).

Sears made a turnaround because it became aware of its problems in time. Executives conducted research to identify what the problems were and how to go about solving them. As a manager, you will probably have to deal with a situation that requires you to identify a trouble area and develop possible solutions. Unless you can conduct research, you will be a part of the problem instead of the solution.

KNOWING THE CHARACTERISTICS OF REPORTS

Hello, Jim. This is Ramon in customer services. The boss wants to know how things are going with the 400-case Sleepwell order. Are we going to make the 4 p.m. shipping deadline?

Oh hi, Ramon. We are going to make the deadline, with time to spare. We have about 250 cases on the loading dock, 100 on the box line, and 50 going through the labeling process. They'll all be ready for the loader at two o'clock.

LEARNING OBJECTIVE 1

This brief exchange illustrates a simple reporting task. A question has been posed; the answer given (along with supporting information) satisfies the reporting requirement. Although Jim may never have studied report preparation, he did an excellent job; so Ramon, in turn, can report to his supervisor. Jim's oral report is a very simple illustration of four main characteristics of reports:

What are the four characteristics of reports?

1. *Reports typically travel upward in an organization because they usually are requested by a higher authority.* In most cases, people would not generate reports unless requested to do so.
2. *Reports are logically organized.* In Jim's case, he answered Ramon's question first and then supported the answer with evidence to justify it. Through your study of the organization of letters, you learned the difference between deductive and inductive organization. Jim's report was deductively organized.

If Jim had given the supporting evidence first and followed that with the answer that he would meet the deadline, the organization of his reply would have been inductive and would still have been logical.

3. *Reports stress objectivity.* Because reports contribute to decision making and problem solving, they should be as objective as possible; when nonobjective (subjective) material is included, the report writer should make that known.

4. *Reports are generally prepared for a limited audience.* This characteristic is particularly true of reports traveling within an organization and means that reports, like letters, can be prepared with the receivers' needs in mind.

What Is a Report?

Based on the four characteristics, a workable definition of a **report** is an orderly, objective message used to convey information from one organizational area to another or from one institution to another to assist in decision making or problem solving. Reports have been classified in numerous ways by management and by report-preparation authorities. The form, direction, functional use, and content of the report are used as bases for classification. However, a single report might be included in several classifications. The following brief review of classification helps explain the scope of reporting and establishes a departure point for studying reports and reporting.

FORMAL OR INFORMAL REPORTS

The formal-informal classification is particularly helpful because it applies to all reports. A **formal report** is carefully structured; it stresses objectivity and organization, contains much detail, and is written in a style that tends to eliminate such elements as personal pronouns. An **informal report** is usually a short message written in natural or personal language. The internal memorandum generally can be described as an informal report. All reports can be placed on a continuum of formality, as shown in Figure 15-1. The distinction among the degrees of formality of various reports is explained more fully in Chapters 16-18.

THINK IT OVER
In groups, write a simple oral report such as the one illustrated based on your own personal experience. Identify its four characteristics.

THINK IT OVER
Define the term *report* in your own words. Share your definition in small groups and with the class.

Formal reports are structured; informal reports are short and use casual language.

FIGURE 15-1
Report formality
continuum.

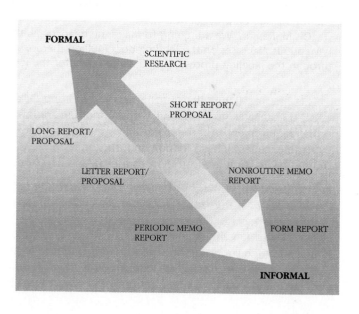

SHORT OR LONG REPORTS

Reports can be classified generally as short or long. A one-page memorandum is obviously short, and a report of twenty pages is obviously long. What about in-between lengths? One important distinction generally holds true: As it becomes longer, a report takes on more characteristics of formal reports. Thus, the formal-informal and short-long classifications are closely related.

How are the formal-informal and the short-long classifications related?

INFORMATIONAL OR ANALYTICAL REPORTS

An **informational report** carries objective information from one area of an organization to another. An **analytical report** presents suggested solutions to problems. Company annual reports, monthly financial statements, reports of sales volume, and reports of employee or personnel absenteeism and turnover are informational reports. Reports of scientific research, real-estate appraisal reports, and feasibility reports by consulting firms are analytical reports.

THINK IT OVER
What are the purposes of an informational report and an analytical report? Provide an example based on your own personal experience.

VERTICAL OR LATERAL REPORTS

The vertical-lateral classification refers to the directions reports travel. Although most reports travel upward in organizations, many travel downward. Both represent vertical reports and are often referred to as *upward-directed* and *downward-directed* reports. The main function of vertical reports is to contribute to management *control*, as shown in Figure 15-2. Lateral reports, on the other hand, assist in *coordination* in the organization. A report traveling between units on the same organizational level, as between the production department and the finance department, is lateral.

THINK IT OVER
What purpose does a vertical and a lateral report achieve in an organization? Provide an example of each report; refer to the Citizens' Bank organization chart and the discussion of flow of communication in an organization in Chapter 2.

INTERNAL OR EXTERNAL REPORTS

An **internal report,** such as a production and a sales report, travels within an organization. An **external report**, such as a company's annual report to stockholders, is prepared for distribution outside an organization.

PERIODIC REPORTS

A **periodic report** is issued on regularly scheduled dates. They are generally upward directed and serve management-control purposes. Daily, weekly, monthly, quarterly, semiannual, and annual time periods are typical for periodic reports. Preprinted forms and computer-generated data contribute to uniformity of periodic reports.

FUNCTIONAL REPORTS

A **functional report** serves a specified purpose within a company. The functional classification includes accounting reports, marketing reports, financial reports, personnel reports, and a variety of other reports that take their functional designation from the ultimate use of the report. For example, a justification of the need for additional personnel or for new equipment is described as a justification report in the functional classification.

Proposals

A **proposal** is a written description of how one organization can meet the needs of another; e.g., provide products or services or solve problems. Businesses issue "calls for bids" that present the specifications for major purchases of

A proposal is a special report that attempts to convince a potential customer/client that the company responding to the "RFP" can meet the specifications established.

FIGURE 15-2
The general upward flow of reports.

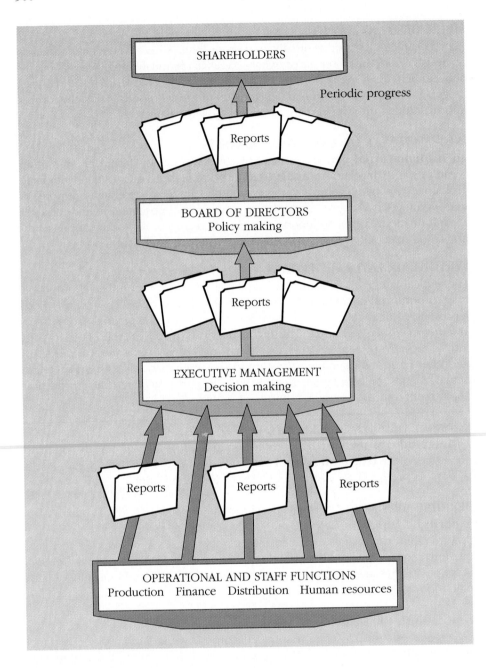

FIGURE 15-2
The general upward flow of reports.

goods and certain services. Most governmental agencies issue "requests for proposals," or RFPs. Potential suppliers prepare proposal reports telling how they can meet that need. Those preparing the proposal create a convincing document that will lead to their obtaining a contract.

In our information-intensive society, proposal preparation is a major activity for many firms. In fact, some companies hire consultants or designate employees to specialize in proposal writing. Chapter 17 presents proposal preparation in considerable detail.

As you review these report classifications, you will very likely decide—correctly—that almost all reports could be included in most of these categories. A

Basically, reports are classified based on flow, time, and use. Review the classifications to see this trend for yourself.

COMMUNICATION MENTOR

Research (information gathering) is the single most important tool in communications. You must answer these questions:

- Who is your audience? What are its perspective and specific needs?
- What is your audience's level of understanding, interest, and receptivity to your message?
- Whom are you competing against and what are their strengths and weaknesses?

If you are in the information business, you will never run out of issues that need to be researched. The challenge is to do it in a manner that is efficient as well as effective.

David Martin, President
INTELECO

report may be formal or informal, short or long, informational or analytical, vertically or laterally directed, internal or external, periodic or nonperiodic, functionally labeled, a proposal, or some other combination of these classifications. These report categories are in common use and provide necessary terminology for the study and production of reports.

Basis for a Report: A Problem

The upward flow of reports provides management with data that someone may use to make a decision. The purpose is to use the data to solve a problem. Some problems are recurring and call for a steady flow of information; other problems may be unique and call for information on a one-time basis. A problem is the basis for a report.

What is the basis for a report?

The following steps are used for finding a solution:

1. Recognize and define the problem.
2. Select a method of solution.
3. Collect and organize the data.
4. Arrive at an answer.

Reports communicate how problems were solved using the four steps in problem solving. What are these steps?

Only after all four steps have been completed to solve the problem is a report written for presentation. Reports represent an attempt to communicate how a problem was solved. These problem-solving steps are completed *before* the report is written in final form.

Is a report written before or after the problem has been solved?

RECOGNIZING AND DEFINING THE PROBLEM

Problem-solving research cannot begin until the researchers define the problem. Frequently, those requesting a report will attempt to provide a suitable definition. Nevertheless, researchers should attempt to paraphrase to ensure they will be on the right track.

LEARNING OBJECTIVE 2

The important *first* step to problem solving is to pinpoint the problem and the purpose.

Research studies often have both a statement of the problem and a statement of the purpose. For example, a real-estate appraiser accepts a client's request to appraise a building to determine its market value. The problem is to arrive at a fair market value for the property. The purpose of the appraisal, however, might be to establish a value for a mortgage loan, to determine the feasibility of adding to the structure, or to assess the financial possibility of demolishing the structure and erecting something else. Thus, the purpose may have much to do with determining what elements to consider in arriving at an answer.

In other words, unless you know why something is wanted, you might have difficulty knowing what is wanted. Once you arrive at the answers to the *what* and *why* questions, write them down. You will be on your way to solving the problem.

Using Hypotheses and Statements of Purpose

A hypothesis is a statement to be proved or disproved through research.

What is the value of stating the hypothesis in the null form?

A **hypothesis** is a statement to be proved or disproved through some type of research. For example, a study of skilled manufacturing employees under varying conditions might be made to determine whether production would increase if each employee were part of a team, as opposed to being a single unit in a production line. For this problem, the hypothesis could be formulated in this way:

Hypothesis:

Productivity will increase when skilled manufacturing employees are members of production teams rather than single units in a production line.

Because the hypothesis tends to be stated in a way that favors one possibility or a prejudice toward a particular answer, many researchers prefer to state hypotheses in the null form. The **null hypothesis** states no relationship or difference will be found in the factors being studied, which tends to remove the

Before you can attempt to solve a problem, you must first realize what the problem is. K-Mart's recent slump in the retail market could be due to any number of reasons: ineffective advertising, competition from other stores, an unappealing image, or the selection of merchandise. Until managers and marketing personnel carefully define the exact nature of the problem, sales will probably continue to decline.

COMMUNICATION   MENTOR

Perhaps the greatest failure of researchers is in recognizing the real issues to be addressed. When beginning any information-gathering process, be sure you know *what* the real issue is and *how* the information you are gathering will be used in addressing this issue.

David Martin, President
INTELECO

element of prejudice toward an answer. The null hypothesis for the previous example could be written as follows:

Null Hypothesis:

No significant difference will exist in productivity between workers as team members and workers as individual production line units.

The hypothesis posed as a problem and purpose statement might read:

Statement of the Purpose:

The purpose of this study is to determine whether production will increase when employees are organized as teams as compared with their working as individuals in a production line.

Using the hypothesis approach or the problem-purpose approach is optional. In many ways, the purpose of a study is determined by the intended use of its results.

Limiting the Scope of the Problem

A major shortcoming of research planning is the failure to establish or to recognize desirable limits. Assume, for instance, that you want to study salaries of office support staff. Imagine the scope of such a task. Millions of people are employed in office support jobs. Perhaps a thousand or so different types of jobs fall into this classification. To reduce such a problem to reasonable proportions, use the *what, why, when, where,* and *who* questions to limit the problem. Here are the limits you might derive as the human resources manager at a metropolitan bank:

What:	A study of salaries of office support staff.
Why:	To determine whether salaries in our firm are competitive and consistent.
When:	Current.
Where:	Our metropolitan area.
Who:	Office support staff employees in banks.

COMMUNICATION   MENTOR

An effective report begins with understanding the objectives and expectations of a client. This understanding should be confirmed and reconfirmed as a finding early in the process might change the entire thrust of the project. For example, a client was interested in acquiring a Russian legal entity. Throughout our initial discussions of the project scope, the client continually referred to necessary "due diligence" and "purchase investigation" procedures. After we presented the report, the client clarified a need for an audit of the financial statements in accordance with generally accepted auditing standards—an entirely different report than the one we prepared. Ultimately, we solved the client's problem while learning a valuable lesson about the importance of effective communication in preparing a report that meets a client's needs.

Larry E. Wilson, Partner
Arthur Andersen, Moscow

Now you can phrase the problem this way:

Statement of the Purpose:

The purpose of this study is to survey salaries of office support staff in local banks to determine whether our salaries are competitive and consistent.

Note that this process of reducing the problem to a workable size has also established some firm limits to the research. You have limited the problem to current salaries, to the local area, and to a particular type of business. Note, too, how important the *why* was in helping establish the limits. Limiting the problem is "zeroing in on the problem."

Defining Terms Clearly

Vague terms contribute greatly to faulty communication. Clearly, in the study of office support staff salaries, a comparison of one bank's salaries with those paid by others would be meaningful only if the information gathered from other banks relates to identical jobs. A job description defining the duties performed by an administrative assistant, for example, would help ensure that all firms would be talking about the same job tasks regardless of the job title.

In addition, the term *salary* requires definition. Is it hourly, weekly, monthly, or yearly? Are benefits included? A conversion table would probably be necessary to provide consistency in converting amounts to appropriate pay periods. In all research, terms must be defined if they could be misleading.

SELECTING A METHOD OF SOLUTION

After defining the problem, the researcher will plan how to arrive at a solution. You may use secondary and/or primary research methods to collect necessary information.

Secondary Research

Secondary research provides information that has already been created by others. Researchers save time and effort by not duplicating research that has already been undertaken. They can access this information easily through the aid of computer databases, bibliographic indexes, and catalogs. Suppose that a marketing manager has been authorized to investigate the feasibility of implementing a strategic information system. The manager knows other companies are utilizing this technology. By engaging in library research, the manager can determine the boundaries of knowledge before proceeding into the unknown.

Figure 15-3 illustrates the constant development of knowledge. Certain truths have been established within the confines (white area) of a field of knowledge. These truths are treated as principles and reported in textbooks and other publications. However, because knowledge is constantly expanding, the researcher knows that new information is available. The job, then, is to become familiar with the library, canvass the literature of the field, and attempt to redefine the boundaries of knowledge (shaded area). This redefinition is the function of secondary research. Researchers then explore the unknown (dark area). Through redefinition of boundaries, library research accomplishes the following objectives:

What is secondary research?

How does secondary research save time and effort?

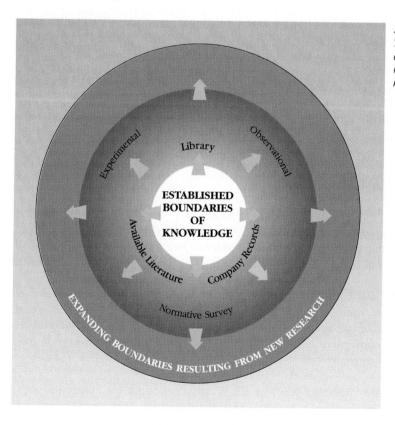

Figure 15-3
The constant
expansion of the
boundaries of
knowledge.

COMMUNICATION   MENTOR

Reports should communicate the authors' findings, conclusions, and recommendations based on the work performed and the data analyzed and not simply rehash the data. When preparing reports

- Determine the purpose of the report. Include sections and topics only if they support this purpose. Exclude extraneous thoughts regardless of how interesting they may be. Stay focused!
- Know and prepare the report for your audience(s). Determine what they expect and gear the report to meet these expectations. If the report is the result of a long project or investigation, provide interim updates.
- Plan your work. Be organized and thorough in your research and analysis. As soon as possible, determine if you will need assistance and identify the sources of information and data.
- Report your findings as unbiased as possible. Nothing is as important as your credibility and integrity. Do not compromise these qualities by skewing the report to meet your agenda.

Sajan K. Thomas
Vice President
Prudential Institutional Investors

In what ways can secondary research facilitate research?

- Establishes a point of departure for further research.
- Avoids needless duplication of costly research efforts.
- Reveals areas of needed research.
- Makes a real contribution to a body of knowledge.

LOCATING SECONDARY DATA

Protect yourself against too much information.

When beginning to collect secondary data, beware of collecting too much information—one of the major deterrents to good report writing. Although you want to be thorough, you do not want to collect and record such a large amount of information that you will hardly know where to begin your analysis. Suggestive or cue notes or a card system will help you keep the volume at a minimum.

THINK IT OVER
Consult an English composition textbook or library research books to reacquaint yourself with techniques for recording information from secondary sources.

SUGGESTIVE OR CUE NOTE.   A **suggestive** or **cue note** is a reminder of something you want to recall. Whether you put these reminders on a single sheet of paper or on separate sheets or cards, the goal is to reduce bulky material to small, convenient-to-use data. Develop a system that satisfies your own needs.

CARD SYSTEM.   Standard 3 x 5 or 4 x 6 cards are useful for library research. When library information is needed, go first to catalogs, bibliographic indexes, or electronic databases to compile a basic bibliography. Become familiar with sources such as those shown in Figure 15-4. By preparing a complete bibliographical entry for each reference on a separate card, you may save a trip to the library or your database. Then you can use the abbreviated bibliographical entry on each note card, as shown in the samples in Figure 15-6.

Printed Indexes

Business Periodicals Index
Education Index
New York Times Index
Readers' Guide to Periodical Literature
Social Science and Humanities Index
The Wall Street Journal Index

Electronic Sources

ProQuest
Business Dateline
DIALOG Information Services
ERIC (educational)
Internet
Lexis/Nexis (news and business)
Moody's International Company Data
Westlaw (legal)

General Facts and Statistics

Statistical Abstract of the United States and other Bureau of the
   Census publications (available on statistical databases)
Dictionary
Encyclopedia (*Americana* or *Britannica*)
Fortune Directories of U.S. Corporations
World Atlas
Almanacs

Biography

Who's Who in America (and a variety of similar directories for
specific geographic areas, industries, and professions)

Report Style and Format

American Psychological Association. (1994). *Publication manual of
the American Psychological Association.* (4th ed.). Washington, DC:
Author.

Campbell, W. G., Ballou, S. V., & Slade, C. (1990). *Form and style:
Theses reports and term papers.* (8th ed.). Boston: Houghton Mifflin.

Gibaldi, J., & Achtert, W. S. (1995). *MLA handbook for writers of
research papers.* (4th ed.). New York: Modern Language Association.

University of Chicago Press. (1993). *The Chicago manual of style.*
(14th ed.). Chicago: Author.

Turabian, K. L. (1987). *A manual for writers of term papers, theses,
and dissertations.* (6th ed.). Chicago: University of Chicago Press.

FIGURE 15-4
Useful reference and source books.

The availability of computer-assisted data searches has simplified the time-consuming task of searching through indexes, card catalogs, and other sources. Note the list of major computer databases for business users listed in Figure 15-4. Weekly and monthly updates keep electronic databases current, and they are easy to use. For example, suppose by inputting the key term *cross-cultural*, you received the computer printout shown in Figure 15-5, which contains information to facilitate your research. First, you can quickly evaluate the relevance of each reference by simply reading the brief summary provided and

THINK IT OVER
Can you proficiently conduct computer-assisted data searches? If not, have a college librarian, an instructor, or a friend help you master this time-saving technique right away.

FIGURE 15-5
A sample computer-assisted data search.

Access No:	00732403 ProQuest ABI/INFORM
Title:	Cross-cultural communication for managers
Authors:	Munter, Mary
Journal:	Business Horizons (BHO) ISSN: 0007-6813 Vol: 36 Iss: 3 Date: May/June 1993 p: 69-78
Subjects:	Management development; Skills; Communication; Multiculturalism & pluralism; Guidelines; Implementations
Geo Places:	US
Codes:	9190 (United States); 9150 (Guidelines); 6200 (Train- ing & development); 2200 (Managerial skills)
Abstract:	Managers must become proficient cross-cultural communicators if they wish to succeed in today's global environment . . . . To be effective in any given culture, managers should consider the following 7 issues before they begin to communicate: 1. setting communication objectives, 2. choosing a communication style, 3. assessing and enhancing credibility, 4. selecting and motivating audiences, 5. setting a message strategy, 6. overcoming lan- guage difficulties, and 7. using appropriate nonver- bal behaviors.
Access No:	00860414 ProQuest ABI/INFORM
Title:	Toppling the cultural tower of Babel
Authors:	De Vries, Manfred F R Kets
Journal:	Chief Executive (CHE) ISSN: 0610-4724 Iss: 94 Date: May 1994 p: 68-71
Subjects:	Multiculturalism & pluralism; Impacts; Corporate culture; Corporate planning; Foreign investment
Geo Places:	US
Codes:	9190 (United States); 2500 (Organizational behavior); 2310 (Planning); 1300 (International trade & foreign investment)
Abstract:	Chief executives with interests abroad must assess the big picture and ensure that their companies' culture is flexible enough to work successfully in countries where they do business. EuroDisney is a good example of what can go wrong when a company tries to create a new venture in a foreign country without taking the context of the national culture into consideration . . . .

highlighting each reference that appears to have merit. The next task is simple: locate each *useful* (highlighted) reference using the complete bibliographic information included in the printout. Databases such as Lexis/Nexis and the Internet have full-text retrieval capability, meaning you can retrieve the entire reference into your word-processing program so that you can review and/or print a copy. A research process that may have taken several hours can be completed in a matter of minutes.

ORGANIZING AND SUMMARIZING SECONDARY RESEARCH

After you have located the relevant sources, you can begin taking notes using various methods. Because your aim is to *learn*, not to accumulate, the following technique for taking notes is effective: (1) read an article rapidly, (2) put it aside,

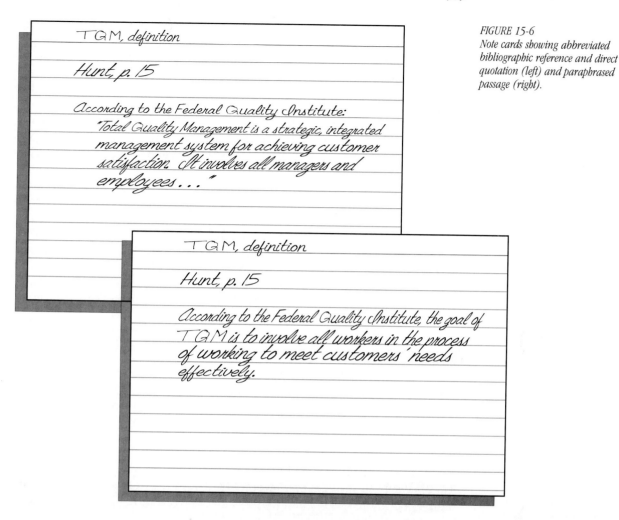

FIGURE 15-6
Note cards showing abbreviated bibliographic reference and direct quotation (left) and paraphrased passage (right).

(3) list main and supporting points *from memory,* and (4) review the article to see whether all significant points have been included. Rapid reading forces concentration. Taking notes from memory reinforces learning and reduces the temptation to rely heavily on the words of others. If you really learn the subject matter of one source, you will (as research progresses) see the relationship between it and other sources. You will see yourself growing toward mastery of the subject.

Traditionally, researchers have read the article and immediately written notes on note cards. With photocopiers so readily available, many researchers prefer highlighting important points on a photocopy of the article; and then from the highlighted material, they write note cards or compose notes at the keyboard. In addition, some researchers are using portable computers to facilitate library research. Rather than spending time and money photocopying large volumes of information, researchers compose notes at the keyboard in the library and then return the reference material to the shelf. This efficient method of gathering secondary data will grow as the price of portable computers decreases.

You can use two kinds of notes: direct quotation or paraphrase. The **direct quotation method** involves citing the exact words from a secondary source. This method is useful when you believe the exact words have a special effect or

THINK IT OVER
How does the statement, "Become an expert before becoming an author" apply to summarizing secondary research?

you want to give the impact of an expert. The **paraphrase method** involves summarizing information in your own words without changing the author's intended meaning. Put direct quotations in quotation marks as a reminder. Indicate on a note card the page numbers from which cited material is taken and the call number of the reference. This information may save you another trip to the library.

THINK IT OVER
Is it necessary to write a citation for quoted material? paraphrased material? What is the consequence of failing to do so?

Plagiarism is the presentation of someone else's ideas or words as your own. To safeguard your reputation against plagiarism charges, be certain to give credit where credit is due. Specifically, provide a citation (footnote, endnote, or in-text parenthetical reference) for each (1) direct quotation and (2) passage from someone else's work that you stated in your own words rather than using the original words (the words are your own, but the idea is not). Regardless of the note cards you choose to use in your report—the direct quotation shown at left in Figure 15-6 or the paraphrased version shown at right—you must include a citation in your report so that the author receives credit for the idea.

After identifying the text that must be credited to someone else, develop complete, accurate citations and a references page. Documentation guidelines are discussed in Chapter 18.

Primary Research

After reviewing the secondary data, you may need to collect primary data to solve your problem. **Primary research** relies on firsthand data; e.g., responses from pertinent individuals or observations of people or phenomenon related to your study. Recognized methods to obtain original information are normative surveys, observational studies, and experiments.

NORMATIVE SURVEY RESEARCH

What is the primary purpose of normative survey research?

Normative survey research determines the status of something at a specific time. Survey instruments such as questionnaires, opinion surveys, checklists, and interviews are used to obtain information. Election opinion polls represent one type of normative survey research. The term *normative* is used to qualify surveys because surveys reveal "norms" or "standards" existing at the time of the survey. An election poll taken two months before an election might have little similarity to one taken the week before the election.

Surveys can help verify the accuracy of existing norms. The U.S. Census is conducted every decade to establish an actual population figure, and each person is supposedly counted. In effect, the census tests the accuracy of prediction techniques used to estimate population during the years between censuses. A survey of what employees consider a fair benefits package would be effective only for the date of the survey. People retire, move, and change their minds often; these human traits make survey research of human opinion somewhat tentative. Yet, surveys remain a valuable tool for gathering information on which to base policy making and decision making.

THINK IT OVER
Explain the terms *validity* and *reliability* in your own words.

VALIDITY AND RELIABILITY.   Whether a survey involves personal interviewing or the distribution of items such as checklists or questionnaires, some principles of procedure and preplanning are common to both methods. These principles assure the researcher that the data gathered will be both valid and reliable. **Validity** refers to the degree to which the data measures what you intend for it to measure. **Reliability** refers to the level of consistency or stability over time; that is, the data are reasonably accurate.

Validity generally results from careful planning of the questionnaire or interview questions (*items*). Cautious wording, preliminary testing of items to detect misunderstandings, and some statistical techniques are helpful in determining whether the responses to the items are valid.

Reliability results from asking a large enough sample of people so that the researcher is reasonably assured the results would be the same even if more people were asked to respond. For example, if you were to ask ten people to react to a questionnaire item, the results might vary considerably. If you were to add 90 more people to the sample, the results might tend to reach a point of stability, where more responses would not change the results. Reliability would then be assured.

SAMPLING.   Researchers normally cannot survey everyone, particularly if the population is large and the research budget is limited. **Sampling** is a survey technique that eliminates the need for questioning 100 percent of the population. Sampling is based on the principle that a sufficiently large number drawn at random from a population will be representative of the total population; that is, the sample will possess the same characteristics in the same proportions as the total population. For example, a company collecting market research data before introducing a new low-fat food product would survey only a few people. The data are considered *valid* if the sample of people surveyed has the same percentage of ages, genders, purchasing power, and so on as the anticipated target market.

A number of sampling methods are available that you will study in research and statistics courses. Presently, you will learn two common sampling proce-

> What steps can you take to ensure that your data are valid and reliable?

> **LEARNING OBJECTIVE 4**
>
> What is sampling and what purpose does it serve?
>
> **THINK IT OVER**
> How large is the United States population, according to the U.S. Census? Would sampling be effective?

A major factor affecting the value of a survey is the way in which it is conducted. The results of any survey are only as valid and reliable as the methods the researchers use to select and question a representative sample of the population.

dures that ensure that each person has a known chance of being selected—random sampling and stratified random sampling.

1. *Random sampling.* Selecting a random sample using a random number generator program is the easiest sampling technique. To determine the career plans of a college student body, a researcher could use a random number generator program from the university's computer system to select the students to be included in the survey. Because the entire student body is included in the computer system, each student would have an equal opportunity to be selected.

2. *Stratified random sampling.* Stratified random sampling involves dividing the population into subgroups. In surveying the student body using this method, you would divide the population into student classifications; e.g., seniors, juniors, sophomores, and freshmen. Suppose the total student body of 10,000 is composed of 30 percent freshmen, 27 percent sophomores, 23 percent juniors, and 20 percent seniors. If you want to survey 1,000 students, you would randomly select students from each classification until you have 300 freshmen, 270 sophomores, 230 juniors, and 200 seniors. Stratified samples are useful for comparing responses between subgroups.

The researcher must be cautious about drawing conclusions from a sample and generalizing them to a population that might not be represented by the sample. For example, early-morning shoppers may differ from afternoon or evening shoppers, young ones may differ from old ones, men may differ from women. A good researcher defines the population as distinctly as possible and uses a sampling technique to ensure that the sample is representative.

OBSERVATIONAL RESEARCH

Observational research involves observing and analyzing statistically certain phenomena to assist in establishing new principles. For example, market analysts observe buying habits of certain income groups to determine the most desirable markets. An EDP manager tabulates the number of input-operator errors made to assess the effectiveness of a computer-training program. Executives analyze the frequency of ethical misconduct to determine the effectiveness of a comprehensive ethics program.

Developing an objective system for quantifying observations is necessary to collect valid data. For example, to gain insight on the effect of a comprehensive ethics program, a researcher might record the number of incidents of ethical misconduct reported or the number of calls made to an ethics helpline to seek advice about proper conduct.

EXPERIMENTAL RESEARCH

Experimental research involves two samples that have exactly the same components before a variable is added to one of the samples. The differences observed are due to the variable. Like scientists, businesses use experimental research.

As a simple example, assume that a company has a great number of machinists doing the same routine job. Management decides to research the effects of work groups on productivity (problem statement discussed earlier in this chapter). The study involves the machinists in two plants with similar

COMMUNICATION IN ACTION

David Martin, INTELECO

Whether gathering information for a small research project or working with an international corporation, David Martin of INTELECO understands the value of good research. His firsthand experience establishes that a company's investment in conducting valid research can yield literally millions of dollars in savings. He cites one specific example of an international cellular company entering an emerging South American market that saved substantially. Martin's research expertise has helped him build two successful marketing research companies primarily involved in conducting corporate marketing research, political polling, and public opinion surveys.

Martin stresses the importance of selecting an appropriate research method. A client hired Martin to conduct focus groups to investigate a problem in the company. After gaining a clear understanding of *what* information the client wanted and *how* the client would use the information, Martin recommended another research method. "Focus groups are not always an appropriate research method for obtaining the information you need for the decision you want to reach," he told the client.

Martin also believes no one research method will give a complete perspective on information gathering. "For example, focus groups are a good research tool but cannot be used in and of themselves," he states. "Nor should telephone surveys, historical sales records, customer satisfaction surveys, and other methods such as comment cards or complaints be used alone," he adds. Martin urges the researcher to integrate many research methods to complete the information-gathering picture.

To emphasize his point, Martin relates an example of a recent political campaign. A client asked Martin to conduct a telephone survey and find *everything* about the electorate. "First, no one will stay on the phone long enough to tell you *everything* and second, obtaining broad, general information is usually not necessary," he adds. To get the kinds of information the client needed, Martin suggested trying other research sources before conducting a telephone interview.

For instance, before surveying public opinion for a political campaign, Martin analyzes the results from previous political races retrieved from databases to gain a historical perspective. "Obtaining this 'precinct-by-precinct' analysis from databases is more cost effective than a telephone survey," he said. The researcher utilizes a number of tools to meet client needs. "Information is not limited to a one tell-all, be-all, and end-all survey."

Applying What You Have Learned

1. Why is research so important to many of the clients with whom Martin works?
2. Why does Martin believe no one research method gives a complete perspective on information gathering?
3. Assume that Martin asked you to conduct research, describing political party affiliations in your community. What research methods would you consider using in gathering this information?

previous productivity rates. The machinists in one plant are organized in work groups; each machinist in the other group continues to work as a single unit on the production line. During the period of the study, the difference in the two groups is noted. Because the work-group organization is assumed to be the only variable, any difference is attributed to its influence.

COLLECTING DATA THROUGH SURVEYS

LEARNING OBJECTIVE 5

Obtaining a low response rate is a primary disadvantage of mailed surveys.

Responses to surveys conducted by mail often represent only a small percentage of the total mailings. In some cases, a return of three to five percent is considered adequate and is planned for by researchers. In other cases, depending on the population, the sample, and the information requested, a return of considerably more than half the mailings might be a planned result. Selecting an appropriate data-collection method and developing a survey instrument are crucial elements of an effective research study.

Selecting a Data-Collection Method

Researchers must consider many factors when selecting an appropriate method for collecting data:

What are the major advantages of mail or telephone surveys? Does a personal interview offer additional advantages or disadvantages?

1. Questionnaire surveys by mail are inexpensive and not limited geographically. Respondents may remain anonymous, which might result in honest answers, and a mailed survey removes difference-in-status barriers—a corporation president may respond readily when the researcher might never succeed in getting a response by telephone or by personal interview. At the same time, mail survey instruments must be concise or they will be discarded. Most people who respond have strong feelings about the topic, so this group of respondents might not be representative of the intended population. Researchers must prepare persuasive transmittal messages that indicate how the respondent can benefit by answering. That persuasion often takes the form of a gift for answering.
2. Personal interviews allow the interviewer to obtain answers in depth and perhaps to explore otherwise sensitive topics. But interviews are expensive in terms of time and money if interviewers are paid, and many people simply don't want to be interviewed.
3. Telephone interviews are inexpensive as a rule. But like mailed questionnaires, a low percentage of total telephone calls will actually provide wanted information.
4. Participant observation is frequently used in consumer research with the observer simply noting how people seem to make selections. A problem, of course, is that observation is sight only and does not give clues about judgment or analytical processes.

Which components of a study are affected by the design of the instrument?

No matter which survey technique or combination of techniques is used, the way in which the survey instrument is designed and written has much to do with response validity and reliability, percentage of response, and quality of information received.

Developing An Effective Survey Instrument

Even when the sampling technique results in a representative sample, the construction of the survey instrument—usually a questionnaire or interview guide—is critical to obtaining reliable and valid data. Before formulating items for a questionnaire or opinion survey, a researcher should visualize the ways responses will be assembled and included in a final report. Here are some suggestions for effective questionnaires:

1. *Arrange the items in a logical sequence.* If possible, the sequence should proceed from easy to difficult items. Easy, nonthreatening items involve respondents and encourage them to finish. You might group related items such as demographic data or those that use the same response options (multiple choice, rating scales, open-ended questions).

2. *Ask for factual information whenever possible.* Opinions may be needed in certain studies, but opinions may change from day to day. As a general rule, too, the smaller the sample, the less reliable are conclusions based on opinions.

3. *Ask for information that can be recalled readily.* Asking for information going back in time may not result in sound data.

4. *Strive to write clear questions that respondents will interpret in the same way.* Follow these suggestions:

    a. *Provide brief, easy-to-follow directions.* Explain the purpose of the study in the cover letter or in a brief statement at the top of the questionnaire so that the respondents understand your intent.

    b. *Avoid words with imprecise meanings (e.g., several, usually) and specialized terms and difficult words that respondents might not understand.* Be sure you have used accurate translations for each concept presented if other cultures are involved. Provide examples for items that might be difficult to understand.

    c. *Use short items that ask for a single answer to one idea.* Include only the questions needed to meet the objectives of your study; questionnaire length affects the return rate.

    d. *Avoid "skip-and-jump" instructions.* Questions such as "If you answered *yes* to 4, skip directly to 9; if you answered *no*, explain your reason under 5 and 6" are confusing.

5. *Avoid questions that may be threatening or awkward to the respondent.*

Have you stopped humiliating employees who question your management decisions?

☐ Yes

☐ No

☐ Undecided

6. *Design questions that are easy to answer and to tabulate.* Suppose you want to determine the most pressing problems facing employees in a production line. You could ask them to list the problems, but the responses might be so ambiguous that tabulating them would be impossible. A rating scale such as the following one would be an improvement:

THINK IT OVER
In groups, discuss the guidelines for developing effective questionnaires. Add other items to this list based on your personal experience.

THINK IT OVER
List three other words with imprecise meanings. For each word, write a word(s) that respondents would likely interpret as you intend.

Ease your own workload by making tabulating easy.

Circle the degree to which each of the following factors affects your job satisfaction:

Acceptance by others

1	2	3	4	5	6

Little
effect

Moderate
effect

Great
effect

Interest in job

1	2	3	4	5	6

Little
effect

Moderate
effect

Great
effect

Does convergence toward
the middle say something
about human nature?

Note that six numbers have been used to indicate how respondents feel. When an odd number of choices, such as five, is provided, responses tend to converge toward the middle number. This tendency to converge may create a bias in the responses.

Similar information could be obtained by listing the potential problems and by asking respondents to rank the problems in order of their importance:

Rank the following factors in order of their importance to you. Place a 1 in the space following the most important problem, a 2 in the space following the second most important problem, and so on until all have been ranked. Two blank lines have been left for you to write in problem areas that may have been omitted.

Acceptance by others   _____
Interest in job   _____
Economic security   _____
Health   _____
_____   _____
_____   _____

To determine which factor is most critical to a production employee, a *forced answer* question can be used:

Of all the problems listed, which is the *single* most critical problem for you personally?

_____

7. *Provide all possible answer choices on multiple choice and rating scale questions; add an "undecided" or "other" category so that respondents are not forced to choose a nonapplicable response.* Note the following examples:

Should city taxes be levied to fund a city recreational complex?

☐ Yes

☐ No

☐ Undecided

Which of the following factors is the single most critical factor for you personally? Place a check in the space provided.

a. Acceptance by others   _____

b. Interest in job   _____

c. Economic security   _____

d. Health   _____

e. Other (specify)   _____

8. *Allow respondents to select among ranges if possible.* Checking a range is especially useful when the respondent may have difficulty remembering the exact information requested or the information is sensitive; e.g., age and income. Tabulating information in ranges requires less effort from the respondent. Questions about age might be arranged in the following manner:

Indicate your age group:

☐ 20-29   ☐ 50-59

☐ 30-39   ☐ 60-69

☐ 40-49   ☐ 70 and over

In this example, respondents whose ages are between 20.0 and 29 years would check 20-29, and the assumed average age for everyone in that group would be the midpoint, 25.0.

9. *Provide enough space for respondents to answer open-ended questions.* "What effect would an additional tax on oil and natural gas have on the economy?" may require a lengthy answer.

10. *Test the instrument by asking others to complete and/or critique the questionnaire; consider conducting a pilot study involving a small group of the population.* This process will allow you to correct problems in clarity, ease of answering, and quality of answers. A pilot study may uncover factors affecting your results, which you can incorporate into the final research design.

What steps can you take to test the clarity of your instrument?

11. *Include a postage-paid envelope with a mailed questionnaire.* A higher percentage of questionnaires is returned when this courtesy is provided. Include your name and address at the bottom of the questionnaire in the event the envelope is misplaced.

12. *Create an appealing, easy-to-comprehend design using word processing or desktop publishing software.* Use print enhancements such as typefaces, bold, underline, and italics to emphasize important ideas and graphic lines and boxes to partition text so that the reader can identify and move through sections of a questionnaire quickly.

Researchers must select from among the several formats available the one best suited to the situation. Criteria for selecting one alternative over the others might include the following items: Which format leaves the least chance for misinterpretation? Which format provides information in the way it can best be used? Can it be tabulated easily? Can it be cross-referenced to other items in the survey instrument?

How do you determine the appropriate format for collecting information?

COMMUNICATION MENTOR

Clients typically push for the research to do more than it can be reasonably expected to do. As a researcher, you must constantly guard against promising too much. Instead, remind your client that research is but *one* source of information. The same principle applies to building a house. You wouldn't try to use a hammer as the only tool in constructing a home. Neither should a survey be the only tool in gathering information on any given issue.

David Martin, President
INTELECO

ARRIVING AT AN ANSWER

LEARNING OBJECTIVE 6

Even the most intelligent person cannot be expected to draw sound conclusions from faulty information. Sound conclusions can be drawn only when information has been properly organized, collected, and interpreted.

Organizing the Data

Having decided on a method, researchers must outline a step-by-step approach to the solution of a problem. The human mind is susceptible to digressions. Although these digressions may be short lived, they distract from the job at hand; and, if given free rein, they can lead you to demolish the real object of the study.

Therefore, *keep on the right track*. Plan the study and follow the plan. Question every step for its contribution to the objective. Keep a record of actions. In a formal research study, the researcher is expected to make a complete report. Another qualified person should be able to make the same study, use the same steps, and arrive at the same conclusion. Thus, a report serves as a guide.

Does tabulating serve the same purpose as cue cards in secondary research?

Tabulation techniques should be used to reduce quantitative data such as numerous answers to questionnaire items. Suppose you have made a survey and have collected several hundred replies to a 20- or 30-item questionnaire in addition to many cards or notes from library sources. What do you do next? As shown in Figure 15-7, the report process is one of reducing the information collected to a size that can be handled conveniently in a written message.

THINK IT OVER
Explain the process of compressing information into a report in your own words.

Visualize the report process as taking place in a huge funnel. At the top of the funnel, pour in all the original information. Then, through a process of compression within the funnel, take these steps:

1. Evaluate the information for its usefulness.
2. Reduce the useful information through the use of suggestive notes, card systems, or learning.
3. Combine like information into understandable form through the use of tables, charts, graphs, and summaries. (See Chapter 16.)
4. Report in written form what remains. (See Chapters 17 and 18.)

Is reading 300 separate questionnaires easier than reading a few tables?

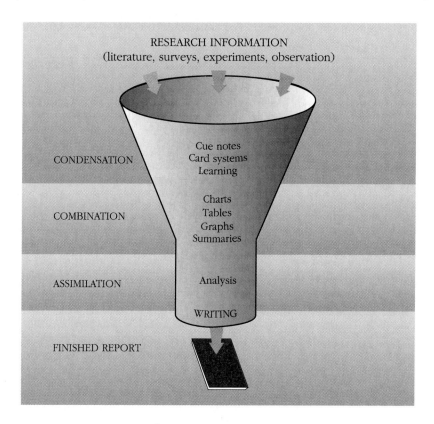

FIGURE 15-7
The report process.

Collecting the Appropriate Data

If acceptable data-gathering techniques have been used, data will measure what they are intended to measure (have validity) and will measure it accurately (have reliability). Some common errors at the data-gathering stage that seriously hamper later interpretation are

- Using samples that are too small.
- Using samples that are not representative.
- Using poorly constructed data-gathering instruments.
- Using information from biased sources.
- Failing to gather enough information to cover all important aspects of a problem.
- Gathering too much information and then attempting to use all of it even though some may be irrelevant.

> Poor sampling and ineffective design of the survey instrument are major data-collection problems.

Interpreting the Data

If you avoid data-collection errors, you are more likely to collect valid and reliable data and reach sound conclusions. However, if you interpret valid and reliable data incorrectly, your conclusions will *not* be sound.

Your ethical principles affect the validity of your interpretations. Through all steps in the research process, you must attempt to maintain the integrity of the research. Strive to remain objective, design and conduct an unbiased study, and

> **THINK IT OVER**
> In groups, discuss how your ethical principles can affect the validity of your interpretations of research data. Provide examples.

resist any pressure to slant research to support a particular viewpoint (e.g., ignoring, altering, or falsifying data).

Common errors that seriously handicap the interpretation of data include

1. *Trying, consciously or unconsciously, to make results conform to a prediction or desire.* Seeing predictions come true may be pleasing, but objectivity is much more important. Facts should determine conclusions.

2. *Hoping for spectacular results.* An attempt to astonish supervisors by preparing a report with revolutionary conclusions can only have a negative effect on accuracy.

3. *Attempting to compare when commonality is absent.* Concluding that a certain product would sell well in Canada because it sold well in the United States is risky. Disney executives presumed company policies successful in the U.S. would be equally as successful at their French theme park, EuroDisney. This *faulty logic* caused immediate problems. Employees resisted Disney's disregard for national customs—the unpopular dress code prohibiting facial hair and limiting make-up and jewelry and the no-alcohol-in-the-park policy (the French generally include wine with most meals) (Kets de Vries, 1994).

The women's basketball team has won every game since you began attending school. Is this record a coincidence or your influence?

4. *Assuming a cause-effect relationship when one does not exist.* A company president may have been in office one year, and sales may have doubled. However, sales might have doubled *in spite* of the president rather than *because* of the president.

5. *Failing to consider important factors.* Learning that McDonald's was considering closing its restaurants in Kassel, Germany, a manager of an industrial supply company recommended that the company reconsider its plans to expand its operation into Germany. The manager failed to recognize that the adverse impact of a new tax on disposable containers, not an unfavorable German economy or government, was the reason McDonald's was considering closing its restaurants (Kinzer, 1994).

6. *Basing a conclusion on lack of evidence.* "We have had no complaints about our present policy" does not mean that the policy is appropriate. Conversely, lack of evidence that a proposed project will succeed does not necessarily mean that it will fail.

THINK IT OVER
In small groups, brainstorm to identify a real-world example of at least one of the common errors in interpreting data. If necessary, use a computer database to locate these examples.

7. *Assuming constancy of human behavior.* A survey indicating 60 percent of the public favors one political party over the other in March does not mean the same will be true in November. Because some people paid their bills late last year does not mean a company should refuse to sell to them next year. The reasons for slow payment may have been removed.

Keep in mind the differences in meaning of some research terms as you analyze your material and attempt to seek meaning from it.

A **finding** from a research study is a specific, measurable fact:

Nearly 75 percent of the recruiters responding indicated they were more likely to hire a candidate who was involved in extracurricular activities.

Only 16 percent of the consumers interviewed knew that Hanson's Toy Company sells educational computer software.

A **conclusion** is derived from findings:

C O M M U N I C A T I O N   M E N T O R

No research is perfect! You can always find ways to challenge research if your objective is to discredit the study. You should also remember that the same is also true if it is *your* study that you are trying to use on your own behalf.

My experience has been that the most common errors include (1) using inadequate sample sizes, (2) asking biased questions, (3) surveying the wrong audience, and (4) drawing inappropriate conclusions.

David Martin, President
INTELECO

Active involvement in extracurricular activities is an important job-selection criterion.
Few consumers are knowledgeable of our line of educational software.

When you are evaluating viable alternatives, you may have findings about each related to cost, weight, manufacturer service after the sale, and any number of other criteria. Your conclusion from these findings may be "Item G meets my needs best."

A **recommendation** is a suggested action based on your research. Possible recommendations for the previous examples include

Students should be involved in several extracurricular activities prior to seeking a job.
An advertising campaign focusing on educational software should be launched.

Recommendations are not a part of every report and should be included only when requested or when they seem to be a natural outcome of the research. A finding is factual, a conclusion is drawn from findings, and a recommendation evolves from the conclusions and the nature of the problem.

SUMMARY

1 The basis of a report is a problem that must be solved through data collection and analysis. Reports are usually requested by a higher authority, are logically organized, highly objective, and prepared for a limited audience. Reports can be classified as formal/informal, short/long, informational/analytical, vertical/lateral, internal/external, or proposal.

2 The four steps in the problem-solving process that must be followed to arrive at a

sound conclusion follow: (1) Recognize and define the problem, (2) select an appropriate secondary and/or primary method for solving the problem, (3) collect and organize the data, and (4) interpret the data to arrive at an answer.

3 Locate information from secondary sources to identify any research that has already been completed on your topic and then collect primary data needed to solve the problem. Then, design effective instruments or experiments for obtaining primary data using one or more recognized research methods:

- **Normative surveys**—involves collecting standard information from a sample to determine the status of something at a specific time.
- **Observational research**—observing and analyzing certain phenomena to assist in establishing new principles.
- **Experimental**—involves identifying the differences between two samples observed when a different treatment is administered to each group.

4 **Selecting a sample that is representative of the entire population affects the validity and reliability of the data.** Valid data measure what they are supposed to measure; data are reliable when they give assurance that they measure accurately. *Random sampling* ensures that all individuals in a population have an equal and independent chance of being selected as a member of the sample. *Stratified random sampling* ensures that certain subgroups in the population will be represented in the sample in proportion to their numbers in the population.

5 **Developing an effective questionnaire is critical to obtaining valid and reliable data.** Effective questionnaires are clear, ask for information the respondent can recall and is willing to answer, and are easy to complete and to tabulate. A pilot test involving a small group of the population provides feedback for improving the survey instrument and redesigning the study.

6 **Valid and reliable data can be worthless if the researcher allows human errors to affect the collection and interpretation of the data.** Common errors in collecting errors include (a) using samples that are too small or not representative, (b) using ineffective survey instruments, (c) using data from biased sources, and (d) gathering too little or too much information. Common errors made in interpreting data include (a) trying to make results conform to a prediction or desire, (b) hoping for spectacular results, (c) attempting to compare when commonality is not present, (d) assuming a cause-effect relationship, (e) failing to consider important facts, (f) basing a conclusion on lack of evidence, and (g) assuming constancy of human behavior.

REFERENCES

Chandler, S. (1994, August 15). Sears' turnaround is for real. *Business Week*, p. 102.

Kets de Vries, M. F. R. (1994). Toppling the cultural tower of Babel. *Chief Executive, 94*, p. 68.

Kinzer, S. (1994, August 22). Germany upholds tax on fast-food restaurants. *The New York Times*, p. 2.

REVIEW QUESTIONS

1. How do informational and analytical reports differ?
2. Why do reports generally travel upward in an organization?
3. In a bank, the internal auditing division performs semiannual audits of each branch. Then the audit reports are sent to the bank's chief executive officer and chief financial officer and to the manager of the audited branch. The purpose of the audits is to determine whether policies and practices are properly followed. Into what report classifications might the audit report fall? Explain.
4. How do the four steps in problem solving apply when the driver of an automobile realizes a tire is going flat rapidly?
5. How might a null hypothesis be stated for a research study attempting to determine whether television or newspaper advertising has greater influence on cereal sales?
6. How does library research make a contribution to all studies?
7. Gathering so much information that the researcher is "snowed under" by the amount is often a barrier to good reporting. How might researchers protect themselves against this possibility?

8. Distinguish between reliability and validity.
9. What is meant by random sampling?
10. What type of research is characterized by efforts to measure the effect of a variable added to one of two samples?
11. What questions might you ask of someone who wants assistance in planning a questionnaire survey to determine automobile-owner satisfaction with certain after-the-sale services provided by dealers?
12. Why is an even number of rating scale responses supposedly better than an odd number?
13. Which data-collection errors are directly related to construction of data-gathering instruments?
14. How does the assumption that human beings behave in consistent ways over time present a danger in data interpretation?

EXERCISES

1. Complete each of the THINK IT OVER activities that your instructor assigns.
2. **Classifying Business Reports.** Classify each of the following reports in one or more of the ways described in this chapter:
   a. Your company's two-year study of traditional classroom training versus satellite classroom training is to be written for publication in an industrial training journal.
   b. You have surveyed company personnel on their perceptions of the need for a company cafeteria. You are preparing a report for the president that conveys the results.
   c. You have completed your department's weekly time sheets to send to payroll.
   d. As department head, you have sent a report to the vice president for finance requesting additional funding for an equipment acquisition.
   e. You have prepared an article on product updates for publication in your consumer newsletter that is mailed out free of charge to customers who request it.
   f. As director of end-user computing, you have prepared a report for circulation to all departments. The report summarizes hardware, software, and training offerings available through your department.
3. **Writing a Hypothesis.** Write a positive hypothesis and then restate it as a null hypothesis for each of the following research topics. Hypotheses for Topic a are given as an example.

   a. A study to determine functional business areas from which chief executive officers advanced in their organizations. Functional areas are legal, financial, accounting, marketing, production, and other.
   Positive Hypothesis: Chief executives advanced primarily through the legal area.
   Null Hypothesis: No relationship exists between chief executives' advancement and the functional field backgrounds.
   b. A study to determine whether a person's net worth at age 50 is directly related to education.
   c. A study to determine the relationship existing between the Fog Index readability rating of business textbooks and student interest in courses using the textbooks.
4. **Limiting the Scope of the Problem.** What factors might limit or influence your findings in any of the studies in Exercise 3? Could you apply the findings of Exercise 3 studies to a broader population than those included in the studies? Why or why not?
5. **Selecting a Research Method.** What research method would you use for each of the research problems identified in Exercise 3?
6. **Using Sampling Techniques.** If you were to conduct a survey of residents' attitudes toward recycling in a town of 35,000 people, describe how you might construct a sampling procedure to avoid having to survey the entire population.

E-MAIL APPLICATION

 This activity will allow you to perform an electronic search of a business research topic. It involves the use of the Veronica index that is accessed through a gopher server on the Internet. Veronica is an index and retrieval system that contains about 10 million items from approximately 5,500 gopher servers. Veronica finds resources by searching for words in titles; it does not do a full-text search of the contents.

1. Select a business topic for investigation; e.g., computer viruses.
2. Access the Internet on your university computer and enter the gopher server. Veronica is listed as a gopher option on most college and university computer systems.
3. Choose a Veronica server site from those listed on the screen. Ideally, it does not matter which server you use as all will give the same responses.

Some servers will return an answer faster than others, depending on load and network traffic. Some Veronica-access menus offer a simple entry rather than a list of servers. In this case, simply select the search type desired and submit your query in the dialog box.

4. Select to search keywords in titles. In the query box, key the word or phrase you wish to search; e.g., computer viruses. The search is *not* case sensitive. A multiple-word query does not require that the words be adjacent in the title nor do they appear in any particular order.
5. Instruct Veronica to search. By default, Veronica will deliver only the first 200 items that match your query unless you specify "-mX" in your query, with X being the number of items you wish. Specify 50 titles.
6. Print the list of 50 titles you located.

APPLICATIONS

1. **Designing a Research Study.** Prepare a one-page description of your plan to solve the problem for each of the following research studies. Use the following headings for the problem assigned: (1) Statement of the Problem, (2) Research Method and Sources of Information, (3) Nature of Data to Be Gathered and Analyzed, (4) Hypothesis or Hypotheses to Be Proved or Disproved (if feasible).

   a. Investigate a problem occurring on your campus (inadequate parking, long cafeteria lines, ineffective career services, limited number of internships and value-added experiences available) or in a job or student organization position you hold.

   b. Pacific Electronics initiated a bulletin board service via the Internet to provide answers to frequently asked questions and product update information. Customer response has been outstanding, freeing up the company's toll-free telephone lines for calls about more technical, nonrecurring problems, a primary goal of the service. As marketing manager, you are considering the possibility of allowing customers to order computer accessories and software packages via the Internet.

   c. Karen's Frozen Foods, Inc., is considering adding frozen breakfast pizza to its product line in an effort to overcome the flat profit line it has experienced for several years. The marketing staff intends to target the product to teenagers and working couples whose busy schedules require foods that can be heated quickly. Because all production facilities are currently operating at full capacity, introducing the frozen pizza will require adding production capacity.

   d. As research director of George-Parsons & Associates, a stock brokerage firm, you have mailed a highly professional newsletter containing tax-saving strategies to your investment clients. Although you know that these clients are in a financial position to take advantage of the strategies you are recommending, very few clients have scheduled appointments to seek additional information or to initiate these more aggressive investment plans.

   e. For the first time, Allied Pharmaceutical Company held a national conference for its entire sales force—three days filled with new product information, sales training, and numerous social activities. Eight months following the conference, sales have not increased significantly, and the time is near when you must decide whether to schedule this conference for the coming year.

2. **Developing a Survey Instrument.** Design a survey instrument for one of the research studies you analyzed in Application 1.

Effective research is vital if a business is to respond to the changing requirements of customers and other interest groups. Various methods exist for obtaining necessary information. Secondary research yields results of information that already exists; primary research reveals new information that cannot be obtained elsewhere. Primary research can be obtained in a variety of ways, each possessing advantages and limitations. Questionnaire design is critical to effective data collection. Random sampling assures that the results obtained are representative of the larger population.

The written report brings all the elements of effective research into a readable format. Careful attention to organization, conciseness, visual presentation, and objectivity is essential as the report is the basis on which the research will be judged. The report must respond to the readers' needs.

Discussion Questions

1. David Martin and Bruce Brown mention several primary research methodologies. List five and for each give a major consideration in choosing it for data collection.
2. How are the concepts of sampling and validity related?
3. What role do computers play in research report preparation?
4. List four characteristics of a well-designed questionnaire.
5. Explain the role of visual and written presentation in producing an effective research report.

Application

You are conducting marketing research on consumers of Jennas, an all-natural, low-fat yogurt. You are interested in the characteristics of typical purchasers and the reasons for their purchasing the product. Design a one-page questionnaire that might be used in a mall-intercept survey.

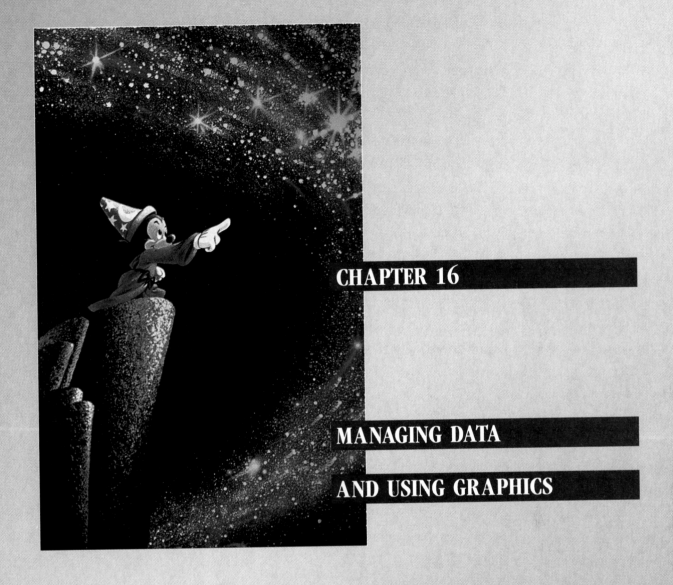

CHAPTER 16

MANAGING DATA

AND USING GRAPHICS

OBJECTIVES

When you have completed Chapter 16, you will be able to

1 Learn ways to manage quantities of data efficiently.

2 Analyze quantitative data using measures of central tendency.

3 Design and integrate graphics within reports.

For many people, classical music is an elevated art form, removed from the realm of public life. Some people feel it is outdated, with no relevance to life in the twentieth century. Still others are puzzled by its abstractions and complexities; they feel as if they just cannot "understand" it. Walt Disney fought ideas like this as he developed his film *Fantasia*. Perhaps he realized that many people, especially children, were missing out on classical music. After all, classical music has had a reputation for being boring. In *Fantasia*, however, Disney showed how fascinating this music could be by setting it to clever animation. This film interpreted the music through animated graphics, thus bringing concrete images to abstract musical themes. In much the same way, you can use creative organization and clever graphics to interpret complex numerical data or highlight important ideas in your business reports and presentations.

If you plan to be involved in virtually any business, you will be writing reports and presentations. A report's success depends largely on how well you have accessed information through research, processed the information through careful study of the data, and organized that information into a comprehensible format. What techniques can keep you from being overwhelmed by your data? How can you make important points stand out and complex data easy to understand?

MANAGING QUANTITATIVE DATA

LEARNING OBJECTIVE 1

Before you can interpret the data, you must classify, summarize, and condense it into a manageable size. This condensed information is meaningful and can be used to answer your research questions. For example, assume that you have been given a large stack of completed questionnaires. This large accumulation of data is overwhelming until you tabulate the responses for each questionnaire item by manually inputting or optically scanning the responses into a computer. Then, you can apply appropriate statistical analysis techniques to the tabulated data.

The computer generates a report of the total responses for each possible response to each item. For example, the tabulation of responses for employee training needs from 300 questionnaires might appear like this table:

Activity-based costing	15
Written communication	54
Computer technology	102
Just-in-time inventory	51
Human behavior	24
Legal environment	24
Workplace diversity	30
	300

You must condense large amounts of data into meaningful information that can be analyzed and interpreted.

The breakdown reduces 300 responses to a manageable size. The tabulation shows only seven items, each with a specific number of responses from the total of 300 questionnaires. Because people tend to make comparisons during analysis, the totals are helpful. People generally want to know proportions or ratios, and these are best presented as percentage parts of the total. Thus, the numbers converted to percentages are

COMMUNICATION MENTOR

If you want your report to be read, then make it readable. Research reports should be as inviting and easy to read as *USA Today*. To accomplish this goal, use ample visuals (charts, graphs, illustrations, and photographs) and train yourself to write for the reader.

David Martin, President
INTELECO

Training Need	Number	Percentage
Activity-based costing	15	5
Written communication	54	18
Computer technology	102	34
Just-in-time inventory	51	17
Human behavior	24	8
Legal environment	24	8
Workplace diversity	30	10
	300	100

Now analyzing the data becomes relatively easy. Eighteen percent of the employees selected written communication, and ten percent selected workplace diversity. Another observation, depending on how exactly you intend to interpret percentages, could be that just over one-third of the employees selected computer technology and approximately a quarter of the employees desire inventory-related training (activity-based costing and just-in-time inventory).

When research results of people's opinions, likes, preferences, and other subjective items are tabulated, rounding off statistics to fractions helps paint a clear picture for readers. In actuality, if the same people were asked this question again a day or two later, a few probably would have changed their minds. For example, an employee who had not indicated a desire for communication training may have received a negative rating on written communication skills during an annual performance appraisal; the next day, the employee might indicate a desire for training in written communication.

THINK IT OVER
How does the description "snapshot view" apply to survey data?

Common Language

Fractions, ratios, and percentages are often examples of **common language**. In effect, common language reduces difficult figures to the "common denominators" of language and ideas. Although "102 of 300 prefer computer technology training" is somewhat easy to understand, "34 percent prefer computer technology training" is even easier, and "approximately one out of three prefers computer technology training" is even more understandable.

Use "common language," such as fractions, percentages, broad terms, or word pictures to help the reader visualize difficult figures or ideas.

THINK IT OVER

Assume that you earned 84 points out of a possible 150 on an exam. Present these data using the most understandable terms. How could you describe the storage capacity of a hard drive or a CD-ROM so that a computer novice could understand? In groups, generate other examples of using common language.

Common language also involves the use of indicators other than actual count or quantity. The Dow Jones Industrial Averages provide a measure of stock market performance and are certainly easier to understand than the complete New York Stock Exchange figures for 2,000 stocks. "Freight car loadings" are weight measurements used in railroad terminology rather than "pounds carried," and oil is counted in barrels rather than in the quart or gallon sizes purchased by consumers. Because of inflation, dollars are not very accurate items to use as comparisons from one year to another in certain areas; for example, automobile manufacturers use "automobile units" to represent production changes in the industry. The important thing for the report writer to remember is that reports are communication media, and everything possible should be done to make sure communication occurs.

Measures of Central Tendency

LEARNING OBJECTIVE 2

The mean, median, mode, and range are measures of central tendency.

The mean is the arithmetic average and the most stable measure of central tendency.

Measures of central tendency are simple statistical treatments of distributions of quantitative data that attempt to find a single figure to describe the entire distribution. The four most commonly used measures are the mean, the median, the mode, and the range.

THE MEAN

The **mean** is the figure obtained when all the values in a distribution (table of values) are totaled and divided by the number of values. If, for example, eight people score values of 60, 65, 70, 75, 80, 85, 90, and 95 on a test, the total of these values is 620. Dividing 620 by 8 gives a mean of 77.5. Most people would call 77.5 the "average" score, but *mean* is a more accurate term.

When material is tabulated by classes, such as "10 people scored between 80 and 89," statisticians would take the midpoint—84.5—and multiply it by 10 to get a total score for that class. Doing the same for other classes would provide a total for all scores in the tabulation. Dividing the total scores of all classes by the number of scores would provide a group mean. Grouping scores (placing them in classes) is not much different from totaling them separately. Determining the mean is simply the process of totaling all values and dividing by the number whether totaled by classes or by individual scores.

THE MEDIAN

The median is the midpoint in a group of figures.

The **median** is the middle value in a distribution. For example, the median for the values 20, 65, 70, 75, 80, 85, and 100 in a distribution would be 75. Half the values are above 75 and half are below 75. In this case, the median is more descriptive than the mean because the very low score of 20 does not skew the measure of central tendency.

When values are counted in classes, find the middle value by counting from the top down or from the bottom up to the class containing the middle value. The class is described as the *median class*.

THE MODE

The mode is the value that occurs most frequently.

The **mode** is the value found most frequently in a distribution. For example, ten test scores of 65, 70, 75, 75, 75, 80, 85, 90, 90, and 100 would have a mode of 75—the most frequent score. The mean would be the total, 805, divided by 10, or 80.5. The median would be halfway between 75 and 80—the fifth and sixth scores of the ten—or 77.5. In this case, either the mean or the median would be an acceptable and more desirable measure than the mode.

In general, the mean is more stable than the median or the mode and usually fluctuates less than the other two measures. The mean is extremely reliable when distributions are large. In small distributions, the median is often a good indicator, especially when some very high or very low extreme values would influence the mean.

THINK IT OVER
Which measure of central tendency would you recommend for a small distribution with several extreme sources? Provide an example.

The mean, median, and mode are statistical measures that help report writers describe the content and meaning of tables and graphs. These measures are part of the common language of statistics and are especially efficient and effective in reporting to people who understand their meanings. Good judgment on the part of the report writer should determine which measure to use or whether to use one at all.

THE RANGE

When researchers first glance at a distribution, they probably look for the **range**— the difference between the lowest and highest values. For example, test scores of 20, 30, 75, 75, 75, 80, 85, 90, and 95 would have a range of 20 to 95, or 76 points (95 – 20 + 1, to count both the 20 and the 95).

Range = High – low + one

The range helps a researcher determine how many classes should be used in tabulating large numbers of values. In general, a first glance at the range reveals the extremes of values and assists in data analysis.

Some researchers use the **interquartile range**—the spread of the middle 50 percent of the values—as a form of central tendency measurement. For example, in a distribution such as 7, 19, 21, 23, 24, 25, 29, and 41, the interquartile range is 21 to 25. Because eight items are included, two are in each quarter of the distribution. The two middle quartiles, the middle half, have the figures 21, 23, 24, and 25. Even though the total range is 7 to 41, the interquartile range shows that most figures are grouped tightly. Thus, the extreme values of 7 (the low) and 41 (the high) become less important.

USING GRAPHICS

Managing data effectively protects a report writer from being overwhelmed by the data. To protect readers from being overwhelmed, report writers must select appropriate means of presenting the data. Data reported in a table, picture, graph, or chart will make your written analysis clearer to the reader.

LEARNING OBJECTIVE 3

Effective graphics (1) clarify complicated statistics and ideas, (2) offer welcome breaks in long sections of text, and (3) increase the overall appeal of the page.

Imagine trying to put in composition style all the information available in a financial statement. Several hundred pages might be necessary to explain all material that could otherwise be contained in three or four pages of balance sheets and profit and loss statements. Even then, the reader would no doubt be thoroughly confused! Graphics go hand in hand with the written discussion to achieve clarity. As you proceed through the remainder of this chapter, ask yourself if the discussion would be effective if the accompanying graphic figures were not included.

Throughout this chapter, the term *graphics* will be used to refer to all types of illustrations. In reports, the most commonly used graphics are tables, bar charts, line charts, pie charts, pictograms, maps, flowcharts, diagrams, and photographs. These graphic presentations are often used as aids during oral reports

You can convert a graphic created using computer software to an overhead transparency or slide to support an oral report.

C O M M U N I C A T I O N   M E N T O R

As accountants, we are obligated to communicate clearly, not only with words, but with numbers. The numbers must be organized to present as clear a picture as possible of the economic activities they describe. This clarity benefits those who use the information, whether they are internal managers or external investors or creditors. In the same way that a "picture is worth a thousand words," well-organized financial reports can significantly enhance a narrative communication.

Dennis R. Beresford, Chairman
Financial Accounting Standards Board

THINK IT OVER
Review the "Using Visual Aids" section of Chapter 3 if your instructor requires you to prepare visuals for an oral report.

What questions will help you determine if a graphic is appropriate for presenting specific information?

as well. In both written and oral reports, several questions can help you determine whether using a graphic presentation is appropriate and effective:

1. Does the graphic presentation contribute to the overall understanding of the subject? Would a graphic assist the reader?
2. Can the material be covered adequately in words rather than in visual ways? Graphics, both in written and oral reports, should be saved for data that are difficult to communicate in words alone.
3. Will the written or spoken text add meaning to the graphic display?
4. Is the graphic easily understood? Extreme use of color, complicated symbols, confusing art techniques, and unusual combinations of typefaces detract from the impact of the material presented.
5. Is the graphic honest? As you studied in Chapter 6 and will discover later in this chapter, data can be distorted easily.
6. If the visual presentation is part of an oral report, can it be seen by the entire audience? Handouts, flip charts, overhead projector transparencies, and

Just as Music Television, or MTV, uses video to illustrate music, rides such as this one at Six Flags use sound, vibration, movement, and video to make the "experience" of being in space come alive for the viewer. Likewise, in your reports, use graphics to illustrate points that are important or difficult to explain with numbers or words alone.

on-screen computer presentations are the visual means most often used to accompany oral reports.

The greatest advantage of computer graphics is their value to the individual decision maker who formerly had to battle through a maze of computer-printed output. With the proper software programs, managers can now use computer software to perform the data-management functions discussed in this chapter and to produce highly professional graphics. The information can be reproduced in a variety of ways for inclusion in reports. A variety of graphics commonly used in reports is illustrated in Figures 16-1 through 16-12.

These figures illustrate acceptable variations in graphic design: placement of the caption (figure number and title), with and without grid lines, the Y-axis labeled at the top of the axis or turned sideways, and others. When designing graphics, adhere to the requirements in your company policy manual or the style manual you are instructed to follow. Then be certain that you design all graphics consistently throughout a report. When preparing a graphic for use as a visual aid (transparency or on-screen display) in an oral presentation, you may wish to remove the figure number and include the title only.

Tables

A **table** presents data in columns and rows, which aids in clarifying large quantities of data in a small space. Clear labeling techniques make the content clear. Some helpful practices in preparing an effective table follow:

1. Number tables and all other graphics consecutively throughout the report. This practice enables you to refer to *"Figure 1"* rather than to "the following table" or "the figure on the following page." Incidentally, the term *figure* should be used to identify all tables, graphs, pictures, and charts. Note that all illustrations in this chapter are identified as figures.
2. Give each table a title that is complete enough to clarify what is included without forcing the reader to review the table. Table titles may be quite long and even extend beyond one line. A two-line title should be arranged on the page so that neither line extends into the margins. The second line should be shorter than the first and centered under it. Titles may contain sources of data, numbers included in the table, and the subject; for example, "Base

THINK IT OVER
If you have not yet learned to operate a computer graphics program or create graphics with spreadsheet software, set a goal to gain that important skill before the end of the semester.

THINK IT OVER
Skim the 12 graphics to identify these variations in style. How do you determine which style to use in a report assigned by your supervisor?

What value does a table add to a report?

Detailed titles help the reader understand the exact data being presented.

A multiple-line title should resemble an inverted pyramid—begin with the longest line and continue with each line shorter than the preceding line.

Salaries of Chief Executives of the 200 Largest Financial Institutions in the United States." Titles may be written in either uppercase or upper-and-lower-case letters.

3. Label columns of data clearly enough to identify the items. Usually, column headings are short and easily arranged. If, however, they happen to be lengthy, use some ingenuity in planning the arrangement.

4. Indent the second line of a label for the rows (horizontal items) requiring more than one line two or three spaces. Labels that are subdivisions of more comprehensive labels should be indented, and summary labels such as *total* should also be indented. The sample table shown in Figure 16-1 illustrates effective layout.

FIGURE 16-1
Effective table layout identifying captions, labels, footnote, and source.

Figure 1

WAL-MART STORES, INC.
Market Price of Common Stock

Fiscal Years Ended January 31

Quarter	1994		1993*	
	High	Low	High	Low
April 30	$34.00	$26.38	$27.75	$25.69
July 31	28.50	24.88	27.94	25.75
October 31	27.25	23.50	31.00	27.94
January 31	29.88	24.38	32.88	29.50

* Reflects the two-for-one stock split distributed on February 25, 1993.

Source: Wal-Mart Stores, Inc., *Annual Report*, 1994.

Bar Charts

Use a bar chart to compare quantities.

A **simple bar chart** (also called a *single-range bar chart*) is an effective graphic for comparing quantities. The length of the bars, horizontal or vertical, indicates quantity, as shown in Figures 16-2 and 16-3. The quantitative axis should always begin at zero and be divided into equal increments. The width of the bars should be equal, or the wider bar will imply that it represents a larger number than the narrower bar. Further suggestions include

1. Shadings (or cross-hatchings) or variations in color can be used to distinguish among the bars.
2. Printing the specific dollar or quantity amount at the top of each bar assists in understanding the graph. Readers tend to skim the text and rely on the graphics for details. Omit actual amounts if a visual estimate is adequate for understanding the relationships presented in the chart. Excluding nonessential information such as specific amounts, grids, and explanatory notes

THINK IT OVER
Should specific quantities and grids be included in graphics? Provide an example to justify your answer.

actually increases the readability of the chart by reducing the clutter. Use your judgment in listing specifics in graphics.

3. Include enough information in the scale labels and bar labels to be understandable but not so complicated that readers will skip over the graph. The horizontal bar chart in Figure 16-2 shows unit sales for five departments in a retail store. Amounts appear in the horizontal scale labels; departments, in the bar labels.

4. If some quantities are so large that the chart would become unwieldy, the bars may be broken to indicate omission of part of each bar, as shown in Figure 16-3.

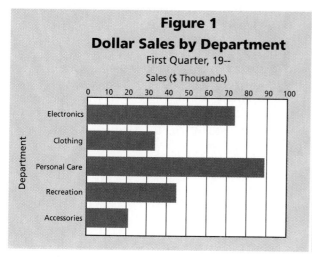

FIGURE 16-2
Horizontal bar chart.

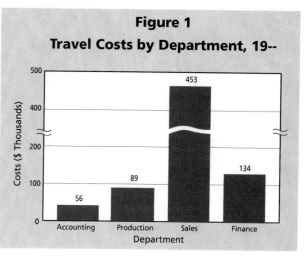

FIGURE 16-3
Vertical bar chart with broken-bar indicating omission of part of the bar.

MULTIPLE-RANGE BAR CHART

A **multiple-range bar chart**, also called a *comparative* or *cluster bar chart*, is useful for comparing more than one quantity (set of data) at each point along the x-axis. The frequency of defects in three product lines over the four quarters of a fiscal year are compared in Figure 16-4. Because the chart was printed using a color printer, each quantity appears in a specific color to facilitate comparison. Cross-hatchings differentiate the quantities if a color printer is not available.

STACKED-BAR CHART

The **stacked-bar chart**, also called a *component, 100 percent,* or *segmented bar chart,* is shown in Figure 16-5. When you want to show how different facts (components) contribute to a total figure, the stacked-bar chart is desirable. This graphic is particularly useful when components for more than one time period are being compared. Figure 16-5 shows the relative amount of sales earned from products in the various stages in the product life cycle. The actual percentage of each component is displayed in this example; however, these numbers can be omitted to reduce excessive clutter if you believe the reader's visual assessment of the proportions is adequate. Because this graph was printed using a color printer, colors distinguish the components, with a key included at the bottom of the chart.

How does a multiple-range bar chart differ from a simple bar chart?

THINK IT OVER
Based on the data in Figure 16-4, in which of the three product lines should the Quality Control Department concentrate its efforts to reduce defects?

THINK IT OVER
Suppose management is considering allocating fewer dollars to product research and development. Use the data in Figure 16-5 to justify your decision to support or reject this decision. Write a brief statement.

FIGURE 16-4
A multiple-range bar chart is
useful for comparing more than
one quantity over time.

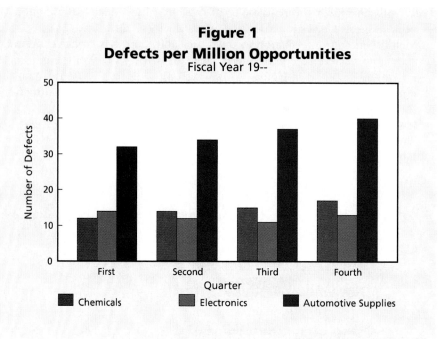

FIGURE 16-5
A stacked-bar chart shows how
proportional relationships change
over time.

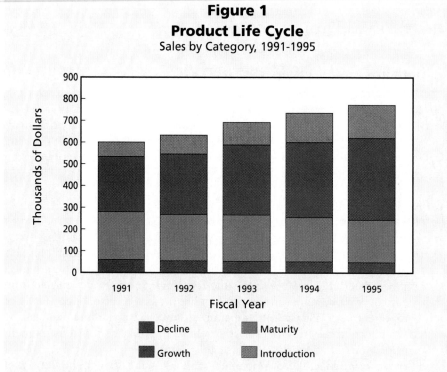

Line Charts

A **line chart**, such as the one shown in Figure 16-6, depicts changes in quantitative data over time and illustrates trends. When constructing line charts, keep these general guidelines in mind:

1. Use the vertical axis for amount and the horizontal axis for time.
2. Begin the vertical axis at zero. If the height of the chart becomes unwieldy, break it the same way the vertical scale was broken in Figure 16-3.
3. Divide the vertical and horizontal scales into equal increments. The vertical or amount increments, however, need not be the same as the horizontal or time increments so the line or lines drawn will have reasonable slopes. (Unrealistic scales might produce startling slopes that could mislead readers.)

Use a line chart to emphasize changes in quantities over time.

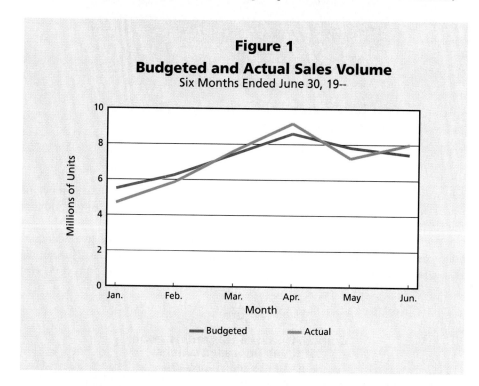

Figure 1
Budgeted and Actual Sales Volume
Six Months Ended June 30, 19--

FIGURE 16-6
A line chart expresses changes over time.

An **area chart**, also called a *cumulative line chart* or a *surface chart*, is similar to a component bar chart because it shows how different factors contribute to a total. An area chart is especially useful when you want to illustrate changes in components over time. For example, the area chart in Figure 16-7 illustrates the changes in the components of a company's retail sales over a fiscal year. The cumulative total of the five departments is illustrated by the top line on the chart. The amount of each component can be estimated by visual assessment. Colors add visual appeal and aid the reader in distinguishing the components.

Unlike bar charts, which show only the total amount for a time period, line charts show variations within each time period. In oral presentations, an area chart can be made more effective by having a separate transparency or graphic screen made for each component. During the presentation, each transparency could be laid over the previous one or each screen displayed in progression for a cumulative

Use an area chart to illustrate changes in components over time.

THINK IT OVER
Compare and contrast an area chart with a stacked-bar chart.

Show each component separately to build impact when the entire area chart is displayed.

FIGURE 16-7
*An area chart shows how
proportional relationships change
over time.*

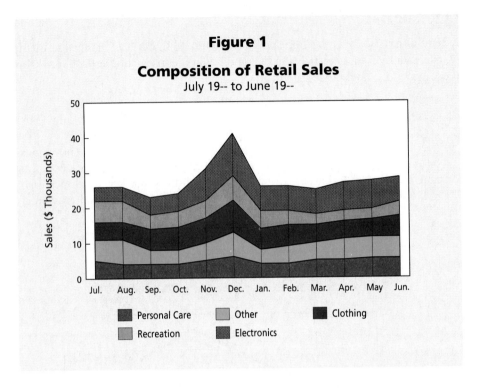

Figure 1

Composition of Retail Sales
July 19-- to June 19--

effect. In the example shown in Figure 16-7, for instance, the first transparency or screen may show only the personal care; the second, recreation; the third, clothing; the fourth, electronics; and accessories, the completed chart.

The chart in Figure 16-8 poses a particular challenge because the two quantities (sales and number of representatives) require scales of different intervals. The graphic is designed so that the reader can interpret the data easily, using the correct interval

A combination bar and
line chart is useful when
scales of different intervals are needed to plot
more than one quantity.

FIGURE 16-8
*A combination bar and line chart
facilitates interpretation of two
quantities requiring different
intervals.*

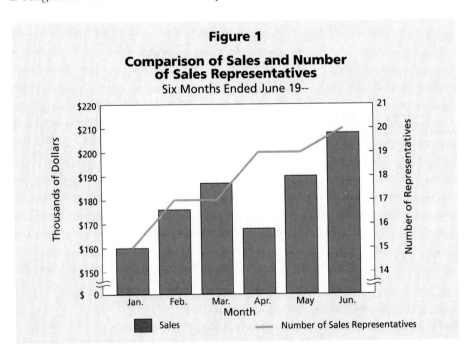

Figure 1

**Comparison of Sales and Number
of Sales Representatives**
Six Months Ended June 19--

for each quantity. The bars use the left vertical axis to depict sales, and the line uses the right vertical axis to show the number of sales representatives. A line graph or a multiple-range bar chart could be used; however, this combination line and bar chart provides the contrast needed to interpret the relationship between sales and the number of sales representatives clearly.

Pie Charts

A **pie chart**, like stacked-bar charts and area charts, shows how the parts of a whole are distributed. As the name indicates, the whole is represented as a pie, with the parts becoming slices of the pie. Pie charts are effective for showing percentages (parts of a whole), but they are ineffective in showing quantitative totals or comparisons. Bars are used for those purposes.

Some generally used guidelines for constructing pie charts follow:

1. Position the largest slice or the slice to be emphasized at the twelve o'clock position. Working clockwise, place the other slices in descending order of size or some other logical order of presentation. Typically, software programs automatically arrange the slices following their own guidelines. For example, if the pie contains many small slices, the program may intersperse the small slices with the larger slices to increase readability and enhance appearance. Some software programs allow you to organize the slices following your guidelines.
2. Label each slice and include information about the quantitative size (percentage, dollars, acres, square feet, etc.) of each slice. Note the labeling in Figure 16-9.
3. Draw attention to one or more slices if you wish by (a) exploding the slice(s) to be emphasized, (that is, removing it from immediate contact with the pie) or (b) displaying or printing only the slice(s) to be emphasized.

Use a pie chart to show the proportions of parts of a whole.

What other graphics show how the parts of a whole are distributed?

THINK IT OVER
Given the fact that 25 percent of the company's total sales is database software, what conclusions might a user documentation manager draw from the pie chart in Figure 16-9?

FIGURE 16-9
A pie chart with exploded section and three-dimensional effect shows percentages of a whole.

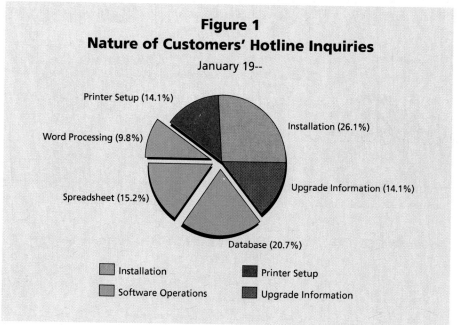

Figure 1
Nature of Customers' Hotline Inquiries
January 19--

Printer Setup (14.1%)
Installation (26.1%)
Word Processing (9.8%)
Spreadsheet (15.2%)
Upgrade Information (14.1%)
Database (20.7%)

Installation   Printer Setup
Software Operations   Upgrade Information

4. Use color or patterns (cross-hatchings) to aid the reader in differentiating among the slices and to add appeal.

THINK IT OVER
Can you think of other situations that might warrant slight deviations from the rules presented in this chapter?

Use your own judgment in constructing a pie chart. Your software may limit your ability to follow rules explicitly. Likewise, the nature of the data or the presentation selected may require slight deviations to increase the clarity of the graphic. For example, if you intend to explode the largest slice, placing it in the twelve o'clock position may not be desirable because the slice is likely to intrude into the space occupied by a title positioned at the top of the page. If your style manual or company policy requires that titles be positioned above the graphic, starting with a slice other than the largest is acceptable. For dramatic effect, many periodicals and reports vary from these general rules.

Pictograms

THINK IT OVER
Clip a pictogram from *USA Today* and share with groups in class. Discuss the effectiveness of the symbols used and the ethical presentation of the data.

A **pictogram** uses pictures to illustrate numerical relationships. For example, the pictograms in Figure 16-10 use coins instead of bars to depict additions to personal savings. However, pictograms can be more dramatic than meaningful if they are not planned properly. For example, doubling the height and width of a picture increases the total area four times. Therefore, all symbols must be the same size so that true relationships are not distorted. Note that the relative sizes of the coins in the pictogram on the left in Figure 16-10 are misleading and make the actual amounts and relationships hard to understand. In the pictogram on the right, using the same size coins makes both amounts and relationships instantly clear. Refer to Chapter 6 ("Communicating Decisions Ethically and Responsibly") for additional discussion of the ethical implications of graphical presentation.

Using inappropriate scales or designing confusing graphics that hide significant information are unethical communication practices.

Maps

Maps allow readers to obtain specific information quickly.

A **map** shows geographic relationships. A map is especially useful when a reader may not be familiar with the geography discussed in a report. The map shown in Figure 16-11 is taken from an annual report. It effectively presents sales growth by state and shows the locations of the home office, distribution centers, and

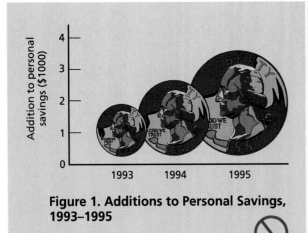

Figure 1. Additions to Personal Savings, 1993–1995

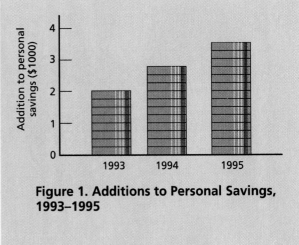

Figure 1. Additions to Personal Savings, 1993–1995

FIGURE 16-10   Relative-size symbols (left) distort data; same-size symbols (right) depict relationships accurately.

COMMUNICATION MENTOR

Absorption and retention of information are unquestionably enhanced by the use of graphics, whether you have time and budget to produce video or computer-generated 35mm slides, elect to hand-draw graphics on a flip chart, or use an overhead projector. (Perhaps you are considering graphics right now to support a term paper or research project.)

Don't be afraid to use graphics to present simple information. On the contrary, be afraid *not* to use them when you are tackling a complex subject. Readers and audiences expect them and will consistently reward you for your extra work.

James F. Hurley
Executive Vice President
California Federal Bank

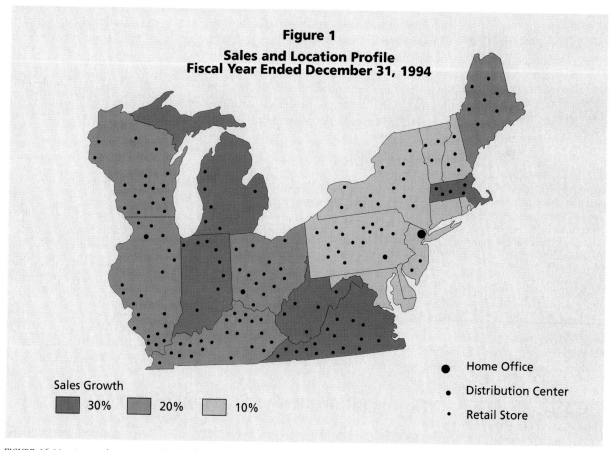

FIGURE 16-11   *A map depicts geographical relationships.*

retail stores within the geographic region. The map gives the information visually and thus eliminates the difficulty of explaining the information in words. In addition to being less confusing, a map is more concise and interesting than a written message would be.

Flowcharts

Supplementing written
instructions with a flow-
chart minimizes the
chance of errors.

A **flowchart** is a step-by-step diagram of a procedure or a graphic depiction of a system or organization. A variety of problems can be resolved by using flowcharts to support written analysis. For example, most companies have procedures manuals to instruct employees in certain work tasks. Including a flowchart with the written instructions minimizes the chance of errors.

THINK IT OVER
Draw a flowchart outlining the
procedure shipping dock employees should follow when shipping
packages. Decisions may include
priority of package, destination
(in-state or out-of-state), and
weight of package.

A flowchart traces a unit of work as it flows from beginning to completion. Symbols with connecting lines are used to trace a step-by-step sequence of the work. A key to a flowchart's symbols may be included if the reader may not readily understand standard symbols. For example, the flowchart in Figure 16-12 illustrates the procedures for processing a telephone order. If this information had been presented only in a series of written steps, the customer service manager would have to rely not only on the input operator's reading ability but also on his or her willingness to read and study the written procedures.

THINK IT OVER
Locate an organizational chart
of a company with a flat
organizational structure.
Compare it with the tall structure shown in Figure 2-1.

Organizational charts, discussed in Chapter 2, are widely used to provide a picture of the authority structure and relationships within an organization. They provide employees with an idea of what their organization looks like in terms of the flow of authority and responsibility. Recall the organizational chart of The Citizens' Bank presented in Figure 2-1 (Chapter 2) as part of the discussion of the interdependence of individuals and units within an organization. When businesses change (because of new employees or reorganization of units and responsibilities), organizational charts must be revised. Revisions are simple if the organizational chart is prepared using graphics software and stored to be retrieved when changes must be made.

Other Graphics

Advances in technology
allow writers to prepare
sophisticated graphics that
give readers a concrete
image of the concept being
discussed.

Other graphics such as floor plans, photographs, cartoons, blueprints, and lists of various kinds may be included in reports. The increased availability of graphics and sophisticated drawing software is leading to the increased inclusion of these more complex visuals in reports and oral presentations. Because managers can prepare these visuals themselves less expensively and more quickly than having them prepared by professional designers, these sophisticated graphics are being used increasingly for internal reports. Photographs are used frequently in annual reports to help the general audience understand a complex concept and to make the document more appealing to read.

Frequently, you must include some material in a report that would make the narrative discussion unwieldy. In this case, the material might be placed in an appendix and only referred to in the report, as explained in Chapters 17 and 18.

Why must graphics be
introduced before they are
included in a report?

INTRODUCING TABLES AND GRAPHS IN THE TEXT

Always introduce and interpret a graphic in the textual material immediately preceding the graphic. Text and graphics are partners in the communication

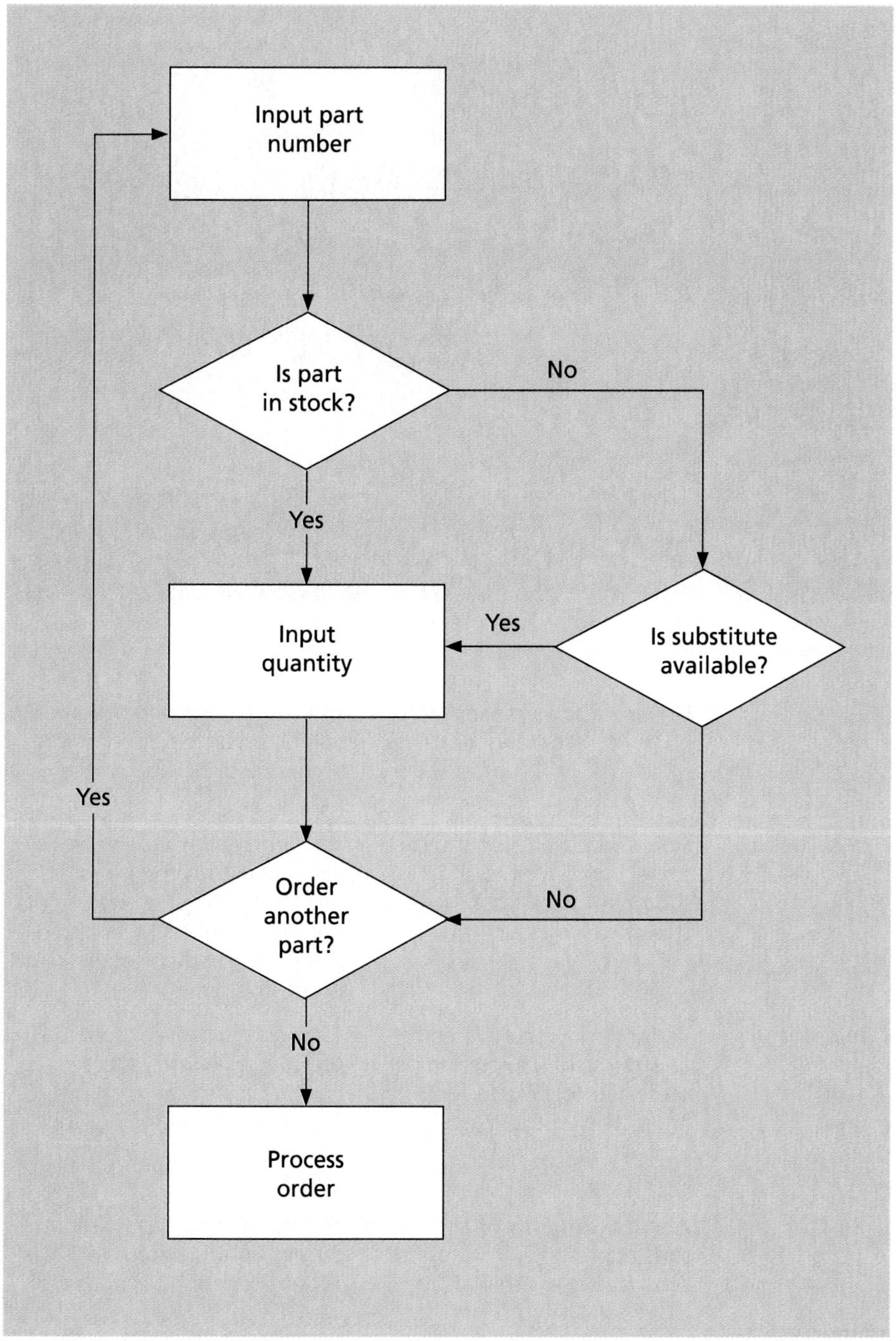

FIGURE 16-12
A flowchart simplifies understanding of work tasks.

process. If graphics appear in the text before readers have been informed, they will begin to study the graphics and draw their own inferences and conclusions. A graphic that follows an introduction and brief interpretation will supplement what has been said in the report.

Note how the language in the following sentences introduces graphic or tabular material:

Does the reader get the point before turning to the graphic?

Stockholders reading Wal-Mart's annual report can easily visualize the company's international expansion as they look at this photograph of company executives and associates interacting in Wal-Mart's new Supercenter in Monterey, Mexico.

Poor:	Figure 1 shows reader preferences for shopping locations.	This sentence is poor because it tells the reader nothing more than would the title of the figure.
Acceptable:	About two-thirds of the consumers preferred to shop in suburban areas rather than in the city. (See Figure 1.)	This sentence is acceptable because it does the job of interpreting the data, but it puts the figure reference in parentheses rather than integrating it into the sentence.
Improved:	As shown in Figure 1, about two-thirds of the consumers preferred to shop in suburban areas than in the city.	Although improved over the previous examples, this sentence puts reference to the figure at the beginning, thus detracting from the interpretation of the data.
Best:	About two-thirds of the consumers preferred to shop in suburban areas than in the city, as shown in Figure 1.	This sentence is best for introducing figures because it talks about the graphic and also includes introductory phrasing, but only after stressing the main point.

THINK IT OVER

Assume that a graphic has been introduced on p. 8 of a report, but the graphic will not fit on the page. Where should you place the graphic? What should you do with any blank space on p. 8?

Ideally, a graphic should be integrated within the text material immediately after its introduction. A graphic that will not fit on the page where it is introduced should appear at the top of the following page. The previous page is filled with text that would have ideally followed the graphic. In this chapter, figures are placed as closely as possible to their introductions in accordance

COMMUNICATION IN ACTION

Paul Lehman, Macom Corporation

When he earned his general engineering degree from the University of Illinois, Paul Lehman had learned how to work with technical concepts and jargon. Communicating these complex concepts so that nonengineers could understand, however, presented another challenge. Thus, he later earned an MBA degree. As president of Macom Corporation, he capitalizes on his technical expertise and business knowledge to develop land and to market property in the Chicago area. Lehman's company spearheaded the development of a large residential community around an Arnold Palmer Signature Golf Course near Chicago.

"Presenting data in graphic form is the key to communicating the technical information required in my business," says Lehman. "For example, putting statistical information about property values in clear, honest graphics enables prospective buyers to see and understand the perceived value of the land they wish to purchase."

"Developers market perceived value—not technical or absolute value. Using visuals to communicate perceived value has worked successfully for Macom Corporation," asserts Lehman. For example, some people desire the majestic view of living on a golf course and the exclusive privilege of observing golfers making shots, golf carts passing by, and even golf balls landing on their lawn. Other people like to be a part of a golf course community but do not want to be a member of the golf club or to own a lot adjacent to the course. A comparable lot in another residential community will sell for less. Because the perceived value of a lot adjacent to an Arnold Palmer golf course is higher, buyers are willing to pay a premium price.

The following stacked-bar (segmented bar) chart compares the cost of three lots: Lot A is located in another Macom development without a golf course; Lot B, in a golf course development but not on the course; and Lot C, adjacent to the golf course with a view of a green. The buyer can visualize the relative price difference of the three lots and, therefore, the value attached to the attributes of each lot. Thus, Macom will sell a lot on the golf course when the buyer perceives that the benefits of living on the course are worth at least $30,000.

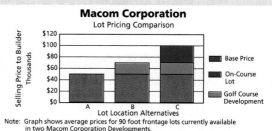

Note: Graph shows average prices for 90 foot frontage lots currently available in two Macom Corporation Developments.

Lehman also uses a stacked-bar chart to assess the progress of each builder. The chart contains crucial information such as the number of homes constructed, the number of homes under construction, and the number of vacant lots. By keeping abreast of his builders' progress, Lehman stays competitive. "A stacked-bar chart gives me the comparisons I need to make competitive decisions. Pie charts, tables of percentages, or absolute numbers will not accurately describe these comparisons."

Applying What You Have Learned

1. Prepare a stacked-bar chart Lehman could use to explain price variations for lots along the golf course. Factors such as proximity to lakes, a green, a tee, the clubhouse, and a fairway affect the perceived value of a lot. Assume that lot prices range from $100,000 to $150,000.
2. Why is a stacked-bar chart appropriate for assessing the progress of Lehman's builders?
3. Prepare a stacked-bar chart using first-quarter data. In January, Lehman's top builder (provide name) had 80 completed homes, 20 homes under construction, and 50 vacant lots. In February, the builder had 95 completed homes, 15 under construction, and 40 vacant lots. In March, the builder had 105 completed homes, 20 under construction, and 25 vacant lots. Provide a descriptive title. What topics does the graph suggest Lehman should discuss with the builder at tomorrow's meeting?

with these suggestions. However, in some cases, several figures may be introduced on one page, making perfect placement difficult and sometimes impossible.

THINK IT OVER
Discuss the two numbering systems for report graphics. Which system would you use if you were writing a report for your supervisor?

Throughout the discussion of tables and graphics, the term *graphics* has been used to include all illustrations. Although your report may include tables, graphs, maps, and even photographs, you will find organizing easier and writing about the illustrations more effective if you label all items as "Figure" followed by a number and number them consecutively. Some report writers like to label tables consecutively as "Table 1," etc., and graphs and charts consecutively in another sequence as "Graph 1," etc. When this dual numbering system is used, readers of the report may become confused if they come upon a sentence saying, "Evidence presented in Tables 3 and 4 and Graph 2 supports. . . ." Both writers and readers appreciate the single numbering system, which makes the sentence read, "Evidence presented in Figures 3, 4, and 5 supports. . . ."

SUMMARY

1 **Graphics complement written text by clarifying complex figures and helping readers visualize major points.** An important aspect of writing effective reports is protecting yourself against a deluge of data. Tabulating data, analyzing data using measures of central tendency, aid in summarizing or classifying large volumes of data into manageable information you can interpret. You can then communicate this meaningful data using common language—fractions, ratios, and percentages—that the reader can easily understand.

2 **Measures of central tendency identify a single figure to describe the entire distribution.** These measures and their purpose follow:
- **Mean**—The arithmetic average and the most stable measure of central tendency.
- **Median**—the middle value in a distribution; especially good indicator when extremely high or low values would influence the mean.
- **Mode**—the value that occurs most frequently.
- **Range**—the difference between the lowest and highest values (add one to include the high and low values).

3 **Use the following questions as a guide for determining whether a graphic is needed for presenting a particular idea:** (1) Would a graphic assist the reader in understanding the subject? (2) Can the material be covered adequately in words rather than in visual ways? (3) Will the written or spoken text add meaning to the graphic display? (4) Is the graphic design uncluttered and easily understood? (5) Does the graphic display the information honestly? (6) Is the graphic large enough to be seen by an audience if it is supporting an oral presentation?

Choose the appropriate type of graphic to communicate the information most effectively. Tables present data in systematic rows and columns. Bar charts (simple, multiple-range, and stacked) compare quantities for a specific period. Line charts depict changes in quantities over time and illustrate trends. Pie charts, pictograms, stacked-bar, and area charts show the proportion of components to a whole. Maps help readers visualize geographical relationships. Flow charts visually depict step-by-step procedures for completing a task; organizational charts show the organizational structure of a company. Floor plans, photographs, cartoons, blueprints, and lists also enhance reports.

Always introduce and interpret a graphic before presenting it. The graphic will then reinforce your conclusions and discourage readers from drawing their own conclusions before encountering your ideas. Place the graphic immediately after the introduction if possible. If the graphic will not fit on the page where it is introduced, position it at the top of the next page, filling the previous page with text that would ideally have followed the graphic. An effective introduction for a graphic interprets the graphic and then refers the reader to a specific figure number.

REVIEW QUESTIONS

1. In what ways does managing data help protect researchers from being overwhelmed by their material?
2. What is meant by common language? Provide several examples.
3. Which measure of central tendency do most people describe as the average? How is it calculated?
4. Which measures of central tendency would be appropriate for the following distribution: 12, 65, 68, 72, 73, 79, 81, 85, and 85? Why?
5. What basic rules are used to determine whether a graphic should be used to present certain information?
6. Discuss the major principles involved in preparing effective tables.
7. Why should increments on the vertical axis be equal in a graphic? Is variation in the sizes of horizontal increments acceptable?
8. Describe a broken-bar chart.
9. What is the difference between a stacked-bar (component) chart and an area (cumulative line) chart? Give an example of how each might be used.
10. Why can pie charts and simple line charts not be used to depict the same type of data effectively?
11. Can the design of a graphic deviate from basic rules (graphic title at the top or bottom, slice the pie beginning at twelve o'clock, and so on) to accomplish a specific purpose? Explain.
12. Why does a lack of consistency in the sizes of symbols create misleading pictograms?
13. Where should a graphic be placed in a report?
14. Should every graphic be introduced in a report? Is interpreting a self-explanatory graphic necessary? Explain.
15. Discuss the appropriate way to introduce a graphic in a report.

EXERCISES

1. Complete each of the THINK IT OVER activities that your instructor assigns.
2. **Computing Measures of Central Tendency.** The following figures represent salaries earned in thousands of dollars by chief financial officers of 25 local high-tech firms.
   a. Compute the mean, median, and mode of the following distribution:

36	48	66	74	82
38	49	68	74	87
38	53	70	78	90
42	57	74	80	92
42	62	74	82	96

   b. Tally the scores in Excerise 2a in seven classes beginning with 30-39, 40-49, and so on to 90-99. When you have tallied the scores, compute the mean, median, and modal class.
3. **Preparing a Table.** Prepare a table for the data used in Exercise 2 and indicate the appropriate percentages for each class. Write a sentence to introduce the table in a report.
4. **Selecting Graphics.** Select the most effective graphic means of presenting the following data. Justify your decision.
   a. Data showing the functional areas of a company from the CEO to the vice presidents to the line supervisors.
   b. Figures showing the total number of minorities employed at Haggard Industries during the past ten years.
   c. Predicted wheat harvest by state for 1996.
   d. Company sales earned in each of five countries during the last fiscal year.
   e. Figures comparing the percentage of total income of a company's three product lines for the past five years.
   f. Instructions for loan officers approving loans for new business ventures.
   g. Figures showing the volume of flood insurance policies by state.
5. **Improving Introductions to Graphics.** Improve the following statements taken from reports:

a. As can be seen in Table 5, the correlation between verbal scores on admission tests and
   achievement in English was .57.
b. Land values in the southern part of the state
   have increased about 32 percent while those
   in the northern portion have increased 19 percent. (See Figure 6.)

c. Take a look at Figure 3, where a steady decline in the price of farm products during the
   past quarter is shown.
d. The data reveal (Figure 4) that only one of
   seven voters is satisfied with the performance
   of the City Council.

E-MAIL APPLICATION

Use the annual report obtained for
Application 7 to critique a graphic
in the report. Complete the following steps:

1. Identify *one* graphic that violates one or more of
   the principles presented in this chapter. For example, the graphic type may be inappropriate to
   present the data meaningfully, may be drawn incorrectly, may distort the true meaning of the data,
   have too much clutter, contain typographical or
   labeling errors, or contain other ineffective design elements.

2. Revise the graphic, incorporating your suggestions. Send your instructor an e-mail message
   outlining the major weaknesses in the graphic
   and your suggestions for improving it. Attach the
   computer file containing your revised graphic.
3. Be prepared to present an oral report to the
   class. To support your report, prepare a transparency of the poor and revised graphic and a
   list of the weaknesses if your graphic contained
   several errors.

APPLICATIONS

1. **Drawing a Bar Chart.** Prepare a bar chart showing the frequency of injuries reported at each of
   Southport Manufacturing's three plants (Memphis,
   Knoxville, and Joliet) for each quarter in the last
   fiscal period. The number of injuries by quarter
   follow: Memphis: 1, 2, 6, 8; Knoxville, 3, 4, 3, 4;
   Joliet: 6, 5, 3, 1. Write a title that clearly identifies
   the data depicted in the chart. Write a sentence
   to introduce the graphic and emphasize the most
   important idea(s) in the graphic.
2. **Drawing a Stacked-Bar Chart.** Prepare a stacked-
   bar chart comparing the results of operation for
   Arlington Fitness Connection for the following
   years in millions of dollars:

	1993	1994	1995
Cost of goods sold	47.9	58.7	67.1
Operating expenses	24.2	28.8	32.0
Interest expense	5.1	4.7	3.9
Pretax income	12.8	17.8	12.0

3. **Drawing a Line Chart.** Prepare a line chart showing the total number of injuries at Southport Manufacturing for each of these years: 1995, 43; 1994,
   51; 1993, 58; 1992, 62. Write a title that clearly
   identifies the data depicted in the chart. Write a
   sentence to introduce the graphic and emphasize the most important idea(s) in the graphic.
4. **Drawing a Pie Chart.** Prepare a pie chart showing the percentage of city tax dollars spent on
   education (55%), fire (8%), police (15%), administration (12%), parks and recreation (4%), and
   other (6%). Write a title that clearly identifies the
   data depicted in the chart. Write a sentence to
   introduce the graphic and emphasize the most
   important idea(s) in the graphic.
5. **Selecting and Drawing an Appropriate Graphic.**
   Prepare an appropriate graphic to show the
   total employer health insurance contribution for
   a fiscal period. The following monthly premiums were paid by Express Printing for employee
   health insurance during the last fiscal period:

single employees and no dependents, $45; employees and one dependent, $54; employees and two dependents, $60; employees and three or more dependents, $72. Express Printing employs 32 employees with no dependents; 26 with one; 18 with two; and 29 with three or more.

6. **Evaluating and Revising Graphics.** Evaluate the effectiveness of each of the following graphics. Revise the graphic, incorporating your suggestions for improvement. Write a title and a sentence to introduce the graphic and emphasize the most important idea(s) in the graphic.

a. Dollar sales (in thousands of dollars) over a six-year period. Graphic is being prepared for inclusion in the annual report.

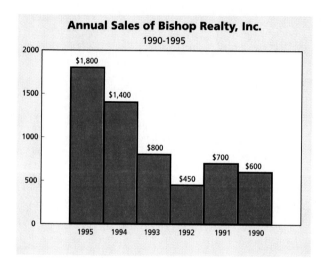

c. Number of customers by sales representatives during October 19--.

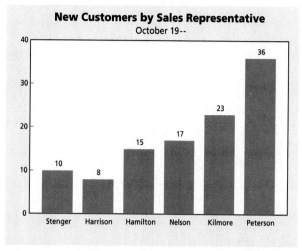

7. **Evaluating Graphics in Annual Reports.** Obtain a copy of a corporate annual report. Prepare a one-page memorandum that evaluates the appropriateness of each graphic in the report, its effectiveness in clarifying or reinforcing major points, and the ethical presentation of information.

b. Unit production per plant during the third quarter of 19--.

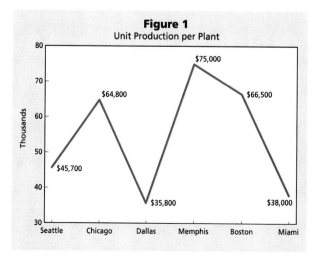

CHAPTER 17

ORGANIZING AND WRITING

SHORT REPORTS

AND PROPOSALS

OBJECTIVES

When you have completed Chapter 17, you will be able to

1 Identify the parts of a formal report and the contribution each part makes to the overall effectiveness of a report.

2 Prepare short reports in letter and memorandum formats.

3 Prepare proposals for a variety of purposes.

Many homeowners, when faced with repairs or renovations, choose to make these improvements themselves instead of hiring a professional. For some, the motivation is money; they believe they can do the job more economically. Others, however, tackle the task for the enjoyment of it and for the satisfaction of being self-reliant. Regardless of the motivation, everyone who begins such a project must plan carefully, follow instructions, use common sense, and follow through. If these general rules are not followed, disaster could result. That lovely garden bench you wanted so badly may turn into an eyesore of scrap lumber, or that simple plumbing repair could flood your house.

Like a home improvement/carpentry project, a business report also consists of several components or tasks. Each part must be carefully "worked" and then reviewed to make sure it is as perfect as possible. If a part is missing, the report is incomplete and will not be effective. After gathering information for your report, be sure to check the style manual approved by your company to make sure that your report has all the required components and to see how to assemble those parts into a clear, complete whole.

PARTS OF A REPORT

The differences between a formal report and an informal report lie in the format and possibly in writing style. The type of report you prepare depends on the subject matter, the purpose of the report, and the readers' needs. At the short, informal end of the report continuum described in Chapter 15, a report could look exactly like a brief memorandum. At the long, formal extreme of the continuum, the report might include most or all of the parts shown in Figure 17-1.

A business report rarely contains all of these parts. They are listed here simply to name all possible parts. The preliminary parts and addenda are mechanical items that support the body of a report. The body contains the report of the research and covers the four steps in the research process. The organization of the body of a report leads to the construction of the contents page.

Because individuals usually write to affect or influence others favorably, they often add parts as the number of pages increases. When a report exceeds one or two pages, you might add a cover or title page. When the body of a report exceeds four or five pages, you might even add a finishing touch by placing the report in a plastic cover or ring binder. Reports frequently take on the characteristics of the formal end of the continuum simply by reason of length. Note how the preliminary parts and addenda items shown in Figure 17-2 increase in number as the report increases in length. Notice, also, the order in which report parts appear in a complete report.

Memo and letter reports are seldom longer than a page or two, but they can be expanded into several pages. As depicted, long reports may include some special pages that do not appear in short reports. The format you select—long or short, formal or informal—may help determine the supporting preliminary and addenda items to include.

To understand how each part of a formal report contributes to reader comprehension and ease of access to the information in the report, study the following explanations of each part in the three basic categories: preliminary parts, report text, and addenda. Figure 17-1 illustrates how these three sections are combined to prepare a complete formal report. In Chapter 18, you will study a

FIGURE 17-1
Parts of a formal report: preliminary parts, report text, and addenda.

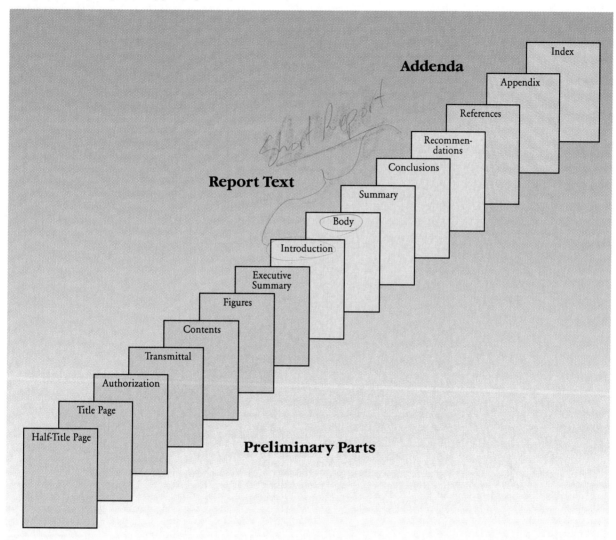

sample long report to help you visualize the selected report parts and the order in which they will appear in a complete report.

Preliminary Parts

Preliminary parts are included to add formality to a report, repeat report content, and aid the reader in locating information in the report quickly and in understanding the report more easily. These parts include the half-title page, title page, authorization, transmittal, contents, figures, and executive summary. Preliminary pages are numbered with small roman numerals (i, ii, iii, and so on).

Why are the preliminary parts added? List the preliminary parts.

Preliminary parts are numbered with small roman numerals.

FIGURE 17-2
The number of assisting items increases as the length of a report increases.

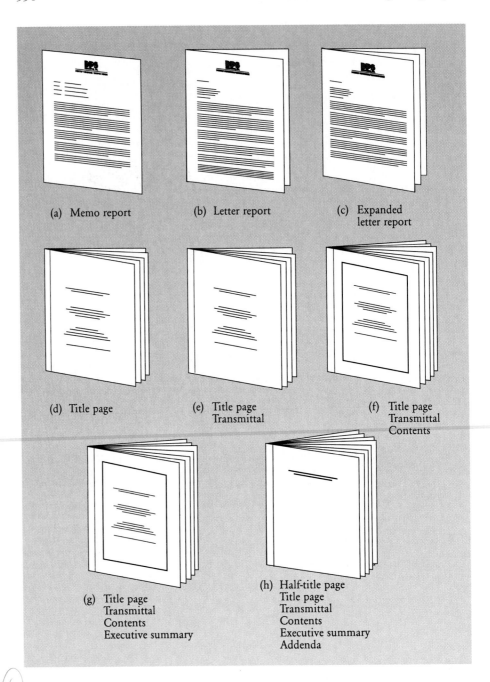

(a) Memo report

(b) Letter report

(c) Expanded letter report

(d) Title page

(e) Title page
Transmittal

(f) Title page
Transmittal
Contents

(g) Title page
Transmittal
Contents
Executive summary

(h) Half-title page
Title page
Transmittal
Contents
Executive summary
Addenda

HALF-TITLE PAGE

What purpose does the half-title page serve?

A **half-title page**, often called a *title fly*, is a single page containing only the report title. This page simply adds formality and enhances the appearance of a report. In less formal reports, including letter and memorandum reports, the half-title page is omitted.

TITLE PAGE

What basic information is included on a title page?

The **title page** includes the title, author, date, and frequently the name of the person or organization that requested the report. A title page is often added when the writer opts to use a formal report format rather than a memorandum or a letter arrangement.

Select a title that is descriptive and comprehensive; its words should reflect the content of the report. Avoid short, vague titles or excessively long titles. Instead, use concise wording to identify the topic adequately. For example, a title such as "Marketing Survey: Noncarbonated Beverages" leaves the reader confused when the title could have been "Noncarbonated Beverage Preferences of College Students in Boston." To give some clues for writing a descriptive title, think of the "Five Ws": *Who, What, When, Where,* and *Why.* Avoid such phrases as "A Study of. . . ," "A Critical Analysis of. . . ," or "A Review of. . . ."

Follow company procedures or a style manual to place the title attractively on the page. If the title is longer than one line, arrange it in the inverted pyramid format; that is, make each succeeding line shorter than the line preceding it. Arrange the title consistently on the half-title page, title page, and the first page of a report. The inverted pyramid format also should be used in titles of graphics. Note the arrangement of the following title of a graphic:

Incorrect:	AVERAGE PER CAPITA INCOME IN 1995 FOR TEN STATES
Incorrect:	AVERAGE PER CAPITA INCOME IN 1995 FOR TEN STATES
Correct:	AVERAGE PER CAPITA INCOME IN 1995 FOR TEN STATES

AUTHORIZATION

An **authorization** is a letter or memorandum authorizing the researcher to conduct a specific research project. The authorization is included as a formal part of the report and follows the title page. If no written authorization is provided, authorization information may be included in the letter of transmittal or the introduction. This information might include a clear description of the problem, limitations restricting the research, resources available, and deadlines.

TRANSMITTAL ~ Preface or Foreword.

As a report becomes more formal, the writer may attach a **letter or memorandum of transmittal**. The transmittal serves two purposes: (1) to present the report to the one who requested it and (2) to provide the conclusion from an analytical study or highlights from an informational report. If the writer has prepared a report for a person or a department inside the company, the writer uses the memorandum format for the transmittal. A consultant preparing a report for another company arranges the transmittal in a letter format.

The transmittal letter or memorandum is the writer's opportunity to speak directly to the reader in an informal tone. Thus, the writer may include first- and second-person pronouns in the transmittal. If the report includes a synopsis or a detailed introduction, the transmittal is short. Use the deductive approach and follow these suggestions:

1. Let the first sentence present the report and remind the reader that he or she requested it.
2. Explain the subject of the report in the first paragraph.
3. Present brief conclusions and, if called for, the recommendations.
4. Close cordially. The closing paragraph also expresses appreciation for the cooperation given by the company.

What are several suggestions for writing an effective title?

THINK IT OVER
Write an effective title for a report to select an automobile type to replace company cars driven by a real estate company's sales staff.

Explain the inverted pyramid format for titles.

What information should be included in the transmittal?

Is using first- and second-person pronouns acceptable in a transmittal?

What is the main idea to be presented in a transmittal? In what position does it appear?

CONTENTS —or Lists

THINK IT OVER
How does the contents page contribute to the coherence of a formal report?

The **contents** provides the reader with an analytical overview of the report and the order in which information is presented. Thus, this preliminary part aids the reader in understanding the report and in locating a specific section of it. The list includes the name and location (beginning page number) of every report part except the half-title page, title page, and contents. Include the list of figures and include the transmittal, executive summary, report headings, references, appendixes, and index. Placing spaced periods (leaders) between the report part and the page numbers helps lead the reader's eyes to the appropriate page number.

Word-processing software simplifies the time-consuming, tedious task of preparing many of the preliminary and addenda report parts including the contents. Because the software can generate these parts automatically, report writers can make last-minute changes to a report and still have time to update preliminary and addenda parts.

FIGURES

To aid the reader in locating a specific graphic in a report with many graphics, the writer might include a list of figures separate from the contents. The contents and the figures can be combined on one page if both lists are brief. Word-processing software can be used to generate the list of figures automatically.

EXECUTIVE SUMMARY — Sinopsis, Abstract

Ability to summarize complex, lengthy reports is a critical skill needed to advance in your career.

The **executive summary** (or *abstract*) summarizes the essential elements in an entire report. This overview simplifies the reader's understanding of a long report. The executive summary is positioned before the first page of the report.

Typically, an executive summary is included when the writer believes it will assist the reader in understanding a long, complex report. Because of the increased volume of information that managers must review, managers tend to require an executive summary regardless of the length and complexity of a report.

THINK IT OVER
Using your library's online database, locate an article about effective report writing. Write an executive summary of the article and be prepared to share with the class.

The executive summary presents the report in miniature: the introduction, body, and summary as well as conclusions and recommendations if they are included in the report. Thus, an executive summary should (1) introduce briefly the report and preview the major divisions, (2) summarize the major sections of the report, and (3) summarize the report summary and any conclusions and recommendations. Pay special attention to topic sentences and to concluding sentences in paragraphs or within sections of reports. This technique helps you write concise executive summaries based on major ideas and reduces the use of supporting details and background information.

THINK IT OVER
Browse through several practitioner journals in your field to determine whether they include executive summaries with each article. If so, how effectively does the executive summary present the gist of the article?

To stay up to date professionally, many busy executives require assistants to prepare executive summaries of articles they do not have time to read and conferences and meetings they cannot attend. Many practitioner journals now include an executive summary of each article. Reading the executive summary provides the gist of the article and alerts the executive of pertinent articles that should be read in detail.

Report Text — Can be used stand-alone!

The report text and addenda are numbered with arabic numerals.

The report itself contains the introduction, body, summary, conclusions, and recommendations. Report pages are numbered with arabic numerals (1, 2, 3, and so on).

COMMUNICATION MENTOR

The executive summary is probably the most important part of reports being presented to top management. Summaries should be prepared with the needs of specific executive readers in mind. For instance, a technically oriented executive may require more detail; a strategist, more analysis.

Executive summaries should "boil down" a report to its barest essentials, yet without brevity so severe that the summaries are incomprehensible. If appropriate, the summary should offer a view or conclusion reached by a report. Essentially, summaries should enable top executives to glean enough information and understanding to feel confident making a decision.

Cynthia Pharr
President & CEO
C. Pharr Marketing Communications

Most appraisal clients are primarily interested in the value conclusion. Therefore, appraisers often provide an executive summary, which presents the highlights of a report and the property value estimate. An executive summary may satisfy the reader's needs, but a full report with details is required.

Bernard J. Fountain
1993 President, Appraisal Institute

INTRODUCTION

The introduction orients the reader to the problem. It may include the following items:

1. What the topic is.
2. Why it is being reported on.
3. Scope and limitations of the research.
4. Where the information came from.
5. A preview of the major sections of the report to provide coherence and transition through the report:
   a. How the topic is divided into parts.
   b. The order in which the parts will be represented.

What information in included in the introduction?

BODY

The **body**, often called the heart of the report, presents the information collected and relates it to the problem. To increase readability and coherence, this section contains numerous headings to denote the various divisions within a report. Refer to "Organizing Report Findings" later in this chapter and the "Using Headings Effectively" section in Chapter 18 for an in-depth discussion of preparing the body.

Why is the body referred to as the heart of the report?

SUMMARY, CONCLUSIONS, AND RECOMMENDATIONS

An informational report ends with a brief **summary** that serves an important function: it adds unity to a report by reviewing the main points presented in the body. A summary includes only material that is discussed in a report.

Why is new information inappropriate in the summary?

Introducing a new idea in the summary may make the reader wonder why the point was not developed earlier. It may suggest that the study was not adequately completed or that the writer did not adequately plan the report before beginning to write. Finally, a summary, which is expected to be fairly short, does not provide enough space for developing a new idea.

Analytical reports include conclusions and sometimes recommendations; informational reports contain only a summary.

Analytical reports, designed to solve a specific problem or answer research questions, may also include a summary of the major research findings, particularly if the report is lengthy. Reviewing the major findings prepares the reader for the conclusions that follow. An analytical report also includes **conclusions**, inferences the writer draws from the findings. If required by the person/organization authorizing the report, recommendations follow the conclusions. **Recommendations** present the writer's opinion on a possible course of action based on the conclusions. Review the examples of findings, conclusions, and recommendations presented in Chapter 15 if necessary.

Is placing the summary, conclusions, and recommendations in separate sections acceptable?

For a long report, the writer may place the summary, the conclusions, and the recommendations in three separate sections. For shorter reports, conclusions and recommendations can be combined into one section, or all three sections can be combined.

Addenda

How are addenda parts numbered?

The addenda to a report may include all materials used in the research but not appropriate to be included in the report itself. The three basic addenda parts are the references, appendixes, and index. Addenda parts continue with the same page numbering system used in the body of the report.

REFERENCES ~Sources, Works Cited, Bibliography

Should you include references consulted but not cited in the references?

The **references** (also called *works cited*) are an alphabetical listing of the sources used in preparing the report. Because the writer may be influenced by any information consulted, some reference manuals require all sources consulted to be included in the references list. When the references list includes sources not cited in the report, it is referred to as a *bibliography* (or *works consulted*). If a report includes endnotes rather than in-text parenthetical citations (author and date within the text), the endnotes precede the references. Using word-processing software to create footnotes and endnotes alleviates much of the monotony and repetition of preparing accurate documentation. Refer to "Documenting Reports" in Chapter 18 or a style manual for specific guidelines for preparing references and citations.

APPENDIXES

How do you decide whether to include an item in the report text or in an appendix?

An **appendix** contains supplementary information that supports the report but is not appropriate for inclusion in the report itself. This information may include questionnaires and accompanying transmittal letters, summary tabulations, verbatim comments from respondents, complex mathematical computations and formulas, legal documents, and a variety of items the writer presents to support the body of the report and the quality of the research. Placing supplementary material in an appendix prevents the text from becoming excessively long.

If the report contains more than one appendix, label each with a capital letter and a title. For example, the four appendixes in a report could be identified as follows:

Appendix A: Cover Letter Accompanying End-User Questionnaire
Appendix B: End-User Questionnaire
Appendix C: Means of 20 Technology Competencies
Appendix D: Number and Percentage of Ratings Given to 20 Technology Competencies

Each item included in the appendixes must be mentioned in the report. References within the report to the four appendixes mentioned in the previous example follow:

> A copy of the end-user questionnaire (Appendix A), a cover letter (Appendix B), and a stamped, pre-addressed envelope were mailed to 1,156 firms on February 15, 19--.
>
> Means were computed, and the total means were ranked to establish an order of importance for the 20 technology competencies as shown in Table 10. The means are shown in Appendix C, and the frequency distribution from which these means were computed is provided in Appendix D.

Mention in the text each item you include in the appendix.

INDEX

The **index** is an alphabetical guide to the subject matter in a report. The subject and each page number on which the subject appears are listed. Word-processing software can generate the index automatically. Each time a new draft is prepared, a new index with revised terms and correct page numbers can be generated quickly and easily.

How can computer software help you prepare an index?

ORGANIZING REPORT FINDINGS

Because the body of a report discusses the four steps in problem solving—usually the items of most interest to readers—it represents the core of the presentation. Within the body, the purpose and method of the solution are minor items in terms of space and are considered part of an introduction to a report. The findings leading to the conclusion or conclusions should consume the major portion of space.

Assume that you must select a personal computer from among three comparable brands from three vendors—IBM, Compaq, and Gateway. You must select the computer that will best serve the computing needs of a small office and present your justification and recommendations in a **justification report**.

You gather all information available from suppliers of the three computers, you operate each computer personally, and you compare the three against a variety of criteria. Your final selection is the Gateway. Why did you select it? What criteria served as decision guides? When you write the report, you will have to tell the reader—the one who will pay for the equipment—how the selection was made in such a way that the reader is "sold" on your conclusion.

If you organize your report so that you tell the reader everything about the IBM, the Compaq, and then the Gateway, the reader may have trouble making comparisons. Your content outline might look like this:

LEARNING OBJECTIVE 2

What report part represents the most significant component of the report? Why?

THINK IT OVER
The purpose of the report is to convince the reader your choice of a computer (your conclusion) is accurate. Would this report be classified as informational or analytical?

COMMUNICATION MENTOR

To write a convincing report, an appraiser begins with a simple outline of steps: (1) define the purpose of the report; (2) describe the methods to be used and include any necessary assumptions and definition; (3) present and analyze the data gathered; and (4) arrive at a conclusion. These steps form the rough framework for the report contents. Complex reports may be several hundred pages long.

Because many appraisal reports are used in court proceedings, they must provide details about sources of information, the methods applied and the steps taken in gathering and compiling data, and the techniques of analysis used. Such documentation demonstrates that another competent appraiser given the same information should arrive at essentially the same conclusion.

Bernard J. Fountain
1993 President, Appraisal Institute

```
I.   Introduction
     A.  The Problem
     B.  The Method Used
II.  IBM
III. Compaq
IV.  Gateway
V.   Conclusion
```

How is the previous outline divided? Why is this outline inappropriate?

Note that this outline devotes three roman numeral sections to the findings, one to the introduction that presents the problem and the method, and one to the conclusion. This division is appropriate because the most space must be devoted to the findings. However, the reader may have difficulty comparing the expansion capacity of the computers because the information is in three different places. Would discussing the expansion capacity of all three in the same section of the report be better? Would prices be compared more easily if they were all in the same section? *Most reports should be divided into sections that reflect the criteria used rather than into sections devoted to the alternatives compared.*

Divide report sections into criteria evaluated rather than alternatives compared.

If you selected your computer based on cost, service/warranties, and expandability, these criteria (rather than the computers themselves) might serve as divisions of the findings. Then your content outline would appear this way:

THINK IT OVER
What criteria might you use to select a company car for realtors?

```
I.   Introduction
     A.  The Problem
     B.  The Method Used
II.  Compaq Is Least Expensive
III. Service/Warranties Favor Gateway
IV.  Expandability Is Best on Gateway
V.   Availability of Software Is Equal
VI.  Gateway Is the Best Buy
```

With page numbers added, the outline could be a contents page.

The outline now has six major sections and two subsections. Four major sections are devoted to the findings. When the report is prepared in this way, the features of each computer (the evaluation criteria) are compared in the same section, and the reader is led logically to the conclusion.

Note the headings used in Sections II-VI. These are called **talking headings** because they talk about the content of the section and even give a conclusion about the section. Adding page numbers after each outline item will convert the outline into a contents page. Interestingly, the headings justify the selection of the Gateway. As a result, a knowledgeable reader who has confidence in the researcher might be satisfied by reading only the content headings.

In addition to organizing findings by criteria, report writers can use other organizational plans. The comparison of three computers was an analytical process. When a report is informational and not analytical, you should use the most logical organization. Treat your material as a "whole" unit. A report on sales might be divided by geographic sales region, by product groups sold, by price range, or by time periods. A report on the development of a product might use chronological order. By visualizing the whole report first, you can then divide it into its major components and perhaps divide the major components into their parts. Remember, a section must divide into at least two parts or it cannot be divided at all. Thus, in an outline you must have a "B" subsection if you have an "A" subsection following a roman numeral or you should not have any subsections.

A final caution: Beware of overdividing the sections. Too many divisions might make the report appear disorganized and choppy. On the other hand, too few divisions might create a problem for the reader. Note how the four steps of research have been developed through headings to the roman numeral outline and to a contents page for a report, as shown in Figure 17-3.

When developing content outlines, some report writers believe that readers expect the beginning of the body to be an introduction, so they begin the outline with the first heading related to findings. In our example, then, Section I would be "Compaq Is Least Expensive." Additionally, when they reach the contents page, readers may eliminate the roman numeral or other outline symbols. A contents page for a report without the "Introduction," "Problem," and "Method" headings would look like this:

> **THINK IT OVER**
> Write talking headings for a report designed to select an automobile type to replace company cars driven by a real-estate company sales staff.

> Analytical reports are organized by criteria. How are informational reports organized?

> Should "Introduction" appear on the contents page?

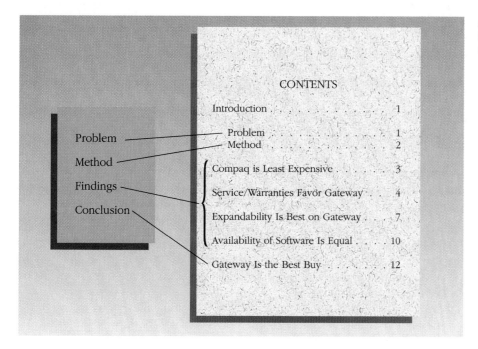

FIGURE 17-3
The basic outline expands into a contents page.

CONTENTS

Problem
Method
Findings
Conclusion

CONTENTS

The research process consists of inductively arranged steps:

1. Problem
2. Method
3. Findings
4. Conclusion

Inductive is indirect: the conclusion is presented last. Deductive is direct: the conclusion is presented first.

When the report is organized in the same order, its users must read through the body to learn about the conclusions—generally the most important part of the report to users. To make the reader's job easier, report writers may organize the report deductively, with the conclusions at the beginning. This sequence is usually achieved by placing a synopsis or summary at the beginning:

I.   Conclusion Reported in the Synopsis
II. Body of the Report
     A. Problem
     B. Method
     C. Findings
III. Conclusion

This arrangement permits the reader to get the primary message early and then to look for support in the body of the report. The deductive arrangement contributes to the repetitious nature of reports, but it also contributes to effective reporting.

FORM REPORTS

Form reports meet the demand for numerous, repetitive reports. College registration forms, applications for credit, airline tickets, and bank checks are examples of simple form reports. Form reports have the following benefits:

What are the benefits of form reports?

1. When designed properly, form reports increase clerical accuracy by providing designated places for specific items.
2. Forms save time by telling the preparer where to put each item and by preprinting common elements so the person filling in the form need not do any narrative writing.
3. In addition to their advantages of accuracy and time saving, forms make tabulation of data relatively simple. The nature of the form is uni*form*ity.

COMMUNICATION   MENTOR

Use headings to draw your reader into a report. Readers prefer headings, so give them what they want. Most researchers follow a linear path of writing. They begin at *A* and continue to *Z*. However, most readers want to know *what* you found out—not how. In other words, tell your reader what time it is—not how to build the watch.

At INTELECO, we begin all reports with an executive summary that uses a "bullet point" style to highlight key findings of the study. The complete report contains typical divisions—objectives, methodology, detailed findings, and conclusions and recommendations.

David Martin, President
INTELECO

Most form reports, such as a bank teller's cash sheet, are informational. At the end of the teller's work period, cash is counted and totals entered in designated blanks. Cash reports from all tellers are then totaled to arrive at period totals and perhaps verified by computer records.

In addition to their informational purpose, form reports assist in analytical work. A residential appraisal report assists real-estate appraisers in analyzing real property. With this information, the appraiser is able to determine the market value of a specific piece of property.

Many form reports are computer-generated. For example, the flowchart in Figure 17-4 illustrates a hospital's automation of repetitive patient reports. The admission clerk inputs the patient information using the carefully designed in-

Do forms also tend to improve the quality of routine reports?

THINK IT OVER
In small groups, discuss another example of computer-generated reports you have encountered through work or other experience. How does this procedure increase the efficiency of report writing? the image of the company?

Form reports are useful when numerous, repetitive reports are necessary. They may be preprinted, which saves time and preserves accuracy.

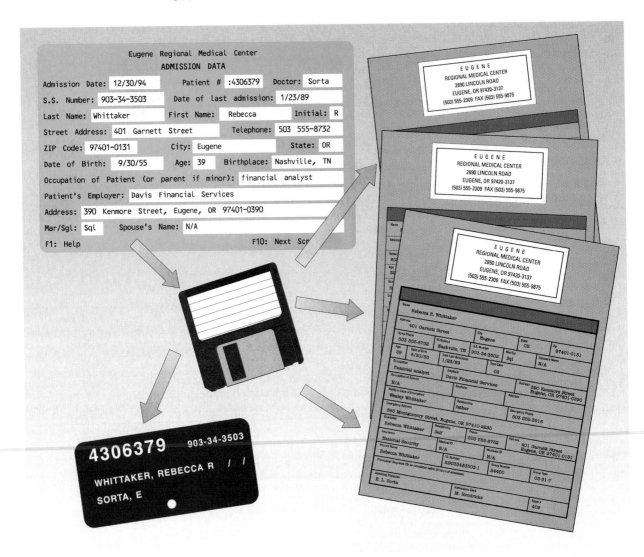

FIGURE 17-4   Computer-generated reports increase efficiency and accuracy.

put screen beginning with the patient's social security number. If the patient has been admitted previously, the patient's name, address, and telephone number are displayed automatically; all the clerk must do is verify the accuracy of the information. When the clerk inputs the patient's date of birth, the computer calculates the patient's age, eliminating the need to ask a potentially sensitive question and assuring accuracy when people cannot remember their ages. All data are stored in a computer file and retrieved as needed to generate numerous reports required during a patient's stay: admissions summary sheet, admissions report, pharmacy profile, and even the addressograph used to stamp each page of the patient's record and the identification arm band.

Using the computer to prepare each report in the previous example leads to higher efficiency levels and minimizes errors because recurring data are input only once. Preparing error-free reports is a critical public relations tool because even minor clerical errors may cause patients to question the hospital's ability to delivery quality health care.

COMMUNICATION MENTOR

Consider the audience to whom you are directing a report. Choose language your audience will understand yet will convey the message adequately. The majority of our reports are directed to the Boards of Directors of the banks our agency regulates. While these directors may be well versed in business jargon, they are not familiar with the special terms and acronyms used in the banking industry. If your audience does not understand your report, either (1) you will lose valuable time and possibly effectiveness if you have to write another report to clarify a previous one or (2) you will lose your audience.

Gabriel Swan
National Bank Examiner

CHARACTERISTICS OF SHORT REPORTS

Most **short reports** include only the minimum supporting materials to achieve effective communication. Short reports focus on the body—problem, method, findings, and conclusion. In addition, short reports might incorporate any of the following features:

What features are frequently found in short reports?

1. Personal writing style using first- or second-person. Contractions are appropriate when they contribute to a natural style.
2. Graphics to reinforce the written text.
3. Headings and subheadings to partition portions of the body and to reflect organization.
4. Memorandum and letter formats when appropriate.

Various types of short reports are illustrated in the examples that follow. The commentary in the left column will help you understand how effective writing principles are applied.

The report in Figure 17-5 communicates the activity of a company's childcare services during one quarter of the fiscal period. This periodic report is formatted as a memorandum because it is prepared for personnel within the company and is a brief, informal report. Outside consultants present their audit of a company's software policy in the letter report in Figure 17-6.

The report in Figure 17-7 is written deductively. Effective nonverbal communication is presented as the key ingredient in the success of the client's expansion into the Kuwaiti market. The consultant briefly describes the procedures used to analyze the problem, presents the findings in a logical sequence, and provides specific recommendations. The letter format is appropriate because a consultant is writing to a client (external audience).

PROPOSALS

A **proposal** is a written description of how one organization can meet the needs of another; e.g., provide products or services as defined in Chapter 15. Managers prepare **internal proposals** to justify or recommend purchases or

LEARNING OBJECTIVE 3

[1] Includes headings to serve the function of the transmittal and a title page in a formal report.

[2] Includes a horizontal line to add interest and to separate the transmittal from the body of the memo.

[3] Uses deductive approach to present this periodic report requested by management on a quarterly basis.

[4] Uses headings to highlight standard information; allows for easy update when preparing a subsequent report.

[5] Includes primary data collected from a survey completed by parents.

[6] Attaches material to the memorandum. The attachment would be an appendix item in a formal report.

TELCO CHILDCARE SERVICES
8300 Lincoln Green
Jacksonville, FL 32203-8300
(904) 555-9340   Fax (904) 555-3087

TO: M. L. Irvin, Director, Human Resources

[1] FROM: Janice Simms, Coordinator, Childcare Services   *J.S.*

DATE: July 14, 19--

SUBJECT: Quarterly Report on In-House Childcare Center, Second Quarter, 19--

[2] _____

[3] The in-house childcare center experienced a successful second quarter. Data related to enrollment and current staffing follow:

[4] **Enrollment:** June 30—92 children, up from 84 at end of first quarter.

Staff: Nine full-time staff members, including five attendants, three teachers, and one registered nurse.

Registration for the upcoming school year is presently underway and is exceeding projected figures. Current staff size will necessitate an enrollment cap of 98. Further increases in enrollment will be possible only if additional personnel are hired.

The payroll deduction method of payment, instituted on January 1, has assured that operations remain profitable. It has also eliminated the time and expense of billing. Parents seem satisfied with the arrangement as well.

Full license renewal is expected in August as we have met and/or exceeded all state and county requirements for facilities, staff, and programs.

[5] Favorable results were obtained to the employee satisfaction poll which was administered to parents participating in the childcare program. Ninety-one percent indicated that they were very satisfied or extremely satisfied with our in-house childcare program. The most frequently mentioned suggestion for improvement was the extension of hours until 7 p.m. This change would allow employees time to run

M. L. Irvin, Director
Page 2
July 14, 19--

necessary errands after work, before picking up their children. We might consider this addition of services on an hourly basis. A copy of the survey instrument is provided for your review.

Call me should you wish to discuss the extended service hours idea or any other aspects of this report.

[6] Attachment

FIGURE 17-5   Short, periodic report in memorandum format.

STERNE BUSINESS CONSULTANTS

1800 RBC Parkway, North
Seattle, WA 98109-3933
(206) 555-9087   Fax (206) 555-3872

September 17, 19--

Ms. Grace Engstrom, CEO
Spectrum Analysis, Inc.
P. O. Box 993
Portland, OR 97238-0993

Dear Ms. Engstrom:

[1] The personal computer software audit for Spectrum Analysis has been completed according to the procedures recommended by Software Publishers Association. These procedures and our findings are summarized below.

[2] PROCEDURES

Specific procedures involved

[3] 1. Reviewing the software policy of the organization and its implementation and control.

2. Reviewing the organization's inventory of software resources, including a list of all personal computers by location and serial number. Using SPAudit, we obtained a list of all the software on the hard disk of each computer.

3. Matching purchase documentation with the software inventory record we had established. This procedure included reviewing software purchase records such as invoices, purchase orders, check registers, canceled checks, manuals, diskettes, license agreements, and registration cards.

FINDINGS

In the area of software policy and controls, we found that the organization owns a total of 432 copies of 11 applications from seven vendors. No record of registration with the publisher was available for 81 of the programs owned. In addition, we identified 47 copies of software programs for which no corresponding purchase records existed and, therefore, appear to be illegal copies.

FIGURE 17-6   Audit report in letter format, page 1.

Margin notes:

[1] Introduces the overall topic and leads into procedures and findings.

[2] Uses side heading to denote the beginning of the body.

[3] Uses enumerations to add emphasis to this important information.

---

changes in the company; e.g., installing a new computer system, introducing telecommuting or other flexible work schedules, or reorganizing the company into work groups. Written to generate business, **external proposals** are a critical part of the successful operation of many companies.

Proposals may be solicited or unsolicited. A **solicited proposal** is generated when a potential buyer submits exact specifications or needs in a request for proposal, commonly referred to as an *RFP*. Governmental agencies such as the Department of Defense solicit proposals and place orders and contracts based on the most desirable proposal. The RFP describes a problem to be solved and invites respondents to describe their proposed solution.

A proposal includes the way a problem will be solved and the price.

4 Formats data in four-
column table to facilitate
reading and uses a clear
title and column headings.
Summarizes major point
in the table and refers the
reader to it. Does not
number this single figure.

5 Uses side heading to
denote the beginning of
the recommendation
section.

6 Uses enumerations to
emphasize the recommen-
dations.

Ms. Grace Engstrom, CEO
Page 2
September 17, 19--

Of the 113 personal computers, we found 14 machines with software
that had been brought from home by employees.

A summary of the software license violations identified follows:

Software	Total Copies Found	Legal Copies	Copies in Violation
WordPerfect 6.0	56	52	4
Lotus 1-2-3	48	45	3
Windows	115	75	40

We have deleted all copies in excess of the number of legal copies, and
you are now in full compliance with applicable software licenses. We
have also ordered legal software to replace the necessary software
that was deleted.

CONCLUSIONS AND RECOMMENDATIONS

Although some departments had little or no illegal software, others
had significant violations. Therefore, the following recommendations
are made:

1. Institute a one-hour training program on the legal use of software
   and require it for all employees. Repeat it weekly over the next
   few months to permit all employees to attend. Additionally, require
   all new employees to participate in the program within two weeks
   of their start date.

2. Implement stricter software inventory controls, including semiannual spot audits.

Thank you for the opportunity to serve your organization in this
manner. Should you wish to discuss any aspects of this report, call me.

Sincerely,

Craig W. Sterne

Craig W. Sterne
Software Consultant

mdy

FIGURE 17-6   Audit report in letter format, page 2.

An **unsolicited proposal** is prepared by an individual or firm who sees a
problem to be solved and submits a proposal. For example, a business consultant is a regular customer of a family-owned retail store. On numerous occasions
he has attempted to purchase an item that was out of stock. Recognizing that
stockouts decrease sales and profits, he prepares a proposal to assist the business in designing a computerized perpetual inventory with an automatic reor-
dering system. For the business to accept the proposal, the consultant must
convince the business that the resulting increase in sales and profits will more
than offset the cost of the computer system and the consulting fee.

GLOBAL CONCEPTS
9000 Delaware Street
New Orleans, LA 70126-9000
(504) 555-8700   Fax (504) 555-7581

November 2, 19--

Mr. Stephen Thames
Vice President of Operations
Unipro Corporation
1700 Gentilly Boulevard
New Orleans, LA 70126-1700

Dear Mr. Thames:

Recommendations for Communicating with the Kuwatis

Thank you for allowing us to assist you in preparing for your expansion into the Kuwaiti market. Your concern about how your company's personnel might be received in the Middle East is certainly warranted. Effective nonverbal communication is a vital element in overall business success.

Procedures

In preparing this report, a variety of books, newspaper and magazine articles, and government documents were examined. Additionally, interviews were conducted with 12 business persons from a variety of organizations, all of whom had lived and worked in the Middle East. Nonverbal communication patterns throughout the culturally complex Middle East vary because of the huge distances and different nationalities residing there. However, the following general advice related to eye contact, gestures, and proxemics applies throughout the Muslim world.

Differences in Eye Contact

Several important differences exist in the interpretation of nonverbal communication patterns of North Americans and those of Middle Easterners. One important difference occurs in the interpretation of eye contact and gaze, as summarized in the following table:

FIGURE 17-7   Short report in letter format, page 1.

A proposal includes (1) details about the manner in which the problem would be solved and (2) the price to be charged. Often the proposal is a lengthy report designed to "sell" the prospective buyer on the ability of the bidder to perform. However, a simple price quotation also constitutes a proposal in response to a request for a price quotation.

Parts of a Proposal

The format of a proposal depends on the length of the proposal and the intended audience report:

What is the appropriate format for proposals?

6 Mr. Stephen Thames
Page 2
November 2, 19--

7

Differences in Nonverbal Communication Between North Americans and Middle Easterners		
Eye Movement	North American	Middle Easterner
Stare	Rude, a threat	Contact with other's soul
Gaze (between strangers)	Sexual interest	Intimacy, sexual, and non-sexual interest
Gaze (conversational)	Speaker gazes to and away from listener	Speaker and listener hold gaze
Avoiding gaze	Hiding something	Rude in conversation
Lowering gaze	Submission; expected between strangers in a crowd	Submission; expected with religious person; strangers of different genders
Hand covers eyes	Possible headache	Swearing by one's eyes

8 Source: Argyle, 1988, p. 26

Obviously, a North American could inadvertently offend or confuse a Middle Easterner through poorly executed eye contact.

Differences in Gestures

9 A second area of concern in nonverbal communication is that of gestures. According to Axtell (1990), "in this area of the world, the left hand is customarily used for bodily hygiene; therefore, it should not be used for eating, handing over gifts or business cards, or other such gestures" (p. 52). Kissing on the cheek is a common business practice among men, as is the taking of another's hand or walking hand in hand. When seated, be careful that the sole of the shoe is not visible; this is considered highly offensive to the Middle Easterner, as the foot is considered the lowliest and dirtiest part of the body (Walker, 1981).

FIGURE 17-7   Short report in letter format, page 2.

Format	Proposal Length and Intended Audience
Memorandum report	Short; remains within the organization
Letter report	Short; travels outside the organization
Formal report	Long; remains within the organization or travels outside the organization

What is the objective of a proposal?

    Writers have much flexibility in preparing proposals. When they find a particular pattern that seems to be successful, they no doubt will adopt it as their basic plan. The ultimate test of a proposal is its effectiveness in achieving its

Mr. Stephen Thames
Page 3
November 2, 19--

Differences in Proxemics

Middle Eastern men typically stand much closer to one another than do North Americans. Conversational distance may shrink to 10 inches or less (Ruch, 1989). Standing close to or touching a woman in public is unacceptable behavior for a man unless he is part of the immediate family (Chuck, 1993).

Summary

Unipro's international operations depend to a large extent on the ability to communicate effectively. The following guidelines are offered to assure better nonverbal communication in the Middle East:

[10] 1. Assemble a reading library containing books and articles about Kuwaiti culture and customs. Require all employees departing for Kuwaiti assignments to familiarize themselves with these materials.

2. Employ a native Kuwaiti in a support role to advise Unipro personnel concerning appropriate verbal and nonverbal communication in Kuwait.

3. Include elements of appropriate nonverbal communication in the language training required of all personnel assigned to Kuwait.

[11] These suggestions should assist you in establishing effective verbal and nonverbal communication in the Middle Eastern culture. Please let us know how we can assist you further with this project or with other international endeavors.

Sincerely,

Janet C. Starns

Janet C. Starns
Consultant

ksm

Enclosure: Reading list

[10] Uses enumerations to highlight recommended guidelines.

[11] Closes with a courteous offer to provide additional service.

FIGURE 17-7   Short report in letter format, page 3.

READING LIST

Argyle, M. (1988). *Bodily communication.* New York: Methuen & Co. Ltd.

Axtell, R. (1990). *Do's and taboo's around the world.* New York: Parker Pen Company.

Chuck, L. (1993, February 22). Converts to Islam say they gain belief system, new way of life. *Austin (Texas) American Statesman,* pp. 1A, 5A.

Ruch, W. V. (1989). *International handbook of corporate communications.* Jefferson, NC: McFarland & Company, Inc.

Walker, S. (1981). *Business traveler's handbook: A guide to the Middle East.* New York: Wiley.

FIGURE 17-7   Short report in letter format, page 4.

purpose. The writer's task is to assemble the parts of a proposal in a way that persuades the reader to accept its proposal.

The following general parts, or variations of them, may be used as headings in a proposal:

Problem or Purpose	Qualifications and Recommendations
Purpose	Follow-up and/or Evaluation
Scope	Cost or Budget
Method and Procedures	Summary
Materials and Equipment	

In addition to these parts, a proposal may include preliminary report parts such as the title page, transmittal message, and contents and addenda parts such as references, appendix, and index.

To put the proposal together expeditiously, determine the parts to include, select one part that will be easy to prepare, prepare that part, and then go on to another. When you have completed the parts, you can arrange them in whatever order you like, incorporate the transitional items necessary to create coherence, and then put the proposal in finished form. As with most report writing, first prepare the pieces of information that you will later assemble as the "whole" report. Trying to write a report by beginning on line one, page one, and proceeding to the end may prove to be frustrating and time consuming. Keep in mind that you should complete the research and planning before you begin to write.

Proposals often are written collaboratively as a team effort.

If you become part of a collaborative-writing team producing a proposal of major size, you probably will be responsible for writing only a small portion of the total proposal. For example, a proposal team of sixteen executives, managers, and engineers might be required to prepare an 87-page proposal presenting a supplier's plan to supply parts to a military aircraft manufacturer. After the group brainstorms and plans the proposal, a project director delegates responsibility for the research and origination of particular sections of the proposal. Finally, one person compiles all the sections, creates many of the preliminary and addenda parts, and produces and distributes the final product.

Let us examine a few parts of a variety of proposals to see how they might eventually fit into a total proposal.

PROBLEM AND/OR PURPOSE

Problem and *purpose* are often used as interchangeable terms in reports. Study this introductory statement, called "Project Description," in a proposal by a firm to contribute to an educational project:

Project Description

Mainline Community College has invited business and industry to participate in the creation of *Business Communication*, a television course and video training package. These materials will provide effective training in business communication skills to enhance the performance of individuals in business and contribute to organizational skills and profitability. In our rapidly evolving information society, skill in communication is integral to success.

Many government agencies award contracts and orders to companies that submit the most desirable proposals. To earn contracts in this highly competitive market, managers quickly learn to prepare proposals that are well-written, detailed, and effectively organized.

Note how the heading "Project Description" has been used in place of "Purpose." In the following opening statement, "Problem" is used as the heading:

Problem

The Board of Directors of Heatherington Village Association has requested a proposal for total management and operation of its 1,620-unit permanent residential planned development. This proposal demonstrates the advantages of using Central Management Corporation in that role.

The purpose of the proposal may be listed as a separate heading (in addition to "Problem") when the proposal intends to include objectives of a measurable nature. When you list objectives such as "To reduce overall expenses for maintenance by 10 percent," attempt to list measurable and attainable objectives and list only enough to accomplish the purpose of selling your proposal. Many proposals are rejected simply because writers promise more than they can actually deliver.

Ethical Issue: When writing a proposal, promise only what you can deliver.

SCOPE

When determining the scope of your proposal, you can place limits on what you propose to do or on what the material or equipment you sell can accomplish. The term *scope* need not necessarily be the only heading for this section. "Areas Served," "Limitations to the Study," and "Where XXX Can Be Used" are examples of headings that describe the scope of a proposal. Study this "scope" section from a consulting firm's proposal to conduct a salary survey:

COMMUNICATION MENTOR

We've learned over the years that a written document, and especially a proposal, faces a great deal of competition for the reader's attention. It must compete, first of all, with other proposals; then it must compete with all other papers on the reader's desk, ringing telephones, visitors, and many other distractions. This document, which we may have labored over for weeks, might get five minutes of the reader's attention. Thus, above all, the proposal must be cleanly written: very easy to read, free of jargon and buzz words, and to the point!

H. Devon Graham, Jr.
Southwest Regional Managing Partner
Arthur Andersen & Co.

Are problem, purpose, and scope related and introductory?

What the Study Will Cover

To assist ABDEC, Inc., in formulating its salary and benefits program for executives, Property Appraisers, Inc., will include an analysis of compensation (salary and benefits) for no fewer than 20 of ABDEC's contemporaries in the same geographic region. In addition to salaries, insurance, incentives, deferred compensation, medical, and retirement plans will be included. Additionally, Property Appraisers, Inc., will make recommendations for ABDEC's program.

Another statement of scope might be as follows:

Scope

Leading figures in business and industry will work with respected academicians and skilled production staff to produce fifteen 30-minute television lessons that may be used in courses for college credit or as modules dealing with discrete topics for corporate executives.

METHOD AND PROCEDURES

After scope tells "what," method tells "how" the research was conducted.

The method used to solve the problem or to conduct the business of the proposal should be spelled out in detail. In this section, simply think through all the steps necessary to meet the terms of the proposal and write them in sequence. When feasible, you should include a time schedule to indicate when the project will be completed.

MATERIALS AND EQUIPMENT

For large proposals, such as construction or research and development, indicate the nature and quantities of materials and equipment to be used. In some cases, several departments will contribute to this portion. When materials and equipment constitute a major portion of the total cost, include prices. Much litigation arises when clients are charged for "cost overruns." When contracts are made on the basis of "cost plus XX percent," the major costs of materials, equipment, and labor/personnel must be thoroughly described and documented.

QUALIFICATIONS AND RECOMMENDATIONS

Assuming your proposal is acceptable in terms of services to be performed or products to be supplied, your proposal must convince the potential buyer that you have the expertise to deliver what you have described and you are a credible individual or company. Therefore, devote a section to presenting the specific qualifications and special expertise of the personnel involved in the proposal. You may include past records of the bidder and the recommendations of its past customers, and the proposed cost. Note how the brief biography of the principal members in the following excerpt from a proposal contributes to the credibility of the proposer:

Following "what" and "how," proposals describe "who."

Principals

Engagement Principal: Harold M. Jones, M.B.A., M.A.I. Partner in Property Appraisers, Inc., consulting appraisers since 1974. Fellow of the American Institute of Appraisers, B.A., M.B.A., Harvard University. Phi Kappa Phi and Beta Gamma Sigma honorary societies. Lecturer and speaker at many realty and appraisal conferences and at the University of Michigan.

In another related section, the proposal might mention other work performed:

Major Clients of Past Five Years

City of Denver, Colorado; Dade County, Florida; City of San Francisco, California; City of Seattle, Washington; Harbor General Corporation, San Francisco; Gulf and Houston, Incorporated, Houston, Texas. Personal references are available on request.

FOLLOW-UP AND/OR EVALUATION

Although your entire proposal is devoted to convincing the reader of its merit, clients are frequently concerned about what will happen when the proposed work or service is completed. Will you return to make certain your work is satisfactory? Can you adjust your method of research as times change?

Follow-up and evaluation provide feedback.

If your proposal is for a research grant, do not promise more than you can deliver. Not all funded research proves to be successful. If you propose to make a study in your firm's area of expertise, you may be more confident. A public accounting firm's proposal to audit a company's records need not be modest. The accountant follows certain audit functions that are prescribed by the profession. However, a proposal that involves providing psychological services probably warrants a thoughtful follow-up program to evaluate the service.

BUDGET, COST, AND SUMMARY

The budget or cost of the program should be detailed when materials, equipment, outside help, consultants, salaries, and travel are to be included. A simple proposal for service by one person might consist of a statement such as "15 hours at $200/hour, totaling $3,000, plus mileage and expenses estimated at $550." Present the budget or cost after the main body of the proposal.

THINK IT OVER
In selling, do you introduce price after you have convinced the reader to buy?

In addition to a cost or budget, you might conclude the proposal with a summary. This summary may also be used to open the total proposal to put it in deductive sequence.

Summary - Optional; If lengthy.

Most work resulting from proposals is covered by a working agreement or contract to avoid discrepancies in the intents of the parties. In some cases, for example, users of outside consultants insist that each consultant be covered by a sizable general personal liability insurance policy that also insures the company. Many large firms and governmental organizations use highly structured procedures to assure understanding of contract terms.

ADDENDA ITEMS

When certain supporting material is necessary to the proposal but would make it too bulky or detract from it, include the material as addenda items. A bibliography and an appendix are examples of addenda items. References used should appear in the bibliography or as footnotes. Maps, questionnaires, letters of recommendation, and similar materials are suitable appendix items.

Sample Short Proposal

A short, informal proposal that includes several of the parts previously discussed is shown in Figure 17-8. This proposal consists of three major divisions: "The Problem," "Proposed Course of Instruction," and "Cost." The "Proposed Course of Instruction" section is divided into five minor divisions to facilitate understanding.

Wanting to increase the chances of securing the contract, the writer made sure the proposal was highly professional and had the impact needed to get the reader's attention. In other words, the writer wanted the proposal to "look" as good as it "sounds." To add to the overall effectiveness of the proposal, the writer incorporated appealing, but not distracting, page-design features. Printing the proposal with a laser printer using proportional fonts of varying sizes and styles resulted in a professional appearance and an appealing document. The reader's positive impression of the high standards exhibited in this state-of-the-art proposal is likely to influence his or her confidence in the writer's ability to present the proposed communication seminar.

PROPOSAL FOR STAFF DEVELOPMENT SEMINAR: INTERPERSONAL COMMUNICATION SKILLS FOR SUPERVISORY AND MIDDLE MANAGEMENT

by Rebecca E. Avery, Staff Development Coordinator

September 1, 19--

The Problem

Management has perceived a need for improved communication performance on the part of supervisory and middle-management personnel to strengthen relationships among them and their employees. The proposed training course is designed to help participants develop effective interpersonal communication skills.

Proposed Course of Instruction

Based on our experience, the following concepts should be effective in improving understanding and improved performance:

Teaching-Learning Method

The acquisition of interpersonal skills results from an activity-oriented training program where participants apply theory through role playing, case discussion, and feedback.

In this approach, the instructor is a learning facilitator rather than a lecturer. Frequent use of video feedback accompanied by instructor and group feedback reinforces learning.

Content

The following topics constitute the content core of the program:

- Perception and self-concept.
- A positive communication climate.
- Sending, receiving, and nonverbal skills.
- Reducing communication barriers.
- Resolving conflict.
- Interviewing.
- Small-group communication.

[1] Describes the nature of the problem and presents the proposed plan as a solution to the problem.

[2] Uses headings to aid the reader in understanding the organization of the proposal. Larger, boldface font adds emphasis.

[3] Describes the course content, instructional method, and design in detail. Divides the "Proposed Course of Instruction" section into five minor divisions for easier comprehension.

[4] Uses bullets to highlight components of the course content.

FIGURE 17-8   Short proposal in memorandum format, page 1.

5 Includes a subsequent-
page heading to identify
the second page. The
horizontal line is added
to increase the profes-
sional appearance.

6 Itemizes costs so the
reader understands
exactly how the total cost
was calculated. Disclosing
this detailed breakdown
gives the reader confi-
dence that the cost is
accurate.

---

5 **Staff Development Proposal**   **September 1, 19--**

Learning Materials

Because participants seem to feel more comfortable when they have a
textbook to guide them, we use the Verderber book, *Interact*. Additionally, case problem handouts are provided for role playing and
discussion.

Length of Course

This course consists of 12 two-hour sessions over a six-week period.

Number of Participants

Because of the activity orientation of the program, a maximum of 12
participants is desirable.

Cost

All teaching-learning materials will be provided by us and include
textbooks, handouts, and video camera and recorder. Based on a 12-
session, 12-participant program, the total cost is $2,172. When two
courses are offered on the same day, the total cost is reduced to
$4,200. Exact charges:

6 *Interact* (12 copies @ $25)	$ 300
Case Problem Handouts (12 copies at $6)	72
Professional Fees (24 hours' instruction at $75/hr., travel, meals, and lodging)	1,800
Total	$2,172

FIGURE 17-8   Short proposal in memorandum format, page 2.

COMMUNICATION IN ACTION

Jim Ratchford,
Cherry, Bekaert & Holland

Jim Ratchford knows the value of having specialized accounting knowledge. He earned his CPA after graduation from Appalachian State University and has worked since 1979 with Cherry, Bekaert & Holland, a regional top 30 accounting firm headquartered in Richmond, Virginia, with offices throughout the Southeast. More than having technical accounting knowledge, Ratchford also understands that successful accounting firms must communicate well with clients by selling ideas and services through proposals.

"The first inside look a prospective client often gets of our firm is the proposal," Ratchford observes. "These proposals usually determine whether we secure the account or even get on a short list." Increasingly, his firm secures work through the bidding process, which has directed the firm toward greater specialization and competitiveness. "Cost consciousness and government requirements drive this process," he explains. "We work primarily through the bid process." As a result, Ratchford's firm emphasizes the kinds and quality of proposals they submit to prospective clients.

Cherry, Bekaert & Holland secures a large volume of governmental work with cities, counties, and local school boards. Typically, these proposals include "hot buttons," which are current accounting changes, terminology, or issues of interest to the client. "The firm that knows the market and knows the industry has an advantage over other firms," Ratchford explains. "For instance, a client may be aware of a new accounting pronouncement. If our firm bids on a job for that client, we must communicate our knowledge of that pronouncement in the proposal."

At Ratchford's firm, proposal formats vary little and are usually determined by the RFP. Governmental RFPs follow a highly structured and standardized format. "Depending on the size of the client and the fees involved, proposal formats are similar," he says. "Basically, prospective clients want to know the background and qualifications of our firm, our audit strategies, who will work on the audit, and what it will cost. In addition, we always include resumes of the engagement team," Ratchford says. "The main item of interest to the prospective client is the cost and the number of hours involved."

During the 40 years Cherry, Bekaert & Holland has been in business, writing proposals and communicating current changes through them has worked successfully. "The superstars in our firm are the ones who know more than technical accounting," he concludes. "They are the ones who can communicate and sell ideas and services."

Applying What You Have Learned

1. Why are proposals so important to Cherry, Bekaert & Holland?
2. Generate an idea for an unsolicited proposal you might write for providing a service in your chosen field (e.g., an architect major might develop a proposal for renovating an old building) or recommending a change in your work environment or your university (e.g., change in procedures or work schedule). Consider "hot buttons" or key issues in your field requiring specialized services that you could promote to a prospective client through an unsolicited proposal. Develop an outline for the proposal and describe briefly the information you would develop within each major section.

SUMMARY

1 As reports increase in length from one page to several pages, they also grow in formality with the addition of introductory and addenda items. As a result, reports at the formal end of the continuum tend to be repetitious. These report parts and their purposes are summarized below:

Preliminary Parts

Half-title Page (Title Fly)–contains title of report; adds formality.

Title Page–includes title, author, writer, and date; adds formality.

Authorization–provides written authorization to complete report.

Transmittal–presents the report to the reader and summarizes the conclusions or major points.

Contents–provides an overview of report and order in which information will be presented; contains headings and page numbers.

Figures–includes number, title, and page number of tables and graphics.

Executive Summary–summarizes essential elements in a report.

Report Text

Introduction–orients the reader to the topic and previews the major divisions.

Body–presents the information collected.

Summary–reviews main points presented in the body.

Conclusions–draws inferences based on the findings.

Recommendations–presents possible actions based on the conclusions.

Addenda

References–includes an alphabetical list of sources used in preparing the report.

Appendix–contains supplementary information that supports the report but placing this information in the report would make the report bulky and unmanageable.

Index–includes an alphabetical guide to the subjects in the report.

2 Organizing the content of a report involves seeing the report problem in its entirety and then breaking it into its parts. Because reports are written after the research or field work has been completed, writers may begin writing with any of the report parts and then complete the rough draft by putting the parts in logical order. Short reports usually are written in memorandum or letter format. They are called "short" because they simply are not long enough to require the many supporting preliminary and ending parts of longer reports. Nevertheless, short reports require the same organizing and writing skills as long reports.

3 Proposals call for thorough organization and require writing methods that will be not only informative but convincing. Proposals often are written by teams; in this way, they typify the nature of reports as having discrete parts that writers can prepare in any order and then assemble into whole reports.

REVIEW QUESTIONS

1. What four terms could probably be used as headings for many reports?
2. What is meant by the concept that as reports become longer they grow in formality?
3. List each of the parts of a formal report and briefly discuss the purpose of each one.
4. Discuss the proper format for arranging multiple-line titles for a report or graphic. Should a report title be presented in this style each time it is used in a report? Explain.
5. Provide guidelines for writing an effective report title.
6. How does a report writer determine which preliminary or addenda parts to include in a report?
7. How are the pages of the three sections (preliminary, report text, and addenda) of a report numbered?
8. Briefly discuss the primary principles involved in writing a transmittal.
9. Describe how word-processing software can be used to simplify production of the preliminary and addenda parts of a report.
10. Briefly discuss the primary principles involved in writing an executive summary. What are other names given to this preliminary report part?
11. Discuss the major items that should be included in an effective introduction.
12. Should new ideas be presented in the summary? Explain.
13. Distinguish between findings, conclusions, and recommendations. Can the report summary, conclusions, and recommendations be presented in separate sections, or must they be combined into one section? Explain.
14. Differentiate between a references page (works cited) and a bibliography (works consulted).
15. Explain how appendixes are identified when more than one appendix item is included. Must the writer mention each item within the report text?
16. Explain why a report comparing alternatives should be divided into sections that reflect the criteria used to judge the alternatives.
17. How does an inductive organization become deductive when applied to reports?
18. How do form reports increase the accuracy of information?
19. Discuss how using the computer to generate form reports can increase a company's efficiency and accuracy.
20. Discuss several features that are incorporated into a short report.
21. What factor(s) determines whether memorandum or letter format should be used for short reports?
22. What is the primary purpose of a proposal? What is meant by RFP?
23. What factor(s) allows a writer to begin writing a report or a proposal with any part of the report?
24. When a lengthy, complex proposal is prepared in industry, is the original writing done by one person? Explain.
25. Complete each of the THINK IT OVER activities that your instructor assigns.

E-MAIL APPLICATION

 Your instructor has provided detailed instructions for completing a short report or proposal in groups of three or four. Send your instructor a weekly progress report via e-mail. The report should contain the following information about each meeting held during the week: date, place, and duration of meeting; members present; report of work accomplished since the last meeting; brief description of work accomplished during the current meeting; and work allocated to be completed before the next meeting.

APPLICATIONS

Informational Reports

PROFESSIONAL DEVELOPMENT

1. **Summarizing a Professional Meeting.** Attend a professional meeting of a campus or community organization. Take notes on the program presented, the issues discussed, etc. Submit a report to your instructor summarizing the events of the meeting, and include a section that describes the benefits that might be derived from membership in that organization.

TECHNOLOGY

2. **Researching the Information Superhighway.** Read three articles on the information superhighway. Submit a report to your instructor that explains what it is, who its users are, and some of its potential applications.

CAREER DEVELOPMENT

3. **Evaluating a Career Field.** Select a career field in which you have some interest. Study government handbooks, yearbooks, and other materials that project the outlook of that career. Submit a report to your instructor that includes the following sections: (1) The career you have chosen with reasons, (2) the relative demand for that career over the next 5-10 years, and (3) the pay scale and other benefits that are typical of that career.

MANAGEMENT/Technology

4. **Auditing a Computer Lab.** Visit the computer lab on your campus. Through observation and interviews, prepare an audit report of the lab's offerings. Include the following items in your report: (1) The types of equipment available (e.g., IBMs and compatibles, Macs, mainframe terminals), (2) the number of each type, (3) the operating systems and applications software available (product, version). Submit the report to your instructor.

FINANCE

5. **Evaluating the Performance of a Stock Portfolio.** Select ten stocks listed on the New York Stock Exchange and reported in your daily newspaper or in *The Wall Street Journal*. Assume that you will purchase 100 shares of each of the ten stocks at the prices listed at the market close on a particular day. You are going to keep a record of changes in the stocks for a one-week period—five trading days.

Required: Submit a memorandum to your instructor on the purchase date reporting your ten stocks according to the following format:

Name of Stock Price per Share Total Cost (x 100)

At the end of the five-day period, submit another memorandum to your instructor detailing how your investments fared during the week. Record the Dow Jones Industrial Average of thirty stocks for both your purchase date and the end of the five-day period. Compare your total performance—percentage gain or loss—with that of the Dow Jones average.

Analytical Reports

MANAGEMENT/Technology   GMAT

6. **Protecting Against Computer Viruses.** Prepare a report on computer viruses and protection against their intrusion. Include the following parts in your report: (1) What are viruses and how do they function? (2) What is the risk from viruses? (3) What protective measures are available? End your report with a recommendation to your organization as to how to best protect itself from damage caused by computer viruses.

FINANCE   GMAT

7. **Comparing the Merits of Franchising vs. Starting an Independent Business.** You and a silent partner plan to open a restaurant in your town. You are unsure whether to obtain a franchise for a fast-food outlet or to start your own independent restaurant. A franchise for Stafford's, a solid organization similar to McDonald's, would yield about $50,000 a year for an owner who does not work actively in the operation and about $100,000 for one who does. Capital required is $150,000;

you have $50,000 and have made arrangements for the remainder from financing sources. The franchiser will supply initial staff training, the additional financing for the physical structure, and financial management advice. Stafford's has had few franchise failures; it operates on a percentage of the gross income of each franchise.

Required: Prepare a proposal for your intended silent partner that compares the options of franchising versus independent ownership. Make a recommendation as to the more desirable action to take.

MANAGEMENT   GMAT

8. **Assessing the Feasibility of Constructing a Recreational Complex.** Southport University has established a committee to study the feasibility of constructing a recreational center for students, faculty, and staff. To help determine the interest of faculty and staff, the committee has administered a questionnaire. The findings will be combined with other aspects of the feasibility study in a presentation to the president. The committee believes the 668-person sample is representative of the faculty and staff. The results of the survey follow:

1. On average, how often do you exercise each week?

   136   0-1 day
   274   2-3 days
   197   4-5 days
    61   6-7 days

2. During a week, in which of the following activities do you participate? Check all that apply.

   171   Aerobic exercise
   157   Jogging
   147   Weightlifting
   299   Walking
    67   Tennis
    42   Other

3. If you had access, in which of the following activities would you participate? Check all that apply.

   196   Racquetball
   361   Swimming
    72   Basketball
   126   Run or walk on an indoor track
   165   Exercise machines

4. If a recreation center were constructed for employees, what is the maximum amount you would be willing to pay *per month* to provide use of the center to your immediate family members?

   125   $0-$10
    69   $11-$20
   156   $21-$30
   261   $31-$40
    57   $41-$50

Required: As a member of the committee, prepare a short report for the president, Michelle Karratassos. You asked respondents to estimate the amounts they would be willing to pay a month for their family to use the center as $0 to $10, $11 to $20, and so on. If you were to do mathematical computations, you would probably use midpoints such as $5, $15.50, $25.50, and so on as values for each class. In this case, however, write in generalities simply using percentages. Measures of central tendency are not necessary.

CROSS-DISCIPLINE

9. **Preparing an Analytical Report.** Prepare a short report on the selection of an alternative in *one* of the following cases. Make any assumptions and create any background information needed to make an informed decision. Reviewing this list may help you identify a business-related problem you have encountered that you would like to investigate; evaluate possible alternative solutions, and make a recommendation.

MANAGEMENT/Technology   GMAT

a. Recommend one of three laptop computers for use by the company's sales representatives to update accounts, process orders, prepare sales proposals, etc. The computer must have the ability to connect by modem to the central office for transmitting daily reports.

FINANCE   GMAT

b. Recommend how you would invest $2 billion of excess cash that the company will not need until the plant expands in two more years.

MANAGEMENT/Technology   GMAT

c. Recommend a printer for a company installing a microcomputer-based information system.

The company will use the printer for both internal and external correspondence; some correspondence requires graphics.

HUMAN RESOURCES MANAGEMENT   GMAT

d. Recommend whether a bank should require its employees to wear uniforms.

MANAGEMENT/Technology   GMAT

e. As director of human resources, recommend the type of network configuration that would best serve the needs of the department's 26 employees. Your computers are presently not networked, and only three can access the company mainframe. Investigate the advantages and disadvantages of the star, ring, and bus configurations. Make a recommendation to upper management.

ACCOUNTING/Legal   GMAT

f. You and six other investors are considering opening a restaurant in your city. Determine the most desirable form of organization for your business: sole proprietorship, partnership, or corporation. Consider the legal, tax, and other implications of each alternative.

MANAGEMENT   GMAT

g. Your government agency has always purchased the automobiles used by its social workers. The cars are typically driven approximately 30,000 miles a year and are sold for about 10 percent of their purchase value at the end of three years. Consider the cost effectiveness of the current policy and a car dealer's offer to lease the cars. Recommend whether the agency should purchase or lease the automobiles.

MANAGEMENT/Technology   GMAT

h. One of your sales representatives has provided literature that claims a sales representative's productivity can increase by as much as 30 percent when a cellular telephone is used to make sales calls. Recommend whether the company should invest in the installation and use of cellular telephones.

MANAGEMENT   GMAT

i. A family-owned business, having had substantial growth, is considering WATS-line service. The company currently incurs $3,000 in long distance telephone charges a month. Evaluate the feasibility of the WATS-line service.

MANAGEMENT   GMAT

j. You have noticed a substantial increase in the number of employees who spend their lunch hour exercising at one of several health clubs in your community. Furthermore, your insurance agent has reported that claims of your company are increasing at less than the national average. Attributing this positive fact to your employees' commitment to physical fitness, you are considering either (1) installing exercise equipment in underutilized areas of your plant or (2) subsidizing membership dues. You are also thinking about extending the lunch hour to make exercising more convenient. Weigh the alternatives and make a recommendation.

MANAGEMENT   GMAT

k. As vice president of production, investigate whether introducing background music would improve productivity in a manufacturing environment.

MANAGEMENT/Technology   GMAT

l. Office support staff in each department of your company make all photocopies on convenience copiers in their departments. Weigh the benefits and expenses of establishing a central copy center.

CROSS-DISCIPLINE

10. **Analyzing Legal and Ethical Issues.** Select from the "Cases for Analysis" at the ends of Chapters 9-12 additional topics requiring research to solve a particular business problem. Turn to the appropriate case and read the complete case problem.

ACCOUNTING/Legal   GMAT

a. *Chapter 10, Case 3.* Determine what action is appropriate when an accountant has knowledge that a client has filed a fraudulent tax return. Use a formal framework for analyzing ethical issues. You must determine the ethical and legal implications of this case: What behavior is ethical according to the standards in the Code of Professional Conduct of the American Institute of Certified Public Accountants? What action, if any, does the Internal Revenue Service require? Communicate this analytical decision to your supervisor and the client.

MARKETING/Legal   GMAT

b. *Chapter 11, Case 1.* Identify the legal implications of using another person's photograph in a television advertisement. Write a memorandum to your supervisor providing a summary of your research to assure the supervisor that your actions are legally defensible. Based on your research, write the appropriate letter to the person whose photograph you wish to use.

MANAGEMENT/Ethics   GMAT

c. *Chapter 6, Case 1.* Analyze the dilemma of whether hiring the homeless to purchase concert tickets is ethical. Communicate this analytical decision to your business partner and write a news release to the general public (content will vary depending on your decision).

MANAGEMENT/Ethics   GMAT

d. *Chapter 6, Case 2.* Analyze the dilemma of whether management compensation should be restricted at the Golden Value Stores. Consult the case for specific information about the company's financial condition and compensation history and the document you are to write.

MANAGEMENT/Ethics   GMAT

e. *Chapter 6, Case 3.* Analyze the dilemma of whether reducing the quality of engine parts to cut costs is ethical. Communicate this analytical decision to two audiences: your supervisor and engineers or quality control personnel.

MANAGEMENT/Ethics   GMAT

f. *Chapter 6, Case 4.* Analyze the dilemma of whether replacing humans with robotics to cut

production costs is ethical. Communicate this analytical decision to the company president.

FINANCE/Ethics   GMAT

g. *Chapter 9, Case 1.* Analyze the ethical dilemma involved in accepting a boat captain's offer to make an "unapproved" charter that is sure to cinch several sizable investment clients. Then communicate this analytical decision to superiors.

MANAGEMENT/Ethics   GMAT

h. *Chapter 9, Case 3.* Determine whether prior products produced with less-than-adequate materials should be recalled using a formal framework for analyzing ethical issues. Then communicate this analytical decision to superiors.

ACCOUNTING/Ethics   GMAT

i. *Chapter 10, Case 3.* See description in Item a.

MARKETING/Ethics   GMAT

j. *Chapter 11, Case 2.* Using a formal framework for analyzing ethical issues, determine whether a company's donating bottled water to U.S. military troops stationed abroad as a public relations maneuver is ethical. Then communicate this analytical decision to supervisors and/or to the public in a news release.

ACCOUNTING/Ethics   GMAT

k. *Chapter 12, Case 3.* Analyze the dilemma of whether overlooking a vendor's error to your advantage is ethical. Then communicate this analytical decision to superiors.

Proposals

MARKETING/Public Sector

11. **Bidding for a Convention Site.** The National Insurance Appraisers Association is planning an upcoming convention. This association of 500 members conducts a three-day conference during late October that includes at least one general session and as many as five breakout groups

of 50-75 participants. The chair of this group's convention site committee has invited your city to submit a proposal bidding for the convention's 1999 national convention.

Required: As the executive director of the Economic Development Council, write a proposal including specific information to convince the group that your city can provide the needed meeting facilities, hotel accommodations, economical transportation from major U.S. cities, and a variety of social and recreational activities for members and guests.

MANAGEMENT

12. **Applying for a Franchise to Open a Miniature Golf Course.**   Interested in opening a miniature golf course, Vicente Cruz wrote Treasure Island, Inc., a franchiser of a popular miniature course, soliciting franchise information. In answer to his request, Vicente received an extremely receptive letter requesting standard information designed to help Treasure Island determine the economic viability of the proposed location. After analyzing this preliminary information, Treasure Island will decide whether to accept Vicente's franchise application.

    Treasure Island has requested preliminary information regarding the economic and social environment of the proposed site. Specifically, Vicente must provide valid, objective data concerning the population of the service area, the economic status of the population, the impact of the climate on the operation of an outdoor business, the nature and extent of competing entertainment businesses, the local tourist industry, and any other information that would support the economic success of the proposed franchise.

Required: As Vicente Cruz, prepare a proposal to the franchiser. Address it to Treasure Island, 9700 Gulfside Drive, Pensacola, FL 32501-9700.

MANAGEMENT/Technology

13. **Proposing to Install an Office System.**   As sales manager of Office Innovations, you are preparing a proposal to automate the Mortgage Department of City National Bank. The Mortgage Department consists of five office support staff, who prepare all mortgage forms and correspondence manually. Five loan officers advise customers on the implications of selecting various options available in making the loan such as interest rate, points, fixed versus variable rates, and term.

Required: Write a proposal that includes the following information: (1) an explanation of how the system described in your proposal would increase the efficiency and effectiveness of the Mortgage Department; (2) complete specifications for the hardware and software you believe will solve the Mortgage Department's problem; (3) a description of the installation procedures including a time line, if necessary, and the training included with the purchase; and (4) a budget for each item proposed in the system.

CASES FOR ANALYSIS

MANAGEMENT/Technology   GMAT

Case 1.   Are Cellular Telephones Affecting Sales at Cannon Engineering?   Today you received the following electronic message from the president and CEO concerning the impact of cellular telephones on gross profit. Firmly convinced that cellular telephones can increase the company's financial picture, you decide to take a closer look at last quarter's sales activity. Specifically, you want to compare the sales performance of each sales representative with his/her use of the cellular telephone. Hopefully, this analysis will help explain the decrease in gross profits and give you the objective evidence you need to convince Mr. Cannon to change his mind.

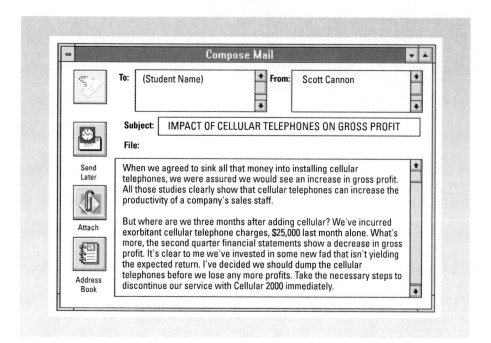

Required:

1. Study the accompanying spreadsheet carefully.
2. Compute the following calculations to help you analyze the data. To increase your efficiency, use an electronic spreadsheet. If software is not available, compute these calculations manually.
   a. Calculate the increase or decrease in gross profit from the first to second quarter without considering the effect of the cellular telephones. Multiply the difference between first- and second-quarter sales by the company's 20-percent gross profit rate.
   b. Calculate the increase or decrease in gross profit including the cost of cellular telephones. Calculate the difference between the first- and second-quarter gross profit.
   c. Calculate the total of each column.
   d. Sort the information in the table in ascending order by each sales representative's telephone minutes.

```
  H 4: +D14*0.2-F14                                                READY
```

	A	B	C	D	E	F	G	H
1	Cannon Engineering							
2	Analysis of Sales by Sales Representative							
3	for the Two Quarters Ended June 30, 19--							
4								
5	Sales Representative		Net Sales		Cellular Phone		Gross Profit	
6			First	Second	Phone		First	Second
7	Number	Name	Quarter	Quarter	Minutes	Cost	Quarter	Quarter
8								
9	14	Davis, S.	$55,200	$78,600	4.190	$2,724	$11,040	$12,997
10	5	Evans, C.	$64,100	$84,900	7,895	$5,132	$12,820	$11,848
11	12	Franks, F.	$62,300	$61,200	1,322	$859	$12,460	$11,381
12	16	Greco, B.	$58,600	$60,400	917	$596	$11,720	$11,484
13	18	Holt, J.	$64,700	$62,200	480	$312	$12,940	$12,128
14	8	Milliard, P.	$63,600	$82,800	3,390	$2,204	$12,720	$14,357
15	9	Peters, R.	$60,600	$77,200	7,745	$5,034	$12,120	$10,406
16	6	Reategui, V	$52,300	$69,500	8,802	$5,721	$10,460	$8,179
17	10	Schwartz, W.	$58,500	$53,000	475	$309	$11,700	$10,291
18	21	Stephens, R.	$52,700	$58,100	800	$520	$10,540	$11,100
19	11	Wang, J.	$65,300	$84,900	3,922	$2,549	$13,060	$14,431

3. Prepare a combination bar-line chart using the spreadsheet completed in Step 2 or graphics software. If spreadsheet or graphics software is *not* available, your instructor will provide you with a printed copy of the graph. Follow these instructions to prepare the graph:

x-axis	Identify each salesperson by number. Begin at the left, listing staff in ascending order according to cellular telephone use.
y-axis, left side	Plot the change in gross profit from the first to second quarter excluding and including cellular telephone costs; use comparative (multiple-range) bars.
y-axis, right side	Plot cellular telephone use in thousands of minutes using a line graph.

Input a descriptive title for the graph labels (x-axis and y-axis, left and right), and a legend (identify the data shown in the two bars and the line). Input an explanatory note denoting the installation of cellular telephone use at the beginning of the second quarter.

4. Analyze the data in the graph prepared in Step 3 to determine the impact of cellular telephones on gross profit.

5. Write a short memorandum report explaining your analysis to Mr. Cannon. Integrate the graph into the memo to support your recommendation.

CHAPTER 18

WRITING A

FORMAL REPORT

OBJECTIVES

When you have completed Chapter 18, you will be able to

1 Specify writing techniques that enhance the credibility and formal writing style of a report.

2 Identify formal report-writing procedures that are effective for you.

3 Use appropriate levels of headings.

4 Use appropriate documentation methods.

5 Write effective formal reports in an acceptable format and writing style.

"Aliens Meet with President, Discuss World Takeover"; "Bat-Boy Found in New Mexico Cave"; "Woman Gives Birth to Pig"; "Devil's Skull Found in Australia." These are just a few of the outrageous (and humorous) tabloid headlines you can read while standing in a checkout line of a grocery store. The headlines are often accompanied with "actual" photos: the president shaking hands with an "alien," a photo of a child whose ears have been rotated to resemble bat ears, or a cow's skull modified to suit Satan himself. When people read those headlines, they laugh because they know the headlines simply are not true. The photos are supposed to be proof that the stories are true, but even a child can tell that the illustrations are bogus. The authors of these tales have no documentation to support their claims, so they make their own support. Hopefully, absolutely no one believes them.

When you write reports, often you will need to conduct research to find quotes, statistics, or ideas from others to back up your own ideas. This information is called *support*; the outside sources serve to bolster or support your research as well as your credibility. Doing research and taking notes, however, are only parts of the process of putting together a well-documented, acceptable report. Whenever you use ideas, thoughts, words, or statistics that were generated by someone other than yourself, you must document that information accurately. Most companies have a style manual that gives examples of acceptable formats for documentation and assembly of reports. Take care to read your company's manual thoroughly, be sure to document your report carefully, and assemble all its parts into a cohesive and attractively formatted final document.

WRITING A CONVINCING AND EFFECTIVE FORMAL REPORT

LEARNING OBJECTIVE 1

After you have solved a problem, the next step is to write a convincing, unbiased report. The report must also adhere to the principles of formal writing style.

Guidelines for Enhancing Credibility

Readers are more likely to accept your research as valid and reliable if you have designed the research effectively and collected and interpreted the data in an objective, unbiased manner. The following writing suggestions will enhance your credibility as a researcher as well:

1. *Avoid emotional terms.* "The increase was fantastic" doesn't convince anyone. However, "The increase was 88 percent—more than double that of the previous year" does convince.
2. *Identify assumptions.* Assumptions are things or conditions taken for granted. However, when you make an assumption, state that clearly. Statements such as "Assuming all other factors remain the same, . . ." informs the reader of an important assumption.
3. *Label opinions.* Facts are preferred over opinion, but sometimes the opinion of a recognized professional is the closest thing to fact. "In the opinion of legal counsel, . . ." lends conviction to the statement that follows and lends credence to the integrity of the writer.

Use sound sources; readers may check your references.

4. *Use documentation.* Citations and references (works cited) are evidence of the writer's scholarship and honesty. These methods acknowledge the use of secondary material in the research.

COMMUNICATION MENTOR

Objectivity is critical to all research and reports. Report writers demonstrate objectivity in their organization and writing style. Objectivity is enhanced by avoiding the use of emotional or persuasive terms and first-person pronouns. Opinions or judgments always must be identified as such. The presentation of definitions early in the report and the recognition of underlying assumptions will assist the reader in understanding the message.

Bernard J. Fountain
1993 President, Appraisal Institute

Writing Style for Formal Reports

The writing style of long, formal reports differs from the personal style used when writing memorandums, letters, and short reports. The following suggestions should be applied when writing a formal report:

1. *Avoid first-person pronouns as a rule.* In formal reports, the use of *I* is generally unacceptable. Because of the objective nature of research, the fewer personal references you use the better. However, in some organizations the first person is acceptable. Certainly, writing is easier when you can use yourself as the subject of a sentence. People who can change their writing by avoiding the use of the first person will develop a genuine skill.

2. *Use active voice.* "Authorization was received from the IRS" might not be so effective as "The IRS granted authorization." Subjects that can be visualized are advantageous, but you should also attempt to use the things most important to the report as subjects. If "authorization" were more important than "IRS," the writer should stay with the first version.

3. *Use tense consistently.* Because you are writing about past actions, much of your report writing is in the past tense. However, when you call the reader's attention to the content of a graphic, remember that the graphic *shows* in the present tense. If you mention where the study *will take* the reader, use a future-tense verb.

4. *Use transition sentences to link sections of a report.* Because you are writing a report in parts, show the connection between those parts by using transition sentences. "Although several advantages accrue from its use, the incentive plan also presents problems" may be a sentence written at the end of a section stressing advantages and before a section stressing problems.

5. *Use a variety of coherence techniques.* Just as transition sentences bind portions of a report together, certain coherence techniques bind sentences together: repeating a word, using a pronoun, or using a conjunction. If such devices are used, each sentence seems to be joined smoothly to the next. These words and phrases keep you from making abrupt changes in thought:

COMMUNICATION   MENTOR

Your personal success is dependent not just on what you know, but on how well you can convey that knowledge to others in an effective report. Ask yourself these questions about your report:

- Is it as concise as possible?
- Have I made valid assumptions about the readers?
- Are the key points readily identifiable?
- Does the report reveal fact, not feelings?
- Are emotional words avoided?
- Is the report error-free (remember even a grammatical error can cause the reader to question the content)?
- Is an executive summary needed? (My personal bias is *yes* if the report exceeds 15 pages.)

Shirley F. Olson
Vice President & Chief Financial Officer
J. J. Ferguson Sand and Gravel/Prestress/Precast

Time Connectors	Contrast Connectors
finally	although
further	despite
furthermore	however
initially	in contrast
meanwhile	nevertheless
next	on the other hand
since	on the contrary
then	yet
thereafter	
while	
at the same time	

Similarity Connectors	Cause-and-Effect Connectors
for instance	but
for example	conversely
likewise	as a result
in the same way	because
just as	consequently
similarly	hence
	therefore
	thus

Refer to Chapter 7, "Link Ideas to Achieve Coherence," to review a detailed discussion of coherence techniques.

6. *Use tabulations and enumerations.* When you have a series of items, give each a number or a bullet and list them consecutively. This list of writing

COMMUNICATION IN ACTION

James F. Hoobler, Ph.D.
U.S. Small Business Administration

In a place as large as Washington, D.C., Jim Hoobler simply cannot have one-to-one meetings with all the constituencies his office serves. As a result, written reports must fill the gap. Hoobler, Inspector General at the Small Business Administration (SBA), was appointed in 1991 by the President and confirmed by the Senate. As head of an independent office within the SBA, he reports directly to the Administrator of the SBA, but he is also held equally accountable by the U.S. Congress. The numerous reports his office produces *must* compete with large volumes of written materials from other departments in the Federal Government. Because of the *oversight* nature of the Office of Inspector General (OIG), Hoobler's reports are distributed widely.

Hoobler stresses the importance of audience analysis. "We target senior Government officials, including the head of the SBA, the director of the Office of Management and Budget (OMB), and Members of Congress. Typically, these policy-level officials will only read the executive summary," he said. "On the other hand, SBA program managers and Congressional and OMB staff officers will pick the report apart." In short, one has to place a premium on both accuracy and presentation.

"SBA's credibility is on the line every time we produce a report," Hoobler said. Consequently, he understands the importance of articulating findings clearly and writing sensible recommendations. "Consider our audit and inspection reports. They must be anchored in hard research with appropriate empirical support," he emphasizes. "In Washington, a report that does not make sense or is poorly or sloppily written will go to the bottom of the heap."

Hoobler's office has three principal functions: audit, evaluation (inspection), and investigation. Having responsibility for all auditing conducted within the SBA, his office shares its audit reports with a wide array of audiences. The Office of Inspector General also evaluates SBA's program performance in terms of its effectiveness and efficiency. As with audit reports, the target audiences for these evaluation or inspection reports include SBA employees and managers, small business men and women using SBA's services, Members of Congress, and other Government officials. In addition, Hoobler's office produces criminal investigation reports. These fact-based reports reach unique audiences in the U.S. Department of Justice; e.g., its legal divisions, the U.S. Attorneys, and the FBI, and form the basis for both criminal and civil prosecutions.

In stressing the importance of including the right parts of a report for the target audience, Hoobler tells how his investigative reports differ. "Our 'Best Practices' type of report, for example, is the end product of an extensive program evaluation. This report always features an executive summary—the section most read by our program managers." An evaluative report also reveals the details of the evaluation, including any supporting tables and appendices. While audit reports also include an executive summary, he notes that they differ in presentation by addressing a more specific problem, articulating any material findings, and offering recommendations for correcting any problem(s) uncovered.

On the investigative side of the OIG, Hoobler frequently presents evidence to the various U.S. Attorneys. "These reports are factual and, therefore, must be communicated clearly and be wholly defensible. Again, your credibility as a member of the law enforcement community is on the line. What you are trying to communicate must be crystal clear," Hoobler asserts. "If the prosecuting U.S. Attorney is mislead or gets the wrong impression, our office, investigator, and case lose credibility." Although the presentation may not be as formal as that found in an audit or an evaluation report, Hoobler also includes a summary in all investigative reports.

Applying What You Have Learned

1. How will a reader be affected by a sloppily written Small Business Administration report?
2. Explain how Hoobler adapted formal reports to various audiences.

suggestions is easier to understand because it contains numbered or bulleted items.

7. *Define terms carefully.* When terms might have specific meanings in the study, define them. Definitions should be written in the term-family-differentiation sequence: "A dictionary (*term*) is a reference book (*family*) that contains a list of all words in a language (*point of difference*)." "A sophomore is a college student in the second year." Refer to Chapter 15 for additional information on defining terms in a research study.

8. *Check for variety.* While you write, most of your attention should be directed toward presenting the right ideas and support. When reviewing the rough draft, you may discover certain portions with a monotonous sameness in sentence length or construction. Changes are easy and well worth the effort.

These stylistic techniques become habitual through experience; you can apply them while concentrating primarily on presenting and supporting ideas at the first-draft stage. Make necessary improvements later.

CREATING AN ENVIRONMENT CONDUCIVE FOR WRITING

A writing procedure that works well for one person may not work for another; however, consider the following general suggestions:

1. *Begin writing only after you have reached a conclusion and prepared a suitable outline.*
2. *Select a good writing environment.* Avoid distractions.
3. *Start planning early and give yourself more time than you anticipate using.* "Burning the midnight oil" is sometimes necessary, but it does not always produce your best work.

Writing a formal report is a major project. For the report to be a success, you must begin planning early, work at a steady pace, and allow time after you finish your draft to edit and rewrite. If you underestimate the amount of effort required (or overestimate your abilities), you may share the fate of the overconfident hare in the fable, losing the race to the slow-but-steady tortoise.

COMMUNICATION   MENTOR

Clear, effective writing is usually the result of a great deal of rewriting. Rarely is the first draft the best that writing can be. Use a first draft just to transfer mental notes to paper. Then edit and rewrite stringently. When you've reached the point where almost every word works as well as possible, leave the text alone for a while. Later, go back and see if you can still find improvements. The best writing is almost always a product of many revisions.

Cynthia Pharr
President & CEO
C. Pharr Marketing Communications

4. *Begin with an easy section.* The confidence gained from completing this section may help prepare you for more difficult ones.
5. *Set aside long, uninterrupted blocks of writing time.*
6. *Write rapidly and plan to revise later.* Do not attempt to edit as you go—you only waste time and lose your train of creative thought.
7. *Skip difficult places when composing and return to them later.* Usually you won't find these sections so difficult then.
8. *Set aside the first draft for a day or two. Editing and rewriting immediately may not pay off.* A report you have just written may look great; tomorrow you may see that it needs some improvement.
9. *Review for possible improvement.* Some points might need more supporting evidence. Reading your writing aloud reveals awkward grammatical construction and poor wording. Silent reading often misses these errors.
10. *Rewrite where necessary.* Rewriting is more than editing; sometimes you may have to rewrite weak material completely without reference to the original.

USING HEADINGS EFFECTIVELY

Headings are signposts informing readers about what text is ahead. Headings take their positions from their relative importance in a complete outline. For example, in a roman-numeral outline, "I" is a first-level heading, "A" is a second-level heading, and "1" is a third-level heading:

LEARNING OBJECTIVE 3

How do headings aid a reader in understanding a report?

    I. First-level Heading
        A. Second-level Heading
        B. Second-level Heading
            1. Third-level Heading
            2. Third-level Heading
    II. First-level Heading

Two important points about the use of headings also relate to outlines:

1. Because second-level headings are subdivisions of first-level headings, you should have at least two subdivisions (A and B). Otherwise, the first-level heading cannot be divided—something divides into at least two parts or it is

If an outline contains an "A," must it also contain a "B"?

not divisible. The same logic applies to the use of third-level headings following second-level headings.

2. All headings of the same level must be treated consistently—physical position on the page, and appearance (typestyle, underline), and grammatical construction as shown in Figure 18-1.

As you review Figure 18-1, note that one blank line precedes first- and second-level headings. This method is not universal; identify the format specified by the documentation style you are using and follow it consistently to aid the reader. A further suggestion, as you will observe in Figure 18-1 and in the sample report that follows, is to avoid placing two headings consecutively without any intervening text. For example, always write something following a first-level heading and before the initial second-level heading.

With word-processing programs, you can develop fourth- and fifth-level headings simply by using boldface, underline, and varying fonts. In short reports, however, organization rarely goes beyond third-level headings; thoughtful organization can limit excessive heading levels in formal reports.

DOCUMENTING REPORTS

A crucial part of honest research writing is documenting sources fairly and accurately. Although time consuming and tedious, meticulous attention to documentation marks you as a respected, highly professional researcher. The *Publication Manual of the American Psychological Association* (1994, p. 175) points out the importance of documentation with a forceful quote by K. F. Bruner: an inaccurate or incomplete reference "will stand in print as an annoyance to future investigators and a monument to the writer's carelessness."

An important first step is to pledge that you will not, for any reason, present someone else's ideas as your own. Then, develop a systematic checklist for avoiding plagiarism. Carelessly forgetting to enclose someone else's words within quotation marks or failing to paraphrase another's words can cause others to

Two consecutive headings with no intervening text is unacceptable.

Plagiarism can diminish your professional reputation and result in costly lawsuits. As a judgment in a plagiarism suit, Michael Bolton will pay the Isley Brothers $18 million for his hit "Love is a Wonderful Thing," an Isley Brothers' song he produced without giving them credit (DeRosa, 1994).

1 1/2" (Line 10)   **REPORT TITLE**
DS
      xxxxxxxxxxxxxxxxxxxxxxxxxxxxxxxxxxxxxxxxxxxxx xxxxxx xxxx
xxxxxxxxx xxxx xxxxxxxxx xxxxxxx. xxxxxxxx xxxxxxxx xxxxxxxxxxxxxxx
xxxxxxxx xxxxxx xxxxxxxxx xxxxxxxxx xxxxxxxx.
      xxxxxxxxxxxxxxxxxxxxxxxxxxxxxxxxxxxxxxxxxxxxx xxxxxxxx xxx
xxxxxxxxxxx xxxxxxxx xxxxxxx. xxxxxxxx xxxxxxxx xxxxxxxxxxxxxxx
xxxxxxxx xxxxxx xxxxxxxxx xxxxxx xxxxxxxxx.
DS
First-level Heading
DS
      xxxxxxxxxxxxxxxxxxxxxxxxxxxxxxxxxxxxxxxxxxxxx xxxxxxx xxxxx
xxxxxx xxxxx xxxxx xxxxx xxxxx xxxxxxxxx.
DS
<u>**Second-level Heading**</u>
      xxxxxxxxxxxxxxxxxxxxxxxxxxxxxxxxxxxxxxxx xxxxxxxxxx xxxxxxxxx
xxxxxx xxxxxxxxx xxxxxxx. xxxxxxxx xxxxxxxxxxxxxx xxxx.
DS
<u>**Second-level Heading**</u>
      xxxxxxxxxxxxxxx xxxxxxxxxxxxx xxxxxxxxxxxxxxxxxxxxxx xxxx xxxx
xxxxxxxx xxxxxxxxx xxxxx xxxxxxxxxxxxxx xxxxxxxx xxxxx.
      <u>**Third-level heading**</u>. xxxxxxxx xxxxxxxxxxx xxxxx xxxxx xxxx
xxxxxxxxxxxx xxxxxxxxxxxxx xxxx xxxxxxx xxxxxxxx.
      <u>**Third-level heading**</u>. xxxxxxxxxx xxxxxxxx xxxxxxxxx xxxxxx
xxxxxxxxxxx xxxxxxxxxxx xxxxxxxxxxxxxxx xxxxxxxxx. xxxxxxx
xxxx xxxxxxx.
DS
First-level Heading
      xxxxxxxxxxxxxxxxxxxxxxxxxxxxxxxxxx xxxxxxxxxxxxxxxxxxxxxxxxxx
xxxxxxxxxxxx xxxxxxxxxxxxxxxxx xxxxxxxxxxx xxxxx xxxx.

Approximately 1"

FIGURE 18-1   Effective headings formats for reports divided into three levels.

question your ethical conduct. When you feel that the tedious work required to document sources fairly and accurately is not worth the time invested, remind yourself of the following reasons for documentation:

1. *Citations give credit where it is due—to the one who created the material.* People who document demonstrate high standards of ethical conduct and responsibility in scholarship. Those exhibiting this professional behavior will gain the well-deserved trust and respect of peers and superiors.
2. *Documentation protects writers against plagiarism, which occurs when someone steals material from another and claims it as his or her own writing.*
3. *Documentation supports your statements.* If recognized authorities have said the same thing, your work takes on credibility; and you put yourself in good company.

THINK IT OVER
Discuss in your own words why you should document your research meticulously.

4. *Documentation can aid future researchers pursuing similar material.* Documentation must be complete and accurate so that the researcher can locate the source.

Many style guides are available to advise writers how to organize, document, and produce reports and manuscripts. Refer to Figure 15-4 for a list of the most popular authoritative style manuals.

The APA method is widely used in the social sciences.

The *Publication Manual of the American Psychological Association* (APA, 1994) has become the most-used guide in the social and soft sciences and in many scholarly journals. The *MLA Handbook for Writers of Research Papers* (Gibaldi, 1995) is another authoritative source in the humanities. In business reports and college papers, any of the various documentation methods is suitable. As you read professional literature and write business reports, you may need to become familiar with many methods.

Follow these general suggestions for preparing accurate documentation:

What guidelines will help you in documenting your report?

1. *Decide which authoritative reference manual to follow for preparing in-text parenthetical citations or footnotes (endnotes) and the bibliography.* Some companies and most journals require writers to prepare reports or manuscripts following a particular reference manual. Once you are certain you have selected the appropriate style manual, follow it precisely as you prepare the documentation and produce the report.
2. *Be consistent.* If you are carefully following a format, you shouldn't have a problem with consistency. For example, one style manual may require an author's initials in place of first name in a bibliography; another reference requires the full name. The placement of commas and periods and other information varies among reference manuals. Consult the manual, apply the rules methodically, and proofread carefully to ensure accuracy and consistency. If you cannot locate a format for an unusual source in the reference manual you are using, use other entries as a guide for presenting information consistently.
3. *Follow the rule that it is better to include more than enough than too little when you are in doubt about whether to include certain information.*

Citations

Two major types of citations are used to document a report: source notes and explanatory notes. Depending on the authoritative style manual used, these notes may be positioned in parentheses within the report, at the bottom of the page, or at the end of the report.

SOURCE NOTES

What are source notes?

Source notes acknowledge the contributions of others. These citations might refer readers to sources of quotations, paraphrased portions of someone else's words or ideas, and quantitative data used in the report. Source notes must include complete and accurate information so that the reader can locate the original source if desired.

EXPLANATORY NOTES

What are explanatory notes?

Explanatory notes are used for several purposes: (1) to comment on a source or to provide information that does not fit easily in the text, (2) to support a statistical table, or (3) to refer the reader to another section of the report. The following sample footnote describes the mathematics involved in preparing a table:

> *The weighted opinion was arrived at by assigning responses from high to low as 5, 4, 3, 2, 1; totaling all respondents; and dividing by the number of respondents.

In this case, the asterisk (*) was used rather than a number to identify the explanatory footnote both in the text and in the citation. This method is often used when only one or two footnotes are included in the report. If two footnotes appear on the same page, two asterisks (* *) or numbers or letters are used to distinguish them. An explanatory note that supports a visual or a source note that provides the reference from which data were taken appears immediately below the visual.

THINK IT OVER
How would you format an explanatory note explaining a specific figure in a visual?

Citation Methods

In-text parenthetical citations are the preferred citation method for source notes in business. The latest editions of the *Publication Manual of the American Psychological Association* (APA) and the *MLA Handbook for Writers of Research Papers* (MLA) require in-text parenthetical citations. You may use traditional citation methods—bottom-of-the-page and end-of-report—if you choose a documentation method that permits traditional citations (e.g., *MLA*, 3rd Edition). The major differences among the methods are presented in the following discussion.

IN-TEXT PARENTHETICAL CITATIONS

The *APA Manual, MLA Handbook,* and other documentation references eliminate separate footnotes or endnotes. Instead, an **in-text citation**, which contains abbreviated information within parentheses, directs the reader to a list of sources at the end of a report. The list of sources at the end contains all publication information on every source cited in a report. This list is arranged alphabetically by the author's last name or, if no author is provided, by the first word of the title (excluding articles). The reader uses the information in an in-text parenthetical citation to locate the original source in the list of sources.

The citations contain minimal information needed to locate the source in the complete list. In-text citations prepared using the *APA Manual* include the author's last name and the date of publication; the page number is included if referencing a direct quotation. The *MLA Handbook* includes the author's last name and the page number but not the date of publication. Note the following citations shown in APA and MLA style:

How does a citation help the reader locate a specific source? What information is included in an in-text parenthetical citation?

THINK IT OVER
Write an APA and MLA in-text parenthetical citation for your business communication text.

One author not named in the text, direct quotation

APA: "Good Ethics, simply, is good business . . . will attract good employees . . ." (Perrella, 1991, p. 7).

Include a page number only when referencing a direct quotation.

MLA: "Good ethics, simply, is good business . . . will attract good employees . . ." (Perrella 7).

THINK IT OVER
Write an in-text citation for the following source: Robock, S. H., & Simmons, K. (1983). International business and multinational enterprises (3rd ed.). Homewood, IL: Irwin. Assume the authors' names were not included in this paraphrased text.

Multiple authors or sources not included in the text

APA: These founders firmly believed . . . (Langley & White, 1994).

"A study of motivation. . . ." (Hansen et al., 1989, p. 21).

For sources by more than six authors, use et al. after the name of the first author. For works by fewer than six authors, cite all authors the first time the work is referenced; use "et al." for subsequent references.

MLA: These founders firmly believed . . . (Langley & White 25).

"A study of motivation. . . ." (Hansen et al. 21).

For sources by more than three authors, use et al. after the name of the first author.

More than one source documenting the same idea

APA: . . . as the reward (Yost, 1990; Correro, 1993).

MLA: . . . as the reward (Yost 25; Correro 56).

More than one source by the same author documenting the same idea

APA: Past research (Taylor, 1989, 1994) shows. . . .

MLA: Past research (Taylor, "Performance Appraisal" 6), ("Frequent Absenteeism" 89) shows. . . .

THINK IT OVER
Rewrite the Robock and Simmons citation assuming the authors' names are mentioned in the text.

Reference to author(s) or date in the text

APA: Marshall McLuhan (1965) coined the phrase. . . .

In 1991, Smith and Brown concluded. . . .

MLA: Marshall McLuhan coined the phrase . . . .

In 1991, Smith and Brown concluded . . . (31).

Omit a page number when citing a one-page article or nonprint sources.

No author provided

APA: . . . guidelines for effective writing ("A Case for Clear," 1992).

MLA: . . . guidelines for effective writing ("A Case for Clear" 3).

One of two or more works by the same author(s) in the same year

APA: Taylor (1994a) advocated. . . .

MLA: Taylor ("Performance Appraisal" 6) advocated. . . .

BOTTOM-OF-THE-PAGE CITATION METHOD

Placing citations at the bottom of the page on which they are cited is the **bottom-of-the page citation method.** It is often referred to as the *traditional method* because of its long use. The reader can conveniently refer to the source if the documentation is positioned at the bottom of the page. An example of a traditional footnote documenting a direct quotation using MLA style (3rd Edition) follows:

Bottom-of-the-Page Citation (Footnote)—MLA Style

"In a Total Quality Management context, the standard for determining quality is meeting customer requirements and expectations the first time and every time."[1]

———————

[1]V. Daniel Hunt, Managing for Quality (Homewood, Ill.: Business One Irwin, 1993) 15.

The APA method does not permit the use of footnotes or endnotes.

Review the citations for a variety of publications using the Modern Language Association (MLA) style (3rd Edition) shown in Figure 18-2. Although MLA style (4th Edition) *requires* in-text parenthetical citations, you may use traditional bottom-of-the-page citations when following MLA style (3rd Edition).

Sophisticated word-processing programs have changed the tedious task of preparing footnotes to a simple matter of instructing the computer to create a footnote. The software inserts the superscript number identifying the footnote and provides a special footnote-entry screen for keying the footnote. The software calculates how much space is needed at the bottom of each page for the footnotes and paginates each page automatically. The software also renumbers the notes automatically any time you add, delete, or move footnotes. The procedures for creating a footnote are illustrated in Figure 18-3.

THINK IT OVER
If you have not learned to use the automatic footnoting feature of your word-processing software, take the time to master that feature now.

END-OF-REPORT CITATION METHOD

The **end-of-report citation method** lists all citations in a list called "Notes" at the end of a report. A list of citations at the end of a report is obviously easier to prepare than footnotes. However, readers will be forced to turn to the end of a report rather than glance at the bottom of the page to locate a source.

End-of-report citations or endnotes are listed in the order in which citations appear in a report. Indicate the in-text citation by placing a superscript number above the text line as in the bottom-of-the-page method. The 4th Edition of the *MLA Handbook* does not allow endnotes. Examples of the citation within the text and the endnote formatted in MLA style (3rd Edition) follow:

Endnotes appear at the end of a report in the order the citations (superscripted numbers) appear in the report.

Citation Within Text

[2]
"In a Total Quality Management context, the standard for determining quality is meeting customer requirements and expectations the first time and every time."[1]

Endnotes—MLA Style (3rd edition)

NOTES

[1]V. Daniel Hunt, Managing for Quality (Homewood, Ill.: Business One Irwin, 1993) 15.

FIGURE 18-2
Traditional footnotes, MLA style
(3rd Edition).

Guide to Preparing Traditional Footnotes
MLA Style (3rd Edition)

A book reference with two authors and edition

Stefan Hyman Robock and Kenneth Simmons, <u>International Business and Multinational Enterprises</u>, 3rd ed. (Homewood: Irwin, 1983) 107.

[For more than three authors, use et al. (meaning "and others") after the name of the first author.]

An edited book

Frederick D. S. Chi, ed., <u>Handbook of International Accounting</u> (New York: J. Wiley, 1991) 15-17.

A chapter in a book or section within a reference book

Stephen R. Covey, "Habit 4 Think Win/Win," <u>The 7 Habits of Highly Effective People</u> (New York: Simon & Schuster, 1989) 204.

"Northland Cranberries, Inc.," <u>Standard & Poor's Corporation Records</u>, vol. 4 (New York: Standard & Poor's), 1994.

A report, brochure, or book from a private organization, corporate author

Wal-Mart Stores, Inc., <u>Annual Report</u> (Bentonville: Wal-Mart Stores, 1994) 8-9.

<u>Common Sense & Everyday Ethics</u> (Washington: Ethics Resource Center, 1980) 7-9.

A periodical article paginated by issue

Gordon Shea, "A Case for Clear Writing," <u>Training & Development</u> 46.1 (1992): 63-66.

A periodical article without an author

"How to Interview, Hire, and Bring New Employees on Board," <u>Supervisory Management</u> May 1994: 7-8.

An article in a newspaper

Lisa Brenner, "The Job Outlook for Current Graduates," <u>The New York Times</u> 12 June 1994: 14WC, p. 1.

A government publication

Equal Employment Opportunity Commission, <u>Minorities and Women in Institutions of Higher Education</u> (Washington: EEOC, 1991) 2.

Unpublished interviews and letters

Richard L. Wang, personal interview, 27 June 1994.

M. Allen Kline, letter to Donna Carlson, 31 Nov. 1994.

Article from online source

Format is not available in 1988 <u>MLA Handbook</u>; adapt the bibliographic entry on p. 602.

Abstract on CD-ROM

Format is not available in 1988 <u>MLA Handbook</u>; adapt the bibliographic entry on p. 602.

Computer software

<u>Microsoft Word 6.0</u>, computer software, Microsoft Corporation, 1994.

Films, filmstrips, slide programs, and videotapes

<u>Communicating Nondefensively</u>, videocassette, CRM Films, 1994.

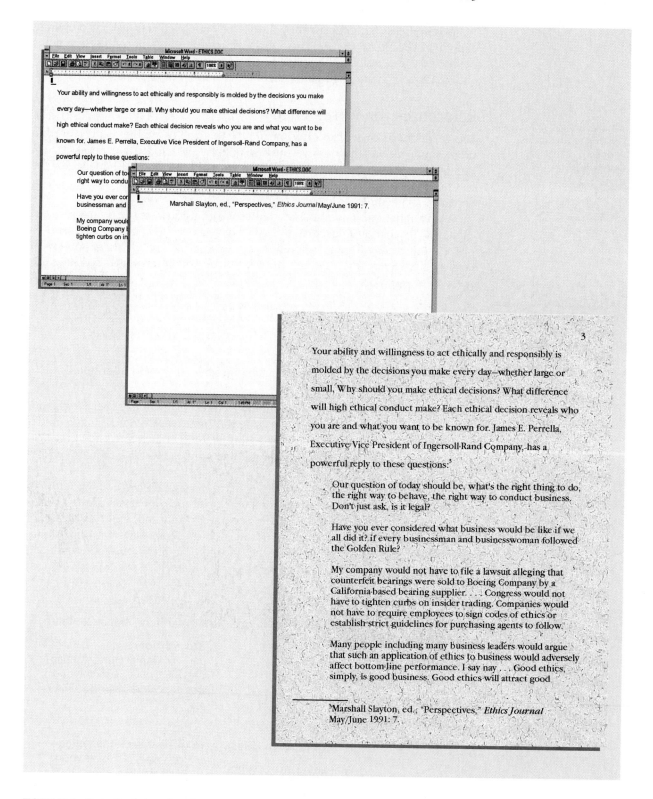

FIGURE 18-3   Footnoting feature of word-processing software simplifies report documentation.

Word-processing software programs have simplified the task of preparing endnotes. The process is similar to that of preparing bottom-of-the-page notes except that you instruct the software to print the endnotes in the correct sequence on a separate page rather than at the bottom of each page.

References (or Works Cited)

A bibliography is an alphabetized list of sources.

The **references** or **works cited** is an alphabetized list of the sources used in preparing a report. Each entry contains publication information necessary for locating the source. In addition, the bibliographic entries give evidence of the nature of sources the author consulted. *Bibliography* (literally "description of books") is sometimes used to refer to this list.

A researcher often uses sources that provide information but do not result in citations. To acknowledge that you may have consulted these works and to provide the reader with a comprehensive reading list, include these sources in the list of sources. The APA and MLA styles use different terms to distinguish between these types of lists:

How do APA and MLA distinguish between a list of sources cited in a report and a list of sources consulted?

	APA	MLA
Includes only sources cited	References	Works Cited
Includes works cited and consulted	Bibliography	Works Consulted

Your company guidelines or authoritative style manual may specify whether to list works cited only or works consulted. If you receive no definitive guidelines, use your own judgment. If in doubt, include all literature cited and read and label the page with the appropriate title so that the reader clearly understands the nature of the list.

As noted earlier, in-text parenthetical citations contain just enough information to locate the source in the list of sources (author's last name, date of publication, and sometimes page number). Footnotes and endnotes, on the other hand, include complete publishing information in a form different from bibliographic entries. Note the difference between the traditional footnote/endnote, in-text parenthetical citations, and bibliographic entries:

	APA	MLA
Footnote or endnote	Not acceptable	**4th Edition:** Not acceptable
		3rd Edition: [1]V. Daniel Hunt, <u>Managing for Quality</u> (Homewood: Business One Irwin, 1993) 15.
In-text paren-thetical citation	(Hunt, 1993)	(Hunt 15)
References	Hunt, V. D. (1993). <u>Managing for Quality</u>. Homewood, IL: Business One Irwin.	Hunt, V. Daniel. <u>Managing for Quality</u>. Homewood: Business One Irwin, 1993.

Three major differences exist between footnotes/endnotes and bibliographic entries:

1. Footnotes and endnotes are listed in the order in which they are cited in the text; bibliographic entries appear in alphabetical order.
2. Footnotes present given names of authors first; bibliographies use surnames first. In a bibliography, the alphabetical list of surnames aids the reader in locating an entry.
3. Bibliographic entries refer to the entire work cited and not simply to the specific page or pages from which the material came. Thus, an in-text citation or a footnote might cite a specific page, but the bibliographic entry includes the entire work. A bibliographic entry for a periodical includes the beginning and ending pages of the article.

To aid the reader in locating sources in lengthy bibliographies, include several headings denoting the types of publications documented; for example, books, articles, unpublished documents and papers, government publications, and nonprint media.

Bibliographic styles for a variety of publications prepared using the MLA style are shown in Figure 18-4. The same entries prepared using the APA style appear in Figure 18-5. Note that the APA format includes several distinct variations from the MLA and other traditional formats:

1. List the last names of all authors. Use initials for first and middle names. Use an ampersand (&) rather than "and" before the name of the last author in a series.
2. Place the date in parentheses after the author's name.
3. In titles of books and articles, capitalize only the first word of the title, the first word of the subtitle, and proper names. All other words begin with lowercase letters. In titles of journals, capitalize *all* significant words. Underline the titles of books and journals. Do not use quotation marks around the titles of articles.
4. Use a shortened form for the name of publishers. For example, omit "Co." and "Inc."
5. Double-space all entries. Indent the first line of each entry; begin subsequent lines at the left margin.

Word-processing programs can be used to convert the endnotes into a properly formatted reference list. Simply use the block command to make another copy of the endnotes page. By inputting the necessary revisions on the copy (change the title to "References," reverse the order of the authors' names, add page numbers, and so on), you avoid having to re-key all the publication information. Finally, use the sort feature to put the entries in alphabetical order by author's last name or the first word of the title if no author is provided.

ANALYZING A FORMAL REPORT

A complete, long report is illustrated following the chapter summary. The notations next to the text will help you understand how effective presentation and writing principles are applied. APA styles require that reports be

What are the major differences between footnotes/endnotes and entries for the references (works cited)?

Describe the major differences between APA references and MLA works cited entries.

What general procedures are used to convert footnotes/endnotes to bibliographic format? Look up the commands for your word-processing program.

LEARNING OBJECTIVE 5

FIGURE 18-4
Works cited, MLA style
(4th Edition).

Guide to Preparing Works Cited MLA Style (4th Edition)

A book reference with two authors and edition

Robock, Stefan Hyman, and Kenneth Simmons. International Business and Multinational Enterprises. 3rd ed. Homewood: Irwin, 1983.

[For more than three authors, use et al. (meaning "and others") after the name of the first author.]

An edited book

Chi, Frederick D. S., ed. Handbook of International Accounting. New York: J. Wiley, 1991.

A chapter in a book or section within a reference book

Covey, Stephen R. "Habit 4 Think Win/Win." The 7 Habits of Highly Effective People. New York: Simon & Schuster, 1989. 204-234.

"Northland Cranberries, Inc." Standard & Poor's Corporation Records. 6 vols. New York: Standard & Poor's Corp., 1994.

A report, brochure, or book from a private organization, corporate author

1994 Annual Report. Bentonville: Wal-Mart Stores, 1994.

Common Sense & Everyday Ethics. Washington: Ethics Resource Center, 1980.

A periodical article paginated by issue

Shea, Gordon. "A Case for Clear Writing." Training & Development 46.1 (1992): 63-66.

A periodical article without an author

"How to Interview, Hire, and Bring New Employees on Board." Supervisory Management May 1994: 7-8.

An article in a newspaper

Brenner, Lisa. "The Job Outlook for Current Graduates." The New York Times 12 June 1994: 14WC, p. 1.

A government publication

United States. Equal Employment Opportunity Commission, Minorities and Women in Institutions of Higher Education. Washington: EEOC, 1991.

Unpublished interviews and letters

Wang, Richard L. Personal interview. 27 June 1994.

Kline, M. Allen. Letter to Donna Carlson. 31 Nov. 1994.

Article from online source

Harnad, Stevan, "Levels of functional equivalence in reverse bio-engineering: The Darwinian turing test for artificial life." Artificial Life 1.3 (in press). Online. Internet. Available FTP: pub/harnad/Harnad: harnad94.artlife 2.

[The electronic address used to access the document is optional.]

Abstract from CD-ROM

Feliu, Joseph M., and Harry Aldstadt. "The Address Managment System: Improving Customer Information Flow." Journal of End User Computing 6.1 (1994): 26–32. Proquest. CD-ROM.

[Cite the electronic publication date at the end of the citation if available.]

Computer software

Microsoft Word 6.0. Computer software. Microsoft Corporation, 1994.

Films, filmstrips, slide programs, and videotapes

Communicating Nondefensively. Videocassette. CRM Films, 1994.

FIGURE 18-5
References, APA style
(4th Edition).

Guide to Preparing References APA Style (4th Edition)

A book reference with two authors and edition

Robock, S. H., & Simmons, K. (1983). <u>International business and multinational enterprises</u> (3rd ed.). Homewood, IL: Irwin.

An edited book

Chi, F. D. S. (Ed.). (1991). <u>Handbook of international accounting</u>. New York: Wiley.

A chapter in a book or section within a reference book

Covey, S. R. (1986). Habit 4 think win/win. In S. R. Covey, <u>The 7 habits of highly effective people</u> (pp. 204-234). New York: Simon & Schuster.

Standard & Poor's. (1994). Northland Cranberries, Inc. In <u>Standard & Poor's corporation records</u> (p. 3093). New York: Author.

A report, brochure, or book from a private organization, corporate author

Wal-Mart Stores, Inc. (1994). <u>1994 annual report.</u> Bentonville, AR: Author.

Ethics Resource Group. (1980). <u>Common sense & everyday ethics</u>. [Brochure]. Washington, DC: Author.

A periodical article paginated by issue

Shea, G. (1992). A case for clear writing. <u>Training & Development, 46</u>(1), 63-66.

A periodical article without an author

How to interview, hire, and bring new employees on board. (1994, May). <u>Supervisory Management,</u> pp. 7-8.

An article in a newspaper

Brenner, E. (1994, June 12). The job outlook for current graduates. <u>The New York Times,</u> p. 14WC1.

A government publication

<u>Minorities and women in institutions of higher education</u>. (1991). Washington, DC: Equal Employment Opportunity Commission.

Unpublished interviews and letters

[Cite *interviews* and *letters* in text as personal communications; do not include in references.]

FIGURE 18-5
References, APA style, continued.

Article from online source

Harnad, S. (in press). Levels of functional equivalence in reverse bioengineering: The Darwinian turing test for artificial life. <u>Artificial Life</u> [Online serial], <u>1</u> (3). Available FTP: Hostname: princeton.edu Directory: pub/harnad/Harnad: harnad94.artlife2

[Specify the method used to locate the source (FTP), the hostname (princeton, edu), the directory (pub/harnad/Harnad), and the file name (harnad94.artlife2).]

[Omit the period at the end of electronic sources; inputting stray punctuation will hinder accurate retrieval.]

Abstract on CD-ROM

Feliu, J. M., & Aldstadt, H. (1994). The Address Management System: Improving customer information flow [CD-ROM]. <u>Journal of End User Computing, 6</u>(1), 26-32. Abstract from: ProQuest File: Access No. 00820979

Computer software

<u>Microsoft Word 6.0.</u> (1994). [Computer software]. Redmond, WA: Microsoft Corporation.

Films, filmstrips, slide programs, and videotapes

<u>Communicating nondefensively.</u> (1994). [Videocassette]. Carlsbad, CA: CRM Films.

double-spaced and that the first line of each paragraph be indented five spaces; however, a company's report-writing style manual may override this style and stipulate single spacing without paragraph indents. The sample report in Figure 18-6 is single-spaced, and paragraphs are not indented to save space and give a more professional look. The report may be considered formal and contains the following parts:

Title page
Transmittal
Contents
Executive summary
Figures
Report text (introduction, body, summary, conclusions, and
  recommendations)
References
Appendix

This example should not be considered the only way to prepare reports, but it is an acceptable model. Following the sample report, the "Check Your Writing" section provides a comprehensive checklist for use in report writing.

C O M M U N I C A T I O N   M E N T O R

Even for the most formal reports, simple writing is best. In the practical, goal-oriented world of business, reports with high "fog factor" no doubt impress the author, but they will rarely impress readers of even the highest intelligence and sophistication. Use technical terms sparingly, avoid long, intricate sentence construction and big words, and edit diligently to make the report as concise as possible.

R. D. Saenz
Business Consultant

SUMMARY

Although reports grow in formality as they increase in length, writers determine whether to prepare a report in formal style and format before they begin writing. As they organize and make tentative outlines, writers learn quickly the format and style best able to communicate the intended message. This chapter presented general suggestions for writing effective formal reports.

1 **Use a writing style that presents the findings and interprets the data clearly and fairly, convincing the reader to accept your point of view, but in an unemotional manner.** Be certain you have labeled your opinions clearly and identified any assumptions. Lay the first draft aside long enough to get a fresh perspective. Then revise the report with a genuine commitment to making all possible improvements.

2 **You must develop specific writing procedures that work best for you.** After conducting complete, accurate research, attempt to write the report during long, uninterrupted writing sessions; begin with an easy section and write as quickly as possible knowing you will revise later.

3 **Include headings in a formal report to label the paragraphs in which certain topics are discussed and to lead the reader from one division to another.** The position of headings on the page indicate the level of importance in the outline; e.g., roman numerals are first-level headings; "A",

second-level headings; and "1", third-level headings. Guidelines for using headings effectively include (1) never divide a section of a report into fewer than two parts; (2) treat all headings of the same level consistently—position, format, and grammatical construction; and (3) never position two headings consecutively without intervening text.

4 **Document any idea that is not yours (direct quotation or paraphrased text) to avoid plagiarism, to demonstrate your high ethical standards, to add credibility to your research, and to assist others in replicating your research.** Follow an authoritative style manual for writing complete documentation that allows readers to locate your sources and portrays the work of a professional. Use a source note to acknowledge the work of others and an explanatory note to provide information that does not easily fit in the text. The style manual you use will indicate whether you use the in-text parenthetical, the bottom-of-the-page, or the end-of-report citation method. Each method requires that an alphabetized list of all sources cited in a report appear at the end of a report.

5 **The writing procedures, techniques, and documentation methods presented in this chapter and illustrated in the sample report also apply to short reports and proposals.** Compare your report with the report-writing checklist shown in the "Check Your Writing" checklist on pages 628-629.

Content:
Provides specific title to give reader overview of topic covered in report. Arranges title in inverted pyramid format; will use same format on page 1 of report.

States the name and title of reader—person who authorized report.

Includes the name and title of person and/or organization that prepared report. Including address is a matter of preference and company requirements.

Includes date report was submitted, for later reference.

Format:
Omits page number but counts the page.

Graphic design to enhance appearance and effectiveness:
· All capital letters and boldface, large font size to emphasize title.
· Different font for remaining items to add interest and to distinguish them from title.
· Double border to add professional flair.

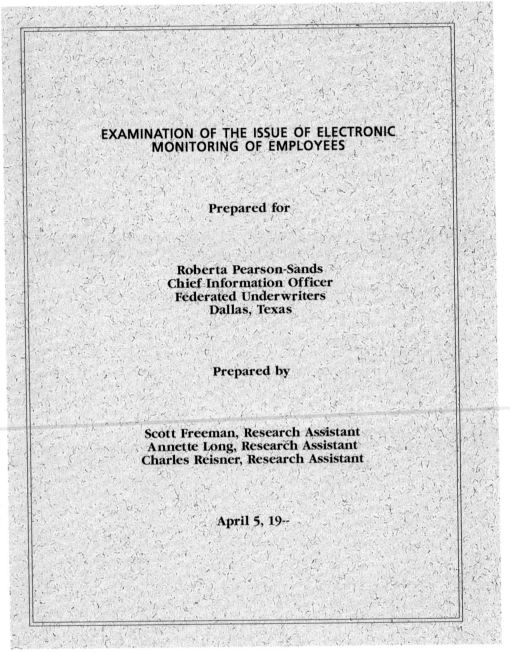

EXAMINATION OF THE ISSUE OF ELECTRONIC
MONITORING OF EMPLOYEES

Prepared for

Roberta Pearson-Sands
Chief Information Officer
Federated Underwriters
Dallas, Texas

Prepared by

Scott Freeman, Research Assistant
Annette Long, Research Assistant
Charles Reisner, Research Assistant

April 5, 19--

FIGURE 18-6   Good example of a long, formal report.

FEDERATED UNDERWRITERS
1340 Johnson Avenue, North
Dallas, TX 75260-1340
(214) 555-3193 Fax (214) 555-9783

TO: Roberta Pearson-Sands, President

FROM: Scott Freeman, Research Assistant   S.F.
          Annette Long, Research Assistant   A.L
          Charles Reisner, Research Assistant C.R

DATE: April 5, 19-

SUBJECT: Report on Electronic Monitoring of Employee Activity

The report on electronic monitoring of employees that you authorized on February 15 is now complete.

The report presents the case both for and against electronic monitoring and makes recommendations about its use to the company. Current business literature was examined to form a conceptual basis for the study. A survey was conducted of 98 business managers representing various segments of the business community; results revealed how and why firms are using electronic monitoring.

Electronic monitoring offers advantages for objective performance appraisal but must be used with caution. Issues related to employee privacy, information access and dissemination, and staff morale must be addressed.

Thank you for allowing us the opportunity to participate in this worthwhile study. We are confident that this report will aid you in making appropriate decisions about the use of electronic monitoring, and we will be happy to discuss the findings with you.

Attachment

ii

FIGURE 18-6, continued.

Uses informal, natural tone that involves reader. Note personal pronouns.

Content: Presents the report and reminds reader that she authorized it.

Discusses the methods used (secondary and primary data) to solve the problem.

Summarizes major conclusions; expresses willingness to discuss the results.

Format: Uses an acceptable memorandum format for a report submitted to someone inside the company.

Adds enclosure notation to indicate report is included.

Centers page number in small roman numerals at bottom of page; may omit page number but count as a page.

Content:
Omits the outline numbering system (I, II, A, B) but arranges the outline to indicate the importance of the headings (main heads placed at left margin; minor ones indented).

Presents each heading exactly as it appears in the report except for "Introduction," which is omitted from the report.

Prepares the contents after completing the report; allows word-processing software to generate contents so it can be updated quickly with each draft.

Omits the word "table," an obvious fact.

Format:
Adds leaders (spaced periods) to guide the eyes from the heading to the page number.

Includes the page number on which each major and minor section begins.

1½"   **CONTENTS**
                          DS.

iii

FIGURE 18-6, continued.

FIGURES

iv

FIGURE 18-6, continued.

Content:
Includes the list of figures on a separate page. If the contents and figures are short, they can be placed on one page.

Omits the word "list," an obvious fact.

Format:
Includes the page number on which each figure appears.

Content:
Uses "Executive Summary," the term commonly used in business, rather than "Abstract" APA recommends.

Provides needed background and explains problems leading to need for the study. Presents purpose of study and identifies person authorizing it.

Describes method used to solve the problem.

Synthesizes major findings, focusing on specific findings needed to support conclusions that follow.

Highlights the conclusions and recommendations based on analysis of the findings.

Format:
Centers heading in all capital letters using a larger, boldface font for emphasis.

EXECUTIVE SUMMARY

Federated Underwriters, a large, full-service insurance company, maintains offices throughout the 48 contiguous states. Roberta Pearson-Sands, Chief Information Officer, oversees the management information systems mainframe functions as well as end-user computing. In her efforts to improve productivity and increase efficiency of information control and dissemination, electronic monitoring of employees has been considered. Current capabilities of the mainframe and network systems would allow electronic logging of user identification, file usage, file manipulation, online user time, etc. In essence, the computer user leaves an "electronic fingerprint" that could be traced and analyzed in a number of ways. Pearson-Sands authorized a study to examine issues related to the electronic monitoring of employee computer activities.

Research was conducted in two ways: (1) current business literature was examined and (2) 98 business managers were surveyed concerning the use of electronic monitoring in their work settings.

The report addressed the following issues: (1) What is the frequency of electronic monitoring within organizations? (2) What are the advantages and disadvantages of monitoring? (3) What are the legal and ethical issues related to monitoring? (4) What factors are related to successful electronic monitoring? (5) Should Federated Underwriters institute a electronic monitoring procedure? Legal, ethical, and productivity issues were examined, and guidelines were developed for the effective utilization of electronic monitoring.

The study concluded that electronic monitoring does offer some advantages that justify its use by Federated Underwriters. Certain safeguards should be applied to its use, however, including the protection of employee privacy, development of policies for access and dissemination of information, and maintenance of staff morale.

v

FIGURE 18-6, continued.

EXAMINATION OF THE ISSUE OF ELECTRONIC MONITORING OF EMPLOYEES

Monitoring of worker activities is not new. Nearly a century ago, Frederick Taylor used detailed worker monitoring through time-and-motion studies to find the most efficient methods of carrying out tasks. Today's technology provides employers with the means to gather information about employees' work activities in unprecedented detail (Ottensmeyer & Heroux, 1991). Mainframe and network capabilities allow electronic logging of data such as user identification, file usage, file manipulation, and online user time. In essence, the computer user leaves an "electronic fingerprint" that can be traced and analyzed in a number of ways.

Purpose of the Study

The purpose of the study was to determine whether Federated Underwriters should implement electronic monitoring of employees. Answers were sought to the following questions:

1. What is the frequency of electronic monitoring within organizations?

2. What are the advantages and disadvantages of electronic monitoring?

3. What legal and ethical issues are raised by the use of computer monitoring?

4. What factors are related to successful electronic monitoring?

5. Should Federated Underwriters institute electronic monitoring?

Methods and Procedures Used

Secondary research was conducted through a thorough search of periodicals, books, and government documents. Interviews were conducted with 98 conveniently selected business managers from throughout Texas. The sample represented a cross-section of business types (See Appendix, Figure 4). Interviewees were asked a set of

1

FIGURE 18-6, continued.

Content:
Omits heading "Introduction" because introduction obviously is the first text reader encounters.

Gives purpose of study. Provides methods and procedures and sources of information used to add credibility.

Refers reader to Appendix and figure listing types of businesses surveyed.

Coherence:
Uses side head-ing to denote the minor divisions of the introduction.

Format:
Sinks first page to 1¹/₂" for added appeal.

Centers title in all capital let-ters with larger, boldface font; overrides APA format (upper and lowercase) as directed in company style manual.

Uses centered and side head-ings in boldface font slightly larger than text through-out report. Note capitalization style for each level.

Centers arabic numeral 1 inch from bottom.

Content:
Uses in-text citations to indicate ideas paraphrased from secondary sources. Page numbers required for direct quotes only.

Coherence:
Uses centered heading to denote the next major division. Follows with a lead-in paragraph that previews the information to be presented and separates a major and a minor heading (text must separate two headings).

Uses side headings to indicate the minor divisions.

Format:
Numbers page 2 and remaining pages with an arabic numeral at the top right margin 1 inch from the top.

Single-spaces final copy of report for cost efficiency; APA style requires double-spacing.

Ensures the page does not begin or end with a single line of a paragraph.

1 "   2

questions dealing with the application of electronic monitoring in their respective companies.

Background of Electronic Monitoring

Although monitoring of employees is common, widespread disagreement exists over its scope and effectiveness.

Frequency of Monitoring

Determining the extent to which electronic monitoring is occurring is difficult because workers, in many cases, may not be aware of it. A study conducted by the National Association of Working Women examined data processing, word processing, and customer-service operations in 110 work sites and found that 98 percent used computers to track the movements of workers (Computer monitoring, 1988). The National Institute of Occupational Safety and Health estimates that two-thirds of users of visual display terminals are monitored (Bible, 1990).

Advantages and Disadvantages of Monitoring

Electronic monitoring can count the number of keystrokes per hour and indicate how often an employee performs certain activities or uses a terminal. Keeping tabs on the quality of service, enhancing productivity, and detecting dishonesty are the most common reasons employers monitor. Some workers are pleased that their work is being observed because they want to be rewarded for their efforts. When monitoring is used to evaluate work, the machine can be fairer than a person because machines are color-blind and do not recognize gender. Electronic monitoring can make data about performance available more quickly and more frequently, thereby increasing employee awareness of personal productivity (Bible, 1990).

Monitoring may, however, be counterproductive, given the animosity and stress that it prompts in employees. Judging by complaints from employees and unions, the general feeling among workers is that monitoring threatens their privacy, intrudes on their personal work in progress, and leads to their being evaluated on criteria that they

FIGURE 18-6, continued.

1 "   3

do not understand. Workers tend to feel that "Big Brother" is always watching, and the fact that everyone is subject to the same scrutiny does little to relieve that sense of exposure (Ottensmeyer & Heroux, 1991). Some companies have implemented monitoring and then stopped because they discovered how counterproductive it could be (Bible, 1990).

Employees frequently find ways to counter attempts at monitoring. When keystrokes are monitored, for example, a key can be held down continuously to make the count go up (although some software programs can detect this deception). Some employees, offended by what they perceive as a sudden lack of trust, reduce their work efforts to the bare minimum needed to get by. Middle managers foil monitoring attempts by filling in their electronic schedules with meetings because employers may tend to think managers are productive if they are in meetings (Bible, 1990).

Legal and Ethical Considerations in Monitoring

Courts and legislatures have historically allowed employers broad rights of observation and record-keeping when monitoring workers. These rights are based on employer ownership of the premises at which the work is done and on the basic right of management to control the work process (U.S. Congress, 1987). Currently, no federal laws ban or restrict electronic monitoring of work performance. One law that vaguely relates to the issue of electronic monitoring is the Omnibus Crime Control and Safe Streets Act of 1968, which was designed to protect the privacy of wire and oral communications. Advances in technology have rendered the wording of the act outdated and thus inapplicable to electronic monitoring (Cooney, 1991).

Congress is considering legislation that would have considerable effect on the future of monitoring. This legislation, the Privacy for Consumers and Workers Act, would limit the use of electronic devices in monitoring employees' activities. The act would require employers to provide employees with prior written notice of electronic monitoring and to signal them orally or visually when monitoring is being performed. Furthermore, it would require that employees

FIGURE 18-6, continued.

Content:
Uses in-text citations to indicate ideas paraphrased from secondary sources.

Summarizes major section before moving to the next one.

Coherence:
Uses centered heading to denote the next major division. Follows with transition sentence that introduces the information to be presented.

4

be informed of the forms of electronic monitoring to be used, the personal data to be collected, the frequency of monitoring, and the use of the data (Smith, 1993). In addition to action pending at the federal level, many states, including Connecticut, Massachusetts, Minnesota, New Jersey, Oregon, Rhode Island, New Mexico, and New York are developing their own comprehensive monitoring bills (Nussbaum, 1989).

In the absence of existing legislation related to electronic monitoring, the Department of Justice in Washington has ruled it legal. The Justice Department, however, strongly advises system administrators to inform users of monitoring. If keystroke monitoring is used—even for purposes of detecting intruders—they should "ensure that all system users, authorized and unauthorized, are notified that such monitoring may be undertaken" (Smith, 1993, p. 204).

Organizations that represent employees have expressed strong reservations about the use of electronic monitoring. The 1987 AFL-CIO Convention adopted the following resolution on the issue:

> Electronic surveillance invades workers' privacy, erodes their sense of dignity, and frustrates their efforts to do high-quality work, by placing a single-minded emphasis on speed and other purely quantitative measurements. Numerous studies have shown that monitoring creates high levels of workplace stress that results in a variety of adverse health conditions (Lund, 1991, p. 197).

In general, opponents of monitoring argue that it undermines customer service, teamwork, and the quality of work life (Grant & Christopher, 1989).

As surely as workers need to be protected against abuses in electronic monitoring, business has the legal right to ensure that it provides a safe working environment. Proponents of monitoring point out that businesses need it to investigate criminal activity and misuse of company property; therefore, the right to unobstructed monitoring is essential to business security. Under current law, monitoring that serves a legitimate business purpose could

FIGURE 18-6, continued.

5

be vigorously and probably successfully defended. However, possible new legal developments should be carefully watched. Electronic monitoring of employees is, for at least some purposes, legal. A more difficult question is whether it is desirable; and if so, under what conditions? Impressive gains in productivity must be carefully weighed against potential damage to quality of work life.

Guidelines for the Use of Electronic Monitoring

Research into work environments where electronic monitoring is used reveals interesting information about worker acceptance of the procedure. The following guidelines help ensure cooperation:

- <u>Reasonable Work</u>. Work standards must be perceived by employees as reasonable and attainable. This feature is essential to a perception of fairness in the process. Furthermore, time spans must be set for measurement performance (Angel, 1989).

- <u>Relevant Tasks</u>. Only relevant tasks should be included in an electronic monitoring system. Overwhelming insignificant data do not usefully serve employees or employers. Further, excessive monitoring can increase the cost of employee performance appraisal while providing few additional benefits (Henriques, 1986).

- <u>Timely Intervals</u>. Evaluation intervals should be appropriate. Production of continuous reports is not only resource-consuming but rarely necessary (Henriques, 1986).

- <u>Employee Access</u>. Employers should have access to their computer-monitored records, which can be used for improving performance and eliminating errors (Henriques, 1986).

- <u>Specified Standards</u>. Specific, well-defined standards should be set for each monitored task. Under such conditions, workers know exactly what is expected of them (Angel, 1989).

- <u>Measurable Tasks</u>. Chosen tasks must be measurable and definitive (Angel, 1989).

FIGURE 18-6, continued.

Content: Summarizes major section before moving to the next one.

Coherence: Uses centered heading to denote the next major division. Follows with transition sentence.

Format: Uses bullets to emphasize the guidelines; would use numbers if the sequence were important.

6

- <u>Results-Oriented Output</u>. Output from the system should be results-oriented. The important element is the measuring of output, not the means of achieving it (Angel, 1989).

- <u>Congruent Pay</u>. The monitoring system should include a pay schedule congruent with different performance levels. This procedure ensures that those who consistently perform above predetermined standards are appropriately compensated (Angel, 1989).

- <u>Mutual Goals.</u> Computerized monitoring is an effective aid only if benefits to employer and employees are explicitly stated. Procedures that appear to advance only the employer's best interest will not be successful (Angel, 1989).

- <u>Effective Supervision.</u> Grant and Christopher (1991) found that supervisors played a critical role in determining whether monitoring would be stressful and whether data feedback would undermine or promote employee satisfaction.

Thus, when safeguards are incorporated into the electronic appraisal process, the result can be better satisfied and more efficient workers. Employees will experience less work-related anxiety, will be more gratified and content, will be objectively evaluated for work performed, and will be properly compensated for output produced. Positive impact on employers will include low-cost, effective, and meaningful evaluation tools; methods to identify unique, individual problems; procedures for providing direction and guidelines for employees; and improved training programs (Angel, 1989).

Survey of Businesses Concerning Electronic Monitoring

Of the 98 managers who participated in the current study, 66 (67%) indicated that their companies engaged in some type of electronic monitoring of employee activities. These respondents provided information related to the uses of monitoring and employee access to the data collected.

FIGURE 18-6, continued.

1"   7

Reported Uses of Monitoring

When asked about the types of computer activities that were monitored in their companies, respondents included log-on identification,
files accessed and changed by users, user time on the system,
electronic mail, and random checks of file accuracy. Respondents
were also asked how monitoring results were used in their respective
organizations. Results of electronic monitoring were used in a variety
of ways, with the setting of standards and comparative data analysis
being the most common uses as shown in Figure 1.

Figure 1

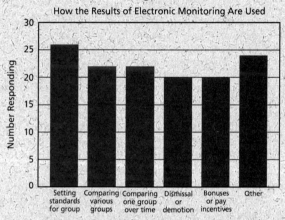

How the Results of Electronic Monitoring Are Used

Employee Access to Monitoring Data

Managers in the current study were asked to what extent employees
were informed of the company's monitoring activities. In nearly one-
half of the cases, employees were informed either orally or perhaps
orally in addition to one of the other means such as in writing or
with a message on the computer. In 18 percent of cases, employees
were not informed of the monitoring activity, as shown in Figure 2.

FIGURE 18-6, continued.

Content:
Summarizes
major points in
the bar chart and
the table and
refers the reader
to the figures.

Provides title
specific enough to
assist readers who
skim the report.

Format:
Centers figure
number and title
on separate lines
separated by a
double space.
(Refer to Chapter
16 for specific
guidelines for
formatting graphs
and tables.)

Places Figure 1
immediately
following its
textual references.

Places Figure 2 at
top of next page.

Content:
Summarizes
major points in
the tables and
refers the reader
to the figures.
Provides title
specific enough to
assist readers who
skim the report.

Format:
Places Figure 3
immediately
following its
textual reference.

Centers figure
number and title
on separate lines
separated by a
double space.
(Refer to Chapter
16 for specific
guidelines for
formatting tables.)

Labels a bar chart
and a table as
figures and
numbers consecu-
tively with one
numbering
system.

1"   8

Figure 2

Extent that Employees Are Informed of Monitoring

Method of Informing	Number Responding	Percent
Orally, as to possibility	32	48
By the system during monitoring	18	27
In writing, as to possibility	14	21
Other means	8	12
Not informed	12	18

Two-thirds of the companies performed continuous monitoring, one-
fourth used random monitoring, and the remainder reported inter-
mittent monitoring at set intervals. Respondents were also asked to
indicate the ways in which the data acquired through monitoring
were reported. More than one-half said that the method of reporting
was group or department data; 42 percent used individual reporting
and 18 percent used company-wide data reporting. Some businesses
used a combination of the reporting methods. In a related item,
managers were asked who sees the results of the electronic monitoring. Upper-level management is most likely to see the results of
monitoring. In only one-third of the organizations surveyed do
employees see their own data, as reported in Figure 3.

Figure 3

Who Sees the Results of Electronic Monitoring

Party Who Views Data	Number Responding	Percent
Upper-level management	46	70
Immediate supervisor	38	58
Employee	22	33
Peers of employee	20	30
Other	14	21

1"

FIGURE 18-6, continued.

1"   9

Summary, Conclusions, and Recommendations

Consideration of primary and secondary research has led to a thorough analysis of the monitoring issue:

Summary

Electronic performance monitoring evokes strong and often contradictory responses among the parties concerned with its use. The potential for impressive gains in productivity must be carefully weighed against possible damage to the quality of work life. Managers who choose to use electronic monitoring must consider effective and fair system design carefully. They must demonstrate that the data generated through electronic monitoring help them see the positive as well as the negative aspects of employee performance, and individual performance must be tied to salary incentives or performance ratings.

Issues in data reporting must be considered. The need for timely system data must be balanced against the risk that information overload will occur. Dissemination of data is an issue; low producers find the comparison of their performance with that of co-workers demoralizing, and even high performers can find the public display of their productivity to be undesirable.

Finally, which tasks should be monitored? Monitoring a task may confirm a belief that a task is important while failure to include a task or behavior can be interpreted as a signal that management does not consider that factor worth watching.

Conclusions

Based on the findings of this research, the following conclusions were drawn:

1. The most significant result of the study was the realization that companies need to address the issue of electronic monitoring and develop a policy for its use.

FIGURE 18-6, continued.

Content:
Combines "Summary, Conclusions, and Recommendations," an appropriate heading for a report designed to solve a problem.

Coherence:
Provides a lead-in sentence to introduce conclusions; enumerates for emphasis and clarity. Includes broad generalizations drawn from the findings and does *not* repeat specific findings.

Format:
Uses centered heading to indicate major division. Includes side headings to divide summary, conclusions, and recommendations into minor divisions.

2. While the current legal structure permits the use of electronic monitoring, informing employees of its use seems advisable.

3. Each organization must examine issues of morale and productivity in order to determine whether electronic monitoring will be a worthwhile means of assessment.

Recommendations

Federated Underwriters should institute an electronic monitoring program that includes the following features:

1. A study should be undertaken to identify the activities that should be monitored.

2. All computer users should be notified in writing that their computer activities are subject to monitoring.

3. Individual data derived from monitoring should be available to employees.

4. Data derived from monitoring should be used as only one indicator of employee performance.

Electronic monitoring is a controversial and complicated issue with implications for performance appraisal, worker productivity, and employee privacy. A promising tool in the managerial process, it is not without its dangers. The challenge to Federated Underwriters is to develop acceptable procedures and guidelines for managing this electronic capability successfully.

FIGURE 18-6, continued.

11

REFERENCES

Angel, F. N. (1989). Evaluating employees by computer. *Personnel Administrator, 34* (11), 67-72.

Bible, J. D. (1990). *Privacy in the workplace.* New York: Quorum Books.

Computer monitoring and other dirty tricks. (1988). New York: National Association of Working Women.

Cooney, C. M. (1991). Who's watching the workplace? The electronic monitoring debate spreads to Capitol Hill. *Security Management, 35* (11), 26-35.

Grant, R. & Christopher, H. (1989, Spring). Monitoring service workers via computer: The effect on employees, productivity, and service. *National Productivity Review,* pp. 101-112.

Grant, R. & Christopher, H. (1991, November). Computerized performance monitors: Factors affecting acceptance. *IEEE Transactions on Engineering Management,* pp. 306-316.

Henriques, V. E. (1986). In defense of computer monitoring. *Training, 23* (12), 120.

Lund, J. (1991). Computerized work performance monitoring and production standards: A review of labor law issues. *Labor Law Journal, 43* (4), 195-203.

FIGURE 18-6, continued.

Format:
Continues page numbering used in the report.

Centers heading in all capital letters with larger, boldface font used for similar headings in the report (title, contents, executive summary, and appendix).

Content:
Presents in-text parenthetical citations formatted in APA style. Italicizes titles of books and periodicals and volume numbers because software supports the feature.

Indents first line of each entry and double-spaces according to APA style.

1   12

Nussbaum, K. (1989). Computer monitoring: A threat to the right to privacy? Speech delivered to the Computer Professionals for Social Responsibility Annual Meeting, Washington, D.C., 1989. In DeJoie, R., Fowler, G., & Paradice, D. (Eds.), *Ethical issues in information systems*. Boston: Boyd and Fraser, 1991.

Ottensmeyer, E., & Heroux, M. (1991). Ethics, public policy, and managing advanced technologies: The case of electronic surveillance. *The Journal of Business Ethics, 10* (7), 519-526.

Smith, L. B. (1993, June 28). Electronic monitoring raises legal and societal questions. *PCWeek*, p. 204.

U.S. Congress, Office of Technology Assessment (1987, September). *The electronic supervisor: New technology, new tensions.* (OTA-CIT-333). Washington, DC, U.S. Government Printing Office.

FIGURE 18-6, continued.

1   13

APPENDIX

DEMOGRAPHIC DATA

Figure 4

Types of Businesses Surveyed

Type of Business	Number Responding	Percent of Total
Banking/Finance	20	20.4
Manufacturing/Construction	16	16.3
Wholesale/Retail Sales	14	14.3
Miscellaneous Services	14	14.3
Agriculture/Drilling/Mining	10	10.2
Communication/Transportation/Utility	10	10.2
Insurance	8	8.2
Education/Government	4	4.1
Legal	2	2.0
	98	100.0

FIGURE 18-6, continued.

Content:
Includes Figure 4 that was referenced on page 1.

Format:
Continues page numbering used in the report.

Centers "Appendix" and title in all capital letters; uses larger, boldface font to add emphasis and to ensure consistency with similar headings (title, contents, executive summary, and appendix).

CHECK YOUR WRITING

The following checklist provides a concise, handy guide for your use as you prepare a report.

TRANSMITTAL LETTER OR MEMORANDUM

Use the following points for a letter-style transmittal in reports going outside the organization. For internal reports, use a memorandum transmittal.

- ☐ Carry a warm greeting to the reader.
- ☐ Open with a "The report you requested is complete" tone.
- ☐ Establish the subject in the first sentence.
- ☐ Follow the opening with a brief summary of the study. Expand the discussion if a separate summary is not included in the report.
- ☐ Acknowledge the assistance of those who helped with the study.
- ☐ Close the letter with a thank you and a forward look.

TITLE PAGE

- ☐ Include the title of the report.
- ☐ Provide full identification of the authority for the report (the person for whom the report was prepared).
- ☐ Provide full identification of the preparer of the report.
- ☐ Include the date of the completion of the report.
- ☐ Use an attractive layout. (If the items are to be centered, leave an extra half-inch on the left for binding. The point from which the items are centered is a little to the right of the actual center of the paper.)

CONTENTS PAGE

- ☐ Use *Contents* as the title.
- ☐ Use a tabular arrangement to indicate the heading levels used in the report.
- ☐ List numerous figures separately. (Otherwise, figures should not be listed because they are not separate sections of the outline but only supporting data within a section.)
- ☐ Center the entire contents outline horizontally; allow $1^1/_2$" top margin.

EXECUTIVE SUMMARY

- ☐ Use a concise title, such as *Executive Summary, Synopsis,* or *Abstract.*
- ☐ Provide a condensation of the major sections of the report.
- ☐ Use effective, generalized statements that avoid detail available in the report itself. Simply tell the reader what was done, how it was done, and what conclusions were reached.

REPORT TEXT

In writing style, observe the following guidelines:

- ☐ Avoid the personal *I* and *we* pronouns. Minimize the use of *the writer, the investigator,* and *the author.*
- ☐ Use active construction to give emphasis to the *doer* of the action; use passive voice to give emphasis to the *results* of the action.
- ☐ Use proper tense. Tell naturally about things in the order in which they happened, are happening, or will happen. Write as though the reader were reading the report at the same time it is written.
- ☐ Avoid ambiguous pronoun references. (If a sentence begins with *This is,* make sure the preceding sentence uses the specific word for which *This* stands. If the specific word is not used, insert it immediately after *This.*)
- ☐ Avoid expletive beginnings. Sentences that begin with *There is, There are,* and *It is* present the verb before presenting the subject. Compared with sentences that use the normal subject-verb-complement sequence, expletive sentences are longer and less interesting.
- ☐ Enumerate lists of three or more items if tabulation will make reading easier. For example, a list of three words such as *Ivan, George,* and *Diana* need not be tabulated; but a list of three long phrases, clauses, or sentences would probably warrant tabulation.
- ☐ Incorporate transition sentences to ensure coherence.

In physical layout, observe the following guidelines:

- ☐ Use headings to assist the reader by making them descriptive of the contents of the section. Talking headings are preferred.
- ☐ Maintain consistency in the mechanical placement of headings of equal degree.
- ☐ Use parallel construction in headings of equal degree in the same section of the report.
- ☐ Incorporate the statement of the problem or purpose and method of research as minor parts of the introduction unless the research method is the unique element in the study.

☐ Use the picture-frame layout for all pages. Recommended margins depending on the bindings are

Unbound: 1" for all margins (top, bottom, left, and right).

Leftbound: $1^{1}/_{2}$" left margin; 1" for other margins.

Topbound: $1^{1}/_{2}$" top margin; 1" for other margins.

Begin first page $^{1}/_{2}$" lower than other pages to add appeal to the first page.

☐ Number all pages, with the first page of the body of the report being page 1. For page 1, omit the number or place it in the center approximately 1" from the bottom of the page. For all other pages, place the number 1" from the top of the page at the right margin.

In using graphics or tabular data, observe the following guidelines:

☐ Number consecutively figures (tables, graphics, and other illustrations) used in the report.

☐ Give each graph or table a descriptive title.

☐ Refer to the graph or table within the text discussion that precedes its appearance.

☐ Place the graph or table as close to the textual reference as possible and limit the text reference to analysis. (It should not merely repeat what can be seen in the graph or table.)

☐ Use effective layout, appropriate captions and legends, and realistic vertical and horizontal scales that help the table or graph stand clearly by itself.

In reporting the analysis, observe the following guidelines:

☐ Question each statement for its contribution to the solution of the problem. Is each statement either descriptive or evaluative?

☐ Reduce large, unwieldy numbers to understandable ones through a common language such as units of production, percentages, or ratios.

☐ Use objective reporting style rather than persuasive language; avoid emotional terms. Identify assumptions and opinions. Avoid unwarranted judgments and inferences.

☐ Tabulate or enumerate items when it will simplify the reading or add emphasis.

In drawing conclusions,

☐ State the conclusions carefully and clearly, and be sure they grow out of the findings.

☐ Repeat the major supporting findings for each conclusion if necessary.

☐ Make recommendations grow naturally from the conclusions if they are required.

CITATIONS

If citations are used:

☐ Include a citation (in-text reference, footnote, or endnote) for material used from another source.

☐ Adhere to an acceptable, authoritative style or company policy.

☐ Present consistent citations including adequate information for readers to locate the source in the bibliography.

REFERENCES

☐ Include an entry for every reference cited in the text.

☐ Adhere to an acceptable, authoritative style or company policy.

☐ Include more information than might be necessary in cases of doubt about what to include in an entry.

☐ Present the references in alphabetic sequence by authors' surnames.

☐ Include separate sections (e.g., books, articles, and nonprint sources) if the references (works cited) section is lengthy.

APPENDIX

☐ Include cover letters for survey instruments, the survey instruments, maps, explanations of formulas used, and other items that should be included but are not important enough to be in the body of a report.

☐ Label each item beginning with *Appendix A, Appendix B,* and so on.

☐ Identify each item with a title.

REFERENCES

American Psychological Association. (1994). *Publication manual of the American Psychological Association* (4th ed.). Washington, DC: Author.

DeRosa, R. (1994, May 3). Courting plans go ape. *USA Today.* p. 1D.

Gibaldi, J., & Achtert, W. S. (1995). *MLA handbook for writers of research papers* (4th ed.). New York: The Modern Language Association.

Note: Case for Analysis 1 was extracted with permission from Lehman, C. M. & Spencer, B. A. (1991). Creative thinking: An integral part of effective business communication, *Bulletin of the Association of Business Communication, 54* (1), 21-27.

REVIEW QUESTIONS

1. Give two or three examples of emotional terms. Why should you avoid them in a formal report?
2. Why is the use of the pronoun *I* generally unacceptable in formal report writing?
3. What is meant by "transition" in composition? By "coherence"?
4. Identify each of the following terms as time, contrast, similarity, or cause-and-effect connectors: "because," "for example," "then," and "although."
5. When using word-processing software, a writer should always expect to prepare final copy without working with a rough draft. Is this statement true? Discuss.
6. Why is reading your writing aloud an effective way to review?
7. Explain the relationship between the content outline of a report and the placement of headings within the body of a report.
8. List four primary reasons for documenting reports.
9. List three suggestions for preparing accurate documentation.
10. Discuss the two major types of citations used to document a report.
11. How can you document a report if you are not using bottom-of-the-page and end-of-report citations? Explain this documentation method briefly.
12. What are the three major differences between a traditional (bottom-of-the-page or end-of-report) citation and a bibliographic entry?
13. Must formal reports be organized in only one way? Must they contain all the preliminary, report text, and addenda parts?
14. Should the contents outline and the figures always be placed on separate pages?
15. Is the heading "Introduction" essential on the first page of the report? Explain.
16. How many levels of headings does the sample report contain? Describe how each level of heading is presented to denote the various divisions within the report.
17. Explain how the graphics in the sample report are positioned, numbered, and introduced.
18. Summarize the techniques used to move the reader from one section of the sample report to the next.
19. List at least three ways the desktop publishing capabilities of sophisticated word-processing software can be used to enhance the appearance of a report and to increase the efficiency of preparing the report.
20. Complete each of the THINK IT OVER activities that your instructor assigns.

E-MAIL APPLICATION

 Your instructor has provided detailed instructions for completing a formal report in groups of three or four. Send your instructor an e-mail message containing your evaluation of each member of the group. Rate each member on a five-point scale or assign a percentage indicating the contribution each member made to the group. Ideally, each member should contribute 100%. However, assume that a group consisted of four members, and one person contributed more than his or her equal share, and one person contributed less. You might rank these two members 120% and 80% respectively and rank the other two members 100%. Note the total percentages awarded equal 400% (100% x 4 members). Write a brief statement justifying the rating you assigned each member; provide specific, verifiable evidence.

APPLICATIONS

MIS/Technology

1. **Shareware vs. Commercial Software.** Your company, Support, Inc., is considering the possibility of using shareware for its software needs rather than commercial software. You have been asked by the owner and president of your organization to research the issue of shareware and to conduct a business survey of the use of shareware and the satisfaction of users. You have surveyed 66 companies that have used shareware and have obtained the following results:

1. What type(s) of shareware have you used? (Check all that apply)

34	Word Processing
26	Spreadsheet
20	Database
24	Graphics
23	Communications
28	Other

2. In general, how would you rate the quality of shareware as compared with software products sold commercially? (Check one)

4	Shareware quality is very inferior to that of commercial software.
31	Shareware quality is somewhat inferior to that of commercial software.
26	Shareware quality is about the same as that of commercial software.
3	Shareware quality is somewhat better than that of commercial software.
2	Shareware quality is much better than that of commercial software.

3. What, if any, problems have you encountered with the use of shareware that you have registered with the owner? (Check all that apply)

26	Inadequate documentation.
25	Glitch(es) in the program.
9	Virus in the program.
22	Lack of technical support.
2	Other problems.
16	No problems.

4. Where have you used shareware? (Check one)

22	Used only at home.
17	Used only at work.
27	Used at both home and work.

5. How did you obtain your shareware? (Check all that apply)

34	Obtained from a friend or acquaintance.
21	Obtained from a computer bulletin board.
18	A copy was provided on my job.
16	Purchased it.
3	Other.

6. How much would you be willing to pay to register a copy of a shareware program? (Check one)

10	Nothing.
28	Under $25.
21	Between $25 and $50.
4	Between $50 and $75.
3	Over $75.

7. What is your opinion of a company purchasing shareware products instead of commercial software for employee use? (Circle one)

(11)	(4)	(15)	(19)	(6)	(10)
1	2	3	4	5	6

Definitely   Definitely
would not   would
recommend   recommend

Required:

As director of information systems, write a report with findings, conclusions, and recommendations. Prepare any preliminary and addenda parts you believe will enable the reader to understand the report.

MANAGEMENT

2. **Merits of Mentoring.** Your company, Ultron Oil, is considering implementing a formal mentoring program as a means for developing managerial talent. Your supervisor, the division director, has commissioned you to prepare a report on the effectiveness of mentoring. As a part of the study, you have surveyed 70 managers representing a variety of businesses; 64 were male, and 6 were female. They ranged in age from 22 to 69, with the median age being 45. Their responses are as follows:

1. In your career development, have you ever had a mentor?
   - 66 — Yes. Answer all items.
   - 4 — No. Skip to Item 6.
2. Which of the following describes your mentoring relationship(s)?
   - 6 — Formal; my mentor(s) was/were appointed or assigned to me.
   - 38 — Informal; the relationship(s) just evolved.
   - 22 — One or more was formal, and one or more was informal.
3. How long did the typical mentoring relationship last?
   - 12 — Less than one year.
   - 12 — One to two years.
   - 16 — Three to five years.
   - 14 — More than five years.
   - 14 — Varying lengths of time (answers varied from one month to life).
4. Did you perceive that you benefited from the mentoring relationship?
   - 6 — Yes.
   - 0 — No.
5. Did you perceive that your mentor benefited from the relationship?

   - 62 — Yes.
   - 4 — No.
6. Have you ever been a mentor to another person?
   - 54 — Yes.
   - 16 — No.
7. Does your present company have a mentoring program in place?
   - 32 — Yes.
   - 38 — No.

Required:

Prepare the report for the division director. Present your findings, draw conclusions, and make recommendations. Prepare any preliminary and addenda parts you believe will enable the reader to understand the report.

INFORMATION SYSTEMS/Technology/Ethics/Legal

3. **Attitudes Toward Software Piracy.** You are conducting a study of college seniors concerning their awareness of and attitudes toward software piracy. You have surveyed 100 students as a part of your project. The first category of questions dealt with their knowledge of software piracy. The correct answer to each of these questions is "true." Their responses are as follows:

1. Purchased software is covered by copyright law and generally allows for only a backup copy to be made by the purchaser.
   - 84 — True
   - 16 — False
2. Making copies of copyrighted software for distribution to others (software piracy) is a federal crime.
   - 94 — True
   - 6 — False
3. Making a copy of a software program owned by my company for use at home, unless expressly allowed, is a violation of copyright law.
   - 82 — True
   - 18 — False
4. Software piracy is punishable by both fine and imprisonment.
   - 92 — True
   - 8 — False

The second category of questions dealt with specific situations. To each, students were instructed to give their **honest** responses. Their responses are as follows:

a. Your employer has purchased WordPerfect 6.0 for use on your computer at work. You have a computer at home and would like to have a copy of the program for you and your family's personal use. You would

   _38_   Make a copy of the disk for use at home and buy a manual from Waldenbooks.

   _50_   Make a copy of the disk and photocopy the manual for home use.

   _12_   Wait until you could afford to purchase a copy yourself.

b. You visit a local computer software store and see WordPerfect 6.0 with a price of $495. You would

   _100_   Buy it now or, if money is short, come back later to buy.

   _0_   Shoplift the software.

c. You obtain a copy of WordPerfect 6.0. A friend asks you for a copy of it. You would

   _58_   Give your friend a copy of the program.

   _22_   Trade your friend a copy of WordPerfect 6.0 for a copy of Lotus 1-2-3.

   _6_   Sell your friend a copy for $25.

   _14_   Tell your friend that he/she must purchase a copy.

Required:

Present your findings, conclusions, and recommendations in a formal report to your college administrators. Prepare any preliminary and addenda parts you believe will enable the reader to understand the report.

MANAGEMENT

4. **Spiraling Health Costs: Do Employee Assistance Programs Help?** As director of human resources management of Soto, Inc., you receive the following voice mail message from Pablo Soto, president of the company:

Hi. I just finished reading your quarterly analysis of benefits and compensation costs. Frankly, I'm overwhelmed with the consistent increase in health claims since last year. If this trend continues, we'll have to eliminate employee health coverage or go out of business. What are the other companies doing to curtail health-care costs? Do these employee assistance programs really work? Please complete a thorough investigation so that we can make an informed decision if the situa-

tion worsens. Let's schedule a meeting to discuss this issue later this month.

Required:

1. To help you focus your research, select a particular business with which you are familiar. Then identify the major health problems that you believe employees in this type of company might have. Among the problems you might list are heart disease, high cholesterol, diabetes, poor physical fitness, substance abuse, stress and burnout, and physical problems caused by using computers or being exposed to other hazardous materials or equipment.

2. Using the problems you listed in Step 1, conduct the necessary research to answer the president's questions; provide accurate, useful, and well-documented information. Specifically, review the research related to employee assistance programs or methods of reducing health-care costs. In addition, read current general business magazines and practitioners' journals to learn about employee assistance programs at other companies and other relevant issues.

3. As director of human resources, write an informational report relating your research about employee assistance programs (relevant to Soto's employee health problem profile) to the president. Include complete and accurate documentation of your sources; use in-text parenthetical citations unless your instructor requires another citation method.

4. Prepare the following preliminary and addenda parts to support the report prepared in Step 3: Title page, executive summary, transmittal memorandum to President Soto (mention the attached references page), and references page. Provide complete, accurate references so that you can readily relocate the information if the president requests a copy.

MANAGEMENT/International

5. **Intercultural Misunderstandings.** McClarney's, a successful fast-food restaurant in the United States, has expanded its operations to Hong Kong, Paris, and now Moscow. In almost every case, U.S. managers were transferred to open and manage restaurants in the company's international operations. These highly competent managers continually make unintentional, yet costly,

mistakes because they are unfamiliar with the differences among the customs, culture, and business practices of these countries and the United States. The price being paid for these innocent mistakes is high: damaged or lost goodwill of customers, employees, and suppliers and, eventually, reduced profits.

When the company decided to expand its operation to Moscow, management agreed unanimously to establish an International Assignments Division. This division is charged with preparing managers transferring to overseas operations for functioning in a new culture. Although some misunderstandings cannot be avoided, a carefully designed orientation program is sure to improve intercultural understanding.

Required:

1. As director of the International Assignments Division, one of your first tasks is to prepare an informational report to the U.S. managers transferring to *one* of the company's three international locations: Hong Kong, Paris, or Moscow. Your purpose is to highlight the major cultural differences and business practices between the United States and the country you select. Conduct the research needed to provide these managers with accurate, useful, and well-documented information. Use in-text parenthetical citations unless your instructor requires another citation method. Use the following suggestions to help you organize your report:

   a. Consider the specific information that managers would need to know to manage a fast-food restaurant in the country you select.

   b. Consider whether the information can be classified. If it can, would headings be appropriate to subdivide this section? How would you present headings in the report?

2. Prepare the following preliminary and addenda parts to support the report prepared in Step 1: (a) title page, (b) contents page if the report is long enough to require one, (c) executive summary, (d) transmittal letter addressed to a manager (provide name and address) in the country you selected in a format acceptable to the country selected, (e) references page (provide complete, accurate references so that managers are able

to locate your sources for additional study if needed).

CROSS-DISCIPLINE

6. **A Business Problem To Be Solved.** Select one of the following problems to solve. Provide the necessary assumptions and background data. Then write a formal report of your analysis, conclusions, and recommendations. Include preliminary and ending parts you believe appropriate. You may need to design a questionnaire and administer it to an appropriate sample. Reviewing this list may help you identify a business-related problem you have encountered during your employment or cooperative education and intern experiences. If you choose to solve your own problem, provide the necessary assumptions and background data.

CROSS-DISCIPLINE

a. Choose from the five research studies presented in Chapter 15, Application 1.

MANAGEMENT

b. While touring the manufacturing plant of a professional friend, you observe the use of universal product code (UPC) symbols to track the movement of inventory through the plant. Propose how UPC symbols could monitor the movement of employees within the manufacturing plant and investigate the implications of this action.

MIS

c. Your data processing department soon will begin to analyze the current manual information system used in your department. Investigate effective methods of preparing your employees for the impending investigation (people asking drilling questions about their work) and later for the conversion to a computer-automated information system—a major change in employees' primary work tasks.

MANAGEMENT/Ethics   GMAT

d. Your department handles highly sensitive information and, as a result, requires extremely reliable user identification. You are considering ocular scanning or perhaps some other type of biometric identification. Investigate the advantages and disadvantages of such a system and recommend whether your organization should pursue it.

MANAGEMENT

e. For some time you have recognized that drug abuse is present in your plant. The problem is becoming increasingly worse, and the company is paying the price in extra health-care costs, lost productivity, and absenteeism. Investigate strategies for coping with this problem.

MANAGEMENT

f. A committee of employees has recommended that the company establish a recycling center where employees can deposit recyclable items when entering the parking lot. The president has asked you to think the idea through and present a report of the cost, public relations implications, employee relations, and logistics of operating the recycling center.

MANAGEMENT

g. Present a report on the cost and logistics of establishing a recycling procedure for computer paper used to prepare internal reports. Select a real or fictitious company.

MANAGEMENT/Ethics

h. You have received reports that several of your major competitors have installed electronic surveillance devices to monitor employees' performance. The president wants your immediate attention on this issue. Investigate the implications of using technology to monitor employees' performance. Will employees consider this procedure an invasion of privacy? Anticipate all possible problems and present strategies for dealing with them.

MANAGEMENT/Ethics

i. Although no employees have made formal complaints of sexual harassment in the workplace, information from the grapevine has convinced you that the company needs a formal policy concerning sexual harassment. To develop this company policy, research the legalities related to this issue and gather information (strategies) from other companies with sexual harassment policies.

MANAGEMENT

j. The upcoming downsizing of your company will result in the displacement of approximately 10 percent of your middle- and upper-level managers. Investigate strategies for supporting these managers in their search for new employment. Many of these managers have worked for your company 15 to 20 years; therefore, they are quite apprehensive about the job-search process.

ACCOUNTING

k. You are in charge of recruiting accounting graduates for entry-level positions in your firm. You believe your current approach needs improvement because too many of the top-notch students interview with you on campus but do not accept office interviews. Investigate the problem and identify effective strategies for recruiting quality students. For example, consider the following thoughts and anticipate many others: Should you hold a formal reception or casual party to get to know the interviewees? Should you take the accounting faculty to lunch to increase your contact with them? What can you do to make your recruitment effort cost effective?

MANAGEMENT

l. Investigate the possibility of hiring senior citizens to fill selected positions in your company.

ECONOMICS/FINANCE

m. A client has $10,000 to invest for her children's college education. Their ages are 12, 9, and 4. Investigate alternatives and prepare a proposal for her consideration.

CROSS-DISCIPLINE

7. A Business Problem with International, Ethical, Legal, or Interpersonal Implications. Refer to the "Cases for Analysis" at the ends of

Chapters 9-14 for additional topics requiring research to solve a particular business problem. Turn to the appropriate case and read the complete case problem.

MANAGEMENT/Interpersonal

a. *Chapter 9, Case 2.* Review research related to employee motivation and current practitioners' journals to identify ways to solve a company's problems with low morale and productivity and write an informational report. A basic scenario is provided. To make the case more meaningful to you, identify an employee group and environment with which you are familiar.

MANAGEMENT

b. *Chapter 10, Case 1.* Review research related to crisis communication to prepare for communicating information about a financial crisis to employees and write an informational report. You may vary this case; for example, communicating financial crisis information to stockholders or negative information about defective products, product tampering, environmental hazards, or ethical misconduct to clients and other groups.

MANAGEMENT

c. *Chapter 10, Case 2.* Review research related to communicating crisis information to prepare for writing a letter to customers announcing the recall of a faulty product. Write an informational report to your supervisor.

MANAGEMENT/International

d. *Chapter 12, Case 1.* Research the cultural differences between business executives in the United States and Mexico. Write a memoran-

dum report communicating this information to U.S. managers working in Mexico. Write another memo to the director of international assignments persuading the director to develop other ways to promote international understanding in the company. You may vary this case by selecting a country of your choice.

PUBLIC SECTOR

e. *Chapter 12, Case 2.* Prepare an analytical letter report evaluating the feasibility of building a plastics recycling plant in your town. Prepare a letter to community leaders, a news release to the general public, or a brochure to gain support for the plastics recycling plant and to educate the public about the benefits of recycling.

HUMAN RESOURCES MANAGEMENT

f. *Chapter 13, Case 1.* Review current research related to preparing winning job credentials. Based on your research, prepare an informational report addressing the needs of a particular group (top- and middle-level managers outplaced by recent downsizing). If you wish, you may vary this case by writing guidelines for entry-level employees or others.

MANAGEMENT/Legal

g. *Chapter 14, Case 1.* Research current legal guidelines of the Equal Employment Opportunity Commission related to job interviewing. Write a memorandum report to store managers reviewing the major guidelines and focusing on recent changes.

CASE FOR ANALYSIS

MANAGEMENT

Case 1.   The Riverside Cafe. Around eight o'clock on a warm, summer evening, you and a friend arrive at the Riverside Cafe and stop for a moment to watch a barge slowly make its way down the Arkansas River. You are eagerly greeted by Mr. James Becker, the owner, who has asked you to visit the restaurant and recommend some changes.

Mr. Becker explains, "I opened the restaurant two years ago with the purpose of attracting the young singles market. You know, a group who will come in around seven in the evening, have several drinks and some appetizers, and visit with their friends until about midnight. We're earning a reasonable rate of return, but I'm concerned that our earnings are falling short of projections."

As you find a table facing the river, you notice about six young couples with children ranging from tot-size to about ten years. While you are munching on your hamburger, a disc jockey starts playing music, but no one goes to the dance floor. In addition, your friend brings to your attention the provocative pictures hanging on the wall over the bar.

Around ten o'clock, the restaurant is practically empty except for a lone couple. Mr. Becker returns to see if you have any questions and says, "I'm leaving tomorrow on a camping trip in the Ozark Mountains—no phones, a great getaway. Could we meet as soon as I return? I'm eager to get some feedback."

Required:

1. What is Mr. Becker's problem? You can look at this situation in several ways. What do you think is wrong here? Write your answer in the form of a problem statement using clear, specific language.

2. What are three alternative solutions to the problem you defined in Step 1? In developing your solutions, be open minded and consider every idea presented—even what may seem to be the most bizarre, off-the-wall idea. Use the following guidelines to evaluate each solution:
   a. Does each alternative solution solve the problem as defined?
   b. Is each alternative solution different, or has the solution simply been rephrased using different language?

3. Write an analytical report to Mr. Becker including the following points:
   a. State the problem as you see it.
   b. Describe briefly the three alternative solutions you identified.
   c. State the solution you believe will best solve the problem, based on your objective analysis of each solution.
   d. Discuss the factors that led to your decision.
   e. List and explain several recommendations Mr. Becker should take to implement your solution. Explain each recommended change thoroughly.

4. Prepare a title page and transmittal letter. Address the letter to Mr. James Becker, Riverside Cafe, 151 Riverside Road, Little Rock, AR 72204-0151.

5. Congratulations! Mr. Becker was very impressed with your recommended changes and wants to get started right away. Although you may not be able to develop every aspect of your recommended solution, you can help Mr. Becker communicate these recommendations to the appropriate group(s). You may use any technology available to you; for example, word processing, spreadsheet, desktop publishing presentation, graphics, sign/ banner maker, and other software programs.
   a. Develop your solution.
   b. Write a letter of transmittal to Mr. Becker explaining how each item relates to the solution. Use your professional judgment to determine the manner in which you will physically present the letter and the documents to Mr. Becker.

6. You have arranged to present your ideas to Mr. Becker tomorrow at 8 a.m. in his office at the Riverside Cafe. Develop a ten-minute oral presentation to explain your recommended changes to Mr. Becker. Carefully follow these pointers:
   a. Have I analyzed my audience and designed my message accordingly?
   b. Do my nonverbal communication cues agree with my worded messages?
   c. Have I prepared the visual aids needed to present my message effectively?

DOCUMENT FORMAT AND LAYOUT GUIDE

First impressions are lasting ones, and the receiver's first impression of your letter is its appearance and format. Preparing an error-free, attractive document is a basic requirement for maintaining credibility with your receiver. This section presents techniques for producing an appealing document. In addition, you will learn the standard and special parts of a letter, punctuation styles, the standard letter formats, and envelope addressing formats.

APPEARANCE

To convey a positive, professional image, a letter should be proofread carefully, prepared on high-quality paper, and balanced attractively on the page. Other factors that affect the overall appearance of your document are justification of margins, spacing after punctuation, abbreviations, and word division. Review the following guidelines to ensure that your documents are accurate in these areas.

Proofreaders' Marks

Carefully proofread for three overall factors: (1) organization, content, and style; (2) grammatical errors; and (3) format errors. In addition, check your document with the electronic spellcheck. Refer to Chapter 8 for a detailed explanation of systematic proofreading procedures. Become familiar with standard proofreaders' marks shown in Figure A-1.

Paper

The quality of paper reflects the professionalism of the company and allows a company to control communication costs effectively. Paper quality is measured in two ways: cotton-fiber content and weight.

High-cotton bond paper has a crisp crackle, is firm to the pencil touch, is difficult to tear, and ages without deterioration or chemical breakdown. The weight of paper is based on the weight of a ream consisting of approximately 500 sheets of 17- by 22-inch paper (equivalent to 1,000 sheets of $8^1/_2$- by 11-inch paper). If the ream weighs 20 pounds, the paper is said to be 20-pound weight. The heavier the paper, the higher the quality. Most business letters are produced on company letterhead that is printed on 16- or 20-pound bond paper.

Extremely important external documents such as reports and proposals may be printed on 24-pound bond paper with 100-percent cotton content. Memorandums, business forms, and other intercompany documents may be printed on lighter-weight paper with lower cotton-fiber content. Envelopes and plain sheets to be used for the second and successive pages of multiple-page letters should be of the same weight, cotton-fiber content, and color as the letterhead.

The standard paper size for business documents is $8^1/_2$ by 11 inches. Some top executives use executive-size ($7^1/_4$ by $10^1/_2$ inches) letterhead printed on 24-pound bond paper with 100-percent cotton content. However, this smaller size could easily be misfiled and may require special formatting that adds to the document cost.

Capitalize	Jim Neal, public relations director, Lincoln Enterprises, will direct the press conference.
Close up	Weekly staff meetings begin at 9 a. m.
Delete	Word-processing software available today is capable ....
Insert	This system can accomodate .... (computer, m)
Insert space	Managers address this problem everyday.
Insert comma	Clear concise messages save time and money.
Insert period	The agenda will be released on Friday
Insert apostrophe	The managers perspective ....
Insert hyphen	Easy to understand instructions are included.
Move copy as indicated	Today your June payment was received.
Change copy as indicated	Responsible for work crews of six to ten employees, monitored .... (Supervised)
Lowercase	Jin Ahiman, an Assistant Manager of a large retail store, is ....
Paragraph	Begin here.
No new paragraph	Do not begin here. (no new)
Start a new line	Proofread for three factors: (1) organization, content, and style; (2) mechanics; (3) ...
Align type vertically	DATE: May 21, 19-- SUBJECT: INTERNATIONAL ASSIGNMENTS AVAILABLE
Spell out	8 boxes of No. 10 envelopes (Sp)
Transpose	The Japanese beleive ....
Center line	ctr Systematic Proofreading Procedures
Use italics	ital Business Communications
Use bold	bf SITE SELECTION FOR MEMPHIS PLANT
Let the original material stand	stet Schedule an intercultural communication seminar .... (cross)
Move down; lower	June 2, 19--
Move up; raise	May 15, 19--
Move to left	1. Begin the date on line 10.
Move to right	Indent paragraphs within double-spaced text.
Single-space	Mr. Jay R. Albright SS President
Double-space	Enclosures DS c Mr. Keith Chan
Quadruple-space	October 1, 19-- QS Mrs. Sandra Pierce

FIGURE A-1   *Standard proofreaders' marks.*

Another characteristic of high-quality paper is the watermark, a design imprinted on the paper. Hold the paper up to the light to see this mark clearly. The watermark may be the trademark of the company using the paper or the brand name of the paper. Watermarked paper has a right side and a top edge; therefore, it must be placed in the printer correctly. The watermark is positioned so that it can be read across the sheet in the same direction as the printing.

Placement of Text on the Page

Letters should be balanced on the page with approximately equal margins. Companies using word-processing software set standard line lengths. To increase efficiency, the standard line length is often the same as the default margins set by the software. One-inch side margins, which produce a $6^1/_2$-inch line of writing, is a typical standard line. The date is printed on lines 14-16, depending on the length of the letter. Side margins are usually adjusted to improve the appearance of extremely short letters.

Many software programs will allow you to center a page of text vertically with one simple command; in that case, execute the center page command. This placement, which creates approximately equal margins on all sides of the letter, is often referred to as fitting the letter into a picture frame. With the proper equipment, the exact centering process is simple and creates a highly professional effect.

Justification of Margins

Word-processing software makes justified margins possible; that is, all lines start at the left margin and end flush at the right margin. Extra spaces are added between words so that the line ends exactly on the right margin. These extra spaces are visually distracting and make the document difficult to read. Research has shown that receiver comprehension is reduced when the copy is justified. In addition, justified margins give the document a computer-generated appearance, as if it were just another form letter. For these reasons, use the unjustified right margin as shown in the examples throughout this text.

Justified documents look very professional when they are printed with proportional spacing (the size of the letters varies and the extra space between words is minimized). Proportional printing and scalable fonts (different print styles whose size and appearance can be altered) are available with many laser printers. These enhancements increase your ability to prepare highly professional letters, reports, and proposals.

Jagged Right (Left Justified)

ESSENTIAL COMPUTER SKILLS

Currently, employees at all levels of our organization are using primary computer applications to increase their productivity and are eager to expand their knowledge to other more advanced areas. A primary need is to implement a telecommunications system that will allow our staff to transmit reports from the field to the home office. Other areas of interest include desktop publishing and electronic mail.

Justified Margins (Left and Right) Without Proportional Print

ESSENTIAL COMPUTER SKILLS

Currently, employees at all levels of our organization are using primary computer applications to increase their productivity and are eager to expand their knowledge to other more advanced areas. A primary need is to implement a telecommunications system that will allow our staff to transmit reports from the field to the home office. Other areas of interest include desktop publishing and electronic mail.

Justified Margins Using Proportional Print with Scalable Fonts

ESSENTIAL COMPUTER SKILLS

Currently, employees at all levels of our organization are using primary computer applications to increase their productivity and are eager to expand their knowledge to other more advanced areas. A primary need is to implement a telecommunications system that will allow our staff to transmit reports from the field to the home office. Other areas of interest include desktop publishing and electronic mail.

Special Symbols

To give documents the appearance of a professional typesetter, learn to create the following special symbols with your word-processing software:

En dash	Use in compound adjectives (Minneapolis–St.Paul) or to separate words indicating a duration (May–June).
Em dash	Use instead of a dash (--) to indicate an abrupt change in thought (statement—that is,)
Hyphen	Use to indicate word division (nega-tive)
Quotation marks	Use instead of the inch (") and foot (') symbols ("Today" or 'today').
Fractions	Create ½ and ¼ rather than key 1/2 and 1/4. Special symbols are available for other common fractions.
Bullets	Use a variety of special symbols to highlight enumerated items (o, ● , □, ■, ✦, ✔, ∅)
Other symbols	Learn the codes for printing symbols: ©, ®, ¢, £, ‰, ¶, and others.

Spacing

Proper spacing after punctuation is essential in preparing a professional document.

1. Space *once* after a period, question mark, or exclamation point (terminal punctuation) when using a proportional font. The proportional font automatically adjusts the white space; therefore, adding an extra space to separate the sentences as you have traditionally done is not necessary. However, space *twice* after terminal punctuation if you use a monospaced font (a "typewriter-like" font with characters of *one* width) or a typewriter.

Proportional: When will he arrive? Regardless of the time . . . .
Monospaced: **Step two was completed.   Then . . . .**

One space follows the terminal punctuation in the examples in this text. Because some writers advocate that extra space aids readability regardless of the font used, you should learn your instructor's preference before submitting documents.

2. Space twice after a colon except in the expression of time:

We have three questions: (1) When is . . . .
Please cancel my 9:15 a.m. meeting with Ann Morse.

3. Space once after a comma or a semicolon.

When the end of the month comes, we will be prepared.
The operator left at three o'clock; he was ill.

4. Space once after a period following an initial and abbreviations.

No., Co., and *Corp.*   Mr. Warren H. Ragsdale

Word Division

Often, word division is necessary to avoid extreme variations in line length. Word-processing software automatically wraps words that will not fit within the margins to the next line. If a long word is wrapped to the next line, the previous line will be extremely short (jagged right margin) or will have large spaces between words (justified right margin). In either case, the result is distracting. A divided word at the end of the line would be less distracting.

Try to avoid dividing words at the ends of lines. If words must be divided, follow acceptable word-division rules. Word-processing software will allow you to make hyphenation decisions. In addition, upgrades to industry's most popular word-processing programs are now capable of automatic hyphenation based on accepted word-division rules. These rules do not necessarily apply in the printing of books, magazines, and newspapers. Apply the following word-division rules:

1. Divide words between syllables only. (Words with only one syllable cannot be divided: *through, hearth, worked*).
2. Do not divide a word if it has fewer than seven letters. (Lines on a printed page can vary as much as six or seven letters in length; therefore, dividing short words such as *letter* or *report* is pointless.)
3. Do not separate the following syllables from the remainder of a word:
   a. A syllable that does not include a vowel: *would/n't.*
   b. A first syllable that contains only one letter: *a/greement.*
   c. A last syllable that contains only one or two letters: *pneumoni/a, apolog/y, complete/ly.*
4. Divide a word after a single-letter syllable: *situ-ation, congratu-late, extenu-ate.*
5. Divide hyphenated words after the hyphen: *self-employed, semi-independent.*

6. Do not divide proper names, abbreviations, or most numbers:
   George Martin, AICPA, 3,189,400
7. Avoid dividing a word at the top or bottom of a page.

PUNCTUATION STYLES AND LETTER FORMATS

Page layout (format) affects the effectiveness of the message. Many companies have policies that dictate the punctuation style and the letter format used.

Mixed and Open Punctuation

Two punctuation styles are customarily used in business letters: mixed and open. Letters using **mixed punctuation style** have a colon after the salutation and a comma after the complimentary close. Letters using **open punctuation style** do not have a colon after the salutation and a comma after the complimentary close. Mixed punctuation is the traditional style; however, cost-conscious companies are increasingly adopting the open style (and other similar format changes), which eliminates unnecessary keystrokes.

Mixed Punctuation	Open Punctuation
January 24, 19--	January 24, 19--
Mr. Lewis R. Moser 1938 South Welch Avenue Northwood, NE 65432-1938	Mr. Lewis R. Moser 1938 South Welch Avenue Northwood, NE 65432-1938
SALUTATION Dear Mr. Moser:	Dear Mr. Moser
COMPLIMENTATY CLOSE Sincerely, *Michele Laird* Michele Laird Program Chair	Sincerely *Michele Laird* Michele Laird Program Chair

Letter Formats

The three letter formats that are commonly accepted by businesses include block, modified block, and simplified block.

BLOCK

Companies striving to reduce the cost of producing business documents adopt the easy-to-learn, efficient block format. All lines (including paragraphs) begin at the left margin; therefore, no time is lost setting tabs and positioning letter parts. Study carefully the letter in block format with open punctuation shown in Figure A-2.

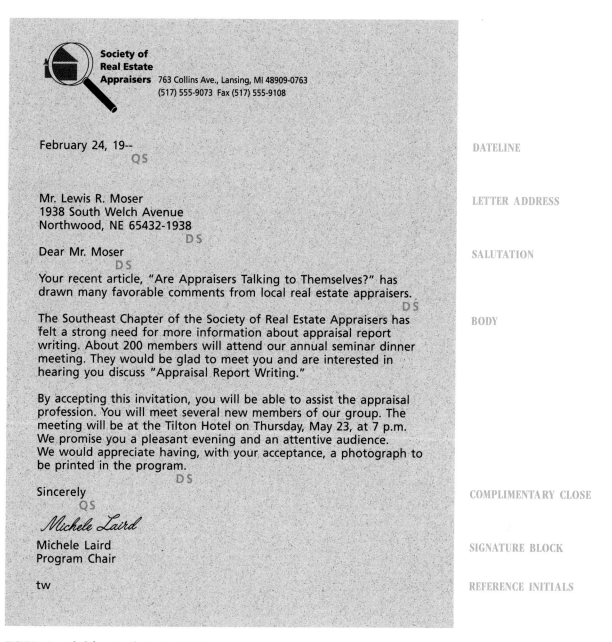

FIGURE A-2   Block format with open punctuation.

MODIFIED BLOCK

Modified block is the traditional letter format still used in many companies. The dateline, complimentary close, and signature block begin at the horizontal center of the page. Paragraphs may be indented five spaces if the writer prefers or the company policy requires it; however, the indention creates unnecessary keystrokes that increase the cost of the letter. All other lines begin at the left margin. Study carefully the letter in modified block format with block paragraphs and mixed punctuation shown in Figure A-3.

Mark's Small Engines
405 South Ridge Road
Macon, GA 31213-0405
(912) 555-1497

DATELINE   February 4, 19--
QS

LETTER ADDRESS   Mr. Wallace Ladner
4513 East Colton Street
Macon, GA 31213-8328
DS

SALUTATION   Dear Mr. Ladner:
DS

Johnson Motors are among the most dependable small electric motors manufactured in the United States today. Here at Mark's Small Engines, we believe that the right size Johnson engine for the particular job is critical.
DS

BODY   The three-month warranty with the Johnson Motors applies only if the motor is used under normal operating conditions. Your pipe size (3/15 inch), the large distance between your pool and the filtering system (100 feet), and the size of your pool (50 by 60 feet) placed undue stress on the 2.5-horsepower motor. Your sales receipt indicates that a 3.5-horsepower motor was recommended based on our evaluation of your needs.

Our sales force will be happy to show you a 3.5-horsepower Johnson motor. This powerful motor should provide clear, sparkling water for outdoor enjoyment for your family.
DS

COMPLIMENTARY CLOSE   Sincerely,
QS

Robin Tilson

SIGNATURE BLOCK   Robin Tilson
Manager
DS

REFERENCE INITIALS   ms

FIGURE A-3   Modified block format with mixed punctuation.

SIMPLIFIED BLOCK

The simplified block format is an efficient letter format. Like the block format, all lines begin at the left margin; but the salutation and complimentary close are omitted, and a subject line is required. Place the subject line a double space below the letter address and a double space above the body. Study carefully the letter in simplified block format shown in Figure A-4.

Strobel Cable Television
8310 Greenbriar Road
Santa Barbara, CA 93102-8310
(805) 555-6540 Fax (805) 555-0943

February 15, 19--
QS

DATELINE

Ms. Iris Cruz
2987 West Wakefield Court
Santa Barbara, CA 93116-8871
DS

LETTER ADDRESS

Changes in Cable Service
DS

SUBJECT LINE

Some important changes in your cable television service will begin
March 1, 19--. We will rearrange our channel line-up and institute a
rate change. These changes are necessary to maintain quality service
and to meet new federal guidelines for programming selection.
DS

BODY

Our new monthly rates are as follows:

Basic Service $12.50
Expanded Service $18.00
Premium Service $32.00

With these changes, the cost of our expanded package (all channels
except premium) is still only 60 cents a day, less than the cost of a
cup of coffee.

Our employees are committed to providing you with the best
quality and variety of cable television, including education, sports,
religion, and public affairs programming. Please call us if we can be
of additional service to you.
QS

Dennis G. Hunter

Dennis G. Hunter
Systems Manager

SIGNATURE BLOCK

yc

REFERENCE INITIALS

FIGURE A-4   Simplified block format.

STANDARD LETTER PARTS

Business letters include seven standard parts. Other parts are optional and may
be included when necessary. The standard parts include (1) heading, (2) letter
address, (3) salutation, (4) body, (5) complimentary close, (6) signature block,
and (7) reference initials. The proper placement of these parts is shown in Figures A-2, A-3, and A-4; a discussion of each standard part follows.

Heading

When the letterhead shows the company name, address, telephone and/or fax number, and logo, the letter begins with the dateline. Use the month-day-year format (September 2, 19--) unless you are preparing government documents, writing to an international audience who uses the day-month-year format, or company policy requires another format. Abbreviating the month or using numbers (9/2/--) may portray a hurried attitude.

If a letter is prepared on plain paper, the writer's address must be keyed immediately above the dateline; otherwise, the recipient may be unable to respond if the envelope is discarded. The **heading** consists of three single-spaced lines: (1) the writer's street address; (2) the writer's city, two-letter postal abbreviation, and 9-digit ZIP Code; and (3) the dateline. The writer's name is omitted because it appears in the signature block.

Letter Address

The **letter address** includes a personal or professional title (e.g., Mr. or Ms.), the name of the person and company to whom the letter is being sent, and the complete address. It begins a quadruple space after the dateline. Refer to Figure A-5 for appropriate formats for letter addresses.

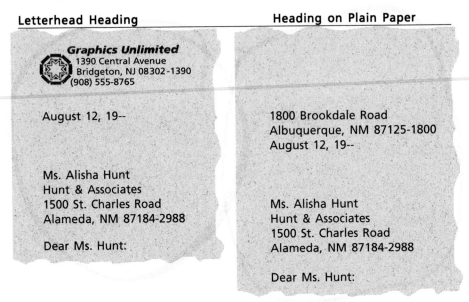

Letterhead Heading

Graphics Unlimited
1390 Central Avenue
Bridgeton, NJ 08302-1390
(908) 555-8765

August 12, 19--

Ms. Alisha Hunt
Hunt & Associates
1500 St. Charles Road
Alameda, NM 87184-2988

Dear Ms. Hunt:

Heading on Plain Paper

1800 Brookdale Road
Albuquerque, NM 87125-1800
August 12, 19--

Ms. Alisha Hunt
Hunt & Associates
1500 St. Charles Road
Alameda, NM 87184-2988

Dear Ms. Hunt:

Salutation

The **salutation** is the greeting that opens a letter and is placed a double space below the letter address. The salutation is omitted in the simplified block format shown in Figure A-4.

To show courtesy for the receiver, include a personal or professional title (Mr., Ms., Dr., Senator). Refer to the *first line* of the letter address to determine an appropriate salutation; use the *second* if the letter includes an attention line as shown in Figure A-5. In the previous example, "Dear Ms. Hunt" is an appropriate salutation for this letter addressed to Ms. Alisha Hunt (first line of letter address). If the first line of the letter address were "Hunt & Associates," "Ladies and Gentlemen" would be an appropriate salutation. To avoid use of

Letter address	Appropriate Salutation	Explanation
A Specific Person Mr. Shawn Tate, President Bank of Commerce P.O. Box 3902 Lincoln, NE 68506-3902	Dear Mr. Tate:	If the person is a business associate, use a courtesy title and the last name.
	Dear Shawn:	If you know the person well, use the person's first name or the name you would use greeting the person face to face.
	Dear Shawn Tate: or use the simplified block format (Figure A-4) that omits the salutation.	If you do not know whether the person is male or female, use the whole name or omit the salutation to avoid offending the receiver.
A Company Bank of Commerce P.O. Box 3902 Lincoln, NE 68506-3902	Ladies and Gentlemen: or use the simplified block format (Figure A-4) that omits the salutation.	This salutation recognizes the presence of males and females in management. Do *not* use "Dear Ladies and Gentlemen." You may use "Ladies" if you are sure that management is all female or "Gentlemen" if you are sure that management is all male.
A Company and Directed to a Specific Individual Attention Mr. Shawn Tate Bank of Commerce P.O. Box 3902 Lincoln, NE 68506-3902	Ladies and Gentlemen: or use the simplified block format (Figure A-4) that omits the salutation.	The letter is officially written to the company; therefore, "Dear Mr. Tate" is *not* acceptable. The salutation matches the second line of the letter address when you direct attention to a specific person.
A Specific Position Within a Business Purchasing Officer United Brokerage Firm 876 Addison Road Toledo, OH 43692-7832	Dear Purchasing Officer: or use the simplified block format (Figure A-4) that omits the salutation.	Because the name of the person is unknown, the simplified block format would be especially useful. A subject line is used rather than the salutation.
A Group of People Institute of Public Accountants 2958 Central Avenue Baltimore, MD 21233-2958	Dear Accounting Professionals:	When form letters are merged with available databases, the letter is personalized by inserting the recipient's letter address and a specific salutation such as "Dear Mr. Moser." This automated procedure eliminates the need for less personal salutations.
Form letter to a potential customer or policyholders (letter address may be omitted)	Dear Customer:	

FIGURE A-5   Appropriate formats for letter addresses and salutations.

Letter address	Appropriate Salutation	Explanation
A Public Official		
The Honorable (first and last name of U.S. Senator)	Dear Senator (last name):	
The Honorable (first and last name of U.S. Representative)	Dear Mr. or Ms. (last name):	This form is also used for state senators and representatives.
The Honorable (first and last name of state governor)	Dear Governor (last name):	
Refer to an up-to-date reference manual or professional protocol guide when writing to other public officials.		

FIGURE A-5   Appropriate formats for letter addresses and salutations, continued.

the impersonal salutation, "Ladies and Gentlemen," format the letter in simplified block that omits the salutation. Use the examples shown in Figure A-5 as a guide when selecting an appropriate salutation.

Body

The **body** contains the message of the letter. It begins a double space below the salutation. Paragraphs are single-spaced with a double space between paragraphs. Because a double space separates the paragraphs, indenting paragraphs, which requires extra startup (setting tabs) and keying time, is not necessary. However, some companies may require paragraph indention as company policy. If so, you must use the modified block style (Figure A-3) with indented paragraphs.

Complimentary Close

The **complimentary close** is a phrase used to close a letter in the same way that you say good-bye at the end of a conversation. To create goodwill, choose a complimentary close that reflects the formality of your relationship with the receiver. Typical examples are "Yours truly," "Sincerely yours," "Sincerely," "Cordially," and "Cordially yours." "Sincerely" is considered neutral and is thus appropriate in a majority of business situations. Capitalize only the first word of the complimentary close and position it a double space below the body. The complimentary close and the salutation are omitted in the simplified block format (Figure A-4).

Signature Block

The **signature block** consists of the writer's name keyed a quadruple space (three blank lines) below the complimentary close (or body in the simplified block letter). The writer's name is signed legibly in the space provided. A female may include a courtesy title to indicate her preference (e.g., Miss, Ms., Mrs.), and a female or male may use a title to distinguish a name used by both males and females (e.g., Shane, Leslie, or Stacy) or initials (E. M. Goodman). A business or professional title may be placed on the same line with the writer's name or directly below it. Use the following examples as guides for balancing the writer's name and title:

Title on the Same Line	Title on the Next Line
Ms. Shawn Tate, President	Ms. E. M. Goodman Assistant Manager
Paul Warner, Manager Quality Control Division	Raymond Fitzpatrick Human Resources Director

Reference Initials

The **reference initials** consist of the keyboard operator's initials keyed in lowercase a double space below the signature block. The writer's initials are not included because the name appears in the signature block. The reference initials and the signature block identify the persons involved in preparing a letter in the event of later questions. Reference initials are omitted when a letter is keyed by the writer—a common practice now that many executives compose documents at a computer terminal both in the office and at remote locations. However, company policy may require that the initials of all people involved in writing a letter be placed in the reference initials line to identify accountability in the case of litigation.

SPECIAL LETTER PARTS

Other letter parts may be added to a letter depending on the particular situation. These parts include (1) mailing notation, (2) attention line, (3) reference line, (4) subject line, (5) second-page heading, (6) company name in signature block, (7) enclosure notation, (8) copy notation, and (9) postscript.

Mailing Notation

A **mailing notation** provides a record of how a letter was sent. Examples of this type of mailing notation include REGISTERED, CERTIFIED, OVERNIGHT DELIVERY, or FACSIMILE. Other mailing notations such as CONFIDENTIAL, PERSONAL, and PLEASE FORWARD give instructions on how a letter should be handled. Key a mailing notation in all capitals a double space below the dateline at the left margin. Key the letter address a double space below the mailing notation as shown in Figure A-6.

Attention Line

An **attention line** directs a letter to a specific person (Attention Ms. Laura Ritter), position within a company (Attention Human Resources Director), or department (Attention Purchasing Department). An attention line appears as the first line of the letter address; the company name appears on the second line as shown in Figure A-6. The appropriate salutation in a letter with an attention line is "Ladies and Gentlemen" as shown in Figure A-5. Because the envelope format also requires the attention line to appear on the first line of the letter address, the envelope can be prepared without rekeying the address.

Reference Line

A **reference line** (Re: Contract No. 983-9873) directs the receiver to source documents or to files. Key a reference line a double space below the letter address, as shown in Figure A-6.

Subject Line

A **subject line** tells the receiver what a letter is about and sets the stage for the receiver to understand the message. The simplified block format requires a subject line; in other letter formats, the subject line is optional. Key the subject line a double space below the salutation, as shown in Figure A-6. Use either lowercase and capitals or all capitals for added emphasis. If modified block format is used, a subject line can be centered for added emphasis. To increase efficiency, the word *subject* is omitted because its position above the body clearly identifies its function.

The mailing notation, attention line, reference line, and subject line are illustrated in Figure A-6.

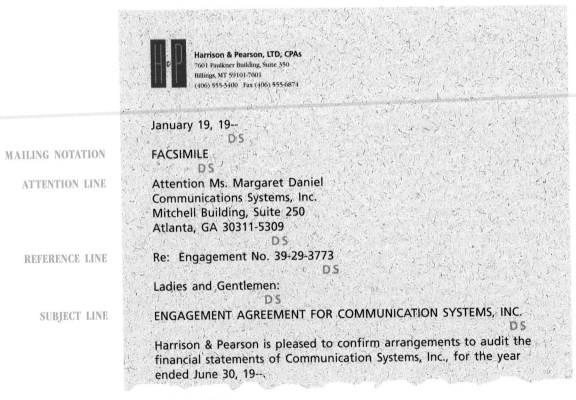

FIGURE A-6   *Special letter parts.*

Second-Page Heading

The second and successive pages of multiple-page letters and memorandums are keyed on plain paper of the same quality as the letterhead. A **second-page heading** is used on the second and successive pages to identify them as a continuation of the first page. A three-part heading includes (1) the name of the person or company to whom the message is sent (identical to the first line of the letter address), (2) the page number, and (3) the date.

Place the heading one inch (six lines) from the top edge of the paper. Double-space after the heading to continue the body of the letter. Both vertical and horizontal formats are acceptable.

With all three lines beginning at the left margin, the vertical format is compatible with all letter formats. The horizontal format is more complex to keyboard but looks attractive with the modified block style and is especially effective when using the vertical heading would force the letter or memorandum to additional pages:

Vertical Format

Mr. Lewis R. Moser   1-inch
Page 2
January 24, 19--
                          D S
We would appreciate having, with your acceptance, a photograph to be printed in the program.

Sincerely,

Michele Laird

Michele Laird
Program Chair

Horizontal Format

                                                                1-inch

Mr. Lewis R. Moser   2   January 24, 19--
                                                              D S
We would appreciate having, with your acceptance, a photograph to be printed in the program.

Sincerely,

Michele Laird

Michele Laird
Program Chair

Company Name in Signature Block

Some companies prefer to include the **company name** in the signature block. However, often the company name is not included in the signature block because it appears in the letterhead. The company name is beneficial when the letter is prepared on plain paper or is more than one page (the second page of the letter is printed on plain paper). When the writer wishes to emphasize that the document is written on behalf of the company, a company name may be useful. For example, the company name might be included when the nature of the letter is a contract such as an engagement letter to a newly acquired client. Key the company name in all capitals a double space below the complimentary close and a quadruple space (three blank lines) above the signature block, as shown in Figure A-7.

Enclosure Notation

An **enclosure notation** indicates that an additional item(s) (brochure, price list, resume) is included in the same envelope. Key "Enclosure" a double space below the reference initials (or the signature block if no reference initials appear), as shown in Figure A-7. Key the plural form (Enclosures) if more than one item is enclosed. You may identify the number of enclosures (Enclosures: 3) or the specific item enclosed (Enclosure: Bid Proposal). Avoid the temptation to abbreviate (Enc.) because abbreviations may communicate that you are in a hurry or that a thorough job is not necessary for this particular person. Some companies use the word "Attachment" on memorandums when the accompanying items may be stapled or paperclipped and not placed in an envelope.

Copy Notation

A **copy notation** indicates that a copy of the document was sent to the person(s) listed. Include the person's personal or professional title and full name after keying "c" for copy. Key the copy notation at the left margin a double space below the signature block, reference initials, or enclosure notation (depending on the special letter parts used).

Postscript

A **postscript**, appearing as the last item in a letter, is commonly used to emphasize information. A postscript in a sales letter, for example, is often used to restate the central selling point; for added emphasis, it may be handwritten or printed in a different color. Researchers have noted an increased trend toward handwritten postscripts of a personal nature as individuals attempt to keep in touch with people in today's high-tech society. Postscripts should not be used to add information inadvertently omitted from the letter. Instead, edit the document and reprint an effectively organized letter.

Key the postscript a double space below the last notation or signature block if no notations are used, as shown in Figure A-7. Treat the postscript as any other paragraph; indent only if the other paragraphs in the letter are indented. Because its position clearly labels this paragraph as a postscript, do not begin with "PS."

The second-page heading, reference initials, company name, enclosure notation, copy notation, and postscript are illustrated in Figure A-7.

MEMORANDUM FORMATS

Memorandums are messages sent to offices or individuals *within* a business. To increase productivity, companies use formats that are easy to input and will

Communications Systems, Inc.   1-inch (Line 6)   SECOND-PAGE HEADING
Page 2
January 19, 19--
        D S
Sharon Hampton has been assigned as the audit manager in charge
of your audit examination. Please review the enclosed preliminary
time schedule she has developed and direct your questions to her at
555-3095, extension 25.

We at Harrison & Pearson look forward to providing these and other
quality professional services to you.
                        D S
Sincerely,
        D S
HARRISON & PEARSON, LTD, CPAs   COMPANY NAME
                    Q S

Jerome S. Fuja

Jerome S. Fuja
Audit Partner

ek   REFERENCE INITIALS
    D S
Enclosure: Audit Agreement   ENCLOSURE NOTATION
                    D S
c Mr. David Banks   COPY NOTATION
            D S
Our annual tax update has been scheduled for March 5-6, 19--. You POSTSCRIPT
will receive an agenda from the tax department just as soon as all
details have been finalized.

FIGURE A-7   *Special letter parts.*

save time. Memorandums, or memos, may be prepared on preprinted memorandum forms, plain paper, or letterhead depending on the preference of the company. Follow these general guidelines in formatting memos:

1. Set one-inch margins or the default set by your word-processing software.
2. Follow these guidelines for determining the starting line:
   Plain paper: $1\frac{1}{2}$ inches (Line 10).
   Letterhead: A double space below the letterhead.
3. Single-space paragraphs and double-space between paragraphs. Do *not* indent paragraphs.

4. Include a subject line in all memos to facilitate quick reading and filing. Key the subject line in all capitals for added emphasis or begin the first word and all other words except articles, prepositions, or conjunctions with capital letters.

5. Omit personal and professional titles (Mr., Mrs., Dr.) on the *TO* and *FROM* lines because of the informality of this intercompany communication. Include job titles or department names.

6. Handle reference initials, enclosure and copy notations, and postscripts just as you would in a letter.

7. Include a second-page heading on the second and successive pages of a memorandum just as you would in a multiple-page letter.

8. Place memos in special envelopes designated for intercompany mail or in plain envelopes. If you use plain envelopes, key COMPANY MAIL in the stamp position so that it will not be inadvertently stamped and mailed. Key the recipient's name and department in the address location and any other information required by company policy. Large companies may require use of office numbers or other mail designations to expedite intercompany deliveries.

Many variations of memorandum formats are used in business. The formal and the simplified memorandum are illustrated in Figures A-8 and A-9 respectively.

Formal

The **formal memorandum format** begins with a standard heading that contains the writer's name, receiver's name, date, and subject. To save input time, some companies use a preprinted form that identifies the document as a memorandum and contains the basic information: *TO, FROM, DATE, SUBJECT*. The writer's initials are typically handwritten to the right of the writer's name. Double-space after each line of the heading and before the beginning of the body. Headings may be added to help the receiver move smoothly from one major section to another. Figure A-8 is an example of the formal memorandum format.

Simplified

The **simplified memorandum format** is designed to save input time. The guide words (*TO, FROM, DATE, SUBJECT*) are omitted, and all lines begin at the left margin. Key the subject line in all capitals or cap/lowercase a double space below the receiver's name and a double space above the body of the memorandum. Key the writer's name a quadruple space below the body, leaving enough space for the writer's signature. Figure A-9 is an example of a simplified memorandum format.

ENVELOPES

The U.S. Postal Service recommends a specific format for addressing envelopes so that the address can be read by optical character readers used to sort mail quickly. The recommended format requires that the envelope address be keyed in all capital letters with no punctuation (all caps, no punctuation).

Watt's Fabrics & Supply
763 East Commerce Street
Toledo, OH 43601-7530
Phone-4195553310 Fax-4195551037

D S

TO: Erin W. Lutzel, Vice President

FROM: Isako Kimura, Marketing Director   *I. K.*

DATE: June 30, 19--

SUBJECT: Marketing Activity Report for June

The marketing division reports the following activities for June:

D S

<u>Advertising</u>

Three meetings were held with representatives at the Bart and
Dome agency to complete plans for the fall campaign for Fluffy
Buns. The campaign will concentrate on the use of discount coupons
published in the Thursday food section of sixty daily newspapers in
the Pacific states. Coupons will be released on the second and fourth
Thursdays in June and July.

Estimated cost of the program is $645,000. That amount includes 2.2
million redeemed coupons at 20 cents each ($440,000).

A point-of-sale advertising display, shown on the attached sheet,
was developed for retail grocery outlets. Sales reps are pushing
these in their regular and new calls. The display may be used to
feature a different product from our line on a weekly basis.

<u>Sales Staff</u>

We have dropped one sales rep from the northern California section
and divided the area between the southern Oregon and Sacramento
reps.

Attachment

FIGURE A-8   Formal memorandum format.

Proper placement of the address on a large envelope (No. 10) is shown in
Figure A-10 and a small envelope (No. 6³/₄) in Figure A-11. Note these specific
points:

- The address matches the letter address.
- The address contains at least three but no more than six lines.
- All lines of the return (writer's) address and the letter (receiver's) address are
  keyed in block form (flush at the left).
- All lines are single-spaced.

January 15, 19--   1½ inches (Line 10)
QS

All Sales Representatives
DS
PLANS FOR ANNUAL SALES MEETING
DS
Just as many of you have requested, this year's sales conference will
be held in Orlando, Florida, March 15-20. The conference will begin
with a reception and awards banquet—a time to recognize those of
you who have earned record-breaking sales for the year. Please
review the enclosed agenda of the informative, energizing sales
sessions and the entertainment planned for free time.

This conference will give you an opportunity to learn about new
products, to renew old friendships, and to meet the ten new reps
hired this year. For the first time at this year's sales conference, we
are including representatives from our engineering division. This
joint meeting will allow you to share with them your first-hand
knowledge of product performance and to recommend ways for
improving our current product line.

Please make your travel arrangements to arrive at the Orlando
International Airport prior to 3 p.m. on Wednesday, March 15.
Magic Carpet Limousine Service will transport you to the Lakeside
Resort. Call Janice Petre at (203) 555-1534 to reserve your place for
our Saturday afternoon recreation.
QS

Clyde N. Collier

Clyde N. Collier
Vice President of Sales
DS
Enclosure

FIGURE A-9   *Simplified memorandum format.*

- A personal or professional title (Mr., Ms., Dr.) is included on the envelope as well as in the letter address.
- The last line contains *only* three items of information: (1) city; (2) two-letter abbreviation for state, territory, or province; and (3) 9-digit ZIP Code.
- One space appears between the two-letter abbreviation for state, territory, or province and the ZIP Code.
- The writer's name is keyed in the half-inch of space above a preprinted company letterhead.
- Place special notations for the addressee (PLEASE FORWARD, HOLD FOR ARRIVAL, PERSONAL) a double space below the return address. Place mailing

FIGURE A-10
Large envelope (No. 10) format
and folding instructions

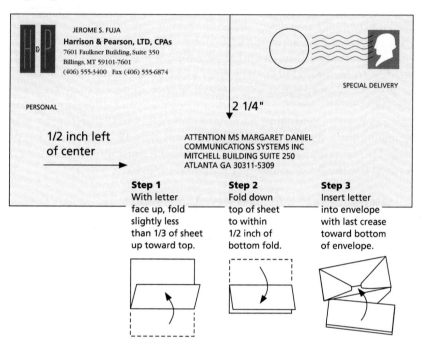

FIGURE A-11
Small envelope (6¾) format and
folding instructions

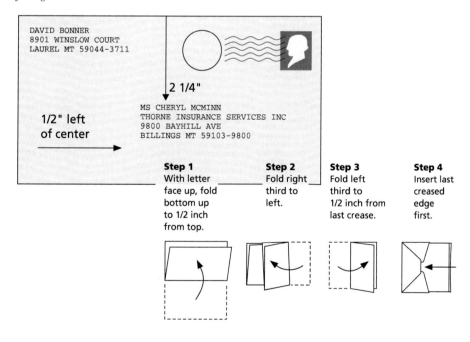

notations for postal authorities (OVERNIGHT and REGISTERED) a double space below the stamp position. Use all capitals for special notations.

Many businesses use word-processing software to print envelopes and mailing labels using the letter address in the letter. To eliminate the need to key the address twice—once for the letter and again for the envelope (all caps, no punctuation)—some authorities recommend keying the letter address in the all caps, no punctuation format. Obviously, if a letter is to be inserted into a window envelope, this format will assist the U.S. Postal Service in processing and delivering it quickly. The all caps, no punctuation format would also be appropriate for quantity mailings of a routine nature. However, because this format may make documents look like form letters and is only beginning to gain acceptance, the traditional upper- and lowercase letters with appropriate punctuation should be used for the letter address in nonroutine business letters.

Routine Letter with Letter Address Keyed in All Caps, No Punctuation

Northside Insurance Co.
1249 Heritage Drive
Norfolk, VA 32511-1249
(804) 555-3700

January 19, 19--

MS MAJORIE VAN DYKE
215 NORTH THIRD STREET
NORFOLK VA 23511-3100

RE: Life Insurance Policy No. 89-392-12

Dear Ms. Van Dyke

The two-letter abbreviations for states, territories, and Canadian provinces (see Figure A-12) and the 9-digit ZIP Code assigned by the U.S. Postal Service should be used for all letters. The first digit in a ZIP Code represents one of ten national areas. Within these areas, each state is divided into an average of ten smaller geographic areas, identified by the second and third digits. The fourth and fifth digits identify a local delivery area. The U.S. Postal Service now uses an extended ZIP Code called *ZIP+4*, which adds a hyphen and four additional numbers to the existing five-digit ZIP Code. These "+4" digits permit automated equipment to sort mail for faster delivery. The first two of the "+4" digits denote a delivery section of blocks, streets, several office buildings, or a small geographic area. The last two numbers denote a delivery "segment," which might be one floor of an office building, one side of a street, a firm, a suite, or a group of post office boxes.

State or Territory	Two-Letter Abbreviation	State or Territory	Two-Letter Abbreviation
Alabama	AL	Ohio	OH
Alaska	AK	Oklahoma	OK
Arizona	AZ	Oregon	OR
Arkansas	AR	Pennsylvania	PA
American Samoa	AS	Puerto Rico	PR
California	CA	Rhode Island	RI
Canal Zone	CZ	South Carolina	SC
Connecticut	CT	South Dakota	SD
Delaware	DE	Tennessee	TN
District of Columbia	DC	Texas	TX
Florida	FL	Trust Territories	TT
Georgia	GA	Utah	UT
Guam	GU	Vermont	VT
Hawaii	HI	Virginia	VA
Idaho	ID	Virgin Islands	VI
Illinois	IL	Washington	WA
Indiana	IN	West Virginia	WV
Iowa	IA	Wisconsin	WI
Kansas	KS	Wyoming	WY
Kentucky	KY		
Louisiana	LA	**Canadian Province**	**Two-Letter Abbreviation**
Maine	ME		
Maryland	MD		
Massachusetts	MA	Alberta	AB
Michigan	MI	British Columbia	BC
Minnesota	MN	Labrador	LB
Mississippi	MS	Manitoba	MN
Missouri	MO	New Brunswick	NB
Montana	MT	Newfoundland	NF
Nebraska	NE	Northwest Territories	NT
Nevada	NV	Nova Scotia	NS
New Hampshire	NH	Ontario	ON
New Jersey	NJ	Prince Edward Island	PE
New Mexico	NM	Quebec	PQ
New York	NY	Saskatchewan	SK
North Carolina	NC	Yukon Territory	YT

FIGURE A-12   *State, district, territory, and province two-letter abbreviations.*

GRAMMAR REVIEW AND EXERCISES

If messages do not meet high standards of grammar and mechanics, they have negative consequences. The receiver may (1) misunderstand the message, (2) lose time by stopping to review the message, (3) think more about the error than the message, (4) think negatively about the sender's background, or (5) lose respect for the sender.

The following pages review some of the common problems that confront business writers. Regardless of job level (from the lowest entry-level to the highest managerial level), a knowledge of basics is beneficial. The rules and principles on the following pages should be mastered by both executive personnel and administrative personnel.

The following review of basics seeks to answer frequently encountered questions about word usage, grammar, spelling, and punctuation. For more thorough reviews, consult standard reference books on grammar or transcription.

SELF CHECK

To measure your knowledge of grammar, spelling, and punctuation, follow these steps: Cover the answer that appears below each numbered sentence. Identify the grammatical error(s) in the numbered sentences. Then, slide the cover sheet down and check your answer against the correct sentence.

1. Only 1 of the applicants have completed the employment tests; but 3 have submitted resumes.

Only one of the applicants has completed the employment tests, but three have submitted resumes.

2. Neither vice president Cox nor secretary Smith are ready to present their recommendations.

Neither Vice President Cox nor Secretary Smith is ready to present recommendations.

3. One applicants' employment test was postponed for two hours, this may have effected the test score.

One applicant's employment test was postponed for two hours; this delay may have affected the test score. (Nouns other than "delay" can be used.)

4. Matthew's grin and bear it attitude is his fundamental principal of survival.

Matthew's grin-and-bear-it attitude is his fundamental principle of survival.

5. Supervisors discussed one criteria for promotion during annual performance interviews with full time personal.

Supervisors discussed one criterion for promotion during annual performance interviews with full-time personnel.

6. I appreciate you writing a proposal, and sending it directly to the controller and I.

I appreciate your writing a proposal and sending it directly to the controller and me.

7. A short intensive review will be conducted on April 14, 1995 at 10:00 A.M.

A short, intensive review will be conducted on April 14, 1995, at 10 a.m.

8. If you can complete the survey before July 1, 1995 please proceed, otherwise ask the superintendent for a new set of questionaires.

If you can complete the survey before July 1, 1995, please proceed; otherwise, ask the superintendent for a new set of questionnaires.

9. Did the Controller really use the words "get out of my office?"

Did the controller really use the words, "Get out of my office"?

10. Please try to quickly review these documents, it's to be returned before October 21st.

Please try to review these documents quickly; they must be returned before October 21.

After completing the Self-Check, identify your problem areas and complete the pertinent sections of this review. For best results, follow these suggestions for studying Appendix B:

1. Read the principle and examine the illustrations that follow. Reread the principle to reinforce learning.
2. Complete the exercises positioned throughout this review. They are designed to test your understanding of the principles.
3. Complete the Self-Check exercise and Review Quiz designed to assess how well you have mastered the grammar principles presented in Appendix B. Analyze any questions you may have answered incorrectly to identify specific areas in which you need further study. Then reread these principles.

NOUNS

Nouns are words that name people, places, things, or ideas.

1. **Use specific nouns for most business writing because they let a receiver see exactly what is meant.** "The dean objected" gives a clearer picture than "An administrator objected"; "A $2^1/_2$-ton truck is missing" is clearer than "One vehicle is missing."
   Use general words when you do not want (or need) to convey a vivid mental picture. "I appreciated your letting me know about the accident" is less vivid (and better) than ". . . about your sprained ankle, your broken ribs, and the smashed-up car."

2. **Use concrete nouns as sentence subjects normally because they help to present ideas vividly.** "Joe explained the procedure" is more vivid than "Explanations were given by Joe." Because "explanations" are harder to visualize than "Joe," the idea in the second sentence is more difficult to see. *Concrete* nouns are word labels for that which is solid—something that can be seen, touched, and so on. *Abstract* nouns are word labels for that which is not solid—something that cannot be seen, touched, and so on. *Tree* is a concrete noun. *Thought, confrontation*, and *willingness* are abstract nouns.
   Use an abstract noun as the subject of a sentence if you do not want an idea to stand out vividly. "His weakness was well known" is less vivid than "He was known to be weak."

EXERCISE 1

Write the letter for the better sentence and provide a reason for your answer.

1. a. Mr. Edwards called me yesterday.
   b. A man called me yesterday.

2. a. George was driving 40 mph in a 25-mph zone.
   b. George was exceeding the speed limit.

3. a. We appreciate the explanation of your financial circumstances.
   b. We appreciate the information you gave about your losses from bad debts and your shrinking markets.

4. a. An explanation of the procedures was presented by Mary Lewis.
   b. Mary Lewis explained the procedures.

> 5. a   Authorization of payment is the responsibility of the controller.
>   b.   The controller authorizes all payments.

PRONOUNS

Pronouns (words used in place of nouns) enable us to make our writing smoother than it would be if no pronouns were used. For example, compare these versions of the same sentence:

Without pronouns:	**With pronouns:**
Mr. Smith had some difficulty with Mr. Smith's car, so Mr. Smith took Mr. Smith's car to the corner garage for repairs.	Mr. Smith had some difficulty with his car, so he took it to the corner garage for repairs.

1. Make a pronoun agree in number with its *antecedent* (the specific noun for which a pronoun stands.)

   a. Use a plural antecedent when a pronoun represents two or more singular antecedents connected by *and*.

      The secretary <u>and</u> the treasurer will take <u>their</u> vacations.

      ["The" before "treasurer" indicates that the sentence is about two people.]

      The secretary <u>and</u> treasurer will take <u>his</u> vacation.

      [Omitting "the" before "treasurer" indicates that the sentence is about one person who has two sets of responsibilities.]

   b. Parenthetical remarks (remarks that can be omitted without destroying the basic meaning of the sentence) that appear between the pronoun and its antecedent have no effect on the form of the pronoun.

      Daniel Brown, <u>not the secretaries</u>, is responsible for <u>his</u> correspondence.

      [Because "his" refers to Daniel and not to "secretaries," "his" is used instead of "their."]

   c. Use a singular antecedent with *each, everyone, no,* and their variations.

      <u>Each</u> student and <u>each</u> teacher will carry <u>his or her</u> own equipment.

      <u>Everyone</u> is responsible for <u>her or his</u> work.

   d. Use a singular antecedent when two or more singular antecedents are connected by *or* or *nor*.

      <u>Neither</u> David <u>nor</u> Bill can complete <u>his</u> work.

      Ask <u>either</u> Mary or Sue about <u>her</u> in-service training.

   e. Use a singular antecedent when a noun represents a *unit* composed of more than *one* person or thing.

      The <u>company</u> stands behind <u>its</u> merchandise.

      The <u>group</u> wants to retain <u>its</u> goals.

f. Use pronouns that agree in number with the intended meaning of collective nouns.

The accounting <u>staff</u> has been asked for <u>its</u> contributions.

["Staff" is thought of as a unit; the singular "its" is appropriate.]

The accounting <u>staff</u> have been asked for <u>their</u> contributions.

["Staff" is thought of as more than one individual; the plural "their" is appropriate.]

2. **Use the correct case of pronouns.** *Case* tells whether a pronoun is used as the subject of a sentence or as an object in it.

a. Use nominative-case pronouns (*I, he, she, they, we, you, it, who*) as subjects of a sentence or clause.

<u>You</u> and <u>I</u> must work together. ["You" and "I" are subjects of the verb "work."]

Those <u>who</u> work will be paid. ["Who" is the subject of the dependent clause "who work."]

b. Use objective-case pronouns (*me, him, her, them, us, you, it, whom*) as objects of verbs and prepositions.

Mrs. Kellegher telephoned <u>him</u>. ["Him" is the object of the verb "telephoned."]

The increase in salary is for the manager and <u>her</u>. ["Her" is the object of the preposition "for."]

To <u>whom</u> should we send the report? ["Whom" is the object of the preposition "to."]

Tip: Restate a subordinate clause introduced by *who* or *whom* to determine the appropriate pronoun.

She is the type of manager <u>whom</u> we can promote.

[Restating "whom we can promote" as "We can promote her (whom)" clarifies that "whom" is the object.]

She is the type of manager <u>who</u> can be promoted.

[Restating "who can be promoted" as "She (who) can be promoted" clarifies that "who" is the subject.]

Tip: Change a question to a statement to determine the correct form of a pronoun.

<u>Whom</u> did you call? [You did call "whom."]

<u>Whom</u> did you select for the position? [You did select "whom" for the position.]

c. Use the nominative case when forms of the linking verb *be* require a pronoun to complete the meaning.

It was <u>he</u> who received credit for the sale.

It is <u>she</u> who deserves the award.

["It was he" may to some people sound just as distracting as the incorrect "It was him." Express the ideas in a different way to avoid the error and an expletive beginning.]

He was the one who received credit for the sale.
She deserves the award.

d. Use the possessive form of a pronoun before a *gerund* (a verb used as a noun).

We were delighted at <u>his</u> (not him) taking the job.

["Taking the job" is used here as a noun. "His" in this sentence serves the same purpose it serves in "We are delighted at *his* success."]

3. **Place relative pronouns as near their antecedents as possible for clear understanding.** A *relative* pronoun joins a subordinate clause to its antecedent.

Ambiguous:	Clear:
The <u>members</u> were given receipts <u>who</u> have paid.	The <u>members</u> <u>who</u> have paid were given receipts.
The agreement will enable you to pay <u>whichever</u> is lower, <u>6 percent or $50</u>.	The agreement will enable you to pay <u>6 percent or $50</u>, <u>whichever</u> is lower.

Restate a noun instead of risking a *vague* pronoun reference.

Vague:	Clear:
The <u>patrolman</u> captured the suspect even though <u>he</u> was unarmed.	The <u>patrolman</u> captured the suspect even though the <u>patrolman</u> was unarmed.

4. **Do not use a pronoun by itself to refer to a phrase, clause, sentence, or paragraph.** *A pronoun should stand for a noun, and that noun should appear in the writing.*

Incorrect:	Correct:
He expects to take all available accounting courses and obtain a position in a public accounting firm. <u>This</u> appeals to him.	He expects to take all available accounting courses and obtain a position in a public accounting firm. <u>This plan</u> appeals to him.

EXERCISE 2

Select the correct word.

1. The president and the chief executive officer reported (his, their) earnings to the employees.
2. Everyone was asked to share (his or her, their) opinion.
3. The production manager, not the controller, presented (his, their) strongly opposing views.
4. Sally and Helen were recognized for (her, their) contribution.
5. Neither Sally nor Helen was recognized for (her, their) contribution.
6. Our company is revising (their, its) statement of purpose.

7. The committee presented (its, their) recommendation to the president yesterday.
8. The instructor asked Dan and (I, me) to leave the room.
9. Lucille requested that proceeds be divided equally between Calvin and (her, she).
10. It was (she, her) who submitted the recommendation.
11. The speaker did not notice (me, my) leaving early.
12. (Who, Whom) is calling?
13. She is an employee in (who, whom) we have great confidence.
14. He is the one (who, whom) arrived twenty minutes late.
15. Mr. Smith forgot to retain his expense vouchers; (this, this oversight) caused a delay in reimbursement.

VERBS

Verbs present problems in number, person, tense, voice, and mood.

1. **Make subjects agree with verbs.**

   a. Ignore intervening phrases that have no effect on the verb used.

   Good material <u>and</u> fast delivery <u>are</u> (not *is*) essential.

   <u>You</u>, not the carrier, <u>are</u> (not *is*) responsible for the damage. [Intervening phrase "not the carrier" does not affect the verb used.]

   The <u>attitude</u> of these people <u>is</u> (not *are*) receptive. [The subject is "attitude"; "of these people" is a phrase coming between the subject and the verb.]

   <u>One</u> of the clerks <u>was</u> (not *were*) dismissed. ["One" is the subject.]

   b. Use a verb that agrees with the noun closer to the verb when *or* or *nor* connects two subjects.

   Only one or <u>two</u> questions <u>are</u> (not *is*) necessary.

   Several paint brushes or <u>one</u> paint roller <u>is</u> (not *are*) necessary.

   c. Use a singular verb with a plural noun that has a singular meaning.

   The <u>news</u> <u>is</u> good.

   <u>Economics</u> <u>is</u> a required course.

   <u>Mathematics</u> <u>is</u> to be reviewed.

   d. Use a singular verb with a plural subject that is thought of as singular unit.

   Twenty <u>dollars</u> <u>is</u> too much.

   Ten <u>minutes</u> <u>is</u> sufficient time.

   e. Use a singular verb for titles of articles, firm names, and slogans.

   "Understanding Computers" <u>is</u> an interesting article.

   Stein, Jones, and Baker <u>is</u> the oldest firm in the city.

   "Free lunches for all" <u>is</u> our campaign slogan.

2. **Choose verbs that agree in *person* with their subjects.** *Person* indicates whether the subject is (1) speaking, (2) being spoken to, or (3) being spoken about.

First person: I am, we are. **[Writer or speaker]**

Second person: You are. **[Receiver of message]**

Third person: He is, she is, they are. **[Person being discussed]**

> <u>She</u> <u>doesn't</u> (not <u>don't</u>) attend class regularly.
>
> <u>They</u> <u>don't</u> attend class regularly.

3. **Use the appropriate verb tense.** *Tense* indicates time. Tenses are both simple and compound.

Simple tenses:

Present: I <u>see</u> you. **[Tells what is happening now.]**

Past: I <u>saw</u> you. **[Tells what has already happened.]**

Future: I <u>will see</u> you. **[Tells what is yet to happen.]**

Compound tenses:

Present perfect: I <u>have seen</u> you. **[Tells of past action that extends to the present.]**

Past perfect: I <u>had seen</u> you. **[Tells of past action that was finished before another past action.]**

Future perfect: I <u>will have seen</u> you. **[Tells of action that will be finished before a future time.]**

a. Use present tense when something *was* and *still is* true,

> The speaker reminded us that Rhode Island <u>is</u> (not *was*) smaller than Wisconsin.

b. Avoid unnecessary shifts in tense.

> The carrier <u>brought</u> (not *brings*) my package but <u>left</u> without asking me to sign for it.

Verbs that appear in the same sentence are not required to be in the same tense.

> The contract that <u>was prepared</u> yesterday <u>will be signed</u> tomorrow.

4. **Use active voice for most business writing.** *Voice* is the term used to indicate whether a subject *acts* or whether it *is acted upon*. If the subject of a sentence acts, the verb used to describe that action is called an *active verb*.

> The keyboard operator <u>made</u> an error.
>
> The woman <u>asked</u> for an adjustment.

If the subject of the sentence is acted upon, the verb used to describe that action is called a *passive verb*.

> An error <u>was made</u> by the keyboard operator.
>
> An adjustment <u>was asked</u> for by the woman.

Active voice is preferred for most business writing. Refer to Chapter 7 for a discussion of appropriate uses of passive voice.

5. Use subjunctive mood when speaking of conditions that do not necessarily exist and when suggesting doubt, supposition, probability, wishfulness, or sorrow.

a. Use *were* for the present tense of *to be* in the subjunctive mood, even with a singular noun.

I wish the story <u>were</u> (not *was*) true.

If I <u>were</u> (not *was*) he, I would try again.

b. Consider the subjunctive mood for communicating negative ideas in positive language.

I wish I <u>were</u>.   [More tactful than "No, I am not."]

We <u>would</u> make a refund if the merchandise had been used in accordance with instructions. [Implies "we are not making a refund" but avoids negative words.]

EXERCISE 3

Select the correct word.

1. If he (was, were) over 18, he would have been hired.
2. Only one of the graphs (was, were) usable.
3. The typesetters, not the editor, (was, were) responsible for these errors.
4. Neither the coach nor the players (was, were) invited.
5. Both John and Steven (was, were) promoted.
6. The news from the rescue mission (is, are) encouraging.
7. *Ten Steps to Greatness* (has, have) been placed in the company library.
8. A child reminded me that the earth (rotates, rotated) on its axis.
9. Tim (don't, doesn't) ask for favors.
10. The president studied the page for a minute and (starts, started) asking questions.

Change each sentence from passive to active voice.

1. The booklet was edited by Susan Woodward.
2. The figures have been checked by our accountant.
3. Ms. Jackson was recommended for promotion by the supervisor.
4. The applications are being screened. (When revising, assume that a committee is doing the screening.)
5. Your request for a leave has been approved. (When revising, assume the manager did the approving.)

ADJECTIVES AND ADVERBS

Adjectives modify nouns or pronouns. **Adverbs** modify verbs, adjectives, or other adverbs. Although most adverbs end in *ly*, some commonly used adverbs do not end in *ly*: *there, then, after, now, hence,* and *very*. Most words that end in *ly* are adverbs; but common exceptions are *neighborly, timely, friendly,* and *gentlemanly*. Some words are both adjective and adverb: *fast, late,* and *well*.

1. Use an adjective to modify a noun or pronoun.

   She wrote a <u>long</u> letter.

   I prefer the <u>little</u> one.

2. Use an adjective after a linking verb when the modifier refers to the subject instead of to the verb. (A linking verb connects a subject to the rest of the sentence. "He *is* old." "She *seems* sincere.")

   The salesperson seemed <u>enthusiastic</u>. [The adjective "enthusiastic" refers to "salesperson," not to "seemed."]

   The president looked <u>suspicious</u>. [The adjective "suspicious" refers to "president," not to "looked."]

3. Use an adverb to modify a verb, an adjective, or another adverb.

   The salesperson looked <u>enthusiastically</u> at the prospect. ["The adverb *enthusiastically* modifies the verb "looked."]

   The committee was <u>really</u> active. [The adverb "really" modifies the adjective "active."]

   Worker A progressed <u>relatively faster</u> than did Worker B. [The adverb "relatively" modifies the adverb "faster."]

4. **Use comparatives and superlatives carefully.**

   She is the <u>faster</u> (not *fastest*) of the two workers.

   He is the <u>better</u> (not *best*) of the two operators.

   Exclude a person or thing from a group with which that person or thing is being compared.

   He is older than <u>anyone else</u> (not *anyone*) in his department. [As a member of his department, he cannot be older than himself.]

   "The XD600 is newer than <u>any other machine</u> (not *any machine*) in our department." [The XD600 cannot be newer than itself.]

Exercise 4

Select the correct word.

1. Our supply is being replenished (frequent, frequently).
2. Marcus looked (angry, angrily).
3. The server moved (quick, quickly) from table to table.
4. Of the two people who were interviewed, Jane made the (better, best) impression.
5. Benito is faster than (any, any other) keyboarder in his department.

SENTENCE STRUCTURE

1. State the subject of each sentence (unless the sentence is a command).

   <u>I received</u> (not *received*) the supervisor's request today.

   Return the forms to me. [The subject ("you") is understood and can be omitted in this imperative sentence.]

2. Rely mainly on sentences that follow the normal subject-verb-complement sequence.

> <u>Jennifer</u> and <u>I</u> <u>withdrew</u> for three <u>reasons.</u>
> (subject) (verb)   (complement)

People are accustomed to sentences stated in this sequence. Sentences that expose the verb *before* revealing the subject (1) slow down the reading, (2) present less vivid pictures, and (3) use more words than would be required if the normal sequence were followed.

Original:	Better:
There are <u>two reasons</u> for our withdrawal.	<u>Two reasons</u> for our withdrawal are. . . . <u>Jennifer and I</u> withdrew for two reasons.
<u>It</u> is important that we withdraw.	<u>Our withdrawal</u> is important. <u>We</u> must withdraw.

There, it, and *here* are called *expletives*—filler words that have no real meaning in the sentence.

3. Do not put unrelated ideas in the same sentence.

> The <u>coffee break</u> is at ten o'clock, and the company plans to purchase additional <u>parking spaces</u>. [These ideas have little relationship.]

4. Put pronouns, adverbs, phrases, and clauses near the words they modify.

Incorrect:	Correct:
Belinda put a new type of <u>gel</u> on her hair, <u>which</u> she had just purchased.	Belinda put a new type of <u>gel, which</u> she had just purchased, on her hair.
He <u>only</u> works in the toy department for <u>$3.25</u> an hour.	He works in the toy department for <u>only $3.25</u> an hour.
The <u>secretary</u> stood beside the fax machine <u>wearing a denim skirt.</u>	<u>The secretary wearing a denim skirt</u> stood beside the fax machine.

5. Do not separate subject and predicate unnecessarily.

Incorrect:	Correct:
<u>He</u>, hoping to receive a bonus, <u>worked</u> rapidly.	Hoping to receive a bonus, <u>he worked</u> rapidly.

6. Place an introductory phrase near the subject of the independent clause it modifies. Otherwise, the phrase dangles. To correct the dangling phrase, change the subject of the independent clause, or make the phrase into a subordinate clause by assigning it a subject.

Incorrect:	Correct:
<u>When</u> a little boy, <u>my mother</u> took me through a milk-processing plant. [Implies that the mother was once a little boy.]	<u>When I was a little boy, my mother</u> took me through a milk-processing plant. <u>When</u> a little boy, <u>I</u> was taken through a milk-processing plant by my mother.

Incorrect:	Correct:
<u>Working</u> at full speed every morning, <u>fatigue</u> overtakes me in the afternoon. [Implies that "fatigue" was working at full speed.]	<u>Working</u> at full speed every morning, <u>I</u> become tired in the afternoon. <u>Because I work</u> at full speed every morning, <u>fatigue</u> overtakes me in the afternoon.
<u>To function</u> properly, <u>you</u> must oil the machine every hour. [Implies that if "you" are "to function properly," the machine must be oiled hourly.]	<u>If the machine</u> is to function properly, <u>you</u> must oil it every hour. <u>To function</u> properly, the <u>machine</u> must be oiled every hour.

7. Express related ideas in similar grammatical form (use parallel construction).

Incorrect:	Correct:
The machine operator made three resolutions: <u>(1) to be punctual, (2) following</u> instructions carefully, and <u>third, the reduction of waste</u>.	The machine operator made three resolutions: <u>(1) to be punctual, (2) to follow</u> instructions carefully, and <u>(3) to reduce</u> waste.
The human resources manager is concerned with <u>the selection</u> of the right worker, <u>providing</u> appropriate orientation, and <u>the worker's</u> progress.	The human resources manager is concerned with <u>selecting</u> the right worker, <u>providing</u> appropriate orientation, and <u>checking</u> the worker's progress.

8. Do not end a sentence with a needless preposition.

Where is the plant to be <u>located</u> (not <u>located at</u>)?

The worker did not tell us where he was <u>going</u> (not <u>going to</u>).

End a sentence with a preposition if for some reason the preposition needs emphasis.

I am not concerned with what he is paying <u>for</u>. I am concerned with what he is paying <u>with</u>.

The prospect has everything—a goal to work <u>toward</u>, a house to live <u>in</u>, and an income to live <u>on</u>.

9. **Avoid split infinitives.** Two words are required to express an infinitive: *to* plus a *verb*. The two words belong together. An infinitive is split when another word is placed between the two.

Clumsy:	Improved:
The superintendent used <u>to</u> occasionally <u>visit</u> the offices.	The superintendent used <u>to visit</u> the offices occasionally.
I want <u>to</u> briefly <u>summarize</u> the report.	I want <u>to summarize</u> the report briefly.

EXERCISE 5

Identify the weakness in each sentence and write an improved version.

1. It is essential that you sign and return the enclosed form.
2. When a small girl, my brother taught me to play basketball.
3. I am submitting an article to *Time*, which I wrote last summer.
4. Almost all of my time is spent in planning, organizing, and the various aspects of control.
5. We want to quickly bring the project to a conclusion.

ABBREVIATIONS

Avoid abbreviations because they are visually distracting to the reader, are difficult to understand, and may send the mistaken message that you are too hurried to do a complete job. Certain abbreviations are standard:

1. **Abbreviate**

   a. Titles that come before and after proper names.

      Dr., Mr., Mrs., Ms.

      D.D.S., Esq., Jr., M.D., Ph.D., Sr.

   b. Commonly known government agencies, organizations, businesses, or institutions.

      FDIC, FCC, FHA, TVA

      NEA, UN, GE, IBM, MIT

   c. Commonly used business expressions: f.o.b., C.O.D., a.m., p.m. (Note: Use a.m. and p.m. only when a specific time is mentioned. Small letters—a.m. and p.m.—are preferred.)

      Come to the office at 10:15 <u>a.m.</u> (not *this a.m.*)

   d. The names of businesses when their own letterheads contain abbreviations:

      Smith & Company; Maynord and Tran, Inc.; The Gene Roudebush Co.

   e. The word *number* when it is used with a figure to designate something.

      Go to Room <u>No.</u> 7.

      May we have a carton of <u>No.</u> 10 envelopes.

      Refer to Policy <u>No.</u> 384862.

   f. The names of states when they appear as parts of envelope addresses or inside addresses. Use the two-letter abbreviations recommended by the U.S. Postal Services (shown in Appendix A, Figure A-12).

2. **Do not abbreviate**

   a. The names of cities, states (except in an envelope and letter address), months, and days of the week.

b. Points on the compass.

Tom has been in the <u>West</u> for seven years.

Go <u>east</u> one block and turn <u>south</u>.

CAPITAL LETTERS

Capitalize

1. Names of people, animals, places, geographic areas, days of the week, months of the year, holidays, deities, publications, documents, historical events, and other special names.

2. The principal words in the titles of books, magazines, newspapers, articles, reports, movies, plays, songs, and poems.

    "The Story of My Life"   [Article]

    The Prince and the Pauper   [Book]

    Cost of the Land   [Heading in a report]

3. The names of specific academic courses and those that are proper nouns.

    The student is taking French, mathematics, science, and English.

    The student is taking Math 101 and Science 1003.

4. The names of seasons only when they are personified.

    We make most of our profits during the winter.

    When a season is used to designate a particular school term or semester, the season is ordinarily capitalized.

    Summer Session 1996

5. Titles that come before a name.

    Editor Smith   Uncle Fred

    President Lopez   Professor Senter

    Do *not* capitalize titles appearing alone or following a name unless they appear in addresses.

    The manager approved the proposal submitted by the editorial assistant.

    He has taken the position formerly held by his father.

    Address all correspondence to Major Michael Anderson, Production Manager, 109 Crescent Avenue, Baltimore, MD 21208.

6. Most nouns followed by numbers (except in page, paragraph, line, and verse references).

    Policy No. 8746826   Chapter 9

    Figure 17-9   Model L379

7. Only the first and last words in salutations and only the first word in complimentary closes.

    My dear Sir: Sincerely yours,

8. The first word of a direct quotation.

> The sales representative said, "We leave tomorrow."

Do *not* capitalize the first word in the last part of an interrupted quotation or the first word in an indirect quotation.

> "We will proceed," he said, "with the utmost caution." [Interrupted quotation]

> He said that the report must be submitted by the end of the week. [Indirect quotation]

9. The first word following a colon when a formal statement or question follows.

> Here is an important rule for report writers: Plan your work and work your plan.

> Each sales representative should ask himself or herself this question: Do I really look like a representative of my firm?

EXERCISE 6

Copy each of the following sentences, making essential changes in abbreviation and capitalization.

1. When I was interviewed during interviewing 101, the first question was "why do you want to work for us?"
2. The summer season is much slower than the rest of the year, according to the Sales Manager.
3. We paid for *The Power of Ethical Management* with check no. 627 on Dec. 10.
4. The N.C.A.A. meeting, moderated by president Marla Stanton, will be held in N.Y.
5. A retirement ceremony is being planned for president Schwada.

NUMBERS

Businesspeople use quantitative data often, so numbers appear frequently in business writing. *Accuracy* is exceedingly important. The most frequent problem in expressing numbers is whether to write them as figures or spell them out as words.

1. **Use figures**

   a. In most business writing because (1) figures should get deserved emphasis, (2) figures are easy for readers to locate if they need to reread for critical points, and (3) figures can be keyed faster and in less space than spelled-out words.

   Regardless of whether a number has one digit or many, use figures to express dates, sums of money, mixed numbers and decimals, distance, dimension, cubic capacity, percentage, weights, temperatures, and chapter and page numbers.

May 10, 19--   165 pounds

$9 million (or $9,000,000)   Chapter 3, page 29

25% (or 25 percent)

With the preceding exceptions, numbers one through ten are normally spelled out if no larger number appears in the same sentence.

Only <u>three</u> people were present.

We need <u>five</u> machines.

Send <u>5</u> officers and <u>37</u> soldiers.

b. With ordinals (*th, st, rd, nd*) only when the number precedes the month.

The meeting is to be held on <u>June 21</u>.

The meeting is to be held on the <u>21st of June</u>.

c. With ciphers but without decimals when presenting even-dollar figures, unless the figure appears in a sentence with another figure that includes dollars and cents.

He paid <u>$30</u> for the cabinet.

He paid <u>$31.75</u> for the table and <u>$30.00</u> for the cabinet.

d. Without a colon when expressing times of day that include hours but not minutes, unless the time appears in a sentence with another time that includes minutes.

The reception began at <u>7 p.m.</u>

The award program began at <u>6:30 p.m.</u> with a reception at <u>8:00 p.m.</u>

2. **Spell out**

a. Numbers if they are used as the first word of a sentence.

<u>Thirty-two</u> people attended.

b. Numbers that represent time when *o'clock* is used.

Please be there at <u>ten o'clock</u>.

Meet me at <u>10:15 p.m.</u>

c. Names of streets up to and including twelve.

<u>Fifth</u> Street, <u>Seventh</u> Avenue

d. One of two adjacent numbers, preferably the smaller of the two.

The package required <u>four</u> <u>32-cent</u> stamps. [A hyphen joins the second number with the word that follows it, thus forming a compound adjective that describes the noun "stamps."]

We shipped <u>nine</u> <u>180-horsepower</u> engines today.

e. Numbers that are indefinite or approximate.

<u>Several hundred</u> boxes were shipped.

The incumbent won by about <u>ten thousand</u> votes.

f. Numbers in legal documents, following them with figures enclosed in parentheses.

For the sum of <u>four hundred dollars ($400)</u>, . . .

For the sum of <u>four hundred (400)</u> dollars, . . .

. . . including <u>forty (40)</u> acres, more or less.

Exercise 7

Correct the number usage in the following sentences taken from a letter or a report.

1. The question was answered by sixty-one percent of the respondents.
2. The meeting will be at 9:00 a.m. on February 21st.
3. Three figures appeared on the expense account: $21.95, $30, and $35.14.
4. Go to the service station at 5th Street and Hardy Drive.
5. We ordered five sixteen-ounce hammers.
6. This MIS manager ordered 10 40-mb hard drives.
7. 21 members voted in favor of the motion.
8. The cost will be approximately $1,000,000.00.
9. Mix two quarts of white with 13 quarts of brown.
10. Examine the diagram on page seven.

PUNCTUATION

Punctuation is basically the same in business writing as in other writing. Clarity is a primary consideration.

1. **Use an apostrophe**

   a. To form the possessive singular. Add an apostrophe and an *s*.

   firm, firm<u>'s</u>   worker, worker<u>'s</u>

   b. To form the possessive plural. Add an apostrophe after the *s*.

   managers, managers<u>'</u>   dealers, dealers<u>'</u>

   c. To form the possessive of a proper noun in which the last letter is not an *s*. Add an apostrophe and an *s*.

   Mr. Wilson<u>'s</u> supervisor   Mr. Bostrom<u>'s</u> interview.

   d. To form the possessive singular when the last letter in a proper noun is an *s*. Determine the placement of the apostrophe by the number of syllables in the noun.

   When the singular form of a one-syllable noun ends in *s*, form the possessive by adding *'s*.

   Jones, Jones<u>'s</u>   Ross, Ross<u>'s</u>

When the singular form contains more than one syllable and ends in *s* or in an *s* sound, form the possessive by adding an apostrophe only.

Ms. Richards, Ms. Richards'   **Mr. Gonzalez, Mr. Gonzalez'**

e. In expressions that indicate ownership. The apostrophe shows omission of a preposition.

Last year's reports. . . .   **Reports of last year. . . .**

f. When the noun presents time or distance in a possessive manner.

an hour's visit   **three weeks' vacation**

g. When a noun precedes a gerund.

Ms. Bowen's receiving the promotion caused . . . .
Mr. Green's taking the gavel indicated . . . .

h. To show whether ownership is joint or separate.

To indicate joint ownership, add an *'s* to the last name only.

Olsen and Howard's accounting firm

To indicate separate ownership, add an *'s* to each name.

Olsen's and Howard's accounting firms

2. **Do not use an apostrophe**

a. In the titles of some organizations. Use the name as the organization uses its name.

National Sales Executives Association

b. To form the possessive of a pronoun (most pronouns become possessive through a change in spelling; therefore, an apostrophe is not used).

Yours [not *your's*]
Ours [not *our's*]

3. **Use brackets**

a. To enclose words that are inserted between words or sentences of quoted material.

"How long will the delay be? No longer than this: [At this point, the speaker tapped the lectern three times.] That means no delay at all."

b. As required in certain mathematical formulas.

c. To enclose parenthetical material that contains parentheses.

The motion passed. [The vote (17 for and 4 against) was not taken until midnight.]

d. To explain, clarify, or correct words of the writer you quote.

"To [accounting] professionals, the ability to express themselves well is more than a hallmark of educated persons," was quoted from a study conducted by the American Institute of Certified Public Accountants.

4. Use a colon

a. To suggest that a list will follow a statement that appears in complete-sentence form.

Three factors influenced our decision: an expanded market, an inexpensive source of raw materials, and a ready source of labor.

We need to (1) expand our market, (2) locate an inexpensive source of materials, and (3) find a ready source of labor. [A colon does not follow to because the words preceding the list do not constitute what could be a complete sentence.]

b. To stress an appositive (a noun that renames the preceding noun) at the end of a sentence.

His heart was set on one thing: promotion.

Our progress is due to the efforts of one person: Mr. Martin.

c. After the salutation of a letter (when mixed punctuation is used).

Dear Dr. Gorga:

d. After a word or phrase followed by additional material in ads or signs.

No Parking: Reserved for executives

For Rent: Two-bedroom apartment

e. Between hours and minutes to express time in figures.

5:45 p.m.   11:05 a.m.

EXERCISE 8

Select the correct word in parentheses.

1. This (company's, companies, companys') mission-and-scope statement is excellent.
2. The workers earned three (week's, weeks') wages.
3. Two service stations were cited: (West's and Johnson's, West and Johnson's).
4. I will appreciate (Pablo's, Pablo) calling before the 15th.
5. Mr. (Morris's, Morris') letter of acceptance had been received.

Correct the use of colons. Write *correct* if you find no errors.

1. The program has one shortcoming: flexibility.
2. Our meetings are scheduled for: Monday, Tuesday, and Friday.
3. We liked this car because of: its price, durability, and appearance.
4. We liked three features of Ms. Cole's resume: her experience, her education, and her attitude.
5. We are enthusiastic about the plan because: (1) it is least expensive, (2) its legality is unquestioned, and (3) it can be implemented quickly.

5. Use a comma

a. Between coordinate clauses joined by *and, but, for*, and other coordinate conjunctions.

He wanted to pay his bills on time, <u>but</u> he did not have the money.

b. After introductory participial phrases or dependent clauses. Sentences that begin with prepositions or such words as *if*, *as*, and *when* almost always need a comma.

<u>Believing that her earnings would continue to increase</u>, she sought to borrow more money.

<u>Under the circumstances,</u> we think you are justified.

<u>To get the full benefit of our insurance plan,</u> just fill out and return the enclosed card.

<u>If you can meet us at the plane</u>, please plan to be there by six o'clock.

c. To separate words in a series.

You have a choice of gray, green, purple, and white.

Without the comma after "purple," no one can tell for sure whether four choices are available, the last of which is "white," or whether three choices are available, the last of which is "purple and white."

You have a choice of purple and white, gray, and green. [Choice is restricted to three, the first of which is "purple and white."]

d. Between coordinate adjectives (two separate adjectives that modify the same noun).

New employees are given a long, difficult examination. [Both "long" and "difficult" modify "examination."]

We want quick, factual news. [Both "quick" and "factual" modify "news."]

Do not place a comma between two adjectives when the second adjective may be considered as part of the noun that follows.

The supervisor is an excellent public speaker. ["Excellent" modifies the noun "public speaker."]

e. To separate a nonrestrictive clause (a clause that is not essential to the basic meaning of the sentence) from the rest of the sentence.

Mr. MacMurray, who is head of the collection department, is leaving for a vacation. [The parenthetical remark is not essential to the meaning of the sentence.]

The man who is head of the collection department is leaving for a vacation. [Commas are not needed because "who is head of the collection department" is essential to the meaning of the sentence.]

f. To separate parenthetical expressions from the rest of the sentence.

Ms. Watson, speaking in behalf of the entire department, accepted the proposal.

g. Before and after the year in month-day-year format.

On July 2, 1995, Mr. Kababik made the final payment.

h. Before and after the name of a state when the name of a city precedes.

   I saw him in Kansas City, Missouri, on the 12th of October.

i. After a direct address.

   John, I believe you have earned a vacation.

j. After the words *No* and *Yes* when they introduce a statement.

   Yes, you can count on me.
   No, I will have to decline.

k. To set off appositives when neutral emphasis is desired.

   The group heard a speech from Mr. Matthew Welch, a recruit.
   Mr. Herbert Jackson, former president of the Jackson Institute, spoke to the group.

l. Between contrasted elements.

   We need more money, not less.
   The job requires experience, not formal education.

m. To show the omission of words that are understood.

   Ms. Reno scored 96 percent on the employment examination; Mr. Mehrmann, 84 percent.

n. Before a question that solicits a confirmatory answer.

   It's a reasonable price, isn't it?
   Our bills have been paid, haven't they?

o. Between the printed name and the title on the same line beneath a signature.

   Roy Murr, President
   No comma is used if the title is on a separate line.
   Cathryn W. Edwards
   President of Academic Affairs

p. After an adverbial conjunction.

   The check was for the right amount; however, it was not signed.

EXERCISE 9

Insert needed commas; delete unneeded commas.

1. The man who came in late, has not been interviewed, but all other applicants have been interviewed.
2. Margie Harrison a new member of the board, remained silent.
3. Ammonium sulfate which is available at almost all home-supply stores is ideal fertilizer for citrus.
4. This carpet is available in three colors: brown, tan and blue.
5. We had a long bitter discussion.

6. Costs have doubled in the last two years, as the following graph illustrates:

7. By the time I arrived at the meeting the issue had been discussed thoroughly and put aside.

8. If you approve of the changes on page 3 please place your initials in the margin.

9. We surveyed the entire population but three of the responses were unusable.

10. Because only 21 percent of the members were present the motion could not be considered.

11. John was awarded $25; Bill $40.

12. We have lost our place in the production line haven't we?

13. We should be spending less money, not more.

14. On November 20 1995 all related documents were submitted.

15. Yes I agree that the meeting in Oxford, Tennessee should be scheduled in April.

6. **Use a dash**

   a. To place emphasis on appositives.

      His answer—the correct answer—was based on years of experience.

      Compare the price—$125—with the cost of a single repair job.

   b. When appositives contain commas.

      Their scores—Mary, 21; Sally, 20; and Jo, 19—were the highest in a group of 300.

   c. When a parenthetical remark consists of an abrupt change in thought.

      The committee decided—you may think it's a joke, but it isn't—that the resolution should be adopted.

7. **Use an ellipsis to indicate that some words have been omitted from a quotation.**

      Mr. Thomas said, "We believe . . . our objectives will be accomplished."

      Mr. Thomas reported, "The time has come when we must provide our employees with in-service training. . . ."

   Insert a space between the three periods or insert the typesetter's symbol for ellipses (. . .). Use four periods in ellipses at the end of a quotation; one period indicates the end of the sentence.

8. **Use a hyphen**

   a. In such compound words as *self-analysis* and *father-in-law.*

   b. Between the words in a compound adjective. (A *compound adjective* is a group of words joined together and used as a single word to describe a noun that follows.)

      An <u>attention-getting</u> device

      A technical, <u>hard-to-follow</u> lecture

Each hyphenated expression precedes a noun. Hyphens are not required when descriptive words follow a noun.

A device that is <u>attention getting</u>.

A lecture that was <u>hard to follow</u>.

An expression made up of an adverb that ends in *ly* and an adjective is not a compound adjective and does not require a hyphen.

<u>commonly accepted</u> principle

<u>widely quoted</u> authority

c. To prevent misinterpretation.

A <u>small-business</u> executive [An executive who operates a small business]

A <u>small business</u> executive [An executive who is small]

<u>Recover</u> a chair [To obtain possession of a chair once more]

<u>Re-cover</u> a chair [To cover a chair again]

<u>Eight inch</u> blades [Eight blades, each of which is an inch long]

<u>Eight-inch</u> blades [Blades eight inches long]

d. To join the numerator and denominator of fractions.

A <u>two-thirds</u> interest

<u>Three-fourths</u> of the respondents agreed.

Figures are acceptable for expressing fractions: "a 2/3 interest."

e. In spelling out compound numbers.

<u>Thirty-one</u>   <u>Ninety-seven</u>

f. To avoid repetition of a word.

<u>Short-, medium-,</u> and <u>long-range</u> missiles

"Short-range, medium-range, and long-range missiles" have the same meaning; but repetition of "range" is not necessary. The hyphens after "short" and "medium" show that these words are connected to another word that will appear at the end of the series.

g. To divide words at the end of a line. (See the discussion of word division in Appendix A.)

h. In a nine-digit ZIP Code.

83475-1247

9. Use parentheses

a. For explanatory material that could be left out.

Three of our employees (Mr. Bachman, Mr. Russo, and Mr. Wilds) took their vacations in August.

All our employees (believe it or not) have perfect attendance records. [Note that a parenthetical sentence within a sentence neither begins with a capital letter nor ends with a period.]

Use commas before and after parenthetical material for neutral emphasis; dashes for added emphasis.

b. For accuracy in writing figures.

> For the sum of three thousand five hundred dollars ($3,500) . . . .

c. Both before and after that which is parenthetical.

Incorrect:	Correct:
. . . authority to 1) issue passes, 2) collect fees.	. . . authority to (1) issue passes, (2) collect fees. . .

d. *After* a period when an entire sentence is parenthetical; *before* a period when only the last part of a sentence is parenthetical.

> The board met for three hours. (The usual time is one hour.)

> Success can be attributed to one person (Earl Knott).

10. **Use a period after declarative and imperative sentences and courteous requests.**

> We will attend. [Declarative sentence.]

> Complete this report. [Imperative sentence.]

> Will you please complete the report today. [Courteous request is a question but does not require a verbal answer with requested action.]

11. **Use quotation marks**

a. To enclose direct quotations.

> The supervisor said, "We will make progress."

> "We will make progress," the supervisor said, "even though we have to work overtime."

Note that the period and comma appear within the quotation marks. Other punctuation marks appear outside—unless the mark is part of the quotation.

b. Before the first word and after the last word of a multiple-sentence quotation.

> The president said, "Have a seat, gentlemen. I'm dictating a letter. I should be through in about five minutes. Please wait."

c. To enclose titles of songs, magazine and newspaper articles, and themes within text.

> "There's a Hero"

> "Progress in Cancer Research"

d. To define terms.

> As used in this report, *syntax* means "the branch of grammar that has to do with sentence structure."

e. To enclose slang expressions.

> We can describe the attacks against our policies with one word—"hogwash."

    f. To enclose nicknames.

And now for some comments by Ray "Skinny" Johnson.

    g. To imply that a different word may be more appropriate.

Our "football" team. . . . [Hints that the team appears to be playing something other than football.]
Our football "team" . . . . [Hints that "collection of individual players" would be more descriptive than "team."]
. . . out for "lunch." [Hints that the reason for being out is something other than lunch.]

    h. To enclose quoted material that contains other quoted material.

The budget director said, "Believe me when I say 'A penny saved is a penny earned' is the best advice I ever had."

A quotation that appears within another quotation is enclosed in *single* quotation marks.

    i. In their proper position within a sentence. Place periods and commas *inside* quotation marks.

"Take your time," she said, "and the work will be easier."

Place semicolons *outside* quotation marks.

The manager said, "That's fine"; his facial expression conveyed an entirely different message.

Place question marks *inside* quotation marks when the question is within the quotation.

The contractor asked, "When will we begin?"

Place question marks *outside* quotation marks when the question is not within the quotation.

Did the contractor say, "We will begin today"?

EXERCISE 10

Describe the difference in meaning caused by the use of a dash, ellipsis, hyphen, parentheses, period, or quotation marks for each pair of sentences.

1. a. Have you read *The Power of Ethical Management?*
    b. Have you read "The Power of Ethical Management"?
2. a. His accomplishments are summarized on the attached page.
    b. His "accomplishments" are summarized on the attached page.
3. a. Tim said the firm plans to establish a sinking fund.
    b. Tim said, "The firm plans to establish a sinking fund."
4 a. A party is being planned for the ten-game winners.
    b. A party is being planned for the ten game winners.
5. a. Our accountant said, "Such expenses . . . are not justified."
    b. Our accountant said, "Such expenses are not justified."

12. Use a semicolon

a. When a conjunction is omitted.

Our workers have been extraordinarily efficient this year; they are expecting a bonus.

b. In a compound-complex sentence.

As indicated earlier, we prefer delivery on Saturday morning at four o'clock; but Friday night at ten o'clock will be satisfactory.

We prefer delivery on Saturday morning at four o'clock; but, if the arrangement is more convenient for you, Friday night at ten o'clock will be satisfactory.

c. Before an adverbial conjunction.

The shipment arrived too late for our weekend sale; therefore, we are returning the shipment to you.

Other frequently used adverbial conjunctions are *however, otherwise, consequently,* and *nevertheless.*

d. In a series that contains commas.

Some of our workers have worked overtime this week: Smith, 6 hours; Hardin, 3; Cantrell, 10; and McGowan, 11.

e. Before illustrative words, as in the following sentences.

We have plans for improvement; for example, we intend to . . . .

The engine has been "knocking"; that is, the gas in the cylinders explodes before the pistons complete their upward strokes.

EXERCISE 11

Insert a semicolon where needed.

1. Expense tickets were not included, otherwise, the request would have been honored.
2. The following agents received a bonus this month: Barnes, $400, Shelley, $450, and Jackson, $600.
3. The bid was not considered, it arrived two days late.
4. This paint does have some disadvantages, for example, its drying time is too long.
5. Soon after the figures have been received, they will be processed, but a formal report cannot be prepared before June 15.

13. Use symbols

For convenience in completing forms such as invoices and statements, but not in letters and reports. The dollar sign ($), in contrast with such symbols as %, ¢, @, and #, should be used in letters and reports.

Spell out terms rather than use symbols in sentences of letters and reports.

31 percent (not *31%*)

80 cents a foot (not *80¢ a foot*)

21 cases <u>at</u> $4 a case (not 21 cases @ $4 a case)

Policy <u>No.</u> 468571 (not *Policy #468571*)

14. **Use an underscore or italics**

a. To indicate words, letters, numbers, and phrases used as words.

The word *effective* was used in describing his presentation.

He had difficulty learning to spell *recommendation.*

b. To emphasize a word that is not sufficiently emphasized by other means.

c. To indicate the titles of books, magazines, and newspapers.

Managing for Quality   *The New York Times*

The Reader's Digest

Underscore or italicize the titles of books, magazines, and newspapers within text. Refer to documentation style manuals for correct treatment of these titles in footnotes/endnotes and bibliographic references.

WORDS FREQUENTLY MISUSED

1. *Accept, except.* *Accept* means "to take what is offered," "to accede," "to assent"; *except* means "to exclude," or "with the exclusion of."

I <u>accept</u> your offer.

All columns have been added <u>except</u> one.

2. *Advice, advise.* *Advice* is a noun meaning "suggestions or recommendations about a course of action." *Advise* is a verb meaning "to give advice; to caution or warn."

The supervisor's <u>advice</u> to John was to abide by safety rules.

Supervisors <u>advise</u> employees of the consequences of safety rules violations.

3. *Affect, effect.* *Affect* is a verb meaning "to influence"; *effect* is a noun meaning "result"; *effect* is also a verb meaning "to bring about."

The change does not <u>affect</u> his pay.

What <u>effect</u> will the change have?

The manager wants to <u>effect</u> a change in the schedule.

4. *Among, between.* Use *among* to discuss three or more, *between* to discuss two.

Divide the earnings <u>among</u> the six workers.

Divide the earnings <u>between</u> the two workers.

5. *Amount, number.* Use *amount* when speaking of money or of things that cannot be counted; use *number* when speaking of things that can be counted.

The <u>amount</u> of grumbling has been troublesome to the supervisors.

The <u>number</u> of workers has been increased.

6. *Capital, capitol. Capital* is money, property, or a city in which a state or national government is located. A *capitol* is a building in which the government meets.

> One business partner provided the <u>capital</u>; the other provided the expertise.

> The <u>capitol</u> is at the intersection of Jefferson Street and Tenth Avenue.

7. *Cite, sight, site. Cite* means to quote or mention. *Sight* refers to the sense of seeing, the process of seeing, or a view. *Site* is a location.

> Marianne <u>cited</u> several authorities in her report.

> Working at the computer is affecting her <u>sight</u>.

> Market Avenue is the <u>site</u> of the new store.

8. *Complement, compliment. Complement* means "to complete" or "that which completes or suits another." *Compliment* means "words of praise."

> This shipment is a <u>complement</u> to our latest series of orders.

> The clerk was <u>complimented</u> for his success.

9. *Continual, continuous.* If an action is *continual* it will have planned-for breaks in continuity; if an action is *continuous,* it will be constant, without breaks.

> The mechanism for raising and lowering the garage door has given <u>continual</u> service for four years.

> The clock has run <u>continuously</u> for four years.

10. *Council, counsel. Council* means "an advisory group." *Counsel* means "advice," "one who gives advice," or "to advise."

> <u>Council</u> members will meet today.

> First, seek legal <u>counsel</u>.

> The defendant and his <u>counsel</u> were excused.

> An attorney will <u>counsel</u> the suspect.

11. *Credible, creditable. Credible* means "believable." *Creditable* means "praiseworthy" or "worthy of commercial credit."

> The explanations were <u>credible</u>.

> Mr. McKay did a <u>creditable</u> job for us.

12. *Criteria, criterion.* A *criterion* is a standard for judging, a yardstick by which something is measured. The plural form is *criteria.*

> The most important <u>criterion</u> was cost.

> Three <u>criteria</u> were developed.

13. *Data, datum. Datum* is a singular noun meaning "fact," "proposition," "condition," or "quantity" from which other facts, etc., may be deduced. *Data* is the plural form.

> This <u>datum</u> suggests . . . .

> These <u>data</u> suggest . . . .

Use of *data* as a singular form is gaining some degree of acceptance. Some people use the word in the same way they use *group*. Although composed of more than one, *group* is singular.

The group has decided.

Until *data* becomes generally accepted as a singular, the word should be used carefully. Instead of "This data is," or "These data are," such expressions as "This *set* of data is," or "These *facts* are," can be used to avoid the risk of alienating certain readers or listeners.

14. *Different from, different than.* *Different from* is correct; *different than* is to be avoided.

    That machine is different from mine.

15. *Each other, one another.* Use *each other* when referring to two people; use *one another* when referring to more than two.

    The two employees competed with each other.
    The members of the group helped one another.

16. *Eminent, imminent. Eminent* means "well known." *Imminent* means "about to happen."

    An eminent scientist will address the group.
    A merger seems imminent.

17. *Envelop, envelope. Envelop* is a verb meaning "to surround" or "to hide." *Envelope* is a noun referring to a cover for a letter.

    A fog was about to envelop the island.
    Just use the enclosed envelope for your reply.

18. *Farther, further.* Use *farther* when referring to distance. Use *further* when referring to extent or degree.

    Let's go one mile farther.
    Let's pursue the thought further.

19. *Fewer, less.* Use *fewer* with items that can be counted; use *less* with items that cannot be counted.

    Fewer than half the employers approved the proposed pay plan.
    Maria spent less time writing the report than Michael because she had spent more time organizing her data.

20. *Formally, formerly.* Use *formally* when discussing that which is ceremonious or done according to an established method. Use *formerly* in discussing that which has preceded in time.

    The award will be formally presented at tomorrow's convocation.
    Tom formerly worked for the department of revenue.

21. *Infer, imply. Infer* means "to draw a conclusion"; readers or listeners infer. *Imply* means "to hint" or "to set forth vaguely"; speakers and writers imply.

I <u>infer</u> from your letter that conditions have improved.

Do you mean to <u>imply</u> that conditions have improved?

22. *Insure, ensure.* To *insure* is to contract for payment of a certain sum in the event of damage or loss. To *ensure* is to make certain that a specified event or result will occur.

> We plan to <u>insure</u> the house for $50,000.
>
> To <u>ensure</u> a passing score, study systematically.

23. *Irregardless.* Avoid using this word. Use *regardless* instead.

24. *Its, it's. Its* is a possessive pronoun; *it's* is a contraction for "it is."

> The phrase has lost <u>its</u> meaning.
>
> <u>It's</u> time to quit.

25. *Lend, loan. Lend* is a verb meaning to let another use something temporarily. *Loan* is a noun referring to the thing given for the borrower's temporary use.

> The bank has agreed to <u>lend</u> us the money.
>
> The bank has approved our <u>loan</u>.

26. *Lose, loose. Lose* means "to fail to keep"; *loose* means "not tight."

> Don't <u>lose</u> the moneybag.
>
> The cap on the pen is <u>loose</u>.

27. *Media, medium.* A *medium* is a means for transmitting a message. Letter, telephone, radio, and newspaper are examples. The plural form is *media.*

> The best <u>medium</u> for advertising this product is the radio.
>
> The news <u>media</u> are very objective in their coverage.

28. *Personal, personnel. Personal* means "concerned with a person" or "private." *Personnel* means "people" or "employees."

> Omit the questions about family background and musical preference; they're too <u>personal</u>.
>
> All advertising <u>personnel</u> are invited to participate in the workshop.

29. *Principal, principle. Principal* means "a person in a leading position," "main," or "primary"; *principle* means "rule" or "law."

> The <u>principal</u> scheduled an all-day faculty meeting.
>
> The <u>principal</u> purpose is to gain speed.
>
> The <u>principal</u> plus interest is due in thirty days.
>
> The theory is based on sound <u>principles</u>.

30. *Reason is because. Because* means "for the reason next presented"; therefore *reason is because* is a redundancy.

> **Not:** The reason is because losses from bad debts tripled.
>
> **But:** The reason is that losses from bad debts tripled.
>
> **Or:** Profits decreased because losses from bad debts tripled.

31. *Stationary, stationery.* *Stationary* means "without movement" or "remaining in one place." *Stationery* is writing paper.

> The machine is to remain <u>stationary</u>.
>
> Order another box of <u>stationery</u>.

32. *That, which.* Use *that* when a dependent clause is essential in conveying the basic meaning of the sentence. Use *which* when a dependent clause is not essential in conveying the basic meaning of the sentence.

> The books <u>that</u> were on the shelf have been sent to the bindery. [The clause identifies certain books sent to the bindery; therefore, it is essential].
>
> Multigrade oil, <u>which</u> is only slightly more expensive than one-grade oil, will serve your purpose better. [Purpose of sentence is to convey the superiority of multigrade oil; therefore, "which is only slightly more expensive than one-grade oil" is not essential.]

33. *Their, there, they're.* *Their* is the possessive form of "they." *There* refers to "at that place" or "at that point." *They're* is a contraction for "they are."

> The president accepted <u>their</u> proposal immediately.
>
> The final copy must be <u>there</u> by May 1.
>
> <u>They're</u> eager to complete the renovation in time for the spring selling season.

34. *To, too, two.* *To* is a preposition or the beginning of an infinitive. *Too* is an adverb meaning "also" or "excessive." *Two* is a number.

> José organized the campaign <u>to</u> initiate flexible scheduling.
>
> Twenty-percent overtime is <u>too</u> demanding.
>
> The entire department shares the <u>two</u> laser printers.

35. *While.* *While*, meaning "at the same time that," should not be used as a synonym for such conjunctions as *but, though, although, and*, and *whereas*.

> You complete the appendixes <u>while</u> I key a transmittal letter. [Concurrent activities]
>
> One man likes his work, <u>but</u> the other does not.
>
> <u>Although</u> we realize your account is overdue, we think you should not pass up this opportunity.

EXERCISE 12

Select the correct word.

1. All questionnaires were returned (accept, except) one.
2. Exactly how will the change (affect, effect) us?
3. The consultants' (advice, advise) is to downsize the organization.
4. The commission is to be divided equally (among, between) the three sales agents.
5. We were astonished by the (amount, number) of complaints.

6. The (cite, sight, site) of Jim's receiving the service award was exhilarating.

7. I consider that remark a (compliment, complement).

8. Because the suspect's statements were (credible, creditable), no charges were filed.

9. The three panelists were constantly interrupting (each other, one another).

10. The issue will be discussed (further, farther) at our next meeting.

11. Limit your discussion to five or (fewer, less) points.

12. From his statements to the press, I (infer, imply) that he is optimistic about the proposal.

13. (Regardless, Irregardless) of weather conditions, we should proceed.

14. The storm seems to be losing (its, it's) force.

15. Please, (lend, loan) me a copy of today's *Wall Street Journal*.

16. Employees are entitled to examine their (personal, personnel) folder.

17. The system's (principal, principle) advantage is monetary.

18. (Their, There, They're) planning to complete (their, there, they're) strategic plan this week.

19. The supervisor expects us (to, too, two) complete (to, too, two) many unnecessary reports.

20. (Although, While) my findings are similar, my conclusions are dissimilar.

Complete the Self-Check and the Review Quiz to test your understanding of grammar, spelling, and punctuation principles.

✓ SELF CHECK

Cover the answer that appears below each numbered sentence. Identify the error(s) in a sentence; then, slide the cover sheet down and check your answer against the correct sentence. Refer to the pages listed in parentheses to review the reasons for each correction. The first number is a page number in Appendix B; the second number or letter identifies a certain place on the page.

1. I will appreciate you sending next months report too my home address.

   I will appreciate your sending next month's report to my home address. (5, d) (16, b; 17, f) (30, 34)

2. Only one of the participant's were willing to ask "what do you think"?

   Only one of the participants was willing to ask, "What do you think?" (16, 1a) (6, 1a) (14, 8) (23, 11a; 24, 11i)

3. While Jan's request for promotion had been denied three times her morale was high.

   Although Jan's request for promotion had been denied three times, her morale was high.

   Jan's request for promotion had been denied three times, but her morale was high. (30, 35) (18, a; 19, b)

4. On March 1st, 1995, we moved to a five room suite, it was formally occupied by Woodson Travel Agency.

   On March 1, 1995, we moved to a five-room suite; it was formerly occupied by Woodson Travel Agency.

   On March 1, 1995, we moved to a five-room suite, which was formerly occupied by Woodson Travel Agency. (14, a; 15, b) (19, g) (21, 8a) (25, a; 18, e) (28, 20)

5. Neither Joe or Phil have planned to attend the three day conference, however, the director has issued instructions to do so.

   Neither Joe nor Phil has planned to attend the three-day conference; however, the director has issued instructions to do so. (6, b) (21, 8b) (25, c)

6. The box which was in room C has been prepared for mailing all other boxes are to be wrapped with heavy paper, and returned to room D.

   The box that was in Room C has been prepared for mailing; all other boxes are to be wrapped with heavy paper and returned to Room D.

   The box that was in Room C has been prepared for mailing, but all other boxes are to be wrapped with heavy paper and returned to Room D. (30, 32) (13, 6) (25, a; 18, 5a)

7. If I completed this long complicated questionnaire my time would be wasted.

   If I completed this long, complicated questionnaire, my time would be wasted. (19, b, d)

8. While the company has lost their first place position this year next years predictions are promising.

   Although the company has lost its first-place position this year, next year's predictions are promising. (30, 35) (3, e; 29, 24) (21, 8b) (19, b) (17, f)

9. The request has been rejected, inadequate funding is the reason for the rejection.

   The request has been rejected; inadequate funding is the reason for the rejection.

   The request has been rejected because of inadequate funding. (25, a) (29, 30)

10. Two thirds of the members thinks the criteria should be revised because of it's ambiguity.

    Two-thirds of the members think the criterion should be revised because of its ambiguity. (21, d) (6, a) (27, 12) (29, 24)

11. For you and I that price seems very low, however for a recently-hired assistant, it probably seems very high.

    For you and <u>me</u>, that price seems very low<u>;</u> however<u>,</u> for a recently<u> </u>hired assistant, it probably seems very high. (4, 2b) (19, b) (25, c; 20, p) (21, 8b)

12. The spellcheck was not able to detect all errors, for example, derive was keyed incorrectly as drive.

    The spellcheck was not able to detect all errors<u>;</u> for example, <u>derive</u> was keyed incorrectly as *drive*. (25, e) (26, a)

13. The following have worked 7 hours of overtime this week; Welch, 4, Redford, 6, and Woods, 11.

    The following <u>employees</u> have worked <u>seven</u> hours of overtime this week: Welch, 4<u>;</u> Redford, 6<u>;</u> and Woods, 11. (9, 1) (14, a) (18, 4a) (20, m; 25, d)

14. Helen made a higher score than any one in her work unit but her promotion was denied because of habitual tardiness.

    Helen made a higher score than <u>anyone else</u> in her work unit<u>,</u> but her promotion was denied because of habitual tardiness. (10, 4) (18, 5a)

15. The commission is too be divided equally between Ray, Coleen, and I.

    The commission is <u>to</u> be divided equally <u>among</u> Ray, Coleen, and <u>me</u>. (30, 34) (26, 4) (4, b).

REVIEW QUIZ

To test your understanding of the grammar, spelling, and punctuation principles presented in Appendix B, identify the error(s) in each sentence.

1. Will you please find out whether first and second year students are eligible too receive that scholarship.

2. George was once in charge of security at the capital building, he is not impressed with our firms security system.

3. The questionaires which were mailed on June 1 have been returned; but only a few of those mailed later in the month have been returned.

4. Our stockbroker has written an article on fiscal policy, the article will appear in the March 21st issue of "Newsweek".

5. While the committee agreed with Ms. Sims conclusions; several members raised serious questions about the questionnaire, which was used as an information gathering instrument.

6. John has submitted more suggestions than anyone in his department but he has yet to receive an award.

7. While the procedure has been highly successful it is not popular in our department.

8. The man, who came late to the meeting, is the new Sales Manager for the southwest region.

9. The 3 applicants were waiting to interview for the same job, therefore they had little to say to each other.

10. Only one of my recommendations were considered, this was very disappointing to the superintendent and I.

11. The majority of the discussion was devoted to personal benefits but that topic has not been listed on the agenda.

12. After you have completed your term please write to me, we have some highly-important matters to discuss.

13. When you rewrite the final draft, please change the word charge to debit.

14. Each of our assistants are required to take a short intensive training course.

15. 13 respondents thought the company was losing sight of it's objectives.

16. On June 3, 1995 the Jackson, Tennessee location was officially approved.

17. John insisted on us listening to his play by play recap of the game.

18. No the comforter comes in these colors only, burgundy, hunter green, and khaki.

19. The sight for the new plant is 5 blocks East of E. Lampkin St.

20. While presenting the proposed change in distribution, an emergency call required the manager to leave abruptly.

GRADING SYMBOLS

Organization and Development
Word Choice and Style
Punctuation
Mechanics
Format

Your instructor may use the following grading symbols to mark corrections on your writing assignments. The instructor may write the abbreviation (highlighted to the right of the numbers) to identify the major area needing improvement. To provide additional feedback on all or selected errors, the instructor may write the number and letter designating the *specific* principle violated. To review the principles marked on your paper, refer to the pages indicated within the parentheses.

ORGANIZATION AND DEVELOPMENT

1. **seq**   Organizational Sequence
   a. Deductive approach to convey good or routine news (193, 245)
   b. Inductive approach to convey bad news (193, 286)
   c. Persuasive approach if reader must be persuaded (193, 322)
   d. Special letters (Chapter 12, refer to specific document)
2. **ss**   Sentences
   a. Normal subject-verb-complement sequence (195; B-10,#2)
   b. Related ideas in sentence (B-10,#3)
   c. Avoid expletive beginnings (223; B-10,#2)
   d. Avoid split infinitives (B-11,#9)
3. **¶**   Paragraphs
   a. Topic sentence presents central idea (201-202)
   b. Coherence; ideas connect logically (201-203)
   c. Unity; has beginning, middle (systematic sequence), and ending (203)
4. **trans**   Transition
   Transition between sentences and paragraphs so that ideas connect; avoid choppy sentences (203-204)

WORD CHOICE AND STYLE

5. **read**   Readability
   a. Use plain, simple words; use jargon only if reader will understand (219-221)
   b. Use short sentences (224-227)
   c. Avoid long, complicated paragraphs (204, 224-227)
6. **clear**   Clarity
   a. Include relevant ideas; develop logically (191-193)
   b. Specific vs. general word choice (214; B-2, #1)
   c. Concrete vs. abstract nouns—word choice (214-215; B-2,#2)
   d. Active voice for vivid writing (197-198; B-7,#4)
   e. Plain, simple language (219-220)
   f. Action-oriented ending paragraph (see example of specific document)
   g. Cite reference for source (505-508; 596-598)
   h. Verify accuracy of names, places, dates, amounts, etc. (see case problem)
7. **concise**   Conciseness
   a. Redundancies (225-226)
   b. Clichés (215-217)
   c. Brevity (unnecessary words and ideas) (224-227)
8. **tone**   Tone
   a. Reader's viewpoint; overuse of first person—I (175-179)
   b. Emphasize positive ideas: use active voice (189, 197-198) second person (188), and positive words (186-188)
   c. De-emphasize negative ideas: use passive voice (188-189; B-7,#4), positive words (186), and subjunctive mood (189; B-8,#5); avoid second person (188),
   d. Use bias-free language (179-182)
   e. Condescending (182) and demeaning tone (184)
   f. Misuse of euphemistic tone (185-186) and connotative tone (184-185)
   g. Expressions of surprise, doubt, and judgment (185-186)
9. **agr**   Agreement
   a.   Number: subject and verb (B-6,#1)
   b.   Person: subject and verb (B-7,#2)
   c.   Tense (B-7,#3)
   d.   Mood (B-8, #5)
   e.   Pronoun and antecedent (B-3,#1; B5, #3-4)
10. **case**   Case
   a. Nominative (B-4,#2a,c)
   b. Objective (B-4,#2b)
   c. Before a gerund (B-5,#2d)
   d. Relative pronouns—who, whom (B-4, #2b; B-5,#3)
   e. Possessives (B-5, 2d)

11. **adj or adv**   Adjectives and Adverbs
    a. Adjectives; use correct degree, avoid superlatives and overly strong adjectives (218-219; B-8, 9,#1,2,4)
    b. Adverbs; use correct degree, avoid superlatives, and overly strong adverbs (218-219; B-9,#3)
    c. Double negatives
12. **frag**   Sentence Fragments (196; B-9,#1)
13. **ro**   Run-on Sentences
    Review the punctuation of sentence types (195-197)
14. **ref**   Pronoun Reference
    a. Ambiguous pronoun reference (B-5,#3)
    b. Misuse: using a pronoun to refer to phrase, clause, sentence, or paragraph (B-5,#4)
    c. Use of you when the meaning is not clear
15. **shifts**   Shifts
    a. Person and number (See agreement)
    b. Tense and mood (See agreement)

16. **mm/dm**   Misplaced and Dangling Modifiers
    a. Misplaced and dangling modifiers (221-223; B-10-11,#6)
    b. Relative pronouns (B-5,#3)
    c. Do not separate subject and verb unnecessarily (B-10,#5)
17. **//**   Parallelism (223-224; B-11,#7)
18. **emph**   Emphasis
    a. Sentence structure (198)
    b. Position: first and last positions for emphasis (199)
    c. Numbers or tabulated enumerations (200)
    d. Include positive idea in sentence (190)
19. **var**   Variety
    a. Sentence length (204)
    b. Sentence structure (204)
    c. Paragraph length (204)

PUNCTUATION

20. **. ? !**   Terminal Punctuation (B-23, #10)
21. **,**   Comma
    a. Coordinate conjunction—*and*, *but*, and *for* (B-18,#5a)
    b. Introductory clause or phrase (B-19,#5b)
    c. Items in a series (B-19,#5c)
    d. Coordinate adjectives (B-19, 5d)
    e. Nonrestrictive clauses and parenthetical expressions (B-19,#5e-f)
    f. Date, city, and state (B-19-20,#5g-h)
    g. Appositive (B-20,#5k)
    h. Adverbial conjunction (B-20,#5p)
    i. Other rules (B-19-20,#5)
22. **;**   Semicolon
    a. Omitted conjunction (B-25,#12a)

    b. Compound-complex sentence (196; B-25,#12b)
    c. Adverbial conjunction (B-25,#12c)
    d. Within series that contains a comma (B-24,#12d)
    e. Other rules (B-25,#12)
23. **'**   Apostrophe
    a. Rules for using apostrophes (B-16,#1)
    b. Rules for not using apostrophes (B-17,#2)
24. **[ ] : -- . . . - ( ) " "**   Other Marks
    a. Brackets (B-17,#3)
    b. Colon (B-18,#4)
    c. Dash (B-21,#6)
    d. Ellipses (B-21,#7)
    e. Hyphen (B-21,#8); compound adjective (B-21,#8b)
    f. Parentheses (B-22-23,#9)
    g. Quotation Marks (B-23-24,#11)

MECHANICS

25. **caps**
    a. Capitals (B-13-14, #1-9)
    b. Envelope address: all caps and no punctuation (A-18, A-22)
26. **ital**   Italics (Underline if software does not support italics.)
    a. Words named as words (B-26,#14a)
    b. Emphasis (B-26,#14b)
    c. Titles of books and magazines (B-26,#14c)
27. **ab**   Abbreviations
    a. Abbreviate (B-12,#1)
    b. Do not abbreviate (B-12-13,#2)
    c. Two-letter ZIP Code abbreviation (A-23)
28. **num**   Numbers
    a. Use figures (B-14, #1)

    b. Spell out (B-15-16,#2)
29. **div**   Word Division (A-5-6,#1-7)
30. **sp**   Spelling
    a. Use a spellcheck or proofread carefully for omitted or repeated words
    b. Frequently misused words; locate the correct usage from text pages or a dictionary (B-26-30)
    c. Verify names, places, dates, amounts, etc. (see case problem)
31. **# or >**   Spacing
    a. Once after terminal punctuation, a comma, and a semicolon (A-4,#1)
    b. Twice after a colon (A-5,#2)
    c. Proper vertical spacing in letters (A-6-9)

FORMAT

32. **App**   Appearance
    a. Poor print quality
    b. Not balanced attractively on page
    c. Unprofessional (submitted with perforated edges; crumpled, etc.)
33. **fmt**   Format

Letters and Memos
    a. Letter style: block (A-6, 7), modified block (A-7, 8), simplified block (A-8, 9)
    b. Punctuation style: mixed (A-6), open (A-6)
    c. Include return address on letter if plain paper is used (A-10)
    d. Appropriate salutation (A-10-12)
    e. Acceptable memo style: traditional (A-18-19), simplified (A-18, A-20)
    f. Second-page heading for letters/memos (A-14, 15)
    g. Appropriate special parts—enclosure, copy, etc. (A-13-16)
    h. Envelope format (A-18-22)
    i. Letters signed and memos initialed legibly

Reports
    j. Report title page (see sample report)
    k. Contents and list of figures (see sample report)
    l. Executive summary (see sample report)
    m. Report text (see sample report)
    n. Citations: In-text parenthetical APA (599-600); bottom-of-the-page or end-of-the-report, MLA (600-604)
    o. Bibliography or references page (604-605)

Other Documents
    p. Resume (421; 423-427)
    q. References Page—employment credentials (422)
    r. News release (376-378)

INDEX

Part 4

Pay, Benefits, Terms and Conditions of Employment

- Wages

- Benefits

- Unions

- Safety and Health

Part 5

Managing Performance

- Appraisals

- Training

- Development

- Privacy

Part 6

Terminating Employment

- Employment at Will with Exceptions

- Just Cause

- Due Process

- Downsizing